NATIONAL GEOGRAPHIC
TRAVELER
Spain

NATIONAL GEOGRAPHIC

TRAVELER
Spain

Fiona Dunlop

National Geographic
Washington, D.C.

Contents

How to use this guide 6–7 About the author 8
The regions 53–340 Travelwise 341–90
Index 391–397 Credits 398–99

Page 1: Girl in traditional dress, Valencia
Pages 2–3: Junior flamenco dancer on the Plaza de España, Madrid
Left: Flamenco steps

How to use this guide

See back flap for keys to text and map symbols

The *National Geographic Traveler* brings you the best of Spain in text, pictures, and maps. Divided into three main sections, the guide begins with an overview of history and culture. Following are ten regional chapters with featured sites selected by the author for their particular interest. Each chapter opens with its own contents list for easy reference.

The regions, and sites within them, are arranged geographically. Some regions are further divided into smaller areas. A map introduces each region, highlighting the featured sites. Walks and drives, plotted on their own maps, suggest routes for discovering an area. Features and sidebars offer intriguing detail on history, culture, or contemporary life.

The final section, Travelwise, lists essential information for the traveler—pre-trip planning, communications, money matters, getting around, and emergencies—plus offers a selection of hotels, restaurants, shops, entertainment, and activities.

To the best of our knowledge, all information is accurate as of the press date. However, it is always advisable to call ahead when possible.

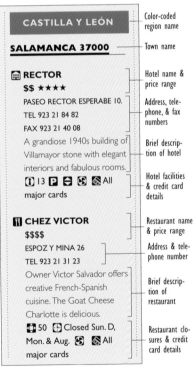

Place-names

In regions where local languages are spoken, for example Galicia, Euskadi (Basque country), Catalunya, Valencia, and the Balearic Islands, the local name is given first with the Castilian name in parentheses afterward.

Color coding

Each region is color coded for easy reference. Find the region you want on the map on the front flap, and look for the color flash at the top of the pages of the relevant chapter. Information in **Travelwise** is also color coded to each region.

130

Museu Picasso

- 155 E3
- ✉ Carrer de Montcada 15–23
- ☎ 93 319 63 10
- 🕐 Closed Sun. p.m.
- 💲 $
- 🚇 Metro: Jaume I, Line 4

Visitor information

Practical information for most sites is given in the side column (see key to symbols on back flap). The map reference gives the page number of the map and grid reference. Other details are the site's address, telephone number, days closed, entrance charge in a range from $ (under $6.50) to $$$$$ (over $25), and public transportation. Other sites have visitor information in italics and parentheses in the text.

TRAVELWISE

CASTILLA Y LEÓN — Color-coded region name

SALAMANCA 37000 — Town name

🏨 **RECTOR** — Hotel name & price range
$$ ★★★★

PASEO RECTOR ESPERABE 10. — Address, telephone, & fax numbers
TEL 923 21 84 82
FAX 923 21 40 08

A grandiose 1940s building of Villamayor stone with elegant interiors and fabulous rooms. — Brief description of hotel

🛏 13 🅿 ⊟ 🅾 🅾 All major cards — Hotel facilities & credit card details

🍴 **CHEZ VICTOR** — Restaurant name & price range
$$$$

ESPOZ Y MINA 26 — Address & telephone number
TEL 923 21 31 23

Owner Victor Salvador offers creative French-Spanish cuisine. The Goat Cheese Charlotte is delicious. — Brief description of restaurant

🍴 50 🕐 Closed Sun. D, Mon. & Aug. 🅾 🅾 All major cards — Restaurant closures & credit card details

Hotel & restaurant prices

An explanation of the price ranges used in entries is given in the Hotels & Restaurants section (see p. 348).

REGIONAL MAPS

Important point of interest

Road number

Important featured town

Map reference

- A locator map accompanies each regional map and shows the location of that region in the country.
- Adjacent regions are shown, each with a page reference.

WALKING TOURS

Walk route

Direction of walk route

Start point

Red numbered bullets link site on map to descriptions in the text

Featured site (in bold) on walk route

Point of interest not on walk route

Building outline

- An information box gives the starting and finishing points, time and length of walk, and places not to be missed along the route.

DRIVING TOURS

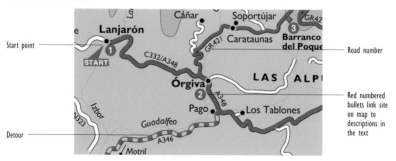

Start point

Detour

Road number

Red numbered bullets link site on map to descriptions in the text

- An information box provides details including starting and finishing points, time and length of drive, and places not to be missed along the route.

NATIONAL GEOGRAPHIC

TRAVELER

Spain

About the author

Fiona Dunlop's peripatetic life has led her from the Australian beaches of her birth to an upbringing in London and subsequent jobs in Italy and Monte Carlo. During 15 years spent in Paris she was strongly involved in the arts before moving into travel journalism. She has written widely for numerous international art and interior design magazines and national newspapers (including the *Observer, Sunday Telegraph, Guardian, Financial Times,* and *CNN Traveler,* among others). A taste for the tropics and ancient cultures has led Fiona to spend long research periods in developing countries. These have produced travel guides to India, Indonesia, Singapore & Malaysia, Vietnam, Mexico, Costa Rica, and southern Africa. Other publications include *In the Asian Style* (on Asian design), *New Tapas,* a book on the Spanish tapas bar tradition, *Medina Kitchen* (exploring the home-cooking of North Africa), and *Viva la Revolucion!,* a food-travel book on Mexico. She has regularly visited Andalucía to write articles and books in what she considers to be the optimum conditions, combining *sol y sombra* (sun and shade), not to mention tapas. Her main base is now in London.

London-born Tomasina Wilson, who has lived and worked in Alicant (Alicante) and in Andalucía, wrote the original Travelwise chapter. Further updates have been researched by Alexander Fraser, who lives in Mojácar.

History & culture

Sevilla's Feria brings out the whole flamenco wardrobe.

Spain today

THE STEREOTYPICAL SPANIARD DISAPPEARED LONG AGO. BACK IN THE 19TH century, writers and artists wove images of a land inhabited by voluptuous, black-haired, fiery-eyed women and dubious-looking, mustachioed men. Look for them today and you will be disappointed as Spain is firmly within the net of globalization. Yet beneath the surface lies a web of regional differences and deeply embedded traditions that even mobile-phone-clutching young professionals have not forsaken.

Whether Catalan, Basque, Galician, Asturian, Cantabrian, Castilian, Aragonese, Extremaduran, Valencian, Manchegan, Murcian, Andalusian, or from the Balearics or the Canaries, the Spaniard of the 21st century clings adamantly to his or her roots, a habit illustrated in local fiestas and by language itself. After long suppression under the dictator General Franco, who died in 1975, regional identities have undergone an explosive revival, given impetus by the powers granted to the 17 autonomous communities set up in the new constitution of 1978. Spain is now Europe's most devolved country. Separatism has reached extremes and provoked terrorist attacks in Euskadi (Basque country), while Catalunya maintains a more pragmatic approach. Regional loyalty fragments further, from province to province, from town to town, and from village to village. There is no Spain or Spaniard as such. Instead, a passionately local spirit is cloaked in the dominant Castilian culture—and in a love of excess that fizzes in the action-packed calendar.

Spain is on the move. You find Andalusians working in Catalunya, unemployed Castilian farmers migrating to Euskadi, and Madrid embracing incomers from every region. Yet, deep in the rural countryside, unadulterated relics of distant invaders exist. Descendants of the Romans live in Asturias, and those of the Swabians on the borders of Extremadura and Castilla. Even more distinct and determinedly set apart from the mainstream is the 500-year-old Gypsy community, visible above all in Andalucía. Gypsies provoke waves of intolerance, and in the 1990s so did Spain's other highly visible minority—North African migrant workers. However, a vast increase in immigration since 2000 has resulted in far greater racial tolerance.

Language is equally diverse. The language called "Spanish" is actually Castilian, from the central part of Spain. The Basque, Catalan, and Galician languages are utterly distinctive, as are regional accents. Each Canary island has its own accent, and the slurred tones of Andalusians are quite different from the crisp, machine-gun fire of Madrileños, the people of Madrid. This is something that you might not be aware of in Spain's bland coastal resorts, where signs are as likely to be in English and German as in Spanish. The onward march of tourism since the 1960s has created yet another division of Spain, that between the Mediterranean *costas* (coasts) invaded by northern European retirees and summer sunseekers, and the vast, underpopulated interior. It is in the latter that the reactionary heart of Spain beats, where rural inhabitants may barely know the next town and where population densities descend below 30 inhabitants per square mile. Catholicism rules in these areas—the two Castillas, Aragón, and Extremadura—and the bells peal daily.

In the big cities, it is another story entirely. Barcelona, capital of Catalunya, is one of Europe's top cultural hubs, and its inhabitants exude a prosperity, confidence, and sophistication seen nowhere else in Spain. Although they do not readily embrace foreigners, they exemplify the old adage: Once you get to know them, they are friends for life. Madrid, the capital and Spain's largest city (with a mere three million population), has caught up in avant-gardism and style, while its businesses bustle and art collections blossom. Its more tolerant and relaxed inhabitants have a talent for nocturnal intensity and living on the edge: They were the ones who spearheaded the *movida*, a cathartic surge of hedonism and creativity that seized Spain in the early 1980s. Sex, drugs, and

Antoni Gaudí's Parc Güell in Barcelona epitomizes the architect's bent for fantasy.

rock and roll boomed, in tandem with a new wave of artists, filmmakers, and musicians. Spain's third largest city is Valencia, whose people adeptly combine southern laissez-faire with Catalan dynamism. As the site for the America's Cup, it has experienced massive regeneration. Sevilla, Zaragoza (home to Expo 2008), Málaga, and Bilbao follow, each with a distinct flavor, culture, and attitude, swinging from high southern exuberance to intelligent urbanism and industrial savvy.

Altogether, Spaniards number 45 million, but a sign of the times is demographic aging. The declining birthrate would make Spain home to the world's oldest population by 2050. However, this has been compensated for by high immigration numbers. Eleven percent of the population is now foreign-born. Other issues have also improved. Unemployment, over 20 percent in the 1990s, is now about 8 percent. On the environmental front, Spain is now a front-runner in alternative energies.

Bronze "Winged Victory" gazes over Madrid from atop the neoclassic Metropolis.

Spain as a nation has undergone a greater social, political, and economic transformation than most other Western European nations. And, despite drinking and smoking with joyous abandon, Spaniards enjoy an exceptionally high life expectancy. The secret could well be that around 87 percent of the population declares itself happy—the key to Spanishness?

FESTIVALS

The fiesta of a village or town is the excuse for everyone to let their hair down. This is the zenith of the year, when normally dignified, well-mannered people (which means most Spaniards) take to the streets and dance the night away. Tradition still pulls the heartstrings, despite the radical social upheavals of recent decades, and this is unlikely to change in the near future. Patron saints' days are the most common fiestas, but you also find a multitude

of idiosyncratic celebrations stemming from seasonal, historic, or religious events, each one requiring costumed participants, food, drink, music, and dance. Stylized battles between Moors and Christians, wine-battles in Rioja, the running of the bulls in Iruña (Pamplona), bonfires and satirical figures in Valencia, towering human pyramids in Catalunya, horse-branding in Galicia, coffin races in La Mancha, men disguised in animal skins and masks in Mallorca, whip-brandishing bogeymen in Extremadura, and a hedonistic pilgrimage to Rocío, in Huelva province, of nearly one million people from all over Andalucía—all are permanent fixtures on the calendar.

Dominating the religious calendar is Semana Santa (Holy Week, see pp. 272–73), the week leading up to Easter at its best in Seville, Malaga, and Zamora. Corpus Christi a few weeks later, sees processions of devils, dance groups, dwarfs, giants, and mythological creatures. Sometimes they follow a route of stunningly patterned carpets of flowers, salt, or sawdust. Medieval mystery plays are performed at this and other festivals. Christmas (Navidad), Los Mayos (a spring celebration of love and nature), San Juan (St. John, when pagan rites and bonfires celebrate the summer solstice), and September 8 (an autumn festival) feature among the other general celebrations. Carnival, which takes place around Mardi Gras, brings exceptional outbursts of color, costumes, and offbeat customs, above all in Cádiz, throughout Galicia, and in Santa Cruz de Tenerife, which approaches Rio de Janeiro's Carnival in scale and exuberance.

BULLFIGHTING

Bulls are the best known animal participants in Spain's festivals. From Easter to October, every town has a bullfighting season during its *feria* (annual fair)—look out for posters advertising the events. Matador prowess reaches a height in the bullrings of Madrid and Sevilla with heroes such as El Juli (Julián López) topping the bill. *Encierros*—the running of the bulls, when bulls are let loose to charge through the streets—lie at the heart

The Catalans are acrobatic experts at creating human pyramids (castellers), seen here in Tarragona.

of local festivals from Peñafiel to Iruña (Pamplona) and beyond. Bullbaiting is still practiced by Basques. Devotees of bullfighting (primarily Andalusians) are called *aficionados,* and for them bullfighting is not a sport, but an art, both ritualistic and ceremonial, with primitive origins and echoes of Roman gladiatorial combat and medieval jousting.

The national passion of bullfighting is considered art rather than sport.

The *corrida de toros* (bullfight) begins with a procession around the ring of the participants, accompanied by stirring music from the band. After testing how aggressive the bull is, the matador and his team on the ground leave center stage to the *picadores,* who ride out and encourage the bull to charge. The horses are padded to prevent serious injury, and their riders pierce the bull's neck and shoulders with their lances. Next, the *banderilleros* (bullfighters on foot, carrying *banderillas* or colored darts) enter and run at the bull trying to stick their banderillas into his shoulders. With the bull's energy depleted, the matador enters alone, to demonstrate his skill in making passes with his red cape and steering the bull expertly within inches of his body. Finally, in an intensely dramatic moment, he drives his sword between the bull's shoulders for the kill.

Long reviled by sensitive foreigners and by many Spaniards, the bullfight is nonetheless

the most perfect expression of Spanishness: pomp and ceremony, *sol y sombra* (sun and shade), a deep sense of drama, tragedy, and fatalism, all orchestrated by the fearless *furia española*—the legendary Spanish fury that made Spain's enemies tremble. Spaniards are not fazed by death, as history from the conquistadores and Inquisition to the Civil War ably demonstrates. Theatricality and pushing to the limit are enduring elements in the national psyche.

THE LAND

Spain is a vast, multifaceted expanse. From lush green valley to craggy granite rockface or barren scrub, the Spanish landscape always forms a powerful absolute. No other European country can rival the splendor, wildness, and intensity of Spain's landscapes, whether shimmering in scorching heat, softened by drizzle, or swept by glacial winter winds. Space dominates, horizons seem infinite, towns are rare, and the climate revels in extremes. In January

Ubrique's whitewashed buildings and surrounding sierra characterize Andalucía.

you can swim in the Canaries while Basques soak in *sirimiri* (misty drizzle), Castilians bend double against a blistering wind, Andalusians bask in gentle sunlight, and Catalans whiz down ski runs.

From the natural barrier of the Pyrenees and its westerly extension, the Sierra Cantábrica, 197,323 square miles (505,957 sq km)

unfold southward through the central *meseta* (tableland) of Castilla to the peaks of the Sierra Nevada and the limestone desert of eastern Andalucía. Mountain ranges—*sierras*—zigzag across the peninsula: Spain's average altitude is second only to that of Switzerland among European countries. It has the continent's highest road and highest village, both in the Sierra Nevada. This predominance of often spectacular sierra is one of the reasons for the strength of tradition in Spain, as isolated mountain communities once had little contact with the sociocultural advances of the cities. Massive improvements in communications and infrastructure over the last 20 years have made most, though not all, of these hidden communities far more accessible.

Like everywhere, the climate is changing: Pyrenean glaciers are melting; snow is less common in the Sierra Nevada, and rainfall is notoriously sparse except in the far north. Water shortages and desertification are a major cause of concern in Andalucía. Only five large rivers course across this generous peninsula: the Ebro, Guadalquivir, Guadiana, Tagus, and Duero, each sprouting branches that end in pathetic trickles and often dry up completely. Yet, once again, Spain surprises, for it boasts one of Europe's most fertile regions: the rice fields and *huerta* (irrigated land) of Valencia. Verdant havens are found in the undulating meadows and orchards of Cantabria and Asturias, and lusher pockets of the Costa del Sol.

FLORA & FAUNA

An estimated 90 percent of Spain's prehistoric forests disappeared long ago. They gave way to wheat fields, vineyards, olive groves, and fruit orchards, but also to vast tracts of uncultivatable scrub and barren shale where only cactuses dare to grow. The remaining pockets of forest harbor over 500 species, making it a European hotspot for bird-watching. After decades of low visibility, wolves and brown bears are multiplying again in the north-west (Galicia and Castilla-León) and Cordillera Cantábrica respectively. You are more likely to glimpse chamois, deer, and possibly wild boars among the oak, beech, ash, and lime trees that cover the lower slopes. Birds of prey also favor mountainous areas, and Spain is home to about 25 species, including red kites, griffon vultures, and the endangered imperial eagle. Southern Spain is a stopping point on migration routes between Europe, Africa, and Asia, and bird-watchers can spot the greatest number of species in the pine forests of the Sierra de Cazorla, near Úbeda, and in the sand dunes and marshes of the Parque Nacional Doñana, southwest of Seville. On inland waters you may see migrating flamingos and European cranes, while hoopoes, golden orioles, cuckoos, woodpeckers, and bee-eaters frequent the riverbanks and woods.

Flora is another attraction, above all in spring: Spain has about 7,000 species of which one tenth are endemic. Many of these are alpine varieties that thrive in the highest mountains.

FOOD & DRINK

Although Spain was never traditionally a gastronome's destination, things have changed radically in recent years, and Ferran Adriá (Catalunya's revolutionary chef) has become an international star. Cuisine is not treated as

Playa de la Frayata, in Sitges near Barcelona, offers the sun, sea, and sand that make Spain so popular with vacationers.

reverently as in France, but its increasingly refined ingredients are as rich and varied as the climate and terrain. An intimate knowledge of the quality of basic products—for example extra virgin olive oil, *jamón* (ham), ewe's cheese, anchovies, tomatoes, seafood, and the most succulent of lamb—is part of the traditional heritage that

even city dwellers share. Just as wine has leapt up the quality scale (see pp. 134–35), cooking is fast developing from simple, hearty fare into far more sophisticated and inventive preparations.

Leading this gastronomic revolution is a new generation of chefs. Everyone knows San Sebastian's veteran nueva cocina chef, Juan Marí Arzak, but there are others such as his fellow-Basques Pedro Subijana of Akelarré, Martin Berasategui at Lagarte, and the up-and-coming Antoní Luis Aduriz at Mugarit. The Catalans,

beyond Adrià, feature towering figures like Santi Santamaría in Sant Celoni, Joan Roca in Girona, and Carme Ruscalleda in Sant Pol de Mar. Madrid boasts Sergi Arola at La Broche and the avant-garde Darrio Barrio, while Valencia trumpets Ca Sento's seafood king, Raúl Aleixandre, an Adrià disciple. With such a galaxy of star chefs, the overall standard has soared and firmly established Spain on the world gastro-map.

One of Spain's greatest contributions to international eating habits is the tradition of *tapas* (known in the Basque Country as *pintxos*), appetizers that you eat with glasses of beer, wine, or sherry at the end of the early evening *paseo* (stroll). Tapas let you sample regional specialties, and keep you going until dinner (which rarely occurs before 10 p.m.), or even replace it. They are served in small *porciones* and larger *raciones:* Typical tapas are *morcilla* (black pudding), *mojama* (air-dried tuna), local hams or cheeses, broad beans cooked with bacon and mint, kidneys sautéed in sherry, or skewers of

A paella of this size, made for a festival in L'Hospitalet de Llobregat, is exceptional.

grilled meat or seafood. Tapas exemplify the Spanish character, as consumption is invariably linked to socializing in an impromptu, informal way. Customers often move from bar to bar, eating, drinking, and chatting, though many bars are now quite sophisticated with sit-down areas.

Lunch is the most important meal of the day, starting after 2 p.m. In restaurants the *menú* *del día* (menu of the day) is usually a good choice, and daily specials have the freshest ingredients. Regional specialties include *cochinillo* (roast suckling pig) in Castilla, *rabo de toro* (ox tail) in Andalucía, *fabada* (pork and beans) in Asturias, paella in Valencia, and *pulpo a la Gallega* (octopus in sauce) in Galicia. From a basic peasant cuisine, the peninsula's food is evolving into an array of finely orchestrated gastronomic indulgences—all taken with an inimitable Spanish dose of enjoyment. ■

History of Spain

THE NAME IBERIA FIRST CROPPED UP IN THE SIXTH CENTURY B.C. WHEN A
Greek writer referred to the people living along the River Ebre, or Ebro (Iberus). Spain's
history goes back a lot further, to the time when early people first crossed the narrow
Straits of Gibraltar from Africa.

Evidence has been found in Andalucía of
human presence (and that of elephants and
carnivorous mammals) more than one million
years ago. By around 25,000 B.C., Paleolithic
hunter-gatherers were creating cave paintings
of bison and deer. The finest Paleolithic
paintings known are in the caves of Altamira
in Cantabria and date from around 15,000
B.C., long before the dolmens of Antequera
(see p. 282) or the *talayot* of the Balearics (see
p. 329) were built.

Settled culture appeared with the Iberians
themselves, who are thought to have originated in North Africa. They were later joined
by Celts to become Celtiberians. Galicia's
castros (fortified hill villages) are relics of their
advanced hybrid culture. Elsewhere, Spain had
little sign of an ordered society other than the
legendary Tartessos in Andalucía. This was
the Biblical Tarshish, a sophisticated, hierar-
chic society between the lower Guadalquivir
and Guadiana rivers, reported by Phoenician
traders in the first millennium B.C.

PHOENICIANS, GREEKS, & CARTHAGINIANS

Change came in the first millennium B.C.
through the trading network of more sophisticated peoples from the eastern Mediterranean—Phoenicians and Greeks. Spain's
extensive mineral resources first attracted
Phoenicians to Cádiz in the eighth century
B.C. They were followed by Greeks, who
spread inland from numerous points on the
Mediterranean coast. The potter's wheel, currency, and iron technology were among Greek
contributions to Iberian society. Spain's oldest
works of art—La Dama de Elche and La Dama
de Baza (both fifth to fourth century B.C.)
display clear eastern Mediterranean influence.

When the sun set for the Phoenicians it rose
in turn for their cousins, the Carthaginians
(based at Carthage, in modern Tunisia). Rome
and Carthage were at loggerheads over control

of the Mediterranean, and the Iberian peninsula was a pawn in their game. Greek influence
ended as the Carthaginians moved into
Tartessos, but native Iberians continued to
flourish, exporting wine, olive oil, grain, and
their rich mineral deposits. During the Punic
Wars (third century B.C.) between Rome and
Carthage, Iberians were employed in Hannibal's
army, which eventually crossed the Alps into
Italy. The Roman response was to obliterate
Carthage in 202 B.C. This announced Rome's
long hold over Europe—including Hispania,
as Roman Spain was known.

ROMAN SPAIN

For the next 500 years Rome imprinted its
mark on Spain, still distinct today in straight-
as-a-die roads, bridges, aqueducts, amphi-
theaters, urban layouts, and the Latin-based
Spanish language. The towns of Córdoba
(Corduba), Tarragona (Tarraco), and Mérida
(Augusta Emerita) became capitals of the
three Roman provinces of Baetica, Tarraconensis, and Lusitania. Numerous other
urban settlements—Sevilla (Hispalis), León
(Legio), Pamplona (Pompaelo), Zaragoza
(Caesar Augusta)—are also Roman. Spain's
mines continued to yield gold and silver in
vast quantities, much of which was shipped
back to Rome in an ironic reversal of Spain's
own plundering of the New World more than
a thousand years later. As Roman control
strengthened, the process of colonization
became Romanization. Waves of immigrant
Romans settled permanently in Hispania and
established their customs alongside those of
the Iberians. Resistance to Romanization was
strongest in the north and northwest, and
Galicia's Celtiberians were allowed to preserve
their traditions and names.

The ruins of a prehistoric Celtic-Roman
castro **(fortified village) at Monte Santa
Tecla, in Galicia**

Under Roman rule, fish products (salted anchovies, spicy garum sauce) and fish (tuna, mackerel, and sardine) joined the Iberians' already prolific production. Culture blossomed: Hispania produced illustrious Roman emperors such as Trajan and Hadrian, scholars such as the Senecas (father and son), Martial, Quintilian, and the geographer Mela. Yet although born and bred in Hispania, they were all undoubtedly of Roman stock, for the Roman elite kept its distance from the Iberians. Stability and prosperity lasted almost three centuries, until, in the third century A.D., cracks began to appear in the Roman armor as the empire went into decline. Spain's weakness was exposed by roving northern tribes of Franks, Vandals, and, in the fifth century, Suebi (Swabians), and Visigoths. Through sporadic raids they gradually broke up the carefully constructed social and political fabric. The Roman Empire was in its death throes, and Hispania's economy disintegrated as defense

Mezquita Mosque, built between the 8th and 10th centuries, stands beyond the Roman bridge.

budgets spiraled. Finally in 409 the ruthless, nonliterate Visigoths moved in.

VISIGOTHS

For the next 300 years, the history of Spain became a complex series of regional and monarchic battles for supremacy, consoli-

dated to a certain extent when the Visigothic kings established their capital in Toledo and the country was unified under King Leovigild in 584. In 654 King Recceswinth established a single code of law based on that of the Romans. Exceptions to this were the mountain people of the north (Cantabrians, Asturians, and Basques), who managed to retain their independence, and the south, which had a long period of Byzantine rule. Christianity had arrived in the late third century, and the emergence of church councils under the Visigoths established a link between Church and State that was crucial to Spain's subsequent history.

This was a dark period in Spain. The Roman system of huge estates *(latifundios)* owned by the aristocracy and worked by virtual slaves continued under the new invaders.

a northern African Islamic province of the Caliphate of Damascus. Its Arab rulers sent a Berber army across the strait, and after a decisive victory over the Visigothic king Roderic, they took barely three years to complete their conquest. Berbers settled in arid areas that resembled their native Atlas Mountains and intermarried. By the ninth

Cities declined to become mere fortified clusters of churches and convents. Jewish people, who had emigrated to Spain under the Romans, were forced to convert or become slaves, a situation exacerbated by the Erwigian code of 681. This legalized anti-Jewish measures and enforced the return of slaves to their masters. Famine, dynastic disputes, and an absence of law and order created a fragile, easily exploitable situation. In 711 an army of Berbers (the indigenous people of North Africa) landed at Gibraltar. This was to be the beginning of a new era that lasted more than seven centuries.

MOORISH CONQUEST

Since the death of the prophet Mohammed (570–632), much of Arabia and northern Africa had come under the sway of Islam, a new, egalitarian religion. News of rich pickings in anarchic Spain—known as al-Andalus, meaning "isle of Vandals"—reached Ifriqiya,

Granada's Alhambra, with its backdrop of the snowcapped Sierra Nevada, is the most sophisticated and dreamlike of Spain's Moorish constructions.

century, Arabic and the local Romance language had replaced Latin. This rapid success is not hard to explain, for Islam espoused religious tolerance, allowing Jews and Christians complete freedom of worship, and the end of Roman law brought liberty for Iberian slaves. Not least, Visigothic opponents of the Moors were embroiled in divisive conflicts that offered little to the average citizen but arbitrary bloodshed.

The one reversal in this astounding military advance was the battle of Covadonga in 718, when the Asturian prince Pelayo gave the army of the crescent its first whipping. This Moorish defeat was significant, as it left a chink of non-Muslim territory. Over the next century this expanded to cover all northern

Spain, from where it gradually spread south to culminate in the victory of the Catholic Monarchs (see pp. 31–33).

AL-ANDALUS & CÓRDOBA

The Arab conquerors and their Berber soldiers adopted an important Muslim ruler: Abd ar-Rahman of the Ummayad dynasty of Damascus, the successors of Mohammed himself. Fleeing the overthrow of his family, he arrived in Córdoba in 756 and established the emirate of al-Andalus, covering territory as far as the Pyrenees. Thus began the golden period of Islamic Spain, with Córdoba at its heart, seconded by Sevilla and Málaga. Agriculture diversified and prospered as sophisticated irrigation systems were installed. Rice, saffron, cotton, citrus fruits, figs, and dates were successfully introduced. Scholarly pursuits flourished among the philosophers, scientists, and writers who came to Córdoba from all over the Muslim world, and also among Jews, Christians (known as *Mozárabes*), and local converts to Islam. This socioreligious tapestry was extended by thousands of slaves brought from eastern and northern Europe and the Sudan, who were able to take on important roles in the ruling classes if they converted to Islam. What could have been a hornets' nest actually fused to create one glorious civilization—that of al-Andalus.

In some respects this newly urbanized society was an embellished version of its Roman precursor. Roman foundations were used to rebuild towns that had crumbled under the Visigoths, but Islamic artistry went far beyond mere restoration. Palaces, fortresses, public baths, schools, mosques, fountains, and gardens of incredible beauty were created. At its zenith in the tenth century, when its population reached 100,000, Córdoba was rivaled only by Constantinople and Baghdad. Even today, the Great Mosque (Mezquita, see pp. 288–89) is unsurpassed in vision.

Not all was milk and honey in the land of al-Andalus. Sporadic raids were made on the infidels of the north in order to exact taxes and tributes under threat of death. Under the despotic rule of al-Hakem I (R.796–822), dissenters were decapitated, and violence spiraled. After an intervening period of cultural enrichment, unrest and revolts returned at the turn of the tenth century. Once again, a precarious situation was saved by an enlightened ruler—Abd ar-Rahman III (R.912–961), whose red hair and blue eyes were inherited from his Basque (or Frank) mother. Severing all ties with Baghdad, he assumed the title of Caliph in 929, took strategic points in north Africa (Melilla, Ceuta, and Tangiers) to preempt territorial threats, and reasserted his military strength against the Christian kingdoms of northern Spain. His palatial complex outside Córdoba, the Medina Azahara (see p. 291), became another of the glories of al-Andalus.

This great show of strength was followed by a period of dynastic weakness under Hisham II (R.976–1013), who relied on his Yemeni prime minister, ruthless Al-Mansur (R.940–1002), to such an extent that the latter even took the caliph's mother as his mistress. Al-Mansur's military ambition knew no bounds either, and León, Barcelona, and Santiago de Compostela all bowed temporarily to his might. By the early 11th century, after Al-Mansur's death, the caliphate had fallen prey to factional conflicts that led, in 1031, to its complete breakup into petty *taifas* (kingdoms). In the 300 years since its foundation al-Andalus had seen many peaks and troughs, and now a new wave of Muslim invaders, the Almoravids, appeared on the horizon.

The Almoravids were a fanatical group of Muslim Berbers who had established a kingdom stretching across North Africa from Morocco to Senegal. The taifa rulers invited them to Spain to help combat the increasingly successful Alfonso VI of Castilla y León, who conquered Toledo in 1085. The Almoravid leader, Yusuf, took a liking to al-Andalus. After defeating Alfonso in 1086, he decided to stay, so initiating the next Moorish dynasty.

Yet Moorish dominance over Spain was in decline, and for the next 400 years it was the Christians of the north who took the initiative. Raiding Muslim territory from their front lines of castles along the Ebro and Duero Rivers, they gradually extended Christian dominion southward. Christianity was strengthening its resolve, too, thanks to the Way of St. James pilgrimage route (see pp. 88–89), which brought a stream of foreign pilgrims to Spain. This stimulated a network of new churches and monasteries, and produced a unifying architectural style—the Romanesque.

CHRISTIAN SPAIN OF THE NORTH

A band of non-Muslim territories ran across northern Spain. The easternmost was Catalunya, which Charlemagne had established as an essential buffer zone against the independent kingdom ruled by ambitious Fernando I, one of Sancho III's four sons. Castilla absorbed León, and Fernando enthroned one of his brothers as puppet-ruler of Navarra. He also made vassals of the Muslim kingdoms of Toledo and Zaragoza. In 1085, Alfonso VI of Castilla y León took the prestigious city of Toledo from the Moors

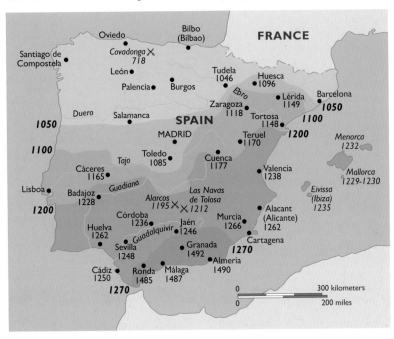

Map showing the Christian reconquest of Spain from the Moors. Dates in bold and color shading show the Christian advance.

Moors at the turn of the ninth century. Its five counties were ruled by the Counts of Barcelona under a feudal system that concentrated property in the hands of civil and religious authorities. By the 12th century the Catalan identity had crystallized and its French-influenced language had taken root. Aragón, too, was developing under its own count, and in the early ninth century became linked with neighboring Navarra through marriage. Under Sancho III (R.1005–1035), Navarra attained political preeminence, but lost it after his death to Aragón and nascent Castilla. The latter was a newly created

and assumed the title Emperor of the Two Religions—a sign of things to come.

RECONQUEST

As the Almoravids were settling comfortably into Andalusian ways, a revivalist Muslim movement led by the the Almohads, from the Atlas Mountains, started threatening their control. By the mid-12th century the Almohads had moved into al-Andalus, bringing a crusading spirit that recovered Extremadura from the Christians and temporarily halted the Christian advance. Christian forces were disorganized and fraught by dynastic crises, and military challenges to the Almohads were left to King Alfonso I of Aragón. He countered their religious zeal with his own, backed up by the newly introduced Knights Templar, an order of soldier-monks founded in 1118 during the First Crusade, and resolved to defeat Islam. Zaragoza was one of several Moorish towns to fall into his net, and when his daughter Petronila married Ramón Berenguer of Barcelona, a solid alliance was created.

remained of the taifas was Granada, a kingdom that stretched from Tarifa east to Almería.

This period, too, saw the Church peaking in strength and status, represented by the massive Gothic cathedrals of Burgos, Toledo, and León. Parallel to this ecclesiastical power came that of the Knights Templar and the Order of Santiago.

A major turning point in the Reconquest came in 1212 at the battle of Las Navas de Tolosa, when Castilla's Alfonso VIII trounced the Almohads with help from Aragón, Navarra, and France. Yet nothing was straightforward during this period of warlords, mercenaries, knightly orders, militant monks, and warring princes, and the Reconquest moved into its penultimate stages under three different Christian rulers. In the east, Jaume I of Aragón and Barcelona expanded his territory south to incorporate Valencia, Alicante, and the Balearics by 1238. Meanwhile, Fernando III led the armies of Castilla and León to capture Córdoba, Jaén, and Sevilla. Cádiz and Murcia were swept up by his son, Alfonso X (known as the Wise for his intellectual and poetic aptitude). Now all that

"The surrender of Granada" by Francisco Pradilla (1846–1921) depicts the final stage of the Reconquest by Fernando and Isabel.

In Granada the Almohads had been replaced in the 1240s by the Nazrids, an aristocratic Moorish family driven south from Zaragoza. They oversaw Granada's cultural zenith, epitomized by their palace at the Alhambra (see pp. 300–305). Cunning diplomacy ensured Castilla's protection for Granada, and until the mid-14th century most of the peninsula prospered, with Muslims, Jews, and Christians coexisting in a tolerant, cosmopolitan society. In eastern Spain, the *cortes* (chamber of representatives) of Catalunya, Aragón, and Valencia instigated a fair system of civil rights accorded by their

king in exchange for allegiance. Mozárabes (Christians from formerly Muslim territory) and Muslims were moved to repopulate newly conquered regions, sometimes provoking social tensions. Roman-style large-scale estates, or latifundios, were allocated to nobility or given as rewards to military orders and prominent knights *(hidalgos)*, whose social code was exploited by Cervantes in *Don Quixote* (see pp. 238–39). The nefarious latifundio system, where large estates are often run by absentee landlords using low-paid laborers, still endures, mainly in Andalucía.

This was the period of Catalan expansion across the Mediterranean, bringing mercantile prosperity reflected in Barcelona's great 14th-century building boom. In 1348 bubonic plague struck, soon followed by famine. The combination drastically reduced Catalunya's population and, to a lesser extent, those of Aragón, Valencia, and the Balearics. By 1412 Castilla's hegemony was complete, and a branch of its ruling Trastámara family provided a new dynasty for eastern Spain.

Unrest continued into the 15th century. Dynastic wars resulted in outright civil war between supporters of Enrique IV's daughter, Juana, and his sister, Isabel, in 1474. Isabel's greatest ally was her husband, Fernando of Aragón. After winning the Battle of Toro in 1476, their collaborative rule transformed the face of Spain, culminating in the momentous events of 1492. That year saw Christopher Columbus landing in the New World, opening up a completely new chapter in Spanish history. Gold and silver were to pour into the national coffers for centuries, while the New World was taken over by Catholicism and the Spanish language. Equally important in 1492 was that after ten years of sieges and rural devastation, Muslim Granada was conquered by Fernando's army. Once Navarra had been annexed, Spain's unification was complete.

CATHOLIC MONARCHS

Fernando and Isabel's crusade against the Moors was heavily financed by the Church. In return they instigated a long period of

Christopher Columbus's ornate tomb in Sevilla Cathedral shows the preeminent role this navigator played in Spanish history.

An engraving by John Pine portrays Felipe II's Invincible Armada being trounced by the English navy in 1588.

religious intolerance, first expelling Jewish people from Spain and soon after threatening the remaining Muslims. Both groups were offered the choice of conversion or exile, but converts could still suffer persecution. Muslim converts, known as *moriscos*, were moved into designated rural areas, and confiscated properties were handed out to nobility, military orders, and town councils. Mosques and synagogues were demolished and rebuilt as churches, and the Inquisition (introduced in 1478), became the central instrument of Catholic and monarchical power.

Fernando and Isabel also expanded their overseas territories. Naples fell to their greatest general, Gonzalo Fernández de Córdoba (known as El Gran Capitán), and Christopher Columbus's pioneering voyage across the Atlantic began to reap rich rewards. Although gold was the chief attraction of the Americas, the conversion of native peoples to Christianity earned Fernando and Isabel the title of *los Reyes Católicos* (the Catholic Monarchs) from the Pope himself, a Spaniard of the Borgia family. Apart from this spiritual justification, the Spaniards were also aided by the Castilian language in their expansionism: It had been codified into Europe's first vernacular grammar and became the lingua franca of the Americas. As the conquistadores extended their New World net, indigenous peoples fell before them—prey to Old World diseases and to the sword.

Isabel's death in 1504 announced a completely new twist in Spanish history. Fernando reigned until his death in 1516, by which time his grandson, Carlos, was old enough to inherit the Crown. When Carlos I (R.1516–1556) arrived on Spanish soil in 1517, he faced a country wracked by

Americas—an unwieldy but unrivaled empire. His loyalties were divided, and regional *cortes* had to lobby intensely to obtain recognition and funds. Insurrections and revolts, notably those of the Castilian *comuneros* and Valencian and Mallorcan *agermanats* (brotherhoods), were brutally crushed by Carlos's German troops. He nonetheless dealt successfully with invasion by France, and his astute marriage to Isabel of Portugal brought further immense wealth to the Spanish Crown and an able replacement during his many absences abroad. Inevitably, the cost of his many wars mounted, so, weary of the worries of his vast empire, Carlos V abdicated in 1556 and retired to the monastery of Yuste, in Extremadura (see p. 249). He left a virtually bankrupt kingdom to his son.

Felipe II (Philip II, *R.*1556–1598), fanatically religious and highly cultivated, intensified the Inquisition's activities from his palace-monastery, El Escorial (see pp. 79–81). Protestants were killed in spectacular autos-da-fé (trial and execution ceremonies), and anyone "tainted" with Jewish blood was persecuted, as were moriscos. Felipe II won an important naval victory over the Turks in 1571, and in 1588 he sent the Invincible Armada to invade Protestant England. Instead the Spanish fleet suffered catastrophic losses, and lost international credibility.

Under Felipe III (*R.*1598–1621), the last 275,000 Moors were expelled from Valencia, a move that ruined local agriculture. This ruthlessness was echoed in Spain's New World activities, where indigenous populations were virtually wiped out by disease and slavery.

Inbreeding was a Habsburg habit, and as a result Felipe IV (*R.*1621–65) appeared only slightly more in control than his easily manipulated father. He was an astute patron of the arts, however. Despite his reformist tendencies, his reign saw increasing internal dissent, the loss of Portugal, and the defeats of the Thirty Years War, culminating in the independence of the Netherlands in 1648. Spain's loss of prestige was underlined in the reign of the last and most degenerate Habsburg king, Carlos II (*R.*1665–1700), whose 35-year rule saw further territorial losses. Spain became an economic wasteland: Once thriving and densely populated Castilla was a bankrupt

disastrous harvests, plague, and widespread social discontent. Speaking no Castilian, this Habsburg king was far from ready to manage the complex and disorderly society he had inherited. Yet a new era had begun.

HABSBURGS & THE GOLDEN AGE
The Habsburg dynasty ruled Spain for nearly 200 years. Their monarchs presided over the arrival of untold amounts of bullion from the Americas, and ruled Europe's largest empire since that of Charlemagne, but the term "Golden Age" is questionable. Culturally Spain prospered, producing an impressive line of Renaissance artists and dramatists. Politically, however, it was another story. Two years after acceding to the Spanish throne, Carlos inherited the Holy Roman Empire through his father. As Carlos V (Charles V), he ruled a large part of northern Europe (the modern Netherlands, Belgium, Austria, and part of Germany), in addition to Spain and the

desert. The only element still to prosper was the Church, and the heavily gilded baroque altarpieces of the time bear witness to its immense wealth.

WAR OF SPANISH SUCCESSION

Carlos II died childless, but he had appointed an heir: Philippe Bourbon, grandson of his sister María Teresa and the French king Louis XIV. Once again, Spain was faced with a foreign ruler, and in 1701 this French 17-year-old entered Madrid as Felipe V. However northern Europe and England supported his rival, the Austrian Archduke Charles, and joined Catalunya, Aragón, and Valencia in the 12-year-long War of Succession. England eventually accepted the Bourbon king when it was given the territorial concessions of Gibraltar (still a thorny point in Anglo-Spanish relations) and Menorca. Stimulated by childhood memories of Versailles, Felipe V (R.1701–1746) spent much of his long reign building sumptuous French-style palaces, a habit continued by more enlightened Carlos III (R.1759–1788).

Other than reveling in baroque artistry, Carlos III continued a centralizing tendency instigated by Felipe V. Steadily, Spain was regaining its lost prosperity, agriculture was recovering, coastal trading companies thrived, and the population expanded. A significant economic move was the Free Trade Act (1778) for the American colonies. Although bread riots ignited Spain in the 1760s, Carlos III found a scapegoat in the Jesuits, who were expelled in 1766. His great love for the arts was expressed by the building of the Prado Museum (see pp. 62–67), Palacio Real (see pp. 56–57), and San Ildefonso de la Granja (see p. 226), near Segovia, monuments to the final moments of an all-powerful monarchy.

WAR OF SPANISH INDEPENDENCE

Weak and indifferent Carlos IV (R.1788–1808) left governing to his wife, María Luisa, and her adviser Don Manuel Godoy. Spain soon found itself enmeshed in the aftermath of the French Revolution. Catapulted into war with Britain, France's arch rival, Spain tumbled into defeat at the Battle of Trafalgar (1805). On land, however, Napoleon was carrying the day. In 1808 he engineered the abdication of Carlos IV, and put his own brother Joseph (José I) on the throne. By now the people of Spain had had enough, and the Madrid uprising of May 2 was the spark that ignited Spain's five-year War of Independence against Napoleon.

The War of Independence produced Spain's first popular united front against a common enemy. Peasant guerrilla fighters played a major role, fragmenting the Napoleonic armies and their supply systems. Guerrillas also cooperated with Spain's former enemies, the British, led by the Duke of Wellington, whose many victories culminated in the Battle of Vitoria in 1813. As a result, José I fled back to France (taking with him considerable artistic booty). Church properties had been heavily targeted, and Spain's infrastructure lay in ruins, devastated by both French and British troops.

CARLIST WARS

In 1812 the cortes of Cádiz had worked out a new, liberal constitution, the Constitution of Cádiz, investing power in a democratically elected chamber. This was soon canceled when despotic Fernando VII (son of Carlos IV) took the throne. As Spain sank yet again under the whims of its king, its American colonies won independence. In 1820 the Constitution of Cádiz was temporarily revived, but a massive French army came to help the king suppress it. On his death in 1833, civil war broke out (the First Carlist War) between supporters of his conservative brother, Carlos, and the liberal promoters of his young daughter, the Infanta Isabel. Isabel's camp won, but her reign (1843–1868) was a troubled one, plagued by successive crises, including the Second Carlist War. In 1874, with Isabel's son Alfonso XII in the driver's seat, the army was assuming increasing power. As a result, Spain's oppressed workers began to organize themselves into trade unions. This was the germination of social conflicts that, around 60 years later, resulted in the rule of the dictator, General Franco.

SOCIAL TRANSFORMATIONS

In the late 19th century and early 20th century, Spain experienced a period of relative calm and prosperity. Yet in 1898 its last

The British fleet's triumph at the 1805 Battle of Trafalgar ran parallel to Napoleon's victories on land, leaving Spain caught between the two rival powers.

overseas possessions were lost to the United States, notably the Philippines and Cuba, and famines and disease wracked the south. Huge numbers emigrated: 1.5 million moved to Latin America between 1886 and 1913. The demographic face of the country was changing with a drift to the cities, although Catalunya, Euskadi, and Asturias were the only truly industrialized regions. Ideological differences became more marked, as did regional variations in wealth, and more than half the population was illiterate. Although the 20th century started with a dazzling cultural renaissance, this was limited to a tiny section of society—the majority languished in poverty.

Barcelona had seen workers' unrest in the mid-19th century, and by the 1880s both Andalucía and Castilla were home to widespread anarchist movements. Marxist-Socialism made advances in Madrid, where the PSOE (Socialist party) was born in 1888. After winning its first parliamentary seat in 1910, it widened its membership in the industrialized north. During World War I Spain remained neutral, and its industry profited for a while from exports to both sides, but in 1917 recession and a draining war in Morocco helped fuel a momentous general strike, which was violently repressed. In 1923 further social unrest caused General Miguel Primo de Rivera to stage a military coup, in cooperation with the king. This led to a military dictatorship until world depression precipitated the general's resignation in 1930. Within two years, anti-monarchist forces won a resounding success in municipal elections, and hapless Alfonso XIII went into exile.

SECOND REPUBLIC & CIVIL WAR

Euphoria greeted the establishment of the
Second Republic on April 14, 1931. At last,
Spain was falling into step with democratic
movements elsewhere. A new Republican
government led by Manuel Azaña soon
introduced land reform and civil marriage
among other sweeping changes, but political
loyalties were becoming dangerously polar-
ized between extreme Republicanism and
extreme conservatism. The Church, army, and
landowners still wielded enormous economic
power. As Socialists, Anarchists, Radicals, and
Marxists bickered among themselves, their
opponents became organized around the
Falange, a youth movement founded by José
Antonio Primo de Rivera (son of the dictator).
Elections in 1933 gave power to the Right—
including the Falange and the Monarchists—
who revealed their true nature the following
year in the bloody suppression of a miners'
strike in Asturias.

**Decades of social unrest, unionization, and
political movements preceded the tragic
hostilities of Spain's civil war that broke
out in 1936.**

By 1936, Spain was spiraling into chaos
with almost daily assassinations, riots, militia
attacks on churches, strikes, and seizures of
estates. When victory in the election was won
by the leftist Popular Front, it took only five
months for the army's response. In July 1936,
the troops of General Francisco Franco were
airlifted from their garrisons in Morocco by
German transport planes and dropped into
Spain. The Civil War had begun.

Spain's Civil War was the bloodiest, most
tragic period that the country ever lived
through, dividing families, devastating the
countryside, ruining the infrastructure, and
leaving half a million dead and millions
starving. Helped by Moroccan mercenaries,
Franco's Nationalist army rapidly won control

Communists within the Republican ranks. All this contributed to the capitulation of the north, and when Franco's offensive in southern Aragón reached the Mediterranean, the Republican forces in the east were divided in two. In early 1939 Barcelona fell, finally followed by Madrid and Valencia. The game was over, and the Generalísimo took up the reins of power on April 1.

GENERAL FRANCO

Social order and uncontested political authority were the priorities of Spain's new ruler. Franco used firing squads, labor camps, and civic ostracism to quell opposition, and the old adage of "convert or be exiled," used against Jews and Moors centuries before, was now reapplied to other sectors. Many intellectuals fled, about 7,000 teachers were executed, and schoolbooks were rewritten. At the end of World War II, during which Spain remained neutral, Franco was the only Fascist dictator left, ruling over a politically and economically isolated country. Any opposition was stamped upon, censorship was enforced, and the powers of the Catholic church were restored. Divorce became illegal, church weddings were obligatory, and the confessor was invoked as the ultimate adviser in reading matter.

Change came in the 1950s, when Franco received General Eisenhower and agreed to host American military bases in exchange for massive loans. This opened the floodgates, propelling Spain to the forefront of economic growth and into world institutions such as the United Nations (1955), so ending its former isolation. Franco invested in roads, electricity plants, apartment blocks for workers, and other infrastructure. Mass tourism arrived and a booming market economy developed, steered by a new breed of technocrats. Yet Spain's increased prosperity had a flipside: Andalusian peasants worked in miserable conditions, workers continued to flood from the land to the cities and abroad, and political and intellectual repression continued, above all in Catalunya and the País Vasco. Clandestine groups and unions worked behind the scenes, and the Basque separatist group Euskadi Ta Askatasuna (ETA) emerged. In 1973 Franco's expected successor, Admiral Carrero Blanco, was blown sky-high by an ETA bomb.

of eastern Andalucía, Extremadura, and Castilla, but it was rebuffed by Madrid, the east, and the north, where Republican sympathies and forces were strongest. Proclaimed Generalísimo of the armed forces and head of state in Burgos, a city with well-entrenched conservative traditions, Franco soon received massive assistance from his Fascist allies in Europe—Germany, Italy, and Portugal. Meanwhile the Republicans received help only from the Soviet Union. Governments of western democracies such as Britain and France did nothing, although about 35,000 foreign volunteers, including George Orwell, Ernest Hemingway, André Malraux, and Willy Brandt, fought for the Republicans with the International Brigade. The Republicans could not compete with the size and resources of the opposing forces, epitomized by the merciless bombing of Gernika (Guernica) by German planes in 1937. Self-destructive rivalries also existed between Anarchists and

AFTER FRANCO

Franco, the wily old *Caudillo* (Chief), hung on for 40 years. When he died in 1975, a grandson of Alfonso XIII was crowned King Juan Carlos I. Franco had chosen him as successor partly because he thought that Juan Carlos was a malleable character. In this he was wrong, and the new king rapidly set about restoring democ-

Community in 1986. European subsidies improved the infrastructure and transformed the country. In 1992 (500 years after Columbus first set foot in the New World), the Olympics were held in Barcelona, Seville hosted Expo 92, and Madrid was designated cultural capital of Europe. Spain's fortunes seemed to be on a roll.

racy through his able Prime Minister, Adolfo Suárez. Political parties and trade unions were recognized, censorship was lifted, and the 1977 elections brought Suárez and his Christian-Democrat party to power. With a new, ultra-liberal Constitution, parliament set about undoing the knots of Castilian centralism and granting autonomy to the regions.

In 1981, the new government survived an attempted military coup thanks to Juan Carlos's firm stand. The following year, Spain entered a new era with the electoral victory of the PSOE (Socialist Party). This brought the youthful and charismatic Felipe González to power and initiated a frenetically optimistic period when anything and everything seemed possible. Advances on every level brought stability, pride, and dynamism, crowned by Spain's entry into the European Economic

An anti-fascist propaganda poster from the civil war of 1936–39

A youthful King Juan Carlos I and Queen Sofía toured Andalucía in 1976, just one year after General Franco's death.

Nothing and nobody is perfect, however, and corruption finally brought down the Socialist government after 14 years in power. José María Aznar's Partido Popular (a merging of center-right parties) was elected in 1996 and survived two terms until the tragic Madrid train bombs of March 11, 2004. Elections held three days later brought a massive unexpected rejection of Aznar's pro-Gulf War policies and autocratic attitude. He was out, and in came José Luis Rodriguez Zapatero, the new Socialist Prime Minister, who rapidly withdrew Spanish troops from Iraq. Spain still has hurdles to overcome: endemic corruption, ETA terrorism, and the more global credit squeeze. Yet it has gained a high standard of living, cultural dynamism, slick city centers, and a viable federal system. Spain has traversed light years in just a few decades. ■

The arts

SPAIN'S ART HISTORY GOES BACK TO THE EARLY STONE AGE WHEN HUNTERS
started painting on the walls of their caves, but it was during the second millennium A.D.
that a truly Hispanic style of art emerged. Among Spain's long roll call of great artists are
Velázquez, Goya, Zurbarán, and Picasso. Architecture and film are the other major fields
of Spanish creative genius.

PAINTING, SCULPTURE, & ARCHITECTURE

The earliest manifestations of Spanish art are
mysterious, but probably had a ritualistic role
for the Paleolithic hunter-gatherers who
painted polychrome bison, wild boars, wolves,
horses, and deer with amazing anatomical precision on the walls of their Cantabrian caves.
These cave paintings, notably at Altamira, date
from 15,000 to 8500 B.C. Later prehistoric art
takes the form of copper idol plaques from
the fortified settlement of Los Millares, near
Almería. Spain's oldest constructions are
the megaliths (huge stone monuments)
of the Balearics and the dolmens (stone
tombs) of Antequera (circa 2500 B.C.).

Iberian art

The growth of gold, silver, lead, and tin mines
in the Andalusian kingdom of Tartessos, and
the subsequent arrival of Phoenician and Greek
traders, sparked the next stage in the peninsula's iconography. Sculpture (carved limestone
and bronze figurines) is the only relic of the
Iberian civilization in central and southern
Spain, as the Punic Wars between Carthage and
Rome devastated most architectural structures.
The most outstanding work of art from those
centuries is the Dama de Elche (sixth–fifth
century B.C.), a beautiful bust of a serene,
bejeweled lady. Important ceramics, too, have
survived the ravages of time. Although influenced by the Greeks, Iberians found their own
inventive style of abstract, zoomorphic, or
anthropomorphic designs painted on crudely
shaped vessels. In the north, Celtiberians produced the magnificent gold jewelry unearthed
in Galicia's *castros* (fortified villages).

Roman classicism

Five hundred years of Roman rule steered
Hispanic art and architecture into an entirely
new phase. Urban design was paramount.

Towns centered on the forum (marketplace),
around which stood the theater, amphitheater,
and temples. The elite lived in magnificently
decorated villas where mosaic panels, marble
colonnades, and statues created dramatic back-
drops for society. Busts of emperors, magis-
trates, and governors reflected a taste for
realism rather than stylization. At this period
in history, Spain was unique in Europe:

Nowhere else had such a wealth of distinctive cultures contributed to artistic development.

Visigoths

Christianity was the next major ingredient in the Hispanic mix. From the fifth century A.D., the Visigoths introduced their nomadic Scandinavian culture, while southern Spain underwent a century of Byzantine domination (522–621). Outstanding Visigothic craftsmanship is seen in gold- and silverwork of royal crowns and offerings in dignitaries' tombs.

Otherwise all that remains of their 300-year presence in the peninsula is the embryonic

Prehistoric paintings of animals and hunters cover the walls of the Tito Bustillo caves at Ribadesella.

structures of Christianity: The seventh-century hermitage of Quintanilla de las Viñas in northern Castilla has primitive, schematized reliefs in carved friezes, and capitals salvaged elsewhere show stylized figures and birds beside floral motifs. This was a far cry from the classical realism of the Romans, and decorative abstraction continued to dominate Spanish art until the flowering of the Romanesque period.

Pre-Romanesque architecture in Asturias, the only kingdom not conquered by the Muslim invaders, represents a more sophisticated bridging period before the Romanesque style was imported from France. Soaring barrel vaults, horseshoe arches, ashlar (square-cut stone facings), and illusionist murals were developed in a wide network of extraordinary, lavish churches.

Moorish style

Andalucía, above all, fell under the most concentrated Islamic influence (see pp. 268–69). Fortresses (*alcazabas*), palaces (*alcázares*), and mosques (*mezquitas*) became the landmarks of al-Andalus, culminating in Granada's dream-like Alhambra (see pp. 300–305), which so perfectly catered to all the senses. Earlier Islamic legacies date from 8th- to 11th-century Córdoba. The Mezquita (Great Mosque, see pp. 288–89), representing paradise and the holy city, and the Medina Azahara (the caliph's palace, see p. 291) incorporated calligraphic stucco friezes, geometric patterns of brick, stone and marble, and intricately intertwined plant motifs. Since Islam forbade representation of humans, craftsmen channeled all their imaginative effort into

Colorful tiled walls surmounted by intricately carved stucco friezes are typical of the Moorish decorative style. These belong to the Alhambra in Granada.

these extensive and finely executed embellishments (although the rules were sometimes bent—even human figures appear in the decoration of the Medina Azahara).

Horseshoe arches, cupolas, blind arches, tracery, and *artesonado* (intricately carved ceilings) were the most lasting structural elements, but art evolved considerably during the 700-year Moorish occupation. An early taste for decorative details came from Syria. The later Almoravids and Almohads were more conservative but nonetheless introduced multicolored *azulejos* (tiles) and the intricacies

brought Arab techniques and forms with them. Even after Moorish territories had been conquered and their mosques demolished, talented Moorish artisans continued to work for Christian masters. This was the origin of the Mudejar style, whose enduring influence on Hispanic art cannot be overestimated. Among its creations were Aragón's intricate brick and ceramic towers, Sevilla's Reales Alcázares (see pp. 266–67)—an indulgence of carved wood, stucco, and tilework—and the Gothic Mudejar of Toledo's towers and churches. Synagogues, too, were designed by Mudejar craftsmen, and the three that survive in Toledo and Córdoba are a unique conjunction of Hebrew calligraphy with Arab artistry. Mudejar was a profusely decorative style, and from it emerged an aversion to unadorned space that dominated Spanish art for the following centuries. In architecture, Mudejar forms continued in bullrings and railway stations right up to the beginning of the 20th century.

Romanesque

While the Moors were covering walls and arches in stucco and azulejos, Christian Spain was building its own masterpieces in the north: Romanesque structures designed to inspire every pilgrim who set foot on the long road to Santiago de Compostela (see pp. 90–93). From the mid-11th century, French and Italian religious orders set up monasteries and churches, and their artistic forms soon dominated northern Spain. Yet Spain, as usual, distinguished itself from the rest of Europe, as Visigothic, Pre-Romanesque, and Moorish influences all played their role. In Catalunya, the Lombards from Italy were another influence, introducing sobriety of form and lofty bell towers.

The cathedral of Santiago de Compostela (see pp. 90–93) retains its original Romanesque soaring nave, superb reliefs on the Puerta de las Platerías (circa 1100), and, above all, the sculptor Mateo's Romanesque masterpiece, the complex, high-relief statues of the Pórtico de la Gloria (1188). A few years earlier, an equally magnificent portal was created at the Catalan monastery of Ripoll as a visual bible for the illiterate. This teaching-through-pictures produced beautifully decorated capitals, cloisters, and portals: Wonderful examples exist in Girona, Santo Domingo de los Silos,

of artesonado. Palaces and houses were built around patios (courtyards), an intelligent response to the climate that continues today: Wealthier families escape the heat by living on the lower floors in the summer, and then they move to the upstairs in winter to catch all the available sun. Palace gardens had water and fragrant flowers and plants. In all this, the Alhambra represents the zenith of Moorish style, combining unparalleled decorative mastery with perspective and sensuality.

Mozarabic & Mudejar

As the Christians of the north extended their territory south during the period of the Reconquest (see pp. 28–31), their taste was influenced by Mozarabic emigrants—Christians who had lived under Arab rule and who

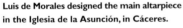

Luis de Morales designed the main altarpiece in the Iglesia de la Asunción, in Cáceres.

Tarragona, San Juan de la Peña, Sangüesa, Leyre, and Santillana del Mar. Altar sculpture was carved in wood and painted, a tradition that endures in the highly realist *pasos* (floats) of Holy Week processions (see pp. 272–73).

Other forms of Spanish Romanesque art are altarpieces and the dynamic, richly colored frescoes in churches such as San Isidoro in León. Examples from Catalunya's remote parish churches are shown in the museums of Barcelona, Vic, and Jaca. Change came when reforming Cistercian monks brought a taste for austerity, and an end to richly carved capitals and portals groaning with apostles. Instead huge monastic complexes devoted to prayer

and work arose, such as Poblet (see pp. 191–92), Santes Creus (see p. 192), and Santa María de Huerta (see p. 151). Secular constructions of the time are the frontier castles of Castilla and towns with narrow winding streets, such as Besalú.

Gothic

By the 13th century, the Gothic was making inroads. This was not just an artistic fashion, but represented a new perception of life in which spirituality and culture were transferred from monastic complexes to medieval cities centered on their cathedrals. The three naves of the Romanesque period became one, and the use of stronger pointed arches rather than round ones meant that walls could rise to increasingly lofty ceilings and domes. Many cathedrals bridged these two major medieval

styles, but the undisputed stars are the 13th-century cathedrals of León, Burgos, and Toledo, which has a marked Moorish influence.

By the following century the building craze had shifted eastward, producing the great cathedrals of Barcelona, Girona, Palma de Mallorca, and Valencia. As the 14th century gave way to the 15th, Gothic architecture acquired the flowery ornamentation known as Flamboyant Gothic. Two main schools developed. The first, in Toledo, was headed by Juan Guas, who designed San Juan de los Reyes. The second, in Burgos, was led by Juan de Colonia and his son, Simón, who was responsible for the lace-like facade of San Pablo in Valladolid. These examples of the Isabelline style crowned the 15th century, combining the height of Flamboyant Gothic with early Renaissance elements.

The *botafumeiro* dispenses incense in the cathedral of Santiago de Compostela.

Sculpture and painting came into their own, their practitioners regarded as fully fledged artists instead of mere artisans. Major influences were absorbed from Italy and France, but by the late 15th century Spanish art had fallen under the sway of Flemish naturalism, a style of remarkably expressive precision. The Catalan Jaume Huguet (circa 1415–1492) was one of its greatest exponents. In sculpture, Gil de Siloé and Pere Joan respectively led the Castilian and Aragonese schools. *Retablos* (altarpieces) became towering painted panels with bas-reliefs, wooden sculptures, and heavily gilded frames—Spain's were the most elaborate of their kind in Europe.

"San Hugo en el Refectorio de los Cartujos" (1633) by Francisco de Zurbarán

Renaissance

When the Reconquest (see pp. 28–31) was complete, the door was definitively closed on medieval Spain and opened to a new philosophy of life—the Renaissance. Scientific discovery and voyages to the New World transformed ideas, and people turned to the classical ideals of ancient Greece and Rome for inspiration. Early Spanish Renaissance architecture, known as plateresque (meaning "resembling silversmith's work"), has delicate, filigree-like reliefs, best exemplified in Salamanca's superb university facade and Toledo's Santa Cruz hospice. Although related to the Isabelline style, plateresque makes greater use of Renaissance elements from Italy, such as gargoyles, pilasters, and medal-

lions. Diego de Siloé in Burgos, Alonso de Covarrubias of Toledo, and Gil de Hontañón in Salamanca represented a transition to the more restrained Renaissance style that emerged in the 1520s, crowned by Pedro Machuca's palace of Carlos V (1526) in Granada, the purest Italianate building in Spain. In the reconquered lands Renaissance mansions mushroomed, with large concentrations in Úbeda and Baeza.

The Italian aesthetic also came to dominate painting and sculpture. Pedro Berruguete (1450–1504), Juan de Borgoña (1470–1536), and Juan de Juanes (much influenced by Raphael) led the field in painting. In sculpture prolific Damián Forment (circa 1480–1540) bridged the Isabelline-Renaissance period with spectacular altarpieces. Alonso de Berruguete's obsession with dramatic realism anticipated the Baroque period, as did the

Valladolid-based Frenchman, Juan de Juni (died 1577). One great difference between Italian and Spanish art of the Renaissance stems from simple economics. The Inquisition imposed a 10 percent tax on any work that did not contain a religious message, which partly explains the preponderance of saintly and monastic subjects in Spanish art before 1783.

By the late 16th century, Felipe II's patronage of the arts had brought many Italian and Flemish artists to Spain, and (despite the Inquisition) portraiture was becoming established. Domenikos Theotokopoulos, or El Greco—The Greek—arrived in Spain in 1577. His free brushstrokes did not meet with royal approval, forcing him to retreat to Toledo to work on ecclesiastical commissions. Architecture was dominated by Juan de Herrera (1530–97), whose austere masterpiece, El Escorial (see pp. 79–81), foreshadowed the next century.

Baroque & the Golden Age

The 17th century saw a profusion of civic building, such as Madrid's Plaza Mayor, but it took several decades for Spain to shake off Herreran influence and embrace baroque. Exuberant Spanish baroque architecture (Churrigueresque) was named after José de Churriguera (1665–1725) and his brothers, Joaquín and Alberto, although another major protagonist was Pedro de Ribera (1683–1742). Andalucía has abundant Churrigueresque works, because it was the arrival point for the riches of the New World. During this Golden Age of Spanish art, the Granadino architect, sculptor, and painter Alonso Cano laid the foundation for a new school of three-dimensional work. His pupil Pedro de Mena (1628–1688) created that period's most emotionally expressive sculptures, and in Castilla, Gregorio Hernández (1566–1636) became the master of depicting pain and sorrow. Baroque gilding, salomonic columns (twisted and entwined), and inverted pilasters were created in a climax of creative delirium, fueled by the profits and optimism of the New World.

The greatest genius of the Golden Age was the painter Diego Velázquez (1599–1660), who emerged from the Sevillian school of Francisco Pacheco (1564–1654). After being appointed court painter by Felipe IV in Madrid, where he also met Peter Paul Rubens

(1577–1640), he made two significant trips to Italy. From still lifes and genre paintings his work matured into courtly portraits and royal themes, before reaching its apogee with Las Meninas (The Maids of Honor) and Las Hilanderas (The Spinners). Master of optical illusions, color, and subtle psychological insights, Velázquez shared the limelight with his contemporaries the Extremaduran Francisco Zurbarán (1598–1664), and the Valencians Francisco Ribalta (1565–1628) and José de Ribera (1591–1652). Ribalta introduced tenebrism (contrasting light and shadow) to Spain, and Ribera took powerful realism to his adopted Naples. Zurbarán's portraits of monks are unsurpassed in their sobriety of composition, compelling the spectator to focus on the subjects' spiritual passion and personality. Sevilla's other great baroque painters were Juan Valdés Leal (1622–1690) and Bartolomé Esteban Murillo (1617–1682), who respectively produced images of the vanity of the world and diaphanous renderings of beatific Virgins surrounded by cherubim.

18th & 19th centuries

Excessive ornamentation characterized the French rococo style that dominated the early 18th century, visible in the palaces of the new Bourbon kings at La Granja, Aranjuez, and Madrid. Decorative arts (porcelain, tapestries, and glass) were fostered in royal factories and workshops. Inevitably, reaction set in. Reason, order, and moderation soon became the ideals of the newly established Academia de Bellas Artes (1752), ushering in the more controlled neoclassic period. In architecture, this was exemplified by Ventura Rodríguez and by Juan de Villanueva, who designed the Prado. In painting, after a period of cold, elegant portraiture, it was Francisco de Goya (1746–1828) who was to make a lasting impact. Rebelling against neoclassic constraints, he developed a style of expressive brushstrokes to depict character and emotions in earthy tones, whether in his series of "black paintings" stemming from personal depression, or in his vivid portraits and political commentaries.

Once the 19th century was in full swing, Goya's influence became apparent as the cult of reason was replaced by the notion of human freedom. With the secular replacing

the religious, a stream of academic painters embraced the melodrama of Romanticism, producing scenes from Spanish history and *costumbrismo* (depiction of local life and customs). It was only by the start of the 20th century that Spain was belatedly noticing French Impressionism.

20th-century modernism

The barriers of conservatism were finally shattered by Catalunya's *Modernista* movement, led by Antoni Gaudí (see pp. 172–75), Lluís Domènech i Montaner, his son Pere Domènech, Josep Maria Jujol, and Juan Martorell. Together they turned architectural tradition on its head with organically inspired structures, extensive use of decorative brickwork, and design "follies." This was Spain's answer to art nouveau.

Spain was resistant to the revolution in art (modernism) that was sweeping Europe, despite being the source of some of its greatest protagonists. Pablo Picasso (1881–1973), a native of Málaga, but brought up in Barcelona before moving to Paris, was unquestionably the figurehead, and in later years he used early Spanish art as inspiration. Another Spanish cubist, Juan Gris (1887–1927) worked with Picasso in Paris. Joan Miró (1893–1983) remained faithful to Catalunya and Mallorca, despite international acclaim for his spontaneous, poetic abstraction. This derived from experiments with surrealism, but the latter movement's most colorful Hispanic representative was Salvador Dalí (see pp. 184–85). In both life and artifice, Dalí perfectly exemplified surrealism's obsession with the irrational. In contrast, sculptors such as Pablo Gargallo, Alberto Sánchez, and Julio González excelled in a more sober, abstract field.

For two decades after World War II, abstract expressionism dominated art in Spain. By the more prosperous 1960s, this was led by a rebellious artists' collective known as El Paso, out of which emerged the powerful gestural works of Antonio Saura and the highly influential canvasses of Antoni Tàpies. Subtle color, geometric symbols, and the incorporation of other media (sand, wax) became the hallmarks of the Tàpies school.

The Nativitat facade of Gaudí's Sagrada Família, in Barcelona, remains unfinished.

Its counterpoint was the pop art of Equipo Crónica and the bold narratives of Eduardo Arroyo. Bridging the two was the work of Tàpies's cousin Modest Cuixart (1925–2007). The late Eduardo Chillida's purist geometrical sculptures became virtually the "official" art of his native Basque country. Today the Mallorcan Miguel Barceló produces imagina-

Pablo Picasso in his studio circa 1920

tive, mixed-media paintings that combine African references with metaphysical concerns. Susana Solano, José María Sicilia, Jaume Plensa, Juan Uslé, and Juan Muñoz have all acquired international profiles, and conceptual work flourishes among younger artists such as Txomin Badiola and Cristina Iglesias.

In architecture, style nose-dived during the Franco era, but reemerged with Josep Luis Sert's modernist homages to Balearic antecedents and with Ricardo Bofill's 1980s postmodernism. At the start of the 21st century, Santiago Calatrava is feted for gravity-defying feats of engineering and many of Valencia's showcase structures, while Pritzker Prize-winner Rafael Moneo is the creator of sensitive, functional,

Gypsy family gatherings in Andalucía inevitably break into spontaneous flamenco.

streamlined buildings that are the perfect symbols of this Spanish renaissance.

MUSIC

Perceived as the quintessential music of Spain, flamenco (see pp. 294–95), in fact, has Gypsy, Arab, and Jewish roots. Before this, Spanish music evolved from polyphonic chants of the early Middle Ages, and reached a high point during the Renaissance, when instruments such as the guitar *(vihuela,* with five strings rather than the modern six) proliferated. Spanish musicians also incorporated tonalities and instruments such as the lute, oboe, and tambourine from the Moors. This distinctive style faded as northern European music became more influential, but a present-day group of musicians called Mudéjar have resurrected its unique sounds and instruments. For centuries, the main forms of homegrown music remained popular ballads and the *zarzuela,* a form of musical play invented by Pedro Calderón de la Barca in the 17th century. However, Spanish music rebounded under the aegis of composers such as Isaac Albeñiz (1860–1909) and Enrique Granados (1867–1916). Manuel de Falla (1876–1946) represented the psychological duality of Spain with *Nights in the Gardens of Spain:* introspection punctuated by violent outbursts. A still more popular classic is Joaquín Rodrigo's (1901–1999) *Concierto de Aranjuez.*

Spain has produced some of the world's

region. One big exception is Manu Chao, a musical revolutionary whose first solo album, *Clandestino* (1998) sold 5 million copies worldwide.

THEATER & LITERATURE

Early playwrights Lope de Vega (1562–1635) and Calderón de la Barca (1600–1681) brilliantly mirrored the exploits and optimism of Spain's Golden Age, and Miguel de Cervantes created its universal protagonist, Don Quixote (see pp. 238–39). In theater, Catalunya has always led the way: Barcelona's Teatre Principal was founded in 1603, and Frederic Soler created modern Catalan theater. An extreme participative form has been perfected by the 1980s Catalan company Fura dels Baus. Theater director Calixto Bieito is known for controversial interpretations of classic operas.

On a more contemplative note, Santa Teresa de Ávila (1515–1582) and Ignatius Loyola (1491–1556, the founder of the Jesuits) wrote mystic works about their spiritual quests. The 19th century saw Spanish literature evolving into the realism and satire of Pedro de Alarcón, Leopoldo Alas, and Benito Pérez Galdós. Galdós's epic *Torquemada* has been compared with the work of Balzac for its social realism and comment. Modern Spanish literature began at the end of the 19th century, when Spain's humiliation by the United States (see p. 35) led a group of intellectuals to explore the identity. This was the Generation of '98, spearheaded by philosopher-essayists Miguel de Unamuno (1864–1936) and José Ortega y Gasset (1883– 1955). The following generation included the great poet Federico García Lorca (1898–1936) and Vicente Aleixandre (1898–1984), who was awarded the Nobel Prize for Literature in 1977. In the late 20th century, new registers of irony, drama, and psychology made up for 40 years of Francoist taboos and repression. Writers to look out for today are Nobel Prize-winner Camilo José Cela, Javier Marías (and his trilogy *Your Face Tomorrow*), Eduardo Mendoza *(City of Prodigies)*, the thrillers of Juan Madrid, the intellectual fireworks of Juan Goytisolo, Javier Cercas on the Civil War *(Soldiers of Salamis)*, and the bestselling author Almudena Grandes whose tomes explore contemporary life. Altogether it is an inspiring spectrum.

top guitar-players, including the classical performer Andrés Segovia and the flamenco artists Paco Peña and Paco de Lucía. The late Pablo Casals took cello playing to its zenith. Many world renowned opera singers are Spanish: Plácido Domingo, José Carreras, Teresa Braganza, Victoria de los Ángeles, Alfredo Kraus, and Montserrat Caballé. On a lighter note, Julio Iglesias and his son, Enrique, have become household names. Spain has yet to produce rock bands of international standing, although flamenco-rock booms (see pp. 294–95), and Galician-Celtic groups are popular. Lack of world status is due more to undeveloped marketing than to absence of talent. Any fiesta is proof of this, and record shops devote large sections to local musicians, categorized, as always, by

Oscar-winning filmmaker Pedro Almodóvar at the Reina Sofia Museum in Madrid (2007)

FILM

Spanish cinema saw its international genesis in two surrealist films by Luis Buñuel and Salvador Dalí, *Un chien Andalou* (1928) and *L'Age d'Or* (1930). Both are known better by their French titles than their Spanish ones, as they were filmed in Paris. With the glorious 1930s, when cinema excelled elsewhere, Spain had dived into a morass of sociopolitical upheaval, followed by decades of Franco's censorship.

However a defiant new wave emerged in the 1950s and '60s. Luis García Berlanga (*Bienvenido, Mr. Marshall,* 1953, and *El Verdugo,* 1964), Juan Bardem (*Muerte de un Ciclista,* 1955), and Carlos Saura (*Los Golfos,* 1959, and *Cría Cuervos,* 1975) created films that artfully sidestepped censorship while maintaining integrity of vision. Buñuel, meanwhile, gravitated between Mexico, Hollywood, and France, writing and directing a succession of masterpieces, including *Viridiana* (1961), which was shot in Spain but also banned there, *The Exterminating Angel* (1962), *Belle de Jour* (1967), and the Oscar-winning *Discreet Charm of the Bourgeoisie* (1972). His eventful life covered the rise, fall, and incipient renewal of the Spanish film industry (he died in 1983).

The next generation of filmmakers includes Oscar-winner Fernando Trueba (*Belle Époque,* 1992, which propelled Penélope Cruz into the spotlight, and *Two Much,* 1995, with heartthrob Antonio Banderas and Melanie Griffith) and Juan Bigas Luna, whose outrageous *Jamón, Jamón* (1992) captivated audiences all over the world. Alejandro Amenabar (*Tesis,* 1995, *Open Your Eyes,* 1997, and *The Sea Inside,* 2004) and Isabel Coixet (*My Life Without Me,* 2003, *The Secret Life of Words,* 2005) represent a younger wave.

However, if one person encapsulates the new Spain it is Pedro Almodóvar, who once declared, "In my own village…the Middle Ages lasted until World War I." Born in 1949 in La Mancha, he emerged when a new spirit was sweeping Madrid. From his first international box-office hit, *Women on the Verge of a Nervous Breakdown* (1988), he projected a quirky, frenetic, multicolor image of Spain onto world screens. His actors Victoria Abril, Carmen Maura, and Antonio Banderas shot to fame, while Almodóvar compounded his success with Oscar-winning *All About My Mother* (1999). Each film is a clever concoction of tragicomedy and high-decibel excess. *Talk to Her* (2002) signalled a more mature, realist approach and gained Almodóvar another Oscar. *Volver* (2006) showcased once again the voluptuous Penélope Cruz. ■

The sizzling nightlife of Madrid is counterbalanced by museums and art collections that create a visual marathon through some of the world's greatest paintings. It is also a city of gastronomic indulgence, good music, and fashion.

In & around Madrid

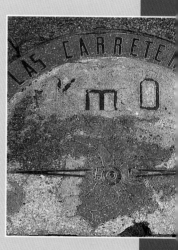

Kilometer Zero (the point from which all distances in Spain are measured) in Puerta del Sol, Madrid

Madrid

SPRAWLING OVER THE MESETA, THE PLATEAU OF CENTRAL SPAIN, MADRID is perfectly placed to play its coordinating role for the nation's 18 autonomous regions. It does not have a lengthy past—it has been Spain's capital only since 1561, when Felipe II moved his court from Toledo. In March 2004 it shot into the world psyche following the devastating train bombings of the Atocha railway station by Islamic extremists.

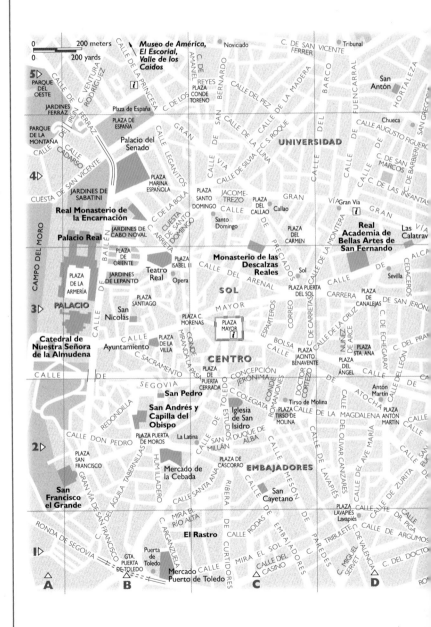

Madrid's cultural identity soars partly thanks to ambitious cultural projects along the Paseo del Arte—the "museum mile." It also is cosmopolitan, with wonderful food, fashion, and nightlife. Add numerous hotels and an excellent transportation system, and you have the ingredients for a very pleasant stay. This is Europe's highest capital at 2,120 feet (646 m), and its climate is

Madrid's emblematic bear and strawberry tree

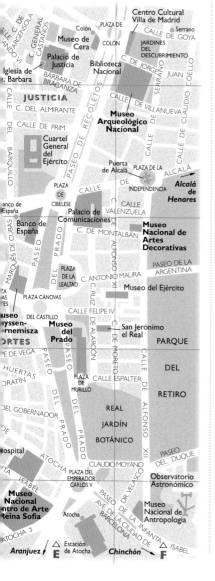

best in spring or autumn. In winter, Madrid suffers from bitter winds straight off the Sierra de Guadarrama; in summer, it is scorchingly hot.

More than anything else, Madrid takes you on a voyage through the history of art. Its oldest treasures are at the Museo Arqueológico, but the finest are at the recently expanded Prado, which has 8,600 paintings from the Middle Ages to the 19th century. The Thyssen-Bornemisza covers the same period into the 20th century, and the Reina Sofía is the most contemporary collection—perhaps to be challenged by Fundación Caja Madrid and the Conde Duque, both still in the pipeline. The latter is another groundbreaking design by the Swiss duo, Herzog & De Meuron. Smaller collections include the wonderful Monasterio de las Descalzas Reales. Among the city's fine buildings, the best is the Palacio Real (Royal Palace)—an ostentatious confection of decorative whimsy and excess.

Chic designer shops line the avenues of Salamanca north of Parque del Retiro. Throbbing clubs and tapas bars fill the narrow streets radiating from Plaza del Ángel. Northeast, modern office blocks rise on the Paseo de la Castellana, which links with Paseo del Prado to form the main city's north–south axis. The main east–west axis is formed by the Gran Vía and Calle de Alcalá. The latter leads to the heart of Habsburg Madrid, the Plaza Mayor. Stay near any of these roads in order truly to enter the spirit of the "city that never sleeps." ∎

The setting
sun lights the
Palacio Real.

Palacio Real

IT IS NOT THE MOST HARMONIOUS OR TASTEFUL OF
Spanish palaces, but the Palacio Real (Royal Palace) drips with regal
opulence. Full of the decorative excesses of the 18th and 19th centuries, it reveals a lot about the royalty that commissioned them. The
palace stands on the site of the Moorish ninth-century fortress. It
became the royal residence in 1561, but was rebuilt after a calami-
tous fire in 1734. Three Italian architects and several French artists
worked to complete the reconstruction, in 1764. The palace is very
much a product of the Bourbon court (see p. 34), and the furnishing
is almost all original 18th-century baroque and rococo. King Alfonso
XIII lived here until he left Spain in 1931 when the Republicans took
control. Today it is used only for state ceremonial purposes.

Palacio Real
www.patrimonionacional.es
/preal/preal.htm

- 54 B4
- Calle de Bailén
- 91 454 88 00
- Closed Sun. p.m. &
  for official
  ceremonies
- $$. Free on Wed.
  for E.U. citizens.
  Guided tours in
  English
- Metro: Ópera

From the entrance in front of the
cathedral (see p. 59), you go into a
vast courtyard, at the back of which
a grand staircase leads up to the
royal apartments. White stone and
granite from the Sierra de Guadar-
rama are the chief building materi-
als, while inside, marble achieves an
impressive acreage. The **Hall of
Halberdiers** (royal guards), with
its ceiling painting by Giovanni
Battista Tiepolo (1696–1770), leads
to the opulent **Hall of Columns**,
where 17th-century Flemish tapes-
tries adorn the walls, and sculptures
symbolize the planets. The dictator
General Franco lay in state in the
hall in 1975, and in 1985, a formal
signing ceremony took place here
when Spain joined the European
Economic Community.

You then enter the most sump-
tuous hall, the Throne Room,
where Tiepolo's ceiling painting
**"Apotheosis of the Spanish
Monarchy"** looks down on
Neapolitan furniture, Venetian
chandeliers, mirrors, and clocks

from San Ildefonso de la Granja (see p. 226), and bronze lions by Benicelli.

You now move on to the **King's Rooms:** the Reception Room, Lunch Room, Dressing Room, and Bedroom, each one full of precious objects and furniture, much of it French. The paintings include portraits by Goya of Carlos IV and his wife, María Luisa. In the **Lunch Room** look out for the astonishing clock made of marble, bronze, and mahogany with a diamond-studded face. The Italian decorator Gasparini designed the rococo extravaganza of the **Dressing Room.** This riot of silk, gold, and silver wall hangings, an inlaid marble floor swirling with floral designs, and an ornately stuccoed ceiling created a fitting stage for the king to undergo the daily ceremony of being dressed in front of his courtiers. The **Bedroom,** now furnished as a sitting room with white-and-gold Empire furniture, has a ceiling painting by Vicente López containing numerous references to the religious and honorific order created by Carlos III.

Next, you see some of the more idiosyncratic rooms, starting with the **Porcelain Room,** a small chamber whose porcelain wall panels were designed for smokers of the time. The Buen Retiro workshop, founded by Carlos III, made the panels, which are decorated with grapes, garlands, and flowers. Next door is the **Yellow Room,** lined with fine tapestries, where ladies sat on marquetry chairs by Dugourc and ate chocolates, while the men puffed away in their adjacent smoking room.

Now comes the pièce de résistance, the vast, ornate **Ballroom,** created in 1879 by Alfonso XII out of three smaller rooms built for Carlos III's wife. On her premature death, Carlos closed them up, and so they remained for more than a

century. Today the room is used as a banqueting hall seating 150 people, who can gaze at the ceiling painting of Christopher Columbus announcing his New World discoveries to Fernando and Isabel. The walls are lined with 16th-century Flemish tapestries and giant vases, both Chinese and French.

The **Music Room** has a rare and unusual collection of stringed instruments by the genius of violin-making, Antonio Stradivari (1644– 1737). The instruments are occasionally used in private concerts organized by the present Queen Sofía, a great music-lover. Watch out, too, for the mother-of-pearl guitar dating from 1796. After the **Silver Room,** displaying a rather motley collection of silver, you reach the **Capilla Real** (Royal Chapel). Colossal marble columns sustain this neoclassic design, gleaming with gilt, by Ventura Rodríguez. The last four, smaller, rooms are the apartments of Queen María Luisa. These include a porcelain smoking room, a chinoiserie room, and an inspiring study with marble marquetry and painted silk ceiling panels. ■

The grand staircase leads to opulent reception rooms and the royal apartments.

Murals watch over the Plaza Mayor, a harmonious arcaded square at the heart of Madrid.

A walk around Plaza Mayor

This walk takes you to the heart of historical Madrid, where winding streets lead past churches and tapas bars, as well as give a glimpse of royal history. Follow the trail by day or night—the ambience changes radically.

Start your walk at the **Plaza Mayor ❶,** a majestic, porticoed square constructed in the early 17th century as the hub of Habsburg Madrid (see p. 33). The work took place under Felipe III, whose equestrian statue gazes over the square, and was directed by Juan Gómez de Mora. The most striking building is the gingerbread-style **Casa de la Panadería** (1672), home of the Bakers' Guild. Its incongruous murals by Carlos Franco are the third to have blanketed the facade. Opposite, the **Casa de la Carnicería** (Butchers' Guild) houses municipal offices and the tourist office. Gone are the weekday markets, bullfights, and autos-da-fé (trials and executions of heretics) that once filled the square: Today it is just a popular place to meet.

Leave the square through the arch in the northeast corner leading to Calle de Ciudad Rodrigo. On the left, you see the green wrought-iron facade of the **Mercado de San Miguel** (*Closed siestas, Sat. p.m. & Sun.*), once

a food market, it is now an upscale food hall. Turn left into the busy Calle Mayor and you soon reach the charming and historic **Plaza de la Villa ❷.** On the right flank of this sloping square stands the **Ayuntamiento** or Casa de la Villa (town hall) designed by Juan Gómez de Mora in 1640 to house the town council and prison. Facing you is the **Casa**

- See area map p. 54
- ► Plaza Mayor
- ⟷ 1.2 miles (2.4 km)
- 1.5 hours
- ► Plaza Mayor

NOT TO BE MISSED
- Plaza Mayor
- Ayuntamiento
- San Pedro
- San Francisco el Grande
- Calle de Cuchilleros

de **Cisneros,** a reconstruction of a 16th-century palace that stood here, and on the left is the 15th-century **Torre de los Lujanes,** the birthplace in 1846 of the composer Federico Chueca and now part of the university. The tower has Mudejar (see p. 43) arches at its summit and, opening onto the narrow Calle del Codo, a horseshoe-arched doorway.

Retrace your steps to Calle Mayor, turn left and continue to the end. As you walk, you see the outskirts of Madrid receding in the distance, reminding you of the height of the city. The massive white forms of the **Catedral de Nuestra Señora de la Almudena** (tel 91 542 22 00) soon appear ahead. It was built in 1985–1992, but the plans were first drawn up a century earlier. Cross the Calle de Bailén if you want to see the interior—an odd mixture of

pure white stone, garish ceiling paintings, and tasteless side chapels. Beside it stands the vast **Palacio Real** (see pp. 56–57). Return to the corner of Bailén and Mayor, and walk down the steps beside the Capitanía General, built as a palace in 1611 and now a military establishment. The city drops steeply here: You soon find yourself gazing back up at the lofty viaduct (1934) of Calle de Bailén. Circle around the back of the palace through the parking lot, and then turn right down Calle de la Villa to reach Calle de Segovia.

Looming opposite is the dome of the 16th-century **Capilla del Obispo** (Plaza de la Paja, tel 91 365 48 71), Madrid's only Gothic chapel and currently being restored. Walk toward it up Costanilla de San Andrés to **Plaza de la Paja,** a pretty residential square

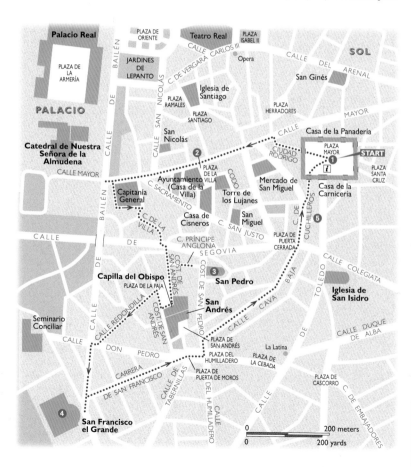

with a few bars and restaurants. In the Middle Ages, this was the commercial heart of Madrid. Turn left into Calle Príncipe Anglona for a closer look at the church of **San Pedro** ❸ *(tel 91 365 12 84)*. Its 14th-century Mudejar tower replaced the minaret of a mosque that once stood here. Return to Plaza de la Paja, cross

Shops and cafés line the arcades below the Casa de la Panadería, Plaza Mayor.

over it and turn into Calle Redondilla. This ends at Calle de Bailén, where you turn left to **San Francisco el Grande** ❹, a neoclassic basilica *(tel 91 365 38 00, closed Sun.–Mon.)*. Built in 1762–1784, it has a Goya painting of San Bernardino and a lavishly painted cupola. The 16th-century choir stalls in the sacristy come from the Carthusian monastery of El Paular.

Walk along Carrera de San Francisco (away from the basilica), to Plaza de Puerta de Moros. Rising to your left is the baroque **Iglesia de San Isidro** *(tel 91 369 20 37)* and the church of **San Andrés** *(Plaza de San Andrés, tel 91 365 48 71)*. Both overlook a peaceful square flanked by a contemporary trompe-l'oeil mural. Go past San Andrés to the tiny Plaza del Humilladero, and turn left down **Calle Cava Baja.** Stop for refreshments at one of the little restaurants and bars with wood-paneled facades that accompany you as far as Plaza de Puerta Cerrada. Or cross to lively **Calle de Cuchilleros** ❺, with more bars and cafés, before going up the arched steps leading into Plaza Mayor. ∎

Coin- and stamp-collectors gather to trade in the Plaza Mayor on Sunday mornings.

Monasterio de las Descalzas Reales

THE ROYAL ORIGINS OF THIS FRANCISCAN CONVENT OF the Royal Barefoot Nuns lie in its conversion from a palace into a convent by Felipe II's sister Juana de Austria, who became a nun. Her sister María also lived in the convent, although without taking orders. Today 28 nuns of the order known as the Poor Clares live in seclusion here, and on your tour you may hear them singing and ringing bells. The magnificent late 15th- to early 16th-century building holds a mass of treasure.

Frescoes by various artists adorn the grand staircase that leads up from the cloisters. The dominant one shows Felipe IV and his family, and opposite is a Crucifixion scene. Off the first-floor cloisters, the remarkable side chapels contain original **Talavera tiled floors,** frescoes, coffered ceilings, and many paintings by anonymous artists. A beautiful recumbent **"Christ"** is the work of 16th-century sculptor Gaspar Becerra. Fra Angelico's masterful "Annunciation" hung here before being moved to the Prado (see pp. 62–67).

The anteroom to the main chapel is packed with silverware, Bohemian crystal crucifixes, and paintings. It leads to the **Choir,** used daily for Mass, where the marble tomb of María stands above that of her daughter, Marguerita. Notice the fabulously realistic and expressive **statue of Mary,** by Pedro de Mena (1628–1688). Back in the cloisters, the next side chapel is devoted to the Virgin of Guadalupe, celebrated in a riot of baroque gilt, with unusual paintings on mirrors. Farther along, look for the **"Madonna and Child"** painted by Bernardino Luini (circa 1480–1532).

From here you are taken upstairs to the vast Hall of Tapestries, lined with 17th-century Flemish tapestries based on cartoons by Peter Paul Rubens (1577–1640), and packed with other treasures—embroidered robes, silverware, and reliquaries (containers for relics of saints and other revered items). In the chapter house overlooking the vegetable garden you'll see more works of art. Two of the more searing are Gregorio Fernández's **sculpture of Mary Magdalen** and Pedro de Mena's **"Ecce Homo."** The tour ends in splendor in a room hung with paintings by Zurbarán, Titian, Caravaggio, Bruegel the Elder, and Rubens. ■

Monasterio de las Descalzas Reales
www.patrimonionacional.es/
    descreal/descreal.htm
🅰 54 C3
✉ Plaza de las
    Descalzas Reales 3
☎ 91 454 88 00
🕐 Closed Fri. & Sun.
    p.m., & Mon.
💲 $. Free on Wed. for
    E.U. citizens with
    passport. 50-minute
    guided tour in
    Spanish
🚇 Metro: Sol, Ópera, &
    Callao

The Monasterio de las Descalzas Reales houses Renaissance and baroque artwork.

Museo del Prado

Marble and bronze sculptures by Leone and Pompeo Leoni stand in a gallery in the new underground extension.

MADRID'S MOST FAMOUS MUSEUM HAS ONE OF THE world's greatest collections of classical paintings, and for many people it is the main reason for visiting the capital. The vast collection of 8,600 works is full of masterpieces, easier to absorb if you focus on a small number of periods. If you can manage only one visit, allow at least three hours, and avoid weekend crowds. An ingenious extension by Rafael Moneo was finally inaugurated in 2007.

Museo del Prado
www.museoprado.mcu.es

🗺 55 E3

✉ Paseo del Prado

☎ 91 330 28 00

🕐 Closed Mon.

💲 $. Free on Sun. 5–8 p.m. & 6–8 p.m. weekdays

🚇 Metro: Banco de España

Opposite: Peter Paul Rubens painted the powerful "Equestrian Portrait of the Duke of Lerma" in 1603, during his Italian period.

This addition includes the cloister of the church of Los Jeronimos which, controversially, was dismantled and rebuilt. It now sits above underground galleries which are linked to the main Villanueva building beneath a roof garden. The extension provides increased space for temporary exhibitions as well as a spacious café and shop area.

Tickets for individual visitors are sold at the Puerta de Goya entrance, and access is either through the front Puerta de Velazquez or through the Puerta de los Jeronimos at the back. Museums often change their displays, so the arrangement described below may change.

The source of this incredible body of works was the Spanish royal family, who, over the centuries, commissioned and collected art with passion. In addition to stars of Spanish painting such as Velázquez, Goya, Ribera, and Zurbarán (see p. 47), the Prado has big collections of Italian (including Titian and Raphael) and Flemish artists. Many of the latter were collected by Felipe II, an astute art-lover whose taste was influenced by his Flemish aunt. Both he and his father, Carlos V, favored Titian (died 1576); Felipe IV chose Diego Velázquez (1599–1660) as court painter, and Carlos III appointed Francisco de Goya (1746–1828). In 1819, Fernando VII opened the collection to the public (in this building designed by Juan de Villanueva, 1739–1811).

ROMANESQUE & EARLY ITALIAN ART

If you enter from the Puerta de Goya (the northern end) on the ground floor, look at **Room 51C** off the rotunda, devoted to Romanesque art. Frescoes here show animals and hunting scenes from San Baudelio, near Soria. Continue to **Room 49** to see early Italian works, including a very delicately painted "Annunciation" (1425–28) by Fra Angelico (died 1455), and three panels by Sandro Botticelli (circa 1445–1510) telling the "Story of Nastagio degli Onesti" (1483). Among several paintings by Raphael (1483–1520) on religious themes, the most striking is his "Portrait of A Cardinal" (1510),

Goya's painting of the "Dos de Mayo" shows Spaniards being shot by French troops during the War of Independence.

with the cardinal in a brilliant red robe. Also in this room, you can see the evolution of Andrea del Sarto's work, from the beautifully expressive "Portrait of a Woman" (1514) to the more baroque "Sacrifice of Isaac" (1528–29).

FLEMISH & GERMAN PAINTING

Rooms 55 to **58** hold 15th- to 18th-century Flemish works, among others. Strong commercial and marriage links between Spain and Flanders produced a style—Spanish but showing Flemish influence—evident in **Room 57,** while **Room 58** houses the "Descent from the Cross" by Rogier van der Weyden (1399–1464). The faces are brilliantly

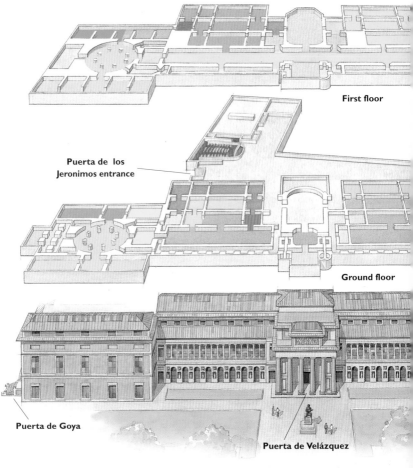

First floor

Puerta de los Jeronimos entrance

Ground floor

Puerta de Goya

Puerta de Velázquez

executed and the whole composition leads the eye to the cross.

In **Room 58** look for Hans Memling's "Adoration of the Kings" (circa 1470). **Room 56A** has works by Bruegel, Joachim Patinir, and Hieronymus Bosch (circa 1450– 1516), whose weird "Garden of Delights" always draws a crowd. Bosch's imagination encompassed both bawdy pursuits and the more mystical. Albrecht Dürer's (1471– 1528) magnificent "Self-portrait" (1498) in **Room 55B,** another masterpiece, is flanked by his full-length paintings of "Adam" and "Eve" (1507). These were the first Renaissance-style paintings to emerge from northern Europe.

EARLY SPANISH WORKS

Room 55 has portraits by Antonio Moro (1519–1576), including one of the English Queen Mary Tudor (1554), painted for Felipe II when he was considering marriage to Mary. **Room 56** contains fine portraits by Juan de Juanes (circa 1523–1579) and his "Last Supper." **Room 56B** shows Sebastiano de Piombo's luminous work—clear blue skies and dazzling white are his hallmarks.

VENETIAN SCHOOL

At this point you enter long **Room 75,** displaying Italian painters of the Venetian school, whose blending of color and light surpassed all other Renaissance schools. Painters include Paolo Veronese (circa

Goya (1746–1828) stands guard outside the Prado.

Italian paintings	
Spanish paintings	
Flemish paintings	
Dutch paintings	
French paintings	
Sculpture	
Drawing & Exhibition halls	
German paintings	
New Areas	
Other	

Close inspection of Velázquez's "The Surrender of Breda"

Puerta de Murillo

Hieronymous Bosch's "The Garden of Earthly Delights" (ca. 1516) hangs in one of the Museo del Prado's galleries.

1528–1588), Jacopo Bassano (died 1592), and Jacopo Tintoretto (1518–1594). Take a good look at Tintoretto's "El Lavatorio," depicting Jesus washing the disciples' feet, a masterpiece of perspective. Titian (died 1576), who worked extensively for both Carlos V and Felipe II, is well represented in **Rooms 61, 61B**, and **63**: Look at his self-portrait, the superb horseback figure of "Carlos V at the Battle of Mühlberg" (1548), and the portrait of "Isabel of Portugal," painted after her death. Titian's fame during his life nearly matched that of Michelangelo, and it is said that Carlos V once did him the honor of picking up a brush he dropped.

EL GRECO & GOYA

El Greco dominates **Rooms 60A,** **62A,** and **61A,** starting with early works and moving into his Spanish period when his figures lengthened and he adopted a very Spanish concern with the division between heaven and earth. Better works, however, are found in Toledo. Classical and Renaissance sculpture complete this floor, but this isn't a must.

Instead, take the stairs to the next level where you are propelled into the world of Goya, whose diverse works fill **Rooms 16B, 19-23, 32,** and **39.** His huge political paintings "El Dos de Mayo" and "El Tres de Mayo" depict scenes from Spain's War of Independence in 1808—unusually for that time he was not working to commission, so the subject matter was his own choice. **Room**

16B has the very strange "black paintings," produced in 1820–23, during a period of deep depression caused by the deaths of his wife and son, and by his own illness. Many of these paintings are grotesque; all are open to interpretation and their titles are conjectural. "Perro" seems completely modern in conception, with its extraordinary spatial arrangement of a dog's head against textured space. Some of the court paintings by Goya which are on display are just as idiosyncratic and often quite unflattering, with an emotional approach to the characterization of his subjects.

VELÁZQUEZ & OTHERS

The long hall off **Room 32** has 17th-century Spanish paintings, with works by Murillo, Ribera, and Zurbarán. **Rooms 14-16** and **26-28** bring you to Velázquez. The Prado has his best pictures, and the greatest of them all, "Las Meninas" ("The Maids of Honor"), is in **Room 27.** Look at it from a distance, and see Velázquez himself observing you from where he stands beside his easel in the picture.

Rooms 8-11 exhibit Peter Paul Rubens (1577–1640), with several paintings of hunting scenes brought from the royal hunting lodge at El Pardo. This floor ends with 17th-century French and Italian paintings. Upstairs, there are several rooms which are devoted to Goya (including selections from a range of his portraits, tapestries, and cartoons). Other rooms have 18th-century European art on display. ■

"Los Borrachos," or "The Drunkards" (1628–29), by Velázquez, one of the few Spanish painters to depict mythological scenes

Museo Thyssen-Bornemisza

Museo Thyssen-Bornemisza

www.museothyssen.org

🗺 55 E3

✉ Palacio de Villahermosa, Paseo del Prado 8

☎ 91 369 01 51

🕐 Closed Mon.

💲 $

🚇 Metro: Banco de España

Opposite: "Swaying Dancer" (1880) by Edgar Degas Below: The Museo Thyssen-Bornemisza showcases Western art of the past 800 years.

MADRID ACQUIRED THIS EXCEPTIONAL ART COLLECTION only in 1993, and its quality gives it equal footing with the Prado across the road. The collection was built by two generations of the Thyssen-Bornemisza family, and it is now overseen by the Spanish Baroness Thyssen-Bornemisza. The collection, housed in a 19th-century neoclassic mansion converted by Rafael Moneo, represents the best of Western art from the last 800 years. In 2004 the museum expanded to exhibit the Carmen Thyssen-Bornemisza Collection concentrating on landscape painting.

For a chronological tour, work your way down from the top floor. Begin in **Room 1** with the oldest paintings, the Italian primitives, among them "Christ and the Samaritan" by Duccio di Buoninsegna (1278–1319), the only artist known to have signed his work at this time. **Room 3** brings you to early Flemish paintings: Best of these are the black-and-white diptych of the "Annunciation" by Jan Van Eyck (1390–1441), which looks like carved stone, and the incredibly detailed "Enthroned Madonna" by Rogier van der Weyden (1400–1464).

In **Room 5,** which has an exceptional display of Renaissance portraits, you touch on early examples of the modern cult of the personality: Look for Domenico Ghirlandaio's "Portrait of Giovanna

Tornabuoni," a representation of perfection, and Hans Holbein's (1498–1543) masterful and much reproduced depiction of a self-satisfied Henry VIII of England. Next to it hangs a delightful portrait of a youthful Catherine of Aragón, Henry's first wife, the "Infanta" (circa 1496) by Juan de Flandes.

The **Villahermosa Gallery,** adjoining, (Room 6) displays Raphael's (1483–1520) "Portrait of a Young Man" in a freer style. **Room 7** brings you to larger format Renaissance paintings. Bernardino Luini's (1486–1532) "Virgin and Child with the Infant St. John" shows wonderful delicacy in the Virgin's face, her veil, and the two babies. "Young Knight in a Landscape" by Vittore Carpaccio (1460–1525) is in a transitional style, part naturalistic, part stylized, and Gothic.

GERMAN & ITALIAN SCHOOLS

A more exaggerated, even caricatural, approach characterizes the paintings of the German school in **Rooms 8** and **9.** Albrecht Dürer's (1471–1528) "Jesus among the Doctors" is a compelling composition that draws the eye to the hands at the center. Next door, in **Room 10,** the "Reclining Nymph" by Lucas Cranach the Elder (1472–1553) has a superbly painted transparent veil.

Edward Hopper's "Hotel Room" (1931) is considered the most important representation of the American figurative school.

Rooms 11 and **12** represent great artists of the Venetian school —Titian, Tintoretto, Bassano— and other Italians. El Greco appears here because he began his career in Italy, and José de Ribera (1591–1652) has a room to himself. This Spaniard, who worked and died in Italy, combines Spanish drama with Italian techniques, as well as displaying a startling realism.

BAROQUE

The early baroque section features anguished sculptures including, "San Sebastián" and "La Piedad" by Bernini (1598–1680); other highlights are Luca Giordano's (1634–1705) "Judgment of Solomon," Francisco de Zurbarán's (1598–1664) "Santa Casilda," and radiant views of Venice by Canaletto (1697–1768). Further Flemish and Dutch paintings are in **Rooms 19, 20,** and **21:** Here you'll find superlative works by Van Dyck, Brueghel, and Rubens, especially his superb "Toilet of Venus." Don't miss Rembrandt's penetrating "Self-portrait."

Dutch 17th-century paintings fill a whole wing of the museum's middle level with beautifully observed and composed scenes of daily life, interiors, and landscapes. An unusual still life by William Claesz Heda (1593–1680) has a magnificent display of silverware and glass standing beside a half-eaten pie.

Rooms 28, 29, and **30** bring you to English and American artists such as Joshua Reynolds (1723–1792), Thomas Gainsborough (1727–1788), and Thomas Cole (1801–1848), an Englishman who emigrated to America and founded the American school. Apart from a rather fine "Portrait of the Duchess of Sutherland" by John Singer Sargent (1856–1925), this section is more interesting intellectually than artistically. After the Spanish, Flemish, and Dutch works, these portraits seem rather stilted and lifeless. Then comes the shock of European Romanticism, with a wall of Goya, Géricault, and Delacroix in **Room 31,** followed by Courbet and Constable.

The Impressionists are in **Rooms 32** and **33:** Make sure you see Renoir's "Woman with Parasol" (1873), Berthe Morisot's "The Cheval-Glass" (1876), and Edgar Degas' "Swaying Dancer" (1880). Vincent van Gogh's "Les Vessenots" (1890), painted in thick impasto, may have been his last painting before his suicide.

MODERNISM

The modern art collection begins in **Room 34** with André Derain (1880–1954) and the other Fauves (wild beasts), so-called because they seemed to break all rules. However, the Thyssen-Bornemisza comes into its own with a superlative collection of German expressionists **(Rooms 35–40)**—Munch, Kokoschka, Nolde, Schiele, and Beckmann are all here, and Otto Kirchner (1880–1938) is especially well represented. Take a look at his radiating composition in "The Bay" (1914) and "Alpine Kitchen" (1918). Franz Marc (1880–1916)

and Wassily Kandinsky (1866–1944) represent the Blaue Reiter group, and the last room has caricatural works by Georg Grosz (1893–1959).

Rooms 41–44 on the ground floor show parallel trends of early modernism, from cubism (Braque, Juan Gris, Picasso) to futurism, constructivism, dadaism and surrealism. The United States rules supreme in **Room 46,** with abstract expressionism by Rothko, O'Keeffe, and De Kooning. **Rooms 47** and **48** round things off with a general survey of post-war figurative work and pop art.

If any criticism can be made of this collection, it is in this last section, which gives a one-sided view of the 1960s and 1970s, completely missing out on the arrival of minimalism and conceptualism. For these two art movements, go to the Reina Sofía (see pp. 74–75). ■

Venetian artist Giovanni Bellini, who painted "Nunc Dimittis" ("Presentation of Christ in the Temple"), helped make Venice an important center of the Italian Renaissance.

Boating on the lake is a popular escape from the city bustle.

Parque del Retiro

MADRID IS NOT BY ANY MEANS A GREEN CITY, BUT IT DOES have a lovely breathing space in this 350-acre (142-ha) park. In the 17th century, the park surrounded Felipe IV's palace. Now it lies conveniently close to the capital's main cluster of museums, and it is the perfect place to recover from the physical and mental rigors of visiting them.

Parque del Retiro
- 55 F2
- Calle de Alfonso XII
- 91 573 62 45
- Metro: Atocha, Retiro, & Ibiza

Real Jardín Botánico
www.rjb.csic.es
- 55 E2
- Plaza de Murillo 2
- 91 420 30 17
- Metro: Atocha & Banco de España
- $

The Conde-Duque de Olivares laid out the park in 1636, and its formal gardens, copses, fountains, statues, and paths remain. All that is left of the palace is the Casón del Buen Retiro, now an annex to the Prado, with a select display of 19th-century Spanish painting and sculpture *(tel 91 330 28 00, closed Mon.; may be closed for renovation)*. It stands at the entrance to the park on Calle de Alfonso XII, just behind the Prado and Iglesia San Jerónimo el Real.

In the park itself, you can take a carriage ride, row a boat on the **Estanque Lake,** watch street theater, hear a concert, visit an exhibition, or just stroll. This is a popular meeting point for Madrileños, especially on Sundays. The **equestrian statue** by the lake portrays Alfonso XII *(R.1874–1885)*, not Spain's most illustrious ruler but one of its youngest—he died at only 28. Jutting out south of the Prado in the far southwest corner of the park is the **Real Jardín Botánico** (Royal Botanic Garden), founded in 1774. It has about 30,000 plants, some of them exotic, and aging greenhouses designed by Juan de Villanueva (1739–1811). Also in the southern half are the **Palacio de Velázquez** *(tel 91 573 62 45, closed Tues.)* and the soaring glass walls of the **Palacio de Cristal** *(tel 91 574 66 14, closed Tues.)*. Both hold exhibitions of contemporary art. Nearby are a pool and grotto, and at the far southern end of the park there are rose gardens. ∎

Museo Arqueológico Nacional

THIS MUSEUM OF ANCIENT ART WAS FOUNDED IN 1895 behind the grandiose Biblioteca Nacional (National Library) building. The Spanish collection is remarkable, and the museum covers ancient Egypt, Greece, Rome, and the Middle East. The museum also displays a partial reproduction of the prehistoric cave paintings of Altamira. Due to renovation works, some rooms may be temporarily closed.

The lower floor covers prehistory and early humans. **Room 6** has the most intriguing exhibits: the Cuencos de Axtroki, hammered gold vessels with circular designs that suggest a cult of the sun in the late Bronze Age. **Room 7** has beautiful gold torques (collars) from northwest Spain, and **Room 9** has Celtiberian silver, mainly from southeast Spain. In the Egyptian section **(Room 13)**, the sarcophagus of Amenemhat is beautifully painted with religious scenes. **Rooms 14–16** display an exceptional collection of Greek pottery.

On the ground floor, start with Iberian and Phoenician works in **Rooms 19–20** (next to the ticket desk) and go around clockwise. Pride of place goes to the limestone bust called the Dama de Elche (late fifth century B.C.). This rare example of Iberian art probably held human ashes in the cavity in her shoulder. It would once have been brightly colored: A few traces of polychrome paint remain, but you get a better idea by looking at the neighboring Dama de Baza (fifth or fourth century B.C.), a seated woman surrounded by the dowry found in her tomb at Baza, near Granada. Older still is another female sculpture, the diminutive Dama de Galera, a seventh-century B.C. Phoenician artifact carved out of alabaster.

In **Room 19,** look for the dazzling Tesoro de Javea (Javea Treasure), a collection of Iberian filigree jewelry. Rising in the middle of these treasures is the tomb from Pozo Moro, a stone tower with traces of bas-reliefs and sculpted lions.

Rooms 21–26 display Roman art, including a fine bronze "Apollo," a marble "Livia," swathed in superbly carved draped clothes, and mosaics, glass, bronze, and pottery. The remaining rooms are devoted to Visigothic, medieval, and Moorish pieces, including an ornate gypsum archway from the Aljafería palace in Zaragoza (see p. 141). Temporary exhibitions are on the upper floor. ∎

Museo Arqueológico Nacional

www.man.mcu.es

⚑ 55 F4

✉ Calle de Serrano 13

☎ 91 577 79 12

⏲ Closed p.m., Sun. & Mon.

💲 $. Free Sat. p.m. & Sun. a.m.

🚇 Metro: Serrano (Line 4) & Retiro (Line 2)

The beautiful Dama de Baza, an Iberian sculpture unearthed in the province of Granada.

Glass elevators spirit visitors to the different levels of Madrid's modern art museum, the Reina Sofía.

Museo Nacional Centro de Arte Reina Sofía

THE NATIONAL CONTEMPORARY ART CENTER AND MUSEUM stands on the southern side of central Madrid, opposite the remodeled station of Atocha. The Reina Sofía, opened in 1986 in tune with Spain's frenetic *movida* spirit of personal and artistic freedom, is home to Picasso's "Guernica" (see p. 125). In 2005, an expansion devised by the acclaimed French architect Jean Nouvel, added a triangular-shaped extension for temporary exhibitions, a library, an auditorium, and a restaurant supervised by celebrity chef, Sergi Arola, around a central atrium topped by a lattice roof.

The main building is a converted 18th-century hospital, with immaculate white walls and transparent external elevators. The permanent collection of 20th–21st-century art is strong on Spanish art, less so on non-Spanish artists.

To start with modernism, go up to **Floor 2,** where exhibition halls take you from the early 20th century up to the outbreak of World War II. At the turn of the century, Spain's two main centers of artistic activity— Euskadi (the Basque country) and Catalunya—nurtured a clutch of artists: Ignacio Zuloaga, Francisco Iturrino, Hermenegildo Anglada-Camarasa, and other Postimpressionists.

Rooms 3 and **4** takes you through constructivism, cubism, and dada: Keep an eye out for the strong colors of Robert Delaunay (1885–1941), his wife Sonia, the Mexican Diego Rivera, and the geometry of Joaquín Torres García (1875–1949). The world-famous names of the period are Juan Gris, Pablo Gargallo, Pablo Picasso, and Joan Miró, who are displayed in interconnecting rooms. **Rooms 5–8** display the stirring context of "Guernica" (1937) through photos, sketches, and works by Picasso's contemporaries: Joan Miró, Alexander Calder, Julio González, and Alberto Sánchez. Finally, you come to the massive work itself in all its tortured, monochromatic splendor. It was painted in a white heat of outrage after German air-crafts bombed the Basque town of Gernika (see p. 125). Spaces nearby behind give a wonderful overview of Miró's career. They include numerous delightful sculptures such as "Pájaro Lunar" (1966), a huge black bronze of a creature.

SURREALISTS

Salvador Dalí's "Cenicitas" (1928) and "El Gran Masturbador" (1929), among other works, tell you unequivocally that you have reached the surrealists whose works monopolize **Rooms 9–12.** Here you will find exhibits related to Spain's pioneering surrealist film-maker Luis Buñuel (1900–1983) and his surrealist films. Paintings

Fernando Zobel. There are some powerful works by Francis Bacon, Henry Moore, and the brilliant French artist, Yves Klein (1928–1962). Next door in **Room 19,** Lucio Fontana (1899–1968), master of the slashed canvas, has equally good coverage. Then come the vigorous canvases of Antonio Saura (1930–1998), followed by Cy Twombly, Jean Dubuffet and, in a different room, Motherwell, Mario Merz, and Jannis Kounellis. One room is devoted to the metal sheet works of Pablo Palazuelo (1916–2007). This is also the world of Antonio Tàpies (b. 1923), Spain's greatest living artist whose textural abstractions dominate two entire rooms. Then in **Room 29** comes

Museo Nacional Centro de Arte Reina Sofía
www.museoreinasofia
.mcu.es

🅰 55 E1
✉ Calle de Santa Isabel 52
☎ 91 774 10 00
🕐 Closed Sun. p.m. & Tues.
💲 $. Free Sat. p.m. & Sun. a.m.
🚇 Metro: Atocha

by the big surrealists such as Max Ernst and René Magritte and pho-tos by Man Ray, are all displayed.

POSTWAR

Take the elevator to **Floor 4** to be plunged into postwar efferves-cence. **Rooms 13–28** offer fasci-nating insight and comparisons between Spanish postwar art within the international scene. Thus works by Rothko, David Smith, Isamo Noguchi, Anthony Caro, and the COBRA group alter-nate with homegrown Eusebia Sempere, Gustavo Tornenr, and

the Pop Art era, showcasing Equipo Cronica and Eduardo Arroyo, before devoting **Rooms 34** and **35** to Eduardo Chillida (1924–2002), the prolific Basque sculptor. American minimalist artists (Barnett Newman, Bruce Nauman, Donald Judd) lead to three rooms of contemporary works, from Ross Bleckner to Georg Baselitz, Guillermo Kuitca, Miguel Barcelo, and Susana Solano. A light installation by Olafur Eliasson, between the elevators, draws the display to a memorable close. ∎

Picasso's famous "Guernica" (1937) is one of the star attractions here.

Museo de América

MADRID HAD NO PUBLIC MUSEUM ON SPAIN'S FORMER colonies in Latin America until the Museo de América opened in 1993, bringing together a huge array of scattered documents and exhibits under one roof. The presentation is slick, but you see the colonies just from the colonist's point of view. No mention is made of the atrocities and exploitation wrought by the Spanish, and indigenous peoples appear as mere exotic curiosities.

This carved and painted tiger's head typifies pre-Columbian Latin American art.

Museo de América

museodeamerica.mcu.es

🅰 54 B5

✉ Avenida Reyes Católicos 6

☎ 91 543 94 37

🕐 Closed p.m., Sun. & Mon.

💲 $. Free on Sun.

🚇 Metro: Moncloa (Line 3)

This said, the 2,500 exhibits are displayed in imaginative ways. The kernel of the collection came from the Royal Cabinet, but other items have been bought or donated: The Colombian government gave the fabulous Quimbayas treasure.

Room 1 is devoted to the voyages of discovery, Spanish chroniclers including Christopher Columbus, a reconstructed 18th-century scientific study room, and fascinating old maps. Also here are engravings, paintings, and stunning artifacts such as Amazonian feathered hats, the fantastic feathered Paracas cape, Costa Rican Diquís gold, and colonial antiques.

The main body of the pre-Hispanic collection fills half the first floor in **Rooms 2** and **3.** It is arranged in themes: birth and death, ceremonies, body ornamentation, dwellings, and tools and implements. You see ceramic figures from Colima in Mexico, Maya sculptures, Olmec jades, lovely pieces from Mexico's Gulf culture, Incan artifacts, Chilean textiles, ceramics from Ecuador, Colombian and Costa Rican gold ornaments, basketware by Hopi and Chumash Indians, and an enormous Amazonian canoe. Whimsical 18th-century Mexican paintings illustrate the Conquest, while Chinese inlaid furniture indicates maritime links with the Philippines, another Spanish colony.

The museum's most precious items concern the religious beliefs of America's pre-Hispanic societies, and are on the **upper floor** (sometimes closed to make way for temporary exhibitions). Here are the Mayan Stela of Madrid (incised stones), the Colombian gold Quimbayas treasure, the Tudela codex manuscript (1553) and, above all, the Trocortesiano codex (13th–16th century), one of only four Mayan manuscripts remaining in the world.

Outside the stately museum stands the surprising **Faro de Moncloa** (Moncloa Lighthouse, *Avenida Reyes Católicos, tel 91 722 04 00, closed Mon.*), a cylindrical steel tower rising 250 feet (76 m), designed by Salvador Pérez Arroyo in 1992. Take the elevator up to the observation platform for fantastic views over Madrid. ■

More places to visit in Madrid

MUSEO NACIONAL DE ARTES DECORATIVAS

This museum of Spanish decorative arts gives you a taste of the lavish interiors of Spain's many castles and palaces. There are six floors covering furniture, costumes, and objects from the 15th to the 20th century. The top floor houses a wonderful tiled Valencian kitchen.

▲ 55 F3 ✉ Calle de Montalbán 12
☎ 91 522 17 40 🕐 Closed p.m. & Mon. 🛇 $
🚇 Metro: Retiro & Banco de España

EL RASTRO

If you are in Madrid on Sunday morning, don't miss this vast flea market. Goods for sale vary from dusty, rusty bric-à-brac to high-quality antiques, in addition to the usual motley array of T-shirts, ethnic imports, cheap shoes, and bags. Stalls invade the streets of La Latina district, stretching from Plaza de Cascorro to the Puerta de Toledo. The best area for antiques and secondhand knickknacks is the Calle Mira el Río Baja and its offshoots. Old books are piled up in the Plaza del Campillo del Mundo Nuevo, and superior antiques are concentrated in the rather soul-less Mercado Puerta de Toledo. A word of warning: As in any market, beware of pick-pockets. The Rastro is notorious for them, although a greater police presence means things have improved a little in recent years.

▲ 54 C1 🚇 Metro: La Latina & Puerta de Toledo

REAL ACADEMIA DE BELLAS ARTES DE SAN FERNANDO

Despite its prime position on the stately Calle de Alcalá, this art museum is often overlooked by visitors intent on the art giants down the road (the Prado and Thyssen-Bornemisza, see pp. 62–71). Housed in the grandiose rooms of the former Palacio Goyeneche, the remarkable collection spans five centuries of Spanish painting, ending with 20 Picasso etchings. Look for Zurbarán's eight superb life-size **portraits of monks,** works by Alonso Cano (1601–1667), and Goya's **"Burial of the Sardine."** Other European artists include Paolo Veronese and Peter Paul Rubens. There are also displays of sculpture and porcelain.

▲ 54 D3 ✉ Calle de Alcalá 13 ☎ 91 524 08 64
🕐 Closed p.m. Sun.–Mon. 🛇 $ 🚇 Metro: Sol & Sevilla

REAL MONASTERIO DE LA ENCARNACIÓN

A few streets west of the Descalzas Reales (see p. 61), this Augustinian convent boasts a collection of religious paintings and sculpture

The Rastro flea market throngs with people every Sunday morning.

from the 16th to 18th centuries. Like the Descalzas Reales, it had a royal founder, in this case Margaret of Austria, wife of Felipe III. A passageway once connected the convent to the Alcázar (now the Palacio Real, see pp. 56–57), and the 17th-century decoration is by artists of the royal court. Look in particular for Ribera's **"John the Baptist"** and the impressive **sculpture of Christ** by Gregorio Hernández on the first floor. Best of all are the hundreds of reliquaries in the **Reliquary Room** attesting to the inspiration of count-less artisans. You could combine a visit here with one to the nearby Palacio Real, and then relax in the **Jardines de Sabatini.**

▲ 54 B4 ✉ Plaza de la Encarnación 1
☎ 91 454 88 00 🕐 Closed Fri. & Sun. p.m., Mon. 🛇 $. Free Wed. for E.U. nationals
🚇 Metro: Ópera ■

Around Madrid

AFTER HOTFOOTING IT AROUND THE SIGHTS OF MADRID, if you feel you need some air, Aranjuez is the place to go. Strawberries and cream are a local specialty sold in season at every corner. Thirty miles (50 km) northwest of Madrid, you enter another world. Built for Felipe II on a personally chosen site, El Escorial is a summer palace, monastery, and mausoleum combined.

Fountains add a touch of French elegance to the Aranjuez Palace.

Aranjuez
www.aranjuez.com
78 B1
Visitor information
✉ Plaza San Antonio 9
☎ 91 891 04 27

Palacio Real
www.patrimonionacional.es
/aranj/aranjuez.htm
✉ Plaza de Parejas
☎ 91 891 07 40
🕐 Closed Mon.
💲 $ guided tour.
Free Wed. for E.U. nationals

ARANJUEZ

This genteel royal town 30 miles (48 km) south of the capital has endless gardens, shady parks bordered by the Tajo and Jarama Rivers, a 200-year-old bullring, and two luxurious royal homes.

Aranjuez may remind you of the French royal palace of Versailles near Paris. The elegant grid pattern of the town, the lateral wings of the royal palace, and the delightful Casa del Labrador were all commissioned by the Bourbon kings of the late 18th century—the heyday of Versailles. Even the formal gardens and the vast park (Jardín del Príncipe, or Prince's Garden) were the work of a French landscape designer. If you don't want to walk, a visitor train *(tel 902 088 089, closed Mon.)* makes regular circuits of the town, starting from the Palacio Real (Royal Palace) and stopping at the main sights.

The **Palacio Real** was originally built for Felipe II by Juan Bautista de Toledo and Juan de Herrera. The grand staircase, the rococo Salón del Trono (Throne Room), the Sala de la China (lined with whimsically decorated porcelain tiles), the Sala Árabe (inspired by the Alhambra in Granada, see pp. 300–305), and the Salón de los Espejos (Hall of Mirrors) are just some of the palace's wonders.

From here you can take a leisurely walk through the 370-acre (150-ha) **Jardín del Príncipe** to the **Casa del Labrador** (Laborer's House), a far more harmonious mansion built for Carlos IV by Isidro González Velázquez.

The most scintillating room is the **Gabinete del Platino** (Platinum Room), with walls encrusted with gold, platinum, and bronze.

EL ESCORIAL

Felipe II's palace-monastery, now a popular excursion from Madrid, looms over the little town of San Lorenzo de El Escorial. The king wanted the palace to reaffirm the glory of the Habsburg dynasty, but also to be a retreat where he could lead a more contemplative existence than was possible in Madrid.

The building was started by Juan Bautista de Toledo in 1563 and rapidly completed by his pupil, Juan de Herrera, in 1584, with constant input from the king himself. It is grandiose, but austere, and suits its bleak setting. The style was to Felipe's own taste, but reflects a wider reaction to the ornate fashions of Carlos V's reign.

If you visit in winter, snow may be on the ground, for you are at 3,370 feet (1,028 m). Whatever the season, the views from the 2,673 windows are sublime, sweeping over manicured hedges to the mountains beyond. The small town of San Lorenzo has a number of hotels and restaurants. You may be glad of these, as the Escorial is a vast labyrinth of patios, corridors, halls, staircases, and chapels, requiring at least three hours to visit.

You have to follow a set route around the building: It is well signed, and information panels give good descriptions in Spanish and English of the main features in each room. Your first sight on entering the palace is the series of tapestries called the **Golden Tapestry** (circa 1502), and also El Greco's massive **"Martyrdom of St. Matthew"** (1580–1582). From here you descend to the Museo de Arquitectura, which has a prodigious display of architectural drawings, plans,

models, and examples of carpentry methods used for the turrets. Next is the **Museo de Pinturas** (Painting Museum), with Italian, Spanish, and Flemish masterpieces: Here are works by Titian, Tintoretto, Veronese, Van Dyck, and Rubens. Among them, look for the powerful light in Luca Cambiaso's (1527–1585) **"Archangel St. Michael,"** and the **triptych** by Michel Coxcie (1499–1592). If you have been to the Prado, you may recognize Rogier van der Weyden's **"Descent from the Cross."** However, this is an inferior copy. Place of honor goes to van der Weyden's **"Calvary,"** which Felipe II inherited from his aunt, Mary of Hungary. Compare the original, with its extraordinary shadows and perspective, with the two Juan Fernández Navarrete (circa 1520–1579) copies flanking it. José Ribera (1591–1652), the great protagonist of tenebrism (depiction of shadows) is well represented by his dramatic and luminous **"St. Jerome Penitent"** and **"Aesop."**

Stairs lead up to Felipe II's palace, partly remodeled by Carlos

The Guadarrama mountains create a magnificent backdrop for the Escorial palace.

Casa del Labrador
www.aranjuez.com/Monumental

✉ Calle de la Reina
☎ 91 891 03 05
🕐 Closed Mon.
💲 $. Free Wed. for E.U. nationals. Reservations required.

San Lorenzo de El Escorial
www.patrimonionacional.es/escorial/escorial.htm
🗺 78 A2
Visitor information
✉ Calle Grimaldi 2
☎ 91 890 53 13

**Real Monasterio
de San Lorenzo de
El Escorial**

🗺 78 A2

☎ 91 890 59 03 or
91 890 59 02

🕐 Closed Mon.

💲 $$. Free Wed. for
E.U. nationals

III. Here you glimpse the more intimate side of royal life, from Isabel Clara Eugenia's apartments to those of Felipe II himself, including the bedroom where he died in 1598. In between is the **Strolling Gallery,** an immense hall with windows on three sides, old maps, and countless paintings of 17th-century battle

confronted by a superb El Greco (1541–1614) painting: **"St. Peter,"** a perfect example of his free brush-work and extraordinary perspective. Here, too, are Titian's **"Last Supper"** and Hieronymus Bosch's **"Christ carrying the Cross"** and **"The Crown of Thorns."** The delicate ceiling paintings of these rooms date from the 1580s.

Next you reach the **cloister,** blanketed with fresh-colored **frescoes,** mainly the work of Pellegrino Tibaldi in the late 16th century, and housing the magnificent main staircase of the monastery. Above hovers a spectacular **ceiling fresco** by Luca Giordano (1632–1705), glorifying the Habsburg monarchy; on the walls are more Tibaldi frescoes. The cloister encloses the

Tibaldi's ceiling frescoes crown the Royal Library.

scenes. The curious sundial inlaid in the floor by the south window is a "solar adjuster," a system for checking clocks made by Wendlingen and Baumgarten in 1755.

Pantheon Real
Ostentation soon returns. You now enter the baroque **Pantheon Real,** where a staircase lined with jasper and gilt leads to a circular chamber full of marble caskets. These contain the remains of nearly all the kings of Spain from Carlos V onward. A series of nine adjoining chambers contains the tombs of princes and princesses.

From the Pantheon, steps rise to the vast **Salas Capitulares** (chapter houses), where you are

Main entrance

College with
four courtyards

Grand entrance

EL ESCORIAL

Evangelist Courtyard, with a temple (designed by Herrera) flanked by four pools.

Basilica & library

The basilica stands at the center of El Escorial and dazzles with its 45 side chapels, as well as a monumental marble **"Christ"** by Benvenuto Cellini (1500–1571). The choir stalls were designed by Juan de Herrera, and the beautiful ceiling frescoes are the work of Luca Giordano and Cambiasso. From the church you cross the Kings' Patio to ascend to the vast **royal library** (above the main entrance), with 45,000 books from the 15th and 16th centuries, and 5,000 Arab, Latin, and Castilian manuscripts. Don't miss the ceiling frescoes, again by Tibaldi. Felipe II's fascination for science and astronomy is well represented by various globes and the **Armillary Sphere,** made around 1582. This is an openwork celestial globe showing the solar system according to Ptolemy, the second-century Greek astronomer —a fitting end to what is a homage to one of Spain's most intellectual and concerned kings. ■

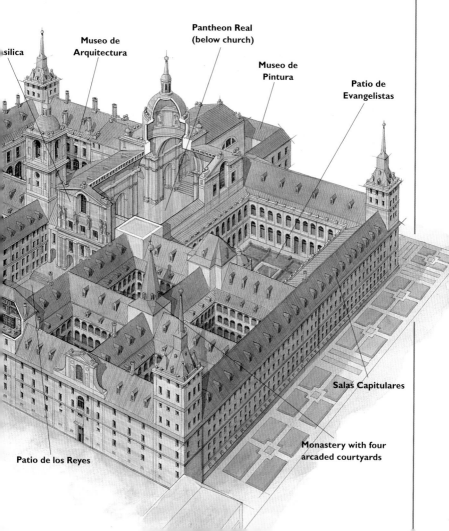

Basilica

Museo de Arquitectura

Pantheon Real (below church)

Museo de Pintura

Patio de Evangelistas

Salas Capitulares

Monastery with four arcaded courtyards

Patio de los Reyes

More places to visit around Madrid

ALCALÁ DE HENARES

The first planned university town in the world lies just 20 miles (33 km) east of Madrid, and is easy to reach by train, bus, or car. In its 16th-century heyday, the university produced the Complutensian Polyglot Bible with four original language texts side by side. Today, despite industrial areas, Alcalá remains a fascinating town, deserving of its World Heritage status accorded in 1998. Three monuments stand out: the **Monasterio de Religiosas Bernardas,** with its baroque extravaganza of a church; the illustrious **university,** centering on the fine plateresque (see p. 45) college of San Ildefonso; and, in contrast, the small **Museum of Miguel de Cervantes,** dedicated to Alcalá's most famous offspring (see pp. 238–39).

🗺 78 B1 **Visitor information** ✉ Callejón Santa María 1 ☎ 91 889 26 94

Chinchón's main square doubles up as a bullring during August festivities.

CHINCHÓN

Chinchón is a quaint, relaxing place, nestling on a hillside 28 miles (45 km) southeast of Madrid. Its only real sight, the **Plaza Mayor,** charms by its total irregularity, with three-story medieval houses rising above porticoes and the church of La Asunción at one end. In August, the square is transformed into a bull-ring, but otherwise life goes on quietly, despite the quantities of anise, gin, and other spirits brewed locally. In the 17th century, the Countess of Chinchón caught malaria in Peru, where her husband was viceroy, and cured herself using the bark of a tropical tree that she subsequently brought back to Spain. This was later named *chinchona* in her honor.

🗺 78 B1 ✉ Plaza Mayor 6 ☎ 91 893 53 23

VALLE DE LOS CAÍDOS

Only 7.5 miles (12 km) from El Escorial (see pp. 79–81) lies this spectacular valley of the Sierra de Guadarrama, chosen by General Franco as the site for his mausoleum. It courts controversy as an ongoing rallying point for right-wing groups, and it has a grim history—Franco's political prisoners of the 1940s and '50s blasted the 804-foot-long (245 m) **basílica** out of the mountainside. A funicular takes you up to the 492-foot-high (150 m) stone cross (La Cruz), said to be the world's largest, above this gloomy church, which contains the tombs both of José Antonio Primo de Rivera, founder of the Falange (see p. 36), and of Franco. The remains of 40,000 soldiers and civilians who died during the Civil War lie in ossuaries beside countless statues of Spanish saints and soldiers. The whole place is a sobering reminder of Spain's dark days.

🗺 78 A2 ✉ Basílica and La Cruz ☎ 91 890 56 11 🕐 Closed Mon. 💲 $ ∎

Guided tours from Madrid

To make life easier, you can visit Aranjuez, El Escorial, Valle de los Caídos, Toledo, Segovia, La Granja, or Ávila on guided day trips from Madrid. Three companies offer comparable services and rates: **Julià Tours** (*Gran Via 68,* *tel 91 559 96 05, Metro: Plaza de España, www.julia tours.es*), **Pullmantur** (*Plaza de Oriente 8, tel 91 541 10 66, Metro: Ópera, www.pullmantur.es*), and **Trapsatur** (*Calle San Bernardo 5, tel 91 542 66 66, Metro: Santo Domingo, www.trapsatur.com*). ∎

Wedged between the Atlantic and the Sierra Cantábrica are the regions of Galicia, Asturias, and Cantabria. Santiago de Compostela is the main magnet; others are pre-historic cave paintings, ancient churches, and exquisite seafood.

Northwest Spain

The ubiquitous scallop shell, the pilgrim's symbol

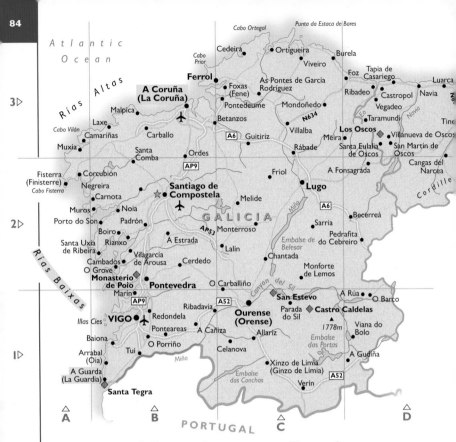

Northwest Spain

IF YOU REMEMBER JUST ONE IMAGE FROM TOURING SPAIN'S NORTHWEST, IT will be that of the humble scallop shell. They are everywhere, on your plate, on pilgrims' staffs, and on roadside signs, pointing the way to Spain's greatest pilgrimage site and westernmost city, Santiago de Compostela. Santiago means "St. James," and pilgrims to his shrine adopted the scallop shell as their symbol. The city named after him is also the magnificent capital of Galicia. Once you have been to Santiago, you understand more about the rest of northern Spain and the spiritual fervor behind its Romanesque churches. You won't be alone either, as in recent years the pilgrimage along the Camino de Santiago (Way of St. James) has undergone an incredible revival.

For pilgrims of yesteryear, much of this part of Spain was quite simply inaccessible due to an awesome mountain chain, the Cordillera Cantábrica. These granite peaks helped protect the region from the Moorish advance, and Asturias and Cantabria are the only part of Spain without any Muslim influence. The northwest does, however, have Paleolithic cave paintings, Celtic, Roman, and Visigothic

remains, and a culture that may remind you of Cornwall in western England, Brittany in western France, or Ireland. Even the climate resembles that of its Celtic cousins: It is mild but often drizzly. Galicia occupies the northwest corner, and is swept by winds straight off the Atlantic.

Weather apart, you can't fail to enjoy the green valleys, apple orchards, meadows, and

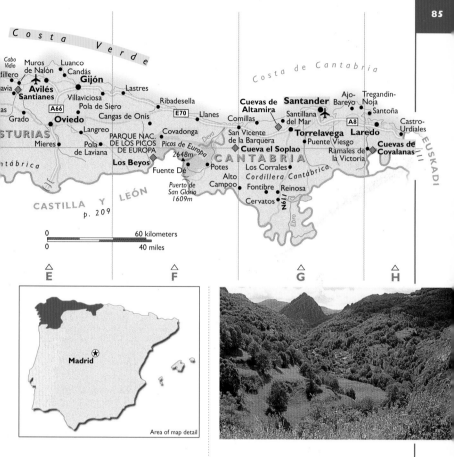

Costa Verde

Costa de Cantabria

Spring wildflowers spangle the lush green foothills of the Picos de Europa.

healthy-looking cows of Asturias and Cantabria; gastronomy is making rapid advances. Cider, rather than wine, is the local tipple in these two regions, and cheese comes in numerous shapes and flavors. The northwest is grain-growing country, and the grain (either corn, originally brought from America, or wheat) ends up in all sorts of dairy-based cakes. Throughout Galicia and Asturias you see picturesque *hórreos*—grain-stores on stilts to keep rodents at bay. For centuries Galicia was the poor cousin of the three, where people painstakingly gleaned a living from fishing or from tiny farms. Hardship prompted extensive emigration to Andalucía and to Latin America. Some emigrants returned once they had made money, and you can easily identify their more gracious houses by the symbolic pair of palm trees growing in front.

The coast is one of high contrast. Galicia has 805 miles (1,289 km) of *rías* (long

sea inlets) and rocky cliffs; Cantabria has long beaches, with the Picos de Europa mountains rising dramatically in the background. Fish, fish, and fish again is the main industry, and Galicia boasts Europe's most important fleet. Hard times came with ecological damage caused by the oil-tanker *Prestige*, which sank off the Galician coast in November 2002, but pristine beaches have now returned.

Relaxed Santander and breezy, glass-balconied A Coruña are the only large coastal towns; otherwise the coast has just a string of fishing villages, low-key resorts, and a handful of industrial towns in Asturias. When touring this region, remember you cross and recross mountains. Journeys might take longer than you expect, but you go through breathtaking scenery. ■

Celtic bagpipes honor local Albariño wine in the August festival at Pontevedra.

Galicia

Spain's most remote region is a wildly beautiful windswept land, squeezed into the peninsula north of Portugal and bordered by the Atlantic on two sides. Celtic culture arrived here around 1000 B.C. Bagpipes are the most obvious sign of Celtic influence, their strident wail still heard in every Galician festival. A deep sense of melancholy and mysticism, a love of poetry, but also a great joie de vivre are present.

Galicians have their own language, *gallego,* a combination of Spanish and Portuguese spoken by nearly 70 percent of the 3 million population. Street names, public information, and museum captions are often only in gallego, which makes this region even more distinctive. Nationalism raised its head in the late 19th century. It was thwarted by the outbreak of the Civil War in 1936, but still simmers today, just as it does in Euskadi (País Vasco) or Basque country and Catalunya.

For centuries Galicia was Spain's poorest region, whose rural inhabitants suffered frequent famines as they eked out a living, either farming on the harsh terrain, or fishing. As a result, Galicians were Spain's most enthusiastic emigrants to Latin America, where the term "Gallego" is interchangeable with "Spanish." Fidel Castro (whose surname derives from the Roman-Celtic word for "fortified village") is probably the most famous Latin American descendant of Galician stock. In the 1980s and '90s, Galicia greatly benefited from E.U. subsidies, and today it has a much more prosperous face, as people give up farms and settle in growing towns on the coast.

Galicia's capital city of Santiago de Compostela has been a magnet for European pilgrims since the Middle Ages. This is a city you must not miss, with its Romanesque architecture and unique atmosphere, but don't ignore charming smaller towns such as Pontevedra, Ourense, and Tui, or the sharply indented coastline and verdant inland hills. Here are remote hermitages, deserted beaches, and dramatic canyons, and all over Galicia you find the region's own wines and divinely fresh seafood. The regional newspaper devotes an entire page to maritime news and the price of 46 types of fish, so variety is assured. ■

A Coruña (La Coruña)

GALICIA'S FORMER CAPITAL WAS DEMOTED IN 1982. IT NOW concentrates its energies on deep-sea fishing and cargo activities. Everything here evokes the sea: The city stands on a peninsula and has salty air, Atlantic beaches, and a Roman lighthouse (the city's emblem). The ill-fated Armada of 1588 set off from here, and its defeat by the English spelled the end of Spanish maritime power.

The most interesting part of the city starts at the well-defined neck of the peninsula, where La Coruña's nickname of "crystal city" originated. Street after street is lined with houses that have several stories of glassed-in balconies, to protect people from the wind while they enjoy the sun. From a distance this looks like modernist architecture of the 1960s, but at closer quarters you can see distinctive 19th-century styles. Here, too, is **Plaza de María Pita,** the arcaded main square, named for a local heroine who saved the town from an English invasion in 1589 by raising the alarm during the night.

Dominating one side of the square is the **Palacio Municipal,** an ornate late 19th-century building that also houses a small **museum of clocks** (*Plaza de María Pita, tel 981 18 42 00, closed a.m. & weekends*). Two blocks south lies the **marina,** and immediately east is the old quarter, which meets the waterfront at **Castillo de San Antón.** This castle is an archaeological museum with exhibits on Galicia's Roman culture, and beautiful Iberian and Celtic metalwork.

Nearby stands the church of **Santiago** (*Plaza de Azcárraga, tel 981 18 98 40*), part Romanesque and part Gothic. Two streets away is the harmonious collegiate church of **Santa María del Campo** (*Calle Damas, tel 981 20 31 86*). Built by the guild of seafarers, it has a beautiful carved Romanesque portal beneath its rose window. In front of the church is a 15th-century

Calvary (representation of the Crucifixion). One mile north of this atmospheric area looms the **Torre de Hércules** (Hercules Tower, *Carretera de la Torre, tel 981 22 37 30*), built by the Romans in the second century A.D., but considerably remodeled in 1790. Said to be the world's oldest working lighthouse, it rises to a lofty 341 feet (104 m). You can climb to the top for the view. The ultramodern building across the cove below is **Domus** (*Ensenada del Orzán, tel 981 18 98 40*), an interactive museum of mankind designed in the 1990s by the Japanese architect Arata Isozaki. ∎

A Coruña (La Coruña)
www.aytolacoruna.es/en
🅰 84 B3
Visitor information
✉ Dársena de la Marina
☎ 981 22 18 22

Castillo de San Antón and Museo Arqueológico
www.sananton.org
✉ Paseo Marítimo del Parrote
☎ 981 18 98 50
🕐 Closed Sun. p.m. & Mon.
💲 $

Coruña's penchant for glassed-in balconies is particularly visible along the seafront.

Way of St. James

For ten centuries pilgrims have been doggedly treading the long path to Santiago de Compostela in a protracted ritual of self-purification. Their goal is the immense cathedral built to house the remains of St. James (Santiago). The remains may or may not be there, but they have had immense symbolic significance for Spain. The apostle preached widely in Roman Spain before returning to Judea to face execution, after which his body was allegedly brought back by followers to Galicia. After long oblivion, its discovery in the ninth century inspired not just a cathedral and pilgrimage route, but also the infrastructure to serve it and the spread of Christian culture throughout northern Spain. In turn, this gave impetus to the fight against the Moors of al-Andalus, and later, a justification (proselytizing) for conquering the New World.

Originally just a simple monastic complex, the subsequent grandiose cathedral of Santiago rapidly became a magnet for pilgrims, bringing them along fixed routes lined with hospices, sanctuaries, and increasingly sophisticated cathedrals. From Tours, Vézélay, and Le Puy in France, pilgrims crossed the Pyrenees via Roncesvalles or Somport, meeting at Puente La Reina to continue together in 13-day stages along the "French Way." This became so popular that in the 12th century a type of pilgrim's guide (Book V of the Liber Sancti Iacobi, or Book of St. James) was written, detailing the characteristics of the regions and people en route. After giving the Basques and people of Navarra a poor press, it becomes more lyrical when describing Castilla and even more so with Galicia—"a land made pleasant by its rivers, meadows and marvelous orchards, its fine fruits and crystal springs…. Abundant too are gold and silver, textiles and furs and other riches, particularly Saracen treasures." With such worldly enticements, pilgrims flocked to Santiago from Portugal, Germany, the Low Countries, Italy, and, by maritime routes, England and Scandinavia. However, the French Way predominated, and it is still followed in today's revival of the medieval trail. Every five years, Holy Year sees participants double in number; the next is 2009, see www.xacobeo.es and www.turgalicia.es.

Along the route villages, bridges were built, and Romanesque and Gothic architecture

The casket at Santiago de Compostela is said to contain the relics of St. James.

Covering a section of the long walk to Santiago de Compostela

blossomed. In addition to hospices and monasteries, pilgrims also needed protection from brigands, and this was provided by castles, forts, and military-religious orders such as the Knights of Santiago. Another offshoot was the proliferation of secondary cults associated with the Way of St. James.

To show their status, pilgrims adopted the scallop shell as a symbol. The Liber Sancti Iacobi explains this by a legend about St. James's arrival. A horseman plunged into the sea from the Portuguese coast at the precise moment when the boat transporting the apostle was sailing by. Miraculously, both steed and rider emerged from the depths, draped in scallop shells—hence the symbol. ∎

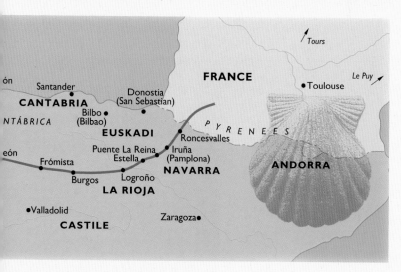

Santiago de Compostela

SANTIAGO HAS BEEN DRAWING PILGRIMS FROM ALL OVER Europe for more than a millennium. Today, visitors still pour in on foot, by bicycle, or even on horseback, but the second-most visited site after the catedral is now the Mercado de Abastos, a cornucopian food market. Santiago exudes an inimitable atmosphere, with wonderful old buildings, great seafood restaurants, and winding medieval streets.

Start at the **catedral,** a massive edifice that rises between four squares. Its ornate towers, carved doorways, and facade are a visual symphony of styles. The cathedral was first built in Romanesque style in the 11th to 13th centuries, but much of it was subsequently modified. Look at the main western facade from the vast **Praza do Obradoiro,** and you see a baroque masterpiece (1750) by Fernando Casas y Novoa. Inside you are faced with the magnificent Romanesque inner facade, the **Pórtico de la Gloria,** which was the work of Master Mateo in 1188. Pilgrims touch the central pillar as they give thanks for safe arrival, and over the centuries their fingers have left imprints. Above the triple-arched doorway, the carvings of the central tympanum show Christ in Majesty flanked by the four evangelists with the 24 Elders of the Apocalypse. Above the central pillar is a seated figure of Santiago (St. James); crouched behind it is the **Santo dos Croques,** meaning "saint of the bumps," which may be a self-portrait of Master Mateo himself. It is said to impart wisdom to those who knock their heads on it.

A long line grows at the **Puerta Santa** (east facade door), which gives direct access to the crypt containing the relics of St. James. To avoid this, go around to the south facade (on **Praza das Praterías),** and enter the cathedral through the stunning **Puerta de las Platerías.** Its low-relief sculptures (1103) illus-trate biblical scenes from Adam and Eve to the flagellation of Christ.

Despite visitors, the cathedral interior has a working atmosphere. During major celebrations the bota-fumeiro, a gigantic incense burner, is suspended from the dome and swung like a pendulum in front of the dazzling baroque high altar.

Don't miss the treasury, the 16th-century cloister, or the crypt museum: one ticket gets you into all three. The **treasury** (off the south aisle, on the right as you face the altar) has a bust (1332) of St. James Alpheus, a lesser apostle, that contains his relics. You reach the 16th-century cloisters from the transept. The upper floors have Flemish tapestries and give wonderful views. The **crypt museum** has contemporary versions of the zithers, fidulas, viols, and lutes played by the Elders on the Pórtico de la Gloria. Best of all is the reconstruction of the original choir structure, destroyed in 1603.

Next to the cathedral is the **Palacio Gelmírez** (Praza do Obradoiro, tel 981 58 35 48, closed Sun. p.m. and siestas), the former archbishop's palace, now exhibition space. Built in the 12th and 13th centuries, it is a rare example of a civil Romanesque building. Inside is the **Salón Sinodal,** over 98 feet (30 m) long, that has unusual rib-vaulting and carved figures illustrating medieval domestic life. On the square outside, admire the facades of the Colegio de San Jerónimo (1501) to the south, the Pazo Raxoi (1766) to the west, now home to the Galician

Santiago de Compostela
www.santiagoturismo.com
📍 84 B2
Visitor information
✉ Rúa do Vilar 63
☎ 981 55 51 29

Catedral
www.archicompostela.org/Catedral/catedral.htm
✉ Praza do Obradoiro
☎ 981 58 11 55

Museos de la Catedral
☎ 981 56 05 27
💲 $ (Treasury, crypt, & cloisters)

The baroque facade of Santiago's cathedral towers overshadows the Praza do Obradoiro.

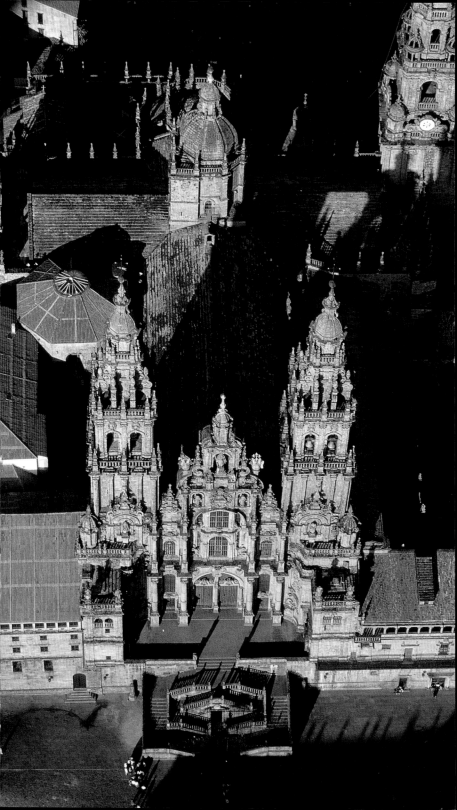

government, and, to the north, the Antiguo Hospital Real, founded in the 16th century to care for sick pilgrims but now a luxury parador.

At the back of the cathedral are two interconnecting squares. **Praza das Praterías** was the home of the silversmiths' guild, and **Praza da Quintana** used to be a cemetery.

You can enjoy the majestic setting at several outdoor cafés: This is a wonderful spot from which to admire the cathedral entrance known variously as the **Puerta Santa** (Holy Door) or **Puerta del Perdón** and its sculptures by Master Mateo.

Behind, is the **Monasterio de**

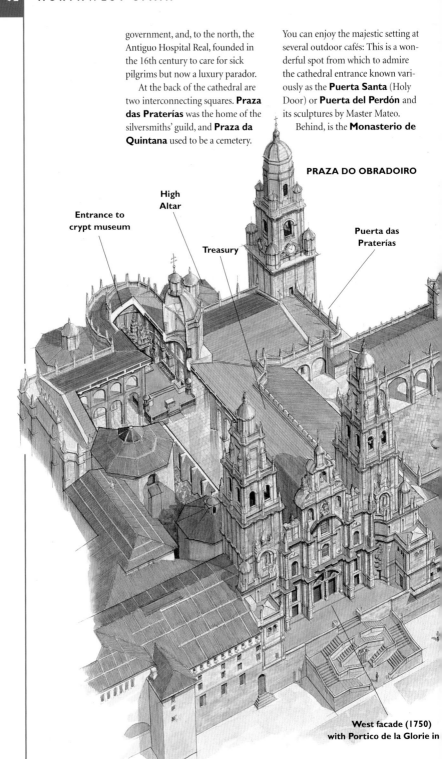

PRAZA DO OBRADOIRO

Entrance to crypt museum

High Altar

Treasury

Puerta das Praterías

West facade (1750) with Portico de la Glorie in

Cloisters

Tapestry museum

rary

San Paio de Antealtares *(Praza da Quintana),* founded in the ninth century to house the tomb of St. James, and its church, dating from 1707. The **Museo de Arte Sacro** *(tel 981 58 31 27, closed Sun. & Oct.–March),* displays sculpture, paintings, gold, and silverwork.

One former monastery, now a museum, is the Convento de Santo Domingo de Bonaval, ten minutes' walk northeast of the center, now the **Museo do Pobo Galego** (Museum of the Galicians, *Convento de Santo Domingo, tel 981 58 36 20, closed Mon. & Sun. p.m.).* Set around verdant cloisters, the rooms are packed with traditional handicrafts, costumes, agricultural implements, and musical instruments. The visit is worthwhile if only to climb the remarkable triple spiral staircase designed by Domingo de Andrade in the 17th century. Next door to the museum, in complete contrast, stands Galicia's contemporary art center, **Centro Gallego de Arte Contemporáneo** *(Rúa Ramón del Valle-Inclán, tel 981 54 66 29, closed Mon.),* built in 1993 to a minimalist design by Portuguese architect Alvaro Siza.

The **Museo de las Peregrinaciones** *(Praza do San Miguel, tel 981 58 15 58, closed Sun. p.m. & Mon.)* sheds light on the fascinating story of the Santiago pilgrimage, and it is partly housed in a Gothic tower. Exhibits illustrate the traditions of the Way of St. James, and include jet jewelry, one of Santiago's traditional crafts. This is still produced and sold on nearby **Calle Azabachería.**

A few yards downhill from the museum you will find the church of **San Martín Pinario** *(Plaza de San Martín),* built in 1597, with gracefully curved steps leading down to its plateresque (see p. 45) facade. Inside are a breathtaking baroque altarpiece and finely carved 17th-century choir stalls. This church is part of the massive monastery of San Martín Pinario.

Just south of the main religious epicenter, a must-visit is the **Mercado de Abastos** *(Praza de Abastos, tel 981 58 34 38, closed Sun.),* the city's main food market which dates from 1873. It is now dynamically run by a local collective. On busy Thursdays and Saturdays, over 4,000 locals come to fill their shopping baskets.

Like the rest of Spain, Santiago de Compostela is gunning for high cultural status with an ambitious mega-project, the **Cidade de Cultura de Galicia.** This is taking shape southeast of town at Monte do Gaias. Designed by the American architect, Peter Eisenman, the 173-acre (70 ha) arts complex of local stone is carved into the hillside. Not without controversy, the budget has more than tripled and building has stopped and restarted. ■

Drive: The hórreo trail from Santiago to Cabo Fisterra

This circuit takes you west to the wild reaches of Galicia's Atlantic coast. It encompasses the characteristic scenes of Spain's most remote province, from rural landscapes to empty beaches and historic fishing villages. You also see plenty of Galicia's *hórreos* (pitched-roof grain-stores on stilts), now more decorative than functional.

Leave Santiago de Compostela (see pp. 90–93) by following signs to Noia (C543), turning right at the unmarked traffic circle on the outskirts. At Bertamiráns, turn right to drive through eucalyptus and pine forests to Negreira, where you turn left toward Muxia (AC443). Rolling farmland, tiny hamlets, and hórreos are the recurring theme of this stretch. At Pereira, the road becomes AC441. On reaching a major junction at Berdoias, turn left on the AC552 to Corcubión.

This takes you past the industrial town of Cée, then 1.8 miles (3 km) farther to

Corcubión ①. This charming fishing village has fine emblazoned houses with glazed balconies. At low tide you see people collecting shellfish.

Continue by following signs to Fisterra (Finisterre), 9 miles (14 km) farther. On the way you round a headland with stunning views through pines to the Atlantic Ocean below, and you pass the half-moon beaches of Praia de Estorde, Praia de Langosteira, and Praia de Sardiñeiro. At **Fisterra ②** itself, follow the sign marked Faro (lighthouse) through the town. Stop at the lovely 12th-

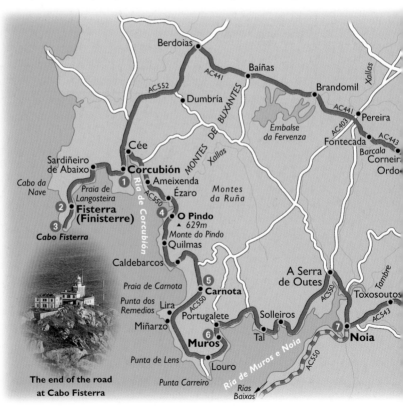

The end of the road at Cabo Fisterra

century church of **Santa María des Areas** (*Closed in winter*), on the main road at the edge of town, to see its much revered statue of Christ with a golden beard, before continuing to the lighthouse. It stands on Europe's westernmost point, **Cabo Fisterra ❸**. Magnificent panoramas open up over the rocky bay, and a path around the lighthouse gives vertiginous views of the surf below.

Retrace your route to Corcubión and Cée to turn right on the C550 towards Muros. After crossing the estuary of Ézaro you reach **O Pindo ❹**, another stunning beach, before passing the rock formations of the 2,063-foot (629 m) **Monte do Pindo,** also known as the Celtic Olympus. The next stop is **Carnota ❺**, which has Galicia's longest hórreo. On entering the village turn right at the main square, circle left around the church, and there it is—a grain-store of 1763 that stretches 78 feet (24 m) in length. Six miles (10 km) farther are Carnota's magnificent wild sand dunes and beach.

Traditional grain-stores or *hórreos*

Go back to the main road, and continue to **Muros ❻** (*Visitor information, Casa del Ayuntamiento, Curro da Praza, tel 981 86 60 50*), a surprisingly grand town with arcaded buildings facing the bay. In 1544, a French fleet was sunk offshore, and in 1809 French troops burned 185 houses in the town. Walk up through the labyrinth of picturesque lanes to see **Santa María do Campo** (1400), a blend of Romanesque and Gothic, then head for the **Pescadería Vella** to see a curious turtle-topped fount.

From Muros, the road snakes around forested promontories overlooking the bay, where you see platforms for collecting mussels. It then crosses a high bridge to make a dramatic arrival at the historic little port of **Noia ❼** (*Visitor information, Casa de la Cultura, Rúa Luis Cadarso 6, tel 981 82 41 69*). Noia's lovely Romanesque church of **Santa María a Nova** (*Carreiriña do E. Ferreiro, closed Sat. p.m. & Sun. p.m.*) was built in 1327 and has a unique collection of more than 300 tombstones from the 10th to the 16th centuries, each one carved with symbols of the deceased's trade. The **medieval quarter** radiates from the Praza do Tapal, dominated by the church of **San Martiño** (1434), an example of Galician Gothic with a magnificent carved portal. It may remind you of Master Mateo's work at Santiago, and Mateo was, in fact, a strong influence. Noia also has many fine old mansions that are well worth seeking out.

From Noia you can return 21 miles (34 km) to Santiago on the AC543 or continue south to the Rías Baixas (see p. 97). ∎

🄽 See area map p. 84
▶ Santiago
🔁 125 miles (200 km)
🕒 1 or 2 days
▶ Cabo Fisterra

NOT TO BE MISSED
- Cabo Fisterra
- Carnota
- Muros
- Santa María a Nova, Noia
- San Martiño, Noia

In & around Pontevedra

Pontevedra
www.concellopontevedra.es/
  ingles/index_i.htm
▲ 84 B2
Visitor information
✉ Calle General
  Gutiérrez Mellado 1
☎ 98 685 08 14

**Museo de
Pontevedra**
www.museo.depontevedra
 .es
✉ Pasantería 10
☎ 98 685 14 55
🕐 Closed Sun. p.m.
  & Mon.

**Part of the
Museo de
Pontevedra faces
Praza de Leña.**

PONTEVEDRA IS ONE OF GALICIA'S MORE SEDUCTIVE small towns. According to legend it was founded by the Greek warrior Teucro, who fought at Troy. More prosaic history records that it prospered on sardine fishing until the mid-16th century, when its port silted up forever.

As a result of its former prosperity, Pontevedra has numerous fine old buildings of local granite, especially in the old town. This is now a lively pedestrianized zone. Pretty little squares such as **Praza do Teucro** and **Praza da Verdura** are still used by traditional specialist markets. The more grandiose **Praza da Herrería** has gardens overlooked by the 14th-century monastery and church of San Francisco. Opposite stands the unusual neoclassic church of the Virgen la Peregrina, built to an elliptical form to house a statue of the city's patron saint. To the west in the old fishermen's quarter stands the plateresque church of **Santa María la Mayor** (*Avenida Santa María 24, tel 98 686 61 85*), erected by the powerful seamen's guild in the 16th century. Low-relief biblical scenes adorn the western facade.

The excellent museum, **Museo de Pontevedra,** housed in five different sites, three of which face the delightful arcaded **Praza da Leña.** The 18th-century mansion of **Castro Monteagudo** displays magnificent Celtic jewelry from 800–700 B.C. and a collection of medieval and Renaissance Spanish, Italian, and Flemish paintings. The museum continues in the beautifully conserved neighboring house of **García Flórez,** with precious metalwork, religious statuary, and reconstructed period interiors, including one of a ship. Galician art and Spanish paintings of the 19th and 20th centuries are displayed in the Edificio Sarmiento and Edificio Fernández López. Don't miss the fifth section, however: This is the evocative Gothic ruin of **Santo Domingo,** next to the leafy gardens of the Alameda, where architectural fragments and sculptures are exhibited. The **Alameda** is a popular spot for the paseo.

Just 4 miles (6 km) west from Pontevedra is the Benedictine **Monasterio de Poio** (*tel 98 677 02 44*). The monastery is medieval and rather forbidding, but the church is a fine example of late Galician classicism, completed in 1708. The 16th-century processional cloister was the work of Portuguese architect Mateo López. ∎

Rías Baixas

THE LONG, FJORDLIKE INLETS OF THE GALICIAN COAST
are known as *rías*. Those between Noia and Vigo are called the Rías
Baixas—the lower rías—to distinguish them from the Rías Altas on
the more exposed northern coast that curves around to A Coruña.
The Rías Baixas have a milder climate, and most of Galicia's tourism.

Fortified Roman-Celtic villages *(cas-tros)* and dolmens (prehistoric slab
tombs), *hórreos* (grain-stores), *pazos*
(mansions), and Romanesque
churches are plentiful. Some spots
are overrated; including the island
of Arousa, despite its bird sanctuary. The resort of O Grove, and the
island of A Toxa have limited appeal.

Head instead for the delightful
town of **Cambados.** Dominating
the main square is the 16th-century
Pazo de Fefiñanes, a Renaissance
palace carved with stone busts and
heraldic arms, and an arched footbridge leading to the San Sadurniño
tower. Across the square stands the
church of **San Benedict.** Vineyards around the town produce
light, slightly fruity and sparkling
white Albariño wine. Bodegas
(wine cellars) abound, and good

local bars face the Pazo de Fefiñanes.

The **Illas Cíes** are a cluster of
beautiful uninhabited islands off
the Ría de Vigo with white beaches,
pine forests where rare seabirds nest,
and Celtic remains. In summer, you
can take a 40-minute boat trip to this
national park and stay at a campsite
(tel 98 643 83 58). The much industrialized fishing port of **Vigo**
(Spain's largest) has pockets of
interest around the harbor, a hilltop
castle with wonderful views, and an
impressive new museum of contemporary art, MARCO *(rua do Principe
54, tel 98 611 39 00, closed Mon.)*.

Baiona, the southernmost
town of the Rías Baixas, has massive
fortified walls of the **Castelo de
Monte Real,** where the towns-
people sheltered from pirate attacks
in earlier centuries. ■

Baiona's Castelo
de Monte Real
(now a parador)
overlooks the
fishing harbor.

Illas Cíes
www.turismodevigo.com

🅰 84 B1

✉ Naviera Mar de Ons,
    Estación Marítima
    de Ría, Vigo

☎ 986 22 52 72

🚢 Boats hourly July—
    mid-Sept. Also Ría
    de Vigo day-cruises

Vigo

🅰 84 B1

✉ Canovas del
    Castillo 22

☎ 986 43 05 77

Baiona
www.baiona.org/org/us/ind
    ex.html

🅰 84 B1

Visitor information

✉ Paseo da Ribeira

☎ 98 668 70 67

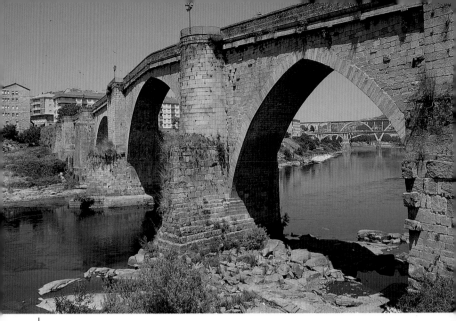

Ourense's pride and joy, its Roman bridge, is in fact almost entirely reconstructed.

In & around Ourense (Orense)

THIS INLAND TOWN RIMMED BY MOUNTAIN RANGES IS noticeably poorer than Galicia's prosperous seaboard, although Ourense is rich in natural resources. Here the Miño River, which crosses Ourense on its way south to the Portuguese border, creates an extensive, fertile valley, the heart of Ribeiro wine country.

Ourense (Orense)
www.turismourense.com
🅰 84 C1
Visitor information
✉ Caseta do Legoeiro, Ponte Romana
☎ 988 37 20 20

Museo Arqueológico
✉ Plaza Mayor
☎ 988 22 38 84
🕐 Closed Mon. & Sun. p.m.

The city of 100,000 inhabitants has a confrontational past: It was attacked by Romans, Visigoths, Swabians (who destroyed the town in A.D. 463), Moors, and Normans (responsible for further destruction in 970). Today, it proudly conserves a **Roman bridge,** rebuilt in the Middle Ages for pilgrims going to Santiago, and other monuments in the pedestrianized **casco viejo** (old town). The **catedral** (*Praza do Trigo, tel 98 822 09 92*), originally Romanesque, has three exceptional portals. The best is the west-facing **Pórtico del Paraíso,** which is decorated with polychrome sculptures. The **interior** has carved choir stalls, suspended lanterns, gilded statues, and carved sar-

cophagi set into niches, all combining to make a harmonious work of art. The high altar has a very ornate retable (1520).

Uphill from the cathedral, beyond lanes of tapas bars, the **Claustro de San Francisco** (*Emilia Pardo Bazán, tel 988 24 03 77, closed Mon.*) has elegant Gothic cloisters with finely decorated capitals on slender columns. Walk east of the cathedral to see the charming **Praza do Ferro,** lined with timbered medieval houses. Then walk down from the cathedral to the sloping, arcaded **Praza Maior.** On one corner, the excellent **Museo Arqueológico** is in a 12th-century archbishop's palace with an ornately emblazoned Renaissance facade. The intelligently laid out collection (with fleeting views over internal patios) is strong on Gallic-Roman pieces, and has Romanesque and Gothic statuary. Notice the fine granite statue of a Roman warrior and the polychrome Romanesque figure of **Nuestra Señora del Refugio,** which shows a strong Byzantine influence. Ourense's steaming thermal springs, known as **Las Burgas,** are on the square of the same name. The water (which heats up to 153°F/ 67°C) erupts into a neoclassic fountain and pools which are surrounded by contemporary sculptures.

It's an easy excursion 18 miles (30 km) west to **Ribadavia,** a pretty riverside town and the center of Ribeiro wine. In 1063, it was capital of the kingdom of Galicia. Old stone houses cluster around Praza Magdalena, once home to a large Jewish community that specialized in the wine trade. Among the churches, 13th- to 14th-century Santo Domingo has a Romanesque-Gothic interior. Rising beside the road, crumbling walls of the **Castillo de los Condes de Ribadavia** enclose tombs and towers.

CANYON DEL SIL

Venture 12 miles (20 km) northeast of Ourense and you could spend an entire day exploring the other-worldly canyon of the Río Sil, whose confluence with the Miño has been tapped to create two reservoirs. This wild, thickly forested region of oaks, pines, and ferns harbors unique historical sights. Hikers follow trails; the more indolent take two-hour boat trips across the river's dark green waters. Of the canyon's three monasteries, **San Estevo,** reachable only by car or on foot, is the most overwhelming in scale, style, and history. It was founded in the sixth century, but the earliest parts are a Romanesque **cloister** and

church. The other two cloisters date from the 16th and 17th centuries, and there is a monumental staircase dating from 1739. This vast edifice has been extensively restored and is now a wonderfully remote and atmospheric parador.

The 9-mile (14 km) drive from Loureiro, 2.5 miles (4 km) east of the monastery, to the village of Parada do Sil gives the most spectacular views over the canyon. Teetering on the brink 3 miles (5 km) north of Parada is the **monastery of Santa Cristina,** which, like San Estevo, stands on the site of earlier wooden structures. What you see dates from the 12th and 13th centuries. Trails make this perfect hiking terrain.

Castro Caldelas is a ruined castle 25 miles (40 km) farther east. Medieval ramparts give huge views, and inside is an illuminating ethnographic museum. Don't miss the **Torre del Reloj** where you get a close view of a 1760 clock that functions with stone weights. ◼

Ribadavia
www.ribadavia.net
▲ 84 B1
Visitor information
✉ Praza Mayor
☎ 98 847 12 75
🕐 Closed Oct.–May

Boat trips along Sil canyon
Viajes Pardo
www.riosil.com
✉ Juan XXIII, I
    Ourense
☎ 98 821 51 00

Canyon del Sil's striking topography has become a favorite with hikers, following in the footsteps of yesterday's monks.

More places to visit in Galicia

BETANZOS

The delightful and historic town of Betanzos, formerly a port (until it became silted up), lies 14 miles (23 km) southeast of A Coruña. By the 14th century the commercial talents of its inhabitants had earned them the nickname the "Genoese of Spain." They used their wealth to build the medieval streets and buildings you see today, including the pleasingly asymmetrical 14th- to 15th-century church of **Santa María del Azogue,** and the neighboring church of **San Francisco** (1387). This lovely Gothic structure has tombs in niches in the walls and sculptures of wild boar. Best of all is the tomb of the town's powerful 14th-century ruler and church founder, Count Fernán Pérez de Andrade. His extraordinary sarcophagus is raised on the backs of his heraldic animals, a boar and a bear. Betanzos holds fairs on the first and sixteenth day of every month, when you see crowds of locals selling and buying homemade baskets, cheese, tables, and all sorts of other things—even socks.

The cathedral of San Telmo dominates the atmospheric cobbled streets of Tui's medieval quarter.

🅰 84 B3 **Visitor information,** www.betanzos .es ✉ Praza de Galicia 1 ☎ 981 77 66 66

A GUARDA (LA GUARDIA)

The local lobsters are excellent, but another reason to venture to this remote town on the Portuguese border is to see **Monte de Santa Tegra.** This legendary hill has the restored remains of a Celtic-Roman *castro* (fortified village) dating back to 600–200 B.C. The rebuilt circular stone dwellings occupy an impressive strategic location, and the *mirador* (viewpoint) that crowns the hill gives fantastic all-around views: The best are south across the Río Miño to Portugal and west across the Atlantic. Just below stands a small **museum** *(tel 98 661 00 00)* with stone inscriptions, Roman amphorae, and other pieces found during excavations. From the castro, a path lined with stone crosses leads to the hermitage of Santa Tegra. 🅰 84 B1

TUI

The medieval quarter of this charming small town is clearly defined by a sharp rise in level along the elegant, tree-lined Rúa Ordoñez. Above lies a web of atmospheric cobbled streets enclosing nine religious structures, dominated by the **catedral San Telmo.** The cathedral dates from 1120 and looks like a fortress because its other role was to fend off attacks from Valença, in Portugal. It incorporates both Romanesque and Gothic styles, and the beautifully sculpted main portal is said to be the earliest example of Gothic in Spain. The **museum treasury** has fine liturgical objects and silverware. It leads to the **cloisters,** from which you reach the corner tower. Climb this to the ramparts for views to Portugal. Opposite the cathedral is the **Museo Diocesano** *(tel 98 660 31 07, closed Oct.–Easter),* with exhibits from the Roman to baroque periods. At the **Convento de las Encerradas** (Convent of the Cloistered Nuns, *Rúa das Monxas*), barely visible nuns sell home-baked cookies through a swiveling counter in the wall. 🅰 84 B1 **Visitor information** ✉ Calle Colón ☎ 98 60 17 89 ∎

The Sierra Cantábrica rises in the distance behind Luarca in Asturias.

Asturias & Cantabria

Squeezed between some of Spain's highest mountain ranges and the Cantabrian Sea, these two regions are a seductive combination of magnificent landscapes richly spiked with history. If you are traveling by car, you are in for momentous driving, with vast vistas over emerald green valleys, precipitous ridges, and narrow, gushing ravines. Lush pastures, contented cattle, and solid stone houses are other hallmarks of Spain's most bucolic region, and it also has sandy beaches, fishing ports, and ski resorts.

About 12,000 years ago, Paleolithic (Old Stone Age) people painted the caves that riddle Cantabria's limestone terrain. The caves of Altamira are world famous but viewing is restricted; at other sites you can gaze at this mysterious art more easily. Millions of years earlier, dinosaurs roamed here and the new Museo Jurasico at Colunga does them imaginative justic. Much later, the mountains that rear behind the Cantabrian coast protected the last Christian enclave in Spain: In 718, a Visigothic nobleman named Pelayo halted the Moorish advance north in the Picos de Europa. These mountains now form Europe's largest national park.

Oviedo is the industrialized Asturian capital, with three beautiful pre-Romanesque churches. The undisputed star of Romanesque in Astrias is at Santillana del Mar, but

Cantabrian roads are dotted with signs pointing travelers to lesser known structures. In contrast, Santander, the Cantabrian capital, is a lighthearted 19th-century resort that makes a relaxing stopover. Westward from here, a string of small coastal resorts dish up generous portions of seafood and shellfish. Try large white beans (*fabes*) with clams, or Asturias's adventurous new cuisine, and wash them down with Asturias's specialty: local cider.

The coast of Asturias is busy with industries based on its coal and iron mines. Move inland and you find age-old traditions such as clog-making, and wild countryside. In Cantabria, 40 percent of the half million inhabitants live in rural communities where livestock farming predominates. You may even see mules loaded with delicious Cabrales cheeses plodding down mountain paths to market towns. ■

Oviedo
www.oviedo.es

🗺 85 E3

Visitor information

✉ Calle Cimadevilla 4

☎ 985 21 33 85

Catedral
www.arsvirtual.com/monum
/oviedo.htm

✉ Plaza de Alfonso II

⊕ Closed Sun. (Cámara
Santa, Claustro, &
Museo Diocesano)

💲 $. Free Thurs. p.m.

☎ 985 20 31 17

**Iglesias
Prerrománicas de
Monte Naranco**

☎ 985 29 56 85 &
676 03 20 87

⊕ Closed Sun. &
Mon. p.m.

💲 $ (30-minute guided
tour); free Mon. a.m.

**Outside Oviedo
lies the church of
Santa María del
Naranco.**

Oviedo

SET IN A BOWL OF LAND THAT IS OFTEN SMOTHERED BY
low, misty cloud, Oviedo is not at first sight the most enticing of
Spanish towns. Yet the modern capital of Asturias is Christian Spain's
oldest city, and a good proportion of the 200,000 inhabitants keep the
cider flowing nightly in the *sidrerías* of the old town.

Rising above the elegant **Plaza
Alfonso II,** named after the ninth-
century founder of the town, is the
catedral, a sprawling edifice in
Flamboyant Gothic style. It towers
over the remains of the church of
San Tirso (its ninth-century prede-
cessor), the former monastery of
San Vicente, now the **archaeological museum** *(Currently closed for
restoration),* and the Benedictine
monastery of San Pelayo. Inside the
cathedral is the vaulted **Cámara
Santa,** which has remarkable statues, capitals, and precious objects.
You reach it from the corner of the
nave that also gives access to the
14th-century cloisters and the
Museo Diocesano. This has
splendid processional crosses, chal-

ices, and Romanesque statues.

A few steps from the cathedral,
the **Museo de Bellas Artes**
*(Palacio de Velarde, Santa Ana 1, tel
985 21 30 61, closed Mon.)* is richly
stocked with art from the 16th to
the 20th centuries. Emphasis is on
Asturian and Spanish painting, but
Flemish and Italian works are here,
too, as are porcelain and glass. In the
web of streets extending south from
here baroque stone mansions are
juxtaposed with Asturian timbered
buildings with projecting first floors.

Just outside Oviedo are its most
prized buildings: three rare pre-
Romanesque churches. Closest to
the center is ninth-century **San
Julián de los Prados** *(tel 607
35 39 99, closed Sun.).* Squeezed
between the Gijón highway and
suburban back streets near the
Campus Universitario, it is a serene,
brick-vaulted structure with well-
restored frescoes and lattice windows. Venture 2.5 miles (4 km)
northwest of Oviedo to Monte
Naranco and you come to **Santa
María,** built in A.D. 848 as the
king's summer palace before being
transformed into a church a
century later. This beautifully
proportioned two-story structure
has open loggias and a vaulted
crypt, originally built as a guard-
room. Immediately uphill stands
its contemporary, **San Miguel
de Lillo.** The capitals and reliefs
are very delicately sculpted. These
two churches are called the
**Iglesias Prerrománicas de
Monte Naranco,** and visits are
by guided tour only. ■

Los Oscos

SPANIARDS FROM FARTHER SOUTH VISIT ASTURIAS FOR one reason: to escape the unrelenting dryness elsewhere. Los Oscos, 60 miles (100 km) west of Oviedo, makes the classic destination. The valleys of these remote mountains have lush, untouched scenery, rivers, and waterfalls, strong folk traditions, and hearty food.

The warmhearted inhabitants who inherit their strong, dark features from Roman ancestors drawn here by gold. Rural tourism is taking off in the region, giving ample opportunities for hiking, horseback riding, and trout fishing, and encouraging traditional crafts. Accommodations are simple, but hospitable.

Three villages bear the name Oscos (Santa Eulalia, Villanueva, and San Martín), but **Taramundi** is the best place to start exploring. It was a center of knifemaking, as iron was worked in local forges using water power. Several old watermills show 18th-century technology, notably that of **Teixois,** a dizzy 20-minute drive southeast. From Taramundi the narrow, often potholed road winds southeast to the three Oscos, passing 3,330-foot

(1,015 m) Pico de Ouroso. **Santa Eulalia** is the most modernized of the three, but has exemplary 18th-century rural architecture and a stunning site. A road through pristine forest (where bears live) leads to **Villanueva,** with its partly ruined Benedictine monastery, where one barrel-vaulted room exhibits information on the region.

The last village, **San Martín,** has the most tortuous access roads, as it lies huddled between two sierra. Next to the church is an impeccable slate-and-thatch-roofed *hórreo* (grain-store), the best of the many in the region. The baroque archway leads to the former palace of the Guzmanes. A few miles on at **Mon** you will find the turreted, emblazoned 16th- to 18th-century palace of the Mon y Velarde family. ■

*Hórreo, or grain-store on stilts, typical of **Galicia** and **Asturias***

Taramundi
www.taramundi.net
🄰 84 D3
Visitor information
✉ Avenida de Galicia s/n
☎ 985 64 68 77
🕐 Closed Mon.

Santa Eulalia
www.asturoccidente.com
🄰 84 D3
Visitor information
✉ Calle Rego del Vale s/n
☎ 985 62 12 61
🕐 Closed winter

San Martín
www.asturoccidente.com
🄰 84 D3
Visitor information
✉ Carretera General s/n
☎ 985 62 60 00
🕐 Closed winter

Fishing boats rest
at low tide at
Lastres's port.

Costa Verde

THE "GREEN COAST" EDGES ASTURIAS, FROM THE RÍO EO
on the Galician border, to Llanes close to the border with Cantabria,
125 miles (200 km) east. Other than the industrialized ports of Avilés
and Gijón, it is characterized by low-key resorts, fishing villages, and
sandy beaches. Traditions remain strong.

Luarca
www.asturisturismo.com
/valdes
🅰 84 D3
Visitor information
✉ Calle Caleros 11
☎ 98 564 00 83

Cudillero
www.cudillero.org
🅰 85 E3
Visitor information
✉ Plaza de la Marina
☎ 98 559 13 77

Muros de Nalón
www.deasturias.com/muros
🅰 85 E3
Visitor information
✉ Parque del Palacio
☎ 98 58 34 85

Moving from west to east, **Luarca**
is the first resort of any importance.
This lively tuna-fishing port is
shaped by the sinuous Río Negro,
which winds through to the harbor below the steep slopes of the
old town. Walk or drive up the
hill at the end of the harbor to the
marine cemetery and lighthouse
for wonderful views. Good clean
beaches are easily reached to the
west and farther east at Cabo Busto.

The lighthouse at **Cabo Vidio**
gives dramatic views before the
next essential stop: **Cudillero,** its
tiny harbor sandwiched between
cliffs in a cove. A cluster of outdoor
restaurants serves seafood and
cider. The beach, Playa de Aguilar,
stretches to a rocky headland.
Immediately beyond that is
Muros de Nalón, which has

large elegant residences of the 15th
and 16th centuries.

At **Colunga,** overlooking the
beaches of Lastres and Griega in
an area rich in dinosaur tracks, an
extensive Jurassic museum opened
in 2004. Shaped like a dinosaur's
footprint, it displays lifesize copies
beside real remains and fossils
*(Museo Jurasico, Colunga tel 90 230
66 00, closed Mon. & Tues.).*

The eastern part of the Costa
Verde has secluded beaches. **Lastres**
is a picturesque clam-fishing port,
with the harbor and noble mansions nestling beneath a cliff. Three
miles (5 km) south of Lastres is the
lookout point of **Mirador del
Fito. Ribadesella** has the paleolithic cave network of Tito Bustillo
which rivals Altamira *(tel 98 586 11
20, closed Mon. & Tues.).* ∎

In & around
Santillana del Mar

IT IS SAID THAT THE NAME OF THIS NOBLE VILLAGE
incorporates three lies. It is not saintly *(sant)*, nor is it flat *(llana)*, nor
is it by the sea *(el mar)*, which is 2 miles (3 km) away. But what does
this matter when a village has a 1,200-year history and a unique, harmonious mix of architecture. Just 12 miles (20 km) west of
Santander, Santillana attracts a lot of visitors. In summer they throng
the narrow cobbled streets; August is best avoided.

The **Colegiata,** once a Benedictine
monastery, was transformed in the
12th century into a Romanesque
masterpiece. Its intricately sculpted
main portal, interior friezes, and
the 42 capitals of the magnificent
cloisters depict lions, doves, snakes,
pelicans, and plant motifs. The
entrance to the **cloisters** is from
the side—don't miss them, nor the
beautifully carved stone **fount** at
the back of the nave, nor the early
16th-century **altarpiece** honoring
the relics of St. Juliana, whose tomb
stands in the transept.

From the Colegiata, the main
street runs through the village to the
Museo Diocesano, in a converted
convent by the road to Santander.
The museum has a fine collection
of medieval and baroque sculptures,
silver, carved ivory, and enamel-
work. Between the Colegiata and
museum a web of delightful streets
show off the best of civil design on
the Gothic towers of Merino and
Don Borja, houses in the Calle del
Cantón, the Renaissance palace of
Velarde behind the Colegiata, and
many baroque mansions.

West of Santillana are Comillas
and San Vicente de la Barquera.
Comillas *(Visitor information
Aldea 6, tel 94 272 07 68)* has the
amazing neo-Gothic **Palacio de
Sobrellano,** designed by Catalan
modernista architect Joan Martorell.
It stands on a hilltop (beside the
marquis's chapel and a folly

designed in 1883 by the architect
Gaudí, (see pp. 172–75), and it is
now a restaurant. Comillas also has
popular beaches.

San Vicente de la Barquera
is an animated fishing port below
a castle, now a museum and exhibition center, and 13th-century
fortified church. The town attracts
hordes of visitors in summer, and
make sure you're among them—
local restaurants serve spectacularly
good seafood. One mile (1.6 km)
south lie the world-famous caves
of **Altamira** (see p. 109). ■

Santillana del Mar
www.santillana-del-mar.com
🅜 85 G3
Visitor information
✉ Calle Jesús Otero 20
☎ 94 281 88 12

**Colegiata, Claustro,
& Museo Diocesano**
☎ 94 281 80 04
⏲ Closed Mon. in
winter
💲 $ (combined ticket)

**San Vicente de la
Barquera**
www.sanvicentedelabarquer
a.org
🅜 85 G3
Visitor information
✉ Avenida del
Generalisimo 20
☎ 94 271 07 97

**Local wedding at
Santillana's
Colegiata**

The dramatic setting of the village of Fuente Dé in the Picos de Europa

Parque Nacional de los Picos de Europa
www.picosdeeuropa.com

🅰 85 F2

National Park Reception Center

✉ Casa Dago, Cangas de Onis

☎ 98 584 86 14

Picos de Europa

CANTABRIA'S IDYLLIC ROLLING PASTURES LEAD TO breathtaking mountains: the limestone massif of the Picos de Europa that borders Asturias. They rise to more than 8,500 feet (2,600 m) just 15 miles (25 km) from the coast. Some 273 square miles (700 sq km) form a national park. Visitors share the mountains with bears, chamois, wild boar, wolves, and royal eagles. In restaurants, game and organic veal top the menu, while cheeses are varied and delicious.

Long isolated by its rim of peaks, the succession of valleys known as **Liébana** successfully repelled Romans, Arabs, and French. Cutting through it is the Río Deva, which has carved a spectacular gorge, the **Desfiladero de la Hermida.** Only one road (N621) runs into Liébana from the Cantabrian coast, and it follows the gorge, so be prepared for tortuous bends. Craggy, eroded pinnacles rise above, and

below is the boulder-strewn torrent of the Deva, teeming with salmon and trout. Two other roads lead into Liébana. The N621 comes from the province of León, south over the San Glorio Pass (5,278 feet/1,609 m). The C627 comes over the lower Piedrasluengas Pass southeast from Palencia. Both have incessant switchbacks and spectacular scenery.

Liébana has lovely churches and hermitages, above all **Nuestra**

Señora de Lebeña *(1.8 miles/3 km north of Cillorigo-Castro, tel 94 274 43 32, closed in winter)*, a tenth-century Mozarabic structure. In the middle of Liébana at the crossroads of four valleys is the lively market town of **Potes,** where a relatively mild climate has resulted in the outlying cherry orchards and grapevines. This center for climbers, mountain bikers, canoeists, and hikers has specialist equipment shops, and guides abound. The restaurants are warm and friendly, and their sausages, cheeses, cheesecakes, and milk-based desserts are evidence of mountain gastronomy.

The road west out of Potes to Fuente Dé (12 miles/19 km) is worth taking. Just outside Potes, turn left at the signpost and go 2.5 miles (4 km) to the Franciscan monastery of **Santo Toribio de Liébana** *(tel 942 73 05 50).* This place of pilgrimage is the most important religious site in the region. It began in the eighth century when a fragment of the True Cross (allegedly) was brought here from Jerusalem. A large gold-plated cross contains the holy relic, in the **Capilla del Lignum Crucis** (Chapel of the Wood of the Cross).

The main road runs on to the village of **Mogrovejo** (with a historic tower house) before coming to an abrupt end at the cluster of restaurants and a parador that form **Fuente Dé,** sitting at the base of a dramatic sheer rock face. A cable car takes you 2,460 feet (750 m) up to a lookout-point at 6,058 feet (1,847 m), with spectacular views. From the lookout, a 1.8-mile (3-km) path leads to the **Puerto de Aliva,** haunt of brown bear, chamois, and capercaillie (a large grouse)—and site of a small hotel.

On the Asturian (western) side of the mountains the most historic site is **Covadonga** (see p. 110), reached by a 7.5-mile (12-km) detour southeast from **Cangas de Onís** (see p. 110)—Spain's first Christian capital 1300 years ago. Driving south on the main N625, you soon come to the gorge of **Los Beyos,** where multiple limestone strata rise on both sides. About 6 miles (10 km) farther south is the **Mirador de Oseja de Sajambre,** one of the region's panoramic lookout points. The road from here to Potes (via the LE 244 and N261) is for diehards only as it entails no fewer than four mountain passes: This is the highest and at times narrowest road of the whole national park. The highlight is the **Puerto de Pandetrave** (5,123 feet/1,562 m), which gives a panorama of three awesome mountain ranges. ∎

Climbers in the Picos de Europa rise above the clouds.

Potes
http://www.liebanaypicosde
europa.com
🗺 85 F2
Visitor information
✉ Plaza la Serna
☎ 94 273 07 87

Fuente Dé
🗺 85 F2
✉ Teleférico (cable car)
☎ 942 73 66 10
🕐 Closed weekdays in Jan.
💲 $$

Santander

THE GENIAL CAPITAL OF CANTABRIA SWINGS AROUND A huge bay. Santander has its own charm, mixing stevedores, chic shoppers, shady bodegas, and stylish pavement cafés. The architectural style, from the late 19th and early 20th centuries, is typified by the wedding-cake casino overlooking the beaches. Much cleaning-up has transformed Santander into a very popular resort.

The Península de la Magdalena separates the elegant resort area of **El Sardinero** from the bustling commercial town and port. It is crowned by the **Palacio Real** (late 19th century), built for King Alfonso XIII and his wife, Victoria Eugenia, by public donation from Santander's citizens, to encourage the king's pioneering habit of sea-bathing in their town. The palace is not open to the public, but the surrounding park is a popular promenade area with a small zoo and restaurants. It is accessible from the beaches on either side.

The **catedral** is in central Santander, and is in fact two

buildings, one superimposed on the other. The lower church dates from the early 13th century, but within a few decades it was joined by the upper one. On one side of the old nave a transparent floor reveals archaeological **excavations** that in 1982–83 unearthed remains of Santander's original Roman settlement and remnants of earlier churches. The **baptismal font** may have had an earlier life as the ritual washing fountain of a mosque. External steps lead up to the upper, more ostentatious, new section. The outer cloister walls date from the 13th-century addition, but the cathedral church was rebuilt in the 17th century and again in 1941, after a house fire, spread by gale-force winds, devastated the old city. This destroyed part of Santander and led to extensive reconstruction.

Don't miss a breezy stroll along Santander's seafront avenue, which edges the pedestrianized shopping area. Note the ornate **Correos** (post office), **Palacete del Embarcadero** (Jetty Mansion) and **Museo Marítimo** (Maritime Museum). The **Museo de Prehistoria y Arqueólogia** (*Calle Casimiro Saínz 4, tel 94 220 71 05, closed Sun. p.m. & Mon.*) gives you an outline of Cantabria's extensive prehistoric past. The small collection includes a number of mysterious circular inscribed stones from the fourth to first centuries B.C. ■

The beach at El Sardinero (above) and the floodlit casino (left)

Santander
www.turismo.cantabria.com
🗺 85 G3
Visitor information
✉ Mercado del Este, Calle Hernán Cortés 4
☎ 94 231 07 08 or 94 231 07 56

Catedral
✉ Plaza Obispo y Trecu
☎ 94 222 60 24

Cantabria's prehistoric cave paintings

The first cave paintings found in Cantabria were those of **Altamira** (1 mile/ 1.6 km inland from Santillana del Mar, see p. 105), in 1879. Altamira is still considered the Sistine Chapel of Paleolithic art, its roof covered with almost a hundred

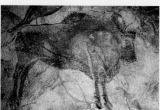

Image of a bison, Altamira caves

expressive renderings of bison, horses, deer, bulls, and wild boars. For conservation reasons, the cave is closed to visitors, but the excellent **Museo de Altamira,** contains an exact reproduction with every crack *(39330 Santillana del Mar, Cantabria, tel 94 281 8815, fax 94 284 01 57, www.museodealtamira.mcu.es, closed Mon., advanced ticket purchase recommended through*

www.bancosantander.es).

The four caves of **Puente Viesgo** are easier to see. Access is in small groups of visitors (no children under 10) with preference given to independent visitors reserving 24 hours in advance *(tel 94 259 84 25, closed Mon.–Tues. in winter).*

The caves are 17 miles (27 km) inland from Santander on the N623. There are more caves at **Covalanas** and near **Cangas de Onís** (see p. 110). At **El Soplao,** you can visit an entire cave system by train *(tel 90 282 02 82, www.elsoplao.es).*

In 1991 archaeologists discovered Paleolithic paintings in the cave of **La Garma,** about 3 miles (5 km) inland from Santander. ■

More places to visit in Asturias & Cantabria

CANGAS DE ONÍS
In the eighth century, Cangas was the capital of Christian Spain, and Pelayo was proclaimed king after he defeated the Moors at Covadonga. The **chapel of Santa Cruz** was built to mark that victory, but was rebuilt in the 15th century. It incorporates a Bronze Age *dolmen* (stone tomb). The town also has a hump backed medieval bridge. Three miles (5 km) east at Cardes is the **Cueva del Buxu** with its Paleolithic cave paintings. Just under 2 miles (3 km) north by the Sella river is the 12th-century Benedictine **monastery of San Pedro,** now a parador.

85 F3 **Visitor information,** www.cangas deonis.com/turismo, ✉ Plaza del Ayuntamiento 1 ☎ 98 584 80 05

COVADONGA
This is a picturesque mountain village and sanctuary on the northern flanks of the Picos

The shrine of the Asturian hero, Pelayo, in the Santa Cueva of Covadonga

de Europa where Pelayo started the Christian Reconquest (see pp. 28–31) in 722. A statue of the hero stands in front of the 1800s **basílica.** Inside the church, the **Museo de la Virgen** displays items given to the Virgin of Covadonga, including a priceless diamond-studded crown. Pelayo's sarcophagus is in the neighboring cave, the **Santa Cueva,** where

he retreated. Here, too, is the much venerated **statue of the Virgin,** patron saint of Asturias. From Covadonga a steep road twists 12 miles (20 km) up to a limestone plateau and the beautiful lakes of Enol and Ercina, a good starting point for mountain hikes.

85 F3 **Visitor information,** www.picode europa.com/es/scripts/covadonga.htm ✉ Explanada de la Basílica ☎ 98 584 60 35

CUEVAS DE COVALANAS
The cave paintings at Covalanas lie 1.8 miles (3 km) from Ramales de la Victoria and 42 miles (68 km) from Santander. The two painted caverns have masterful representations of deer, a horse, cattle, and possibly a stag. Visitors are limited to groups of ten and children under ten are not admitted.

85 H2 ✉ Ramales de la Victoria ☎ 94 264 65 04 🕒 Closed Mon.–Tues. & p.m. in winter. Visits by appointment only.

REINOSA
This lively market town on Santander's main road link with Castilla y León makes a good base, as it lies on the slopes of the Cantabrian Mountains. The ski resort of **Alto Campóo** is 16 miles (25 km) west, just beneath the towering peak of **Pico de Tres Mares** (7,136 feet/2,175 m). You can reach the summit by chairlift for magnificent views over the Picos de Europa.

On the C628 road to Alto Campóo, stop at **Fontibre** where a scenic footpath leads to the source of the Ebro River. This whole lush valley has great natural beauty and numerous dolmens (prehistoric stone tombs) lie hidden in remote corners. Immediately east of Reinosa is the immense **Embalse del Ebro,** a reservoir which attracts a wide variety of waterfowl (and bird-watchers). On its banks cows gently chew the cud. Four miles (7 km) south of Reinosa is **Cervatos,** which has a 12th-century Romanesque **collegiate church** *(tel 942 75 41 42, keys next door).* It has wonderful carvings of lions and more unusual, blatantly erotic figures decorating the capitals of the apse.

85 G2 **Visitor information** ✉ Avenida Puente Carlos III ☎ 94 275 52 15 ∎

From Basque fishing villages
to remote farming commu-
nities, vast sweeps of vineyards,
and the Pyrenees, this is one
of Spain's most diverse regions.
You can ski, hike, taste wine,
visit monasteries, or enjoy
contemporary art in Bilbo.

Northeast Spain

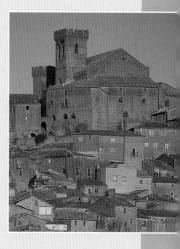

The medieval town of Ujué
at dawn

Northeast Spain

THE MOUNTAIN BARRIER THAT separates Spain from France is nudged by four autonomous regions. They are Euskadi (Basque Country), Navarra, Aragón, and Catalunya (see pp. 180–98). Nestling south of the three is La Rioja. They present very different faces of the Spanish character. The belligerent Basques share a language, culture, and excellent gastronomy with neighboring Navarra. Aragón has historically had closer links with Catalunya and Castilla. In between, the fun-loving Riojans specialize in fiestas and superb wine.

Traditionally, this region never had as many foreign visitors as other parts of Spain, but its main towns are now firmly on the trail. On the coast are the hip resort of Donostia (San Sebastián) and the burgeoning city of Bilbo (Bilbao), experiencing a tourist boom thanks to the Guggenheim Museum. Inland are the monasteries and sierra of La Rioja, Navarra, and Aragón, and the nature reserves of the Pyrenees. In Aragón especially, where the Moors held sway until the 12th century, you find tiny historic towns with elaborate Mudejar architecture, and open, rolling landscapes.

Unspoiled nature is never far away, although Euskadi has a lot of industry, which has contributed to its wealth and self-esteem. Be prepared for a new vocabulary, as the Basques, like the Catalans and Galicians, use their own language on every sign. This doesn't mean that they have a narrow outlook: Basques take pride in being a cultured and educated people. Explore the Basque coastal towns, but go inland to experience rural life and delightful small towns. The best wilderness areas in northeast Spain are in the Pyrenean foothills, and the most beautiful stretch of these is in Aragón's Parque Nacional de Ordesa y Monte Perdido—perfect for long treks.

Navarra has Iruña (Pamplona), world famous for bullrunning, but it also has some of the major stopping points on the Way of St.

James (see pp. 88–89), hence the string of superb Romanesque constructions that continues through La Rioja. Palaces, castles, and churches are scattered through the region. San Juan de la Peña has a medieval royal pantheon and Zaragoza the magnificent Moorish palace used by Fernando and Isabel (see pp. 31–32) (as well as a whole new quarter built for Expo 2008). The fortifications at Gasteiz (Vitoria) were built by a 12th-century Navarrese king, and royal sarcophagi in Jaca and Huesca bear witness to the importance of these towns in Aragonese history. ■

Area of map detail

f Biscay

sca

Zumaia
Getaria
Zarautz
zkoitia
eitia
Tolosa **A15**
Peñas
de Aia
1018m
Altsasu(Alsasua)
**Monasterio
de Iranzu**
A12
Estella(L
izarra)
**nasterio
Irache**

Hondarribia
(Fuenterrabia)
Irún
Donostia (San Sebastián)
A8

Elizondo
(Baztan)
Lekunberri
(Larraun)

Sanctuario de
San Miguel de Excelsis

**Iruña
(Pamplona)**

**Monasterio
de Leyre**
Sangüesa(
Zangoza)
A15
**Castillo
de Javier**
Tafalla
Sos del
Olite   Rey Católico
Uncastillo

FRANCE

Orreaga
(Roncesvalles)

Ansó
Hecho
Berdún

Puerto de
Somport
Canfranc
Torla
Biescas

**Parque Nacional
de Ordesa y
Monte Perdido**

3355m
Monte
Perdido

Pico
Posets
3371m

Pico de
Aneto
3404m

Bielsa
Revilla

Benasque

Jaca
Sabiñánigo

**San Juan
de la Peña**
Gállego

Ainsa

Riglos
**Castillo
de Loarre**

AP68
Marcilla
Calahorra
Arnedo
Alfaro
Corella
Fitero
Tudela

**Monasterio
de la Oliva**
**Bardenas
Reales**
Arguedas
Ejea de los
Caballeros

Sádaba
Ayerbe
Bolea

Almudévar

Alquézar
Graus

Huesca

Barbastro
Monzón

Binéfar

Tarazona
Tauste
Zuera

Sariñena

23 6m
**Monasterio
de Veruela**
AP68
Alagón
Utebo
ZARAGOZA

La Almunia de
Doña Godina
E90

A23

Calatayud
Ateca
E90
**Monasterio de
Santa María de Huerta**
**Monasterio
de Piedra**

Maluenda
Cariñena

Daroca

Fuendetodos

A23

ARAGÓN
Quinto

Los Monegros

A2 **E90**

Bujaraloz

Fraga
A2 **E90**

Embalse de
Mequinenza

Caspe

Híjar

Andorra

Alcañiz

Calanda

Valderrobres

CATALUNYA (CATALUÑA)
p. 177

**CASTILLA-
LA
MANCHA**
p. 233

Calamocha
Montalbán

Monreal
del Campo

Villarluengo

Mirambel
Cantavieja
La Iglesuela
del Cid

Sierra de
Albarracín
Cella

Albarracín
Teruel

Mora de
Rubielos

Sarrión

Sierra de
Javalambre

VALENCIA
p. 177

0 _____ 60 kilometers
0 _____ 40 miles

NAVARRA

Bidasoa

p i r i n e o s

Aragón

Ebro

Ebro

Jalón

Jiloca

N330

Turia

Guadalope

Cinca

Ésera

Ara

Alcanadre

Sierra del
Moncayo

E
F
C
D

Euskadi & Navarra

Euskadi (as the Basques call their country) and Navarra have long been linked by their common language, *euskera*, still widely spoken in varying dialects throughout the region. When Castilla wrested control from the kings of Navarra in the 13th century, the Basque identity and sense of civic rights strengthened. Seven centuries later, with grievances exacerbated by Franco's repression, this became a bitter separatist struggle that continues today. There is generally no threat to visitors, however, as targets are political.

The 2,800 square miles (7,200 sq km) of Euskadi are divided into three historical territories: Vizcaya to the northwest, around Bilbo (Bilbao); Guipúzcoa to the northeast, with Donostia (San Sebastián) as its capital; and the inland region of Álava to the south, surrounding Gasteiz (Vitoria). The latter borders Navarra, 4,056 square miles (10,400 sq km) of diverse landscapes, from Pyrenean peaks through green valleys to southern plains.

You may find Euskadi's prosperous cities of Bilbo and Donostia more exciting than Iruña (Pamplona), the capital of Navarra. The Basque coast has a history of seamanship and fishing. Donostia and Hondarribia (Fuenterrabía) are established resorts; elsewhere are surfing beaches and low-key fishing villages strung along 125 miles

(200 km) of rugged, sharply indented coastline.

Common to both Navarra and Euskadi are rolling green hills and valleys clad in beech, oak, and chestnut forests. Here are nature reserves, solid stone houses, pastoral scenes, and also a lot of history. This is where the Cantabrian Mountains meet the Pyrenees.

Navarra's 56,810 acres (23,000 ha) of vineyards have progressed by leaps and bounds since the late 20th century, and now produce highly regarded wines. Euskadi's *pintxos* (appetizers) and other innovative cuisine are as good as its traditionally excellent wines from the Rioja Alavesa (which neighbors La Rioja). Signature bodegas are the latest development here, part of the renewal that has infused this corner of Spain since Bilbo's massive facelift. ■

Dramatically indented coastline is typical of Vizcaya, the area around Bilbo (Bilbao).

Bilbo (Bilbao)

EVER SINCE THE MUSEO GUGGENHEIM OPENED IN 1997, Bilbo has experienced a cultural renaissance and consequent surge in tourism. Nearly half the population of Euskadi lives in greater Bilbo (one million people), and the city is vital to the Spanish economy. Architectural signatures such as Cesar Pelli, Calatrava, Isozaki, Legorreta, Foster, and Zaha Hadid are all leaving their mark.

In 1300 the city officially came into being. Its site on the navigable estuary of the Río Ibaizabal made it important for exporting Castilian goods. Today the old shipbuilding and dock area of **Abandoibarra** is the cultural hub with a 2-mile sculpture walk, the Guggenheim, Pedro Arrupe's new footbridge, and new hotels. On the other side of Bilbo, the winding streets of the **casco viejo** (old town) around the **cathedral** (*Closed Sat. & Sun.*) have been injected with new life. The **Museo Vasco** (*Plaza Unamuno 4, tel 94 415 54 23, closed Sun. p.m. & Mon.*) gives background on the culture and economy of the Basque region. A few steps away is the lively **Plaza Nueva,** lined with cafés and food shops. Behind rises the hill of

Artxanda, a leisure park, reached by funicular railway. On the river bank beside the Puente del Arenal stands the **Teatro Arriaga.** Most of the casco viejo is pedestrianized and packed with tapas bars.

A new riverside tramway links this quarter with Abandoibarra. In between stretches Bilbo's **19th-century quarter** and the Gran Vía—home to Bilbo's financial institutions and upscale shops. It ends in the west at the **Parque Doña Casilda de Iturriza,** a park next to the renovated **Museo de Bellas Artes** (*Plaza del Museo 2, tel 94 439 60 60, closed Sun. p.m. & Mon.*). The museum has paintings by Zurbarán, Ribera, El Greco, van Dyck, Goya, Gauguin, Chillida, Tàpies, and Bacon. ■

The Nervion River twists through the heart of Bilbo; the Guggenheim stands on the right.

Bilbo (Bilbao)
www.bilbao.net
🔼 112 B6
Visitor information
✉ Rodríguez Arias 3
☎ 94 479 57 60 or
94 479 57 70
🕐 Closed Sat. & Sun. p.m.

Museo Guggenheim
www.guggenheim-bilbao.es

🅰 112 B6

✉ Abandoibarra
Etorbidea 2

☎ 94 435 90 00

🕐 Closed Mon.,
Sept.–June

💲 $$. Free guided
tours in English
daily at 4 p.m.

The bold steel
planes of Frank
O. Gehry's
Guggenheim
(above) and a
vertiginous view
of the interior
(right)

Museo Guggenheim

HOWEVER MANY PHOTOGRAPHS YOU MAY HAVE SEEN OF this building, the reality is still a visual shock. Its curved steel and titanium planes beside the Puente de la Salve reflect the hills, sky, and river of Bilbo in an endless play with light that defies all logic. Architect Frank O. Gehry's masterwork has put Bilbo firmly on the world cultural map and is one of the icons of the new Spain. One million visitors per year now come to admire it!

The idea of the museum arose in the late 1980s when the Basque government decided to diversify the city's economic base by redeveloping the old shipbuilding area. By 1992, the Solomon R. Guggenheim Foundation had been signed up to manage this important new institution, and in October 1997 the daring gamble with Gehry's innovative design paid off: The museum opened to world applause. The nucleus of Gehry's design is a soaring 164-foot-high (50 m) atrium, around which are interconnected blocks housing 19 galleries, an auditorium, a restaurant, and offices, in steel, glass, and limestone. Transparent elevator shafts, curving walkways and terraces all add to the vertiginous sense of excitement in this rule-breaking building—an apt

expression of Basque audacity. Since its inauguration, neighboring structures have matched Gehry's imagination, notably Federico Soriano's new Congress Hall and Music Centre and Ricardo Legorreta's Sheraton Hotel.

The Guggenheim's total floor area is 260,000 square feet (24,000 sq m), and just under half that is exhibition space, including the world's largest exhibition hall, a staggering 426 feet (130 m) in length. This is one of several halls designed for specially commissioned installations and site-specific works.

Along with its sister museums in New York and Venice (the Solomon R. Guggenheim Museum and the Peggy Guggenheim Collection), the Bilbo museum has access to an impressive sweep of 20th-century

Cézanne, and Pablo Picasso, may appear beside Constantin Brancusi, Piet Mondrian, or Joseph Beuys. Works by Max Ernst, Man Ray, and Marcel Duchamp, and those of American abstract expressionists and Pop artists can be seen in Galleries 103 and 105 on the third floor and also on the second floor.

Leading contemporary Spanish and Basque artists are also featured, and an exciting program of temporary exhibitions highlights current trends in Spanish art.

Much emphasis is placed on new forms of medium, bringing installations together with videos and paintings. Multimedia and site-specific commissions include Francesco Clemente, Sol LeWitt, Fujiko Nakaya, Richard Serra, and a witty LED installation by Jenny Holzer in a corner of the atrium. One unmissable piece is the gigantic, flower-studded "Puppy" by Jeff Koons that sits in the museum entrance. Equally arresting is Louise Bourgeois's bronze "Maman." ■

A show of Richard Serra works in exhibition hall (above); pop art (below) plays large role in the Guggenheim collection.

artworks that form a shared permanent collection. These are presented on a rotational basis, and offer contrasting perspectives on seminal movements and artists from the U.S. and Europe. Early radicals, such as Vasily Kandinsky, Paul

Gasteiz (Vitoria)

THE STREETS OF THE OLD PART OF GASTEIZ RING THE
hilltop cathedral, and their picturesque slopes have endless nooks and
crannies to explore. The town was fortified in 1181 by Sancho III,
king of Navarra, as a stronghold against Castilla, and flourished as a
trading crossroads. Gasteiz is the Basque name of Euskadi's capital.

Much of the Basque capital is
pedestrianized, reinforcing the air
of placid provincialism so evident
in the formal gardens of the
Parque de la Florida (1820)
and stately **Plaza de España.**
This square, **Los Arquillos,** and
Plaza del Machete form an
intriguing bridging area between
the medieval hill town and the
flat, largely 19th-century city
below. Just east of here is **Artium,**
the stunning new museum of contemporary art devoted to Basque
and Spanish art *(tel 94 520 90 20,
closed Mon.)*.

Walk from Plaza del Machete
along Calle de Santa María and
you pass the **Palacio de**
Montehermoso (1524), and, a
block to the west, the plateresque
Palacio de Escoriaza-Esquivel.
At the end stands the 14th-century
cathedral of Santa María *(tel
94 525 51 35, daily visits by appointment)*, and a cluster of medieval and
Renaissance buildings.

This historic nucleus includes
El Portalón, built in timber and
brick the **Torre de los Anda** (a
fortified house), the **Museo de
Arqueología,** in the Casa Armera
de los Gobeo, and the exceptional
Museo Fournier *(Palacio de
Bendaña, Calle de Cuchillería, tel
945 18 19 20, closed Sat. & Sun. p.m.
& Mon.)* devoted entirely to tarot
and playing cards. ■

Gasteiz (Vitoria)
www.vitoria-gasteiz.org
/turismo
🅼 112 B5
Visitor information
✉ Plaza de General
   Loma 1
☎ 94 516 15 98

**Museo de
Arqueología de
Álava**
vppx134.vp.ehu.es/mitoi
✉ Casa Gobeo-
   Guevara-San Juan,
   Correría 116
☎ 94 518 19 22
🕐 Closed Sat. & Sun.
   p.m. & Mon.

**View over
Gasteiz's rooftops
toward the Plaza
de Espana**

Basque identity

The mysterious origins of the Basques help to make Euskadi, as they call their country, one of Spain's most beguiling regions. Green valleys and a dramatically indented coastline do not, however, capture the headlines. Far more prominent is the Basque role as a thorn in the flesh of central government.

What is certain about their unique identity is that the Basque language predates Indo-European, and that it has significant links with Caucasian languages of Central Asia and with Berber, the language of the pre-Arab inhabitants of North Africa. Studies in diverse fields from blood groups to morphology eventually produced one common theory: the Basques have inhabited their remote, verdant valleys since the Stone Age, and they could well be the direct descendants of Cro-Magnon man.

Over the centuries, the Basques' fiercely independent nature maintained the last outpost of pagan beliefs in southwestern Europe. Basques converted to Christianity only in the ninth and tenth centuries, and were the last to adopt urban living—as late as the 14th century. Today this is hard to believe when you look at the burgeoning cities of Donostia (San Sebastián) and Bilbo (Bilbao), but the lack of towns did not stop the Basques forging ahead to establish personal liberties and elective assemblies in the provinces of Vizcaya and Guipúzcoa. Their ongoing battle with the central Spanish government dates from the days of the *fueros,* codes of traditional laws that were respected by the Catholic Monarchs and the Habsburgs, but were repeatedly revoked in the 19th century in order to create a more centralized Spain.

The man who catalyzed Basque resentment was Sabino de Arana Goiri (1865–1903), who fortuitously entered the stage at a time of increasing industrialization. After coining the word Euskadi to encompass the four Basque territories of Álava, Guipúzcoa, Vizcaya, and northern Navarra, where Basque is spoken, he founded the Basque National Party (PNV). By his death his avowed aim had swung from independence to autonomy. General Franco (dictator from 1939 to 1975) aroused intense bitterness: He colluded in the bombing of the Basque town of Gernika in 1937, and later repressed Basque identity and abolished all remaining fueros. In 1960 Basque separatists founded ETA (an acronym meaning Euskadi and Freedom), which started a campaign of terrorism against Madrid. Euskadi (País Vasco, or Basque Country) gained autonomy in 1979, but despite that, and despite the ever encroaching lifestyle, language, and immigrants of Castilian Spain, ETA bombs and assassinations continued to make headlines, goading the rest of Spain into massive demonstrations of outrage. Ironically, the March 2004 Madrid train bombings (by Islamic terrorists) produced a new optimism with regard to the Basque issue due to the sense of shock and horror that united the nation.

Politics aside, however, the Basques easily outpace their neighbors economically, with the notable exception of the Catalans. Having been an agrarian society, Euskadi rapidly became Spain's most competitive industrialized region. Yet, like all Spaniards, they cling to their roots. Some of the most genuine expressions of Basqueness come from *bertsolaris,* poets who improvise in local competitions, *pelota* (a ball and bat game), and *harriketa,* a more primitive pastime of lifting massive stones of up to 660 pounds (300 kg).

Closer to the outsider's heart is the renowned Basque gastronomy, which has propelled chefs such as Juan Mari Arzak, Pedro Subijana, and Martín Berasategui to the forefront of Spanish cuisine. Their emphasis on ultra-fresh ingredients, particularly seafood, and innovative combinations of flavors has spread like wildfire. Food has always been important for the Basques, who even have gastronomic clubs (*txokos*) devoted to one product. Despite its apparently inward-looking nature, Euskadi has also been a region of maritime explorers (Sebastián Elcano, Lope de Aguirre) and of spiritual philosophers (Ignatius de Loyola, Francis Xavier). Adventurous and introspective, radical and traditional, stone-hefters and gourmets—Basques may be the most paradoxical people of Spain. ∎

Symbols of Basque identity: pelota and traditional dance (above); red berets (below)

Donostia (San Sebastián)

THE QUEEN OF EUSKADI'S COAST, ALSO CALLED THE "PEARL of the ocean," is a dynamic, outgoing resort surrounding a stunning bay and spanning the estuary of the Río Urumea. A fishing village that grew into a port, it is now a prosperous resort town of 180,000 people. All of them seem to gravitate nightly to the streets of the old quarter, with allegedly the greatest concentration of bars in the world.

After surviving no fewer than 12 major fires since the 13th century, Donostia flourished in the 19th century. Queen Isabel II (R.1843–1868) was the catalyst—she chose this spot when her doctor advised her to frequent the Cantabrian coast. For over 20 years she returned each summer, and in 1863 by agreeing to the demolition of the old town walls, she unleashed Donostia's expansion. The result is the 19th-century city, a harmonious grid of streets stretching south from the old quarter, east along the Bahía de la Concha, and eventually west across the river. Donostia is poor in monuments, but it has plenty of other good things, including excellent cuisine.

The coastline is punctuated by three hills. **Monte Igueldo** has an amusement park and is reached by cable car *(tel 94 321 05 64, cars run every 15 minutes during daylight*

Donostia (San Sebastián)
www.sansebastianturismo .com
🅰 113 C6
Visitor information
✉ Reina Regente 8
☎ 943 48 11 66

hours) from the Plaza del Funicular. The old town grew at the foot of **Monte Urgull,** now a park, with a castle at the top. **Monte Ulía's** whale lookout has fabulous views. Go by bus, car, or taxi from the old town to the base of the hill, then walk or drive about a mile up the hill. A 7-mile (12 km) waterfront promenade takes you the length of the city, and three city beaches give good swimming. Queen Isabel II's favored beach was the lively **Playa de la Concha,** where you can visit her gardens and mock-English manor house, **Palacio de Miramar**.

In the old quarter, one of the nicest strolls is along Paseo del Muelle, at the back of the harbor. At the far end stands the **Aquarium** *(Plaza Carlos Blasco de Imaz, tel 94 344 00 99),* modernized in 1998, with a transparent tunnel for close views of creatures of the deep. Packed into the little harbor are fishing trawlers, tour boats, the fish market, local women selling prawns, and a string of outdoor seafood restaurants. The **Museo Naval** *(Paseo del Muelle 24, tel 94 343 00 51, closed Mon. & p.m. Sun.)* displays items from the city's seafaring past.

Penetrate the labyrinth of streets beside the harbor densely packed with tapas bars and you soon see the heavy baroque facade of the church of **Santa María** *(Calle 31 de Agosto)*. The vaults beneath the organ hold a sculpture by Eduardo Chillida (1924–2002), Euskadi's great artist. (If you enjoy his work drive 10 minutes from town to Hernani and the rural Museo Chillida-Leku —*Caserío Zabalaga 66, Hernani, tel 94 333 60 06, closed Tues.).* On the same street as the Santa Maria there is a side entrance to the **Museo San Telmo** *(Plaza Zuloaga 1, tel 94 348 15 80, closed Sun. p.m. & Mon.)* through a converted Dominican convent. Here are

11 murals by the Catalan artist José María Sert (1876–1945), depicting Guipúzcoa's history. Other post-Renaissance paintings, include a room devoted to Antonio Ortiz Echagüe (1883–1942).

Also in this quarter, is the **Plaza de la Constitución,** site of a farmers' market and outdoor cafés. The square used to be a bullring, and the numbered balconies were the seats for the spectators. Over the river in the art deco quarter of Gros, an old tobacco factory, **Tabacalera,** is now a lively arts center *(tel 67 768 14 57, closed Mon.).* This area is another gastronomic hub. ■

Fish dominates the menu at this old quarter restaurant.

Film festival

Donostia has a flourishing cultural life, but the biggest event of the year is the international film festival in September. It was first held in 1952. Screenings are shared by Rafael Moneo's state-of-the-art congress hall—the Kursaal—whose spectacular translucent cubes rise on the eastern tip of the estuary and the recently restored Teatro Victoria Eugenia. No self-respecting star can stay anywhere but the regal-looking María Cristina hotel next door. ■

Donostia's buildings edge the regal sweep of the Bahía de la Concha, seen here from Monte Igueldo.

Costa Vasca

STRETCHING FROM THE PYRENEES AT THE FRENCH BORDER, an enticing, often wild coastline of nearly 125 miles (200 km) stretches west to Bilbo. Most resorts are small, squeezed between rocky cliffs and the thundering surf of the Cantabrian Sea. Town outskirts may be marred by high-rises and light industry, but the coast has good opportunities for board sailing, surfing, scuba-diving, and sailing.

The prettiest resort by far is **Hondarribia (Fuenterrabía),** a picture-postcard town looking across the Bidasoa estuary to Hendaye in France. This strategic site was heavily fortified, and 15th-century ramparts still enclose the austere **Castillo de Carlos V,** now a parador. The steep narrow streets around it have several Baroque mansions. Down at the **Marina,** painted wooden balconies brimming with flowers overlook lively bars and outdoor restaurants. Toward sunset, drive west about 4 miles (7 km) to the *mirador* (lookout point) at **Jaizkibel,** for polychrome views.

West of Donostia, a string of resorts starts with one of the busiest, **Zarautz,** which has this coastline's longest beach (2 miles/3 km), a favorite with surfers. The access road from the hills goes past modern buildings that do not auger well, but the old quarter claims a 16th-century **Luzea tower, Palacio de Narros,** a Franciscan convent, and grand 19th-century villas.

From Zarautz the coast road (N634) twists around the indented shore to **Getaria,** (*Visitor information, Parque Aldamar 2, tel 94 314 09 57, closed winter*) a real charmer. The old quarter lies on a promontory ending at **Monte San Antón,** nicknamed the "mouse of Getaria." The resort's main attraction is the seafood restaurants lining the lively port, the perfect place to sip a glass of *txakoli* (local white wine) in honor of Getaria's most illustrious

sons—fashion designer Cristobal Balenciaga (1892–1972), and Juan Sebastián Elcano, second-in-command to the Portuguese navigator Ferdinand Magellan on his great voyage round the world. Elcano completed the voyage in 1522 after Magellan was killed. Balenciaga will soon have have a museum devoted to him at the **Palacio Aldamar.**

The corniche road soon comes to **Zumaia** (*Visitor information, Plaza Zuloaga, tel 94 314 33 96, closed winter*), a friendly town on an estuary, with a lovely medieval quarter and a breezy promenade. Zumaia has two good beaches, **Itzurun** and **Santiago;** surfers prefer the pounding surf at **San Telmo,** to the west. Ten miles (16 km) inland of Zumaia are the neighboring towns of Azpeitia and Azkoitia. On the outskirts of **Azpeitia** stands the sanctuary of St. Ignatius de Loyola, philosopher and founder of the Jesuits, and now a major pilgrimage spot. Next to his family's tower-house stands the **Basílica de Loyola** (*tel 94 302 50 00*), designed by Carlo Fontana, a disciple of the Italian sculptor Bernini, with a striking baroque facade and 196-foot (60 m) cupola.

Back on the coast, **Deba** is the next fishing port west of Zumaia, with a good beach and dramatic cliffs. It lies at the mouth of the river of the same name and was important in the heyday of the Castilian wool trade—hence the surprisingly grandiose 16th-century church of **Santa María la Real.**

West of Deba, the coast road becomes increasingly scenic as it edges cliffs with plunging views over **Mutriku,** the rugged **Playa Saturraran,** and **Ondarroa.** Lookout points let you stop to admire the scene in safety, before the road reaches **Lekeitio,** in its lovely bay setting. The protected beaches here have safe swimming and the seafood restaurants are predictably good.

Sixteen miles (25 km) to the west, houses at **Elantxobe**—the attractive marine extension of Ibarrangelu—seem to tumble down the steep hillside to the harbor and fishing boats. West of Elantxobe's rugged headland, **Cabo Ogoño,** are the area's two main sandy beaches, **Playa de Laida** and **Playa de Laga,** both at the mouth of the lovely Mundaka estuary. This was declared a biosphere reserve in 1984 and has a rich plant life and birdlife, beaches, and the prehistoric caves of Santimaiñe. The town of **Gernika (Lumo)** lies at the southern end of the estuary. The name is immortalized by Picasso's painting, and commemorated in Gernika's park with sculptures by Eduardo Chillida and British sculptor Henry Moore. Of vital symbolic importance for Basque political identity is the venerable oak tree under which the medieval Lords of Vizcaya (Biscay) would periodically vow to uphold Basque privileges. The original tree died in early 2004 but an offshoot has been planted; its green shoots represent new hope for the Basques. Nearby stands the neoclassic **Casa de Juntas** where, since 1979, Vizcaya representatives now meet once more. ■

Elantxobe's tiled roofs huddle high above the fishing harbor.

Lekeitio
www.lekeitio.com
🅰 112 B6
✉ Independentzia Enparantza
☎ 94 684 40 17

Gernika (Lumo)
www.gernika-lumo.net
🅰 112 B6
✉ Artekale 8
☎ 94 625 58 92

"Guernica"

Picasso's painting "Guernica" was inspired by the brutal bombing of the little town of Gernika on April 26, 1937. The three-hour raid was carried out on General Franco's orders by a German squadron and killed over 2,000 people, most of whom were in Gernika for the weekly market. "Guernica" hangs in Madrid's Reina Sofia (see pp. 74–75).

The medieval town
of Estella (Lizarra)

Valley towns

Bergara
www.bergara.es

M 112 B6

Visitor information

✉ Ayuntamiento, Plaza
San Martín de
Agirre

☎ 94 377 91 28

Oñati
www.onati.org

M 112 B5

Visitor information

✉ Foruen
Enparantza 2

☎ 94 378 34 53

DESPITE EUSKADI'S HIGH LEVEL OF INDUSTRIALIZATION,
its green valleys encompass vast swaths of unadulterated nature and
fascinating small towns. Northern Navarra has these, too, with the
added bonus of Romanesque relics of the Way of St. James.

In the valley of the Deba River,
34 miles (54 km) southeast of
Bilbo (Bilbao), **Bergara** has harmonious Renaissance buildings
behind its industrialized outskirts.
You may well arrive during one of
its many music festivals.

The heart of Bergara is **Plaza
San Martín Agirre,** where the
arcaded baroque town hall faces the
former royal Jesuit seminary. Also
on the square are three Renaissance
palaces with emblazoned facades.
Immediately uphill, the church of
San Pedro de Ariznoa has a
17th-century statue of Christ by
Juan de Mesa and a painting by José
Ribera. Don't leave Bergara without
tasting the local *errellenoak* and
tostoiak sweets.

Of the 20 hermitages that dot
the surrounding countryside, the
most venerated is that of **San
Miguel de Aritzeta,** 1 mile
(1.6 km) south of Bergara. From
its site it gives wonderful views
over this lush region.

Seven miles (12 km) south
through the hills lies the noble
town of **Oñati.** Its monuments
make it the most historically rich
town in the province of Guipúzcoa,
and the calendar is studded with
local fiestas that usually involve the
populace parading in Basque costumes. **Sancti Spiritu university,** started in 1540, has a beautiful
plateresque facade and a courtyard
decorated in coffered Mudejar style.
On the main square stands the
church of **San Miguel Arcángel,**
originally Gothic but with an 18th-
century baroque-rococo tower, the
work of Martin Carrera, who was
also responsible for the rococo
Casa Consistorial (Town Hall).

The monastery of Bidaurreta (1510) is on the southern edge of town. In the hills about 5 miles (9 km) on is Guipúzcoa's most important shrine—that of **Arantzazu** *(tel 94 878 09 51)*, the region's patron saint. This modern building (1955) was a collaboration between architects Sainz de Oiza and Laorga, and sculptors Eduardo Chillida, Lucio Muñoz, and Jorge Oteiza.

Strong Basque traditions continue 27 miles (43 km) southwest of Iruña (Pamplona) at **Estella (Lizarra),** the 12th-century capital of the kings of Navarra. It became a center of the Carlists (see p. 34) seven centuries later. It flourished because it was on the Way of St. James (see pp. 88–89) and also enjoyed privileges granted by King Sancho Ramirez—hence its fine medieval buildings. The **Palacio de los Reyes de Navarra**—the royal palace—dates from the 12th century and is a rare example of civic Romanesque architecture. It is now the **Museo Gustavo de Maeztu.** Close by stands the 12th-century church of **San Pedro de la Rúa,** built in Cistercian style (see p. 151). Two sides of the cloisters were blown up in the 16th century, but what is left is very beautiful. Cross the Río Ega, by the Puente de la Cárcel, and you find an old quarter of winding medieval lanes, and the Romanesque church of **San Miguel,** with its intricately carved northern portal.

Outside town, in wild, bucolic surroundings, is the Cistercian **Monasterio de Irantzu** *(6.8 miles/11 km north of Lizarra on N120, tel 94 852 00 12)*, now a college. The even older **Monasterio de Iratxe** *(1.8 miles/3 km southwest of Lizarra, tel 94 855 44 64)* is on the old pilgrimage route. It has magnificent, plateresque cloisters and a church combining Cistercian and Romanesque features. It

houses the **Museo Julio Caro Baroja,** named for a Navarrese ethnographer (one who describes human cultures).

Less atmospheric than these, and in the much more arid area bordering Aragón, **Sangüesa (Zangoza)** has a remarkable church, **Santa María la Real** *(Open in summer; for guided visits, call Sangüesa Tour 62 011 05 81)*, which looms above the Aragón River. It was begun in the early 12th century, and final touches, such as the octagonal tower, the south portal, and spire, date from the middle of the 13th century. The highlight is the **south portal,** which contains an astonishing number of sculptures by the master of San Juan de la Peña (see p. 146) and Leodegarius. Close by in Calle Alfonso el Batallador is **Palacio de Vallesantoro,** with an unusual baroque facade: It has projecting carved eaves and elaborately carved columns inspired by Spanish colonial art in Latin America. ∎

Estella (Lizarra)
www.estella-lizarra.com
Ⓜ 113 C5
Visitor information
✉ Calle San Nicolás 1
☎ 94 855 63 01

Sangüesa (Zangoza)
www.navarra.net/pueblos /sanguesa.htm
Ⓜ 113 D5
Visitor information
✉ Calle Mayor 2
☎ 94 887 14 11

One of Oñati's many Basque festivals

Navarra's spiritual lookouts

**Monasterio de
Leyre**
www.monasteriodeleyre.com
🅰 113 D5
✉ 2.5 miles (4 km)
northeast of Yesa
on N240
☎ 94 888 41 50
💲 $

**Sanctuario de San
Miguel de Excelsis**
turismo.navarra.com/sierras
/san_miguel.html
🅰 113 C5
✉ 10 miles (18 km)
southwest of
Lekunberri
☎ 94 837 30 13

**St. Francis
Xavier's festival
brings pilgrims to
his birthplace.**

NORTHERN SPAIN'S MONASTERIES AND OTHER HOLY SITES
are often in remote and beautiful settings, and Navarra's are no exception. The three sites below have a long history as spiritual retreats,
coupled with spectacular positions.

The **Monasterio de Leyre**
stands in the rugged, pine-clad
Sierra Errando, 31 miles (50 km)
southeast of Iruña (Pamplona), and
has sweeping views of the **Yesa
Reservoir.** Benedictine monks
returned here in 1954, and you
should arrive early or stay late in
order to hear their Gregorian chants
*(daily at 7:30 & 9 a.m. and 7 & 9
p.m.)* in the serene Romanesque
church of San Salvador. You can stay
at the monastery, or visit from Sos
del Rey Católico (see p. 152) or
Iruña. The church entrance known
as the **Porta Speciosa** has complex carvings; also in the church is
the mausoleum of the kings of
Navarra. You can visit the unique
crypt (1057), where vaults and

pillars spring from low, carved capitals of extraordinary dimensions—
some are up to 1 yard in width.

A few miles southwest of Leyre,
the much rebuilt **Castillo de
Javier** *(tel 948 88 40 00)* was the
birthplace of the great Jesuit mis-
sionary Saint Francis Xavier (1506–
1552). He is Navarra's patron saint,
and the castle is flanked by a basilica, a Jesuit retreat, and a mission.
Inside the castle, exceptional
exhibits include a Gothic sculpture
of Christ carved in walnut, and a
15th-century wall painting of the
Dance of Death (both in the Holy
Christ Tower). From the crenellated
walls on the terrace you look north
toward Leyre and south to Aragón
(see pp. 139–52). Javier itself has
rather commercialized cafés and
souvenir shops.

To reach the **Sanctuario de
San Miguel de Excelsis,** you
drive through lovely holm-oak and
beech forests, up to wild heath. The
area has dozens of dolmens—the
largest concentration of Stone Age
structures in northern Spain—and
is popular with trekkers. Ask about
trails at the **Casa Forestal** on the
road to the sanctuary. The church is
perched on a promontory with
dizzying views over the Sierra de
Aralar, about halfway between
Donostia and Iruña. It has a
Visigothic (9th-century) apse,
a pre-Romanesque (10th-century)
structure, and an enclosed Romanesque chapel. The fabulous gilded
and enamel 12th-century altar
front, almost certainly from
Limoges, was brought here from
Iruña cathedral in 1765. ∎

Iruña (Pamplona)

IRUÑA, BETTER KNOWN AS PAMPLONA, IS FAMOUS FAR beyond Spain thanks to Ernest Hemingway. He wrote about the bull-running that takes place during Iruña's festival of Sanfermines, and the event now attracts hundreds of thousands of visitors.

At other times, Iruña is a quiet, even colorless little city, where life revolves placidly around the porticoed **Plaza del Castillo** on the edge of the old quarter. North of this are dark narrow lanes that date from when Iruña was the fortified capital of the kingdom of Navarra. Today they are lined with five-story houses and specialist shops. Close to the old city walls, the Gothic **cathedral** has delicately structured cloisters. The old refectory and kitchen (1330) are now the **Museo Diocesano,** which displays religious objects. For an idea of Navarra's long and complex history, visit the **Museo de Navarra** (*Cuesta de Sto. Domingo, tel 848 42 64 92, closed Sun. p.m. &*

Mon.), housed in a 16th-century hospital with an impressive Renaissance frontage. It has Roman mosaics (Pamplona was founded by the Romans in 75 B.C. on the Basque settlement of Iruña), Romanesque capitals from the former cathedral, Renaissance paintings, and frescoes gathered together from all over the province.

The bullring lies immediately southwest of the old quarter on **Paseo Hemingway,** a lovely leafy promenade shaded by lofty plane and chestnut trees. Your next priority should be to follow the example of Hemingway himself and retire to the chandeliered 19th-century splendor of the **Café Iruña** on the Plaza del Castillo. ∎

Iruña (Pamplona)
www.pamplona.net
▲ 113 C5
Visitor information
✉ Eslava 1
☎ 84 842 04 20

cathedral & Museo Diocesano
www.iglesianavarra.org/67c atpam.htm
✉ Dormitalería 3-5
☎ 94 822 29 90
🕐 Closed Sat. p.m. & Sun.
💲 $

Hemingway eternalized Iruña's annual running of the bulls.

Sanfermines

The dates are fixed: Iruña's Sanfermines festival is always July 6–14. This is when the city has the debacle of bullrunning known as the *encierro,* immortalized by Hemingway in *The Sun Also Rises.* The encierro originated to honor Iruña's patron saint, but has since become a test for daredevil locals and visitors alike. It starts daily at 8 a.m., when bulls are let loose to charge along a fenced route through town on their way to the bullring. Hundreds of people run into the street to pit their wits and speed against those of the bulls. Bullfights take place every day and celebrations continue long into the night. ∎

More places to visit in Euskadi & Navarra

OLITE

Olite's castle is a massive affair with crenellated towers and battlements. It dates from 1407 and had numerous Moorish elements such as hanging gardens, *azulejos* (tiles), and stucco work, but much of this vanished during multiple renovations and a devastating fire in 1813. Part of the castle is now a parador. The neighboring 14th-century church of **Santa María la Real** has a Renaissance altarpiece and sculpted doorway. Olite's other medieval church, **San Pedro,** has been altered but still has a Romanesque doorway. From Olite, it's a 19-mile (30 km) drive to the **Monasterio de la Oliva** *(tel 948 72 50 06)*. This was one of the first monasteries built by French Cistercian monks (see p. 151) outside their country. The 12th- to 15th-century church and cloisters have a striking purity of style.
113 C5 **Visitor information** ✉ Galerías de la Plaza Carlos III ☎ 94 871 24 34

ORREAGA (RONCESVALLES)

This mountain pass in the Pyrenees has a special place in history and poetry: It was here that the Navarrese Basques unleashed their terror on the rearguard of Charlemagne's army in A.D. 778.

Over the centuries, thousands of pilgrims trudged through the pass on their way to Santiago de Compostela (see pp. 90–93). Landmarks include a 12th-century **hostelry,** the over-restored **collegiate church,** and its Gothic **chapter house,** which contains the tomb of Sancho VII (1154–1234) beside his queen. Don't miss the **museum** *(tel 948 76 04 80)* in the old stables. Among other wonderful things it contains is an emerald from a Sultan's turban, worn during his last fatal battle against King Sancho at Navas de Tolosa in 1212, and a 14th-century enameled reliquary dubbed **"Charlemagne's chessboard"** because of its checkered design. From the village, you can walk up an easy trail to **Puerto Ibañeta,** the top of the pass (3,466 feet/1,057 m), for good views.
113 D5 **Visitor information** ✉ Antiguo Molino ☎ 94 876 03 01

TUDELA

Navarra's second largest city lies at the center of a fertile agricultural region, the source of Tudela's hearty vegetable soup and its robust red wine, la Ribera. Tudela was ruled by Moors for several centuries and developed intellectual and religious tolerance.

The old Moorish quarter, the **Morería,** is an atmospheric labyrinth of winding lanes lined with Mudejar- style houses; also here is the 12th- to 13th-century **cathedral,** built on the site of a mosque. Its carved **Portada del Juicio** (Last Judgment doorway) fronts a Romanesque-Gothic interior, and the lovely cloisters have columns carved with numerous biblical scenes. Tudela's patron saint, Santa Ana, is honored in an exuberantly decorated baroque side chapel.

Nine miles (15 km) northeast of Tudela is a desert-like region, the **Bardenas Reales,** where ocher-colored rocks have been eroded into extraordinary forms. The best way to see them is by following a hiking trail (GR13) from the hermitage of **Nuestra Señora del Yugo,** 1.8 miles (3 km) north of Arguedas on NA134.
113 C4 **Visitor information** ✉ Juicio 4, Tudela ☎ 94 884 80 58 ■

The rolling landscapes of Navarra end at the Pyrenees.

Spain's Rioja wine tastes soft, full, and warm, with a hint of vanilla.

La Rioja

The word "Rioja" means one thing only to most non-Spaniards—Spain's most prestigious and internationally famous wine. But this small province of 1,950 square miles (5,000 sq km) sandwiched between Navarra and Castilla y León has a lot more. A combination of mountains, fertile farmland, and a mild climate has given rise to a cheerful, generous-hearted population and a rich, delicious cuisine. In between hearty Riojan meals you can explore monasteries, churches, or chase dinosaur paths near Enciso.

The Ebro River marks the northern border with Euskadi (Basque Country), although vineyards continue in the Rioja Alavesa on the Basque side. An Ebro tributary, the Río Oja, gave the province its name, and it is along the Ebro's fertile banks that Rioja's main towns are sited: Logroño, the modern provincial capital, Calahorra, and Haro, the center of the wine industry. To the south loom Rioja's two mountain ranges, the Sierra de la Demanda and the Sierra de Cameros. This mountainous area is the Rioja Alta—Upper Rioja, as opposed to the flatter Rioja Baja in the northeast—with skiing, mountaineering, hunting (red and roe deer, wild boar), and fishing (river trout, crab, and carp). Low-key spas have grown up around the therapeutic springs at Arnedillo and Arnedo to the east on the bank of the Río Cidacos. The peaks have snow from late October until May and good hiking the rest of the year.

The Rioja Alta also has hermitages, churches, and monasteries. The Way of St. James (see pp. 88–89) runs north of the sierra (now the N120 route), and sites here include the magnificent cathedral of Santo Domingo de la Calzada and the monastery of Nájera. As you climb south into the sierra, churches and monasteries multiply. So do the flocks of sheep and cattle—Rioja's cuisine is largely meat based, with succulent lamb the main specialty. Vegetarians won't go hungry: The Ebro valley produces abundant artichokes, asparagus, peppers, and beans, for the famous Riojan vegetable stew. The liveliest fiestas are Logroño's grape-picking festival in September, and Haro's Wine Battle every June 29, when the ammunition is Riojan wine. ■

Sierra de la Demanda

Sierra de la Demanda
www.sierradelademanda
.com
 112 B5
Visitor information
✉ Calle Sagastia 1,
Ezcaray
☎ 94 135 46 79

**Santo Domingo
de la Calzada**
www.lacalzada.com
 112 B5
Visitor information
✉ Calle Mayor 70
☎ 94 134 12 30

**San Millán de
la Cogolla**
www.larioja.com/cultura
 112 B4
Visitor information
✉ Monasterio de Yuso
☎ 94 137 32 59

RISING TO OVER 6,500 FEET (2,000 M) IN WESTERN RIOJA
and western Castilla y León, the Sierra de la Demanda is ruggedly
beautiful. This is a place for hikers, and part of the western side is a
nature reserve. The Way of St. James runs below the northern flanks.

Good walking trails on the Burgos
(western) side start from the villages of **Pradoluengo, Pineda
de la Sierra, Quintanar de la
Sierra,** and **Neila.** The last gives
access to the **Parque de las
Lagunas Altas,** a series of high
altitude lakes in stark, moody
surroundings. The Riojan side is
crowned by the pine forests of **San
Lorenzo** (7,450 feet/2,271 m) and
the ski-resort of **Ezcaray** (*Map
112 B4, tel 94 135 46 79*), also a hub
for Spanish hunters. The nature
reserve of rivers and forest, which
covers 200,800 acres (81,270 ha)
has wolves, deer, mountain cats,
eagles, and wild boars.

Beneath the northern flanks is
the pilgrimage town of **Santo
Domingo de la Calzada,**
situated where a Riojan holy man,
Domingo, built a hospice for

pilgrims. The Romanesque cathedral was completed shortly before
his death in 1109. The ornamental
baroque steeple (1765) that rises
230 feet (70 m) above the cathedral
is actually the third version. Inside
the cathedral is its oddest feature,
a late-Gothic **henhouse,** where
a white cock and hen are kept to
remind worshipers of a miracle
that took place here: A roast
chicken jumped up and crowed to
prove the innocence of the pilgrim
hanged for stealing it (the pilgrim
was also revived).

Across the nave, look for the side
chapel holding the stunning **main
altarpiece,** moved in 1994 to
uncover the Romanesque chapel
that it concealed. The altarpiece is
the last work of the prolific sculptor
Damián Forment (circa 1480–
1540), and is unique in its profuse

depiction of mythological and fantastical figures. The sensitive polychrome painting of this 42-foot (13 m) masterpiece is by Andrés de Melgar. The restored early 14th-century cloisters and Sala Capitular are now a **museum** (Closed Sun.), with treasures such as three Flemish triptychs and mid-17th century Mexican silver. In the Sala Capitular the coffered ceiling and **choir stalls** (1668) were carved by Santiago Allona and his son, Juan Baptista.

Southeast of Santo Domingo is **San Millán de la Cogolla,** named for the sixth-century Benedictine hermit whose legendary posthumous appearance on a white charger halted the Moorish advance against the Christians of this region. Pilgrims on their way to Santiago would make a detour into the hills between Nájera and Santo Domingo de la Calzada to pay homage to him at two monasteries 1.5 miles (2 km) apart. The tenth-century Mozarabic **monastery of Suso** is a pretty, tiered

structure (tel 941 37 32 59, closed Mon.), built above the cave where San Millán had his retreat. Lines are lengthy (only 20 enter at a time) to see its graceful horseshoe arches, Visigothic capitals, and the alabaster tomb of the saint himself.

In complete contrast, the much larger **monastery of Yuso** (tel 941 37 30 49, closed Mon.) in the valley below, also inspired by San Millán, is a massive 16th- to 18th-century hulk, but it's a popular Sunday outing for Riojans, and the Benedictine monks have converted part of the monastery into a four-star hotel. The church itself is an unsuccessful mixture of styles from Renaissance to baroque, but the monastery **treasury** has exceptional pieces, including two carved ivory reliquaries and 12th-century processional crosses. The **library** contains one of Spain's best monasterial collections of medieval books.

Due south of here, over the sierra, lies the **Monasterio de la Valvanera** (tel 941 37 70 44, closed Dec. 20–Jan. 7). Part of its attraction is the access along the winding LR113, which follows every bend of the Río Najerilla. A narrow turnoff snakes 3 miles (5 km) up through oak and beech forest to this peaceful monastery perched on the hillside with terraced vegetable gardens below. Dedicated to Santa María, the patron saint of Rioja, it was rebuilt in the 15th century after the original tenth-century structure burned down, but the lofty vaulted church still contains the precious 12th-century **sculpture of the Virgin Mary.** It is in Byzantine style and was allegedly carved out of an oak tree by a repentant thief. Climb upstairs behind the altar to see the back of the statue. Downhill is a little stone hermitage and the fountain of **Fuensanta.** ■

The monastery of la Valvanera sits in a wooded valley (above). The "100 maidens" festival at Santo Domingo de la Calzada (below)

A Spanish wine renaissance

Spanish wines are undergoing huge changes. Winemakers are using innovative techniques to produce a delectable and highly diverse range that is causing concern among Europe's other big producers. About 2.7 million acres (1,100,000 ha) of vineyards make Spain the country with the largest productive area, and it is the world's third largest producer after France and Italy. From sparkling cava to smooth Riojan vintages, full-bodied Ribera del Duero, and light, fruity Galician whites, the choice seems endless. Spain now has more than 60 official wine-producing areas, each one a Denominación de Origen (D.O.) that may be further diversified by specially selected Reservas or Gran Reservas.

Spanish winemaking dates back to the Phoenicians in Cádiz and to the Romans' need to fuel their legions. According to Roman chroniclers Pliny and Martial, the wine of Tarragona vied with that of Sevilla as the finest wine of the Roman Empire. After centuries of Arab domination, production was revived by thirsty medieval monks and pilgrims on the Way of St. James and was subsequently boosted by English merchants in Galicia and Jerez. The biggest impetus came in the 19th century when Bordeaux vintners were ruined by the grape scourges of oidium and phylloxera. They set up in Rioja instead, where many of their companies still figure among the elite of today's producers.

One of the fundamental differences between French and Spanish wines is the Spanish system of aging. Whereas in France the consumer takes the risk by choosing and investing in young wines, in Spain it is the vineyard that selects wines deemed most promising for aging.

Crianzas must be at least two years old and have spent a minimum of six months in a cask (one year in La Rioja). Reservas undergo a minimum of a year in an oak cask followed by two in the bottle, and Gran Reservas require two years in oak casks followed by at least three years in the bottle. This vigil in shady cellars at constant temperatures intensifies the character of each wine, as the wood adds aromatic qualities while its tannin is blended with that of the wine. For white and rosé wines aging periods are shorter, and oak is replaced by stainless steel vats.

Vintners are now experimenting with mixing native varieties of grapes such as Tempranillo, Garnacha, Graciano, Palomino, and Albariño, with imported ones (Cabernet Sauvignon, Merlot, Pinot Noir, Chardonnay, Syrah), a system that was frowned upon until recently. A revolution in quality has swept Spanish vineyards since the 1980s, and greater use has been made of varieties that were once minorities—notably the Tempranillo grape. Although it has always been Spain's best-known variety outside the peninsula because of its primordial role in Riojan wines, it is no longer exclusive to that region. You now find it figuring in wines from Navarra to La Mancha and forming the basis for almost half Spain's Denominaciones de Origen. This has given rise to the following regional synonyms for cloned varieties adapted to local terrain: Cencibel, Tinto Fino, Tinta de Toro, Tinta del País, and Ull de Llebre. Although the grape is basically the same, wide variations in climate and soil produce quite different personalities.

An example of Spain's new wave wines is the denominación of Priorat, a region of Catalunya where winemaking dates from the 12th century. In the early 1980s, it was looking into an abyss of unproductive despair. Then a group of innovative young vintners came, attracted by the unique slate soil and steeply terraced terrain. For seasoned winemakers such as René Barbier, it provided a perfect combination of ancient Garnacha and Cariñena vines with soil that has no need of fertilizers or chemicals and that easily absorbs water. By introducing Cabernet

Sauvignon, Syrah, and Merlot (and new French barrels), they were producing highly rated wines within a decade.

Other contenders in Spain's new wine stakes include Aragón's lesser known Somontano. In the mid-1980s it was producing bulk wines for export, but it is now

Grapevines are the mainstay of much of Spain's rural economy (left). Tourists taste wine at a bodega (right). A wine cellar in Haro, La Rioja's wine capital (above right)

experimenting with international grape varieties that thrive in its relatively high terrain and cool night temperatures.

Apart from this vastly improved wine produced in the foothills of the Pyrenees near Huesca, Aragon has three other Denominaciones de Origen. Cariñena, the oldest, lies just south of Zaragoza over the Sierra de la Muela and produces remarkable reds; lesser known Campo de Borja to the west uses the Garnacha grape for delicious reds and some rosés, and Calatayud, located between the two, is another resurgent tipple to watch out for (it actually goes back to Roman times).

Increasingly recognized abroad are the reds of Toro and Bierzo, both of which are neighbors of the highly rated Ribera del Duero near Valladolid. Up-and-coming whites may be Rueda in Castilla, Penedés in Catalunya, and the fresh, crisp Albariño wine of Galicia's Rías Baixas. The latter, said to have originated in the Riesling grape, has helped reverse the previous reputation of Spanish white wines.

The latest trend is innovative bodega architecture. The one to hit the headlines is

Preparing barbecues for the feast cooked at Logroño's annual wine festival

at Elciego, near Laguardia, where the new Marqués de Riscal bodega designed by Frank O. Gehry opened in 2006. The building combines a hotel with wine-spa and a restaurant run by Michelin-starred Riojan chef, Francis Paniego. Equally arresting is Santiago Calatrava's cathedral for Bodega Ysios and the ground-breaking zinc and glass Bodega Baigorri by local architect, Iñaki Aspiazu, with its underground restaurant. Near Logroño, Viña Real chose the French architect, Philippe Mazières. In Haro, Zaha Hadid has designed a tasting-room and shop inside the 130-year old López de Heredia vineyard. What is certain is that Spain's innovative bodegas will not stop there. ∎

Laguardia

For aficionados of Riojan wines, one of the most attractive places to sample them is Laguardia. Although politically part of Euskadi (Basque Country), it produces Tempranillos flavored with Mazuelo and Graciano under the Rioja Alavesa label. Bodegas built into the walls of this fortified village give an atmospheric introduction to Spain's most internationally famous wine. ∎

Logroño

THE PROSPEROUS RIVERSIDE CAPITAL OF LA RIOJA IS NOT the most picturesque or historical town, yet it has a dynamism and friendliness that make up for this as well as being king of tapas.

Slicing through the center is the modern Gran Vía, which separates the new city to the south from the pedestrianized old quarter ending at the Ebro River. Just off the access road to the Puente de Hierro (iron bridge) you find Logroño's oldest church, **Santiago el Real** (*Barriocepo 6*), originally a Gothic structure but rebuilt in 1500. Look above the main portal for the **statue of St. James** astride a very chubby horse, slaying Moors. Opposite stands a 16th-century **pilgrims' fountain;** inside the single-naved church is a Renaissance **altarpiece.**

Logroño's cathedral looms a few steps away, **Santa María de la Redonda** (*Plaza del Mercado*). The twin baroque towers, topped by storks' nests, can be admired from sidewalk cafés in front. The third church to see is **Santa María del Palacio** (*Calle Marqués de San Nicolás 30*), remarkable above all for its soaring pyramidal spire, 146 feet (45 m) high. The old **pilgrims' hostel** stands close by on Ruavieja, Logroño's oldest street.

West of here, the **Museo de la Rioja** exhibits ecclesiastical artwork and 19th-and 20th-century paintings. Nobody should leave Logroño without touring the **Mercado San Blas** (*Plaza Espolón, corner of Calle de Sagasta*), an art deco market building that brims with La Rioja's finest and shiniest produce, which you can sample at restaurants and the excellent tapas bars in nearby **Calle Laurel.**

Logroño's grape-picking festival takes place in the second half of September, with bullfights, parades, folklore and night-long tapas bar crawls. ■

Pedestrian streets wind through Logroño's bustling old quarter.

Logroño
www.lariojaturismo.com
▲ 112 B5
Visitor information
✉ Paseo del Espolón, Príncipe de Vergara 1
☎ 94 129 12 60

Museo de la Rioja
www.larioja.org/web/centrales/cultura/museo.htm
✉ Palacio del Espartero, Plaza de San Agustín 23
☎ 94 129 12 59
🕐 Closed Mon.

More places to visit in La Rioja

CALAHORRA

The far east of Rioja province, known as Rioja Baja, is a region of orchards, olive trees, and fields of vegetables watered by the Alhama and Cidacos Rivers. The Romans built Calagurris, and by the fifth century A.D. it had gained episcopal status. The **cathedral,** originally Gothic, has a neoclassic facade. The Renaissance cloisters now contain the **Museo Diocesano** *(Paseo de las Bolas 1, tel 94 113 00 98, closed p.m.).* The remains of the old Roman walls are most visible in the lower town at the **Arco del Planillo,** the only surviving gateway. Go uphill on the Camino Bellavista for scenic views.

Rioja Baja also has Europe's largest number of **dinosaur footprints** *(ichnites).* The best place to see them is near the banks of the Cidacos at Enciso, about 22 miles (35 km) southwest of Calahorra. A new **Centro Paleontologico** *(tel 94 139 60 93)* explains the background.

🅰 113 C4 **Visitor information** ✉ Calle Angel Oliván 8 ☎ 94 114 63 98

HARO

Many of the world-famous crianza Riojan wines originate from the prestigious bodegas

The monastery of Santa María la Real in Nájera, a stop on the Way of St. James

of Haro, a strategic town on the banks of the Ebro, 22 miles (35 km) west of Logroño. Its economy blossomed with the growth of the wine industry in the late 19th century and by 1890, Haro was the first town in Spain to install electric street-lighting. Monuments include the elegant **Casa Consistorial** (1775) designed by Juan de Villanueva, architect of the Prado, and a former Augustinian convent (1741), now a hotel. Visit the impressive Bodega López Heredia *(tel 94 131 02 44)* to see Zaha Hadid's sleek tasting pavilion contrasting with traditional structures. The town makes an atmospheric setting for visiting bodegas (the tourist office publishes a useful guide to them), sampling Riojan cuisine, and enjoying the cafés of the sloping **Plaza de la Paz.** At the southern end of town, the **Museo del Vino** *(Calle Bretón de los Herreros 34, tel 94 131 05 47, closed Sun. p.m. Apr.-Oct.; closed a.m. & Sun. Nov.–Mar.)* illustrates the latest processes of winemaking and aging. Another wine museum, the **Dinastia Vivanco,** is at Briones, just outside Haro *(tel 94 132 23 23).*

🅰 112 B5 **Visitor information** ✉ Plaza Monseñor Florentino Rodríguez, Haro ☎ 94 130 33 66 🕓 Closed Sat.–Mon.

NÁJERA

This industrialized town was once the capital of the kings of Navarra and an important halt on the road to Santiago. The rather unattractive center conceals one architectural gem, the **monastery of Santa María la Real** *(tel 94 136 36 50, closed Mon.).* Legend says it was founded in 1044 by King García Sánchez III after his falcon led him to a statue of the Virgin in a cave, but the present church dates from the mid-1400s. The **royal pantheon** is next to the cave and contains the tombs of kings of Navarra, Castilla, and León. The delicately carved sarcophagi date from the 12th century. A 13th-century **statue of the Virgin** is at the center of the plateresque (see p. 45) altarpiece. Don't miss the masterly choir stalls (1495), or the lacelike stonework of the cloisters.

🅰 112 B5 **Visitor information** ✉ Plaza San Miguel 10 ☎ 94 136 00 41 ∎

Medieval lanes edged with half-timbered houses give old Albarracín a fairy-tale feel.

Aragón

Aragón has incredible diversity: the stark, snowcapped peaks of the Pyrenees in the north, rich green valleys, desolate sierra, and arid plains extending into the central meseta (plain). This vast area of 18,720 square miles (48,000 sq km), nearly one-tenth of Spain, harbors an abundance of artistic riches from Roman, Moorish, and medieval times, when the region reached its zenith. It is often, mistakenly, missed by visitors.

Created in the 11th century and unified with Catalunya in 1150, the kingdom consolidated its power and influence under Jaime I (1213–1276), who drew even Naples, Sicily, and Sardinia into the Aragonese net. This lasted until 1469, when the marriage of King Fernando II of Aragón and Isabel of Castilla led to Spain's virtual unification.

One of Aragón's most outstanding characteristics is its high level of culture and tolerance, assets that led to a fruitful coexistence of Catholics, Jews, and Muslims until the days of the Inquisition. Out of this peaceful coexistence sprang the Mudejar architectural style (see p. 43). The province also has exceptional monasteries, just as diverse, from remote and rocky San Juan de la Peña to peaceful Cistercian-style Veruela. Even Zaragoza, the ungainly and industrialized provincial capital, has unique sights such as the Moorish Aljafería, two vast cathedrals, and several striking Mudejar towers.

The real magic of Aragón however lies in its small towns and villages, which may nestle in verdant valleys beside rushing streams, huddle in the shadow of a ruined castle, or look out over placid artificial lakes rimmed by sierra. Public transportation does not bring you easily to these places, so it is well worth renting a car and heading into the hills to explore the likes of the Sierra del Moncayo, south of Tarazona, the sleepy charms of Sos del Rey Católico, or the walled splendor of Daroca and Albarracín.

Aragón has excellent cross-country and alpine skiing from November to April, followed in the warmer months by canyoning (climbing up and down canyons), kayaking, and hiking. To finish off any day, the province also makes excellent wines. ∎

Zaragoza

Grain dealers at the Plaza del Pilar assure that Zaragoza's pigeons are among the plumpest in Spain.

THE APPEARANCE OF THIS CITY OF MORE THAN 650,000 inhabitants is due to extensive reconstruction in the 19th century, after it was devastated by Napoleon's troops. Industry has played a major role, and until Expo 2008, unattractive outskirts sprawled beside the Ebro River. In the center, you find wide boulevards and squares, a dynamic commercial life, and a large area of shady lanes.

Zaragoza
www.turismo.aytozaragoza
.es

113 D4

Visitor information

Plaza del Pilar

976 20 12 00

Also information booths around city and tourist bus ($) making 14 stops along two different routes, Apr.–Oct.

Zaragoza's history kicked off with the Romans, whose name for their settlement, Cesaraugusta, became today's Zaragoza. Remains from that time include the **Roman Forum** *(Plaza de la Seo, tel 97 639 97 52, closed Mon. & Sun. p.m.)* in front of La Seo cathedral, and parts of the third-century A.D. wall on Avenida César Augusto. The next stage came in 714 when Zaragoza was conquered by the Moors, who remained here for four centuries. This period saw the city flourishing and becoming a cultural hub, of which the most outstanding monument is the beautiful Aljafería palace. Muslims, Jews, and Christians continued to coexist peaceably, leaving the skyline spiked with

Mudejar towers, until the Inquisition arrived (see p. 32). As capital of Aragón Zaragoza continued to prosper, but half the population died in the Napoleonic siege of 1808–1809.

Zaragoza's two cathedrals rise over the vast, paved **Plaza del Pilar,** which lies between the old quarter and the river. The oldest and most interesting of the two, **La Seo,** dominates the eastern end. Its extraordinary mix of styles includes original Gothic, later Mudejar, and finally baroque of the ornate Spanish sort known as Churrigueresque. The gigantic edifice has been extensively restored and its interior gleams. The fantastic altarpiece was initially carved by the Catalan sculptor Pere Johan in 1434–1445, and 30 years later was reworked by Hans Piet d'Anso, a German sculptor who created the magnificent alabaster figures of the central panel. A Mudejar dome crowns the **Parroquieta,** a Gothic chapel in the chancel; also Mudejar is the northern brick facade inlaid with geometric ceramics, in high contrast to the 18th-century baroque of the main western facade.

At the back of La Seo is the entrance to the **Museo de Tapices** and **Museo Capitular** *(tel 97 629 12 31, closed Sun. p.m. & Mon.).* This stunning collection of 60 tapestries, mainly 15th-century Flemish, is one of the best in the world. The huge, fine weavings measure up to 36 feet (11 m) in length, and are displayed beside beautiful antiques. Don't miss the **Arco del Dean** (Dean's Arch), four brick arches spanning the alleyway that were built in Mudejar style in the 16th century.

Dominating the northern flank of the Plaza del Pilar is the other cathedral, **Basílica de Nuestra Señora del Pilar** *(tel 97 629 12 31),* a real hodgepodge of styles and materials built around a legendary pillar on which the Virgin Mary is said to have appeared to St. James in the year A.D. 40. This cathedral has little of interest other than the huge **Capilla del Virgen** where the pillar and a statue of the Virgin are displayed. Her embroidered mantle is ceremoniously changed daily and a constant stream of admirers kiss the pillar. Have a look, too, at the altarpiece carved by Damián Forment (circa 1480–1540) above the central high altar, and frescoes painted by the young Goya (see pp. 47–49) inside the cupolas.

Just east of the basilica and the 20th-century Town Hall stands one of Zaragoza's most important civic buildings, **La Lonja de Mercaderes** *(Exchange Palace, tel 97 639 72 39, closed Mon. & Sun. p.m.),* a Renaissance building with

Mudejar features that symbolized Zaragoza's influential economic role. Among Zaragoza's Moorish monuments, the jewel in the crown is the fully restored fortified **Palacio de la Aljafería,** which stands 2 miles (3 km) west of the old quarter. Originally built in the 9th century, it surrounds a central patio rich in carved stuccowork. The most exceptional sight is the **musallah,** an intimate mosque, which is a visual feast of Moorish craftsmanship. After the Reconquest (see pp. 28–31), Fernando and Isabel could not resist using this stunning palace, and this is reflected in the flamboyant Gothic of the upper floor.

The new infrastructure built for Expo 2008 has transformed this western side of town, connecting it to the center with about 2 miles of riverside gardens and walkway and with a cable-car from the station. Of the Expo structures themselves, most outstanding are the Water Tower and the Aquarium, said to be Europe's largest. ∎

La Seo
- www.redaragon.com/cultura/laseo
- ✉ Plaza de la Seo
- ☎ 97 639 38 56
- ⏱ Closed Mon.

Palacio de la Aljafería
- ✉ Avenida Madrid
- ☎ 97 628 95 28
- ⏱ Closed Fri. a.m. & Thurs., & Sun p.m. in winter
- 💲 $
- 🚌 Bus 32 & 36 from Plaza del Pilar

"Extreme Water" exhibit Expo 2008

The influence of the Moors can be seen in the local architecture—here at Morata de Jiloga, near Daroca.

Mudejar towns

A UNIQUE FUSION OF ISLAMIC AND WESTERN STYLES developed in the wake of the 12th–16th-century Reconquest. This style was created by the remaining community of Arab craftsmen to meet the needs of Catholic Spain. Aragonese Mudejar is characterized by brickwork bell towers, decorated with glazed ceramic tiles.

The delightful little town of **Daroca** huddles beneath the roaring traffic on the N330 southwest of Zaragoza, but remnants of its Moorish origins are still very visible. It has an illustrious past: Symbolic of this is the ruined hilltop castle, originally an 11th-century Moorish fortress of which the keep, the **Torre del Homenaje,** remains, but subsequently much altered. Encircling the town below are 2 miles (4 km) of walls punctuated by towers and three surviving gateways *(puertas).* You can take a scenic three-hour walk around the walls starting at the **Puerta Alta,** climbing to the castle, then continuing round the northern and western perimeters to end at the crenellated and intricately worked **Puerta del Arrabal.** This walk gives wonderful views over Daroca's pretty tiled roofs, pinkish stone houses, and verdant surrounding countryside.

Walk through the **Puerta Baja** to find atmospheric cobbled alleyways and graceful mansions. Also here is Aragón's first Mudejar tower, the belfry of **Santo Domingo.** The upper part was completed in the early 14th century by a Muslim mason, but when much of the church interior was destroyed by fire, the Gothic-Mudejar structure was replaced by 18th-century baroque. Next door is the **Museo Parroquial** *(tel 97 662 02 47, closed Sun. p.m. & Mon.),* displaying gold and silver plate made in Daroca beside other ecclesiastical objects. A few steps northeast is the stunning church of **San Juan,** begun in Romanesque style in

the 12th century on the site of a mosque, and completed by Muslim craftsmen a century later with a flourish of Mudejar brick pilasters.

Northwest of Zaragoza lies **Tarazona,** the medieval home of the kings of Aragón. Between the 13th and 16th centuries Tarazona excelled in Mudejar craftsmanship, and numerous bell towers spike the clifftop site overlooking the Río Queiles. Of these, the one at the church of **La Magdalena** is particularly striking. The complex architecture of Tarazona's **cathedral** makes extensive use of brickwork and inlaid ceramic tiles beside its minaret-like belfry. Don't miss the **cloisters,** where niches are filled with delicate stucco tracery made in the 16th century. Tarazona's other curiosity is its arcaded old bullring, now transformed into a residential square, **Plaza de Toros Vieja.**

Southern Aragón's main town of **Teruel** has its own version of Mudejar towers: square in form, decorated with green and white glazed tiles, and sometimes incorporating a passageway at the base. Teruel stands on a high plateau, and its harmonious group is visible from miles around.

Teruel has five Mudejar towers, four of which are alongside equally exceptional churches. The most impressive are 13th-century **Torre de San Martín** (slightly leaning) and **Torre del Salvador,** both of which rise majestically over streets, leaving access through the arched base. The **cathedral** *(tel 97 861 80 16)* has a magnificent coffered ceiling painted with portraits, hunting scenes, and decorative patterns. The last tower of note, **Torre de San Pedro** is above the mausoleum of Teruel's star-crossed lovers, Diego de Marcilla and Isabel de Segura, the Aragonese Romeo and Juliet. Diego returned from his quest to make his fortune, to find Isabel had been forcibly married to someone else. He died of grief, and at his funeral Isabel kissed his lips and fell dead beside him. ■

The square towers of Teruel's *parador* reproduce local Mudejar-style architecture.

Huesca

Huesca
www.huescaturismo.com

🅰 113 E4

Visitor information

✉ Plaza de Luis López Allué

☎ 97 429 21 70

Cathedral

✉ Plaza de la Catedral

☎ 97 422 06 76

Iglesia de San Pedro El Viejo

✉ Plaza San Pedro

☎ 97 422 23 87

Huesca's cathedral mixes styles from the 13th to the 16th centuries.

THIS UNASSUMING TOWN IS IN FACT A MAJOR CROSSROADS of Aragón, the last of the plains before the Sierra de Guara and the foothills of the Pyrenees. Called Osca by the Romans, Wasqa by the Arabs, and Vesca or Huesca in the local Iberian language, it reached its zenith in the Middle Ages when it was home to the royal court.

Particularly memorable was King Ramiro II (died 1137), formerly a monk, who, goaded by lack of support from his nobles, proceeded to decapitate them all. By 1354 Huesca had its own influential university, but decline followed and it was not until the late 19th century that its prosperity revived. Among its more illustrious recent sons are the artist Antonio Saura and the filmmaker Carlos Saura.

The **old town** lies on a hill at the center. Flanking the Plaza de la Catedral are the **Ayuntamiento** (Town Hall), a striking example of Aragonese Renaissance style, and the **cathedral.** This towering 13th- to 16th-century structure has an ornately carved **portal** (1302) sheltered by a wood and tiled gable that is typical of Aragón (added in 1574). The interior is Gothic and austere, but with an alabaster altarpiece (1533), intricately carved by Damián Forment (circa 1480– 1540) with scenes of the Road to Calvary, the Crucifixion, and the Descent from the Cross.

Another exceptional alabaster altarpiece is in the cathedral's **Museo Diocesano** *(tel 97 423 10 99, closed Sat. p.m., Sun., & p.m. daily in winter);* this one, dating from 1512, is by Gil Morlanes el Viejo.

More poignant still is Huesca's oldest church, **San Pedro El Viejo,** a real marvel of Romanesque style with a beautifully restored cloister, where King Ramiro II spent his final years in retreat. Started in 1116 on the site of a Visigothic church, San Pedro has a fortresslike tower that was once much higher. Inside, it is severe and usually rather dark, but you can see beautifully restored late 13th-century **frescoes** and several impressive Renaissance **altarpieces.** The Romanesque capitals crowning the pillars of the cloisters are carved with themes ranging from the life of Christ to the conquest of Huesca, featuring apocalyptic monsters, devils, musicians, and dancers.

Don't miss the **San Bartholomé chapel,** reached from Calle de Cuatro Reyes, where Ramiro II lies in a Romanesque alabaster sarcophagus opposite Alfonso I. ■

Jaca

LYING IN THE SHADOW OF THE PYRENEES AT AN ALTITUDE of 2,690 feet (820 m), the lively little town of Jaca is Aragón's prime base for winter skiers, with plenty of bars, hotels, and restaurants. If you come from the south, you notice a distinct change in architectural style, with timbered chalet-style interiors and high-gabled houses.

Jaca is well organized for outdoor pursuits, with mountain guides, adventure sports agencies, hunting and fishing equipment, and buses to ski resorts. The town was the first capital of the kingdom of Aragón, and the gateway for the French Romanesque style (see pp. 43–44) that was to spread across northern Spain to Santiago de Compostela. Aragón's first king, Ramiro I, commissioned the **cathedral** *(Calle de la Catedral, tel 97 435 51 30),* built 1076–1130. Unusually, it is not easy to find as the low structure is tucked away in Jaca's narrow streets. The Romanesque portal, with its capitals and complex stone carving shaded by a carved wooden Aragonese overhang at the base of a squat stone tower, is obvious. Inside the Gothic style wins, sometimes rather florid, for example at the doorway to the cloisters. These have been transformed into the exceptional **Museo Diocesano,** with Romanesque and Gothic frescoes transferred for conservation from remote village churches. Some are breathtaking, above all those from Bagüés, and, together with remarkable 12th-century wooden sculptures, form a rare collection.

The otherwise unexceptional church of **San Salvador y San Ginés** *(Calle Mayor, ask for key at adjoining Benedictine convent)* holds the exquisitely carved sarcophagus of the Infanta Doña Sancha, sister of Sancho Ramírez.

Jaca's pride and joy is the late 16th-century **Ciudadela** with its moated-and-walled exterior, the only one still standing in Spain. ∎

The cloisters at Jaca cathedral now function as a museum of frescoes collected from abandoned chapels in the Pyrenees.

Jaca
www.altoaragon.com/jaca
△ 113 D5
Visitor information
✉ Avenida Regimiento de Galicia 2 (corner of Paseo de la Constitución)
☎ 974 36 00 98
⊕ Closed Sun. p.m.

Drive: Castles & eyries

Drive through wheatfields and pine forests to see stunningly sited relics of Aragonese history—both religious and royal—before ending at the influential monastery of San Juan de la Peña.

Leave **Huesca** by following signs to Iruña (Pamplona) (A132) as far as Esquedas, where a signed turnoff to the right leads across farmland to the hill village of **Bolea ❶**. Once under Muslim tutelage, it was reconquered by Pedro I of Aragón in 1101 and was important until the 18th century. Turn into the village and drive up to park on the main square. Walk up to the **Colegiata** *(tel 649 65 51 25)*, a Renaissance church built on the ruins of an Arab castle in 1556. Inside is a main altarpiece of 77 paintings by the anonymous "master of Bolea," with carvings and sculpture by Gil de Brabante. The altar of Santiago (1530) is attributed to the prolific Damián Forment (circa 1480–1540). Just downhill is the church of **Santo Tomás** *(Open only Sat. & Sun. June-Aug.)*, with an old covered fountain in the garden at the back.

Leave Bolea by the same road, then turn right at a junction below the village, following signs to Loarre. The road begins to wind through the hills, passing the occasional shepherd and his flock, fruit orchards, and wheatfields. After 5 miles (8 km) a signed turnoff to the right twists precipitously up to **Castillo de Loarre ❷** *(tel 97 434 21 61)*, a dramatic walled-and-turreted castle perched on a towering rock. Built on Roman walls in the 11th century by the king of Navarra, Sancho Ramírez, it may be the oldest castle in Spain. It was used both as a fortress and royal palace. Exploring it entails climbing narrow staircases in the three towers and crossing ruined ramparts, but it is well worth the effort. The beautiful **Romanesque chapel** is in excellent condition.

Drive back down to the village of Loarre, skirting around it to rejoin the main road (A1206) where you turn right. Continue 4 miles (6 km) to Ayerbe, where you turn right on the A132 (direction of Iruña/Pamplona). Soon, on your right, the intriguing sculptural forms of **Los Mallos ❸** come into sight. These pink, eroded cylindrical rocks dominate the landscape for several miles. For a close view turn right to the village of Riglos, just after the village of Concilio, which nestles at the foot of these startling formations. Return to the A132, which runs through a gorge next to the torrential waters of the Río Gállego, passing the pretty village of Murillo de Gállego, before crossing a bridge over the **Embalse de la Peña** (reservoir). Immediately after, take a right turn marked San Juan de la Peña to embark on a long and winding road (A1205), which, after running parallel to the reservoir, soon starts climbing through beautiful wild pine forests. You may see falcons and eagles soaring above. After 21 miles (34 km), at the village of Bernués, turn left, again following signs to San Juan de la Peña. The road twists upward for 11 miles (18 km) until it finally reaches the grounds of the **Monasterio de San Juan de la Peña ❹** *(tel 97 435 51 19; closed Mon.)*.

The grounds are a highly organized park with hiking trails, a small bar, and picnic tables in front of the partly ruined 18th-century monastery. It makes an ideal place to stop for lunch. You can walk or take a bus half a mile downhill to the much older original **monastery,** set under an enormous projecting rock reminiscent of Buddhist rock temples in India. Although only about a quarter of the original structure remains, this monastery (founded in 1025) has frescoes, an open-air **cloister** with superb capitals sheltered by the rock, the sarcophagi of Aragonese kings (the last, Pedro I, was buried here in 1104), a pantheon of nobles, and a vaulted **Romanesque church.** Much has been restored, but this has been done in a sympathetic way, and it remains an evocative and intriguing spot.

Leave the park by driving downhill past the old monastery (where parking is forbidden) and continuing 3 miles (5 km) to the N240 where you turn right to reach Jaca in 6 miles (10 km). ■

DRIVE: CASTLES & EYRIES

0 — 10 kilometers	
0 — 6 miles	

🗺 See area map
pp. 112–13

➤ Huesca

↔ 76.56 miles (122.5 km)

🕐 6 hours (including visits)

➤ Jaca

NOT TO BE MISSED
- Colegiata de Bolea
- Castillo de Loarre
- Monasterio de San Juan de la Peña

Jaca

Puente la Reina de Jaca

Aragón

N240

1552m ▲

Santa Cruz de la Serós

A1603

Bailo

Monasterio de San Juan de la Peña ④ ● Botaya

Bernués

A1205

SIERRA DE SAN JUAN DE LA PEÑA

A132

Ena ●

SIERRA DE SANTA ISABEL

Santa María

Triste

Gállego

Anzánigo ●

Embalse de la Peña

③ **Los Mallos**

Riglos

SIERRA DE LOARRE

Murillo de Gállego

Linás de Marcuello

Loarre

② **Castillo de Loarre** ▲1597m

Aniés

SIERRA CABALLERA

Concilio

A132

Seco

Sotón

Santa Eulalia de Gállego

Ayerbe

A1206

Riel

Bolea ①

Puibolea ●

N330

Gállego

Biscarrués ●

Plasencia del Monte

Esquedas

Venia

Isuela

A132

Banastás

Chimillas

Lupiñén ●

Alerre

START

Huesca

N330

The truly regal golden eagle

Castillo de Loarre

Pirineos (Pyrenees)

THIS IS THE PLACE TO COME TO ESCAPE ALL IMPRINTS OF modern civilization. The Pyrenees, and particularly the central section that lies in Aragón, have unadulterated wilderness beyond their tiny slate-roofed hamlets, spas, ski runs, and shepherds. This mountain range is Spain's natural barrier with France. Aragón has its highest peaks, the loftiest being Pico de Aneto (11,170 feet/ 3,404 m), and much harsher, more rugged landscapes than the Pyrenees in Navarra or Catalunya. Between the peaks lie wide valleys, lakes, gorges, sculptural limestone outcrops, and sparsely forested foothills. All these landscapes are encompassed by a national park, Parque Nacional de Ordesa y Monte Perdido. Its wild beauty is best in summer and fall. From October to May snow blocks the high roads and they are officially closed, leaving the terrain to climbers and cross-country skiers.

The lowland starting points for exploring these mountains are Jaca (see p. 145) in the west, Ainsa in the center, and Benasque, higher up in the east, near Parque Posets Maladeta. Outside the national park are villages where stone houses still have *cadieras* (wooden benches set around a cooking fire). The area used to be inaccessible, but tourism is making inroads.

PARQUE NACIONAL DE ORDESA Y MONTE PERDIDO

This 38,568-acre (15,608 ha) national park encompasses virtually every aspect of Pyrenean nature, and has unique species of flora and fauna. Rising over its northern perimeter is **Monte Perdido** (11,007 feet/3,355 m), a peak of sharply eroded limestone and glaciers. It overlooks the Ordesa valley, a canyon sliced by the Arazas River whose course is punctuated by waterfalls, notably **Cascada de Tamborrotera** and the 230-foot (70 m) **Cola de Caballo** (Horse's Tail). Beeches, maples, willows, and, higher up, silvester pines and firs are the dominant trees here. Eagles and vultures soar above and trout fill the water below.

This popular hiking area is easily reached by car from Ainsa via the pretty village of Torla. The road ends at Cascada de Tamborrotera, from where several hiking routes are laid out, the easiest along the river.

Parque Nacional de Ordesa y Monte Perdido

Pirineos

Ⓜ 113 E5

Visitor information

www.pirineos.com

✉ Avenida Ordesa 19, Torla

☎ 97 448 61 52

✉ Plaza de Luis López Allué, Huesca,

☎ 97 429 21 70

✉ Avenida Ordesa 1, Broto

☎ 97 448 60 02

Hikers' tips

Before embarking on any long hike, get reliable weather and geographical information from the nearest tourist office or visitor center. The Pyrenees are notorious for potentially dangerous storms and rising river levels. In a storm, do not stay on ridges or isolated outcrops, nor shelter under trees.

Be prepared for cooler temperatures as you rise in altitude, but remember that in summer the karstic (limestone) surrounds increase the aridity of the air, so take plenty of water. Start early, not only to catch the good morning light, but also to grab space at official parking lots. ■

The region's loveliest town, Aínsa was the capital of the ancient kingdom of Sobrarbe.

Aínsa

▲ 113 E5

Visitor information

www.pirineo.com/ainsa

✉ Avenida Pirenaica 1

☎ 97 450 07 67

Detailed route maps are available at the visitor center and cover more strenuous hikes such as the one to **Circo de Soaso,** a full-day trek with steep climbs and fantastic panoramas. Camping in small tents is allowed, but only at the four camping grounds. Refuge huts also provide for overnight treks.

To the east of this valley on the other side of the mountains is the **Cañon de Añisclo,** reached by car from Aínsa via Bielsa. This is a much narrower gorge than Ordesa, and has sheer cliffs striped with gray and red-ocher strata. The walk beside the Río Vellos (allow about five hours) is not difficult and takes you through woods of ilex and beech. Farther east still, on the edge of the park, is the **Valle de Escoaín,** best reached from Revilla

on a turnoff from the A138. You can follow a trail from Revilla down to the Río Yaga, and see the village of Escoaín across the river, high up on the flanks of Mt. Castillo Mayor.

From Bielsa it is also well worth driving beside the Río Cinca to the **Balcón de Pineta,** near the parador (state-run hotel) at the base of Monte Perdido. The views from here are quite spectacular. Beyond lie the French Pyrenees: You can reach them through the **Bielsa tunnel,** 7 miles (11 km) north of Bielsa.

AÍNSA & BENASQUE

The charming old town of **Aínsa** stands on a promontory at the meeting point of the Cinca and Ara Rivers, and of two main roads that twist up through the mountains—

Skiers revel on the slopes of the Pyrenees in the winter (above). A golden eagle, one of Ordesa's specialties (below)

Benasque
🅰 113 F5
Visitor information
www.turismobenasque.com
✉ Calle San Pedro
☎ 97 455 12 89

the A138 to France and the N260. The latter curves through stunning landscapes around the southern edge of Ordesa National Park. Aínsa's houses of golden stone, brimming with geraniums, surround the arcaded, cobbled Plaza Mayor, which is overlooked by the 12th-century church of **Santa María,** a lovely example of Aragonese Romanesque.

Benasque lies farther north and west, in a striking setting at 3,743 feet (1,138 m). The wide Benasque valley opens out at the base of the rugged Maladeta range that includes the Pyrenees' highest

peak, **Pico de Aneto,** with the popular ski resort of Cerler on its slopes. Benasque is a favorite hiking destination, but you should also take a stroll around the old quarter, which is lined with elegant mansions. Immediately west, trails lead into the **Parque Posets Maladeta,** surrounding the Pyrenees' second highest peak, **Pico de Posets** (11,060 feet/ 3,371 m). Lakes abound in this area. To the south, the Ésera River enters the dramatic **Congosto de Ventamillo,** 2 miles (3 km) of sheer limestone cliffs. ■

Pyrenean wildlife

Parque Nacional de Ordesa y Monte Perdido has examples of all the wildlife that haunts these imposing rocky mountains. The rarest of them all, the Pyrenean ibex, once inhabited the higher slopes but was officially declared extinct in January 2000. You may still spot marmots, chamois (a goat-like antelope), foxes, and mink. The cold rivers have otters, trout, and

the Pyrenean newt. Among 65 species of birds nesting here are golden eagles, bearded vultures, lioned vultures, various sorts of falcon, and capercaillies (a large form of grouse). The 1,500 species of Pyrenean flora are a delight, especially in May and June when the snows have melted and brilliantly colored primulas, edelweiss, and gentians carpet the slopes. ■

Cistercian monasteries

THE CISTERCIAN ORDER CAME TO NORTHERN SPAIN FROM France in the mid-12th century to build a series of monasteries in isolated sites. Cistercians devoted themselves to God and physical work. Their architecture is suitably devoid of decoration.

One of Aragón's most beautiful parks harbors the remains of the **Monasterio de Piedra,** a Cistercian abbey built with the stones of a Moorish castle. It lies near the village of Nuévalos about 75 miles (120 km) southwest of Zaragoza. The monks remained in this verdant oasis for 640 years, until the closure of monasteries in 1835. Since then, Piedra has been privately owned, and the monastery has lost all sense of spirituality. It has been converted into a hotel with a motley assembly of wine museum, restaurants, and carriage collection. The vast **church ruins,** open to the sky, are nonetheless impressive, and the surrounding **park** is a magnificent mixture of waterfalls, lakes, grottoes, and woods.

The beautiful **Monasterio de Santa María de Huerta** lies to the west, just over the border of Castilla y León, but it is best visited together with other Aragonese sights. Founded in 1162, it was inhabited continuously by monks until 1835, and was reestablished in 1930. The first sight as you enter is the 16th-century **cloister,** now the monks' quarters. Next are the older Gothic cloister and, behind, the **refectory** and enormous **kitchen.** These two rooms give you a wonderful picture of monastic daily life: You can imagine monks eating in silence while listening to texts being read from the carved stone pulpit, or cooking communal meals in the central oven of the kitchen. On the other side of the cloister is the **church,** whose original purity was enlivened by frescoes (1580) by Bartolomé de Matarana, and gilded baroque altarpieces. The monks' shop sells homemade cakes and liqueurs.

Ten miles (16 km) south of Tarazona (see p. 143) in the verdant Huecha Valley is the fortified Cistercian **Monasterio de Veruela** (1171–1224) *(tel 97 664 90 25, Closed Tues.).* The vast Romanesque and early Gothic church has an unusual green-and-blue **tiled floor** beneath its massive pointed vaults, and the ornate 14th-century **cloisters** writhe with carvings of gargoyles, plant motifs, and human heads. The **chapter house,** a more perfect example of Cistercian sobriety, contains the tombs of early abbots. ∎

Monasterio de Piedra

www.monasteriopiedra.com

⊠ 113 C3

✉ Nuévalos

☎ 90 219 60 52

$ \$ $ (monastery); $ \$\$\$ $ (monastery & park)

Monasterio de Santa María de Huerta

⊠ 113 C3

www.monasteriohuerta.org

✉ Santa María de Huerta (Soria)

☎ 97 532 70 02

$ \$ $

Monasterio de Santa María de Huerta

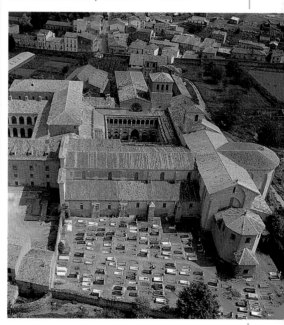

More places to visit in Aragón

ALBARRACÍN

Lower Aragón's most spectacularly sited town lies in the arid Sierra de Albarracín overlooking the Guadalaviar River, 28 miles (45 km) west of Teruel. If you are in Teruel, this is an essential detour. Albarracín has been declared a national monument, and restoration work has been sensitive. The ruined, turreted **ramparts** were originally built by the Moors in the tenth century. They are visible for miles. In the center of the town, cobbled medieval streets twist up past pink, part-timbered houses with projecting upper stories and tiled roofs, then go through archways to eventually reach the Renaissance **cathedral** *(tel 97 871 00 93)*. The cathedral museum has 16th-century Flemish tapestries and beautiful liturgical objects. Around Albarracín are pine forests with good walks, and you can see

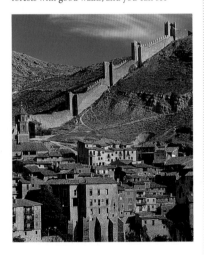

Albarracín's walls date from the 10th-century Moors.

prehistoric **rock paintings** 3 miles (5 km) southeast of town toward Bezas.

🔼 113 C2 **Visitor information,** www.albarracin.org ✉ Diputación 4 ☎ 97 871 02 51 🕐 Closed Mon.

ANSÓ

One of the prettiest Pyrenean towns lies in splendid isolation in northwestern Aragón,

5 miles (7 km) from the Navarra border. This remoteness led to Ansó's own dialect and traditions. The small **Museo Etnológico** *(Inside the church, tel 97 437 00 22)* tells you more. Ansó is in the valley between the equally attractive **Valle del Roncal,** to the west, and **Valle de Hecho,** to the east. **Hecho** (4 miles/7 km from Ansó) is a lovely town, though somewhat marred by its popularity; from there you can take an easy walk to the **monastery of San Pedro,** in Siresa, in the hills to the north. This entire area is ideal for hikes.

🔼 113 D5 **Visitor information,** www.lospirineos.com/mancomunidad/anso.htm ✉ Domingo Miral 1 ☎ 97 437 02 25 🕐 Closed Mon.

SOS DEL REY CATÓLICO

This walled town studded with towering gateways acquired its name because it was the birthplace of King Fernando of Aragón (see pp. 31–32). Sos is in the bleak Sierra de la Peña, and easily visited from the Monasterio de Leyre (see p. 128) and Sangüesa (see p. 127) in neighboring Navarra. The road from the reservoir Embalse de Yesa (A1601, the route from Jaca) has beautiful scenery.

Sos was a medieval stronghold against the kingdom of Navarra, and its shady lanes wind along a strategic hilltop between two promontories. Crowning the eastern end are the ruins of the **castle,** and just below is the 12th-century church of **Sant Esteban.** Inside are amazing things: the late-Renaissance **Capilla del Pilar** (with a stunning baroque altarpiece), Mudejar floor tiles, a 12th-century statue of a swarthy Christ, and an 8th-century font. You can visit the **crypt** *($)*, which has unusual frescoes in Byzantine style and beautifully carved capitals.

Sos also has fine Renaissance houses: the **Palacio de los Sada** where Fernando was born, and harmonious mansions linked by arches around the tiny Plaza Mayor. A few steps north of here, off the Calle Pérez de Biel, the medieval **corn exchange** has graceful pointed arches and a stone well.

🔼 113 D5 **Visitor information,** www.dpz.es/turi/english/comarcas/cinco-villas.asp ✉ Plaza Hispanidad ☎ 94 888 85 24 🕐 Closed winter ∎

This proud, self-sufficient city exudes style. Gothic and early 20th-century architecture combine with sleek contemporary work, enticing shops both old and new, innovative museums, and great restaurants.

Barcelona

Gaudí's Sagrada Familia

Barcelona

CATALUNYA'S VIBRANT CAPITAL ROOTED ITSELF IN THE GLOBAL PSYCHE with its spectacular staging of the Olympic Games in 1992, and since then it has not looked back. Before that, during the long gray years of Franco's dictatorship (1939–1975), it was a city struggling to keep its own culture and politics alive despite vindictive repression from central government. Today Barcelona is among the front-runners of Spanish business, theater, cuisine, and design while Catalan identity is clearly spelled out.

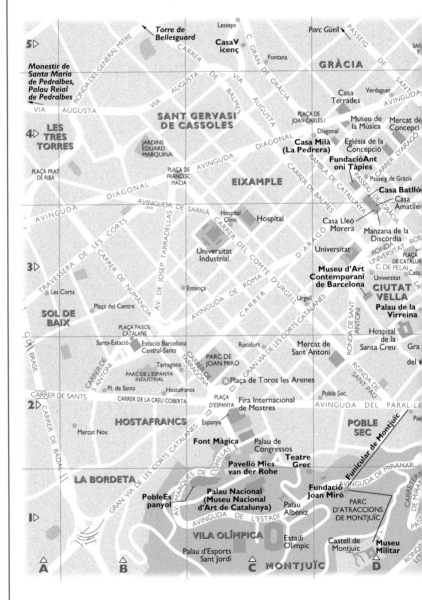

Barcelona's heritage ranges from Roman ruins to state-of-the-art contemporary architecture, with a good dose of Gothic and *modernista* (Catalan art nouveau) mixed in. Twentieth-century greats such as Pablo Picasso, Joan Miró, and Antoni Tàpies each have their museums. The Gran Teatre del Liceu and Rafael Moneo's slick concert hall—the Auditori

Intricate sculpture adorns the top of the Monument a Colom (Columbus).

Municipal—stage memorable performances. For the visitor, the place to start is the Barri Gòtic (Gothic quarter), where the cathedral, palaces, and museums all echo the zenith of Catalan trading prowess. In the 1990s the port area was transformed from a grimy, neglected network of streets into a glossy new window on culture and gastronomy. The main artery in this area is La Rambla, a long avenue stretching from Plaça de Catalunya to the statue of Christopher Columbus by the harbor. South of La Rambla is the newly fashionable Raval district, home to the contemporary art museum (MACBA), while to the north, La Ribera and the Born offer history and innovations. Seafront development continues northward past the Forum Building by Herzog & de Meuron.

To the west lies Eixample's grid of streets. Most of Barcelona's art nouveau monuments are here, standing beside designer shops and restaurants. This, too, is where you see the unmistakable spires of the Sagrada Familia, Gaudí's masterwork, and, farther inland, his Parc Güell. More of Barcelona's 40-odd museums lie in Montjuïc's hilltop setting, which you can reach via a cable car ride from the main harbor. Public transport, notably the metro, is very user friendly, restaurants are of high quality, and the surrounding hills and sea give a clear sense of the city's layout. Enjoy this culturally rich city and enter the heart of Catalan life. ■

Catedral (La Seu)

Catedral (La Seu)

🅰 155 E3

www.catedralbcn.org

✉ Pla de la Seu

☎ 93 342 82 60

💲 $ (choir & elevator to rooftop); $ (chapter house museum)

🚇 Metro: Jaume I

THE IMPOSING FACADE AND SPIRE OF THIS MASSIVE cathedral may look Gothic, but they actually date from the 19th century when they were added to the existing 14th- to 15th-century structure. Luckily the original 1408 designs by Charles Galtès from Rouen were used, which ensured overall visual harmony. Before this Gothic edifice came into existence in 1298, the site was occupied by a Romanesque church, a mosque, and a Roman basilica.

Penetrate the interior and you are in a lofty single nave, whose vast space is broken midway by the elaborate choir. This, in turn, fronts stairs leading down to the **crypt.** Here in a low-vaulted chamber beneath the main altar stands the carved marble sarcophagus of Santa Eulalia, a locally born virgin martyr who was executed by the Romans in the fourth century and who subsequently became Barcelona's patron saint. From the sunken steps you have a magnificent view of the soaring vaulted ceiling supported by ribbed columns. The **choir** is among the cathedral's many masterpieces. Its white marble screen depicts Santa Eulalia's life (sculpted from designs by Bartolomé Ordóñez) and enclose beautifully carved Renaissance choir stalls. These were later decorated with the coats of arms of European kings.

No fewer than 29 side chapels line the nave and apse, nearly every one of them containing an altarpiece or sculpture of interest. On your immediate right as you enter the main doors is the large **Capella del Santissim Sagrament,** whose 16th-century crucifix with its twisted Christ is alleged to have adorned the prow of Don Juan of Austria's flagship during the Battle of Lepanto (1571). In the opposite corner, a side chapel contains a huge marble font (1433) and a historic plaque recording the baptism of six

Carib Indians brought back by Christopher Columbus in 1493.

At the back of the cathedral look at the first side chapel to the left of the altar to see the alabaster tomb of Ramon d'Escales, Count of Barcelona, sculpted by Antoni Canet in 1409. Farther around the ambulatory, **Chapel VI** contains a lovely 1390 painting of St. Gabriel on 18 panels, by Lluís Borrassa. Between these is the **Capella de Sant Benet,** dedicated to the Benedictine Order, which is celebrated by an altarpiece (1452) painted by Bernat Martorell. This corner of the apse also gives access to the elevator for the rooftop. Look for two surprisingly modest coffins attached to the transept wall that belong to Ramon Berenguer I (Count of Barcelona) and his wife.

Another surprise lies in store in the oasislike Gothic **cloister** (1498), which you can also enter directly from Carrer del Bistre through the Porta de Santa Eulalia: A gaggle of geese roams between a palm tree, potted plants, and a fountain mounted with a statue of Sant Jordi (St. George), Catalunya's patron saint. Huge vaulted chapels line the cloister, each dedicated to a saint, and the **chapter house** has a small museum. The purist font that stands in the lobby was salvaged from the original Romanesque cathedral. ■

Recovering from history on the cathedral steps

Soaring rib vaulting leads the eye upward from the crypt.

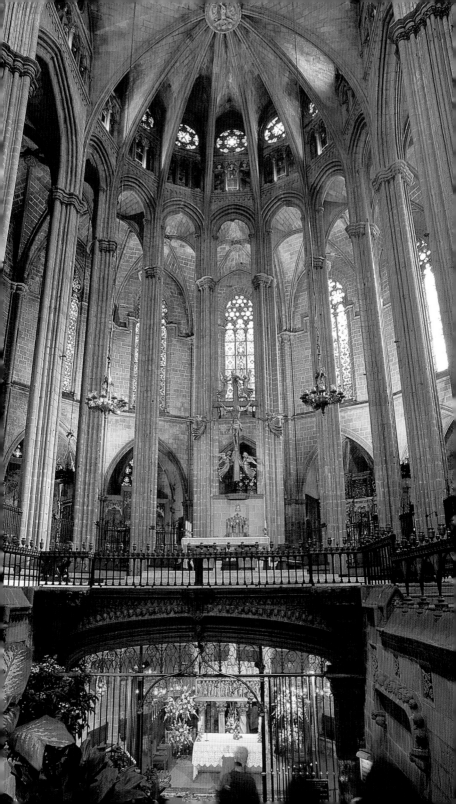

Barri Gòtic walk

This walk takes you through the evocative narrow alleyways of Barcelona's oldest quarter, passing major monuments, such as the cathedral and medieval palace, while touching the pulse of the city.

Leave **Plaça Reial** by the northeast corner, Carrer del Vidre, and then cross Ferran to walk up the alley of Carrer d'en Quintana. Turn right into Boqueria and immediately left to emerge on Plaçeta del Pi. In front of you is the apse of **Santa María del Pi ❶** and its 177-foot (54 m) octagonal tower. Walk around the church to the main plaza, backed by ornately decorated 18th-century houses, and admire the huge rose window. Turn into narrow, tile-studded **Carrer de Petritxol,** then right into Carrer Portaferrissa. Walk straight on to **Plaça Nova,** where the cathedral looms behind the Casa de l'Ardiaca (Archdeacon's house).

Turn right here, past remains of the Roman wall, into Carrer del Bisbe, where ahead of you is a surprising neo-Gothic **covered bridge** (1929) linking the medieval Casa dels Canonges (Canons' Residence) to the Palau de la Generalitat (Parliament Building). Turn right again into Carrer de Montjuïc del Bisbe to see the baroque church of **Sant Felip Neri ❷** on a delightful little square. In the

corner is the idiosyncratic **Museu del Calçat** (Shoe Museum, *tel 93 301 45 33, closed Mon. & p.m.*), a must for shoe fanatics. Returning to Carrer del Bisbe, enter the **Catedral (La Seu) ❸** (see pp. 156–57) through the cloister doorway. Leaving the main door, turn right past the **Museu Diocesa** (*tel 93 315 22 13, closed Mon.*) to walk beside a monumental section of the Roman wall and sections of the medieval royal palace that lead to impressive **Plaça Ramon Berenguer el Gran,** named after

---

- See area map pp. 154–55
- ▶ Plaça Reial
- ↔ 1.25 miles (2 km)
- ⏱ 1–2 hours (without visits)
- ▶ Plaça de Sant Jaume

NOT TO BE MISSED

- Catedral
- Museu d'Història de la Ciutat
- Museu Frederic Marès

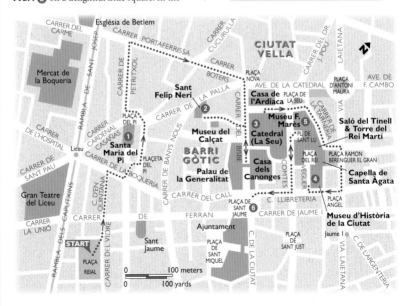

A stamp and coin market adds to Plaça Reial's hubbub on Sundays.

the Catalan ruler who is honored by an equestrian statue. Turn right off the main avenue, Via Laietana, into Carrer Llibreteria, past a candlemakers' shop dating from 1761. Then turn right again into Carrer del Veguer, where you reach the **Museu d'Història de la Ciutat** ❹ *(Plaça del Rei, tel 93 315 11 11, closed Sun. & public holidays p.m., & Mon. Oct.–Apr.).* This Museum of the History of the City overlooks the shadowy 14th- to 16th-century Plaça del Rei. Among the displays are Jewish and Arab artifacts, a large underground section showing Roman foundation walls and water channels, as well as Roman sculptures, the lovely 14th-century **Capella de Santa Àgata,** and, at the back of the square, the vast **Saló del Tinell,** a majestic construction of semicircular arches. Adjoining it is the five-story **Torre del Rei Martí:** Climb this for fine views of the entire Barri Gòtic.

On the left (southwest) of the square stands the Gothic-Renaissance palace used by Catalan viceroys. Walk around this to the back of the cathedral and turn right to reach Plaça de Sant Lu. In front is the **Museu Frederic Marès** ❺ *(Plaça de Sant Iu 5-6, tel 93 310 58 00, closed Sun. & public holidays p.m., & Mon.),* in the Romanesque-Gothic royal palace. This exceptional collection has Spanish sculpture from pre-Roman times to the 19th century. A section called the **Museu Sentimental** exhibits more everyday objects.

Return to Carrer Llibreteria and turn right to reach the administrative heart of Barcelona, the **Plaça de Sant Jaume** ❻. On the right is the **Palau de la Generalitat** *(Plaça de Sant Jaume 4, tel 93 402 46 00, open 2nd & 4th Sun. of month, & by appt. Sat. & Sun.),* a 15th-century structure with a Renaissance facade, now home to the Catalan government. ∎

La Ribera & El Born

IF YOU ENJOY THE GOTHIC QUARTER, THEN NEIGHBORING La Ribera should prove even more fascinating. Carrer de Montcada, with wall-to-wall art galleries, craft shops, Gothic palaces, and museums slices through here to reach the funky Born district.

La Ribera has been a residential quarter since medieval times. Any detour down its shady side streets takes you beneath balconies festooned with laundry, past neighborhood bars and Chinese-owned shops. The entire port area used to look like this before it was transformed for the Olympic Games. Since then, designers and restaurateurs have moved in to make it one of Barcelona's liveliest neighborhoods, especially around Passeig del Born.

The **Museu Picasso** may not have the world's finest or most comprehensive collection of Picassos, but it certainly has the most illuminating. The richest sections here cover Picasso's burgeoning early years, his "Las Meninas" series, and his last burst of creativity, expressed in engravings. All this and more is displayed in the neighboring Gothic palaces of **Berenguer de Aguilar** and **Barón de Castellet.**

At the top of the beautiful courtyard staircase, the collection moves chronologically through Pablo Picasso's life (1881–1973), although unclear directions make backtracking inevitable. His earliest work includes sketches he produced as a ten-year-old prodigy. Start at the far end and work back to see his lively imagination and academic prowess. Skillful life studies, portraits, and oil landscapes of A Coruña, painted when his family

Museu Picasso

⚑ 155 E3

www.museupicasso.bcn.es

✉ Carrer de Montcada 15–23

☎ 93 319 63 10

🕐 Closed Sun. p.m.

💲 $

Ⓜ Metro: Jaume I, Line 4

Museu Barbier-Mueller

⚑ 155 E3

www.amicsmuseupre colombi.org

✉ Carrer de Montcada 14

☎ 93 310 45 16

🕐 Closed Sun.p.m., public holidays p.m., & Mon.

💲 $

The Museu Picasso in La Ribera district

Santa María del Mar, the seamen's favorite church

Tèxtil i d' Indumentària

⚑ 155 E3

www.museutextil.bcn.es

✉ Carrer de Montcada 12

☎ 93 319 76 03

🕐 Closed Sun. p.m., public holidays, & Mon.

💲 $

in perfect condition, so you have a real feast of the best of Latin America's indigenous cultures. Eight rooms take you from Mesoamerica's mother culture, the Olmecs, through the classic period of Teotihuacán, the Aztec, the Maya, as well as rare pieces from Costa Rica, Nicaragua, and Panama to South America. Chavin, Moche, Nazca, and Inca pieces represent Andean culture beside pottery from the Lower Amazon. Admire the complex Zapotec god in feathered headdress, the fearsome, cross-eyed Maya mask of jade, and the strong geometry of Peruvian textiles.

In the adjoining Palau del Marquès de Llió, the **Museu Tèxtil i d'Indumentària** grew out of several private collections of costumes and textiles, including that of the renowned couturier Cristóbal Balenciaga. Starting with Copt, Moorish, and Romanesque textiles, it ends with contemporary designs.

At the end of Montcada you cannot miss the popular Gothic church of **Santa María del Mar** *(Plaça de Santa María del Mar 1, tel 93 319 05 16),* funded by local sailors in the 14th century to rival the extravagance of the bourgeois cathedral and known as the People's Cathedral. It has perfect proportions in its three soaring naves, and the 15th-century **rose window** above the western portal is a good example of Catalan Flamboyant Gothic.

North of here is the Passeig del Born, once used for jousting at the center of a delightful medieval merchants' quarter, **El Born.** Today this forms a maze of enticing fashion and design shops, as well as lively tapas bars and affordable young restaurants. Gourmet stores, art galleries, and more upscale restaurants are now moving in. ■

moved there from Málaga, demonstrate his early application and humor (look for his self-portrait in a wig, 1897). These are followed by stylistic experiments, much influenced by a visit to Paris in 1900.

After a room devoted to his **Blue Period** (1901–1904), the collection leaps to 1917, when Picasso's artistic freedom was in full flower, then to his **Las Meninas series** (1957). These 57 oils, inspired by Velázquez's painting "Las Meninas" (see p. 67), are astounding in their deconstructed abandon. The last rooms on this floor display landscapes of Cannes and ceramics made at Mougins.

Upstairs is the masterpiece of Picasso's old age, **"Suite 156"** (1969–1972). A masterful series of engravings using every possible technique, this is the culmination of both his cultural inspirations and strong erotic impulses.

Virtually opposite, the medieval Palau Nadal houses the **Museu Barbier-Mueller,** which has a choice collection of pre-Columbian art. Every exhibit is a masterpiece

A walk down La Rambla

Soak up the many variations on Barcelona's 21st-century spirit by exploring the animated Rambla and its side streets. These harbor a wealth of historical and contemporary interest in an inspirational mix of styles.

With your back to the modern fountain **"Homenatge a Francesc Macià" ①** on the southwest corner of Plaça de Catalunya (*Visitor information, Plaça de Catalunya 17-S, tel 93 304 31 35*), cross to the central pedestrian walkway of **La Rambla.** This immediately gives you a taste of Barcelona's most famous avenue with sidewalk cafés, street performers, flower sellers, and people strolling. At the sign pointing to Anteneu, cross to the left and take a sharp left into the pedestrianized Carrer de Santa Anna. At No. 32, walk into the courtyard where the charming Romanesque church of **Santa Ana ②** *(tel 93 301 35 76, open a.m. & 6:30–8.30 p.m., closed Sun. p.m.)* now stands jammed between 19th- and 20th-century buildings.

Retrace your steps to La Rambla. Cross to the other side, noting the ornate pharmacy, and walk down Calle d'Elisabets. This street crosses the Plaça del Bonsuccés before reaching a junction at Carrer dels Angels. Immediately visible on your right are the contemporary forms of the **Museu d'Art Contemporani de Barcelona** or **MACBA ③** *(Plaça dels Àngels 1, tel 93 412 08 10, closed Tues., www .macba.es)*, a stone, glass, and metal-plated building designed by Richard Meier, which opened in 1995. The permanent collection starts in the late 1940s with artists such as Jean Dubuffet, Alexander Calder, and Marcel Broodthaers, and ends with contemporaries such as Christian Boltanski, Rosemary Trockel, Richard Long, and Jaume Plensa. The museum has inspired a rash of art and design-related shops in the nearby streets of El Raval.

From here, turn right down tree-lined Carrer dels Angels until you come to Carrer del Carme. Opposite stands the massive Gothic-style **Hospital de Santa Creu,** which currently houses the **Biblioteca de Catalunya ④** *(tel 93 317 07 78)*. It is worth walking around to **Carrer de l'Hospital 56** to enter the courtyard and Gothic patio.

Continue across the pretty little square named for Alexander Fleming (the Scottish bacteriologist who discovered penicillin) and return to La Rambla. On your left is the rusticated baroque facade of the **Església de Betlem.** The interior of the church dates from a 1930s renovation after a fire and is of little interest. Turn right into the lively

View from the Monument a Colom

Rambla de Sant Josep, monopolized by a **bird market,** where caged parrots squawk beneath the chestnut trees.

You soon see on your right the imposing **Palau de la Virreina ⑤** (1778), whose baroque and rococo interior now hosts municipal exhibitions. Next comes the cornucopian **Mercat de la Boqueria** (also called Mercat de Sant Josep), where foodstuffs are sold beneath a wrought-iron and glass roof. Flower stands on La Rambla partly conceal a **Joan Miró design** on the central sidewalk as it widens into Plaça de la Boqueria. Look, too, at the tall, narrow building at **No. 77,** whose facade is decorated in art nouveau mosaics. Almost opposite is a kitsch example of the 1920s chinoiserie craze that bristles with dragons and parasols.

You have now reached **Rambla dels Caputxins.** On the right stands the **Gran Teatre del Liceu 6,** Barcelona's most prestigious theater, reopened in 1999 after extensive renovation. After the Hotel Oriente turn right into Carrer Nou de la Rambla to see Gaudí's extraordinary **Palau Güell 7** *(Carrer Nou de la Rambla 3, tel 93 317 39 74, closed Sun. & public holidays, guided visits only),* built 1885–1890. Back on La Rambla you pass the curved facade of the **Teatre Principal** (1847), opposite which stands a statue of the founder of modern Catalunyan theater, Frederic Soler. You are now in the last stretch, **Rambla de Santa Mònica,** where the 17th-century **Convento de Santa Monica** hides behind the nondescript facade of a cultural center.

Cross over and walk back up La Rambla to No. 42 and enter a covered passageway crossed by a glassed-in bridge. This leads to the elegant mid-19th-century **Plaça Reial 8,** where overpriced cafés overlook palm trees and lampposts designed by Gaudí. ∎

A "living statue" on La Rambla

▲ See area map pp. 154–55
► Plaça de Catalunya
↔ 1.75 miles (2.8 km)
⊕ 1–2 hours (without visits)
► Plaça Reial

NOT TO BE MISSED

- Museu d'Art Contemporani de Barcelona
- Mercat de la Boqueria
- Palau Güell
- Plaça Reial

Waterfront

BARCELONA'S HARBOR HAS BEEN COMPLETELY TRANS-formed since the 1990s and now bristles with marinas, leisure facilities, state-of-the-art museums, restaurants, and plenty of viewpoints. Alongside the spanking new is the illustrious old, nearly all of it connected with Barcelona's maritime history. The Aduana (Customs House), Capitania General (Naval Headquarters), and Gobierno Militar (Military Headquarters) line the harbor.

The Columbus Lookout or **Monument a Colom** (*tel 93 302 52 24*) is no longer the tallest waterfront structure, but it is probably the most symbolic and makes a good starting point. Take the elevator up this 160-foot (50 m) iron column to join the statue of Christopher Columbus surveying the harbor. In front is the mooring for trimarans (*Las Golondrinas, tel 93 442 31 06*) that tour the harbor to the **Vila Olímpica.** You also look down on the world's largest **medieval shipyards,** a unique complex of 13th-century vaulted halls built around a central courtyard large enough to contain galleons. Luckily for Barcelona they were saved from demolition and in their present spectacularly refur-

bished form they make a fitting background for the **Museu Marítim.** Model ships, paintings, prowheads, navigational instruments, maps, and charts illustrate Barcelona's maritime history. Exhibits also give a wider picture of the evolution of seafaring, ending with submarines before you are plunged into an aquatic virtual reality show. After this, you certainly need the café-restaurant, overlooking orange trees in the sunken entrance courtyard.

Another successful conversion houses the **Museu d'Història de Catalunya,** a lively chronological survey of Catalan history using interactive exhibits, information panels, charts, audiovisuals, photos,

Museu Marítim
- 155 E2
- www.museumaritim
  barcelona.com
- Avinguda de les
  Drassanes
- 93 342 99 20
- $$
- Metro: Drassanes,
  Line 3

**Museu d'Història
de Catalunya**
- 155 F2
- www.mhcat.net
- Palau de Mar, Plaça
  Pau Vila 3
- 93 225 47 00
- Closed Sun. p.m.,
  & Mon.
- Metro: Barceloneta,
  Line 4

**The panoramic
view from the
Mirador de Colom
encompasses the
modern marina.**

reconstructions, and models. Texts are in Catalan only, so most foreign visitors must borrow a translation brochure at the ticket desk. The illuminating display covers two remodeled floors of the 1900 **Palau de Mar,** the former main warehouses of the Barceloneta wharf. The most interesting section is on **Floor 2,** showing man's origins in Catalunya, the Iberians, and Romans. It also covers the short Moorish occupation and masses of information on medieval times and the Habsburg Empire. Don't miss **Floor 4,** where the café opens onto a terrace with fabulous port views.

A boardwalk, **Rambla de Mar,** leads from the Monument a Colom across to **Port Vell** and the **Moll d'Espanya** (Jetty of Spain), a reclaimed area flanked by marinas and devoted to entertainment and leisure. The Maremàgnum shopping mall and cinema complex jostle with the **IMAX theater** *(tel 93 225 11 11)* and the **Aquàrium** *(tel 93 221 74 74),* which has a special display of

Mediterranean underwater life and a tunnel for viewing sharks.

La Barceloneta, an 18th-century grid of streets that was traditionally the sailors' quarter, lies between the main harbor and the Vila Olímpica. Beyond a few harbor buildings to the south looms the rusty **Torre de Sant Sebastià** from where you can catch a cable car, **Transbordador Aeri** *(Tele-férico de Miramar, tel 93 298 70 00),* over the harbor to Montjuïc (see pp. 168–69). Seafood restaurants abound in this neighborhood, and 2.5 miles (4 km) of sandy beaches stretch northward. Towering over the Port Olímpic are two high-rises, one of which houses the very avant-garde Hotel Arts, fronted by a giant metallic fish designed by Frank Gehry. The beaches end at the junction with the lengthy Avinguda Diagonal, now graced by Herzog & De Meuron's elegant triangular structure, Edifici Fòrum, which was designed for the cultural events of Fòrum 2004. ■

Catalan pride

At the heart of Catalunya lies Barcelona, "a city of merchants, conquerors and people of good upbringing, refined, well educated and luxurious…." Little has changed since these words were written in a 19th-century travel guide, and Catalunya still spearheads Spain's commercial development, culture, and cuisine. Pride is an integral part of the individualistic Catalan character, and it is manifest first in the language, which stirs Provençal French and Castilian Spanish into a unique cocktail peppered with the letter *x,* and secondly in a strong attachment to regional customs. Whether dancing the *sardana,* a slow-moving circular dance, or creating gravity-defying human pyramids *(castellers),* the six million or so Catalans have defied all attempts to quash their identity. Industrialized, hardworking, solidly white-collar, liberal, and anticlerical, they are very different from the fervent, fun-loving farmers of the south.

The Catalan flag flies high in Barcelona.

This individualism stems from the early ninth century when the French Holy Roman Emperor Charlemagne successfully besieged Barcelona, and then divided the surrounding land into feudal kingdoms ruled by counts. By the 12th century, Catalan had become a written language, and the word "Catalunya" was mentioned explicitly. For two centuries Catalunya remained at its zenith. Its seamen and merchants dominated trade in the Mediterranean, and citizens enjoyed a unique system of privileges. Although Catalan trading prominence was later usurped by Castilian and Andalusian monopolization of New World routes, Catalans never lost their strong sense of civil rights, something that has irritated every Madrid-based ruler since. The 19th and 20th centuries saw decades of industrial

revolt and anarchism, and Catalunya was at its lowest ebb under General Franco's dictatorship (1939–1975), when the Catalan language itself was banned, as were books in Catalan and even the sardana.

Behind the scenes the radical spirit never died, and Catalan entrepreneurs now once more lead the way. Pragmatism (some would say mercantile obsession) is another enduring Catalan characteristic. Although one-third of Spanish wine is produced in Catalunya, it is textiles, chemicals, cars, and planes that form the backbone of the healthy economy.

Culturally, this region long dominated the Spanish avant-garde. Although Madrid and regional cities have caught up since the 1980s, Barcelona still boasts Spain's liveliest cultural calendar and a string of 20th-century luminaries. These examples have affected the activities of even the smallest Catalan towns. It is no surprise that Spain's greatest living writer, Juan Goytisolo, was born—where else?—in Barcelona.

Catalunya's geographical position has helped make it the most cosmopolitan of Spanish states. The proximity of France encourages high standards in gastronomy, art, and design, but French influence is tempered by habits that can only be termed Spanish, such as the relaxed post-meal chat *(sobre-taula),* which can last several hours. On the table itself, refined, painstakingly prepared Mediterranean dishes are served with an elegant flourish, and restaurants may display audacious contemporary architecture and designer furniture. Innovation is an essential component in its identity. Catalan pride is seen as arrogance by some, but its record is nonetheless impressive. With six Catalan newspapers and three TV stations, it is unlikely to fade. ∎

Gaudí's interpretation of the striped Catalan flag over the entrance to Palau Güell (above left); La Diada, the Catalan national holiday (above right); and dancing the Sardana (below)

Montjuïc

**The Fundació Juan
Miró, with its many
indoor and out-
door sculptures, is
housed in a
building designed
by Josep Lluis Sert.**

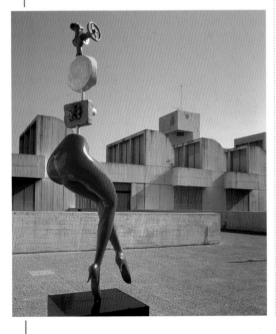

EASILY ACCESSIBLE FROM THE CITY BELOW, MONTJUÏC (meaning "Mount of the Jews") is an essential destination for its cultural sites, pine trees, gardens, and panoramic views. This was the bucolic setting of the 1929 World's Fair, and in 1992 the stadium was remodeled for the Olympics.

You can reach Montjuïc by **cable car** from La Barceloneta (see p. 165) or by **funicular railway** *(Open daily mid-Mar.–Oct. & Christmas holidays; rest of the year open Sun. only)* from Espanya metro station. Another cable car links the Montjuïc funicular station with the castle at the top of the hill, home to the **Museu Militar** *(tel 93 329 8613)*, with its displays of arms, uniforms, and suits of armor, and Montjuïc's best view.

Uphill to the east (nearer the cable car) from the Museu Nacional d'Art is the **Fundació Joan Miró.** One of the pleasures of this exhibition center is its architecture, the work of Josep Luis Sert

in honor of his longstanding friendship with the Catalan artist Joan Miró (1893–1983). The foundation was set up by Miró himself in 1971 to conserve a body of his work for the public and to promote contemporary art. It retains its popularity thanks to excellent temporary exhibitions and a lovely setting overlooking the city. Sert's Mediterranean-style architecture creates free-flowing spaces with changing vistas and forms. The permanent collection is concentrated on the upper floor, leaving most of the ground floor for temporary exhibitions and services.

On entering, cross the courtyard to the back wing to see Alexander Calder's spellbinding **"Mercury Fountain,"** made in 1937 for the Paris World's Fair. Beside this are wonderful, playful Miró sculptures and a large room showing his early work from the 1930s and '40s, with the **"Constellations"** series. Take the ramp upstairs to see the main body of work from the 1950s to '60s. The last, equally revealing section is comprised of works donated by friends, from Henry Moore to Henri Matisse. Look for Arnold Newman's 1979 photograph of Miró, which spells out the intense humanity of this man.

Structures remaining from the 1929 World's Fair include the **Poble Espanyol** *(Avinguda Marquès de Comillas, tel 93 508 63 00)* with its lively nightspots and reproductions of regional Spanish architecture, and the **Teatre Grec,** an open-air theater used in

The Font Màgica performs a stunning display of color and light.

Pavelló Mies van der Rohe

www.miesbcn.com

- 🅰 154 C2
- ✉ Avinguda del Marquès de Comillas
- ☎ 93 423 40 16
- 💲 $
- 🚇 Metro: Espanya Lines 1 & 3

Fundació Joan Miró

- 🅰 154 D1

www.bcn.fjmiro.es

- ✉ Parc de Montjuïc
- ☎ 93 443 94 70
- 🕐 Closed Sun. p.m., Mon. & public holidays
- 💲 $$
- 🚌 Bus 50 or funicular

the summer. The **Palau Nacional** was Spain's national pavilion. This extravagant building is now the **Museu Nacional d'Art de Catalunya,** which has the world's widest collection of Romanesque art, an equally impressive Gothic section, the Cambó collection of Renaissance and baroque paintings, and a large section on Catalan art.

Concentrate on the first two sections, respectively left and right of the entrance hall. The Romanesque part is largely composed of Catalan church interiors reconstructed with original frescoes that have been removed for conservation from the churches themselves. The exemplary display and multilingual explanations give clear indications of the location of each monastery or church and lead you in chronological order. Also look for the late 12th century altar frontals, notably those from Avia and Baltarga.

The Gothic section, dazzling with gilt and multipaneled altar paintings, includes a row of lifesize saints by Pere Llobet (circa 1387). Look out for the fine double portrait of John the Baptist and St. Estève

from Santa Maria de Puigcerdà (1445–1453), the room devoted to Bernat Martorell, and Jaume Huguet's magnificent paintings.

At the base of the wide steps to the Palau Nacional, beside the 1929 **Font Màgica** (Magic Fountain), stand the serene, purist forms of the **Pavelló Mies van der Rohe**—the pavilion designed by modernist Mies van der Rohe for the 1929 World's Fair. When the German government offered it for sale, no one reacted, so this masterpiece was dismantled. In 1983 moves were made by the Mies van der Rohe Foundation to reconstruct it, and in 1986 the pavilion reappeared on its original site. Water is an essential element, and the inner pool comes to life with a copy of Georg Kolbe's sculpture "Morning." Inside are examples of the Barcelona chair. Down the avenue, stands a beautifully restored art nouveau factory that since 2002 has been a showcase for the contemporary art collection of **Caixa Forum** (*tel 90 222 30 40, closed Mon.)*—a bank foundation—and a popular venue for concerts and talks. ■

Eixample

THIS NEAT GRID OF STREETS, WHOSE NAME MEANS "NEW extension," dates from the late 19th century, when booming Barcelona expanded westward from the Barri Gòtic. It is the place to go for designer shopping, art galleries, and sophisticated dining. One side, Gai-Eixample, is the hub for Barcelona's gay community.

Sagrada Familia

🗺 155 E5

www.sagradafamilia.org

✉ Carrer de Sardenya

☎ 93 207 30 31

💲 $$

🚇 Metro: Sagrada Familia, Line 2 & 5

Parc Güell & Casa-Museu Gaudí

🗺 154 D5

www.gaudiallgaudi.com/AA0 10d.htm

✉ Carrer d'Olot 7

☎ 93 219 38 11

💲 $

🚇 Metro: Lesseps, Line 3

Chief among Eixample's architects is Antoni Gaudí (see pp. 173–75), and here you find his unfinished masterpiece, the unorthodox **Sagrada Familia cathedral** (see pp. 174–75), and several other seminal buildings. The cathedral's multiple pinnacle steeples, permanently surrounded by cranes and a builders' site below, have become the emblem of Barcelona's individualism. Like it or not, the story behind the ambitious structure is one of an architect's total, and ultimately tragic, dedication to his greatest work.

Building started in 1882, but was interrupted by World War I. When Gaudí died in 1926, only the **Nativitat** (Nativity) **facade** was complete. Since then, work has continued sporadically, fraught by personality clashes, controversy,

and, above all, by a total absence of plans, as was Gaudí's modus operandi. In 1986 the **Passion** facade was commissioned from Josep Maria Subirachs, who added yet another thorny aesthetic issue with his stiff, unattractive sculptures.

Gaudí is buried in the **crypt,** where services are held, and a small museum relates the complexities of the cathedral's history and Gaudí's role. Best of all, for the moment, are the stunning views from one of the steeples. An elevator takes you up.

Far more successful as a Gaudí memorial is **La Pedrera** or **Casa Milà** *(Carrer de Provença 261–5, tel 93 484 59 00)*, which lies ten blocks southwest in the heart of Eixample. This innovative block of flats was built in 1906–1912. On its vaulted top floor is the **Espai Gaudí,** a brilliantly conceived interactive display of Gaudí's designs, models, and inspiration. This gives access to the extraordinary and much photographed roof terrace crowned with organically shaped sculptures. The Caixa, the dynamic Catalan bank that runs the space, also organizes high-profile art exhibitions on the first floor (the adjoining gift shop and snack bar are excellent, too).

Other Gaudí designs that you can track down in the neighborhood are **Casa Batlló** (1906) at Passeig de Gracia 43, **Casa Calvet** (1899) at Casp 48, the **Torre de Bellesguard** (1909) at Bellesguard 16–20, and **Casa Vicenç** (1888) at Carolines 24.

One of Gaudí's most colorful and expansive designs is **Parc Güell,** 1.5 miles (2.5 km) west of Sagrada Familia at the foot of Mont Carmel, just outside Eixample. This massive project (1900–1914) was originally intended as a garden city for 60 houses, but when the plots did not sell, Count Eusebi Güell, the promoter who was also Gaudí's patron, allowed the architect to let his fantasies fly. The result is a labyrinth of textured viaducts, pavilions, stairways, fountains, benches, curved columns, and arches upon which he developed his characteristic use of randomly fragmented ceramics. The park structures are inspirational, but the **Casa-Museu Gaudí** (designed by Francesc Berenguer, and where Gaudí lived) is of less interest, displaying only limited furniture and drawings. Join a one-hour guided tour of the park at the ticket office to understand the concepts behind it all.

Antoni Tàpies (born 1923) is another Catalan artist with the status of a regional institution. He instigated the **Fundació Antoni Tàpies** (*Aragó 255, tel 93 487 03 15, closed Mon.*) in 1984 to promote contemporary art, preserve

a representative body of his own work, and create an impressive reference library of modern and Oriental art. All this is installed in an extensively converted *modernista* building designed by Lluis Domènech i Montaner (1850–1923). ■

Casa Vicenç by Gaudí

The Fundació Antoni Tàpies displays contemporary works.

Gaudí & modernism

Through his total dedication to organically inspired architecture, Antoni Gaudí (1852–1926) revolution-ized architecture in Catalunya early in the 20th century. When art nouveau swept the Western world, the Catalan version, *modernismo,* became the most extreme form and Gaudí its most controversial and intuitively brilliant pro-tagonist. He originated from Reus, near Tarragona, where he showed a preco-cious fascination with natural forms found in zoology, botany, geology, and anatomy. This, com-bined with a taste for craft techniques inherited from his father (a coppersmith), became the unifying thread running through his work. For Gaudí, structure was inseparable from form, color, and texture, a holistic approach inspired by the English Arts and Crafts movement. He transformed these ideas into reality with the assistance of architec-tural training and an enlightened backer.

organic form and extensive use of fragmented ceramic tiles became the hallmarks of Gaudí's complex, playful style; other examples in Barcelona are in the Casa Batlló, nicknamed the "house of the emaciated tibia," and Casa Milà (La Pedrera), where chimney pots and access staircases on the roof were transformed into colorful, surrealistic sculp-tures. This rooftop fantasy-land is still a popular meeting place for Barcelona's art-oriented youth.

Gaudí's approach to construction was equally unorthodox: He never used plans, instead depending on sketches, elevations, and models. This deliberate nonrationality may have predated the surrealists, but later produced insurmount-able difficulties in complet-ing Gaudí's last project, Barcelona's Sagrada Familia cathedral, after his death. The architect intended this neo-Gothic church to synthesize his deepening sense of spirituality, devel-oped in mystical theories of symbolic structure while he lived as a virtual recluse

Above: Ceiling boss from the Room of a Hundred Towers in the Parc Güell. Below: the magnificent towers of the Sagrada Familia

Gaudí's early designs in the 1880s incorporated Mudejar and Gothic influ-ences, using ornamental brickwork, ceramic tiling, parabolic arches, turrets, and domes. By the 1900s he had developed his inimitable, curvilinear style in ambitious, ground-breaking Parc Güell in Barcelona. This project was financed by Eusebi Güell, a local industrialist who became his faithful patron. Free-flowing,

Casa Batlló, with its lavish baroque face and sensuous ironwork, is a Gaudí redesign of a typical Eixample apartment block.

during the latter part of his life. His work on the Sagrada Familia became so obsessional that when funds were low Gaudí even sold his possessions and begged money from friends. Finally, the life of this eccentric genius came to an end in a tragic, though fittingly unconven-tional way: When he was knocked over by a tram in 1926, Gaudí's appearance was so tramplike that nobody recognized him. Since then his star has risen, and the still incomplete Sagrada Familia has become the architectural symbol of Barcelona. ∎

Towers,
four on each facade
represent the 12
apostles

Nativity facade,
completed in 1904

Passion facade

Main entrance

Sagrada Familia

Begun by Francisco Villar in 1882, this project was taken over by Gaudí a year later. He planned to create a church in the form of the Latin Cross, with four towering spires over each of the three facades to represent the 12 Apostles and a central cluster of five more to symbolize Christ and the Evangelists. In medieval fashion, he worked without plans and remodeled as construction progressed. On his death, 40 years later, just one spire, the crypt, the apsidal walls, and the Nativity facade had been completed. Work on the church ceased temporarily, but it continues once more today. ■

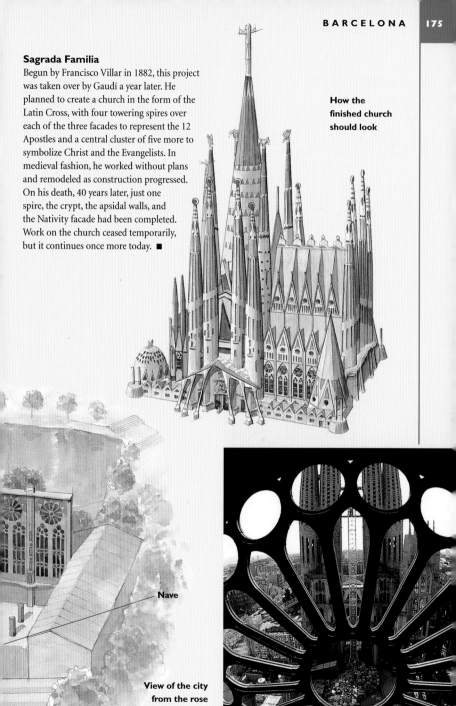

How the finished church should look

Nave

View of the city from the rose window past the towers of the Passion facade

More places to visit in Barcelona

MONESTIR DE SANTA MARIA DE PEDRALBES

Come here to drift back into medieval times, and see a top-notch selection of paintings from the Thyssen-Bornemisza collection in Madrid (see pp. 68–71). The walled Gothic monastery was founded in 1326 by Elisenda de Montcada, the fourth wife of Jaume II. In this serene three-story cloister, a garden and fountains gave solace to the nuns with their tiny cells round the perimeter. Here, you'll find a small, irregularly shaped chapel, **Capella de Sant Miquel,** faced in exquisite frescoes (1346) by Ferrer Bassá, a follower of Giotto.

From the cloister you reach the former dormitory and the Sala de la Reina (Queen's Room), where the 72 paintings from the **Thyssen-Bornemisza** collection hang. The jewel of medieval art and arguably of the

View of Gaudí's Cascada in Parc de la Ciutadella

entire collection is Fra Angelico's **"Virgin of Humility,"** but the collection includes other, masterpieces by Tiepolo, Cranach, Tintoretto, Veronese, Canaletto, Zurbarán, Velázquez, and Rubens.

🗺 154 A4 www.museuhistoria.bcn.es/cat /centres/pedralbes ✉ Baixada del Monestir 9 ☎ 93 203 92 82 🕐 Open Tues.–Sun. a.m. 🟢 $ 🚇 Metro: Maria Cristina, Line 3

PALAU REIAL DE PEDRALBES

This palace was built for King Alfonso XIII in 1919–1929, courtesy of the Güell family. It is in the far southwestern corner of the city, within walking distance of the Monestir de Santa María de Pedralbes. Italian Renaissance style dominates, and the lavish interior flaunts Murano glass chandeliers beside antique furniture, tapestries, and a throne resting on golden lions. Visit the **Museu de Cerámica,** (tel 93 280 16 21), with its rich display of Spanish ceramics, including 12th-century Mudejar work, 18th-century *azulejos* (tiles), and pieces by Miró, Picasso, and contemporary ceramicists.

Here, too, is the **Museu de les Arts Decoratives,** (tel 93 280 50 24), spanning the centuries from medieval days to the present. The surrounding classically designed gardens have plenty of shade. Use any remaining energy to walk around to the **Pavellons de la Finca Güell** (Avinguda de Pedralbes 7, closed Sat.– Sun.), near the crossroads with Passeig Manuel Girona, to see their decorative brickwork. Gaudí designed the buildings in 1887 as a porter's lodge and stables for the Güell estate.

🗺 154 A4 ✉ Avinguda Diagonal 686 ☎ 93 280 13 64 🕐 Closed Sun. p.m. & Mon. 🟢 $ 🚇 Metro: Palau Reial

PARC DE LA CIUTADELLA

Barcelona's largest park lies between the old town and the Olympic area on the site of a citadel developed for the 1888 World's Fair. Some of the original structures remain, such as the **Umbracle** (tropical plants greenhouse) and **Hivernacle** (glasshouse), and the elaborate restaurant building designed by Domènech i Montaner, now home to the **Museu de Zoologia** (tel 93 319 69 12, closed Tue.–Wed. p.m., Fri.–Sun. p.m. & Mon.). Close by stands the **Museu de Geologia** (tel 93 319 68 95, closed Tue.–Wed. p.m., Fri.–Sun. p.m. & Mon.). These two museums together form the Museu de Ciencies Naturals (www.bcn.es/museu ciencies). Also in the park are the Catalan Parliament and the **Parc Zoològic.**

🗺 155 E3 🚇 Metros: Ciutadella-Vila Olímpica, Arc de Triomf, & Barceloneta ■

Spain's prosperous eastern seaboard of Catalunya and Valencia has endless beaches, remote inland sierra, Roman Tarragona, and Spain's third city, Valencia. Juicy oranges, inventive rice dishes, and sparkling *cava* are part of the bargain.

Eastern Spain

Detail of a Roman mosaic

Some of Dalí's most notorious frolics took place at his summer home at Portlligat.

Eastern Spain

FROM THE PYRENEES ON THE FRENCH BORDER SOUTH TO THE CAREFREE beach resorts of the Costa Blanca is a vast swath of land with one obvious trait—the Catalan language. Less obvious, but just as strong is left-wing Republicanism. During the Civil War of 1936–39, this part of Spain endured terrible hardship, resulting in simmering resentment throughout the four decades of General Franco's rule. Eastern Spain's landscapes vary from chilly Pyrenean villages with wandering goats, to mellow sandy beaches, rugged interior sierra, and valleys clad in almond and citrus trees. You can experience huge climatic variations in a day, but almost everywhere, with only a few exceptions, you also sense a burgeoning prosperity.

Of the cities, Barcelona (see pp. 153–76) has the highest profile, but Valencia, Spain's third largest city, was given immense impetus when it hosted the America's Cup in 2007. It is an increasingly strong cultural center, with plenty of spruced-up monuments and dazzling new buildings. Between the two is Tarragona, giving an unparalleled vision of Roman Spain. The design-conscious town of Girona (Gerona) is to the north, and in the deep south the mirage of Alacant (Alicante) rises from arid hills over a generous bay. Seafaring has been king has been since the Greeks and then the Romans crossed the Mediterranean to colonize Spain. Charlemagne left his mark in the ninth century, creat-

ing the County of Barcelona and a feudal system that persisted for several centuries. The Moors came and went fast from the north of this region, but more slowly from Valencia. By 1443, Catalunya, Aragón, Valencia, and the Balearic Islands had created one powerful kingdom including Sardinia, Sicily, and southern Italy and was soon united with Castilla. Many of the monuments date from this Renaissance period, when prosperity soared and huge areas were repopulated by northerners to replace the victims of the Spanish Inquisition. Agriculture remains dominant in the economy —obviously so in Valencia's vast inland *huerta* (orchard, a nickname for its irrigated land),

and more discreetly in Catalunya's sierra. The region is also highly industrialized.

A major source of income is tourism, above all along the *costas*, home to a high proportion of northern Europeans. The most venerable, the Costa Brava, saw its first waves of foreign visitors in the 1950s. The development of the 1960s and '70s now seems to be a mistake, yet vacationers still flock here. Despite this, you still see dramatic natural beauty. If you visit only one stretch of coast, the Costa Brava should be your choice. Farther south, the Costa Blanca, has pockets of outstanding scenery, and its special is that quintessential Spanish dish—*paella*, a fragrant blend (with variations) of rice, saffron, shellfish, meat, and lemon. ■

The Costa Brava, or "wild coast," is named for its rugged, rocky coastline.

Catalunya (Cataluña)

Together with the Madrid region and Euskadi (Basque Country), Catalunya is economically the most dynamic part of Spain and long stood on its own as the most avant-garde. It still clings jealously to its Catalan language and traditions, sometimes to the detriment of universal communication.

This clear sense of identity dates from the ninth century, when Charlemagne established Catalunya as a buffer zone. It has close linguistic and cultural links with southern France, although this did not protect it from destructive French troops during warfare between France and Spain in 1714 and in 1808. Close geographic and cultural links continue today, and for inhabitants of northern Catalunya, France is more easily accessible than the Spanish capital.

The Moorish occupation was short, enabling the counts of this feudal region to finally crystallize Catalan identity in the 12th century, crowned by the marriage of Count Ramon Berenguer IV with the Aragón heiress Petronila in 1137. This was the beginning of a golden age for Catalan merchants that peaked in the 14th century, when Catalunya and Aragón controlled a huge Mediterranean empire. Despite their alliance, each of these regions kept its traditional civic privileges, and the Catalans' proud sense of justice, expressed in strikes and industrial unrest, was one of the biggest thorns in Franco's side.

Catalunya has widely diverse interest, from gastronomy to history, wine to contemporary design, and volcanoes to sun-drenched beaches and crisp ski slopes. Highlights include historic monasteries in Pyrenean valleys and coastal sierra, spectacular Roman remains at Empuries and Tarragona, and Girona—Catalunya's most enjoyable, forward-looking town outside Barcelona. You can pick up the threads of Salvador Dalí's eccentricities in Cadaqués and Figueres, or take a half hour's drive into the hills to hike and taste wine and *cava* (the Spanish equivalent of champagne) before collapsing on a beach to digest it all. On the down side, Catalunya's greatest economic asset, its industry, does not always make for scenic landscapes. ■

Costa Brava

FROM THE FRENCH BORDER AT PORTBOU SOUTH TO Blanes stretch 125 miles (200 km) of rugged coastline, coves, and beaches that still possess magic and beauty despite vigorous development in the 1960s and '70s. Dalí, Picasso, Chagall, and Man Ray were among the many artists captivated by the coast's fishing villages and limpid sky.

The Costa Brava has black spots such as the package vacation resort of **Lloret de Mar,** but its highlights include the inland medieval villages of **Pals** and **Peratallada,** the nature reserve of the **Les Medes** (islands reached by glass-bottomed boat from L'Estartit), and, in the south, the picturesque walled town of **Tossa de Mar.**

Empúries (Ampurias) was the site of a Greek and Roman settlement that held sway over the area for more than seven centuries from 600 B.C. Apart from its archaeological interest, the location encapsulates the original untouched beauty of this coast, with magnificent views across the Golf de Roses and a lovely beach that is accessible from the site. Wander through the Greek and Roman ruins in their landscaped park, look at the mosaics of the villas, then see the dramatic audiovisual show at the **Museu Arqueologia** (L'Escala, tel 972 77 02 08) to get a sense of Catalunya's long history. Even the anchovy industry at neighboring L'Escala dates back to the Romans.

One of the coast's most popular towns is **Cadaqués,** which, unlike more commercialized resorts, still has a distinctive atmosphere out of season. This whitewashed fishing port huddles in a cove at the end of a tortuous road across the hilly promontory and nature reserve of **Cap de Creus.** Seafood restaurants (reservations necessary in summer) and art galleries are abundant, and Salvador Dalí's fascinating house, **Casa-Museu Salvador Dalí** (Portlligat, Cadaqués, tel 972 25 10 15, reservations needed), awaits over the hill.

The most exclusive resort is **Begur,** 30 miles (50 km) east of Girona. Crowned by castle ruins and backed by wooded hills, it lies within a couple of miles of idyllic sandy coves lapped by crystalline water. From here to the lighthouse of Llafranc is arguably the most beautiful stretch of the Costa Brava that you can explore on foot or by car before visiting delightfully well-preserved **Palafrugell,** preferably for its Sunday market. ∎

Costa Brava
△ 179 C5
www.costabrava.org

Cadaqués
△ 179 C5
Visitor information
www.cadaques.net
✉ Carrer Cotxe 2A
☎ 972 25 83 15

Begur
△ 179 C5
Visitor information
www.begur.net
✉ Plaça de
l'Església 8
☎ 972 62 45 20

Cadaqués has been a popular artists' getaway ever since Dalí spent his summers here.

The Onyar River flows past central Girona's colorful houses.

Girona (Gerona)

THE LOVELY OLD TOWN OF GIRONA IS UNDERGOING A minor boom and this, combined with its strategic location, makes it a stimulating base from which to explore the region. In some ways Girona is a mini-Barcelona, its characteristic river frontage replacing the Catalan capital's seafront. It even has its own equivalent of Gaudí, embodied in his contemporary, Rafael Maso (1880–1935), whose *modernista* buildings pepper the center.

Girona (Gerona)
🅰 179 C5
Visitor information
www.costabrava.org
✉ Rambla de la
   Llibertat 1
☎ 972 22 65 75

Iberians built Girona as a military fortress at the confluence of the Ter and Onyar Rivers. Romans, Jews, and Arabs all left their mark, and Charlemagne's army was not the only one to besiege it. The Onyar River clearly divides the medieval town from the 19th- and 20th-century quarter that spreads to the west, and the numerous footbridges give you lovely views of colorful old houses with laundry-draped balconies lining the banks. One of the best viewpoints is the **Pont de Peixateries Velles,** built in 1877 by Gustave Eiffel's company.

Back on the historic east bank, head for the social focal point, porticoed **Rambla de la Llibertat,** with a Saturday flower market, sidewalk cafés, and boutiques. From here it is a gentle uphill climb into the heart of medieval Girona, which culminates at the Roman walls and their highest point, the medieval **Torre Gironella,** where you have panoramic views and a rampart walk. Skirting around the walls you come to the magnificent **Roman north gate,** that opens onto a wide esplanade in front of 90 steps leading up to the **cathedral** *(Plaça de la Catedral).* The baroque facade conceals a Gothic interior of one single nave, an astonishing 94 feet wide (23 m), which caused controversy when it was designed in the 14th century.

The cloister and chapter house museum house the original, Romanesque section. In the trapezoidal **cloister,** look at the beautifully carved capitals and 11th-century bell tower. The museum, the **Tresor Capitular** *(tel 972 21 44 26, closed Sun. p.m. & Mon.)* displays the **Tapestry of the Creation,** a Romanesque masterpiece, alongside religious silverware, manuscripts (look for the Codex del Beatus), and sculptures.

Just outside the north gate stand the 12th-century **Banys Àrabs** (Arab Baths, *Carrer Ferrán el Católic, tel 972 21 32 62, closed Sun. p.m.*), built in Moorish style but based on Roman design. The *frigidarium* (cold bath) has a colonnaded octagonal pool beneath a skylight. Immediately below this, you can't miss the unfinished Gothic bell tower of **Sant Feliu** church, which contains sarcophagi from the Roman and early Christian era, some from Italy. Here, too, is an unusual recumbent statue of Christ (1350) by Mestre Aloi, an example of Catalan Gothic sculpture.

Another major site is the beautiful Romanesque monastery that now houses the **Museo Arqueológico de Sant Pere de Galligants** *(Plaza Santa Lucia, tel 972 20 26 32, closed Sun. p.m. & Mon., $).*

Girona's newest jewel lies in the renovated Jewish quarter, **El Call,** just a few steps south of the cathedral square along Carrer de la Força. In the 15th century, the Jewish community that had lived there for six centuries was expelled, and part of this web of lanes was bricked up. Today, El Call is not only one of the most fashionable places to live, but is also home to the **Bonastruc Ça Porta** *(Carrer Sant Llorenc, tel 972 21 67 61, closed Sun. p.m. & public holidays)*, a study center and museum. It has been rebuilt from a synagogue and named for

Nahmánides, or Bonastruc de Porta, the 13th-century rabbi who symbolizes the importance of Girona's school of the Kabbalah (mystical Judaism). The **Museo de Historia de los Judíos** illustrates rituals and daily life, giving insight into this community's role in Spanish history and on the religious tolerance that existed (most of the time) until the Inquisition.

A final glimpse of Girona's illustrious past can be had in Pujada de Sant Domenec at the **Palau dels Agullana.** The unusual oblique archway of this 14th- to 17th-century mansion flanks a picturesque stairway, one of the city's most photographed corners. ∎

The graceful *frigidarium* of Girona's Arab baths were built to a Roman design.

Salvador Dalí

His image transcended nationality, as did his trademark moustache, dreamlike, liquid landscape paintings, and still unsurpassed megalomania. First and foremost, Salvador Dalí was seduced by fame, a status he expertly cultivated whether in his stage-set garden in Cadaqués, at the Hotel Meurice in Paris, or the St. Regis in New York. In 1958 he wrote, "It is difficult to hold the world's interest for more than half an hour at a time. I myself have done so successfully every day for twenty years." Andy Warhol predicted that everyone would be famous for 15 minutes, but Dalí made his fame last a lifetime, from the day he joined the surrealist movement in Paris in 1929, until his death in 1989. Nor did his cult end there, for Dalí's posthumous legacy was a minefield of unauthenticated works and question marks over his chosen burial place and will that provided headlines for years after.

Portrait of Salvador Dalí and Gala. Dalí sports his trademark moustache.

Dalí had a talent for drama, provocation, and exhibitionism, all held together by an unbridled imaginative genius. These qualities came at the perfect moment, propelling him to the forefront of the surrealist movement, although its founder, André Breton, later labeled him in disgust "Avida Dollars" (dollar greedy). Dalí's principles were questionable: He veered between anarchism, Marxism, monarchism, and Catholicism, and he did not hesitate to embrace Francoism when it suited him. Yet this extravagant opportunist was no empty bubble, and his earlier works, until the 1940s, reveal a consummate draughtsman and expert weaver of Freudian dreams and neuroses. From "Metamorphosis of Narcissus" (1936–37) to "Galarina" (1944–45), he showed off classical oil-painting techniques with mythological, sexual, and psychoanalytical references in a virtuoso body of work. Before that, his talents extended to collaborating with the filmmaker Luis Buñuel on two seminal surrealist films: *Un Chien Andalou* (1928) and *L'Âge d'Or* (1930).

At the center of Dalí's existence and of many of his paintings was his seductive, strong-willed Russian wife, Gala. From 1930 onward they led an unconventional existence between globetrotting winters and summers at their fisherman's cottage at Portlligat, near Cadaqués. In 1970 Gala moved to a transformed castle ruin, Castell Pubol, to which Dalí was admitted only by written invitation. Here she entertained young lovers until her death in 1982, while Dalí dallied with the transsexual Amanda Lear. This arrangement is typical of their offbeat yet impassioned relationship. Dalí's last years were taken up with obsessional work on his museum at Figueres, where he was born. This converted theater was to be a monument to his life, creativity, and "paranoiac-critical" stance, surrealistically blurring the boundaries between fiction and reality. A coin-operated Cadillac that is sprayed by a fountain, articulated bronze sculptures, the Mae West room, a bed from a brothel, and facades studded with models of eggs and bread-rolls provide the context for hundreds of his works. Dalí's tomb is under the central stage, marked by a simple gravestone—unexpected for someone who once declared "I have always considered myself to be a genius." ∎

The exterior of the Dalí Museum in Figueres (above), constructed to the artist's own design, gives visitors a taste of what is to come inside (below).

Pirineos (Pyrenees)

THE PYRENEES IN CATALUNYA ARE DISTINCTLY MORE developed and prosperous than their counterparts in Aragón and Navarra, but you still find fortified medieval villages, remote monasteries and hermitages, and flocks of sheep and cattle grazing in meadows. Looming in the far west is the highest peak, Aneto (11,200 feet/3,408 m), and 83 miles (230 km) east the last bumps descend into the balmy Mediterranean at Portbou, on the French border.

The national park, **Parque Nacional d'Aigüestortes** (*tel 973 62 40 36 or 973 69 61 89, visitor numbers limited in summer*), covers 34,500 acres (14,000 ha) and is a perfect destination for hiking except in winter when entry roads are blocked by snow. The park, whose name means "winding waters," is a heady mountain mix of glacial lakes, waterfalls, and rushing streams, spiked by towering granite peaks with flanks clad in pine and fir forests. One of the most popular places is the **Estany de Sant Maurici** (Estany meaning "lake"), which you can reach by car from Espot (on the C147) in the east. Access from the west is

from Boí (via Pont de Suert on the N230), and a trail connects the two villages. Paths are well marked, and there are refuge huts for longer treks. Driving from the south, on the N260, you can't miss the spectacular **Estret de Collegats,** a narrow gorge gouged by the torrential Noguera River, where a rock face dripping with icy stalactites is named the **Roca de l'Argentaria.**

At the spa town of **Caldes de Boí,** on the western perimeter of Aigüestortes park, you can recover in hot springs. Farther into the valley are many 12th-century churches, where reproductions now replace unique frescoes that

were painstakingly moved to Barcelona's Museu Nacional d'Art de Catalunya (see pp. 168–69). If you are short of time, go straight to **Taüll,** where there are the lovely churches of **Santa Maria** and **Sant Climent,** both with multistory bell towers rising above slate roofs, in a setting of verdant meadows. In winter this area becomes the domain of skiers heading for the slopes of **Boí-Taüll,** which lie between 6,550 feet (2,000 m) and 8,060 feet (2,457 m).

The easternmost area of interest in the Pyrenees is the county of **Ripollès,** where peaks rising to 9,850 feet (3,000 m) dominate two valleys, **Camprodon** and **Ribes.** Their access point is **Ripoll,** a sleepy town at the confluence of two rivers that you will want to visit for its Romanesque monastery, **Monestir de Santa Maria** *(Plaça de l'Abat Oliba, Ripoll, tel 972 70 02 43)*, a landmark in Catalan history. Founded in A.D. 880 by Guifré "the Hairy," first Count of Barcelona, the monastery housed the royal pantheon until the focus moved to Barcelona in 1162. The monastery scriptorium produced illuminated masterpieces such as the Ripoll Bible (1015–1020), now housed in the Vatican. The library was said to be one of Europe's top four in the Middle Ages.

The monastery itself lost all charm during 19th-century alterations, but the **basilica** and **cloister** remain outstanding. Pick up a leaflet at the ticket office to identify countless fascinating details, and be sure to admire the basilica's structure from the garden at the back, where you can see the seven apses that end the single nave, four aisles, and transept. Santa Maria's masterpiece is the **front portal** (built around

Above: A view over the town of Berga from its castle ramparts

Above right: The ski slopes of Cerdanya, west of Núria, are located right on the French border.

1150), a monumental gateway sculpted with a multitude of scenes, figures, and symbols. Take time to sit in the glassed-in lobby and follow its intricacies.

Guifré the Hairy was responsible for another remarkable monastery, **Sant Joan de les Abadesses** *(Plaça de l´Abadia 9, St. Joan de les Abadesses, tel 972 72 05 99)*, only 6 miles (10 km) farther up the Ter River. His daughter Emma became its first abbess. A 15th-century earthquake caused the steeple to collapse, but the pure Romanesque interior remains a serene backdrop to rarities such as the **Santíssim Misteri,** a 13th-century group of sculptures depicting Christ's removal from the cross.

North of Ripoll, the mountain area of **Núria** can only be reached by rack railway (with a cogged rail between the bearing rails), the **Cremallera.** This lifts you 7.5 miles (12 km) from Ribes de Freser to Núria's ski station, **Estació de Montanya Vall de Núria** *(Queralbs, tel 972 73 20 30, www.valdenuria.cat)*, 3,280 feet (1,000 m) higher up. ■

Volcanoes of Olot (Garrotxa)

**Volcanoes of Olot
(Garrotxa)
Visitor information
& botanic garden**
www.turismegarrotxa.com
✉ Casal dels Volcans,
Avinguda Santa
Coloma, Olot
☎ 972 26 62 02

Olot
🗺 179 C5
Visitor information
www.turismegarrotxa.com
✉ Hospici 8
☎ 972 26 01 41

Spain's greatest volcanic landscape is somewhat illusory. Ever since the last eruption took place, over 10,000 years ago, these 46 square miles (120 sq km) of valleys, plains, rivers, and volcanoes have been transformed into well-irrigated cropland and grazing pastures. The craters are mostly visible from the volcano summits, and the walls of river valleys reveal spectacular basalt strata created by lava flows.

In 1985 the **Garrotxa** became a protected natural park, and visitor facilities make it a popular weekend hiking destination—best avoided on Sundays. The starting point is the town of Olot, where you are within easy striking distance of the beech woods of Jordà and the neighboring volcanoes of Croscat and Santa Margarita. The latter, reached by an almost vertical path, has a hermitage that sits picturesquely in its crater. Croscat (17,000 years old) has a less strenuous trail past sections of fissured rock and

lava blocks. Garrotxa's very diverse woodland provides habitats for beech marten, wildcats, genets, badgers, occasional wild boar, otters, and 143 bird species.

Three of the villages are exceptional. **Castellfollit de la Roca** perches dramatically on 197-foot (60 m) walls of basalt prisms and strata eroded by lava flows, with the Fluvia River at its feet. It is best seen from the N260. Head east to explore **Besalú** *(Visitor information, Plaça de la Llibertat 1, tel 972 59 12 40),* a stunning medieval village where a Romanesque bridge and four churches stand beside a Jewish quarter and baths. In **Santa Pau,** walk through cobbled medieval streets to the sloping main square bordered by Gothic arches (each one a different shape) where a cattle market was once held. Looming above the village is an 11th-century baron's castle that was used as a Dominican monastery before later being abandoned. ∎

Figueres

**Dalí Theater-
Museum**
www.salvador-dali.org
✉ Plaça Gala-Salvador
Dalí 5
☎ 972 67 75 00
🕐 Closed Mon. except
July-Sept.
💲 $$

Figueres
🗺 179 C5
Visitor information
✉ Plaça del Sol
☎ 972 50 31 55
🕐 Closed Sun. Oct.-
June, p.m. Oct.-Feb.

This small town is the capital of Catalunya's Salvador Dalí empire (see page 184), since 1974, it has been the location for his provocative **museum,** as well as being the birthplace of this extraordinary, larger-than-life artist, in 1904. Other than that, Figueres is a pleasant stopover on the main highway leading to France and lies only 12.5 miles (20km) from the Costa Brava. An alternative to viewing Dalís is the charming **Museu de Joguets** (Toy Museum)*(tel 972 50 45 85, closed Sun. p.m. and Tues.)* which displays a miniature world of

trains, teddy bears, and doll furniture. Otherwise, enter the megalomaniacal universe of the world's most flamboyant artist, housed in a mid-19th-century theater that was destroyed by fire at the end of the Civil War. Dalí was closely involved in this project from its inception, in 1961, and many of the works were specially created, such as Mae West's Room (her lips a red sofa, her hair yellow curtains, her eyes framed paintings and her nose a fireplace). Don't miss seeing this museum— it's unique. ∎

Vic

AT FIRST SIGHT VIC IS A DARK, UNINVITING INDUSTRIAL town, not helped by an unhealthy climate of high rainfall and fog. Other Catalan towns may appear livelier, but don't be put off—the old town center is undergoing renovation to highlight numerous architectural jewels.

Vic has a long mercantile tradition (and tanning and sausagemaking industries), and the twice-weekly market *(Tues. & Sat.)* has been held on **Plaça Major** for centuries. This porticoed square lined with cafés exemplifies the historical continuity of the town: Gothic houses stand next to baroque and 1900s extravaganzas. The prize for true *modernista* excess must go to the **Casa Comella,** a neo-Gothic folly dominating the southwest corner. Walk in the narrow streets southeast of the square and you come to Vic's oldest building, a restored second-century **Roman temple** that stands beside the ruins of the **Palau dels Montcada.** For centuries this Romanesque palace concealed the temple in its interior patio.

Downhill from here stands the hulk of Vic's **cathedral**—a mixture of styles from Romanesque to neoclassic. What immediately strikes you inside are the theatrical murals in dark gold and red by Josep Maria Sert (1876–1945), painted twice over owing to a devastating Civil War fire, and finally completed shortly before his death. Every surface of the vast nave writhes with Sert's powerful, symbolic figures illustrating both biblical subjects and the history of Catalunya. His modest tomb stands in the lovely Gothic **cloister** that surrounds the ostentatious tomb of Vic's homegrown philosopher, Jaume Balmes (1810–1848).

Other unusual features are the beautiful 10th- to 11th-century capitals of the **crypt** and the main **altarpiece,** which now stands at the back of the apse—feed the light- meter a coin to illuminate Pere Oller's 1427 alabaster masterpiece, carved with scenes of the life of Christ and Mary.

The **Museu Episcopal de Vic** houses one of the most important and complete collections of medieval Catalan art in Spain beside paintings and sculpture from the 16th- to 18th-centuries. It is now housed in a luminous brand new building designed by Federico Correa and Alfonso Milá. ∎

Vic

⚏ 179 C5

Visitor information

www.ajvic.net

✉ Carrer de la Ciutat 4

☎ 93 886 20 91

Cathedral

✉ Plaça de la Catedral

☎ 93 886 44 49

💲 $

Museu Episcopal de Vic

www.museuepiscopalvic.com

✉ Plaça del Bisbe Oliba 31

☎ 93 886 93 60

🕐 Closed Mon., & Sun. p.m.

💲 $

Vic's busy market adds to Plaça Major's hubbub.

Three monasteries

OF EASTERN CATALUNYA'S MANY MONASTERIES, THREE ARE outstanding. Montserrat is the most popular, Poblet the most beautiful, and Santes Creus the most instructive.

MONESTIR DE MONTSERRAT

Whatever way you choose to reach Montserrat (meaning "serrated mountain"), whether by road, cable car, or rack railway from Monistrol, the journey is absolutely unforgettable. For a thousand years pilgrims have been drawn to the spectacular pinnacles crowning the rugged sierra that is home to Catalunya's holiest site: the Benedictine monastery, chapels, and caves of Montserrat. About 80 monks live here, but don't expect a sense of deep spirituality. The entire complex is heavily commercialized and very crowded on Sundays and public holidays. That said, facilities are excellent, with funiculars to the hermitage of Sant Joan and grotto of Santa Cova, a museum, restaurants, hotel, shops, and well-marked paths through the sierra.

The main priority is to see the carved wooden statue of the Virgin of Montserrat, popularly known as **La Moreneta** (the dark one), due to her black face. Legend has it that

Montserrat
www.abadiamontserrat.net

🅰 179 C4

✉ Montserrat

☎ 93 877 77 01

🅂 $ (museum);
    $ (parking)

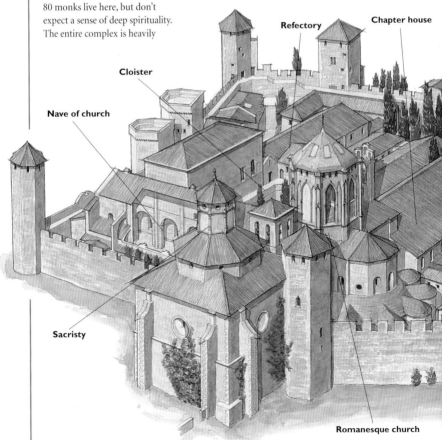

Refectory

Chapter house

Cloister

Nave of church

Sacristy

Romanesque church

the statue was carved by St. Luke and then miraculously found in 880 in Santa Cova, but more scientific testing has proved that it is 12th century. La Moreneta's status was enhanced in 1881 when she became patron saint of Catalunya. You can see her up close by following a passage *(Closed 10:30 a.m.–noon)* to the right of the main doors to her jewel-studded eyrie behind the altar. The basilica itself was much transformed in the early 19th century following destruction by French troops, and the facade dates from 1901. Try to coincide your visit with **L'Escolania** *(Mon.-Sat. 1 p.m. & 7:10 p.m. & Sun. 12 p.m.)*, Europe's oldest boys' choir.

Beneath the esplanade in front of the basilica, the museum *(tel 938 77 77 01)* displays a very mixed bunch of pieces ranging from a 4,000-year-old Egyptian mummy to classical paintings (look for Luca Giordano), Impressionists, and a touching collection of votive offerings to La Moreneta. Walkers can make the gentle climb to the **shrine of Sant Miquel,** or follow the longer **Way of the Rosary,** lined with *modernista* sculptures, to **Santa Cova.** Wilder in spirit but kinder to the leg muscles is the **Cami des Degotalls** that skirts around the mountain. All these paths command magnificent views of the Pyrenees.

The monastery of Montserrat sits in the cleft of the spectacular "serrated mountain."

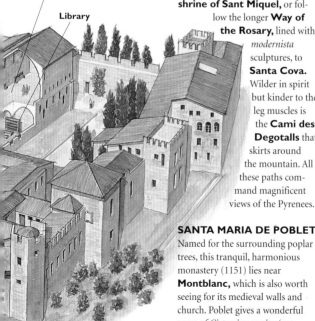

Monks' dormitory

Library

SANTA MARIA DE POBLET
Named for the surrounding poplar trees, this tranquil, harmonious monastery (1151) lies near **Montblanc,** which is also worth seeing for its medieval walls and church. Poblet gives a wonderful sense of Cistercian purity (see p. 44) within its walled precinct.

Monks returned in 1940 after a century-long absence, and parts of the monastery are out of bounds, but you can peer through the library doors, for instance, to see these theologians working at computers. The library hall lies off the beautiful, contemplative Gothic **cloister** enclosing a pretty pavilion with a fountain, as do the kitchen, a vaulted refectory where monks eat and drink in silence, and the chapter house with its palm tree vaults and tombstones of past abbots.

The cloister also leads to the Romanesque **church**, where attention focuses on the altar area. Look at the exceptional alabaster altarpiece carved by Damián Forment in 1527, and the elaborate royal tombs, dating from the 14th century but extensively restored in 1950. The stairs to the left of the altar lead up to the monks' vast dormitory—no longer in use—and out to the upper gallery of the cloister. The tour ends in the **wine cellars** below, a reminder of the Cistercians' involvement in viticulture and agriculture, which in

medieval days gave a huge boost to the local economy.

SANTES CREUS

Founded shortly after Poblet by French Cistercians from Toulouse, Santes Creus has a similar layout to its sister monastery but is no longer in use. The austere **church,** on the other hand, never stopped functioning, and here you see a lovely rose window and royal tombs beneath elaborate Gothic canopies. There are two cloisters. The so-called "old cloister" was built in the 17th century on the site of the original one, and leads to the kitchen, refectory, wine cellars, and royal palace. The 14th-century **Gran Claustro** (Great Cloister) is lined with beautifully carved capitals and leads to the chapter house. Above this, the lofty dormitory is now used for summer concerts. An innovative audiovisual circuit guides you through the monastery, reconstructing its atmosphere and life. If you want the English version, make sure you arrive promptly at either 10 a.m. or 3 p.m. ■

White-robed Cistercian monks inhabit Poblet, a much quieter monastery than Montserrat.

Santa María de Poblet
🄰 179 B4
www.conca.altanet.org
✉ Poblet
☎ 977 87 12 47

Santes Creus
🄰 179 B4
www.altcamp.info/eng/
santescreus.htm
✉ Santes Creus
☎ 977 63 83 29
🕐 Closed Mon.
💲 $. Free Tues.

Costa Daurada & Ebro Delta

COSTA DAURADA IS NOT ONE OF SPAIN'S MOST APPEALING coastlines, but it has long golden *(daurada)* beaches and unusual spots. Cosmopolitan Sitges, an offshoot of Barcelona, is known as the gay beach resort of Spain, Port Aventura is a must for anyone with children, and the Ebre Delta is the second largest in the Mediterranean.

Sitges lies just half an hour's drive southwest of Barcelona airport, and crowds from all over Europe throng its bars and nudist beaches. Its reputation flowered in the 1960s when it nutured an arty counter-culture and antagonized Franco. It lies beside a beautiful stretch of high, rocky coastline. An outrageous February carnival continues the traditions of the heady past. The most enlightening windows on Sitges' history are the **Museu del Cau Ferrat,** once the home of the eccentric painter Santiago Rusinyol (1861–1931), where paintings and wrought ironwork are displayed, and the neighboring **Museu Maricel,** an old hospital that was lavishly refurbished for the American millionaire Charles Deering.

Barely 5 miles (8 km) south of Tarragona lies **Port Aventura** *(Avinguda Pere Molas, Vila-Seca, tel 900 40 44 40, www.portaventura.es),* Spain's largest theme park. Packed with high-adrenaline rides and entertainment, it is perfectly adapted to this balmy climate and ideal for anyone with children in tow.

The string of family resorts fades away in the south at the large, flat peninsula formed by the **Delta de l'Ebre** (Ebro Delta). These 124 square miles (320 sq km) of wetlands, partly protected as a reserve, come third only to France's Camargue and Andalucía's Parque Nacional de Doñana (see p. 274) for Mediterranean aquatic wildlife.

Diverse ecosystems include inland rice fields, lagoons, salt marshes, and dunes, all favored by flamingoes and more than 350 other bird species that rest here while migrating, from April to late August and October to February. The best starting point is the village of **Deltebre** *(Visitor information, Plaça Vint de Maig, tel 977 48 93 09),* site of the **Eco-Museu,** or Ecological Museum *(Visitor information, Carrer Marti Buera 22, tel 977 48 96 79)* and horseback-riding activities. You can rent traditional boats and canoes to tour the waterways. ∎

Sitges
🗺 179 C4
Visitor information
www.sitges.com
✉ Carrer Sinia Morera
☎ 93 894 42 51

Museu del Cau Ferrat & Museu Maricel
✉ Carrer Fonollar s/n
☎ 93 894 03 64
🕐 Closed Sun. p.m. & Mon.
💲 $

One of Europe's most popular resorts, Sitges boasts a palm tree-lined seafront and a picturesque old quarter.

Tarragona

PRONOUNCED "THE MOST PLEASANT SPOT FOR RESTING" by the Roman poet Virgil (70–19 B.C.), Tarragona now has more than 100,000 inhabitants, whose livelihoods oscillate between the petrochemical industry and tourism. Spain's deepest port and Catalunya's most productive fishing harbor first attracted the Romans in the third century B.C. Three centuries later this city, known to the Romans as Tarraco, was capital of the vast Imperial *Hispania Tarraconensis*.

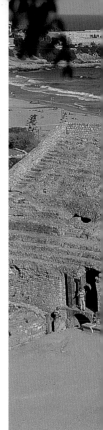

Contemporary Tarragona spreads west of the hilltop cathedral and Roman remains into a grid of 19th- and 20th-century streets. It is very much a provincial town, without the designer buzz of Barcelona or Girona. Archaeologists are still excavating numerous monuments. It was granted world heritage status by UNESCO in 2000. A wonderfully mild climate, sandy beaches, and bountiful seafood are extras on this relaxed city's plate.

Once you climb to the third- to second-century B.C. walls and follow the **Passeig Arqueològic** *(tel 977 24 57 96, closed Sun. p.m. & Mon.)* around their perimeter, you begin to understand the importance of the largest and oldest Roman settlement in Iberia. These fully restored, 40-foot-high (12 m)

sandstone blocks once enclosed three terraced levels: a massive temple, the forum (marketplace), and vast **Circ Romans** (circus or chariot stadium), which could accommodate 30,000 of Tarraco's 40,000 inhabitants. The temple was replaced by a Romanesque cathedral, but much of the lower walls and structures were incorporated into houses and public buildings.

For the best view head for the **Pretori** (Praetorium), a stone tower and former palace of the counts of Barcelona that rises beside the circus at the base of the Rambla Vella. An elevator speeds you to the rooftop, where views open of the entire city. Roman remains lie at your feet, literally—beneath the tower, two of many vaulted tunnels have been excavated to reveal the sophistication of Roman engineering. Don't miss the model of Tarraco displayed here, and stop at the first floor to admire a superbly sculpted sarcophagus showing the legend of Hippolytus, salvaged from the sea. From the rooftop you also have a good aerial view of the scenic but much restored **amphitheater** *(Parc del Miracle, tel 977 24 25 79, closed Sun. p.m. & Mon.)*, where gladiator fights were held.

Anyone bitten by the Roman bug should continue to the neighboring **Museo Arqueològic** *(Plaça del Rei 5, tel 977 23 62 09, closed Sun. p.m. & Mon.)*, to see exceptional Roman artifacts. There is a fine mosaic head of Medusa in Room 3

Left: The soaring interior of La Concepción chapel in the cathedral

Tarragona
⛰ 179 B4
Visitor information
www.tarragona.turisme.es
✉ Carrer Major 39
☎ 977 25 07 95

and, on the top floor, a copy of an articulated ivory doll whose original is exhibited at the **Necropolis** west of town. Tarragona's magnificent **aqueduct** can be seen only by making a dangerous turn marked off the A7 motorway, 3 miles (5 km) north of town.

Back at the summit, the **cathedral** *(Plaça de la Seu, tel 977 23 86 85, closed Sun.)* beckons, its curious facade combining Romanesque and Gothic portals beneath a huge rose window and two unfinished steeples. Enter through the **cloister,** where pointed Gothic arches enclose rounded Romanesque ones with Moorish-inspired tracery above. The museum and sacristy contain some interest, but keep your appreciation for the main **altarpiece** in the cathedral itself.

This 1430 masterpiece of alabaster and wood by Pere Joan illustrates in detail the life of Tarragona's patron saint, Santa Tecla. Look out for minutely carved animals and insects, and extremely realistic human expressions.

The 330-foot-long (100 m) nave has wonderful proportions, enhanced by suspended Flemish tapestries and light through the rose window. When you leave the cathedral, walk around the back to see the beautifully sculpted 12th- to 14th-century arches of the former **hospital of Santa Tecla,** and then go down the wide steps in front. At the bottom is **Carrer La Merceria.** Gothic market arcades that replaced the Roman forum colonnade are still used on Sunday mornings for an antique market. ■

Tarragona's elliptical Roman amphitheater held up to 14,000 spectators.

Pretori & Circ Romans

www.costadaurada.org

⊠ Plaça del Rei, Rambla Vella

☎ 977 24 19 52

🕐 Closed Sun. p.m. & Mon.

💲 $ (combined ticket for Pretori & Circ Romans)

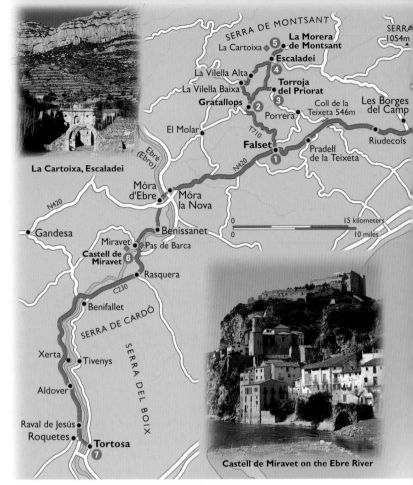

La Cartoixa, Escaladei

Castell de Miravet on the Ebre River

Drive: Priorat vineyards & Templars

This inland circuit takes you through rugged sierra ("serra" in Catalan) to a little-visited wine-producing region and to the impressive castle of Miravet. This was a stronghold of the Knights Templar, a religious military order of knighthood that was originally formed during the Crusades. The drive ends at Tortosa on the Ebre (Ebro) Delta.

Leave Tarragona on the N420 heading toward the airport and Reus, through a fairly uninteresting, flat, semi-industrial area. Once you have entered Reus, turn right onto the beltway (Rondes), following signs to Montblanc, and then, farther on, to Falset and Alcañiz. You soon see the distant outline of the Serra de la Mussara with vineyards in the foreground. After climbing 1,800 feet (548 m), the road winds down through pine-clad limestone hills to **Falset** ❶ (*Visitor information, Avinguda Catalunya 6, tel 977 83 10 23*). Crowned by a

castle, the baroque church of Santa Maria, and arcaded Plaça Quartera, this pretty medieval town is a major wine-producing center. Its impressive **wine-cooperative building** was designed by Cesar Martinell, a disciple of Antoni Gaudí (see pp. 172–75). You can park your car down below the old town and walk uphill from there.

Leave Falset to tour the heart of the Priorat wine-producing area by following the continuation of the access road, now the T710, to Gratallops. Enjoy this good road while it lasts

Cap de Salou

See area map p. 179
▶ Tarragona
🔄 90 miles (144 km)
🕐 Allow a day (including visits)
▶ Tortosa

NOT TO BE MISSED
- Falset old town
- Gratallops wineries
- La Cartoixa, Escaladei
- Castell de Miravet
- Tortosa cathedral

---

civilization. Three miles (5 km) of bends farther you reach the picture-postcard vision of **Torroja del Priorat** ❸, perched high on an isolated hilltop. Cross the bridge to drive up behind the tiny village for a view over its tiled roofs and cobbled streets. It is inhabited by a population of only 140 people. Return to the T711 and turn right toward **Escaladei** ❹, 4 miles (7 km) ahead.

This beautiful village, also written "Scala Dei," is the historic and spiritual focal point of the Priorat area, because monks from the 12th-century Carthusian monastery here introduced the techniques of vine cultivation and wine-aging. Follow the sign beside the bridge (La Cartoixa) to drive half a mile (0.8 km) beyond the village to the picturesquely ruined and very extensive monastery of **La Cartoixa** *(tel 977 82 70 06, closed Mon.).* Escaladei itself is an idyllic little stone village with two restaurants and a well-organized **winery** *(Cellers Scala Dei, Rambla de la Cartoixa s/n, tel 977 82 70 27).* You can taste and buy wine, and don't miss the exquisite Siurana olive oil.

Spain's prehistoric inhabitants scratched then colored these cave paintings on rocks beside the Ebre River.

---

for the next 6 miles (10 km) and, when **Gratallops** ❷ appears on its striking hilltop site, circle around the village to turn right at the sign Centre Urba. You enter Calle Piro, in the shadow of the church, where there are three wine cooperatives, at any of which you can taste and buy different varieties of wine and olive oil. Try the **Celler Cecilio** *(Carrer Piró 28, tel 977 83 91 81),* which still uses time-honored methods. Continue your route on the T710, and then, after 1 mile (1.6 km), turn right onto the much narrower T711, toward Torroja del Priorat.

As the road twists through wild, semiarid landscapes where pine and olive trees grow, with glimpses of the lovely pink-ocher Serra de Montsant in the distance, you feel far from

The ruined Templar castle of Miravet lords over the Ebré River.

There are further stunning landscapes to be seen by following the sign to La Morera de Montsant along a 3-mile (5-km) road. This route takes you up through the hills to the extraordinary village of **La Morera de Montsant** ❺ (*Visitor information, Carrer Major 4, tel 977 82 73 10*), which nestles beneath the 3,660-foot (1,115-m) Seyalets peak. Though the Romanesque church and semideserted village are being renovated, the town is still a popular starting point for hiking and horseback riding in the Serra de Montsant. Return by the same road to Escaladei, where you turn right on the T702 to drive beside the scenic sierra to La Vilella Baixa. Rejoin the T710 back to Falset, 9 miles (15 km) away.

Drive through Falset, following signs for Móra d'Ebre on the N420, to follow a less dramatic but still pretty 20-mile (32-km) road through the agricultural plain. Pass by the unappealing town of Móra la Nova, cross over the Ebre River, and then, at a traffic circle, turn left to Miravet on the T324. On entering the village of **Miravet,** follow the signs to Castell that lead you uphill to the forbidding ruins of **Castell de Miravet** ❻ (*tel 977 40 73 68, closed Mon.*). This was the castle of the Knights Templar, an order of medieval soldier-monks

(see p. 29). There are panoramic views from the castle over the river valley. From here you can either hike down a cliff path to the **Casc Antic** (old quarter), or drive back down, following signs to Casc Antic. Park on the shady, riverside square and walk through the old town, before continuing by car along the river to **Pas de Barca.** Here a simple ferry (*Closed 1–3 p.m. & in bad weather*), powered only by the swift-flowing current, takes up to three cars at a time across the Ebre. On the opposite bank you join the C230, a good road that for 20 miles (32 km) slices through forested sierra, follows the peaceful meanders of the river, and finally passes through extensive groves of orange trees to reach Tortosa.

In **Tortosa** ❼, do not miss a visit to the spectacular Gothic **cathedral** (*tel 977 44 17 52*), built over a mosque. After this go for a well-deserved drink at the hilltop castle of **La Zuda,** now an impressive *parador* (state-run hotel). This magnificent building echoes with the ghosts of three former kings: Abd-ar-Rahman III, who ordered the *zuda* (well) to be built, Count Ramon Berenguer IV, who reclaimed Tortosa from the Moors in 1148; and Jaime I of Aragón, who used it as his royal residence. ■

Crates of Valencia's famed fruit, collected during the orange harvest and ready for shipment

Valencia

Valencia, kingdom of oranges and queen of the Levante (the East), has an indented coast-line backed by hills and the inland *huerta,* said to be Europe's most fertile land. Contrary to what you might expect, this region is not particularly scenic. Agriculture is modern and intensive rather than picturesque, but you do see endless terraced orchards laden with oranges, lemons, and peaches, and rice fields stretching to the horizon. Rice reappears on your plate in countless guises: Paella is ubiquitous, and you also find a close cousin of Italy's more famous risotto. More striking still is the immense palm grove of Elx (Elche), an oasis in the increasingly arid terrain that borders Murcia to the south, and source of the symbolic palm fronds used in Holy Week processions.

For beach lovers the Costa Blanca has highlights at Dénia, Xàbia (Jávea), and Calp (Calpe). Best of all is the seaside capital of Valencia itself, where Renaissance and baroque buildings stand as testimony to the region's long history. Over the last decade the city has reinvented itself through dazzling architecture and a new seaside quarter.

The kingdom of Valencia's first golden age started in 1238 and nurtured the independent streak that remains at its heart. Depression followed in the 17th century when Valencia was forced by Madrid to expel its Jews and Moriscos—baptized Moors—who made up almost one-third of the population. This economic disaster was compounded by the War of Spanish Succession (see p. 34), when Valencia picked the losing side.

The Valencian language may only vary slightly from Catalan, but a quite different, easygoing character comes to the fore in the province's imaginative fiestas. It is here that a whole day is spent pelting friend and foe with tons of ripe tomatoes, producing one giant purée. This takes place at Buñol, 25 miles (40 km) southwest of the capital on the last Wednesday of August. Nor does the capital rest in the wings, for it is here that pyromaniacs take over during Las Fallas, a fiesta of image-burning and fireworks every March. ∎

Valencia city

SPAIN'S THIRD LARGEST CITY IS NOT ENTICING AT FIRST
sight, but with a sunny climate, excellent restaurants, a hopping
nightlife, and the makeover brought by hosting the Americas Cup in
2007 (also in 2009), it is a city on the move. Wide avenues lined with
upscale shops and palm trees eventually lead to the new marina area.
After the sun has set, the superb monuments are spotlit, lending the
city an evocative atmosphere as nightclubs and tapas bars move into
top gear. One-way systems make driving difficult, so if you are in a car,
head for a parking lot then use your feet.

Valencia's history dates back to the
Greeks, Carthaginians, Romans,
Visigoths, and, in A.D. 714, the Arabs.
Legendary El Cid conquered the city
in 1094, but it was retaken by the
Moors (the Almoravids), whose rule
lasted until King Jaime I of Aragón's
conquest in 1238. This marked the
start of a golden age when Valencia
became one of the strongest
Mediterranean powers, prospering
from trading links with possessions
in Italy. Hard times followed, culminating in the Civil War (1936–39),
when Republican forces retreated to
Valencia after Catalunya was taken
by Franco. After intense bombardment, Valencia gave in to the
Nationalists on March 30, 1939.

Today, Valencia's economy is
based on agriculture, industry (with
Ford and IBM factories), and the service industry. Not wanting to be left
behind, Valencia demonstrates a
strong sense of art and design now
crowned by the internationally
acclaimed Ciudad de las Artes y
las Ciencias. Precursors are the
IVAM (Instituto Valenciano de Arte
Moderno), a contemporary art
center (see p. 203) and the glass-
fronted **Palau de la Música y
Congresos,** a congress center
designed in 1977 by British architect

**Locally made
lace trims
the elaborate
traditional dress
of Valencian girls.**

Valencia
🅰 179 A2
Visitor information
www.turisvalencia.es
✉ Plaza del
Ayuntamiento 1
☎ 96 351 04 17
🕐 Closed Sat. & Sun.

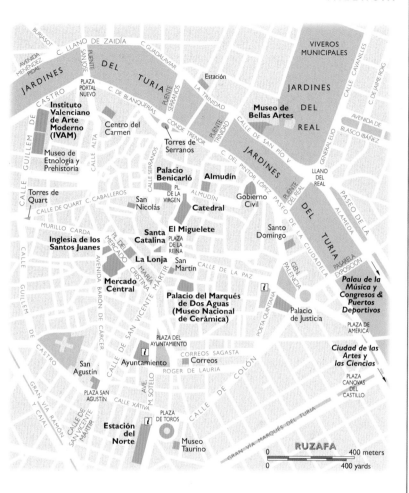

Norman Foster. Despite this dynamism, Valencians retain their traditions, notably the exuberant Fallas (March 12–19), when papier-mâché figures are set alight amid fireworks and festivities. Numerous shops sell ornate mantillas, hand-painted fans, hand-embroidered silk shawls, and ceramics from outlying Paterna. Paella is on every menu, for this is where it originated.

The historic sights lie close to each other, within the area once enclosed by the city walls. Demolished a century ago, only two impressive gateways remain. North of this area are the **Jardines del Turia,** landscaped gardens in the old riverbed that offer a welcome splash of greenery. In the old center, the Gothic **cathedral** *(Plaza de la Reina, tel 96 391 81 27)* is flanked by **El Miguelete,** an octagonal bell tower. Climb to the top of this for wonderful views over Valencia's glazed ceramic domes and labyrinthine streets. The main sight inside the cathedral is the **Capilla del Santo Cáliz** (Chapel of the Holy Grail), a flamboyant Gothic chapel with a superb alabaster altarpiece carved with biblical scenes by the Florentine sculptor Guiliano Poggibonsi. This enshrines the

In the main hall of the 15th-century Silk Exchange, a Latin inscription along the walls reads, "I am a famous building that took fifteen years to build."

cathedral's marvel, a first-century agate goblet said to be the one used by Christ at the Last Supper. Before reaching the cathedral in 1437, it transited via Rome, the monastery of San Juan de la Peña (see p. 146), and Zaragoza (see pp. 140–41). The chapel leads to the museum.

In front of the cathedral overlooking the Plaza de la Reina, you can't miss the baroque bell tower of **Santa Catalina.** Northeast one block lies the beautiful 13th- to 14th-century **Almudín** *(Plaza San Luis Bertran 1, tel 96 352 54 78, closed Sun. p.m. & Mon.),* the city's former granary, now used for art exhibitions. It is worth noticing the sober stone interior enhanced by whimsical 17th-century wall paintings. Outside, a large archaeological site shows Roman and Moorish ruins. A few steps north of the cathedral is the **Palacio Benicarló** *(Calle Santa Ana),* a striking Gothic structure of two arcaded stories—once the residence of the Dukes of Gandia—now the seat of the Valencian parliament.

For a vision of excess, head for the **Palacio del Marqués de**

Dos Aguas *(Poeta Querol 2, tel 96 351 63 92, closed Sun. p.m. & Mon.),* now housing the national ceramics museum. It is a wedding cake of a building, with what is arguably Spain's most ornate domestic facade. The building dates from the 15th century, but was heavily restructured in 1740, and then again a century later. The lower two floors exhibit remarkable original furnishings and decoration: Don't miss the cupola painting by Hipolito Rovira (1693–1765), the Chinoiserie Room, the inlaid ivory and ebony furniture of the Smoking Room, or the marquis's bedroom with carved marble bath.

On the top floor, the **Museo Nacional de Cerámica** gives an excellent overview of the development of Spanish ceramics, from early Arab pieces to the Moorish period, Mudejar, Catholic Spain (which still could not shake off Moorish influences), and on to the 18th century. The collection ends with six superb Picasso works, and contemporary pieces.

Valencia's palatial railway station, the **Estación del Norte,** *(Calle*

Xàtiva), is an artistic treasure of a different sort—a fine example of the use of illustrative *azulejos* (tiles) and decorative woodwork in a purely functional building. It dates from 1910–17, the creative period that also produced the central market.

Valencia's **Mercado Central** (central market) occupies a vast *modernista* (see pp. 172–75) building, and is worth a morning visit to see the incredible wealth of produce from the *huerta*. The **Iglesia de los Santos Juanes** is next to the market and **La Lonja**, the Silk Exchange building, *(Plaza del Mercado, tel 96 352 54 78, closed Sun. p.m. & Mon.),* stands opposite. This was commissioned in the 15th century by the city's wealthy silk merchants. It is an exceptional flamboyant Gothic building, from the imposing crenellated exterior to the vast interior hall of pillars, their twisted spirals rising to tracery high up in the vaults. Take the stairs from the orange-tree patio to the upper floor to admire a masterfully carved and gilded ceiling that has been resurrected from the old town hall.

In the 1980s Valencia's cultural riches were enhanced with the **Instituto Valenciano de Arte Moderno** or IVAM. Split between the Centro del Carmen (a former convent) and modern galleries, the complex stands in the northwest corner of the old town. The permanent collection is devoted to the 20th-century sculptor Julio onzález.

The city's other main art collection is found at the **Museo de Bellas Artes,** on the far side of the old riverbed. This large and important collection has paintings that range from Valencian primitives, through the Renaissance, and up to the early 20th century. Watch for the Valencian painters Juan de Juanes (died 1579) and Francisco Ribalta (1565–1628), and for Hieronymus Bosch, Ribera, van Dyck, Murillo,

Goya, and Velázquez (a wonderful self-portrait).

The neighboring gardens, **Jardines del Real,** make a good place to relax afterward, with the added bonus of a zoo, sculptures, and fountains.

Follow the old riverbed southeast and you soon see the futuristic forms of Santiago Calatrava and Félix Candela's **Ciudad de las Artes y las Ciencias** (City of Arts and Sciences). Completed in 2003, the four components of this ambitious cultural complex are the Hemisféric, showing IMAX films; the Science Museum; the Palace of the Arts, where opera is staged; and finally the Oceanogràfic —Europe's largest seaquarium, a universe of lakes and islands. The entire complex has become a magnet for Valencianos who stroll beside mosaic-clad pools of water or beneath the palm trees of the **Umbracle,** a raised walkway. Besides attracting world attention, the project has successfully regenerated an entire district.

Valencia's transformation has since sprinted toward the port. The area was revamped for the America's Cup in 2007, bringing modern hotels and the **Veles e Vents,** a spectators' building by David Chipperfield and Fermín Vázquez. **Playa Malvarosa,** the popular beach north of the marina, is home to some of Valencia's best paella restaurants, joined by a tapas-bars in the old fishermen's quarter, **El Cabañal.**

Valencia offers great shopping in and around the renovated **Mercado de Colón** *(Jorge Juan 19),* an iconic modernista building now housing select boutiques and cafés. In the traditional center, the **Barrio del Carmen,** northwest of the Plaza de la Reina, fascinating artisan workshops alternate with funky, alternative fashion and bars. Keep an eye, too, on the arty emerging district to the south, the **Barrio Ruzafa.** ∎

Instituto Valenciano de Arte Moderno (IVAM)
www.ivam.es
✉ Calle de Guillem de Castro 118
☎ 96 386 30 00
🕐 Closed Mon.

Museo de Bellas Artes
www.cult.gva.es/mbav
✉ Calle San Pío V
☎ 96 387 03 00
🕐 Closed Mon.

Ciudad de las Artes y Ciencias
www.cac.es
✉ Avenida Autopista de El Saler
☎ 902 10 00 31
💲 $$

The Costa Blanca's sugarloaf, the Peñon de Ifach, towers over the resort of Calp.

Costa Blanca

HALFWAY BETWEEN VALENCIA AND ALACANT ON THE MAP, the Costa Blanca still has immense natural drama. Moody mountains loom just a few miles inland, and the exceptionally mild climate nurtures lush vegetation. Many of the beaches are now full of high-rise hotels. Worst of all is Benidorm, give it a wide berth.

Costa Blanca
△ 179 B1
www.costablanca.org

Warning: Avoid driving along the coast road N332, as its many bends get choked with traffic. Stick to the Autovia and drive in to specific coastal spots from there. ∎

Calp (Calpe) (*Visitor information, Plaça del Mosquit, tel 96 583 85 32, closed Sun. p.m. in winter*) has highrises, but it also has a beautiful wide bay backed by sierra, a sandy beach, a working fishing harbor, and the **Peñón de Ifach,** rising 1,090 feet (332 m) above the Mediterranean. A **nature reserve** (*tel 96 597 20 15, closed on rainy days*) here protects about 300 species of flora and a large number of seabirds that nest there in spring. Just inland is the hilltop **old town,** with the restored remains of a 16th-century castle.

North of Calp is the popular beach resort of Moraira. Far more scenic is **Xàbia (Jávea)** (*Visitor information, Plaça de l'Església 6, tel 96 579 43 56, closed Sun. p.m.*), on the north side of the Costa Blanca peninsula, near its point. El Arenal

beach draws the sun lovers here. The attractive, partly walled old town was built inland around the fortified church of **San Bartolomé** for fear of pirates, and this is where you find its history explained at the small **Museo Arqueológico** (*tel 96 579 10 98*). Today tourism has meant expansion, but the rocky capes and lovely beaches still hold their own. The same goes for **Dénia** (*Visitor information, Plaza Oculista Buigues 9, tel 96 642 23 67, www.communitat-valenciana.com*), 5 miles (8 km) northwest, a popular retirement area for northern Europeans. Its illustrious Greek and Roman past, is illustrated at the **Museo Arqueológico** (*Castillo de Dénia, tel 966 42 06 56, closed Thurs.*), and the Moorish castle still stands. ∎

Alacant (Alicante)

SPRAWLING AROUND A HUGE BAY, ALACANT IS A THRIVING, ever expanding port city with few historic sights other than its magnificent castle. You could spend a happy couple of hours exploring the backstreets of the old town, which burst into long nocturnal life on Friday and Saturday nights. Then head for one of the beaches.

In the **old town,** just behind the marina and beneath the hilltop castle, have a look at the 18th-century **Ayuntamiento,** with its beautiful baroque facade. A few steps away, Alicante's ambitious **MACA (Museo de Arte Contemporáneo)** is taking shape. Sol Madridejos and Juan Carlos Sancho have designed a four-story edifice, which will exhibit a major collection of contemporary art from local artist Eusebio Sempere (1923–1985).

From here, take a stroll south along the **Explanada de España,** with its majestic banyan trees, past the marina to the early 20th-century **Lonja del Pescado** *(tel 96 592 23 06, opening times vary)*. This former fish market, designed in *modernista*

neo-Mudejar style is used for temporary exhibitions.

For a magnificent view, take the elevator to the **Castillo de Santa Bárbara,** a fortress originally built by the Carthaginians. This is reached from the coastal highway via a 225-yard (208-m) tunnel. A large collection of 20th-century sculpture is dotted around the ramparts and in castle halls. The oldest buildings, dating from the Middle Ages, are found at the top of the elevator. Halfway down is the 16th-century section, and the lowest level is 17th century. Don't miss the vaulted exhibition hall, which illustrates the castle's long and momentous history. Walk down the access road, circle left along a path and go down steps that bring you back to the old quarter. ■

Set on a rocky peak, Alacant's old fortress offers a spectacular bird's-eye view of the city.

Alacant (Alicante)
🅰 179 B1
Visitor information
www.alicanteturismo.com
✉ Rambla Méndez
    Núñez 23
☎ 96 520 00 00
🕐 Closed Sun.

Castillo de Santa Bárbara
www.alicante-ayto.es
    /cultura/museos-
    santabarbara.html
☎ 96 516 21 28
🕐 Exhibitions closed
    Sun. p.m. & Mon.
💲 $ (elevator)

Drive: Into Sierra via Guadalest

Leave the coastal crowds behind to head into the welcome emptiness of the sierra (called "serra" in Catalan). The Moors originally carved out the terraced hillsides, now covered in olive and almond trees, and orange and lemon groves. Guadalest attracts visitors from the coast because of its dramatic site, but it is worth visiting for the magnificent views over the surrounding mountains.

Leave the coastal resort of **Altea** on the Valencia road (N332) following the bay. Turn left toward Callosa d'en Sarrià (A150), and then left again onto C3313. The Serra de Guadalest looms ahead, with terraced orange and lemon groves in the foreground. You soon come to **Callosa d'en Sarrià ❶**, an agricultural town with a medieval arch and old walls around **Plaza del Castell.** As an antidote to the dry sierra, make a 2-mile (3.2 km) detour on the CV715 (direction Bolulla) to **Fonts de l'Algar ❷** (*tel 96 597 21 29*), an area of rushing springs with visitor facilities, environmental exhibits, and small restaurants.

From Callosa, follow signs to Guadalest (CV755) and drive 8 miles (12 km) through increasingly rugged limestone hills clad in pine trees and maquis. Your first sight of **Guadalest ❸** is extraordinary: Granite pinnacles topped by towers stand out of the valley, and in fact it was once accessible only through a tunnel. Drive into the village to the parking lot, and from there wander through narrow streets lined with souvenir shops to the tunnel that leads into the old part of Guadalest. (Follow signs to "Museo.") The castle ruins above are reached via 18th-century **Casa Orduña,** Guadalest's noble mansion, now the **Museo Municipal** (*Calle Iglesia 2, tel 96 588 53 93*). This was built after a devastating earthquake in 1644 destroyed most of the original castle, and was subsequently rebuilt after being burnt down during the 1708 War of Succession. Inside, it retains the Orduña family's furnishings, paintings (look at the anonymous double-sided "Ecce Homo"), and vast library. From the garden, steps lead up to the ruins of **Sant Josep castle,** now partly a cemetery, which give fantastic panoramic views. Other sights in this popular village are the church and a small **ethnological museum** (*Opposite church, tel 96 588 52 38, closed Sat.*), with displays on Guadalest's chocolate-making industry.

Leave Guadalest on the same road, which winds around the flanks of the valley through terraced almond trees (a magnificent sight in February when the trees are covered in a mass of pink and white blossom) and tiny villages. When you reach the pretty village of **Confrides ❹** (*Visitor information, tel 96 588 58 04*), source of the Guadalest River, stop to enjoy the magnificent views and the monumental walnut tree on the main square.

Terraced almond groves

From here to Penàguila, the road winds through 6 miles (10 km) of rocky moor and over the 3,170-foot (966-m) pass. Turn left onto the CV781, and then make a stop at **Penàguila ⑤** to look at its medieval gateway and noble mansions.

Leave this village on the CV785 in the direction of Sella (14 miles/22 km), driving through the beautiful, densely forested **Serra de Aitana,** with the 4,626-foot (1,410 m) silhouette of Puig Campana a permanent companion. **Sella ⑥** has Roman ruins and the remains of a medieval castle at the top of the town, and is a good starting point for hikes. Keep going toward Finestrat, where you return to terraced agriculture and orchards. Stop in **Finestrat ⑦** *(Visitor information, Avenida Marina Baixa 14, tel 96 680 12 08)* to

walk up to the church and hermitage of the Remedio, built over a Moorish castle, which gives fine views toward the Mediterranean. The CV758 finally joins the busy CV70, from which you turn off on the N332 to **Alfaz del Pi.** The pretty beach at **Albir ⑧** is overlooked by the rocky outcrop of Serra Helada, another good spot for hiking, this time with a sea breeze. ∎

🅰 See area map p. 179
▶ Altea
⬌ 36.6 miles (58.5 km)
🕐 3 hours (5–6 hours with stops)
▶ Albir

NOT TO BE MISSED
- Fonts de l'Algar
- Guadalest
- Confrides
- Finestrat

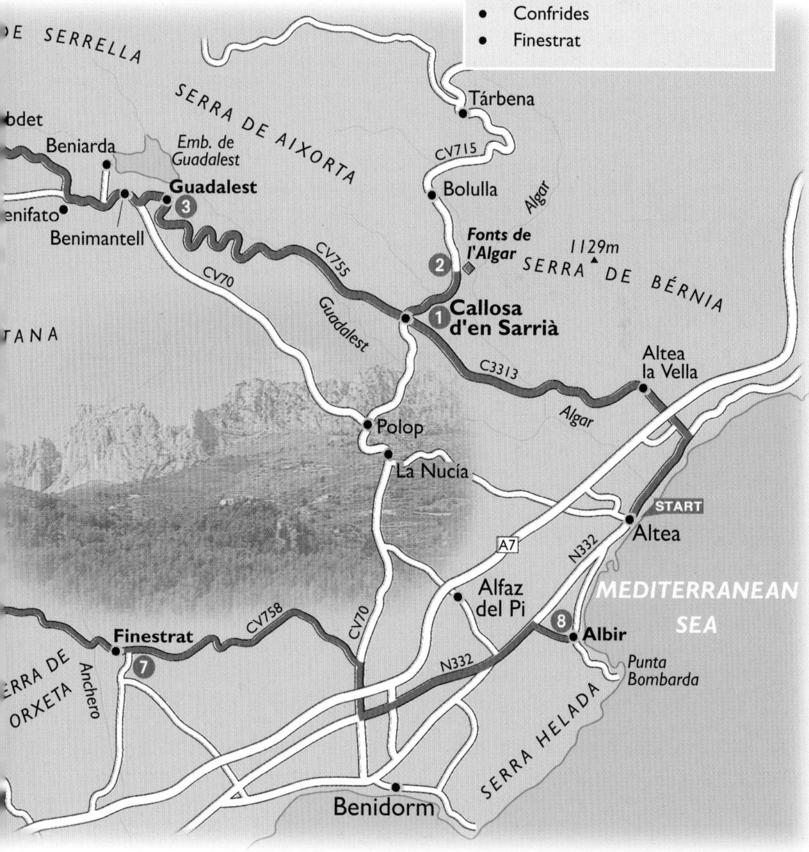

More places to visit in Valencia

ELX (ELCHE)

Twenty-five miles (32 km) southwest of Alacant (Alicante) lies the small town of Elx, known for three things: the much reproduced Iberian sculpture, La Dama de Elche, found here and now displayed at Madrid's Museo Arqueológico Nacional (see p. 73); the medieval mystery play enacted every August 14–15; and, visible year-round, the immense and majestic **palm grove.** With more than 125,000 date palms, it is Europe's largest. It is thought to have been planted by Phoenicians who established trading posts along this coast for several centuries before the birth of Christ. Growing alongside canals of brackish water on the eastern side of the Vinalopo River, the palms reach heights of up to 78 feet (24 m). You see many with branches bound up to create the *ramilletes* (bleached fronds) that are used in Palm Sunday processions. You can get a closer look

Sagunt's restored Roman amphitheater was built after Hannibal attacked the city.

at the **Huerto del Cura** (*Porta de la Morera, tel 96 545 19 36*), one of a series of separate, unenclosed plantations. Reigning supreme here among flowers and cactuses is the bizarre **Palmera Imperial,** which has seven secondary trunks.

🇦 179 A1 **Visitor information** ✉ Plaza Parque 3 ☎ 96 665 81 96

SAGUNT (SAGUNTO)

The story of Hannibal and his elephants crossing the Alps may be the one you know, but in Spain he is better known for his failure to defeat Rome, which led to Roman dominance of the peninsula. Sagunto, a Roman ally, put up an obstinate and heroic fight against Hannibal in 219 B.C. Later the town fell into decay, and by the time the Moors rolled up, it was renamed Murbiter, hardly inspiring as it meant "old walls." Today you can visit the ruins of the old hilltop **fortress** (*tel 96 266 55 81, closed Mon. & Sun. p.m.*). Look, too, at the **Judería,** a maze of alleyways that is one of Spain's oldest Jewish quarters. Remember, though, that the town is also engaged in heavy industry, so not every landscape is a delight. The best of the Roman remains is the controversially restored **amphitheater,** used as a venue during Sagunt's annual drama festival.

🇦 179 A2 **Visitor information** ✉ Plaza Cronista Chabret ☎ 96 265 58 59

XÀTIVA

About halfway between Valencia and Alacant on the inland route lies Xàtiva. A picturesque hill town among vineyards, it was one of Europe's first paper-manufacturing centers. The crenellated ramparts of a ruined 15th-century **castle** give sweeping views toward the sea. Just below, the Mozarabic church of **Sant Feliu** houses Renaissance paintings. In the main historic center, head for **Plaza del Seo,** dominated by the bulky **Colegiata** (1596), standing opposite a delicately decorated plateresque building, the former hospital. The most interesting spot is the **Museo del Almudín** (*Carrer de la Corretgeria 46, tel 96 227 65 97, closed Mon.*), housed in a former granary. Among excellent paintings, one portrait hangs upside down: This depicts Felipe V, who sacked most of the town in 1707. Xàtiva's spirit is also reflected in three remarkable emigrants to Italy: the great painter José de Ribera (1591–1652), and two notorious members of the Borja (Borgia) family who later became pope. One, the debauched Alexander VI, fathered infamous Cesare and Lucrezia Borgia.

🇦 179 A2 **Visitor information** ✉ Alameda Jaume I 50 ☎ 96 227 33 46 ∎

You can almost hear the Moorish and Christian armies thundering across the plains of this tableland punctuated by castles, super-lative cathedrals, numerous monasteries, and golden-stone Renaissance monuments.

Castilla y León

Corner turrets of Castillo de la Mota

Castilla y León

VAST, OFTEN HARSH, BUT ALWAYS MESMERIZING, THIS IS ARGUABLY THE quintessential region of northern Spain. Here you can explore secret villages, contemplate Romanesque monasteries and churches, drive across endless plains of wheat fields, or clamber over medieval battlements. It is not all austerity: Salamanca, Valladolid, and León are convivial, attractive cities to relax in and some of Spain's greatest wines are produced beside the Duero River.

Most of the nine provinces of Castilla y León are on the meseta, an arid, often barren plateau that lies between 2,300 feet (700 m) and 3,600 feet (1,100 m) above sea level. The climate is extreme, with fierce summer tem-

peratures and long harrowing winters. Each province is still touched by the Castilian spirit described by writer V.S. Pritchett in 1954 as "austere, frugal, and inhibited…puritan and grave." In between are simple farming villages

where life has hardly changed in centuries.

Castilla y León is Old Castile, the original kingdom of Madrid. Castilla-La Mancha is New Castile, reconquered much later from the Moors. Dominating the landscape of Old Castile are the castles that gave the region its name in the ninth century, reminders of constant battles between Moors and Christians. In the towns are the emblazoned mansions of the ruling nobles, called *hidalgos,* meaning "free men." Catholicism is still deeply rooted. The Way of St. James (see pp. 88–89) pilgrimage route crossed the north of Old Castile, resulting in the monumental cathedrals of Burgos and León. A string of monasteries and sanctuaries also lines the route.

The kingdoms of Castile and León were first united in 1037, a territorial marriage that was not fully consummated until the 13th century. Old Castile is the proud mother of the purest Castilian Spanish. The purest form of all is spoken in Burgos, seat of the first counts of Castile, and capital of Franco's provisional government

The castle at Arévalo

during the Civil War. This region was also the source of the Spanish culture that conquered the New World. Salamanca has some of Spain's finest Renaissance architecture and its first university. Ávila produced the feminist mystic, Santa Teresa. The legendary hero El Cid came from near Burgos, and Segovia has the archetypal, multiturreted royal castle.

Follow the course of the Duero River, from Zamora in the west to Peñafiel in the east, and you can sample Castilla y León's best wines (see pp. 134–36), organic sausages, cheese, and a wide variety of beans. Despite their reputation, Castilians are welcoming to visitors. With city centers renovated, modern architecture and standards of living vastly improved since the 1980s, Castilians are proud of their heritage. ■

Area of map detail

Numerous stained-glass windows illuminate León cathedral's vaulted brick ceiling.

León

LIVELY AND ATTRACTIVE, LEÓN HAS AN EASILY NEGOTIATED scale. Much of the old walled center—the **casco** *viejo*—is now pedestrianized, and renovation makes it a fabulous showpiece. Historic buildings have been converted into apartments, and bars and restaurants pack the Barrio Humédo quarter. The modern city spreads westward along and over the banks of the Río Bernesga, but still León's population barely tops 150,000.

León

🗺 210 C4

Visitor information

www.turismocastillayleon
   .com

✉ Plaza de Regla 4

☎ 987 23 70 82

Catedral de León

www.catedraldeleon.org

✉ Plaza de Regla

☎ 987 87 57 70

🕐 Closed 1:30-4:00 p.m.

CATEDRAL DE LEÓN

The spires of the mighty Catedral de León, founded by Alfonso IX, are clearly visible, and for centuries they guided weary pilgrims.
Little can prepare you for the visual assault of entering this Gothic masterpiece. Built between the mid-13th and late 14th centuries, it has more than a hundred stained-glass windows covering an area of 19,375 square feet (1,800 sq m) and is considered second only to Chartes Cathedral in France. For searing color, go late in the afternoon, when sunlight pierces the rose window above the magnificently sculpted western portal. Other things to look for are the Renaissance choir, with four

alabaster reliefs by Juan de Badajoz, the Gothic tombs of the ambulatory chapels; and the high altar painting by Nicolás Francés (died 1468).

The lofty vaults of the nave are breathtaking, but they are easily rivaled by the cloisters. Enter through a plateresque (see p. 46) doorway that doubles as the entrance to the **museum** (*Closed Sun.*). Frescoes by Nicolás Francés and 16th-century keystone vaulting in the galleries add to the impact of this monumental courtyard.

BASÍLICA OF SAN ISIDORO

The **Basílica of San Isidoro** abuts the Roman ramparts at the northern perimeter of the old town. Although far less harmonious in style than the cathedral, as its construction ranged from the late 11th century through to a very baroque mid-18th century, it contains the remarkable **Panteón de los Reyes** (Kings' Pantheon) and a selective **museum.** Among other exhibits are the jewel-encrusted gold and agate chalice of Doña Urraca (11th century), and the silver reliquary of San Isidoro. A spiral staircase goes down to the vaulted pantheon, which holds the sarcophagi of 23 kings and queens. Unique 12th-century frescoes blanket the vaults. They illustrate not only the Last Supper and other biblical scenes, but also rural rites and life.

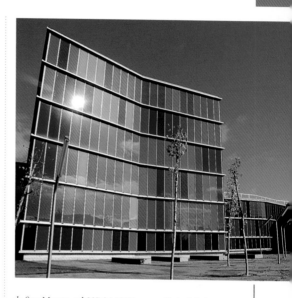

OTHER SITES

Forming the apex of a triangle between these two monuments, the **Palacio de los Guzmanes** *(Plaza de San Marcelo 6, guided tours of upper floors on request)* is one of León's beautiful Renaissance mansions. Completed by the architect Rodrigo Gil de Hontañon in 1560, it has three floors around a typical arcaded patio, with gargoyles peering down from the roof and complex corner towers. Immediately opposite stands the dreadful **Casa de Botines,** a mock-medieval castle designed by Antoni Gaudí (see pp. 172–75), and best left to its present occupier—a bank.

León's other major sight, the Renaissance **Convento de San Marcos,** lies west of the center on the banks of the Río Bernesga. The Convento, founded for the Knights of the Order of St. James, with its profusely decorated facade extends over 109 yards (100 m). Behind are a *parador* (see p. 367), church, cloisters, and an archaeological museum, the **Museo de León** *(Convento de San Marcos, Plaza de San Marcos, tel 987 24 50 61, closed Sun p.m. & Mon.).* Among other dazzling exhibits in the museum, look for the beautiful Visigothic marble statue of Christ and a tenth-century jewel-encrusted cross.

The latest addition (2005) to León's artistic glories is the very lively, innovative **MUSAC** *(Museo de Arte Contemporaneo de Castilla y León, Avenida Reyes Leoneses 24, tel 987 09 00 00, closed Mon., www.musac.es).* The award-winning, multi-colored cubes are by Madrid-based architects, Mansilla & Tuñón, and house diverse activities from art to cinema.

Thirty miles (47 km) north of the city in a mountainous region of waterfalls and forests lie the cave formations of the **Cuevas de Valporquero** *(tel 987 57 64 08, closed Jan.–Feb., Mon.-Thurs. Mar.–mid-May & Oct.-Dec.).* The vast subterranean spaces with stalactites and stalagmites have humidity at over 90 percent and a constant temperature of 45°F (7°C)—so be prepared, and take a sweater. ■

Colorful glass panels of the MUSAC

Basílica San Isidoro
- ✉ Plaza San Isidoro 4
- ☎ 987 22 96 08
  987 87 61 61
- 🕐 Closed Sun. p.m.
- 💲 $, free Thurs. p.m. museum

Zamora

Zamora

🗺 210 B2

Visitor information

www.zamoradipu.es/
patronato

✉ Plaza Arias Gonzolo 6

☎ 980 53 36 94

**Cathedral & Museo
Catedralicio**

www.zamoradipu.es/
patronato

✉ Plaza del Pio XIII

☎ 980 53 06 44

🕐 Closed Mon.

💲 $

**Zamora Holy
Week procession**

SOMETIMES CALLED A LIVING MUSEUM OF ROMANESQUE
art, Zamora predates the Romanesque period. Its history goes back to
the Celts and Romans who occupied this strategic hilltop site overlooking the Duero River. For most of the year, a charming, small-
town atmosphere prevails, but in Holy Week Zamora's unique
collection of *pasos* (sculpted floats) appears in fervent processions.

Zamora's unusually squat 12th-
century **cathedral** has a beautiful
dome clad in scalloped tiles and a
Romanesque bell tower and south
portal. Inside, look at the elaborately carved choir stalls and the
anatomically perfect statue of
Christ in the Capilla de San
Bernardo. The 17th-century
cloisters give access to the
museum, which has remarkable
silverware and exquisite 15th-
century Flemish tapestries, including four illustrating the Trojan War.
Behind the cathedral, peaceful gardens of the former castle abutting
the old city walls give good views.

Zamora also has 16 Romanesque
churches, each one different and
many of them still functioning. All
of the following are in the old town.
At the beautifully proportioned
Santa María Magdalena *(Rúa
de los Francos, closed Mon.),* look at
the delicately sculpted tomb of an
unknown lady (1190) and intricate
carvings in the southern portal. **San
Cipriano** *(Plaza Claudio Moyano,
closed Mon.)* has a purist interior:
a single nave with ornamentation
only in the carved capitals flanking
the altar. Zamora's oldest church,
Santa María la Nueva *(Calle
Motín de la Trucha),* rebuilt in 1158,
played an important role as both a
refuge and a forum for nobles and
their workforce.

Zamora's impressive civic
architecture is later (16th century),
notably the **Palacio de Los
Momos** *(Plaza Zorilla, not open
to the public)* with its exuberantly
decorated Isabelline windows
(now the Palace of Justice). The
masterly Renaissance **Palacio
del Cordón** houses the **Museo
de Zamora** *(Palacio del Cordón,
Plaza de Santa Lucia 2, tel 980
51 61 50, closed Mon.),* which
has displays on local history
and ethnography. ∎

Valladolid

OVERTLY MODERN, FAST-GROWING VALLADOLID PLAYS A leading industrial role as Spain's chief car manufacturer but still has some intriguing secrets tucked away. With a population of 320,000, it is one of northern Spain's larger cities, but the partly pedestrianized center is easy to find your way around, and the shops are excellent. It is now the administrative capital of Castilla y León.

Its history is symbolized by the **Plaza Mayor,** rebuilt in 1631 after a fire, and the dazzling sculpture collection of the **Museo Nacional de Escultura.** The setting, the **Colegio de San Gregorio** is a remarkable example of Spanish Gothic (1496). The entrance gateway is a riot of sculpture thought to be the work of Gil de Siloé, Simon of Cologne, and Juan Guas, and is rivaled in splendor by the patio, staircase, and funerary chapel of Fray Alonso. Sculptures on show, mainly in polychrome wood, cover the 13th to 18th centuries. Some of the finest pieces are Alonso Berruguete's (circa 1488–1561) 16th-century altarpiece for San Benito and the "Burial of Christ" by Juan de Juni (died 1577). Adjoining the museum is the church of **San Pablo,** with a beautiful late Gothic facade by Simon of Cologne.

Valladolid's **cathedral** is a mixture of styles, but it has elaborate baroque decoration by the influential Alberto Churriguera (see p. 47), and a striking altarpiece by Juan de Juni. The **Museo Oriental** (*Paseo Filipinos 7, tel 983 30 68 00 or 983 30 69 00, closed Mon.–Sat. a.m. & Sun. p.m.*), housed in a neoclassic Augustinian seminary, is an excellent antidote to a surfeit of Castilian religious art: It shows a priceless collection of ivory figures, tribal pieces from the Philippines, and Chinese decorative arts. Equally escapist is the **Casa-Museo Colón** (*Calle Colón, tel 983 29 13 53, closed Sun. p.m. & Mon.*) dedicated to Christopher Columbus who died in Valladolid in 1506.

One of Europe's best private collections of African art, the Fundación Alberto Jiménez, is exhibited at the Palacio de Santa Cruz (*Plaza Santa Cruz 8, tel 983 18 45 30, closed Sun.*). On a more hedonist note, every mid-October Valladolid hosts Spain's national tapas competition. ∎

Valladolid
△ 210 C3
Visitor information
www.asomateavalladolid.org
✉ Calle Santiago 19
☎ 983 34 40 13

Museo Nacional de Escultura
www.museoescultura.mcu.es
✉ Colegio de San Gregorio, Calle Cadenas de San Gregorio 1
☎ 983 25 40 83
🕐 Closed Sun. p.m. & Mon.

The Isaballine facade of Colegio de San Gregorio

The ship-shape, white stone castle of Peñafiel sits on a narrow ridge overlooking the Duero River.

Castles in Castilla y León

OLD CASTILE IS LIBERALLY STUDDED WITH CASTLES—OVER 600 of them. Celtiberian fortified settlements were built over by Roman military outposts. Moors built castles to defend their kingdom against the Christians of Asturias. As the Reconquest advanced, Christian nobles rebuilt these and used them as bases for pushing farther south. Others were built completely afresh—nearly 90 survive today in Castilla y León. First the upper Ebré, and then the Duero was the front line between Christian kingdoms to the north and Moorish al-Andalus to the south. Castles proliferated on these demarcation lines, giving rise to the name of the kingdom of "Castilla."

Castillo de Coca
🏰 210 C2
www.coca-ciudaddecauca
.org
✉ Coca, Segovia
province
☎ 921 58 66 22
🕐 Closed first Tues.
of month
💲 $ (40-minute
guided tour)

Castillo de Cuéllar
🏰 210 D2
www.aytocuellar.es/villa/10A
A_qvisitar_cdm.html
✉ Cuéllar, Segovia
province
☎ 921 14 22 03
🕐 Guided visits: call
for an appointment

Castillo de Coca must be the ultimate in brick castles, with crenellated ramparts and polygonal turrets rising majestically from the plains about 30 miles (45 km) northwest of Segovia. It was built in Gothic Mudejar style for Alonso de Fonseca, archbishop of Sevilla, in 1453, and then given to the Marquis of Ayala and later the Duke of Alba (whose family still owns it, although it is used by a forestry training school). An outer square bailey encloses an inner one, both executed in decorative brickwork. The Pedro Mata Tower has a circu-

lar room with a curious acoustic: Whisper a secret into a wall and it is heard on the opposite side. Here, too, the dungeon is a cruel reminder of those days when prisoners arrived through the ceiling, usually breaking their legs before enduring a long, slow death.

Set high on a citadel and incorporated into the town walls, **Castillo de Cuéllar** (mid-15th century) has been much lusted after. The original owner, Juan II, bequeathed the castle to his daughter Isabel, but it was soon grabbed by her stepbrother Enrique IV, who

then passed it to his favorite, Beltrán de la Cueva. Inside the castle is an extensive collection of antique arms.

Castillo de Frías (*Map 211 E4, Frías, Burgos province, www.burgos .net /frias/monumen.htm, 947 35 71 26*) is one of Castilla's most dramatically placed castles: It perches high on a craggy rock that towers over a charming medieval village. Although it is now mainly in ruins, you can climb up to the ramparts for stunning views north over the Ebré River. Construction spanned the 13th to 16th centuries, a period echoed in the church of **San Vicente** at the other end of the village. Below is a medieval fortified bridge.

Castillo La Mota is one of Castilla y León's greatest castles, with crenellated walls and a towering keep on a hilltop. Started by the Moors in the 13th century, it was much extended by Fernando and Isabel (see p. 31) in the 15th century. Their daughter, Juana the Mad, was another royal resident. It became a state prison, and Cesare Borgia was one of its political and military prisoners.

The austere 14th- to 16th-century **Castillo Pedraza de la Sierra** contrasts with one of Castilla's prettiest and best conserved medieval towns, its steep, narrow streets lined with atmospheric mansions, porticoes, and balconies. The castle belonged to the counts of Castile, the Fernández de Velasco family. Its present owners are the descendants of the painter Ignacio Zuloaga (1870–1945), some of whose works are exhibited beside antiques and engravings. The castle moat is cut into the rock, with circular and square towers rising above.

The elongated white stone **Castillo de Peñafiel** looms high above the plain and the charming wine-producing town at its feet. The castle was built in the 15th century, and the keep was remodeled in the following century for the Girón family, with walls 11 feet (3.5 m) thick and eight side-turrets. Visit the castle's **wine museum,** and don't miss the rest of this unusual town. **Plaza del Coso** is surrounded by timbered houses, and the church of **Santa María** has a museum of religious art. ■

Castillo La Mota
🏰 210 C2
www.castillosdejirm.com/la mota.htm
✉ Medina del Campo, Valladolid province
☎ 983 81 13 57
🕐 Closed Sun.

Castillo Pedraza de la Sierra
🏰 210 D2
www.pedraza.info
✉ Pedraza de la Sierra, Segovia province
☎ 921 50 98 25
🕐 Closed Mon. & Tues., & when family is in residence

Castillo de Peñafiel
🏰 210 D3
www.turismopenafiel.com/e lcastilo.html
✉ Peñafiel, Valladolid province
☎ 983 88 11 99
🕐 Closed Mon.

Salamanca

Lofty and elegant, Salamanca's "new" cathedral was built between 1513 and 1733.

SPEND A COUPLE OF DAYS IN SALAMANCA TO GET AN insight into Spain's academic life and a complete picture of the evolution of Spanish architecture. Salamanca's university, one of Europe's earliest, was founded in 1218. Over the centuries, this lively town has hardly stood still, and today its university population combines with a steady flow of visitors and Spanish language students to create a cosmopolitan atmosphere in which traditions are nonetheless respected.

Salamanca
🔼 210 B2
Visitor information
www.salamanca.es
✉ Plaza Mayor 32
☎ 923 21 83 42
   902 30 30 02

Catedral Nueva
www.guia-digital.com/
   salamanca/turismo
✉ Plaza de Anaya
☎ 923 21 74 76
💲 $ (Catedral Vieja)

The Romans founded Helmantica here and built a fine bridge that still spans the Tormes River. In 1102 the medieval city took root on the escarpment of its northern bank. Using a soft stone from nearby quarries whose high iron-ore content rusts into an inimitable golden color, the great men of Salamanca gradually constructed an architectural marvel. At its center is the **Plaza Mayor,** one of the most beautiful squares in Europe. Start your exploration, sitting in a sidewalk café. Savor the majesty of the square, and pay homage to the Churriguera brothers (see pp. 46–47), who designed it in the 1720s. Look for the sculpted portraits of luminaries such as Christopher

Columbus, El Cid, Cervantes, and a string of Spanish kings. At night the square becomes a stage set, invaded by wandering musicians and other street performers.

The main monuments lie west and south of here. The much photographed **Casa de las Conchas,** or House of Shells (*Calle Compañía, tel 923 26 93 17*), was once a palace and is now a public library. The stone Renaissance facade comes alive with 400 sculpted scallop shells, the symbol worn by pilgrims to Santiago de Compostela. Inside the courtyard are delicately carved balustrades and lions' heads. The pedestrianized Rúa Mayor is the most commercial in Salamanca, as it leads straight to the cathedral, which dominates broad Plaza de Anaya. Turn down any side street, however, and you are projected back in time.

The massive cathedral is in fact two adjoining buildings: the Catedral Nueva (New Cathedral), which you enter first beneath the decorative Renaissance stonework of the west facade, and the Catedral Vieja (Old Cathedral). The **Catedral Nueva** dates from 1513, and additions over the next two centuries created a mixture of styles from late Gothic through Renais-sance and plateresque to baroque. What is immediately striking is the immense scale. Visitors become antlike beside soaring

carved arches, ribbed columns, and the ornately carved choir, another work of the Churriguera brothers. Here, too, you see one of Spain's most famous organs, the work of Pedro de Echevarría in 1745.

Go behind the main altar to see the much revered 11th-century figure of Christ set into an exuber-ant Churrigueresque altarpiece. And don't miss the **Patio Chico,** through a door in the south aisle, a terrace which gives an all-encompassing view of the old cathedral, cupola, and baroque tower of the new cathedral.

The entrance to the **Catedral Vieja** *($)* is also off the south aisle. As you step into its Romanesque

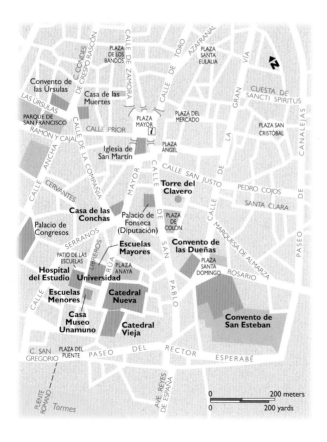

Scallop shells cover the extraordinary front of the Casa de las Conchas in ornate plateresque style.

serenity, the contrast could not be greater. Light stone columns lead your eye to an early Renaissance **altarpiece** comprised of 53 exquisitely painted panels surrounding a bejeweled statue of the Virgin of the Vega, patron saint of Salamanca. This gilded sculpture dates from the late 12th century, as does the cathedral. Other outstanding features are the wall of frescoes (1262) by Antón Sánchez de Segovia, one of Europe's oldest works by a known artist, and the beautiful dome above the transept. You must also look at the part-Romanesque cloisters and **Capilla de Talavera,** with its Mudejar dome.

Back outside Salamanca's glowing edifices, head 200 yards (183 m) east to the church of San Esteban, attached to a Dominican monastery,

and the convent of Las Dueñas. These face each other across a wide street, but if you have time for only one, opt for the **Convento de San Esteban** *(Plaza del Concilio de Trento s/n, tel 923 21 50 00).* The facade (1524–1610) is a stunning example of fine plateresque carving. Inside, the luminous single nave focuses on a fabulous Churrigueresque altarpiece, 98 feet (30 m) in height, that surrounds a painting of the martyrdom of St. Stephen (San Esteban). For an even better view, look from the elevated choir above the nave. You reach this through the **King's Cloister,** which blends Gothic, Renaissance, and plateresque details, and is notable for medallions depicting prophets. Climb the magnificent **grand staircase** to the upper gallery and the **biblioteca** (library), which exhibits lovely 17th-century ivory statues from the Philippines, and then on to the choir viewpoint.

The **Convento de las Dueñas** *(Plaza del Concilio de Trento s/n, tel 923 21 54 42)* is more intimate in scale, and its pretty Renaissance cloisters are the main point of interest. Dominican nuns still live in the convent and run a good business selling homemade cakes. The lattice screens of their cell windows are visible from the well-tended gardens of the cloisters. Go around the side of the convent to see the **Torre del Clavero,** an octagonal tower that is the only remnant of a medieval castle. It has traces of Mudejar decoration.

UNIVERSIDAD DE SALAMANCA

Salamanca's prestige was built upon its university, which opened in 1218 and is one of the world's oldest, a contemporary of the universities of Paris and Bologna. Its various build-ings are clustered around Calle Serranos and Calle Libreros, imme-diately west of Rúa Mayor. The most spectacular facade is that of the **Escuelas Mayores,** a plateresque masterpiece completed in 1533 for the original Gothic university behind. Inside, the modernized patio (with a Mudejar wooden ceiling) is sur-rounded by the old lecture halls where literati such as the philoso-pher Miguel de Unamuno (see p. 51) once held sway. A beautiful carved stone staircase leads to the upper floor, where you can peer at the prodigious library through a glass vestibule. The shelves contain around 2,770 manuscripts, 483 incunabula (early books), and 62,000 pre-19th-century publications.

Flanking this building to the south is the **Casa Museo Unamuno,** the home of the writer Miguel de Unamuno, mostly of interest to

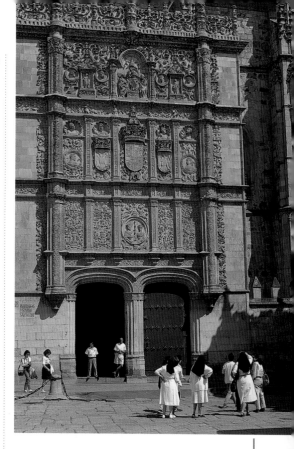

those who know his work. Opposite, overlooking a small square, are the **Hospital del Estudio** (Students' Hospice) and neighboring **Escuela Menores** (for pre-university stud-ies). Here you discover a delightful Gothic patio and, in the **Museo Universitaria,** an extraordinary ceiling decoration, the Cielo de Salamanca (Salamanca Sky), trans-ferred from the old library. Only a third of it is here, but it is enough to convey the finesse of Fernando Gallego's 1473 illustration of the cosmos and celestial beings. Other Renaissance exhibits include a collection of walnut sculptures by Felipe Bigarny, paintings, and dazzling silverwork. Next door, the curious **Sala de las Tortugas** (Tortoise Room) shows the world's second largest fossil collection. ■

Salamanca's Escuelas Mayores, built by order of Fernando and Isabel, bears their figures in its intricate plateresque facade.

Universidad de Salamanca

www.usal.es/webusal/visita/index.htm

✉ Libreros, s/n

☎ 923 29 44 00

🕐 Closed Sun. p.m.

💲 $

Ciudad Rodrigo

Ciudad Rodrigo

◪ 210 B1

Visitor information

www.ciudadrodrigo.net

✉ Plaza de Amayuelas 5

☎ 923 46 05 61

Cathedral

✉ Plaza San Salvador

☎ 923 48 14 24

$ $ (cloisters)

Emblazoned facade of a mansion

OUT ON A GEOGRAPHIC LIMB, THE FORTIFIED TOWN OF Ciudad Rodrigo is one of northern Spain's delightful secrets, redolent with history without being affected by mass tourism. This is changing with new highway connections to Oporto, in Portugal, and to Valladolid. It comes to life every year at the start of the bullfighting season, during Carnival in February, when the *encierro*—the running of the bulls—takes over the streets.

The surrounding agricultural region is by no means prosperous—you might guess this from Ciudad Rodrigo's rather dubious speciality, *el farinato*, a sausage made from flour and lard, generally eaten with fried eggs. Years ago, this was surpassed by

green lizard stew, but protected species status has taken it off local menus. The town's illustrious past is recalled by a string of palaces. The town was named for Count Rodrigo González Girón, who resettled it after driving out the Moors in the 12th century. In 1812, the Duke of Wellington took Ciudad Rodrigo from Napoleon's forces after a bloody siege. Ciudad Rodrigo's strategic position on the frontier is symbolized by its massive ramparts. There are several stairways that follow the 1-mile (1.6-km) sentry path—to very good views.

Rising above the town is the 14th-century **castle of Enrique II de Trastámara**, now a *parador* (see p. 367). The austere stone walls bear traces of Roman foundations, and the crenellated towers are spectacularly illuminated at night. The **cathedral,** has features from the 12th century in addition to a beautiful 13th-century portal, Portada de la Virgen, Isabelline choir stalls exuberantly carved by Rodrigo Alemán, an alabaster Renaissance altarpiece, and cloisters in a mix of architectural styles. Richly ornamented tombs of noblemen and women add to its interest.

Next door the more sober Capilla de Cerralbo is worth a visit for its altar-painting by José Ribero. Walk south to reach the town's main social gathering place, arcaded **Plaza del Buen Alcalde**—then sample a farinato. ∎

Ávila

THE WALLED TOWN OF ÁVILA IS ONE OF SPAIN'S MOST spectacular urban sights, but within Spain it is more famous for just one person. The mystic Santa Teresa was born here in 1515, and convents and churches devoted to her grace its streets. It is a small town of 50,000 inhabitants perched on a spur above the Río Adaja at an altitude of over 3,700 feet (1,130 m). Winters are particularly harsh, but in any other season, it's pleasant to explore on foot.

Ávila's perfectly preserved walls date from the 11th century, when the 88 cylindrical towers and 9 gateways were built to fend off the Moors. You can walk 1.5 miles (2.5 km) beside the walls for panoramic views. Abutting the walls at the older, eastern end is the 12th- to 15th-century **cathedral.** Look for the tomb of El Tostado (a 15th-century bishop nicknamed "the toasted one" for his dark complexion). There are also finely carved plateresque choir stalls, two unusual wrought-iron pulpits, and a Renaissance altarpiece. Don't miss the 13th-century **sacristy** with its octagonal vaulted ceiling. Go through to the **museum,** where you find a gigantic silver monstrance (1571). The delicate Gothic **cloisters** lie next to the museum.

Turn right on leaving the cathedral to reach the Puerta de San Vicente and, just outside the walls, the **Basílica de San Vicente** (*Plaza San Vicente, tel 920 25 52 30*). This Romanesque-Gothic construction has an exceptional sculpted west portal. Inside is the canopied **sarcophagus** of San Vicente and his sisters.

Santa Teresa, one of Spain's patron saints, was a great mystic, rebel, and writer, and founder of the barefoot Carmelite order. Her birthplace in Ávila is marked by the **Convento de Santa Teresa** (*Plaza de la Santa*). The **Convento de la Encarnación** (*Paseo de la Encarnación, 920 21 12 12*), where she lived for 27 years, has a rather dull museum dedicated to her far-from-dull life. ∎

Ávila's surrounding walls, restored in parts, look exactly as they did in the Middle Ages.

Ávila
- 210 C1

Visitor information
- www.avilaturismo.com
- Plaza de la Catedral 4
- 920 21 13 87

Catedral
- Plaza de la Catedral
- 920 21 16 41
- $ (museum)

Segovia's Roman aqueduct, a masterpiece of 118 arches, brought water from the Frio River, several miles away.

In & around Segovia

LIKE A HUGE SHIP MOORED ON THE PLAIN OF OLD CASTILE, Segovia is one of northern Spain's most seductive towns. Depending on where you come from, your first sight may take in the Roman aqueduct, cathedral, and fantasy palace of the Alcázar, all clustered around the prominent limestone outcrop on which the old town stands. In addition to the monuments that have made it a World Heritage city, Segovia has a healthy cultural life and a meat-and-game (and suckling pig) gastronomy produced in capacious brick ovens.

Segovia

🅰 210 D2

Visitor information

www.segoviaturismo.com

✉ Plaza Mayor 10

☎ 921 46 03 34

Cathedral

www.aytosegovia.com/monu
mentos/mo_02.htm

✉ Calle Marqués de
Arco 1

☎ 921 46 22 05

💲 $ (cloisters, chapter
house, museum)

In summer or winter you feel the climate change as you approach the city, for Segovia lies at 3,300 feet (1,000 m). The Romans were the first to recognize the site's attractions: The 95-foot-high (29-m) aqueduct spanning Plaza de Azoguejo still stands as proof of their superior engineering. After Visigothic and Moorish domination, Segovia came into its own in 1088 when the Castilian king Alfonso VI installed his court there and initiated a properous period represented by over 40 Romanesque churches. Segovia reached its zenith in 1474 when Isabel la Católica was proclaimed Queen of Castile in the church of San Miguel. The town

declined under the Habsburg kings (16th and 17th centuries), but enjoyed an 18th-century renaissance.

Segovia's old town is very much a place to explore, so arm yourself with a map from the visitor center and head for the backstreets, all of which contain notable churches, towers, and mansions enlivened by numerous storks. The hub of the old town is semiporticoed **Plaza Mayor,** lined with lively cafés and dominated by the huge, rhythmical hulk of the **cathedral.** This Flamboyant Gothic extravaganza houses some rarities in its lofty interior, notably the baroque main altarpiece by Andrea Sabatini (circa 1480–1530) and the

"Entombment" sculpture by Juan de Juni (died 1577) in a side chapel off the south aisle. The choir stalls and the cloisters were saved from the old cathedral, which was destroyed by fire during the Revolt of the Communeros (1520–1521).

From the Plaza Mayor, follow Calle Infanta Isabel to reach Segovia's most striking square, **Plaza de San Martín.** This terraced area surrounds a statue of local hero Juan Bravo in the shadow of the magnificent church of **San Martín.** Like most of Segovia's churches, this is open only for services, but you can admire the Mudejar tower and Romanesque capitals of the porch. Next door stands the elegant 17th-century **royal prison,** now a public library. Across the square looms a 14th-century tower, the **Torreón de Lozoya** *(Plaza de San Martín, tel 921 46 24 61, open from 7 p.m.),* flanked by the **Museo de Arte Contemporáneo Esteban Vicente** exhibiting works by this abstract expressionist painter who died on Long Island in 2001 *(tel 921 46 20 10, closed Mon.).* Downhill from here is the **Casa de los Picos** *(Calle Juan Bravo 33),* a 15th-century mansion with a remarkable facade of diamond-shaped granite studs. This is now the School of Applied Arts. Facades decorated in plaster relief patterns *(esgrafiados)* abound in this quarter, including that of the **Alhóndiga,** meaning "public granary," now home to the Municipal Archives. Both the Alhóndiga and the neighboring **Palacio de Aspiroz** *(Plaza Platero Oquendo)* are typical of 15th-century local architecture.

Without a doubt, Segovia's greatest landmark is the **Alcázar,** the turreted castle that rises like a mirage at the western tip of the outcrop above the confluence of the Clamores and Eresma Rivers. The

Habsburg king Felipe II was responsible for the building of this unexpected sight. It was during his reign that major additions were made to the original medieval castle, and the roof bristles with slate-roofed turrets. But thank also the 1880s restorers who enhanced the castle's theatricality after a fire. It was then handed over to the Royal Artillery, who have a museum inside. Ask at the ticket office for a leaflet with detailed descriptions of the interior, although the itinerary tends to change. Arrows guide you through, from the medieval entrance hall with original mullioned windows to the elaborate throne room that dazzles with restored Mudejar decoration. Tapestries, antique furniture, paintings, beautiful coffered Mudejar ceilings (look in particular at the one in the chapel), and suits of armor accompany you throughout. Don't miss the panoramic views from the roof of the keep, reached by over 150 narrow steps in a tower beside the ticket office, and notice the half-formed turrets of its ramparts—truly theatrical!

The Torreón de Lozoya dominates the Plaza de San Martín in the heart of the old aristocratic quarter.

Alcázar
www.alcazardesegovia.com
✉ Plaza de la Reina Victoria Eugenia
☎ 921 46 07 59
💲 $. Free on Tues. for E.U. nationals

The whimsical Habsburg-style Alcázar appears like a Germanic mirage in Segovia.

San Ildefonso de la Granja

 210 D2

www.realsitio.com

✉ Plaza de España
San Ildefonso

☎ 921 47 00 19 or
921 47 00 20

🕐 Closed Mon. all year,
& Sun. p.m.
Oct.–Mar.

💲 $$. Free on Wed.
for E.U. nationals

Real Palacio de Riofrío

🗺 210 D1

✉ Bosque de Riofrío

☎ 921 47 00 19 or
921 47 00 20

🕐 Closed Mon. all year,
& Sun. p.m.
Oct.–Mar.

💲 $$. Free on Wed.
for E.U. nationals

ROYAL ENVIRONS

Segovia's environs are also replete with royal memorabilia. The finest is **San Ildefonso de la Granja,** 7 miles (11 km) southeast on the N601, in a stunning location at the foot of the Guadarrama Mountains. Begun in 1721, the palace reflects the nostalgia of the Bourbon king Felipe V for his grandfather's palace—Versailles in France. Several architects contributed to La Granja, producing a blend of Spanish baroque and French neoclassic styles. Marble, gilded stucco, and velvet surround predictably lavish furnishings such as beautiful 16th-century Flemish tapestries and scintillating chandeliers. The latter were made at the nearby glass factory, the **Real Fábrica de Cristales** *(Paseo del Pocillo, tel 921 01 07 00 or 921 47 00 20, closed Sun. p.m.in winter & Mon.),* where you can watch glassblowing and see a display of antique glass. The palace also has exceptional, extensive formal gardens, the work of French landscape gardeners, which, again like Versailles, are strewn with statues and fountains.

Felipe V's second wife, Isabella Farnese, was responsible for the royal retreat at **Riofrío,** 4 miles (7 km) south of Segovia off the N603. More a country mansion than a palace, it is surrounded by 1,700 acres (700 ha) of lovely holm-oak woods. The pink Italianate building houses valuable paintings (by Ribera, Velázquez, and Rubens), plus a museum of hunting.

SIERRA DE GUADARRAMA

Slicing across the border between Madrid and Castilla y León, this 62-mile (100 km) mountain range of granite outcrops, streams, and forests of oak and pine attracts hordes of overheated Madrileños in summer. With its highest peak, **Peñalara,** rising to 7,970 feet (2,429 m), the sierra is also a popular winter skiing destination, with low-key resorts at Navacerrada, Valcotos, Valdesqui, and La Pinilla. Hiking opportunities include the pine forest of **Valsaín,** 5 miles (8 km) south of La Granja, and the slopes around the forbidding fortress of **Manzanares el Real** higher up. ■

Soria

ALTHOUGH NOT THE MOST COMPELLING OF THE PROVIN-
cial capitals, Soria is known for its "liquid gold" garlic soups. Above
all, it lies at the heart of some beautiful landscapes. This province is a
region of transition wedged between Castilla, Aragón, and La Rioja.
Northwest is the magnificent Sierra de Urbión, known for prolific
game and trout. East is the dramatically rugged Sierra de Moncayo.

The red-tiled roofs of golden sandstone houses, lauded by poet Antonio Machado (1875–1939), slot into
the streets of this town center. South
from the formal **Parque Alameda
de Cervantes** through squares
and pedestrian streets is **Plaza
Mayor,** the hub of the town. In the
web of streets that lies between,
centering on **Calle Aduana
Vieja,** emblazoned Renaissance
facades lead you to the Romanesque
church of **Santo Domingo,** with
statues of its founders flanking the
richly carved portal, a rose window,
and tiers of niches.

Other churches lie south, near
the Duero River. The **cathedral
of San Pedro** (Plaza de San Pedro
s/n, closed Apr.-Oct. Mon. p.m., &
Nov.-Mar. Tues.-Sun. p.m. & Mon.)
is mainly Gothic but has pure
Romanesque cloisters. Across the
Duero are the remains of the
**Monasterio de San Juan de
Duero** (Camino Monte de las
Ánimas, tel 975 23 02 18, closed Sun.
p.m. & Mon.), built with Moorish
influence in the 13th century. From
here you can see the **Parque del
Castillo,** a landscaped hill.

The Romans rebuilt
Numancia (4 miles/7 km northeast of Soria) in 133 B.C. after its
Celtiberian inhabitants destroyed it
to avoid capture. The ruins are of
interest only for enthusiasts, but in
town the **Museo Numantino**
(Paseo del Espolón 8, tel 975 23 24
56, closed Sun. p.m. & Mon.), beside
the Alameda de Cervantes park, has
Roman artifacts. ∎

The ruins of the
Monasterio de
San Juan de Duero
include the
curious remains
of a Romanesque
cloister.

Soria
🅰 211 E3
Visitor information
www.sorianitelaimaginas
.com
✉ Plaza Ramón
y Cajal
☎ 975 21 20 52

DRIVE TO ARLANZA: VALLEY OF TOWERS

Monks' graves on the hillside overlook Santo Domingo de los Silos.

Drive to Arlanza: Valley of Towers

From its source in the Sierra de Urbión, the Arlanza River meanders through a dramatic valley west to Lerma. This drive takes you through beautiful, often wild countryside, much of it ideal hiking territory and recently classified as a protected area.

On the way visit jewel-like churches, each one in a different architectural style.

Leave Burgos on the A1/E5 in the direction of Madrid. After 22 miles (36 km), cross the Arlanza River and turn off the highway at the exit marked Lerma–Estacion. Follow the signs into **Lerma ❶,** and then drive through a stone arch, **Arco de la Cárcel.** This is all that remains of the medieval town walls; proceed uphill to Plaza Mayor.

In front stands the **Palacio Ducal,** austere symbol of the extensive political power of Francisco Gómez, Duke of Lerma, who virtually ruled Spain from 1598 to 1618. This is now a parador. The duke created Spain's best example of a 17th-century planned town. The old quarter, with many mansions and porticoes, lies downhill, and is best seen on foot. From the square, walk down Calle de la Audiencia past the former convent of Santa Teresa, now the town hall and tourist office (*Casa Consistorial, Calle de la Audiencia, tel 947 17 70 02, closed Mon., & Sun. p.m.*). The

Plaza de Santa Clara is flanked by the monastery of La Ascensión and a balcony with sweeping views. Lerma's most important ecclesiastical monument, the 1617 church of San Pedro, or **Colegiata** *(by guided tour only)*, houses one of Spain's oldest organs.

Leave Lerma by continuing across the Plaza

- ⓜ   See area map pp. 210–211
- ▶   Burgos
- 🔁   89 miles (142 km)
- ⏱   2.5 hours (excluding visits)
- ▶   Burgos

NOT TO BE MISSED

- Colegiata, Lerma
- Monasterio de Santo Domingo
- Colegiata, Covarrubias
- San Pedro de Arlanza
- Ermita Visigótica

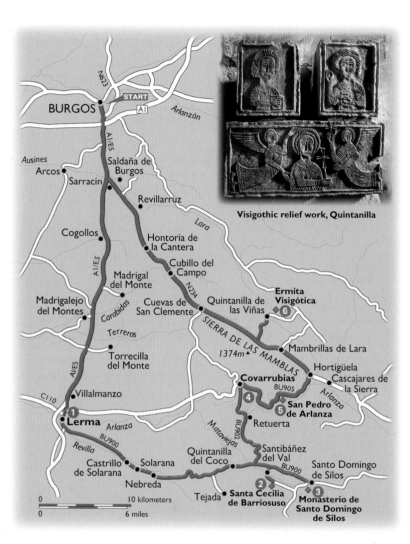

Visigothic relief work, Quintanilla

Mayor (following signs "Todas direcciones"), and turn right downhill to take the left turnoff signed Santo Domingo de Silos. This local road (BU 900) winds gently through rolling hills and wheat fields, passing little stone villages typical of the Arlanza, such as **Castrillo de Solarana,** with a massive rocky outcrop rising to the south. Turn right at the next junction (signed Santo Domingo), and after 1 mile (2 km) turn right into Santibañez del Val. Follow signs for the Ermita Mozárabe, past the village church, and left at a junction to continue beyond the

hamlet, parallel to the Ura River, for half a mile. Cross a bridge to reach the charming little stone hermitage of **Santa Cecilia de Barriosuso** ②, which dates from the 10th to 13th centuries. Below is a restored Roman bridge and a source of spring water (*fuente*).

Return to the BU900 to drive 3 miles (5 km) to **Santo Domingo de Silos.** This idyllic medieval village is the home of the **Monasterio de Santo Domingo de Silos** ③ (*tel 947 39 00 68, www.abadiadesi los.es, closed Sun.–Mon. & public holidays*

4:30 p.m.). As well as boasting one of the world's most beautiful monastery cloisters, it is more famous for the hugely successful recordings made by the monks. You can hear their melodic Gregorian chants during Mass *(Check daily schedule)* in the 18th-century church. Take time to explore the cobbled streets of the village, and then visit the **cloisters.** The lower floor has carved 11th- to 12th-century capitals decorated with harpies, griffons, and other motifs on slender double columns. The ceiling is pure 14th-century Mudejar artistry, and the corner pillars have eight superb Romanesque bas-reliefs illustrating the life of Jesus. Of the many treasures in the **museum,** look for the 11th-century chalice of Santo Domingo, the Romanesque woman's head, the manuscript of the Mozarabic rite (tenth to eleventh century), and the old pharmacy with fine Talavera jars.

From Santo Domingo backtrack 4 miles (6 km) along the BU900, and turn right to Covarrubias. For 7 miles (11 km) the road winds up through forested rocky hills, before descending to the village of **Covarrubias** ④

Exquisitely carved Romanesque capitals surround Santo Domingo's monastery cloisters in the old town of Santo Domingo.

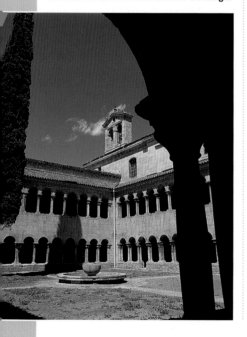

(Visitor information, tel 947 40 64 61, closed Mon. & Sun. p.m., & mid-Dec.–mid-Mar.), huddled at the base of the Sierra de las Mamblas. Wander the streets past impeccably maintained medieval houses, admiring those of Doña Sancha and Doña Urraca that flank squares of the same names. The church of San Cosme y San Damián, or **Colegiata** *(tel 947 40 63 11, closed Tues., guided tour only)* is a harmonious white stone Gothic structure begun in 1474. Numerous tombs include the sarcophagi of Fernán González, count of Castile, his wife Sancha, and three princesses. The 400-year-old organ still functions. The delicately carved cloisters, dating from 1528–1535, surround a lovely patio with a fountain and lead to the museum, a treasure trove of statues, papal bulls (documents), and 150 magnificent bishop's capes. The artworks include a painting by Jan van Eyck (circa 1390–1441) and a high relief triptych of the Adoration of the Magi by an unknown 16th-century artist.

Leave Covarrubias by following signs to San Pedro de Arlanza, 4 miles (6 km) away on the BU905. Now an evocative ruin, **San Pedro de Arlanza** ⑤ *(tel 689 59 60 64, closed Mon.–Tues., & last weekend of month)* was one of Castilla's largest Benedictine monasteries. The church structure dates from 1080 and the entire site is under renovation. The road continues through a delightful valley overshadowed by another towering escarpment, crisscrossing the Arlanza River before joining the N234 at Hortigüela. Turn left here and drive 4.4 miles (7 km) to a turnoff to the right marked Quintanilla de las Viñas. This narrow minor road twists through open wheat fields to reach the village of Quintanilla de las Viñas, where you take a right fork marked Ermita Visigótica. A few more bends and you come to the **Ermita Visigótica** ⑥ *(tel 626 49 62 15, closed Mon.–Tues., & last weekend of month),* the oldest religious structure of this region. It is a simple stone hermitage of the late seventh century, decorated with Visigothic carved friezes of grapes, birds, turkeys, and monograms. Similar whimsical carvings are inside.

Return to the N234, turn right and after 2.5 miles (4 km) pass the cave houses of **Cuevas de San Clemente** before returning to Burgos, reconnecting with the A1/E5 at Saldaña de Burgos. ∎

Burgos

THIS PROSPEROUS AND ULTRACONSERVATIVE CITY ON THE Way of St. James has one of Spain's greatest Gothic cathedrals, and for this alone it is an essential stop in the barren *meseta* (plateau). Its other Gothic treasures are the monasteries of Las Huelgas and Miraflores, just outside town. Burgos also has the ghost of the heroic warrior and mercenary El Cid, whose legendary exploits ended in death at the hands of the Moors in 1099. His body was brought from the monastery of San Pedro de Cardeña, southeast of Burgos, to be entombed in the cathedral in 1921.

Burgos
- 210 D3

Visitor information
www.turismoburgos.org
- Paseo del Espolón 1
- 947 28 88 74

Cathedral
www.catedraldeburgos.es
- Plaza de Santa María
- 947 20 47 12
- $ (cloisters area & chapels)

Burgos is strung out on both banks of the Arlanza River, but the atmospheric old town lies to the north and can be easily toured on foot. Towering above everything are the lacelike steeples of the **cathedral,** commenced in 1221 and extended over the next five centuries by some of Spain's most outstanding craftsmen. Audiophones, available for rent, are helpful for following the cathedral's complexities. Third in size after the cathedrals of Sevilla and Toledo, it presents an overwhelming display of Flamboyant Gothic design, sculpture, funerary art, carved Renaissance choir stalls, baroque wrought iron, and, despite considerable plundering by Napoleon's troops in 1809, a rich treasury. This is housed in the sacristy, the 14th-century **Capilla de Santa Catalina,** and the chapter house (with a beautiful coffered Mudejar ceiling), all of which lie off the cloisters. Admission to this area includes access to the main side chapels and the high altar. Look for the "Virgin and Child" by Hans Memling (circa 1430–1494), Diego de Siloé's "Christ at the Column," and stunning processional crosses made in Burgos.

Each of the side chapels is a work of art. In the **Capilla del Condestable,** designed by Simon of Cologne in 1482, note the star-shaped dome, heavily sculpted walls and altar, and the tombs of the Constable and his wife. The intricately sculpted back of the high altar illustrates the ascent to Calvary. West of the nave in the **Capilla de Santa Ana,** a massive Gothic altarpiece details events from the saint's life, and in the **Capilla de Santa Tecla,** there is a rococo ceiling sheltering an elaborate Churrigueresque (see pp. 46–47) altarpiece dedicated to this martyr. ■

Perched on the banks of the Arlanza River, Burgos has some of Spain's most spectacular medieval architecture.

More places to visit in Castilla y León

EL BURGO DE OSMA

This delightful town has an air of faded grandeur, especially in the medieval streets surrounding the Gothic **cathedral** *(Plaza de San Pedro 2, closed Mon.)*. Originally built for the Cistercians, it acquired late Gothic cloisters and also has a baroque bell tower and ambulatory. The cloisters museum has interesting pieces, but the main attraction of Burgo de Osma is its placid streets, lined with 16th-century porticoes, and majestic emblazoned buildings such as the **Hospital de San Agustín** (1694) on Plaza Mayor. The hospital was built outside the town wall, but in the late 18th century it was incorporated into a new quarter. Today the building is used as an exhibition center. In the arcaded **Calle Mayor,** explore the specialist foodshops for local fare: cakes, pâté de foie gras, blood-pudding, and ewe's cheese, and then join bereted old men on the Plaza Mayor for a coffee.

Surveying the view from Orellán over the red-ocher formations of Las Médulas

⚠ 211 E2 **Visitor information,** www.bur gosma.es ✉ Calle Universidad 39 ☎ 975 36 02 79

LAS MÉDULAS

Added to UNESCO's cultural heritage list in 1997, the Roman gold mines of Las Médulas are this region's most spectacular archaeological sight. These remnants of Roman excavations lie 14 miles (22 km) southwest of Ponferrada, close to the Galician border and the Sil River, and cover a vast, desertlike area, interrupted only by gnarled chestnut trees. The reddish ocher crags are most striking toward sundown, when their contours seem to catch fire. A visitor center explains the sophisticated system of hydraulics, tunnels, and channels set up by the Romans, and you can follow trails or drive effortlessly to a viewpoint at Orellán to admire this surreal landscape.

⚠ 210 B4 **Aula Arqueológica de Las Médulas** www.bierzonet.es/ieb/medulas/aula.html ☎ 987 42 28 48 ⏰ Closed Mon.–Fri. & Sun. p.m. (winter)

TORDESILLAS

Smack in the middle of the wine-growing region between Zamora and Valladolid, the friendly little town of Tordesillas stands at a busy intersection. It is known for the Treaty of Tordesillas, signed here in 1494, which carved up the New World between Spain and Portugal. The sight to head for is **Monasterio de Santa Clara** *(tel 983 77 00 71, closed Mon., guided tour)*—built in 1350 as a royal palace. As the home of Pedro I's Andalucian mistress, it acquired extensive Moorish features, including Sevillian *azulejos* (tiles) and a stuccoed, arched patio. In 1373 a church was built and nuns were admitted; 13 *claustrados* (cloistered nuns) live there today. Outstanding features are the carved Mudejar ceiling (1430) of the church and the 43 paintings of saints, set off by Moorish stuccowork. A Gothic side chapel housed the tombs of the Catholic monarchs, Fernando and Isabel before they were subsequently moved to Granada, and it still has a superb gilded altarpiece by Nicolás Francés. A collection of unusual musical instruments includes a portable organ used by Juana the Mad. After the death of her husband, she was declared insane by Fernando (her father) and Carlos V (her son), and was shut away in Tordesillas for 46 years, from 1509–1555.

⚠ 210 C2 **Visitor information,** www.torde sillas.net ✉ Casa del Tratado, Plaza de la Hispanidad 1 ☎ 983 77 10 67 ■

Out of the bleak plains of La Mancha spring surprises such as Cuenca and Toledo. Extremadura's bucolic hills and valleys lead to the historical Cáceres, Mérida, and Trujillo. This is a region for heading off the beaten track.

Castilla-La Mancha & Extremadura

Conquistador celebrations in Trujillo

Castilla-La Mancha & Extremadura

CASTILLA-LA MANCHA, THAT GREAT SWATH OF LAND THAT LIES BETWEEN
Madrid and Andalucía, is not Spain's most compelling region. Flat, monotonous, and
seemingly devoid of inhabitants, it seems drab compared with its neighboring regions
on all sides—including Extremadura, which is a place of rural delights. For many people
Extremadura represents the last bastion of old Spain, sidelined by the dynamism of the
country's other autonomous communities, but still an enclave of tradition, Catholicism,
and unspoiled countryside. Common to both regions are an audible population of storks,
nesting on every available tower, and reminders of the medieval knights, half-monk and
half-soldier, who fought so fiercely against the Moors.

Castilla-La Mancha does have two points of
major interest: Toledo and Cuenca. Toledo,
just south of Madrid, is one of Spain's great
museum cities. Despite being entirely geared
to tourism, it maintains an affable and still
individualistic attitude. It was the center of
multireligious learning during the Middle
Ages, before a long period of intolerance, and
is one of those places you simply have to see.

A long leap to the east is Cuenca, a much
smaller town perched picturesquely on a cliff
and edged by spectacular rock formations
that resemble a ruined city. Exhilarating for
its setting and for its fantastic museums of
abstract art, it does, however, require a
logistical effort to reach. The area north of
Cuenca has beautiful landscapes and the
charming town of Sigüenza. The central
plains of the region are empty. Interest picks
up again to the south at Almagro and at
several smaller towns scattered through the
Sierra de Alcaraz, which borders Andalucía.
You should sample the local Manchego cheese,

a sharply flavored ewe's milk cheese, accompanied by robust Valdepeñas wine.

Over in Extremadura, the landscapes are
another story entirely. Here you enter verdant
valleys of cherry and olive trees (the locals are
the champion pickers of Spain), rolling wheat
fields, sheep pastures, and wooded hills, an
intensely rural land that in the 16th century
produced the conquerors of the New World.
Two towns are especially redolent of the past:
Cáceres, with its monumental upper town of
silent Renaissance

mansions, and Mérida, once the heart of Roman Lusitania, whose Roman remains are quite exceptional. You can complete a triangular itinerary by also visiting Trujillo, a real charmer of a town where historic monuments are integrated into daily life. Extremadura's big religious center is the magnificent monastery of Guadalupe. Emperor Carlos V spent his last contemplative days in the monastery at Yuste, in the north of Extremadura. This is the most bucolic part, where fertile undulating terrain gives good hiking, and villages have unique rural architecture.

Extremadura is wetter and cooler than other regions of southern Spain, but the plains of La Mancha (whose name derives from the Arabic *manxa,* meaning "dry land") become a furnace in midsummer. Neither region is renowned for innovative gastronomy, but both have an honest cuisine of dishes such as goat or lamb stew, exquisite ham, fresh river trout, game, and La Mancha's vegetable *pisto.* Perhaps the most outstanding characteristic of this part of Spain is its unspoiled, undeveloped nature—here the visitor becomes a benign conquistador. ■ 4▷

A La Mancha windmill

CASTILLA Y LEÓN p. 209

MADRID p. 53

ARAGÓN p. 111

VALENCIA p. 177

MURCIA p. 259

ANDALUCÍA p. 259

2275m Lobo

Sigüenza
Jadraque
Maranchón
Molina de Aragón
Brihuega
Guadalajara
Sacedón
Embalse de Entrepeñas
Béteta
Pastrana
Priego
Embalse de Buendía
Sayatón
Mar de Castilla
Garganta del Júcar-Ventana del Diablo
Ciudad Encantada
Cuenca
Cañete

Talavera de la Reina E90
Esquivias
Torrijos
Tarancón
San Lorenzo de la Parrilla
Oropesa
Ocaña
Villatobas E901
Saelices
Carboneras de Guadazaón
Belvis de la Jara
La Puebla de Montalbán
Toledo E05
Corral de Almaguer
Quintanar de la Orden
Embalse de Alarcón
Embalse de Contreras
Sonseca
Mora
Villacañas
El Toboso
Honrubia
Los Yébenes
Madridejos
Alcázar de San Juan
Belmonte E901
Motilla del Palancar
Minglanilla
Consuegra
Mota del Cuervo A31
Puerto Lápice
Campo de Criptana
San Clemente
Porzuna
Malagón
Socuéllamos
Villarrobledo
Tarazona de la Mancha
Herrera del Duque
Parque Nacional de las Tablas de Daimiel
Argamasilla de Alba
Tomelloso
La Roda
Alcalá del Júcar
Agudo
Daimiel
Barrax
La Gineta
Manzanares
Munera
Albacete N430
Ciudad Real
Almagro
La Solana
Ossa de Montiel
Balazote
Chinchilla de Monte Aragón
Almansa
Almadén
Valdepeñas
Villanueva de los Infantes
Alcaraz
Caudete
Almodóvar del Campo
Puertollano E05
Calzada de Calatrava
Liétor
Tobarra
Castillo de Calatrava
Santa Cruz de Mudela
Hellín
Viso del Marqués
Elche de la Sierra

Cuenca

Cuenca

📍 235 E3

Visitor information

www.cuenca.org

✉ Alfonso VIII 2

☎ 969 24 10 51

Museo de Arte Abstracto Español

www.march.es/cuenca

✉ Calle Canonigos

☎ 969 21 29 83

🕐 Closed Sun. p.m. & Mon.

💲 $

Cuenca's towering houses cling to a rocky precipice.

CUENCA IS CASTILLA-LA MANCHA'S GREATEST SURPRISE. IT is set spectacularly on a cliff between the Huécar and Júcar Rivers, northeast of the central plains, where the Serranía de Cuenca rises to become a natural frontier with Aragón. The equally dramatic surroundings helped lure dozens of artists here in the 1960s.

Equidistant between Madrid (103 miles/165 km/) and Valencia, Cuenca is famous for its vertiginous **Casas Colgadas** (hanging houses), best viewed from the Puente de San Pablo. One contains the **Museo de Arte Abstracto Español,** where paintings by important abstract artists such as Antoni Tàpies and Antonio Saura vie with fantastic views. On the other side

of the bridge stands the **Monasterio de los Paúles,** partly a *parador* (see p. 370) and partly another art foundation, that of Gustavo Torner.

A few steps away looms the beautiful Gothic-Norman and Renaissance **cathedral** (*Plaza Mayor, tel 969 22 25 06, closed Sun. p.m.*). Look for the carved walnut door leading to the chapter house, the work of Alonso de Berreguete (see pp. 45–46), and the stained-glass windows by contemporary artists. Outside is the trapezoidal **Plaza Mayor,** scene of Holy Week processions, and the festival of San Mateo (September 18–21). At the top of town, in a converted 17th-century convent overlooking the ravine, is the fascinating and labyrinthine **Fundación Antonio Pérez** (*Convento de las Carmelitas Descalzas, Ronda de Julián Romero, tel 969 23 06 19*). This exhibits a vast private collection assembled by artist, poet, and art-publisher, Antonio Pérez, who still lives in Cuenca. Artists range from Andy Warhol to Lucio Fontana, Antonio Tàpies, and Miguel Barceló.

Of the many beautiful spots in the Serranía de Cuenca, the most striking is the **Ciudad Encantada** (Enchanted City), 15 miles (25 km) northeast of Cuenca. You can follow a marked path around this surrealistic landscape of eroded rocks. Three miles (5 km) north lies the **Garganta del Júcar** (Júcar Gorge), best seen through a rock opening nicknamed the **Ventana del Diablo** (Devil's Window). ■

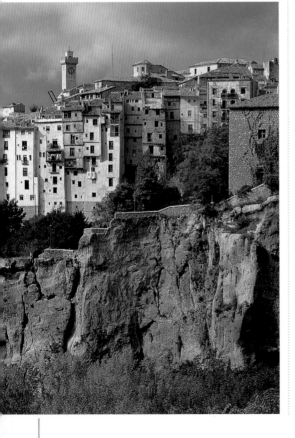

Albacete

ISOLATED ALBACETE, IN EASTERN LA MANCHA, HAS NO great monuments, but lies at a crossroads for routes between central Spain, Valencia on the east coast, and Andalucía. Its name refers to its flat setting, now the scene of intensive cultivation of vines, artichokes, and profitable saffron, introduced by the Arabs between the 8th and 13th centuries.

Arabs also brought the art of knife-making, and the quality of Albacete's steel knives and daggers has long been admired. Workshops use time-honored techniques to make knives in all shapes and sizes, so this is the perfect place to restock your kitchen. The new **Museo de la Cuchilleria** *(Plaza de la Catedral, closed Mon., $)* displaying old and new designs.

Albacete's modern **Museo Arqueológico** was built to house the wealth of finds from surrounding excavations. Prehistoric objects from the caves of Alpera range from an Iberian sphinx from Haches, to a lion from Bienservida, and countless Roman artifacts. Many of the latter were uncovered at the fourth-century necropolis of Ontur.

Exploring Albacete province will take you off the beaten track. Drive 31 miles (50 km) northeast to **Alcalá del Júcar** to see a mini-Cuenca—a village built into a cliff, and dominated by a Moorish castle. South of Albacete is **Liétor,** another spectacularly sited village perched on a dolmitic crag above the Mundo River. Narrow medieval streets reflect the village's not-so-distant Moorish past, and the mountain views are superb. Do not miss **Chinchilla de Monte Aragón,** with its well-conserved medieval quarter, 15th-century castle, noble-men's houses, and Arab baths. An important potterymaking center, it also has a ceramics museum. Try the provincial specialities, notably partridge, hare, and rabbit prepared in about 30 different ways. ■

Dominated by a medieval castle and neoclassic church, Almansa lies between Albacete and Alacant.

Albacete
235 E2
Visitor information
www.albacete.com
Calle Tinte 2
967 21 42 26

Museo Arqueológico de Albacete
www.albaturismo.com/engli sh/albaturismo.htm
Parque de Abelardo Sánchez
967 22 83 07
Closed Sun. p.m. & Mon.
$

Miguel de Cervantes & Don Quixote

Trotting across the plains of La Mancha are the ghosts of Don Quixote and his faithful squire, Sancho Panza, two comical but darkly allegorical figures created by Miguel de Cervantes (1547–1616). From its initial aim to be a parody of traditional romantic ballads and tales of knights errant, this book became a universally popular synthesis of the Renaissance. It is also a racy adventure story crammed with amusing, earthy characters. Superficially it paints a picture of the period in entertaining color, but beneath the surface lie a social critique and symbolism that enchanted Europe in the early 17th century.

Cervantes' own life was a picaresque adventure. Born in Alcalá de Henares, he started adult life as a soldier. He participated in the naval victory of Lepanto (1571) against the Ottoman Turks, where injuries left him with a crippled arm. He then ran into trouble when captured by pirates on his return to Spain in 1575. Enslaved for five years in Algiers, he made several unsuccessful attempts to escape before he was ransomed by his family and could start life again. Between periods of imprisonment for debt and mismanaged accounts, Cervantes led a disillusioned, outsider's life, not helped by an unhappy marriage or the menial jobs with which he made a living. He wrote when he was in prison, and from 1608 he was able to devote himself entirely to literary pursuits while living in Madrid. Little is known about the

Left: Dalí sketch of Don Quixote. Above: The familiar windmills that he perceived as giants

man himself except that he was reserved, cautious, and at times aggressive. He was 50 before he realized his own talent for narrative, first glimpsed in his unsuccessful pastoral novel, *La Galatea* (1585), and later in his short stories, *The Exemplary Novels* (1613).

The multiple dimensions of Don Quixote stretched Cervantes' imaginative powers to the fullest and brought him instant success. Publication of the first part of the book in 1605 was followed rapidly by pirate editions within just a few weeks, and made the public avid for more. This finally appeared ten years later, just one year before the author's death, and was a much deeper and more subtle text. Described at this point by a French visitor as "old, a soldier, a gentleman and poor," Cervantes nevertheless died knowing that his creation had become famous, with translations into French and English.

In Don Quixote's illusory, innocent world, the windmills of La Mancha become giants, and heroic misadventures are inspired by his parallel vision of reality. The knight's noble, eccentric generosity, set against the common-sensical, often skeptical attitudes of his faithful servant, Sancho Panza, becomes an allegory about human perception: Things can be real or ideal, feasible or fantastic, sane or insane. Don Quixote's descent into madness, accentuated by his awareness of it, is finally cured only by death. Ironically it is Sancho who has the hero's return. In the words of the English writer V.S. Pritchett, "The extreme strains of the Spanish nature are celebrated in these two characters: the passionate tendency to fantasy, the fatal reaction into skepticism, realism, and cynicism." Nearly 400 years after the publication of his masterpiece, Cervantes' analysis still holds true. ■

Toledo

Toledo
🗺 235 C3

Visitor information
www.toledoweb.org
✉ Plaza Consistorial I
☎ 925 25 40 30
🕐 Closed Mon. p.m.

✉ Puerta de Bisagra
☎ 925 22 08 43

Cathedral
✉ Calle Cisneros
☎ 925 22 22 41
🕐 Closed Sun. a.m.
& Mon.
$ $$ (museum,
chapter house,
treasury, & choir)

TOLEDO'S PROXIMITY TO MADRID MAKES IT A CLASSIC DAY-trip destination (trains take 75 minutes), but its many monuments and eerie nocturnal atmosphere warrant an overnight stay. It is one of Spain's great historic cities, spectacularly sited on a hilltop and practically encircled by the Tajo River. The Greek painter El Greco lived and worked in Toledo until his death in 1614, and left an overwhelming pictorial legacy.

Toledo became the Visigothic capital in A.D. 554 and played a major role for the next eight centuries. It was a flourishing trading center under Moorish rule, when Jews, Muslims, and Christians worked side by side. After Toledo was captured by Alfonso VI of Castilla y León in 1085, the three communities continued to prosper peaceably under Christian rule until the mid-14th century, when persecution of the Jewish community began. From 1492, decline set in with the expulsion and repression of Jews and Muslims.

Modern Toledo depends above all on tourism, and you may become jaded at the sight of many multilingual menus and tourist souvenir shops.

Plot your route carefully: Toledo is a labyrinth of steep cobbled streets. The extraordinary **cathedral** is the obvious starting point, a symphony of Gothic spires and pinnacles rising over the Plaza del Ayuntamiento. Construction began in 1226, but it took over 250 years to complete, resulting in a bizarre convergence of styles and artists. Look at the **western portal,** consisting of three heavily sculpted doors (Hell, Pardon, and Judgment), the Flamboyant Gothic **spire** to the left, and to the right the Renaissance **dome** by the son of El Greco, Jorge Theotocópuli (who also designed the elegant town hall opposite). Access is from the side, in the Calle Cisneros,

where you should buy a ticket from the shop opposite to visit the cathedral's treasures.

Inside, between the lofty ribbed columns and 800 stained-glass windows, your first sight is the immense, elaborately sculpted choir. The **choir stalls** are masterpieces, especially the lower, 15th-century ones, carved by Rodrigo Alemán with mythical beasts and battle scenes of the conquest of Granada. Above are 16th-century alabaster seats (by Alonso Berruguete and Felipe Vigarny) separated by columns of jasper.

Go around the outer walls of the choir (depicting Old Testament scenes) to the High Altar: the **altarpiece** is a gigantic Flamboyant Gothic polychrome carving of the Life of Christ. To your right is another outsize work, a 30-foot (9-m) mural depicting St. Christopher. Behind the altar is the cathedral's most remarkable architectural and artistic feature, the **Transparente** (1732). This baroque folly was designed by Narciso Tomé to allow light to penetrate from the ceiling and illuminate the tabernacle. It requires a real neck bend to admire the incredible feat of sculptures looking down from the painted dome, where the Virgin evaporates into a cloud of saints and angels.

To the right is the **sala capitular** (chapter house), where both the antechamber and main hall have magnificent coffered ceilings, the main one heavy with gold leaf

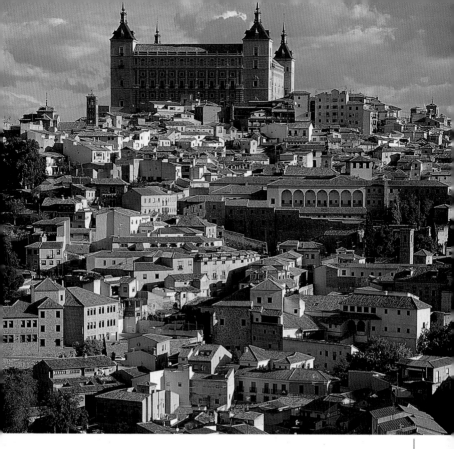

(the work of Diego López de Arenas). Below are lovely frescoes by Juan de Borgoña, and a bottom row of portraits of Toledo's powerful archbishops—leaving space for those of the future. Look, too, at the delicately carved wardrobes in the antechamber. Your next surprise comes in the **sacristy** and **museum.** This is an art galley in itself, rich in El Grecos and work by Zurbarán, Juan de Borgoña, and Goya (note the light and expressions of his "Capture of Christ"). El Greco's dramatic **"El Expolio"** demands attention, but don't miss the exhibits flanking it: a superb Romanesque "Virgin and Child" in silver with a gold filigree crown, and to the right a beautiful 12th-century silver casket that contains the relics of St. Eugenio.

The vestry displays more masterpieces—Van Dyck, Velázquez, Titian, and Rubens—and leads to rooms filled with sumptuous clerical robes, altar dressings (look for the one of silver thread and coral), and embroidered Moorish banners from the 14th century.

If you have any powers of admiration left, visit the **treasury,** where you walk smack into the sight of a 10-foot-high (3-m) gold and silver monstrance made by Enrique de Arfe in the 1520s. Despite its immense weight of almost 400 pounds (180 kg), it is paraded through Toledo during Corpus Christi (May/June). Assorted items around it include the finely illustrated Bible of St. Louis (13th century) and a 15th-century calvary cross painted by Fra Angelico.

Long the spiritual capital of Spain, Toledo rises abruptly from the plain in an upsweep of gates, battlements, and church towers dominated by the Alcázar.

Intricate, delicate Mudejar designs grace the ceiling of the Monasterio de San Juan de los Reyes.

Hospital y Museo de Santa Cruz

✉ Miguel de Cervantes 3

☎ 925 22 14 02

Monasterio de San Juan de los Reyes

www.fundacioniberdrola.org /sanjuan_01.htm

✉ Calle de los Reyes Católicos 21

☎ 925 22 38 02

💲 $

EAST OF THE CATHEDRAL

Dominating Toledo's skyline, the **Alcázar** *(Cuesta Carlos V 2, tel 925 22 16 73, reopening in late 2008)* is a massive fortress. It dates from the Middle Ages, but retains little of its original structure. In the 16th century, both Carlos V and his son Felipe II extended it for use as a royal residence, but successive fires in the 18th and 19th centuries wrought havoc with the fabric. Even greater damage came during the Civil War (see pp. 36–37), when Franco's forces withstood a siege and bombardment for ten weeks.

Since being rebuilt, the Alcázar has become the headquarters of military organizations, and its exhibits demand a keen interest in army history. If you venture to the basement to see the oven that baked 1,735 bread rolls daily during the siege, you pass through a Moorish arch, a relic from an even earlier structure, dated 970.

Just north of the Alcázar, pass through the horseshoe arch on the Plaza de Zocodover to reach Toledo's most beautiful Renaissance building, the **Hospital y Museo de Santa Cruz** (1524), a former orphanage. Its delicately carved facade, cloisters, and staircase are plateresque masterpieces by Alonso de Covarrubias, and the patio garden makes a wonderfully serene retreat. It is now Toledo's main museum of art, industrial arts, and archaeology. The lower floor is worth visiting if only to see the giant tusks of a Paleolithic mammoth; also here are Roman mosaics and pottery. The upper floor has paintings by El Greco, Flemish tapestries, sculptures by Pedro de Mena, and local crafts.

WEST OF THE CATHEDRAL

The west side of Toledo has a cluster of monuments that demonstrate the medieval coexistence of three cultures. The Franciscan **Monasterio de San Juan de los Reyes** is a Flamboyant Gothic construction by Juan Guas (died 1496), with a north portal by Covarrubias (1488–1570). Commissioned by the Catholic Monarchs (see pp. 31–33), it bears many traces of their royal patronage. The **cloisters** are superb, a harmonious mixture of ornate pinnacles, balustrades, and arches with a Mudejar ceiling on the upper gallery. The **church,** much rebuilt following a French attack in 1808, combines royal escutcheons with Gothic stone tracery.

Close by are two synagogue buildings, the only reminders of Toledo's once flourishing Jewish community and Jewish quarter, most of which was destroyed in 1491. The **Sinagoga del Tránsito** was commissioned in 1336–1357 by Samuel ha-Leví, a distinguished court adviser. It finally closed in 1494 after Jews were expelled from Spain. Subsequently it functioned as a hospital and a church, but is now the **Museo Sefardí** (Sephardic Museum). It has been completely restored to reveal its original use, with additional rooms illustrating Jewish traditions and the history of Sephardic Jews. The main worship hall, a sumptuous example of Mudejar artistry, incorporates Hebrew and Kufic inscriptions and heraldic shields. Look in particular at the spectacular cedarwood ceiling and intricate stuccowork around the *hejal* (Jewish altar). Above, in the women's gallery, numerous items from Tunisia, Morocco, France, and Italy illustrate the Sephardic culture, one that is alive today.

In contrast, the **Sinagoga de Santa María la Blanca** *(Calle de los Reyes Católicos 4, tel 925 22 72 57)* has an immaculately restored and whitewashed interior, almost devoid of any exhibits or furnishings. Five aisles are divided by rhythmical horseshoe arches (reminiscent of Córdoba's Great Mosque, see pp. 288–89) with identical capitals adorned with plant motifs. By 1405, the synagogue had been converted into a church and had acquired its present name. The three altars were decorated by Covarrubias.

Just opposite the Tránsito synagogue is the **Casa de El Greco** *(Calle Samuel Leví, tel 925 22 40 46, closed Sun. p.m. & Mon.).* The artist never lived in this house, despite its name, but it is an atmospheric reflection of his life. It is currently closed for restoration until 2010. Uphill from here, the church of **Santo Tomé** *(Plaza del Conde, tel 925 25 60 98)* houses El Greco's masterpiece, the **"Burial of the Count of Orgaz"** (1586), an unmissable site.

A little further out, the **Museo de Escultura Victorio Macho** *(Plaza de Victorio Macho, tel 925 28 42 25, closed Sun. p.m., $),* set in gardens on a promontory overlooking the Tagus River, makes a delightful escape. Inside are sketches, drawings and sculptures by the figurative artist, Victorio Macho (1887–1966), who after political exile in South America, spent the last years of his life in Toledo. ∎

Museo Sefardí
www.museosefardi.net
✉ Calle Samuel Levi
☎ 925 22 36 65
🕐 Closed Sun. p.m.
   & Mon.
$ $. Free Sat. p.m.
   & Sun. a.m.

The Casa de El Greco reconstructs the studio where the mannerist painter worked in the 16th century.

Toledo's center, with the cathedral straight ahead and the Archbishop's Palace to the left

A walk around Toledo

This walk takes you through the characteristically steep, high-walled streets of central Toledo, stopping at intriguing churches, convents, and even a mosque—a synopsis of this once spiritual city.

Start from the main door of the **Cathedral ❶** and walk up the steps beside the **Palacio Arzobispal** (Archbishop's Palace) opposite. On the pretty Plaza Consistorial at the top, turn right and walk up Cuesta del Ordenal, where you turn right and then left into narrow Callejón de Jesus María. At the top turn right, where you will see the imposing baroque facade of **San Ildefonso.** Turn left beside the church into Calle de San Román, which leads to the church of **San Román ❷;** the entrance is around the corner in Calle San Clemente. San Román is Toledo's oldest church. Of Visigothic origin, it was later used as a mosque before being rebuilt in Mudejar style in the 13th century. Now it serves as a museum of Visigothic culture, the **Museo de los Concilios y de la Cultura Visigoda** (*Iglesia de San Román, Calle de San Román, tel 925 22 78 72, closed Sun. p.m. & Mon.*). The unusual interior combines Caliphal arches, Roman columns, Visigothic and Mozarabic

capitals, and, above all, wonderful frescoes that blanket nearly every wall and arch.

On leaving the church, walk down the street opposite and turn left at the bottom into Plaza de Padilla. Cross the square diagonally to descend the steps, and then turn right to skirt the convent and church of **Santo Domingo el Antiguo ❸** (*tel 925 22 29 30, closed Sun. a.m.*). This was Toledo's first convent, founded in 1085 by Cistercians. Today it has about 14

- See area map p. 235
- ► Plaza del Ayuntamiento
- ↔ 1.7 miles (2.7 km)
- ⏱ 1–2 hours
- ► Mezquita del Cristo de la Luz

NOT TO BE MISSED

- San Román
- Santo Domingo el Antiguo
- Mezquita del Cristo de la Luz

nuns, whose work includes guiding tourists around their considerable treasures and selling homemade candies. The church is neoclassic inside and has three paintings by El Greco, as well as several copies. Two of the originals (depicting John the Baptist and San Bernard) are part of the altarpiece; the third is the exceptional **"Resurrection of Christ"** hanging to the right of this area. Switch on the lights to peer through a grille at the coffered ceiling of the chapter house and through the floor at El Greco's modest tomb in the crypt before being led through to the old choir. This magnificent room and adjoining antechamber are full of interest—the superb coffered ceiling, a carved head of John the Baptist by Pedro de Mena (see p. 47), a painting by Luca Giordano (1634–1705), richly embroidered altar dressings, and 12th- to 16th-century documents, including El Greco's contract with the convent, and others signed by King Sancho III (1154) and Alfonso VII (1150).

Walk down Calle de Santa Leocadia and turn right into Calle Real, passing the grandiose provincial council building before turning right and immediately left at the end through a typically narrow, high-sided lane, Calle Buzones. This brings you to the baroque facade of **Santo Domingo el Real,** one of several convents around this square. Walk through the *cobertizo* (a bridged-over passage-way), turn right up another, and you come to the 13th-century Mudejar church of **San Vicente,** dominating a plaza. On your left is **Las Gaitanas,** a cloistered convent; beyond San Vicente is the neoclassic **Palacio de Lorenzana.** Turn left into Calle de los Alfileritos, and then take the third lane on your left, Calle del Cristo de la Luz. This brings you to the **Mezquita del Cristo de la Luz** ❹ (*Calle del Cristo de la Luz, tel 925 25 41 91), a stunning intact mosque dating from A.D. 999, with a 12th-century Romanesque sanctuary. ■

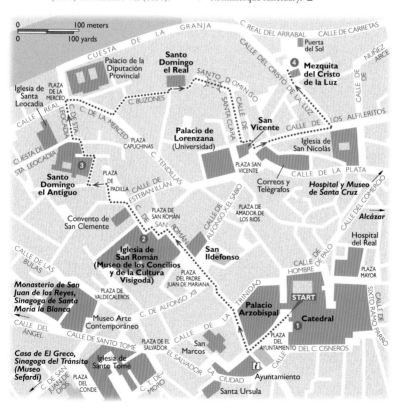

The Monasterio
de Guadalupe's
Gothic and
Mudejar towers
loom above the
medieval town
of Guadalupe.

Guadalupe

MEXICO'S MUCH REVERED PATRON SAINT, THE VIRGIN OF
Guadalupe, and the Caribbean island named for her originated here,
a village in the remote green hills of Extremadura, where a miracu-
lous image of the Virgin was found seven centuries ago. This black-
faced Virgin became the patron of "all Spains," the very essence of
Spanishness, and her shrine continues to attract streams of pilgrims.

Guadalupe

🅼 234 B2

Visitor information

www.puebladeguadalupe.net

✉ Plaza Santa María
   de Guadalupe

☎ 927 15 41 28

**Real Monasterio
de Santa María**

www.monasterioguadalupe.
com

☎ 927 36 70 00

💲 $ (guided
   tours only)

A huge monastery and church
dominate the pretty hillside village,
where medieval streets lined with
flower-filled balconies radiate from
a wide plaza in front of the church.
The 12th-century statue of the
Virgin, allegedly carved by St. Luke,
inspired the building of the
Hieronymite monastery in
1340. It is now run by Franciscans,
who have undertaken extensive
restoration. There is a very pleasant
guesthouse in the Gothic cloisters.

The golden-stone church facade
rises between crenellated towers. In
the church all attention is focused
on the altarpiece and its diminutive, caped figure of the Virgin. You
get a closer look in the Camarín
above, a small, highly decorated
18th-century chapel. This is where

your guide spins the image around
to face the crowd of expectant pilgrims. In the nearby **Relicario** are
the Virgin's rich wardrobe and
crown, reserved for processions.

The **Museo de Bordados**
is an embroidery museum, with
monks' needlework from the 15th
to 19th centuries. In the **Museo
de Pinturas y Esculturas**
(paintings and sculptures), look for
an ivory sculpture of Christ, said
to be by Michelangelo, and the
beautiful small portraits of monks
by Zurbarán. The **chapter house**
has a dazzling collection of illuminated psalmbooks. Structurally
the most interesting section is the
Claustro Mudejar, an unusually
large, two-story cloister of horseshoe arches. ■

Sierra de la Peña de Francia

Looking toward La Alberca from the Sierra de la Peña de Francia

THIS RANGE IS PART OF THE RUGGED CORDILLERA CENTRAL that continues into the craggy Sierra de Gredos, and is a natural border between Castilla y León and Extremadura. The highest peak, Peña de Francia, rises to 5,682 feet (1,732 m), and its tortuous access road gives panoramic views west toward Portugal, east to the Sierra de Gredos, and north over the Castilian meseta.

The most interesting place to head is **La Alberca** in Castilla y León, a charming, restored mountain village of stone and half-timbered houses on cobbled streets. For centuries its remoteness preserved local traditions and religious zeal, but national monument status has resulted in a steady stream of visitors in summer. If you can, time your visit for August 15, when villagers don exuberantly embroidered costumes to enact a mystery play celebrating the triumph of the Virgin over the Devil.

Immediately south, over the Portillo pass, the dramatic road (SA201) descends into the bucolic valley of **Las Batuecas**—protected as a nature park. Rock formations in startling shapes harbor prehistoric cave paintings.

Las Batuecas is on the edge of **Las Hurdes,** a region brought to fame by Luis Buñuel in his 1932 film *Tierra Sin Pan* (Land Without Bread), which portrayed its extreme hardship and poverty. Today life has improved, but there remains a distinctive wildness in the landscape, and a time-warped atmosphere in the tiny whitewashed hamlets and stone farmhouses. Follow the C515 to see attractive **Miranda del Castañar** before reaching **Béjar,** a fortified hilltop town, and then go southeast to **Hervás**. This village preserves a remarkable old **Jewish quarter** among its leaning, half-timbered houses. The maze of narrow streets with a backdrop of snowcapped peaks makes a rewarding stroll. ∎

Sierra de la Peña de Francia
Béjar
🗺 234 B3
Visitor information
www.i-bejar.com
✉ Paseo de
Cervantes 6
☎ 923 40 30 05

Hervás
🗺 234 B3
Visitor information
www.valledelambroz.com
/hervas
✉ Calle Braulio
Navas 6
☎ 927 47 36 18

In & around Plasencia

Almond orchards near Plasencia

DRAMATICALLY SITED ON A HILLTOP ABOVE THE JERTE River, against a backdrop of jagged limestone outcrops, the "pearl of the Jerte" is a fine base for explorations of the beautiful Valle del Jerte. South are the rural delights of the Valle de la Vera, and the monastery to which Carlos V retired in 1556, exhausted from the burden of being Holy Roman Emperor.

Plasencia's star attraction is the **cathedral,** which, like Salamanca's (see pp. 218–220), combines two distinct periods and buildings: the old Romanesque-Gothic cathedral, dating from the 13th and 14th centuries, and, linked to it by cloisters, the new cathedral. Completed in Renaissance style in the early 16th century by some of Spain's best architects of the time, the latter is Extremadura's most ornate church. Look in particular at the dome of the chapel of San Pablo, the beautiful plateresque north portal, the sculptures by Gregorio Fernández for the main altar (1634), and the carved choir stalls (1520).

Handsome mansions line the streets around the **Plaza Mayor,** where every Tuesday sees a bountiful food market dating from the Middle Ages. The Casa del Dean, Palacio Episcopal, and Casa de las Dos Torres are worth finding, and the **Museo la Etnográfico** *(Calle Marqués de la Puebla, tel 927 42 18 43, closed Sun. p.m., Mon., & Tues.)* gives insight into the area's rural traditions.

The beautiful **Valle del Jerte** is rich in oak trees, chestnut trees, and especially cherry trees: Over 30 varieties of cherries are grown here on an estimated one million trees. Imagine the blossom in spring, or, better still, be here to see it. If you are in the region in May, visit the village of **Valdastillas,** where you get a close-up on cherry-related activities: Families pick and sort them, and you can take guided tours

Plasencia
🅰 234 B3
Visitor information
www.aytoplasencia.es
✉ Plaza Torre de Lucia
☎ 927 01 78 40

Valle del Jerte
🅰 234 B3
Visitor information
www.vallecereza.com
✉ Paraje Virgen de Peñas Albas, Cabazuela del Valle
☎ 927 47 21 22

of the cooperatives where cherries are bottled and turned into liqueurs.

Near the village of Jerte is the **Reserva Natural Garganta de los Infiernos,** a stunning nature reserve of torrential waterfalls, that gives really scenic, though tough, hiking. Farther northeast along this valley, **Tornavacas** is the last village before the border with Castilla y León, 4 miles (6 km) away at the Puerto de Tornavacas mountain pass (4,183 feet/1,275 m). Slotted between the towering sierras of Gredos and Bejar, Tornavacas has only one main street, Calle Real. At **No. 23** is the inn where Carlos V spent the night on his way to the monastery at Yuste in 1556, in the fertile La Vera valley.

The **Valle de la Vera** is south of Valle del Jerte. You can reach it on a twisting road from Valdastillas or, more easily, on the C501 from Plasencia. La Vera, riddled with streams, is a major producer of tobacco, vegetables, and goat cheese. The main historical interest is at Jarandilla and Yuste, but you find traditional architecture at any of the rural villages, and the landscapes are wonderfully serene. One of the prettiest villages is **Cuacos,** from where you can walk or drive 1 mile (1.6 km) uphill to the monastery.

Carlos V, depressed with court life and political intrigues, chose to retire to the simple Hieronymite in 1556 **Monasterio de Yuste** *(Cuacos de Yuste, www.yuste.org/ monasterio, tel 927 17 21 97, guided tour only).* He stayed until his death two years later.

Despite the apparent simplicity of the place (heavily restored after damage during the Peninsular War of the early 1800s), Carlos V did have a retinue of about a hundred servants, and had his bedroom built next to the chapel so that he could hear Mass from bed. (He had just retired from being the world's most

powerful man, after all.) The guided tour points out details such as the chair built specially for the gout-ridden emperor.

To complete this imperial tour, visit **Jarandilla,** just 3 miles (5 km) northeast of the monastery, where the magnificent 15th-century **castle** welcomed Carlos V while he awaited the completion of his quarters at Yuste. The **church of Jarandilla,** built by the Knights Templar, contains a baptismal font carved with the ancient Sanskrit sign of the swastika, and the castle stands on the ruins of the Templar fortress. Although austere from the outside, this Renaissance edifice conceals a gracious home centered on a verdant courtyard, and has become, not surprisingly, a *parador* (see p. 371).

Southeast of Plasencia lies the **Parque Natural de Monfragüe,** good for hiking, created to protect the rare flora and fauna of this region, notably Iberian lynxes, boars, badgers, imperial eagles, black storks, and numerous vultures. In 2003, it was enlarged to 453 square miles (1175 sq km) and became a biosphere reserve. ■

Jarandilla's castle, once a Templar fortress, is now a luxurious parador (state-run hotel).

Jarandilla
www.jarandilla.net
✉ Plaza de España
☎ 927 56 04 60

Parque Natural de Monfragüe
🅰 234 B3
Visitor information
www.monfrague.com
✉ Villareal de San Carlos (on Plasencia-Trujillo road)
☎ 927 19 91 34

Above: Steps from the Plaza Mayor lead up through the city walls into the immaculately preserved old town, a UNESCO World Heritage site.

Cáceres

THIS IS STORK CITY, WHERE THE RATTLING OF BEAKS AND voluminous nests are part and parcel of the old town. White storks nest on towers, chimneys, and TV antennae in spring and summer. They are visible all over Extremadura and La Mancha. Cáceres displays its noble past in a walled hilltop quarter where emblazoned facades, lofty towers, archways, and winding cobbled streets create an inimitable atmosphere.

Cáceres

🅜 234 B2

Visitor information

www.turismocaceres.org

✉ Plaza Mayor 3

☎ 927 01 08 34

🕓 Closed Sat. & Sun. p.m.

Museo de Cáceres

www.museosextremadura .com/caceres

✉ Plaza de las Veletas 1

☎ 927 24 72 34

🕓 Closed Sun. p.m., & Mon.

$ $. Free for E.U. nationals

The only drawback today is that the historical center is barely inhabited. To taste real life in this provincial capital you have to explore the **lower town,** which has an appealing, zesty atmosphere. It centers on a generous Plaza Mayor dominated by the town hall, where steps lead up to originally Moorish walls. Some of their rubble masonry towers are intact. At the **Arco de la Estrella,** an arch built by Manuel Lara de Churriguera in the 18th century, you can enter the **Torre de Bujaco** to see an exhibition on Cáceres history and climb to the ramparts for good views *(tel 927 24 67 89, closed Mon.).* Then enter the venerable old quarter at its heart, **Plaza de Santa María.** Go inside **cathedral de Santa María** *(Plaza de Santa María, tel 927 24 52 50)* to admire the Gothic vaulting, serene proportions, and Renaissance details. Just behind is the **Palacio de Carvajal** *(Calle Amargura 1, tel 927 25 55 97, closed Sun. p.m.),* home of the local tourist board. Enter the lovely courtyard, see the garden at the back, and don't miss the Moorish tower with fragments of 16th-century frescoes. In the lobby a model of old Cáceres gives a clear idea of the various palaces, as every detail has been painstakingly crafted.

Facing the cathedral across the square there are three beautiful Renaissance mansions, all of the honey and gray stone that is so typical of Cáceres: the **Palacio de Hernando de Ovando,** the **Palacio de Mayoralgo,** and the **Palacio Episcopal.** The first of these was built by the Ovando family. Nicolás Ovando was appointed governor of the Indies by the Catholic monarchs, taking over from Christopher Columbus and Francisco de Bobadilla. The palace now houses administrative offices and is closed to the public.

Stepped back from the cathedral to the south is the magnificent **Palacio de los Golfines de Abajo,** whose tower, in turn, overlooks Plaza San Jorge. The facade combines late-Gothic and platteresque decoration of the 15th and 16th centuries: Look in particular at the rooftop balustrade of carved birds and the medieval tower. Looming above the souvenir shops of the little plaza is a very different style of building, the whitewashed Jesuit **church of San Francisco Javier** *(Plaza de San Jorge 8, tel 927 24 51 71),* dating from the 18th century. Check out the art and photography exhibitions that are regularly held here.

At the top of the wide steps flanking the church is another delightful square, **Plaza de las Veletas,** centering on the church of **San Mateo** *(Open only for Mass),* built on the site of a mosque. Next to it stands the crenellated tower of **Casa de las Cigüeñas** (House of Storks), the only tower in this quarter not to have been lopped off—a sign that its owner, Diego de Ovando, was a supporter of Isabel in the civil war of the 1470s (see p. 31).

Opposite, on the south side of the square, is the elegant Casa de las Veletas, now the excellent **Museo de Cáceres.** Here you find a good collection of prehistoric and Roman artifacts, even a small

incised menhir (an upright prehistoric monumental stone) from the third millennium B.C., and regional ethnographic exhibits including beautiful weavings, lace, costumes, and ceramics. Downstairs is the star exhibit, an Arab ***aljibe*** (cistern) with perfectly conserved horseshoe arches. Across the garden a modernized annex displays fine art. Etchings by Picasso and Miró hang beside paintings by more recent Spanish artists; downstairs are 12th- to 19th-century works, a rather motley collection including "Jesus Salvador" by El Greco and an awkward "San Andres" by Luca Giordano (1634–1705).

Before leaving this square, notice the ivy-draped **Torre de los Plata,** behind San Mateo, then descend Calle Ancha past more emblazoned palaces to the *parador* (see p. 369), the former mansion of the Marquises of Torreorgaz. This is the perfect place to have a drink or a meal in a setting relevant to everything you have just seen. ∎

Right: Palacio de los Golfines de Abajo on Plaza de San Jorge, with the cathedral in the background

Trujillo

Trujillo
234 B2
Visitor information
www.trujillo.es
✉ Plaza Mayor
☎ 927 32 26 77

THIS DELIGHTFUL LITTLE TOWN IS A PLEASURE TO VISIT, with a network of fine old buildings, exuberant vegetation—cactuses, palms, olives, oranges, and magnolias—and plenty of life. Trujillo's renown, however, is due to one man: the conquistador Francisco Pizarro, who conquered the Incas of Peru. His statue (erected in 1927, and identical to one in Lima) reigns supreme over the Plaza Mayor, surrounded by palaces paid for with plunder from Latin America.

All Trujillo's narrow, winding streets eventually lead to this large, irregular square (actually more of a triangle). **Plaza Mayor** is the social hub of town, lined by sidewalk cafés, restaurants, and illustrious palaces. It is flanked by wide steps leading up to their porticoes, and the rather severe church of San Martín rises in the north corner.

Nuns now inhabit the 17th-century Palacio Carvajal-Vargas.

Opposite the church is the **Palacio Carvajal-Vargas** (or Palacio de Duques de San Carlos), a sober late Renaissance building. It was handed over to Hieronymite nuns (hermits of St. Jerome—a medieval religious order also called Jeronymite) in the 1960s, so public access is unfortunately restricted. Pull the bell chain in the entrance hall and a nun will open up, attempt to sell you cakes, and then wave you across the handsome patio toward the palace's most curious feature. The steps of this 17th-century staircase are not attached to the wall but held together by an interlocking structure, so earning it the name "flying."

At the other end of the square, the more ornate **Palacio del Marqués de la Conquista** was built by Hernando Pizarro, Francisco's brother. Its richly emblazoned corner, added in the 17th century, displays busts of the two brothers and their wives. From here you can walk up to explore the upper town by following the Cañon de la Cárcel, a passageway in the corner of the Palacio de la Justicia next to the Pizarro mansion. Go around the corner to your right and you come to the harmonious facade of the 16th-century **Palacio Orellana-Pizarro,** now a convent school. Francisco de Orellana was another of Trujillo's conquistadores, the first European to explore the Amazon. You can enter the beautiful patio for a small fee

Francisco Pizarro

The actions of this illiterate, illegitimate son of a captain eventually led to the death of an estimated five million Incas. In 1513, Pizarro (ca 1478–1541) accompanied another Extremaduran explorer, Vasco Núñez de Balboa, on his expedition to the Pacific, and from 1524 began searching the coasts of Ecuador and Peru for the legendary Incan empire. He discovered it in 1532, had the Incan emperor Atahualpa treacherously killed in 1533, and founded Lima in 1535. Pizarro's ambition and ruthlessness eventually turned against him, when he was assassinated by the followers of Diego de Almagro, a fellow explorer whom Pizarro had double-crossed. ■

and look for the ghost of Miguel de Cervantes, author of *Don Quixote* (see pp. 238–39), who once stayed here.

By circling this mansion into the Cuesta de la Sangre, you pass another imposing Renaissance palace, before turning left through the archway of Santiago. This brings you to the charming **church of Santiago,** where a Romanesque bell tower stands beside a basically Gothic structure. The scenic path beside the church takes you along the old town walls, built by the Moors in the 13th century to defend their 10th-century castle from Christian attacks. Views take in Trujillo's abundant stork population nesting on every available tower. The **castle** stands above, an imposing sight of crenellated walls and sturdy towers. There is little inside, however, except the revered statue of the Virgen de la Victoria, the patron saint of Trujillo, who can easily be seen from outside in her glassed eyrie.

Take Calleja de los Martires to the left and you soon come to the **Casa-Museo Pizarro** *(tel 927 32 26 77),* a 15th-century house where the conquistador was born. Inside, period furniture and conquistador memorabilia are shown with Inca artifacts. A few steps farther bring you to the Gothic **church of Santa María la Mayor,** which

holds the tombs of Trujillo's explorers. It also has a lovely main altarpiece painted by Fernando Gallegos. Climb the Romanesque bell tower for sweeping views over Trujillo's tiled roofs to the distant Sierra de Guadalupe. ■

Despite his misdeeds, Francisco Pizarro remains Trujillo's local hero.

Mérida

WITH A STREET NAMED AFTER JOHN LENNON, MÉRIDA, capital of the Autonomous Community of Extremadura is not exactly buried in its Roman past. It is a lively town that has been developing on the eastern bank of the Guadiana River ever since its founding in 25 B.C., after which it became capital of the Roman province of Lusitania. It has more Roman remains than any other Spanish town except Tarragona, and since 1986, a superlative museum has displayed the best of its Roman artifacts.

The most impressive sights are the **Teatro Romano y Anfiteatro** (Roman theater and amphitheater), both built of blocks of granite. The majestic colonnaded levels of the theater facing the semicircular terraced seats are absolutely magnificent. Go there in July or August to watch Mérida's theater festival, when the entire structure returns to its original function. It holds 6,000 spectators. A few yards away is the vast amphitheater, with a capacity for 14,000 people. This was used for gladiator combats, chariot races, and mock sea battles, for which the arena was flooded. Close by, the **Casa del Anfiteatro** displays the ruins of a third- to fourth-century villa still being excavated. Note the mosaic floors. Another villa, **Casa de Mitreo** *(Calle Oviedo, tel 924 30 15 04)*, a five-minute walk southwest, displays the beautiful Mosaico Cosmológico, a lyrical mosaic rendering of the Roman gods. The **basilica of Santa Eulalia** dates from the 5th century and contains the relics of the martyr, Santa Eulalia. Since 1990, major excavations have revealed the successive stages of its long history. It stands east of the Plaza de España *(Avenida de Extremadura)*.

The **Museo Nacional de Arte Romano** is opposite the

Mérida

🔼 234 B2

Visitor information

www.merida.es

✉ Paseo José Alvarez
   Sáez de Buruaga

☎ 924 00 97 30

🕐 Closed Sat. & Sun. p.m.

Teatro Romano y Anfiteatro

www.merida.es/nuvo_nuev.
   htm

✉ Paseo José Álvarez
   Sáez de Buruaga

☎ 924 31 25 30

💲 $ ($$ combined
   ticket includes Casa
   de Mitreo, Alcazaba,
   & Santa Eulalia
   excavations)

Built in 24 B.C., Mérida's Roman theater is the best preserved in Spain.

Museo Nacional de Arte Romano

✉ Calle José Ramón Mélida

☎ 924 31 16 90

🕐 Closed Sun. p.m. & Mon.

💲 $. Free Sat. p.m. & Sun. a.m.

The Roman art museum's stately brick building, constructed in 1986, looks as if the Romans themselves had a hand in it.

theater and amphitheater. This brilliantly conceived design by Rafael Moneo evokes Roman architecture in a purist, sympathetic style. Captions are in Spanish, but ask for a leaflet in English at the ticket desk. The vast, skylit main hall exhibits superb sculptures, architectural details, and mosaics, with two mezzanine galleries rising to one side. The first mezzanine concentrates on daily objects (glass, pottery, lamps, coins, dice) and the second, not to be missed, has thematic displays, including an exceptional section of sculpted heads. Huge mosaic panels add to the general impact. In the main hall, don't miss the beautiful seated figure of Ceres, goddess of agriculture, or the trio of the imperial family (Augustus, Tiberius, and Drusus, in the end alcove). In Section IX, look especially for the torso of Thorocatus, with its remarkable depiction of movement in the tasseled strips of his uniform.

End your visit in the **crypt** below, where ruins of first- and second-century houses with murals and tombs were found during construction of the museum. From

here, a tunnel leads directly into the amphitheater precinct.

From the museum, walk downhill (northwest) to the town center and turn left into Calle Sagasta. On your right you soon see the ruins of the **Forum** and then the magnificent **Temple of Diana.** Although named after the goddess of hunting, it was in fact dedicated to the cult of the emperor. Immediately behind is the Renaissance mansion of the counts of Corbos. Two blocks farther is the lovely **Plaza de España,** dotted with orange and palm trees. The **Town Hall** (1883) and the ceramic-faced folly of the **Palacio de la China** are particularly striking. The square has outdoor cafés, and is a good spot to relax before you visit the riverside **Alcazaba** *(Calle Graciano s/n, tel 924 00 49 08),* a ninth-century Moorish fortress incorporating Roman and Visigothic details. It has a majestic cistern built into the rock. From the Alcazaba you get wonderful views of the **Roman bridge,** its 60 arches stretching 866 yards (792 m) across the river. ■

Frontier towns

THE TOWNS OF OLIVENZA, JEREZ DE LOS CABALLEROS, and Zafra in southern Extremadura are close to two borders: that of Portugal across the Guadian River, and that of the vast sweep of Andalucía to the south. History here is inextricably linked to this strategic position and to the Christian Reconquest of Muslim land. As a result this pastoral landscape is dotted with fortresses.

OLIVENZA

Nudging the Portuguese border in a sea of olive groves, the fortified town of Olivenza was actually in Portuguese hands for six centuries. This has left it with an interesting dual character. The castle, with a mighty keep rising nearly 100 feet (30 m), was built by Juan II of Portugal in the 15th century; its royal bakery now houses the **Museo Etnográfico** *(Plaza de Santa María, tel 924 49 02 22, closed Mon., & Sun. p.m.)*. The **church of Santa María Magdalena** is Spain's only example of 16th-century Manueline Gothic, a

The frontier towns display a distinct Portuguese flair, seen here at Jerez de los Caballeros.

Portuguese style. The spiraling columns, slender rib-vaulting, *azulejos* (tiles), and genealogical tree of the Virgin crowning the altar are outstanding features. Close to the Puerta de los Angeles stands the Casa de la Misericordia, notable for a chapel faced in illustrative azulejos.

Seven miles (11 km) north of Olivenza stand the ruins of the 1,246-foot (380-m) **bridge of Ajuda** across the Olivenza River. Built by Manuel I of Portugal, it frequently became a battleground in the wars fought over this region.

JEREZ DE LOS CABALLEROS

About a 50 miles (80 km) southeast, Jerez de los Caballeros became a stronghold of the Knights Templar after being captured from the Moors in 1230. In the hilltop town center, the sumptuously carved bell tower of San Miguel (1749) rises over the Plaza de España. Here, too, is the Templar castle, with Moorish remains still visible in the renovated structure. Other landmarks are the 1759 **church of San Bartolomé** *(Plaza de San Bartolomé)*, a dazzling combination of inlaid ceramic and gilt, and **Santa María** *(Llano de Santa María)*, both with ornate baroque towers. Keys for both churches are at the tourist office. The pretty whitewashed streets produced one of Extremadura's adventurers, Vasco Núñez de Balboa (1475–1517), the first European to cross the Central American isthmus

Left: Zafra's *parador,* **the former Alcázar, has a Renaissance patio by Juan de Herrera.**

Olivenza

 234 A2

Visitor information

www.olivenza.es

✉ Plaza de España

☎ 924 49 01 51

🕓 Closed Sat., Mon. & Sun. p.m.

Jerez de los Caballeros

🅰 234 A1

Visitor information

www.jerezdeloscaballeros.com

✉ Plaza de la Constitución 4

☎ 924 73 03 72

🕓 Closed Sat. & Sun. p.m.

Zafra

🅰 234 B1

Visitor information

www.zafra.es

✉ Plaza de España 8B

☎ 924 55 10 36

🕓 Closed Sat. & Sun. p.m.

and see the Pacific. Jerez is famous for colorful celebrations during Semana Santa (Holy Week), and for its pork festival in May, when sausages and *jamón ibérico* (Iberian ham) abound. Several dolmens (prehistoric stone tombs) are in the area. The most striking is the **Dolmen del Torriñuelo** *(5 miles/8 km northeast of town at La Granja).*

ZAFRA

About 30 miles (50 km) east of Jerez de los Caballeros is Zafra, which some call a miniature Sevilla. Zafra has a wonderfully homogenous 18th-century center full of whitewashed houses, and larger, mansions, their architectural details picked out in saffron yellow.

The town's history started with the Moors, but fame and fortune came in the 1440s following construction of a massive stone castle, the **Alcázar,** by the Dukes of Feria. Although this is now a *parador* (see p. 372), you can visit the vast, graceful Renaissance patio (the work of Juan de Herrera, architect of El Escorial, see pp. 79–81). Ask to see

the superb gilded *artesonado* ceiling of the chapel, and have a drink beneath the more sober Mudejar ceiling of the bar. In front, the **Plaza Corazón de María** descends to a web of streets leading to the interconnecting **Plaza Grande** and **Plaza Chica.** These charming arcaded squares are the sleepy heart of Zafra. Palm trees dominate the former, and the old town hall (1750) the latter.

Rising above the roofs one block west is the unmistakable bell tower of the Renaissance **church of La Candelaria** *(Calle Tetuán, tel 924 55 01 28).* Inside are altarpieces by Francisco de Zurbarán (1598–1664), who was born nearby, and Juan Ramos Castro; also here is a small museum. Zafra's other architectural jewel, **Plaza del Pilar Redondo,** is dominated by the present **town hall** *(tel 924 55 45 01),* which occupies a 16th-century Franciscan convent. Enter the patio to admire the arcaded structure, and then, for a contrast, look at No.14 on the square, an idiosyncratic art nouveau house completely faced in turquoise tiles. ■

More places to visit in Castilla-La Mancha & Extremadura

ALMAGRO

Smack in the middle of Don Quixote country, Almagro is a small town with a long history. Mansions, monasteries, and churches surround the focal point of the **Plaza Mayor,** a beautiful arcaded rectangle. At No. 17 is Europe's oldest continuously used theater, the 16th-century **Corral de Comedias** *(Plaza Mayor 18, tel 926 86 15 39, closed Mon., $).* You can look inside, or, better still, see a play here during the festival of classical drama every July.

In the 13th century, Almagro became the base of the Knights of Calatrava, one of the military orders that fought for the Reconquest (see pp. 28–31). Their seat was the stunning castle of Calatrava la Nueva (19 miles/30 km south of Almagro on Carretera de Calzada de Calatrava, tel 926 22 13 37, closed Mon., $). Extensive vineyards have replaced the battle-

Talavera de la Reina's blue and yellow *azulejos* **(tiles) are justifiably famous, here put to decorative use in the park.**

fields of old, and red peppers, tomatoes, and eggplant are grown for the local specialty, pisto manchego (eggs, peppers, tomatoes, and eggplant fried together in La Mancha style).
🅼 235 D2 **Visitor information,** www.ciudad-almagro.com ✉ Plaza Mayor 1 ☎ 926 86 07 17

SIGÜENZA

In the far north of Castilla-La Mancha, near the border with Aragón, this lovely hilltop town is dominated by its castle (now a hotel), and fortresslike Romanesque cathedral. The old town is a labyrinth, but if you keep going up you eventually reach the 16th-century Plaza Mayor and the **cathedral.** Look for the poignant alabaster sculpture on the tomb of El Doncel, Isabel I's page, and the countless cherubim decorating the sacristy ceiling by Alonso de Covarrubias (1488–1570).
🅼 235 E4 **Visitor information,** www.siguenza.com ✉ Ermita del Humilladero, Paseo de la Alameda ☎ 949 34 70 07

PARQUE NACIONAL DE LAS TABLAS DE DAIMIEL

Nineteen miles (30 km) northeast of the city of Ciudad Real is one of Spain's hidden gems, Tablas de Daimiel, an area of marshy wetlands formed by the Guaiana River. This ornithologists' paradise has breeding aquatic birds from April to July, and huge flocks of migrants from September to January. You might see various species of duck, purple heron, and great crested grebes. Guided visits are on foot or by jeep.
🅼 235 D2 **Visitor information,** www.lastablasdedaimiel.com ✉ Parque Nacional de Daimiel, 11 miles (18 km) north of Daimiel ☎ 926 85 03 71 or 902 52 02 00

TALAVERA DE LA REINA

Talavera is renowned for one thing: ceramics. Be prepared for the feast of color, above all in the form of the *cacharro* (drinking jar). Talavera's production of handpainted glazed *azulejos* (tiles) blossomed in the 15th century, and Talaveran techniques were taken to Mexico by Spanish colonists. West of the center are ceramic workshops where you can buy tiles and domestic ware. Other sights in town include a Roman wall, extended during the Middle Ages, four Gothic-Mudejar churches, and the **Basílica de la Virgen del Prado** *(tel 925 80 14 45),* where almost every surface is blanketed with azulejos.
🅼 235 C3 www.turismo.talavera.org ✉ Ronda de Cañillo ☎ 925 82 63 22 ∎

Sounds of flamenco and echoes of the Moors accompany you through the vast open spaces of Andalucía. Sevilla, Córdoba, and Granada synthesize the past, while the coast draws millions of sun worshippers.

Andalucía & Murcia

Decorative tile in Sevilla

Andalucía & Murcia

WILD, RUGGED SIERRA, VERDANT VALLEYS, ACRES OF OLIVE GROVES, SNOWY peaks, the blue Mediterranean, dazzling white hill villages, and a succession of Moorish castles and Renaissance mansions…these are the seductive ingredients of the vast swath of Andalucía. Together with neighboring Murcia, it covers 38,063 square miles (98,583 sq km), sweeping across from the Portuguese border and the Atlantic Ocean past the towering Sierra Nevada peaks to the lunar landscapes of southeastern Spain and the Mediterranean. Andalucía's southernmost tip is a mere 9 miles (14 km) from Africa, so it is not surprising that its history, climate, and topography have so many African influences.

This was the last part of Spain to be relinquished by the Moors when the Catholic Monarchs, Fernando and Isabel, swept southward. They finally united Spain in 1492 by conquering the Moors' last stronghold, Granada. Non-Christians were driven out of Spain, but the Moors did not all leave, and their skills gave rise to Andalucía's own form of Mudejar architecture.

Well before the first independent Arab kingdom emerged in Córdoba in 756, Phoenicians, Greeks, Romans, and Visigoths had joined the region's original Iberian and Tartassian inhabitants. Archaeological finds at Orce, in eastern Andalucía, turned up a fragment of what could be a 1.5-million-year-old human skull, the earliest human fossil in Europe, still much disputed.

Despite its past, Andalucía remains a laggard in Spain's economic tables, notching up a 12 percent rate of unemployment. This is most visible in

p. 233

the provinces of Cádiz and Almería. *Latifundios* (vast estates) are one reason, the economic downturn and a surfeit of building are others, but climatic duress also contributes to the region's problems. In inland areas, July and August see temperatures over 105°F (40°C), and drought has reached dramatic proportions in recent years. All the stereotypical images of Spain come from Andalucía: fiestas, siestas, flamenco, bullfights, and a relaxed approach to life—and there is some truth in them.

The flip side of an easy-going attitude is corruption, which in Andalucía has spawned Spain's worst coastal eyesores. Nonetheless, Andalucía has a string of unmissable cities: Sevilla, Córdoba, Granada, and Malaga, each with spectacular (and well-maintained) monuments, superb tapas, and modernized services. Smaller towns, too, such as, Jerez de la Frontera, Ronda, Úbeda, and Baeza, not only reflect Spain's so-called Golden Age, when the booty from the New World financed Andalucía, but are also highly rewarding.

When you become monument weary, you can refresh your eyes in this region's virgin landscapes, from the marshes and dunes of Doñana to the Alpujarras (the lovely foothills of the Sierra Nevada), the green Sierra de Cazorla, and the undulating desert of the southeast corner, home of spaghetti Westerns. The high-speed AVE train helps, connecting Madrid with Cordoba, Seville, Malaga, and, in 2010, Cádiz.

Lowland Andalucía divides into two halves,

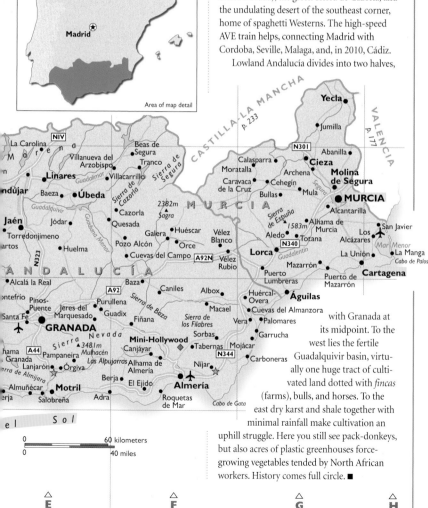

with Granada at its midpoint. To the west lies the fertile Guadalquivir basin, virtually one huge tract of cultivated land dotted with *fincas* (farms), bulls, and horses. To the east dry karst and shale together with minimal rainfall make cultivation an uphill struggle. Here you still see pack-donkeys, but also acres of plastic greenhouses force-growing vegetables tended by North African workers. History comes full circle. ∎

Sevilla (Seville)

Sevilla (Seville)

🅰 260 C3

Visitor information

www.turismo.sevilla.org

✉ Avenida de la
   Constitución 21b

☎ 95 422 14 04

🕐 Closed Sun. p.m.

SEVILLA IS A CITY OF 700,000 EXTROVERTS WHO REVEL IN flamenco, bullfighting, processions, fiestas, and tapas. The town center resembles a mosaic of stage sets, each plaza prettier than the next, with its colorful baroque church and orange trees. Discreet alcove shrines and shady tiled patios point to a more secret life, but the overwhelming characteristic is one of openness and conviviality.

The negative side of Sevilla's charm is the inevitable commercialization of the center. In the Barrio de Santa Cruz district (see p. 265), steer clear of the more touristy restaurants, and watch your wallets, bags, and cameras. That said, relax and take your time. Lose your way in the whitewashed streets, and enjoy the daily life of the shops, markets, music, and bars that boom into the night.

Sevilla's history began with the Romans. Extensive ruins of Itálica, where the emperors Hadrian and Trajan were born, lie 6 miles (10 km) northwest. Remnants of Hispalis, the Roman settlement of Sevilla itself, include the aqueduct (best seen in the Callejón del Agua, in the Barrio de Santa Cruz), and the columns and statues of Hercules and Julius Caesar

on the Alameda. Hercules was Sevilla's legendary founder; Julius Caesar was the real one. The Moors disembarked in 711. It took four centuries for Sevilla to reach its zenith under the rule of the Almohad dynasty, who left a lasting influence on architectural style. From the sumptuous royal palace (Reales Alcázares) and the Casa de Pilatos to endless tiled walls, Sevilla is a dazzling window on an artistry still practiced today.

The end of this golden period came in 1248 when King Fernando III of Castile captured Sevilla from the Moors, but Sevilla soon prospered again following the European discovery of America in 1492. The Atlantic Ocean is only 56 miles (90 km) away down the

Guadalquivir River, and Sevilla's port saw Ferdinand Magellan, Juan Sebastián Elcano, and Christopher Columbus set sail. The immense riches brought back in their holds financed many of the city's monuments. The 20th century had two high points: the 1929 Ibero-American Exhibition and the 1992

World's Fair. The first has survived best. The latter, a motley assembly of postmodern architecture on the Isla de la Cartuja, is best forgotten. Seville's latest innovation is a large pedestrianized area around the cathedral, traversed by tram. Bike lanes are also multiplying; try a saddle-bound guided tour.

Colorfully painted *azulejo* tiles adorn Plaza de España, built for the 1929 Ibero-American Exhibition.

View from La
Giralda over
Sevilla and the
cathedral rooftop

**Catedral de Sevilla
& La Giralda**

catedralsevilla.es

✉ Avenida de la
Constitución
(entrance at Plaza
Virgen de los Reyes)

☎ 95 421 49 71

🕐 Closed Sun. a.m.

💲 $$

CATEDRAL & LA GIRALDA

The cathedral is outwardly ungainly but it has many treasures, not least being the Giralda tower rising majestically on one side. The Giralda, Sevilla's finest relic of the Almohad dynasty, served as the minaret for the Aljama, the mosque on the site of which the cathedral was built.

La Giralda was completed in 1198 by the architect Ali de Gomara. It suffered damage from an earthquake in 1365, then in the 16th century acquired a Renaissance belfry with 25 bells of differing ages, and finally the weather vane, from which its name derives. Inside the 322-foot (98-m) tower is a ramp that enabled the *muezzin,* a Muslim crier whose job is the call to prayer, to go up on horseback to make his call to prayer. Lesser mortals must climb up on foot, but the effort is repaid by stupendous views over Sevilla.

You enter both La Giralda and cathedral through a large patio dotted with orange trees and edged by horseshoe arches on two sides, which is all that remains of the mosque. From here a double arch, one Arab and one Gothic, leads inside the world's third largest cathedral (after St. Peter's in the Vatican and St. Paul's in London), an overpoweringly scaled combination of late Gothic and Renaissance styles. It took more than a century to build, from 1403 to 1506. Start at the **high altar,** a staggering work of Flemish art incorporating 2.5 tons (2.4 tonnes) of gold from Mexico and Peru. This

alone took 35 years to complete. The detailed carving is magnificent but difficult to see from a distance, so take binoculars.

Behind you, the **choir** is another artistic feat, with beautifully carved 15th- and 16th-century choir stalls of Cuban mahogany. Look up into the transept dome to see ornate stonework dating from after the Lisbon earthquake of 1778, when this section collapsed and was rebuilt. The vivid stained-glass windows show that the building period spanned a change in style: The upper row is Gothic and the lower one Renaissance.

To the right of the transept stands the tomb of Christopher Columbus—after years of controversy and rivalry, DNA testing proves his remains lie here, not in the vast mausoleum of Santo Domingo, in the Dominican Republic. In the sacristy rooms is the cathedral's dazzling **treasury.** You see paintings by Murillo, Zurbarán, and Goya (the only Goya in Sevilla), silver and gold chalices, reliquaries, and processional crosses laden with jewels, a beautiful 12th-century portable altar, and a massive monstrance. This later section of the cathedral has an oval **chapter house,** the first such construction in Europe. The cathedral's last surprise is the **Capilla Real,** entered separately from the plaza, which houses the much revered 12th-century statue of the Virgen de los Reyes, the patron saint of Sevilla.

BARRIO DE SANTA CRUZ

Immediately east of the cathedral lies a charming web of streets and little squares. The Barrio de Santa Cruz developed as the Jewish quarter from 1248, when Sevilla was taken from the Moors, and remained so until 1492, when Jews were expelled from Spain. Around 400 families lived here in a self-contained ghetto with their own judiciary and synagogue, although they still paid taxes to the Crown. Today, Santa Cruz has a very different image, firstly being a desirable residential quarter, as it has been since the 17th century, and secondly being heavily geared up for visitors.

It makes an attractive stroll though, and you pass typical flower-covered Sevillian patios on the way, particularly along the **Callejón del Agua.** Head for **Plaza de Santa Cruz,** the site of the main synagogue, which was later converted into a church and, in turn, destroyed by Napoleon's troops. Between this plaza and the cathedral is the impressive baroque **Hospital de los Venerables** *(Plaza de los Venerables, tel 95 456 26 96),* founded as an asylum for priests, with superb frescoes by Valdés Leal and his son Lucas in the church. The hospital is owned by the Focus cultural foundation and stages concerts and exhibitions.

All the world's a stage in Sevilla.

Pools were both extravagant and luxurious in Sevilla's hot, dry climate.

Reales Alcázares
www.patronato-alcazarse
villa.es
✉ Plaza del Triunfo
☎ 95 450 23 24
🕐 Closed Mon.
💲 $

REALES ALCÁZARES

Sevilla's rulers did themselves proud, as this royal palace complex displays a masterful combination of Moorish techniques and Catholic symbols—the ultimate example of Mudejar architecture. One of Europe's oldest royal palaces, it is still used by the king of Spain.

The oldest surviving parts of the Alcázar were built by the Almohad dynasty, but long before that the Roman acropolis was here, then an early Christian basilica, and a Moorish castle. What you see today is essentially the work of Pedro I, who ordered its construction in 1362, about the same time as the Nazrid Palace was being built in Granada's Alhambra (see pp. 300–305). A century or so later Isabel I added a wing, and another

century on Emperor Carlos V built an adjoining palace for his young Portuguese bride.

From the entrance (where it is advisable to rent audioguide headphones), your first sight is the **Patio de las Doncellas,** a beautiful arcaded patio of exquisite cedarwood marquetry, original *zelij* tiling, and intricate stucco. The upper story, now the king's official residence, and the adjacent **Salón de Carlos V,** with its beautiful mahogany *artesonado* (coffered Mudejar ceiling), are both 16th-century additions. Whenever you see red-and-gold paintwork, you are seeing 19th-century restoration. The Moorish and Mudejar palette was essentially blue and green.

The most masterfully worked rooms lie off the far side of the patio, a maze of interconnecting bedrooms and reception rooms. At their center is the stunning **Salón de Embajadores** (Ambassadors' Hall), topped by an exceptional cedarwood cupola with images of the Catholic Monarchs on the balconies. Horseshoe arches lead to a luminous dining room overlooking the garden: Note the more delicate decoration here, the work of Persian artists after the original hall burned down in a fire. Next is the delightful **Patio de las Muñecas** (Dolls' Patio—so-called for its diminutive size), also known as the Patio de la Reina (Queen's Patio) because it has pierced screens for court women to look through, just as harems did. The open upper gallery was for musicians. Off this lie the modest bedrooms of Fernando and Isabel and of their son, Don Juan.

From the tiled chapel flanking Pedro I's palace, you cross gardens to enter **Palacio de Carlos V,** a complete contrast in scale, with lifeless decoration dominated by tapestries (1740) of the Conquest of

Tunisia. Keep moving, however, and you enter the magnificent **Jardines del Alcázar** (gardens) beside Mercury's Pool, backed by decorative volcanic rock. This is the perfect place to wander, among the perfumes of aromatic plants, magnolias or orange trees in flower, and the sounds of trickling water.

PARQUE DE MARÍA LUISA

In 1893, María Luisa, Duchess of Montpensier, gave most of the vast grounds of Palacio San Telmo to the city. The 1929 Ibero-American Exhibition was staged here, so the 94-acre (38 ha) park is riddled with architectural curiosities.

Start at the **Palacio de San Telmo,** built in 1734 as the first nautical school in the world and later the palace of the Dukes of Montpensier. It is now home to the Andalusian government. Just beyond looms the imposing **Fábrica de Tabacos** (Tobacco Factory, now part of Sevilla University), the setting of Prosper Mérimée's story *Carmen* (1845), on which Bizet's opera was based.

The park is crisscrossed with roads and paths connecting the numerous structures that were built here for the 1929 Ibero-American Exhibition. Each building has found a subsequent function, whether as consulate, museum, art school, flamenco school, or police station (the Brazil pavilion). Spain's national pavilion reigns in splendor around the semicircular **Plaza de España.** Designed by Aníbal González, this outsized masterpiece of neo-Andalusian baroque uses brick and handpainted tiles (from Valencia, Toledo, and Sevilla) with generous abandon. Each Spanish province is represented in a tiled illustration of its historical highpoint, and three pretty bridges span the surrounding water channel. Don't miss the fabulous *artesonado*

(marquetry) ceilings above the lateral staircases into the pavilion, and give the Gypsy fortune-tellers a wide berth.

Walk 300 yards (275 m) south to Plaza de América, site of two museums. The **Museo de Artes y Costumbres Populares** in the grandiose Mudejar Pavilion *(Plaza de América, tel 95 471 23 91, closed Sun. p.m.–Tues. a.m.)* is worthwhile for its ceramics exhibit on the lower floor, although the display of costumes and furniture above is rather dull. The **Museo Arqueológico** in the plateresque Pavilion *(Plaza de America, tel 95 429 82 58, closed Sun. p.m.–Tues. a.m.)* has a superb collection ranging from Phoenician statuary and the gold Carambolo Treasure through Roman works to Mudejar ceramics. ■

Sevilla's favorite taxi service: a horse-drawn carriage

Moorish architecture

Although nearly all the mosques of the Moors were demolished after the Christian Reconquest, other structures such as palaces and bathhouses survived. The architectural elements they introduced to Spain became integrated into Hispanic architecture.

VAULTS & DOMES

Domes were a common feature in Moorish architecture, and they are best seen today in the remaining bathhouses. Developed in the Middle East in the eighth century, these single-story structures had domed and vaulted roofs perforated by star-shaped openings for ventilation and light. The most luxurious bathhouse in Spain is that of the Alhambra in Granada (see pp. 300–305), where white marble columns and floors combine with glazed wall tiles, plaster, and timber. Good examples of public baths can also be seen in Ronda, Girona, and Granada's Albaicín.

HORSESHOE ARCHES

The quintessential Moorish arch is horseshoe-shaped, its most memorable example being in Córdoba's Mezquita. Although the Mezquita is based on the Great Mosque of Damascus, its superimposed tiered arches are said to have been inspired by Roman aqueducts. Builders recycled Visigothic and Roman columns and capitals, while creating a sensation of infinite space. Alternating bands of stone and red brick in the arch itself add even greater visual dynamism. Repetitive horseshoe arches can also be seen in Toledo's Santa María la Blanca synagogue, and blind horseshoe arches on facades were extensively used by Mudejar craftsmen. Later extensions brought other arch designs: the trefoil, multilobed, pointed horseshoe, and pointed arch.

Ornate brickwork and blind arches face La Giralda in Sevilla.

MINARETS

The muezzin's call to prayer came from lofty minarets built next to mosques. Spain's most impressive remaining example is that of Sevilla, the main al-Andalus base for the orthodox Almohad dynasty. This was designed by Ahmed ibn Baso, who repeated its form at the Koutoubia Mosque in Marrakesh. The square tower, known as La Giralda, is faced in sebka brickwork, the repetition of small arch forms. The same use of brick patterning was multiplied by Mudejar craftsmen in the intricately faced towers of Teruel and at Zaragoza's La Seo cathedral.

STUCCO

The sculptural quality of plaster combined with powdered marble (stucco) produced acres of walls carved with arabesque and floral patterns, edged by bands of Kufic calligraphy. Stucco's fragility meant that it was applied only to upper walls, archways, and ceilings. The apogee of stucco complexity is found in the Nazrid Palace of the Alhambra, where *muqarnas* (resembling honeycomb and stalactites) dripping from star-shaped domes create a dazzling optical effect.

AZULEJOS

Glazed tiles were extensively used for surfacing dados (lower walls) in Moorish and Mudejar buildings. Their bold colors and geometric patterns create a strong visual contrast with the more delicate appearance of the stucco-faced upper walls. Geometry was one of the Arabs' greatest skills, and their talent for multiplying basic star forms can be seen in the incredible variations of their *azulejo* designs. Ceramics were also incorporated into Mudejar decorative brickwork. ■

Superlative stuccowork on rhythmical arches (above) and intricate tile inlays (right) are examples of the zenith of Moorish decoration reached at the Alhambra. Below left: A typical horseshoe arch of cut stone surrounds a studded wooden door in Granada's Sacromonte. Below right: Stucco, tiles, and arches create a visual feast of receding perspectives.

The ground floor of the Casa de Pilatos showcases Mudejar artistry.

More places to visit in Sevilla

CASA DE PILATOS

Another fantastic example of Mudejar architecture, the intriguing Casa de Pilatos lies northeast of the Alcázar and cathedral. Built by the Marqués de Tarifa in the 15th to 16th centuries, it was erroneously thought to be a copy of Pontius Pilate's villa, hence the name.

The main patio presents an exceptionally harmonious combination of stuccowork, tiles, *artesonado* (coffered) ceilings, and marble and tiled floors. The same artistry continues in deserted rooms that lead to luxuriant gardens on both sides. In the garden to the left of the main patio, an incongruous Italian loggia is the wing of the palace where the 18th Duchess of Medinacelli and her family still live. Here and throughout the palace are numerous very fine Roman busts and statues, most of which were brought from Rome. The peaceful and well-tended garden to the right of the patio makes a wonderful spot for relaxing beside the fountain during Sevilla's long hot afternoons. Don't miss the gilded artesonado ceiling in the neighboring study, nor the spectacularly worked dome above the main staircase. On the upper floor (sometimes closed for private use), wait for a guide to walk you through a completely different universe, that of the Spanish Renaissance.
🅰 263. www.turismo.sevilla.org ✉ Plaza de Pilatos ☎ 95 422 52 98 💲 $$. Free Tues. p.m. for E.U. citizens

HOSPITAL DE LA CARIDAD

The Hospital of Charity is a few steps west of the cathedral, behind the Teatro de la Maestranza, Spain's prestigious operatic and musical venue. In 1625, a repentant, formerly dissolute aristocrat, Miguel de Mañara, became head of the brotherhood of La Caridad and founded the hospital and church. Both are wonderful examples of Sevillian baroque.

In the church you can see the paintings Mañara commissioned: seven superb works by Murillo created for the site (four others were looted by Napoleon's troops), and two compelling paintings by Valdés Leal.
🅰 263. www.santa.caridad.org ✉ Calle Temprado 3 ☎ 95 422 32 32 🕐 Closed Sun. p.m. 💲 $. Free Sun. a.m. for Spanish nationals.

MONASTERIO DE LA CARTUJA

The Isla de la Cartuja, site of Expo '92, is of little interest other than for the vast and venerable Carthusian monastery that has stood here since

1428. Once a visited by every Spanish monarch who came to Sevilla, it lost its function in 1836, when Church property was seized by the state. An Englishman set up a porcelain factory on the site, the result being a line of chimney stacks connected to the kilns, which remained active until 1982. Since then, La Cartuja has become government property and extensive restoration has created a unique place. A pristine contemporary art center installed beside the orchards stages innovative shows, and the Mudejar church successfully displays contemporary paintings (José Manuel Broto, José María Sicilia) beside beautiful original features and the monks' quarters. In 2004 it was the setting for Seville's first biennial of contemporary art.

A patio in the Museo de Bellas Artes

🅐 263. www.turismo.sevilla.org ✉ Isla de la Cartuja, Avenida Américo Vespucio 2 ☎ 95 503 70 96 🕐 Closed Mon. & Sun p.m 💲 $. Free on Tues. for E.U. citizens.

MUSEO DEL BAILE FLAMENCO

Opened in 2006 by Seville with the great flamenco dancer, Cristina Hoyos, this high-tech museum is a real eye-opener on the tradition. Interactive exhibits, costumes, projections, photos, paintings, and soundtracks of the inimitable rhythms and voices all create an evocative universe. Sign up for a class or, less actively, hire a flamenco group for an evening from the museum's extensive database.

🅐 263. www.flamencomuseum.com ✉ Calle Manuel Rojas Marcos 3 ☎ 954 34 03 11 💲 $.

MUSEO DE BELLAS ARTES

This museum, transformed from a 17th-century convent in 1841, displays Sevilla's best painters. It is laid out around three patios with two floors connected by an imperial staircase. The Aljibe cloister is particularly interesting for its central well and Sevillian tilework. Although the nucleus of the collection is the Sevillian school of painting that flourished in the 17th century, you can sidetrack to look at medieval art. Sevilla's 20th-century output is less interesting.

Rooms 3 and **4** on the lower floor are crucial—they hold mannerist works by Francisco Pacheco, who exerted such an influence on his students Diego Velázquez (1599–1660) and Alonso Cano (1601–1667). Cano's wonderful painting of the "Souls of Purgatory" and Velázquez's "La Casulla a San

Ildefonso," in which the Virgin was modeled on Juana Pacheco, his wife and the daughter of his teacher, hang there also. **Room 5** moves into the baroque world of Murillo, perfectly represented in the reconstructed altar of the Convento de los Capuchinos, and the subtly executed "Virgen de la Servilleta" (Virgin of the Napkin, so-called because it was allegedly painted on Murillo's dinner napkin). Head for the upper floor to see the intense, colorful canvases of Juan de Valdés Leal (1622–1690) in **Room 8,** and the master of monks, Francisco de Zurbarán, represented in **Room 10** by monastery altarpieces.

🅐 263. www.cica.es ✉ Plaza del Museo 9 ☎ 95 421 95 00 🕐 Closed Sun. p.m.–Tues. a.m. 💲 $. Free for E.U. nationals. ∎

Semana Santa

Spain's most important festival is not Christmas, but Holy Week (Semana Santa). The entire week from Palm Sunday to Easter Sunday is one long and spectacular demonstration of mourning, enacted with high Catholic color, fervor, and exoticism. In any village of Andalucía you might encounter midnight processions with hooded, torch-bearing penitents, or, in brilliant sunlight, see crowds of villagers clutching palm fronds before a venerated statue of Christ. *Pasos* (floats) of highly realistic figures in theatrical poses are the focal point, although in some places the week culminates in the ceremonial burning or exploding of an effigy of Judas.

In the words of the travel writer Jan Morris, "There are few spectacles on earth to match the holy parades of Malaga or Seville." The main protagonists are parish brotherhoods (*cofradías*), whose penitential origins go back to the 15th century and who spend the preceding year preparing costumes and floats. The sculptures of the elaborate floats, usually focusing on a sorrowful Virgin Mary and a

Easter procession of penitents at Baeza, near Granada

tortured Christ, are life-size figures (some dating from the 16th and 17th centuries) dressed in embroidered robes and surrounded by flowers, palm fronds, and candles. Beneath them labor the cassocked *costaleros* (carriers), accompanied by hooded *nazarenos* (penitents) atoning for their year's errors.

Sevilla has 57 brotherhoods, 116 floats, and more than 50,000 nazarenos, who slowly advance in turn along a preset route from their *barrio* (quarter) to the cathedral. The weeklong commemoration reaches a climax early on Good Friday, when the most venerated statues of the Virgin Mary and of Christ are carried by six specific brotherhoods. With the penitents, worshippers and onlookers come the inevitable bands. Usually composed of wind and percussion instruments led by an obsessive drum beat, these bands are sometimes interrupted by the penetratingly deep wail of a *saeta*, a song that originates in flamenco. Traditionally, these agonized notes from the crowd impose an immediate silence and halt—signs both of respect for the vocalist and solidarity in his or her prayer. However, the saeta is often prearranged, giving the costaleros a break for a drink and cigarette. Although religious passions run deep, the Sevillian Semana Santa is also about enjoyment, a prelude to the hedonistic Feria that takes place two weeks later. ■

Penitents

Although a royal decree in 1777 banned acts of medieval penitence and self-abasement, many have survived. In San Vicente de la Sonsierra (Rioja), you see penitents indulge in self-flagellation using strips of linen to beat their bare backs, pricked to facilitate bleeding and avoid blood congestion. Equally extreme are the acts of the *empalaos* in Valverde de la Vera (Extremadura) who cover their backs, torsos, and arms with thick rope before being bound to a cross-shaped plough and dragged through the stages of the Passion. ■

Hooded penitents follow a *paso* (float), illuminated by candles, that bears a realistic statue of the crucified Christ (above), while other participants (below) take Holy Week in a lighter vein.

Jerez de la Frontera

Cartujano horses and their elegant riders demonstrate intricate dressage techniques. Jerez's Royal Andalusian School of Equestrian Art offers frequent performances.

THIS LIVELY LITTLE TOWN MAY SMACK OF SEVILLA (ONLY 62 miles/100 km to the north), but it has its own raisons d'être: sherry, flamenco, and horses. No fewer than nine sherry bodegas are open for visits, the Royal Andalusian School of Equestrian Art is world famous for equestrian shows, and two Gypsy quarters (San Miguel and Bulería) perpetuate the traditions of the legendary flamenco dancer Lola Flores, a native of Jerez.

These are the things that set Jerez apart, but it also has an impressive old walled **Alcázar** (*Alameda Vieja, tel 956 31 97 98*), containing a well-conserved mosque, beautifully restored baths, and shady gardens. This abuts the baroque **Villavicencia palace,** where you can climb up to a camera obscura projecting a bird's-eye view of the townscape below. The lovely Palacio Atalaya houses a clock museum, the **Museo de Relojes** (*Calle Cervantes 3, tel 902 18 21 00, closed Sun. p.m. & Mon., $$*), where 302 17th- to 19th-century clocks and watches from Italy, Austria, France, and England strike in unison every noon. The surrounding gardens also contain a small sherry museum. The

pedestrianized center has numerous beautiful baroque mansions and interesting old churches to discover as you roam. The **cathedral** (*Plaza de la Encarnación, tel 956 34 84 82, closed Sun. p.m.*) is a dignified combination of baroque styles.

Flamenco (see pp. 294–95) is nurtured at the **Centro Andaluz de Flamenco** (*Palacio Pemartín, Plaza San Juan 1, tel 956 34 92 65, closed Sat. & Sun.*), a dance school and museum where you can see videos of past flamenco stars. Come to Jerez in September to catch the Feria de la Bulería, Spain's greatest flamenco festival, with some of the most renowned practitioners.

Bulls and horses are part and parcel of the Jerez landscape. Jerez

Jerez de la Frontera
⚠ 260 B2
Visitor information
www.turismojerez.com
✉ Alameda Cristina s/n
☎ 956 34 17 11

Real Escuela Andaluza del Arte Ecuestre

www.realescuela.org

✉ Avenida Duque de Abrantes

☎ 956 31 80 08

🕐 Closed Sat.–Sun.

💲 $ (training); $$/$$$ (dressage show)

Bodega González Byass (Tio Pepe)

www.gonzalezbyass.es

✉ Calle Manuel M. González 12

☎ 956 35 70 16

🕐 Closed Sun. p.m.

💲 $$

Sanlucar de Barrameda

www.visitasdonana.com

✉ Fabrica de Hielo, Avenida Bajo de Guia

☎ 956 36 38 13

Almonte

✉ Calle Alonso Pérez

☎ 959 45 06 16

even has a bull museum, **Museo Taurino** (*Calle Pozo del Olivar 6, tel 956 31 90 00, closed p.m. & Sun., $*), but your priority should be the **Real Escuela Andaluza del Arte Ecuestre.** This equestrian academy was founded in 1973 to train dressage riders, all of whom use the Andalusian horse, the Cartujano, originally bred in the 18th century by Carthusian monks. You can watch morning training sessions on Mondays, Wednesdays, and Fridays (plus Tuesdays in winter), and then visit the stables and saddlery. Try to be here for the Thursday performance (also on Tuesdays in summer) of dancing horses mounted by riders in stunning 17th-century costumes. In May, Jerez has its Feria del Caballo (Horse Fair), with horse shows, dancing, and parades of horsedrawn carriages.

Andalucía takes great pride in sherry, as you might guess from the huge sherry barrels (each with with a capacity of 130 gallons/500 liters) sitting outside bars here and in Sevilla. Sherry drinkers already know the names Sandeman, Pedro Domecq, Harvey, and González Byass, all mainstays of Jerez's economy. A visit to a bodega is enlightening. One of the best is **Bodega González Byass** near the Alcázar, where you see a structure designed by Gustave Eiffel (designer of the Eiffel Tower in Paris), and barrels signed by the likes of Orson Welles, Winston Churchill, General Franco, Margaret Thatcher, Steven Spielberg, and the entire Spanish royal family. All visits are followed by a tasting.

PARQUE NACIONAL DE DOÑANA

Just 14 miles (22 km) northwest of Jerez lies the vast expanse of Spain largest's national park. Covering 195 square miles (500 sq km), it was created in 1969 to protect wetlands edging the Guadalquivir river, 31 miles (50 km) of coastal sand-dunes and inland pastures and scrubland rich in wildflowers. There is a rich wildlife population, including endangered mammals (Iberian lynx, mongoose, red deer) beside wild horses and bulls, and rare birds such as the imperial eagle. Spring and autumn bring huge flocks of migratory birds to the lagoons and marshes, perfect for birdwatchers.

Tours can be made by boat, by jeep, on foot, or on horseback. Of the entry points, the most accessible from Jerez is at Sanlúcar de Barrameda and from Seville, Almonte. ■

Sherry

Sherry (the English corruption of 'Jerez') is a blended wine whose origins go back to the Phoenicians. Records show that it was produced by the Moors and exported to England in the 12th century. Although the Koran forbids alcohol, Arabs used it for medicinal purposes. The sherry trade blossomed in the 17th and 18th centuries, when London merchants became closely involved, as they have been ever since. Today, over 30 percent of Jerez's exports go to England. The next biggest markets are Holland and Germany, and lagging far behind is the United States.

Sherry is unique. It is made from palomino grapes that thrive on the chalky soil and local climate, and then aged in casks of American oak, in which old and young sherries are periodically mixed. The four main categories are: *fino*, the driest and lightest in color; *amontillado*, still dry but with greater body and more depth; *oloroso*, medium dry and a rich golden color; and *dulce*, the sweetest of all, whose color resembles a port. ■

The old town of
Cádiz stretches
picturesquely
along the seawall
of a promontory.

Cádiz and Costa de la Luz

CÁDIZ IS TRULY OUT ON A LIMB. IT SITS ON A NARROW
tongue of land curving northward on the Costa de la Luz—the coast
of light. Over the millennia, this seagirt site was much coveted by
Phoenicians, Greeks, Romans, Visigoths, and Arabs. Even today,
Cádiz has an end-of-the-world feel, although recent regeneration is
changing this. The opening of the high-speed AVE train-line, in 2010,
will give more impetus.

Cádiz

ⓜ 260 B1

Visitor information

✉ Avenida Ramón de
Carranza

☎ 956 20 33 91

🕐 Closed Sun.

Museo de Cádiz

www.juntadeandalucia.es
/cultura/museos

✉ Plaza de Mina

☎ 956 20 33 68

🕐 Closed Sun. p.m.
& Mon.

💲 $. Free for E.U.
nationals.

The Phoenicians founded Cádiz
around 1100 B.C., which makes it
Europe's oldest city. Its moment
came in the 18th century, when
Sevilla's port on the Guadalquivir
River silted up and left Cádiz as
Spain's main trading port with the
New World. In 1812, the city had its
moment as Spain's capital when a
republican constitution briefly saw
the light of day there.

Once you have penetrated the
peripheral shell of modernity, you
find a harmonious old center of
baroque churches (stuffed with gilt
altarpieces) and elegant mansions,
many of them painted in delicate

pastel colors and sporting ornate
wrought-iron balconies.

Cádiz has few great monuments
or sights, but it makes a relaxed
stopover where traditions are still
strong. Artisans carve wooden
furniture and gild baroque frames,
cafés align bottles of olive oil to
drizzle over morning toast, and in
the old part of the town, a network
of narrow alleyways reeks of Arab
urbanism, particularly in **Barrio
de la Viña,** an excellent area for
flamenco and seafood restaurants.
The silhouettes of ocean liners
moored in the port have a certain
romance too. In summer, when the

wind drops, head for the beaches of fine white sand on the west coast of the peninsula.

The most visible of Cádiz's churches is the cathedral whose tiled dome towers over the Plaza de la Catedral *(tel 956 28 61 54, museum, closed Mon., Sat., and Sun. p.m., $)* and which took 116 years to complete. The resulting mix of styles is not the most compelling, although it displays some impressive baroque paintings. You can climb the Poniente bell-tower for inspiring views over the city and ocean. Close by are the remains of a first century B.C. Roman theater *(tel 956 26 47 34, closed Tues.),* another sign of the city's great age.

West of here, the sea-wall leads to an unusual bastion with a castle, the Castillo de San Sebastián, jutting out into the sea.

One place you should not miss is the **Museo de Cádiz,** which has an impressive collection of archaeology and fine arts. Head straight for **Room 2** to see a pair of Phoenician marble sarcophagi dating from the fifth century B.C. These magnificent life-size tombs, with distinct echoes of Egypt, were unearthed almost a century apart. They lie in serene splendor beside sophisticated terra-cotta busts of gods, amphorae, and Etruscan pieces. Next door, bright, skylit **Room 4** exhibits fine Roman statues including an imposing one of the emperor Trajan, dating from A.D. 98 to 117. The painting collection on the upper floors has its marvels, too, above all Zurbarán's series of portraits of monks, each one expressing a different personality. Murillo, Zurbarán, Rubens, and a string of 20th-century artists from Joan Miró to Chema Cobo (born in 1952 in Tarifa) occupy the other rooms of this grandiose mid-19th-century building.

The museum overlooks the lush and shady Plaza de la Mina, full of centennial ficus trees. On its southwestern flank stands the birthplace of the great Spanish composer, Manuel de la Falla (1876–1946) whose tomb is in the cathedral crypt. Follow Calle Zorrilla from the northeastern corner to discover some of Cadiz' best tapas bars before ending at the gardens of the Alameda overlooking the Atlantic.

If sleepy most of the year, Cádiz really makes up for it in February—Carnival time. Brimming with ingenuity, satire, and song, costumed carnival groups flock to the more traditional barrios such as La Viña, El Populo, Santa María (near the cathedral), and Mentidero. Cádiz' other big secular moment celebrates the football calendar, at the end of August, with all-night barbecues on the beach.

South of Cádiz stretches a coastline of golden beaches and dunes backed by pine forests and inland pastures grazed by bulls. Kitesurfing (formerly windsurfing) is king in these choppy waters, above all close to Tarifa, the southernmost point, while surf- and bodyboarding come in a close second at El Palmar beach. For hikers there are shady trails cutting through pine-forests with tantalising glimpses of the ocean below. The one drawback is the wind, which at certain times of year becomes irritating. This does not put off hundreds of illegal African immigrants who land at night from tiny fishing-boats, though many drown.

Wind aside, this coast has attractive villages, beautiful scenery, and, as yet, little beach development except around **Conil de la Frontera** and **Tarifa.** Conil, a once elegant, traditional town has spawned a sprawling family resort due to its calm, shallow water. Immediately south stretches the

Conil de la Frontera

✉ Calle Carretera 1

☎ 956 44 05 01

Tarifa

✉ Paseo de la Alameda

☎ 956 68 09 93

Long golden beaches define Costa de la Luz, Andalucía's Atlantic coast south of Cádiz.

Vejér de la Frontera

✉ Avenida de los Remedios2

☎ 956 45 17 36

beautiful **El Palmar** beach where surfers' cafés and a few restaurants nestle behind the dunes. At the southern headland a lighthouse marks **Cabo de Trafalgar** (Cape Trafalgar) where British admiral Horatio Nelson trounced the French-Spanish fleet in 1805 and died in the process.

About 5 miles (8 km) inland from here is the stunning hill village of **Vejér de la Frontera.** Much targeted by Northern Europeans for holiday homes, it has also spawned a whole new town along the ridge. Yet a potent medieval atmosphere prevails in the walled upper part surrounding the old castle and the attractive church of San Salvador. A well-preserved Jewish quarter is on Calle Cobijadas, by the walls. Some aristocratic mansions have become boutique hotels while bars and restaurants are proliferating around the Plaza de España down below. This is the ideal spot to relax in front of an ornately tiled fountain. Just outside town, contemporary art is scenically presented at the NMAC Foundation *(Carretera A48/N340, tel 956 45 51 34, $$)*. You can head due north of Vejér to **Arcos** to connect with the *pueblos blancos* circuit (see pp 280–81).

To the south, between Cabo de Trafalgar and Barbate lies a 4,940-acre (2,000 ha) nature reserve, the **Parque Natural La Breña y Marismas de Barbate,** where pines, junipers, scrub, and salt-flats are much favored by gulls, rock doves, kestrels, barn owls, and cattle egrets. Further south down the coast, beyond another popular resort, **Zahara de los Atunes,** and one of Spain's largest wind-farms, lies **Playa de Bolonia,** a beautiful sweep of beach complete with the Roman ruins of **Baelo Claudia** *(tel 956 68 85 30, closed Mon.)*. Founded in the second century B.C., this town was closely linked with trade with North Africa (visible across the Strait) and with fish-salting.

Overlooking the Strait of Gibraltar, **Tarifa** has seen better days as cheap apartment blocks now rim the outskirts. The plazas and alleys of the old-walled town still have character. Tarifa was actually the first Arab settlement in Spain, in 711. Morocco is only 9 miles (14 km) away and with plans afoot to build a railway tunnel, this may become even closer. The tentative date is 2025. In the meantime, most of the action comes from foreign surfers. There is some good whale- and dolphin-watching through a Swiss research foundation *(tel 956 62 70 08, www.firmm.org)*. ■

Ronda

THIS IS ANDALUCÍA'S GREAT CLIFF-HANGER: RONDA straddles a gorge with a sheer 325-foot (100 m) drop down to the Guadalevín River. Over the gorge (known as El Tajo) stretches the Puente Nuevo, or "new bridge," connecting the old and new parts of town—"new" being only relative, as the latter quarter dates from the 18th century. Ronda is a popular town with extensive facilities for visitors, including numerous antique shops, yet it retains a powerful atmosphere if you avoid the crowded summer months.

The secret plazas and cobbled streets of **Old Ronda** are very evocative, and you can visit several mansions. One of the prettiest and most intimate is the **Palacio de Mondragón** *(Plaza de Mondragón, tel 95 287 84 50, closed Sat. & Sun. p.m.),* now housing a small museum. This was built in 1314 as the residence of the great Moorish king Abb el Malik. Fernando and Isabel stayed here in 1485, and the palace acquired its present facade in the 18th century.

Of the many patios, the most outstanding is the Mudejar courtyard, rich in craftsmanship in brick, marble, tiles, and wood. From there a horseshoe arch leads to a charming garden. A few steps from the mansion is the stately **Parque Duquesa de Parcent,** overlooked by the church of **Santa María la Mayor** *(tel 95 287 22 46),* which was built over a mosque, and the Renaissance **town hall,** with an impressive loggia.

Downhill (east) from here on the main road looms a Nazari-style minaret that now belongs to the church of San Sebastian. To the south stands a section of the old Arab walls with their double gateway: the Moorish **Puerta de Almocabar** and the Renaissance **Puerta de Carlos V.** At the bottom of the hill to the east lie the restored **Baños Árabes** (Arab Baths). If you walk down to them on Calle Santo Domingo, you pass

the beautiful facade of the **Palacio del Marqués de Salvatierra** with its curious sculptures of naked children, thought to be pre-Columbian figures.

In the new town, don't miss the venerated bullring, the **Plaza de Toros,** where man has been pitting his wits against bulls since 1785. On display inside, in the **Museo Taurino,** are dazzling toreadors' jackets and capes encrusted with beading, sequins, and braids, beside photos of historic matadors, fights, deaths, and aficionados such as Orson Welles. ∎

Ronda
🅜 260 C2
Visitor information
www.turismoderonda.es
✉ Paseo de Blas Infante
☎ 95 218 71 19
🕐 Closed Sat. & Sun. p.m.

Baños Árabes
www.turismoderonda.es
✉ Calle San Miguel
☎ 95 287 08 18

Plaza de Toros & Museo Taurino
www.rmcr.org
✉ Calle Virgen de la Paz
☎ 95 287 41 32
💲 $

Bandits held court here from the early 18th to 20th centuries.

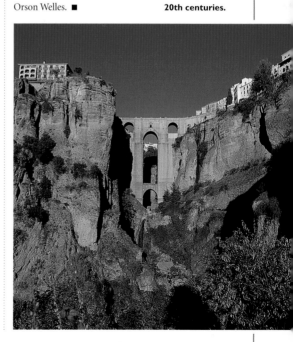

A drive through *pueblos blancos*

This drive takes you through the dramatic Sierra de Grazalema Natural Park from west to east, stopping at typical white villages (pueblos blancos) before arriving at Ronda, the most inviting of them all.

Arcos de la Frontera ① *(Visitor information, Plaza del Cabildo, tel 956 70 22 64),* first settled by the Romans, is the western gateway to this region, with roads radiating in all directions from its spectacular clifftop site. Negotiating the narrow, winding streets of Arcos by car is an art in itself, so allow time to climb up on foot to the main square. On one side is the **church of Santa María,** a beautiful Gothic-Mudejar building with plateresque details; on the other is a *mirador* (lookout point) with views over orchards and olive groves. Here, too, are the Moorish walls of the **Castillo de los Duques** and numerous baroque and Renaissance facades.

Leave Arcos on the beltway by following signs for the A372 to El Bosque, 17 miles (27 km) away. You go through densely farmed land of vegetables, olive groves, and horse ranches, and eventually the Sierra de Grazalema comes into view. Scenery becomes increasingly spectacular as you arrive at **El Bosque** ②,

huddled at the base of the mountains. This center for hikers, rock climbers, trout fishers, and hang gliders consists of a handful of cafés and a waterwheel grouped around a bridge over El Bosque River. Cross this and turn right after the bar to reach the parking lot from where you can walk to the visitor center of the **Parque Natural de la Sierra de Grazalema** *(Oficina del Parque Natural de la Sierra de Grazalema, tel 956 71 60 63).*

Leave El Bosque on the A372 and after 1 mile (1.6 km) watch for a turnoff on the left to Grazalema. From here the road climbs immediately through eucalyptus and pine trees, and the soil becomes chalkier. You soon see the village of **Benamahoma** ③ on your left. Views open up over the valley, and forests alternate with rock. Views of the stark, granite-capped peak of **Monte Simancón** (5,134 feet/1,565 m) accompany you to the pass, the **Puerto del Boyar** ④ (3,618 feet/1,103 m),

Arcos de la Frontera, set on a crag above the Guadalete River

where you can park to admire the superb perspective of mountain ridges receding to the west and buy honey from local vendors. This is classic territory for roe deer, mountain goats, Griffon vultures, and eagles. Also here is the Spanish fir *(pinsapo)*, a rare species that grows only above 3,280 feet (1,000 m) and is a survivor from the forests of the Tertiary era.

As the road snakes down, you catch sight of **Grazalema** ⑤ *(Visitor information, Plaza de España 11, tel 956 13 22 25)*, a dazzling sight of whitewashed houses, tiled roofs, and church towers wedged between the sierras of El Pinar and El Endrinal. Opposite is the rocky outcrop of El Reloj (The Clock). Drive down into the village, cross the main square, and turn right at the church into the parking lot (invaded by a market on Tuesday mornings). Then start exploring this immaculate village, its houses thick with layers of whitewash and its streets well endowed with bars, restaurants, and churches. The neoclassic **church of La Aurora** is the one with the octagonal tower; the other churches are the **Encarnación** and **San José,** which was once a Carmelite monastery and is built over a mosque.

Leave Grazalema by continuing on the A372 marked Ronda (20 miles/33 km). After 1 mile (1.6 km) a turnoff to the left, signed to **Zahara,** is a worthwhile detour if you can face more than an hour of truly tortuous bends. Otherwise continue on the A372 down through a rock-strewn valley with striking views of Grazalema perched high above. Cork- and holm-oak forests line the road as you cross into the province of Málaga, and views gradually open up to farmland dotted with white *fincas* (farms). Turn right toward Ronda when you reach the first junction, and then turn right again onto the A376. As this twists rapidly downward past steep granite cliffs on the right, **Ronda** (see p. 279), set dramatically over a gorge, appears on the horizon. ■

- 🗺 See area map pp. 260–61
- ► Arcos de la Frontera
- 🔄 47 miles (76 km)
- 🕐 3 hours (with short visits)
- ► Ronda

NOT TO BE MISSED
- Arcos de la Frontera
- El Bosque
- Puerto del Boyar
- Grazalema

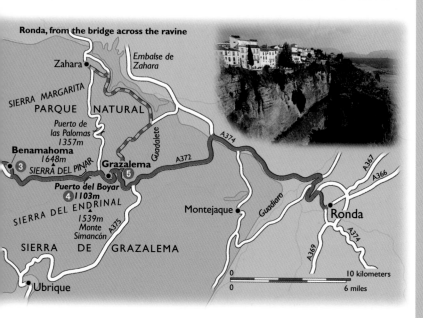

Ronda, from the bridge across the ravine

Zahara

Embalse de Zahara

SIERRA MARGARITA

PARQUE   NATURAL

Puerto de las Palomas 1357m

Benamahoma 1648m ③

Guadalete

Grazalema ⑤

SIERRA DEL PINAR

A372

A374

A367

A366

Puerto del Boyar ④ 1103m

SIERRA DEL ENDRINAL

1539m Monte Simancón

Montejaque

Guadiaro

Ronda

A374

SIERRA   DE   GRAZALEMA

A375

A369

Ubrique

0   10 kilometers
0   6 miles

Antequera

Antequera
🗺 260 D2
Visitor information
www.antequera.es
✉ Plaza San
  Sebastián 7
☎ 95 270 25 05
🕐 Closed Sun. p.m.

El Torcal
🗺 260 D2
Visitor information
www.eltorcal.com
✉ Centro de
  Interpretación
☎ 95 203 13 89

IT SEEMS APT THAT THE TOWN AT THE GEOGRAPHICAL heart of Andalucía also claims the greatest number of churches of any town in Spain. Antequera also lies in an exceptionally beautiful spot, with the spectacular rock formation of El Torcal to the south.

Crowned by the **Alcazaba,** or Moorish castle, the white houses of Antequera spill down the hillside, their tiled roofs spiked with some 30 church steeples. The one you must see is the **church of El Carmen** (*Plaza del Carmen, tel 95*

Eroded limestone shapes at El Torcal create a surreal landscape for hiking.

270 25 05, closed Sun. p.m.), which has delicate 16th- to 17th-century wall paintings, polychrome statues, a Mudejar coffered ceiling, and, best of all, a masterfully carved main altarpiece, one of Andalucía's finest baroque works. Walk uphill, through the 16th-century **Arco de los Gigantes,** to the **Colegiata de Santa María** (*Closed Sat. & Sun. p.m., & Mon.*), an early example of Andalusian Renaissance architecture, with another impressive Mudejar ceiling. From here you can walk up through the landscaped gardens of the Alcazaba to the tower, **Torre del Homenaje** (*Closed Mon.*) for wonderful views.

Back in the center of town, don't miss the graceful Palacio de Nájera, one of many noble mansions, now converted into the **Museo Municipal** (*Plaza Coso Viejo, tel 95 270 40 51, closed Sat. & Sun. p.m., & Mon.*). The main exhibit is a superb first-century Roman bronze statue of a boy. Take the Málaga road out of town to three dolmens (stone tombs). The **Cueva de Menga** and **Cueva de Viera** (*Carretera de Málaga, closed Sun. & Tues. p.m.*), the most impressive, date from about 2500 B.C. One mile (1.6 km) farther on is the slightly younger **Romeral** (*Closed Sun. & Tues. p.m.*), dating from about 1800 B.C.

Older than all of these is **El Torcal,** 8 miles (13 km) south, where 6.5 square miles (17 sq km) of calcareous rock have been eroded into extraordinary shapes. Well-marked hiking trails lead through this fantasy landscape. ∎

Málaga

THIS CITY OF OVER HALF A MILLION PEOPLE HAS AN animation and atmosphere of its own, and Malagueños are known for their exuberance, which peaks during their August feria. The port was frequented by Phoenicians, Romans, and Moors. Cargo ships and ferries still dock there; however, the buzzword today is Picasso.

Crowning a hilltop in the center of town is the Moorish **Alcazaba.** Its many towers and walls enclose the former palace, which is now the **Museo Arqueológico.** Enjoy the views but don't forget to go inside to see the Mudejar-style carved and painted ceilings, fine Roman pottery, mosaics, and Arab ceramics, appropriate echoes of the mixed architectural elements of the fortress. At the entrance below is a **Roman theater**—a venue for summer concerts. Higher still than the Alcazaba, the 14th-century castle of **Gibralfaro** gives sweeping views over the town and the harbor. Part of it is now a *parador* with an inviting panoramic terrace.

Much of Málaga's attraction lies in its easy, breezy walking areas, from the **Paseo Marítimo** beside the town beach to the luxuriant gardens, tiled benches, and duck ponds of the **Paseo del Parque** leading to the leafy **Alameda.** As pony carts trot by, flower vendors set up their stands under towering centennial trees in front of elegant 19th-century buildings. Running north from the Alameda is the marble-paved shopping street, **Marqués de Larios,** which ends at the Plaza de la Constitución. The web of narrow pedestrian streets on both sides bristle with little restaurants, bars, and small stores selling books, clothes, and antiques. Three blocks west of Marqués de Larios, the bustling mock-Mudejar market, **Mercado**

Fountain in the Plaza de la Constitución with the cathedral in the background

Málaga
⬛ 260 D2
Visitor information
www.malagaturismo.com
✉ Pasaje de Chinitas 4 Alameda Principal 23
☎ 95 221 34 45
95 221 60 61
🕐 Closed Sat. & Sun. p.m.

Alcazaba & Museo Arqueológico
✉ Calle Alcazabilla
☎ 95 212 20 20
🕐 Closed Mon.
💲 $

Museo Picasso

✉ Palacio de Buenvista
Calle San Agustín 8

☎ 93 256 30 00
93 256 30 22 (tour reservations)

🕐 Closed Mon.

💲 $

de Atarazanas, has wonderful fresh produce and a real curiosity: a 14th-century stone arch, all that survives of the Moorish arsenal.

The **cathedral** *(Calle Molina Larios, tel 95 221 59 17, closed Sun.)* is a must. Although its second tower was never built (the bishop of the time apparently siphoned the funds to aid the American Revolution), the cool late Renaissance interior has great harmony. Cupolas crown the three naves, with spectacular choir stalls carved by Pedro de Mena. Dazzling white marble sculptures by Juan de Salazar vie with those of the retrochoir (facing the main doors), the work in 1802 of the brothers Pissani. In the **gardens** at the back, the church of **El Sagrario** houses a magnificent plateresque altarpiece by Juan Balmaseda and has an ornate Isabelline-Gothic portal.

A short walk northeast of here is Málaga's latest jewel, the **Museo Picasso,** which opened in 2003. This long-awaited homage to the town's native son, Pablo Picasso (1881-1973) is housed in a beautifully renovated Renaissance mansion, the Palacio de Buenavista. The sleek modern extension was designed by Richard Gluckman (who designed Pittsburgh's Andy Warhol Museum) and Spanish architects Isabel Cámara and Rafael Martín Delgado. The collection stems from Picasso's daughter-in-law, Christine Ruiz Picasso, and his grandson, Bernard, who together donated 155 works by the great man, as well as 89 long-term loans. The result is an electrifying display, hung chronologically starting with "Woman with Mantilla" (1894), moving through his Blue and Pink periods to Cubism, with numerous depictions of the many women in his life, and ending with "Man, Woman and Child" (1972). Many of the works have never been on public display before—look out for "Olga

Seated" (1923) and "Geometrical Still Life with Music Score" (1921). Relevant temporary exhibitions are displayed in a vast hall in the annex. A café and a leafy patio offer welcome respite. This wonderful setting was chosen partly for its proximity to Picasso's childhood home, just five minutes walk away along a winding pedestrianized street. The **Casa Natal de Picasso** *(Plaza de la Merced, www.fundacionpicasso.es, tel 95 206 02 15, closed Sun. p.m.)* is an elegant house on a rather scruffy square. The pristine, renovated interior tells you nothing about his life, but displays ceramics, enlarged photos, and small-scale works (exhibited in rotation). The lower floor is used for art exhibitions.

Málaga's contemporary venue is the **CAC** (Centro de Arte Contemporáneo)*(Calle Alemania, tel 95 212 00 55, www.cacmalaga.org, closed Mon.)*, a dynamic exhibition center modeled out of the old wholesale market building which stands beside the river. Artists featured in the permanent collection include Roy Lichtenstein, Frank Stella, Susana Solano and Juan Uslé, and there is a lively program of exhibitions by younger artists.

Malaga's hotels have multiplied to accommodate a flood of art and business visitors, and with the new high-speed AVE link to Madrid, facilities will expand further. Andalucía's largest shopping-center is already in place.

Four miles (7 km) north of Málaga is a botanical garden, **Finca de la Concepción** *(Carretera de las Pedrizas Km 166, tel 95 225 07 45, closed Mon.)*, a vast collection of palms and exotic plants that was started in the 1850s and has flourished in the mild, humid climate. Pools and Roman statues add to the charm, and a *mirador* (lookout point) gives views across the city to the Mediterranean. ∎

Costa del Sol

STRETCHING FROM GIBRALTAR EASTWARD TO ALMERÍA, this much visited coast has its highs and its lows. The coast west of Málaga has been intensely developed but still has interesting corners, and even glamour at the jet-set resort of Marbella.

Fuengirola
🗺 260 D1
Visitor information
www.fuengirola.org
✉ Avenida Jesús Santos Rein 6
☎ 95 246 74 57

East of Málaga, the coast is less built up, but still has eyesores. One major exception is **Nerja,** *(Visitor information, Puerta del Mar 2, tel 95 252 15 31)* an attractive resort town 3 miles (4.5 km) from Málaga, with a cave complex, **Cuevas de Nerja** *(Carretera de Maro, tel 95 252 95 20).* The chambers, with their stalactites and stalagmites, stretch for 2,625 feet (800 m). Background music dispels the mystery somewhat, but you can see Paleolithic rock paintings in the upper chamber.

Southwest of Málaga is **Torremolinos,** a jumble of high-rises packed with bars, shops, discos, and other facilities for vacationers. **Fuengirola** has more of the same, but it also has the ruins of a Moorish castle and nearly 4 miles (6 km) of beach. If you like water sports, this is a good place to be. Five miles (8 km) inland is the beautiful and well-preserved hill village of **Mijas,** once a haunt of artists but now suffering from a tidal wave of visitors from the coast. Sights include the remains of Arab walls and the 17th-century hermitage of the Virgen de la Peña, but the chief attractions are the town's geranium-laden balconies, craft shops, and wonderful views—all easily seen by donkey taxi.

Next stop west along the coastal highway is **Marbella,** the most glitzy and upscale resort in Spain. A steady flow of top-of-the-range cars cruises along the "Golden Mile" past endless bars and chic hotels. Inside are Marbella's Michelin-starred restaurants where tables are

hot property. The old and pretty center radiates from the Plaza de la Constitución, with a 16th-century town hall and fountain, and a castle, **Castillo de Madera.** Its nightlife is the hottest on the costa, and the gastronomy is highly rated.

San Pedro de Alcántara was the ancient Roman colony of Silniana, destroyed by an earthquake in A.D. 365. You can see well-restored structures and a sixth-century **Visigothic basilica** here. San Pedro also has a lovely beach and several golf courses, and it is the start of the long, tortuous, but magnificent drive of 31 miles (50 km) through rocky landscapes, woods, ravines, and isolated villages up into the Serranía de Ronda. ■

The Sierra de Tejeda looms behind Nerja.

Marbella
🗺 260 D1
Visitor information
www.marbella.com
✉ Glorieta de la Fontanilla
☎ 95 277 14 42

San Pedro de Alcántara
🗺 260 D1
Visitor information
www.sanpedroalcantara.ne/sanpedro
✉ Avenida Marqués del Duero 69
☎ 95 278 52 52

All forms of
transportation
can be found
near Córdoba's
Mezquita
(mosque).

Córdoba

THERE IS SOMETHING SPECIAL ABOUT CÓRDOBA, SLIGHTLY
off the tourism trail between the Sierra Morena to the north and the
Campiña agricultural plains to the south. A plethora of souvenir shops
surrounds the Mezquita, Córdoba's greatest monument, but otherwise
it is very unspoilt. Head through the twisting alleys and strike out
into the backstreets and you find the true spirit of Andalusian life.

Córdoba
🅰 260 D3
Visitor information
www.cordobaturismo.es
✉ Caballerizas Reales 1
☎ 957 20 01 59

With a population of little more
than 300,000, Córdoba is a small
city. It was the capital of Roman
Spain and of a Moorish kingdom,
but ruins of Roman and Moorish
structures remain unexploited due
to lack of funds. The city endures
baking temperatures in July and
August, when shady patios become
essential oases. This climactic
adversity has not prevented a string
of festivities. During Holy Week
(see pp. 272–73) processions invade
the narrow streets. In May, the Feria
(festival) takes place, and the entire
population seems to be involved in
crucifix-decorating, patio contests,
and pilgrimages. Córdoba's
legendary bullfighters and flamenco
dancers spring into action. The
sultry summer months bring long

evenings of flamenco music in
various gardens of the city.
    The Romans founded the town
in 169 B.C., but it was under Islamic
dominance that Córdoba reached
its zenith. In 756, Abd ar-Rahman I
founded Córdoba as capital of
Moorish Spain. By 929, when Abd-
ar-Rahman III declared himself
caliph, it had become the envy of
Europe. About 1,000 mosques, 600
public baths, public street lighting,
and a renowned university graced
the city, where philosophers, poets,
mathematicians, and doctors
(including the great Jewish thinker,
Maimónides) created an intellectual ferment. Decline came in the
11th century after the skillful but
ruthless reign of Al-Mansur. Al-
Andalus fragmented into petty

taifas (kingdoms), although intellectual life continued until 1236, when Córdoba was conquered by Fernando III.

From then on it was a steady downward slide. Ingenious Moorish waterworks were abandoned and every mosque except the Mezquita was replaced by a church. In the 16th and 17th centuries, Córdoba's artisans of embossed leather and silver were much sought after, but plague decimated the population in the 17th century.

It is an easy city in which to orient yourself, although you may get lost in the Judería, the old Jewish quarter. Bordered to the south by the Guadalquivir River, Córdoba radiates from the Mezquita and the labyrinthine Judería. Few sights lie outside this area, but it is worth exploring the barrios to the east: Their modest houses have produced famous bullfighters and flamenco artists. Outside town is the Medina Azahara, epicenter of Córdoba's golden age.

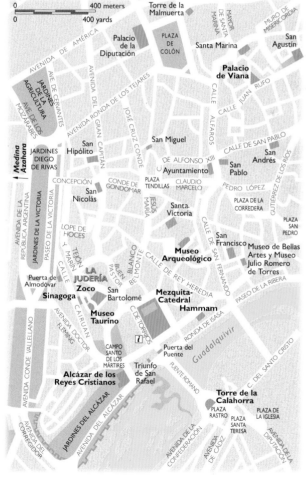

MEZQUITA

Mezquita
www.turismodecordoba.org
/mezquita.htm
✉ Calle Torrijos
☎ 957 47 05 12
🕐 Closed Sun. a.m.
💲 $$

Alcázar de los Reyes Cristianos
www.turismodecordoba.org
/alcazar.htm
✉ Calle Caballerizas Reales
☎ 957 42 01 51
🕐 Closed Sun. p.m. & Mon.
💲 $. Free on Fri.

The jewel in Córdoba's crown is still called by its Arabic name, Mezquita, meaning "mosque," despite the extraordinary intrusion of a Catholic cathedral in its midst. It is the only mosque left from medieval Spain, and it is one of the largest in the world.

The vast, walled Mezquita covers 258,330 square feet (24,000 sq m). Building started in 785, it was extended in 848 and 961, then almost doubled in size in 987. Your first sight is from the **Puerta del Perdón,** an immense gateway beside the baroque belfry that encloses the old minaret. In front is the beautiful **Patio de los Naranjos,** dotted with orange trees whose fragrant blossoms in April are unforgettable. Once you enter the oldest part of the mosque, you understand why Charles V ordered that the building be saved, despite immense pressure from the Church to demolish it. It is a visual masterpiece of rhythmical horse-shoe arches that somehow gives the sense of infinity that underlies Islamic belief. Each of the 824 columns is different, as are their capitals, since they were mostly salvaged from previous Roman and Visigothic structures. The two-tiered arch was copied from Roman aqueducts for structural purposes and to increase the light. Notice the alternating bands of red brick and white stone, and their painted imitations in the later, northern section, built with inferior materials under the aegis of power-crazy Prime Minister Al-Mansur.

Penetrate the interior, passing the cathedral on your left, and you come to the end wall, the **Kibla,** which should face Mecca (southeast of Córdoba) but actually faces due south. The Mezquita's most stunning piece of craftsmanship is here, the **mihrab,** or prayer niche, from which the imam (Muslim prayer-leader) would lead worshippers in prayer. Look carefully at the exquisite mosaics and dome decorated by Byzantine craftsmen, and the entire *maqsura,* the marble-flagged space that was once reserved for the caliph and his courtiers. Koranic texts are engraved into marble cornices, and you can see Spain's earliest stucco tracery—later to become a major feature of Nazrid and Mudejar architecture.

From here you move to the **Tesoro,** a comparatively heavy baroque chapel containing Córdoba's massive silver and gold monstrance, made by Enrique de Arfe in 1516. It weighs 270 pounds (122 kg), and since 1518 has had an annual airing at Corpus Christi. Turn around from here to see the 14th-century **Capilla Real** (Royal Chapel), built under Alfonso X and sympathetically decorated in Mudejar-style stucco. Then you get to the carbuncle of the Mezquita, the Renaissance-baroque **cathedral** (1523–1617) that was plunked down in the center of the mosque, thus destroying much of its unique harmony. The only real interest here lies in the beautifully carved **choir stalls** (1750). On leaving, take time to look at the exquisitely carved outer doorways on Calle de Torrijos (by the Mezquita's western wall), where an elevated walkway once joined the caliph's palace.

A few steps southwest of the Mezquita lies the **Alcázar de los Reyes Cristianos** (Fort of the Christian Kings), which was built in 1328 after the Christian Reconquest

of Córdoba. Fernando and Isabel used this fortified palace as their base in 1491–92 while plotting their attack on Granada, the last Moorish stronghold of Andalucía. After that its functions became less glorious: It was the Court of the Inquisition (see p. 32) until the early 19th century and then a prison. Today, the interior has a few interesting features—including Roman mosaics, an ornately carved Roman sarcophagus, and a Gothic chapel in the tower—and the **water gardens** are superb. They were re-created in Moorish style in the 1960s, and every July are the setting for Córdoba's guitar festival.

Cross the Roman bridge from here to reach the **Torre de la Calahorra** (*Puente Romano, tel 957 29 39 29*), originally an Arab tower that replaced a Roman gateway and was itself rebuilt in 1369. From the roof you have spectacular views of Córdoba across the river; inside is an audiovisual display on Moorish culture that you can follow with headsets. Some rooms are simplistic, but the commentary gives easily accessible information.

**Above left:
The Mezquita's rhythmic interior was designed over a thousand years ago to create a spatial sense of infinity.**

**Above right:
A service at Córdoba's cathedral, built within the walls of the mosque**

**Museo
Arqueológico**

www.turismodecordoba
/museos.htm

✉ Plaza de Jerónimo
Páez 7

☎ 957 47 10 76

🕐 Closed Sun.
p.m.–Tues. a.m.

💲 $. Free for E.U.
citizens

The short-lived
Medina Azahara
once boasted
fantastic whims
such as curtains
of water, domes
of crystal, and
African
menageries.

MUSEUMS & PALACES

Two blocks northeast of the
Mezquita, on one of Córdoba's most
delightful squares, the **Museo
Arqueológico** is as interesting for
its setting as for its collection. The
collection is imaginatively distrib-
uted throughout the four patios and
galleries of a lovely Renaissance
mansion with a magnificent
sculpted gateway. **Patio II** has a
superb Roman statue of a crouching
Aphrodite, copied from a Greek
piece. In **Patio III** the remains of
Roman steps face a mosaic panel
of the Nile River. Fragments of
stone inscriptions, columns, and
capitals in **Room V** lead you to a
model of the Roman temple standing on Calle Claudio Marcelo and
a superb statue of Hermaphrodite.

As you climb the Renaissance
staircase examine the carved *artesonado* ceiling before moving clockwise around the upper galleries
devoted to Moorish artifacts.
Among them are a lovely capital
sculpted with four figures of

musicians and, in **Room VII,** the
incised bronze of a fawn: This and
the surrounding glass and ceramic
all came from Medina Azahara.
Also outstanding is the rare
collection of terra-cotta wells.

Just beside the museum is the
Zoco, or souk, a small artisans'
market where some of Córdoba's
many silversmiths and ceramicists
practice their trade. Opposite, is the
tiny **Sinagoga** *(Calle Judíos, tel 957
20 29 28, closed Mon.),* built in 1315,
one of only two major synagogues
that survive in Spain today.

Opposite the synagogue is the
newly opened **Casa de Sefarad**
(Calle Judíos, tel 957 42 14 04, $) in
which five rooms explain the history of Spain's Sephardic Jews and
exhibit related objects. Fourteenth-
century architectural details reveal
the age of this remarkable street, the
best preserved of Spain's many
medieval Jewish quarters. Watch out
for special events or concerts.

Right by the northeastern corner
of the Mezquita is a renovated

mansion devoted to the craft of leather, the Museo Arte sobre Piel (*Plaza Agrupación de Cofradías 2, tel 957 05 01 31, closed Mon.*). This fascinating Cordoban craft was developed under the Caliphate in the tenth-century and still survives today.

Well outside the Judería but still within walking distance, the **Palacio de Viana** (*Plaza de Don Gome 2, tel 957 49 67 41 closed Sat. p.m. & Sun.*) is a fine and substantial aristocratic mansion. The one-hour guided tour (in Spanish but with an explanatory leaflet in English) whisks you through a labyrinth of halls and rooms, all stuffed with valuable antiques, chandeliers, paintings, and tapestries. Their provenance varies, but they are mainly European with a few Oriental additions. Like the Casa de Pilatos in Sevilla (see p. 270), it makes a fascinating eye-opener on the lifestyle and means of the Spanish nobility. Explore the twelve stunning patios and one garden that surround the mansion, each one perfumed by aromatic plants. If you miss Córdoba's Festival of Patios, held in May, this makes an excellent substitute.

MEDINA AZAHARA

Medina Azahara is one of Spain's most important archaeological sites, and it is a must on your Andalusian journey. It lies 7 miles (11 km) west of Córdoba off the C431. The extensive ruins in front of you are the vast tenth-century palace of Caliph Abd ar-Rahman III, of the Umayyad dynasty. The palace was built in pink, blue, and white marble and decorated with ebony, ivory, and precious stones. It is said that 10,000 workers, 1,500 mules, and 400 camels were employed on the site to build this homage to the Caliph's favorite wife, Al-Zahra ("orange blossom"). The Medina became both the seat of government and a

palatial residence, but it stood for only 70 years before it was destroyed by North African Berbers in 1010.

The most impressive surviving structures are the army barracks and the marble-carved **Salón Rico** (Rich Room), a restored hall of the reconstructed palace. Here you see the relaxed attitude of the Umayyads to representation: Trees, animals, and even human figures appear in the decoration, in a less rigid style than the strict geometry of the Almohads and Almoravids of Granada and Sevilla. Below, the ruins of the mosque are correctly oriented toward Mecca, unlike the Mezquita in Córdoba. The terraced site, with its sweeping view, cypress trees, palms, and wild cactuses, evokes a sense of the power and majesty of Córdoba's caliphate. ■

The Palacio de Viana is known as the Museum of Patios, for its twelve distinctly different patio gardens.

Medina Azahara
www.turismodecordoba.org /medinazahara.htm

✉ Carretera de Palma del Rio (C431)

☎ 957 32 91 30

🕐 Closed Sun. p.m. & Mon.

💲 $. Free for E.U. citizens

Úbeda commands a sweeping view over surrounding olive groves.

Úbeda

JUST 5 MILES (8 KM) APART, ÚBEDA AND BAEZA ARE WORLD Heritage sites of Renaissance architecture in the province of Jaén. Úbeda was founded as Ubbadat al-Arab and was one of the most important towns of the Moorish region of al-Andalus.

Úbeda

🗺 261 E3

Visitor information

www.ubedainteresa.com

✉ Palacio del Marqués de Contadero, Calle Bajo del Marqués 4

☎ 953 75 08 97

🕐 Closed Sat. & Sun. p.m.

After Fernando III captured the Úbeda 1234, it became a base for the struggle against the Muslims. At its peak the 16th century, gold from America was pouring into Spain. The result is a cluster of buildings in the **old town,** untouched by the hurly-burly of modern life. Sit on a bench by the esplanade of **Plaza de Vázquez de Molina,** looking at the church of El Salvador ahead of you, the town hall to the left, and, to your right, Santa María, the Palacio del Marqués de Mancero, and the old granary. **El Salvador** (*Calle Baja del Salvador, tel 953 75 81 50*) has an extravagant baroque altarpiece with a sculpture of Christ by Alonso Berruguete and an inner lobby of carved wood.

Úbeda has long been known for ceramics finished in a deep green glaze. Head for **Calle Valencia,** just north of the Puerta del Losal, one of the old city gates. Here you can watch craftsmen at work. On your way, stop to admire the lovely **church of San Pablo** (*Plaza del 1° de Mayo*) on the old market square, an early Gothic church with beautifully carved portals. A few steps from here is the small **Museo Arqueológico** (*Casa Mudéjar, Calle Cervantes 6, tel 953 75 37 02, closed Sun. p.m. & Mon.*), attractively set out in a 14th-century Mudejar house. On the way to Baeza, stop at Puente del Obispo to learn more about olive oil at the **Museo de la Cultura del Olivo** (*Hacienda de la Laguna, tel 953 76 51 42, www.futurolivabaeza .com, $*). This is part of a complex which includes a hotel, two excellent restaurants, a catering college, and a campsite. ∎

Baeza

THE SLIGHTLY POORER COUSIN OF ÚBEDA, BAEZA HAS A similar inheritance of Renaissance structures, more civic than domestic, and all built in a lovely golden stone. Baeza's monuments are more integrated into the modern town than Úbeda's, which makes it less of a museum and more enjoyable. The olive oil is just as delicious.

In the 13th century Baeza became capital of the High Guadalquivir before Jaén was conquered. Like Úbeda, it reached its zenith in the 16th and 17th centuries, when the university was founded and the cathedral was transformed. The **cathedral** dominates high ground to the east of the center, and is a good starting point for a walk. Inside, climb the bell tower for wonderful views over the town and countryside. Don't miss the Mudejar cloisters with their four chapels inscribed in Arabic, echoes of the mosque that once stood on this site. Outside, stop to admire the oldest elements of the cathedral, the 13th-century Puerta de la Luna and the Gothic rose window. In front is the pretty fountain of Santa María, built in the 16th century by Ginés Martínez, who also designed Baeza's water conduits.

A few steps west on the Plaza Santa Cruz stands Baeza's most exceptional building, the **Palacio de Jabalquinto.** The facade is a masterpiece of delicate Flamboyant Gothic stonecarving, incorporating diamond-shaped studs. It was commissioned by Juan Alfonso de Benavides, a cousin of Fernando V of Aragón. Restoration work will prevent you from visiting the inner patio, but try and get a peep at the sumptuous baroque staircase in one corner.

Across the square, enter the charming little **church of Santa Cruz** (*Plaza de Santa Cruz, open sporadically*), built in 1227 in late Romanesque style. Among the traces of frescoes, look inside the arch to the left of the altar for the one of San Sebastián, still looking saintly despite the cascading arrows. The other impressive building on this square is the old university, founded in 1538.

Baeza's social focus is oval **Plaza de la Constitución,** just downhill. Other Renaissance buildings lie to the north on Calle de San Pablo; another attractive cluster is on **Plaza de los Leones** (Lions' Square). It is named for the fountain at the center, thought to have come from the Roman town of Cantulo. On one side is the distinctive double arch of the **Puerta de Jaén** and **Arco de Villalar.** ∎

Baeza

🅐 261 E3

Visitor information

www.baeza.net

✉ Plaza del Pópulo

☎ 953 74 04 44

🕓 Closed Sat. & Sun. p.m.

The fountain of Santa María stands outside Baeza's imposing cathedral.

Flamenco

Flamenco is a form of song, guitar playing, and dance that epitomizes the complex soul of Andalucía. Arab, Oriental, and Gypsy influences mingled to produce this extraordinarily characteristic sound, which in its rawest, most authentic state is a spontaneous outburst late at night in a backstreet bar. The frills, flounces, castanets, and syncopated hand-clapping of the dancers are more easily accessible to foreigners, but often produce disappointingly mechanical shows laid on for tourists on the *costas*. Nonetheless, true flamenco is alive, well, and, since the 1980s, reinventing itself.

Joaquin Cortés, an innovative flamenco dancer from Cordoba

Most experts believe that the roots of flamenco lie in the 15th century, when Gypsies arrived from north India via Egypt and eastern Europe, and fused their music with that of the Moors and Jews in Andalucía. The word "flamenco" probably derives from the Arabic "felag mengu," meaning "fugitive peasant"—a reference to Gypsies and perhaps also Moriscos (baptized Moors). Since then it has evolved into several branches, notably the *soleá* of Sevilla's Triana district, the *bulería* of Jerez de la Frontera, and the *cantes festeros* (festive styles) of Cádiz. These three towns were the homes of Spain's first flamenco schools. The different styles, or *palos,* have a common rhythmical cycle of 12, like the blues, but differ in key and harmonic progression.

For all its variations, the bottom line of flamenco is to attain *duende,* an intense, interactive communication with the audience, which participates with interjected cries of appreciation. As a nonwritten, oral tradition, flamenco song can be modified according to need and context. The *cante jondo* (deep song), reserved for virtuosos, is the oldest form, in which the singer's emotional expression of loss, grief, or injustice is considered more important than tonal clarity, and is often performed a cappella.

Solo guitar playing evolved from providing the singers with a break to becoming an art in itself. Guitarists such as Paco Peña, Paco de Lucía, and Tomatito have become world famous, often more so than their singing companions. A notable exception was El Camarón de la Isla (1950–1992), part of the nuevo flamenco movement. The total performing art of song, music, and dance came together in the late 19th century and was crowned by Manuel de Falla's flamenco ballet, El Amor Brujo, in 1915. Since the 1950s, *tablaos* (specialized flamenco bars) has encouraged exponents of all three elements.

In dance, it is mesmerizing footwork that is primordial, hence the flounced, long-trained dresses cut high at the front. In the 1970s, the Sevillian dancer Manuela Carrasco carried this technique to its greatest heights. Anyone who saw Carlos Saura's film Carmen (1983) must remember the fabulous footwork of Cristina Hoyos dancing with Antonio Gades. Their generation may be on the wane, but the torch is carried forward by Joaquin Cortés, Eva "La Yerbabuena," and, younger still, Niño de los Reyes. In music itself, flamenco still has traditional interpreters, most of whom are Gypsies. With women singers such as Aurora Vargas and the impetus of *nuevo flamenco* (new flamenco) groups such as Ketama, Pata Negra, Radio Tarifa (fusing flamenco with Arab music), and Ojos de Brujo (mixing in hip-hop) flamenco is gaining wider audiences and, again, evolving. ■

A flamenco group usually includes a guitarist, singer, and hand-clapper, as well as the dancers, both male and female.

The exquisite Alhambra palace and gardens exemplify the apex of Muslim architecture in Spain.

Granada

IT WAS IN THE 19TH CENTURY THAT THE IMAGE OF Granada as the quintessential Oriental town first floated into the Western imagination. This was in part thanks to the American writer Washington Irving, whose *Tales of the Alhambra* inspired a succession of writers and artists to try to capture the wonders of Granada's palace, the Alhambra. Today the Alhambra is the number one sight for visitors to Spain. You are never alone beside the fountains of its cool patios and verdant gardens, though you can always find a relatively secluded corner in which to muse on the past. The rest of Granada is also very rich in monuments and has a lively cultural program, partly because of its burgeoning population of 50,000 students. Behind the city loom the snowcapped peaks of the Sierra Nevada, creating an ethereal atmosphere.

Granada

🗺 261 E2

Visitor information

www.granadatur.com/princi palen.htm

www.dipgra.es

✉ Plaza Mariana Pineda 10

☎ 958 24 71 28

🕐 Closed Sat. p.m. & Sun.

You can divide your sight-seeing neatly into three areas: first, the hilltop Alhambra; second, the steep, rambling lanes of the Albaicín opposite (sprinkled with restaurants that give huge views); and third, the "new" town that sprawls below. The heart of modern Granada beats here, and is far from lacking in interest between specialist shops, graceful avenues, and a good sprinkling of historical musts. A possible fourth area is Sacromonte, the Gypsy cave dwellers' quarter that stretches north into the hills from the Albaicín. Flamenco clubs abound, but they are not authentic. Don't take valuables, or leave anything in your car—better still, leave the car

itself in a downtown parking lot, using your feet or local minibuses to get you uphill.

Granada was ruled by Moors from 731, but it came into its own in 1031, with the collapse of the Córdoban caliphate. Out of centuries of obscurity emerged a kingdom of splendor, wealth, and poetry, ruled by the Almoravids, then by the Almohads, and, from 1238, the Nazrids. Arts and sciences flourished side by side, in an era of brilliance and religious tolerance that drew together thinkers from Europe, North Africa, and the Middle East. The magnificent buildings of the Alhambra arose, culminating in the magical Nazrid palace. During this time, however, the Christian Reconquest (see pp. 28–31) was pushing southward. Granada held out longer than any other Muslim city in Spain.

However, in January 1492, after a six-month siege of the city, the Catholic Monarchs Fernando and Isabel finally rode in victorious. The boy-king Boabdil fled with his mother into exile, famously shedding a last tear as he looked back at Granada from the mountain pass now called El Suspiro del Moro (the moor's last sigh—used by English novelist Salman Rushdie as the title of a book published in 1995). Nearly eight centuries of Muslim rule in Andalucía were over, although it was not until the expulsion of the Moriscos (baptized Moors) in 1570 that Granada wholly lost its true creators.

Granada continued to flourish in the Renaissance: Monuments from then include the massive cathedral, monastery of San Jerónimo, and Hospital Real (Royal

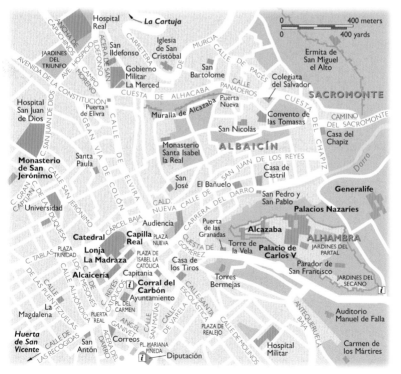

Lavish baroque carving decorates the tabernacle at La Cartuja monastery.

The heart of downtown is **Plaza de Isabel la Católica,** a little square with the cathedral and other sights clustered around it.

The grandiose **cathedral** dominates the southwest corner of Granada. The main building is a Renaissance masterpiece, begun under Diego de Siloé (1495–1563) in 1528, with a facade by Alonso Cano, completed in 1667, the year of his death.

The most impresssive part of it, however, is the earlier **Capilla Real** (Royal Chapel) abutting its southern flank. You enter it through the **Lonja** (Exchange). Commissioned by the Catholic Monarchs to house their tombs, the Capilla Real was built in just 15 years, and the result is a harmonious profusion of Isabelline Gothic, fittingly lavish for its royal incumbents. The superb tombs of Fernando and Isabel are by the Florentine sculptor Domenico Fancelli (1469–1519). Bartolomé Ordóñez (circa 1485–1520) was responsible for those of their daughter Juana ("the Mad") and her husband Felipe. The tombs lie beneath a soaring rib-vaulted ceiling, while their lead coffins lie in the crypt below. Look, too, at the gilded, wrought-iron screen in front, another masterpiece, this one by Maestro Bartolomé de Jaén. The **sacristy museum** dazzles you with chalices, processional crosses, reliquaries, the crown and scepter of Isabel herself, Fernando's sword, and banners carried during the conquest of Granada. Here, too, is Isabel's impressive collection of Flemish and Italian paintings, including works by Memling, van der Weyden, and Botticelli.

In contrast, the main cathedral seems rather a soulless affair, despite its airiness and height. In the **Capilla Mayor** look for Pedro de Mena's praying figures of Fernando and Isabel. You see

Hospital). In the 17th century the monastery of La Cartuja was built, and the city produced artists such as Alonso Cano (1601–1667) and Pedro de Mena (1628–1688). Later the city wove its spell over Eugène Delacroix, the French 19th-century Romantic painter, and on musicians such as Manuel de Falla and Andrés Segovia. Granada's greatest 20th-century writer was the poet Federico García Lorca (1899–1936), shot by Franco's troops in the Civil War. Today, this is a sophisticated, vibrant, city, redolent of the past but not buried in it. However, an expanding Moroccan community is bringing Islam back to the city.

DOWNTOWN GRANADA

The Gran Vía de Colón is the main artery through downtown Granada.

Alonso Cano's works throughout. The cathedral was built on the site of the demolished Great Mosque, the last remnant of which is **La Madraza** (*Closed Sat.–Sun., & Aug.*), opposite the Capilla Real. This was a 14th-century Islamic college, rebuilt in baroque style and now part of Granada University, but it still has a superb prayer hall. You can drop in to admire its magnificent stucco work. Another relic of this period, tucked away behind Calle de los Reyes Catolicos, is the **Corral del Carbón** (*Calle Mariana Pineda, tel 958 22 59 90*), an unusually sober courtyard building that functioned as a storehouse and merchants' inn. Between this and the cathedral lies the old Arab souk, the **Alcaicería,** completely rebuilt following a fire and now full of overpriced souvenirs.

West of the cathedral, follow Calle San Jerónimo to the 16th-century **Monasterio de San Jerónimo** (*Calle Rector López Argüeta, tel 958 27 93 37*). This jewel of Spanish Renaissance architecture has a wonderful two-tiered cloister, the work of Diego de Siloé, architect of the cathedral. In the church are beautiful 18th-century frescoes, and the tomb of the Catholic Monarchs' general, Gonzalo Fernández de Córdoba, known as El Gran Capitán. Nuns still live here: You can buy their cakes and jams at the entrance, and occasionally you hear them singing.

Now take bus No. 18 or Linea C from Gran Vía to the Carthusian monastery of **La Cartuja** (*Paseo de Cartuja, tel 958 16 19 32*), by far the greatest baroque monument in Granada. The Carthusians lived austerely but ornamented lavishly, and this monastery takes the cake. Gold leaf, mirrors, stuccowork, marble, Venetian glass, mural paintings, marquetry, and a pro-

fusion of sculpted cherubim, flowers, and vines set the tone—and that's just in the church **sanctuary.** This exercise in excess was created by Francisco Hurtado Izquierdo from 1704 to 1720 and is rivaled only by the **sacristy,** which he designed later. Here you find a sculpture of St. Bruno by José de Mora, Alonso Cano's "Inmaculada," and cupola frescoes by Tomás Ferrer. The church glitters with the gilt of Churrigueresque altarpieces, doors inlaid with mother-of-pearl, ivory, ebony, and tortoiseshell—the work of a monk, José Manuel Vázquez. Recover from this visual assault in the peaceful **cloisters.**

Poet Federico García Lorca is honored at his family's former summer house, the **Huerta de San Vicente** (*Calle Arabial s/n,*

Designed by Hurtado Izquierdo, the sacristy of La Cartuja dates from 1727 to 1764.

Cathedral
www.granadatur.com/DATA/
   mainMonEN.htm
✉ Gran Vía de Colón 5
☎ 958 22 29 59
🕐 Closed Sun. a.m.
💲 $

Capilla Real
www.capillarealgranada.com
✉ Oficios 3
☎ 958 22 78 48
💲 $

Parque Federico García Lorca, tel 958 25 84 66, closed Mon., www.huertagarcialorca.org). He did much of his writing here; at that time the house stood in an orchard, but it has been swallowed up by suburbs. You see original furnishings, drawings by friends such as Salvador Dalí, manuscripts, and photos. Reserve a place on the guided tour in advance, as numbers are limited.

ALHAMBRA

It is visible from all over the city, reigning in splendor from its hilltop, the simple crenellated towers and walls rising above a cloud of greenery that extends to the white structures of the Generalife beyond. You can walk up the steep incline of Cuesta de Gomérez, through shady pine trees, or ride in a tomato red minibus that drops you near the main entrance. If you are driving, plenty of signs point the way from the center of town. Another, little-used route for walkers is to approach from the Darro riverbank up Cuesta del Rey Chico, where a path brings you to the Generalife.

The Alhambra encompasses four sections: the military fortress of the Alcazaba (the oldest part); the exquisite Nazrid Palace (the ultimate flowering of Moorish architecture); the summer palace of the Generalife; and the Renaissance Palace of Carlos V. Between them lies a labyrinthine garden of paradise, or at least a good earthly semblance of heavenly bliss. Every sense is ignited by the subtle combination of light, color, sound, and smell created by trickling fountains, reflective ponds, high hedges, and an abundance of fragrant flowers—roses, plumbago, honeysuckle, jasmine, and bougainvillea.

The color of the walls, built from a durable mixture of red earth and stone, gave the Alhambra its name, derived from the Arabic word for "red." The walls once enclosed a self-contained town with four gateways, 23 towers, seven palaces, workers' houses, workshops, baths, a *madrasa* (Islamic school), and mosques. Many of these buildings have disappeared, but the surviving palaces continue to exert their magic, just

Patio del Cuarto Dorado in the Nazrid Palace

Alhambra & Generalife
www.alhambra.org
✉ Avenida de los Alixares
☎ 902 44 12 21
🕐 Open for night visits Fri. & Sat. (winter), Tues.–Sat. (summer)
💲 $$. Book your visit to Nazrid Palace at 902 88 80 01 or at www.alhambra-tickets.es

Opposite: The Patio de los Leones, named for the 12 lions bedecking its fountain, embodies the archetypal image of Granada.

Washington Irving

He was not the first or last person to be enamored of the Alhambra, but Washington Irving was the first writer to describe in so humane a fashion the tales and legends of this rambling fairy-tale palace, bringing to life its silent towers and chambers. It was in 1829 that he installed himself in the governor's apartments overlooking the orange trees and fountains of the garden of Daraxa, and over the next few weeks, penned his tribute to the palace's inhabitants, *Tales of the Alhambra*. You can buy it everywhere in Granada. ∎

as they did on Carlos V: He built his own imperial palace here but used it only for ceremonial functions, preferring to live with his family in the more congenial Moorish palaces.

The Alhambra's overwhelming popularity means that in peak season you have to dodge large guided tours. Ideally, make time for a second daytime visit, and also come back at night when lighting brings to the fore elements that you might have missed by day. For the Nazrid Palace you have to book to visit within a given half-hour (try late in the afternoon when crowds have thinned), but you can soak up the sensual atmosphere of the rest of the Alhambra for as long as you want.

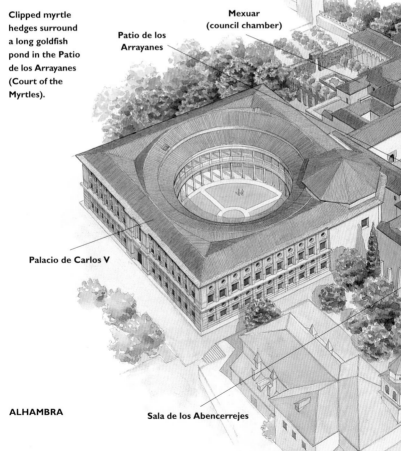

Clipped myrtle hedges surround a long goldfish pond in the Patio de los Arrayanes (Court of the Myrtles).

Patio de los Arrayanes

Mexuar (council chamber)

Palacio de Carlos V

ALHAMBRA

Sala de los Abencerrejes

Alcazaba

This is a good place to start. You can climb to the roof of the Torre de la Vela for a fantastic panoramic view of the entire site, and of the rest of Granada, the Sierra Nevada, and the endless *vega* (plain) to the west. Dating from the ninth century, the Alcazaba was Granada's first major Moorish structure, though the front two towers were built four centuries later. An often deserted garden on the southern side makes a meditative oasis.

Palacios Nazaríes (Nazrid Palace)

Called an earthly paradise by the French poet Théophile Gautier, the palace was built for Yusuf I and

Painted and carved stucco frames an archway of the Nazrid Palace.

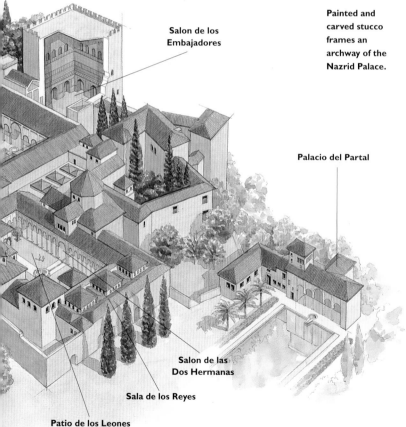

Salon de los Embajadores

Palacio del Partal

Salon de las Dos Hermanas

Sala de los Reyes

Patio de los Leones

Mohammed V in the 1300s, and its two patios, intricately carved stucco ceilings, friezes, capitals and archways, geometric mosaics, fountains, and infinite perspectives constitute the zenith of Moorish style in Spain.

From the beautifully tiled **Mexuar** (Council Chamber) you

enter the Patio del Cuarto Dorado, then the overwhelming **Salón de los Embajadores** (Hall of Ambassadors, inside the Comares Tower). Its complex domed marquetry ceiling is said to consist of more than 8,000 polygonal pieces of cedarwood, and the stuccowork of the walls is masterful. Look at the beautiful *muqarnas* (honeycomb stuccowork used in ceiling, archways, and domes), then admire the wonderful views from the windows. Outside, the **Patio de los Arrayanes** (Court of Myrtles) presents one of the finest perspectives in the Alhambra, accentuated by the myrtle hedges flanking the pool.

From here, a passage leads to the **Sala de los Mozárabes,** an anteroom that opens onto the much photographed **Patio de los Leones** (Court of Lions). This rhythmical, colonnaded courtyard is divided into four sections, in traditional Islamic style, accentuating the fountain and water channels, symbols of the four rivers of life. You have to imagine this patio planted with cypresses, palms, orange trees, pomegranates and flowers. Twelve stone lions hold the fountain basin, whose rim is carved with a poem extolling the beauty of the court, the garden, and the play of water. Written by Ibn Zamrak, Mohammed V's chief minister, it is one of many that are inscribed in the Alhambra's surfaces.

Around the patio are three halls, each one a jewel of delicate craftwork. The most breathtaking is the **Sala de las Dos Hermanas,** (to the left as you enter the patio) where the domed octagonal ceiling has finely worked muqarnas resembling stalactites, lit by natural light filtered through the tracery of windows just below.

Opposite, linked to the Sala de las Dos Hermanas by a water channel, is the **Sala de los Abencerrajes,** with its high domed ceiling and stalactite vaulting. The third hall, the **Sala de los Reyes,** lies behind the main cluster of arches. The ceiling paintings here may be the work of Christian painters commissioned by Mohammed V. North of the Sala de las Dos Hermanas, another hall leads to the **Mirador de Daraxa,** overlooking a lovely garden patio.

Outside the main palace, you come to the **Palacio del Partal,** which was probably the first part to be built. Its arched gallery leads to the Torre de las Damas (Ladies' Tower), reflected in the mirrorlike surface of a large pool. Beyond this, the **gardens** take you through their different levels to cross a bridge to the Generalife.

Left: Running water refreshes the Generalife's luxuriant, shaded gardens. Standing on the Cerro del Sol (Hill of the Sun), the Generalife was the ancient palace of the Nazrid kings.

Generalife

Built on a higher level than the Alhambra, the Generalife is a summer palace that celebrates the outdoors. Its central attraction is an oblong pool edged by fountain jets in the **Patio de la Acequia;** also here are terraced gardens, pergolas, bowers, and cypress trees, providing refreshing shade even at the height of summer. There is little to see in the royal apartments except stupendous views: Don't miss the **Mirador de la Sultana** viewpoint at the very top. In late June, some of the performances in Granada's music and dance festival are held in the Generalife gardens.

Palacio de Carlos V

Carlos V's palace was designed by Pedro Machuca, a disciple of Michelangelo. The vast circular courtyard represents the Universal Empire (the globe) and is unlike anything else in the Alhambra, although it is stunning in its own right. Inside are the **Museo de Bellas Artes** *(tel 958 22 48 43, closed Sun. p.m.–Tues. a.m.)* and the **Museo de la Alhambra** *(tel 958 22 56 40, closed Sun. p.m.– Tues. a.m.).* The latter has beautiful Hispano-Muslim exhibits, including ceramics, carved screens, and fragments of sculpted stucco. Upstairs, the Bellas Artes has a good display of Granadino artists (Diego de Siloé, Alonso Cano, Pedro de Mena, Diego and José de Mora), but it is hard to do them justice after the very different artistry of the Moorish palaces and gardens. ■

The Renaissance palace of Carlos V is an intruder in the midst of an Arabian Nights setting.

Gypsies practice their mercantile charm at the Mirador de San Nicolas in the Albaicín.

A stroll in the Albaicín

The Albaicín district flanks the hill opposite the Alhambra and was the site of the first Arab fortress. This walk leads you through its steep, picturesque lanes, with stupendous views at every turn.

Start from the **Plaza Nueva** and walk north past the pretty church of Santa Ana, following the Darro riverbed. On your left you soon come to **El Bañuelo** ❶ *(Carrera del Darro 31, tel 958 02 78 00, closed p.m. & Sun.)*, 11th-century Arab baths with colonnaded rooms, some with star-shaped ceiling openings. A little farther on stands the **Casa de Castril,** a Renaissance mansion housing the **Museo Arqueológico** ❷ *(Carrera del Darro 43, tel 958 22 56 40, closed Sun. p.m., Mon., & Tues. a.m.)*, with impressive Moorish exhibits in Room 7. Continue past the Convento de Santa Catalina with the walls and towers of the Alhambra looming high above to the right. You come to a large esplanade, **Paseo del Padre Manjón,** packed with bars and cafés. Turn left up Cuesta de la Victoria, left again into Calle San Juan de los Reyes, and then right up steps that plunge you into the Albaicín. Here, many *cármenes* (large walled villas) stand in lush, gardens. Climb to the top,

turn left then right up Calle Carrillo, and then take a sharp left into Carril de San Agustín.

Follow it to the top, passing the 17th-century Convento de las Tomasas, and circle around the church, **Colegiata del Salvador** ❸ *(Plaza del Salvador, tel 958 27 86 44, closed Sun.)*, to reach its entrance. El Salvador was built in 1501 on the foundations of the Albaicín's largest mosque, and has a magnificent Almohad patio of horseshoe arches. The small museum has beautiful religious paintings and sculptures, and the church itself a reconstructed Moorish ceiling. Outside, you could stop for a drink on Plaza del Aliatar, then continue by turning right into Calle Panaderos, which leads to shady Plaza Larga. Cross the square diagonally to admire the restored Arab house on the corner, now an ice-cream parlor, and the beginning of the Arab walls, which are being renovated.

Retrace your steps along Calle Panaderos, then go right on a dogleg turn to reach charming **Plaza Charca,** encircled by typical, geranium-laden houses. Walk up steps opposite, then down an alley to emerge at **Plaza San Nicolás** ❹ with its white-washed brick 16th-century church *(Open only for Mass)*. In front is the quintessential view of the hilltop Alhambra with the peaks of the Sierra Nevada behind. This spot is a favorite with guitar-strumming students and castanet-clicking Gypsies. Behind San Nicolás is Granada's brand new **mosque.**

Walk down the steps beside the viewing terrace to Camino Nuevo de San Nicolás, turn right, and stop to see the **Carmen-Museo Max Moreau** ❺ *(Camino Nuevo de San Nicolás 12, tel 958 29 33 10, closed Sun.–Mon.).* This house belonged to the Belgian painter Max Moreau (1902–1992) and his wife Felice. His studio and their home are full of items from their extensive travels. After leaving, turn left down Calle Gumiel to Placeta del Nevot and keep walking down Cuesta San Gregorio to finally take a sharp left into Placeta de

Porras. The **Casa de Porras** ❻ *(Placeta de Porras, tel 958 22 44 25, closed Sun.)* is a magnificent example of Renaissance-Mudejar wooden architecture and now belongs to Granada University. Return to San Gregorio, turn left, and walk down **Calderería Nueva,** the most Arab part of the Albaicín, full of Moroccan pastry shops. At the bottom, turn left to return to Plaza Nueva. ∎

🄰 See area map pp. 260–61
▶ Plaza Nueva
↔ 2 miles (3 km)
🕐 1.5 hours
▶ Plaza Nueva

NOT TO BE MISSED
- El Bañuelo
- Museo Arqueológico
- Colegiata del Salvador
- Carmen-Museo Max Moreau
- Casa de Porras

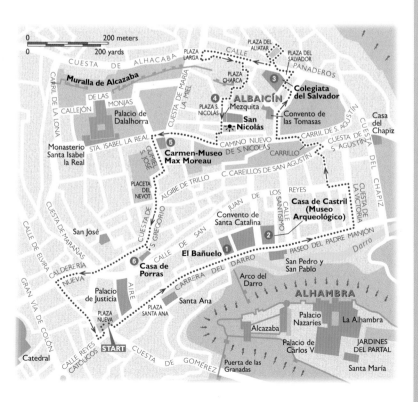

Troglodyte towns

Guadix

⚠ 261 E2

Visitor information

www.andalucia.com/guadix

✉ Avenida Mariana
Pineda s/n

☎ 958 66 26 65

🕐 Closed Sat. p.m.
& Sun.

Baza

⚠ 261 F2

Visitor information

✉ Plaza Mayor 1

☎ 958 86 13 25

🕐 Closed Sat. &
Sun. p.m.

Guadix's cave
district features
some 2,000 caves
carved out of lime-
stone. Far from
being holes , they
are quite cozy.

THE ARID LIMESTONE LANDSCAPE OF ALMERÍA AND
eastern Granada provinces was one of Europe's earliest inhabited
areas more than a million years ago. It is still a land of cave dwellers—
troglodytes—but today TV aerials, satellite dishes, and even burglar
alarms sprout from their pristine, ever expanding houses. A sign of
the times is that foreigners are snapping them up.

The distinctive whitewashed chimneys of cave dwellings stud the
landscape around Guadix, 34 miles
(54 km) northeast of Granada.
They extend north and east to the
Sierra de Baza, to Orce, and beyond
to Cuevas de Almanzora. **Guadix**
is the most accessible of these
towns, but be wary of inhabitants
who do not always take kindly to
ogling tourists. Keep an eye on your
wallet, too. Crowned by a dramatic
Moorish castle, Guadix has a generous sprinkling of 16th- and 17th-
century buildings, but is otherwise
pretty ramshackle. You'll find the
Ermita Nueva, or cave zone,
beyond the whitewashed church of

Santiago. On your way, stop at the
Museo de Alfarería *(Calle San
Miguel, tel 958 66 47 67, closed Sun.
p.m.),* a pottery museum in a renovated cave dwelling. Continue to
the **Cueva Museo** *(Plaza del
Padre Poveda, closed Sun. p.m.),* a
charming reconstruction of a traditional cave dwelling complete with
furniture, antiques, and farming
implements. Then wander around
this extensive troglodyte area to
admire the increasing sophistication of today's dwellings.

Purullena, 4 miles (6 km)
west of Guadix, has numerous cave
houses, their smooth white chimneys punctuating the outskirts of
town. Pottery shops line the main
road selling typical Granadino
green-and-blue ware.

Baza lies 27 miles (44 km)
northeast of Guadix across a stark
landscape of hillocks and esparto
grass. The sculpture known as the
"Dama de Baza," now in Madrid's
archaeological museum (see p. 73),
was found here. Historical sights
include the crumbling **Alcazaba,**
tenth-century **Arab baths**
(Spain's oldest), and the lovely
16th-century church of **Santa
María de la Encarnación.** The
church was designed by Alonso de
Covarrubias and built under the
supervision of Diego de Siloé.

Baza's cave district is on the
eastern side of town. About 25
miles (40 km) northeast is **Galera,**
an Iberian necropolis and an entire
valley of cave dwellings at the back
of town. ■

Sierra Nevada

THIS SPECTACULAR MASSIF, INCORPORATING SPAIN'S newest national park (1999), is a challenge throughout the year, whether you are traveling on foot, skis, or by car. The tortuous road that runs from Granada into the sierra is Europe's highest and defies even the hardiest drivers.

Whatever the season, the **Parque Nacional de la Sierra Nevada** is awesome, and for most of the year is snowcapped. With Mulhacén peak rising to 11,420 feet (3,481 m) and neighboring Veleta to 11,128 feet (3,392 m), it is the highest massif in Western Europe after the Alps. It is also the continent's southernmost ski resort—barely 25 miles (40 km) from the balmy coast.

The mountains have glacier lakes such as **Laguna Altera** around the 10,000-foot (3,000 m) mark and stark tundra landscapes favored by agile mountain goats. Lower down are pine forests where badgers, beech marten, and wild mountain lions roam. Among more than 2,000 botanical species are the Sierra Nevada violet, gentian, aconite, royal camomile, and a rampant honeysuckle. Butterflies include the rare Nevada blue and Glandon blue. Hoopoes whoop and show their flashy plumage, and numerous birds of prey soar overhead. The main **visitor center** for the national park is at Pampaneira in Las Alpujarras (see pp. 310–12).

Skiers can whiz down the slopes of the ski resort of **Solynieve** from November right into May. However, the resort is a truly uninspiring 1970s design. Buses from Granada stop here, and there is a parking lot at the Albergue Universitario. The road beyond, which crosses the national park to the Alpujarras, is only accessible on foot or by bicycle. You can hike to the summit of **Veleta** in about

three hours, allowing two hours for the descent, for a predictably stupendous panorama south to the Mediterranean and north across the sierra. Experienced mountaineers take three to four days to cross the Sierra Nevada, starting in Jerez del Marquesado on the north flank and ending in Lanjarón, in the Alpujarras.

The light in the Sierra Nevada is incredibly clear. So it is understandable why the two Nasmyth telescopes—1.5 and 0.9 m—of the **Observatorio Astronómico** (tel 958 12 13 11, closed to the public), are located at Loma de Dilar at 9,348 feet (2,850 m) above sea level. ■

Sierra Nevada
- 261 E2

Visitor information
- www.cetursa.es
- ✉ Plaza de Andalucía s/n, Granada
- ☎ 958 24 91 00

Centro de Visitantes El Dornajo
- ✉ Carretera de Sierra Nevada, Km 23,
- ☎ 958 34 06 25

Parque Nacional de la Sierra Nevada
- 310–311
- www.mma.es/parques/lared/s_nevada/index.htm
- ✉ Plaza de la Libertad, Pampaneira
- ☎ 958 76 31 27
- ⏱ Closed Sun. & Mon. p.m.

Après-ski at La Veleta ski resort

A drive in Las Alpujarras

This drive makes a circular route through the Alpujarras, the southern foothills of the Sierra Nevada. It passes few specific sights, but the scenery is beautiful, and you may want to allow time for a hike to enjoy the clear air and spectacular views and to get a close look at the wildflowers.

Start your drive in **Lanjarón** ❶, a popular spa town and source of a renowned mineral water. It was a Roman town, but is more famous for the Moorish population's heroic stand against the troops of Fernando and Isabel of Aragón in March 1500. The Moorish castle, downhill from the main road, has been left to slowly crumble, but the scenic view over the valley is special.

Drive out on the C332 toward Órgiva, and you start to enter the dramatic mountain scenery of the Alpujarras. In the market town of **Órgiva** ❷ stop at the main junction to look at the twin-towered baroque church and rather dilapidated Mudejar mansion across the road. The castle of the counts of Sástago stands here, but it has been left to deteriorate.

On Thursday Órgiva's **weekly market** draws northern European expatriates who live in the hills. The large alternative community has spawned a few health-food shops and vegetarian restaurants to join pack mules as part of the townscape. Return to the entrance to Órgiva and turn right onto the GR421 in the direction of Trevélez (21 miles/34 km).

Switchbacks immediately take you uphill into an extraordinary landscape of chasms and glowering mountains with tiny white villages clinging to the slopes. A surprising number of people live here. On this northern side of the valley the road passes numerous isolated houses and *fincas* (farms), many of which are now foreign owned, and the hamlets of Soportújar and Carataunas. As the road

Almond blossoms festoon the Alpujarras.

swings north, you enter the **Barranco del Poqueira** ③, a deep canyon created by the Poqueira River.

At **Pampaneira** ④, park the car and walk into the main square behind the church. This pretty, well-conserved village is a major crafts center, and its shops are draped with hand-woven rugs. Ceramics and jewelry are the other chief attractions. The **Parque Nacional de la Sierra Nevada** (see p. 309) has its main visitor center in the village, and you can pick up detailed trekking maps here—this is one of the best hiking areas. Wander around the pretty streets and enjoy a drink on the little square with its old fountain before continuing. The road now climbs to dizzying heights as you come to a turnoff to the left for **Bubión** ⑤ (2 miles/3.2 km) and **Capileira** (3 miles/4.8 km). These spectacularly sited villages cater to visitors with abundant craftshops and other facilities. The Sierra Nevada's highest peaks rise behind them, and Capileira is a well-trodden meeting point for mountaineers descending from the heights.

Filling water bottles at the local spring

Return to the GR421 and turn left toward Trevélez. Three miles (4.8 km) farther, take a turnoff down to the right to visit the traditional villages of **Mecina Fondales** ⑥, **Ferreirola,** and **Busquistar.** Lying 1 to 2 miles (2–3 km) away from the main road, they still have unspoiled Alpujarras architecture: thick stone walls, often whitewashed, flat roofs, and a few covered bridges between the upper stories. Return to the main road to drive through Pitres and Pórtugos, enjoying the views of stark mountains studded with white hamlets, occasional meadows, oaks, chestnuts, and poplars.

The road then turns north into another deep gorge with a reservoir far below. This is wilder country, favored by goats and

	See area map pp. 260–61
▶	Lanjarón
↔	70 miles (110 km)
⏱	3 hours (excluding stops)
▶	Órgiva or Motril

NOT TO BE MISSED
- Lanjarón
- Órgiva
- Pampaneira
- Bubión

A typical Alpujarras village with terraced farmland

free-roaming pigs—which turn up on your plate at **Trevélez** ❼, the local capital of *jamón serrano* (cured ham). In the Renaissance the town was famous for silk made by Moriscos expelled from Granada. Here you are among mountain pine trees, at a height of 4,820 feet (1,470 m), with the village spilling down the cleft of the mountain to the Trevélez River. The lower part of the village is not particularly picturesque, but it has plenty of watering holes. Walk uphill to see traditional buildings. Trails from here lead up into the mountains or across to Juviles.

The road that you arrived on now backtracks along the opposite side of the gorge, then curves back into the main valley skirting the peak of **Peñabón** (8,310 feet/2,533 m). Ignore turnoffs and follow signs to Bérchules and Ugijar until you come to the attractive village of **Juviles** ❽, also a major silk producer in Renaissance times. This peaceful place is worth another stop before you make the last push to the neighboring villages of Bérchules and Alcútar, through increasingly barren moor dotted with olive trees. As you reach Alcútar you see the road snaking ahead of you across the Guadalfeo River and up again to give more vertiginous views.

Follow signs to Cádiar, then on to Órgiva

(24 miles/39 km), as you turn right down into the valley. **Cádiar** ❾ has become one of the Alpujarras' largest towns because of its strategic setting. Life revolves around the main square dominated by a 16th-century church. The slopes of the Sierra de Contraviesa rising to the south are blanketed in terraced almond trees, with clouds of pink and white blossom in February. Drive out of Cádiar, continue following signs for Órgiva, and after 2 miles (3.2 km), at a small sign for Alquería de Morayma, turn right up a dirt road, which brings you to a magical spot overlooking the valley—perfect for a snack or lunch.

Continue on the A348, which skirts the Sierra de Contraviesa. This is a less tortuous road, with continuous views across the valley of the region you have just driven through. Despite its beauty, this north-facing flank is not much inhabited, and for the next 35 miles you see very few houses. Torvizcón, the only village, is an attractive place clustered around a church tower. From then on, as Órgiva comes into view, the road straightens out considerably and soon brings you down to the bridge with a turnoff to Órgiva (1.5 miles/2.4 km). Alternatively drive straight on through the tunnel towards Motril (18 miles/29 km) on the Costa del Sol. ■

Almería

SEEN FROM THE EYRIE OF THE IMMENSE ALCAZABA, Almería resembles North Africa, with a background of yellow ocher desert and a hodgepodge of traditional flat-roofed houses and concrete high-rise apartment blocks. From the harbor car ferries leave for Melilla, one of Spain's remaining possessions in Moroccan territory.

Dominating the town from its hilltop perch, the Alcazaba, or fortress, echoes Almería's Moorish past and present.

Soak up the atmosphere in the seafront **Parque Nicolás Salmerón,** with its palm trees, fountains, and gardens. Moroccans clad in *djellabas* (loose robes) come here to sip mint tea. Almería's large Moroccan immigrant population is mainly employed in the fruit and vegetable fields around the city, above all at El Ejido, 19 miles (30 km) to the west. You find a more European face to the city in **Paseo de Almería,** the main shopping and social hub. Take a peek at No. 35, the ornate **Círculo Mercantil,** or Traders' Guild, *(tel 609 57 58 02).* In the streets to the west is the fortified **cathedral** *(Plaza de la Catedral, tel 609 57 58 02, closed Sat. p.m. & Sun.),* built in the 17th century. Look out for the Sol de Portocarrero, a large sun carved in the stone facade which symbolizes Almería's privileged climate. A reminder of the port's industrial past is the Cable Inglés, a mineral ore cable loader used for the province's tin mines.

Don't miss the **Alcazaba** (Arab citadel), its crenellated walls and towers dominating the town. Built in 955 to crown Muslim Spain's most prosperous port, it fell to the forces of the Catholic Monarchs in 1490. Today, little remains within its walls, but wander through three enclosures, partly landscaped with aromatic plants, fountains, and water channels. Climb the **Torre de Pólvora** at the far end, and admire the **Muralla de la Hoya,** a fortified wall that dips into the valley and rises to St. Christopher's Hill opposite. ■

Almería
🅰 261 F2
Visitor information
www.almeria-turismo.org
✉ Mirador de la Rambla Avenida F. García Lorca
☎ 950 28 07 48
🕐 Closed Sat. & Sun. p.m.

Alcazaba
www.visitalmeria.com
✉ Calle Almanzor
☎ 950 27 16 17
🕐 Closed Mon.
💲 $. Free for E.U. nationals

Countless spaghetti Westerns have been shot at Mini-Hollywood, a film set near Tabernas, complete with false-fronted buildings and the occasional fake bank raid.

Desert places

THE PROVINCE OF ALMERÍA HAS THE LOWEST RAINFALL IN Spain, barely 16 inches (400 mm) annually. Dryness combines with 3,000 hours of sunshine to create the steppelike semidesert of the province. This torrid climate is exploited at Spain's largest solar-energy installation, which lies between Tabernas and Sorbas.

Sorbas

🅰 261 F2

Visitor information

www.dipalme.org/sorbas

✉ Calle Terraplén 9

☎ 950 36 44 76

Mini-Hollywood

🅰 261 F2

www.hotelesplaya.es

✉ Carretera Nacional 340, Km 138, Desierto de Tabernas

☎ 950 36 52 36

🕐 Shows at noon & 5 p.m.

💲 $$$$

You find spectacular scenery in the **Desierto de Tabernas,** 19 miles (30 km) northeast of Almería, where an undulating lunar landscape is alleviated only by the odd palm tree and cactus. Dramatic hills and canyons, crystalline light, and low production costs have lured many a filmmaker to the area. David Lean made *Lawrence of Arabia* here, and Sergio Leone filmed a string of spaghetti Westerns, including *A Fistful of Dollars* and *The Good, The Bad, and The Ugly.* You can visit old film sets of this Spanish Wild West at the theme-park, **Mini-Hollywood.** Then continue to the village of **Tabernas,** dominated by the ruins of a Moorish castle.

From Tabernas it is 15 miles (25 km) east to **Sorbas,** a dra-matically sited village hanging over a dry gorge. This characteristic little village has long been renowned for its pottery, particularly simple glazed terra-cotta ovenware. Follow signs for *Alfarería* (Pottery) to see potters at work and buy their wares.

Around it is the **Parque Natural de Karst en Yesos,** an eerily white landscape that is the world's largest gypsum karst. Huge subterranean caves with stalactites and stalagmites can be visited on tours *(tel 950 36 47 04, www.cuevas desorbas.com),* which you must reserve in advance. Tours last about two hours and lighted helmets are provided. Alternatively you can walk or drive eastward to **Los Molinos del Río Aguas** for panoramic views. ■

A drive around Cabo de Gata

This route takes you from a village renowned for crafts, through arid and rugged landscapes typical of eastern Andalucía. It includes stops at pretty fishing villages and a succession of wonderful sea and mountain views. Most of this area lies in the Parque Natural de Cabo de Gata-Níjar.

Allow an hour or so to look at crafts in **Níjar** ❶ (*Visitor information, tel 950 61 22 29, Closed Sun. p.m.*), a typical Almeían village of whitewashed houses huddled against the slopes of the Sierra de Alhamilla. Leave the car at the top of the village, dominated by a 15th-century church with a fine Mudejar ceiling. Then you can walk to the **Plaza del Mercado,** or descend to the main street lined with shops selling *jarapas* (woven cotton rugs and blankets), ceramics, and baskets made of coarse esparto grass. Most of the items are made in Níjar.

Back in the car, leave Níjar on the main street, turning right at the bottom, then left following signs to Almería and San Isidro. Don't turn onto the highway but drive straight on through an underpass to emerge into an unappealing plain of *plásticos* (plastic greenhouses) under which tomatoes, asparagus, avocados, and tropical fruits are cultivated. This lasts for 8 miles (12 km) before the scenic landscapes of the **Parque Natural de Cabo de Gata-Nijar** (*Visitor information, Las Amoladeras, tel 950 16 04 35*) begin. Follow signs to San José as the road winds over low sierra through sparse vegetation, mainly yuccas, aloes, prickly pears, and olive trees. As you drive through **Boca de los Frailes,** look for the igloo-shaped stone oven (formerly used for baking bread) on your left. At **Pozo de los Frailes,** stop to look at the mill and old *noria* (water wheel), one of 95 in the park, on your right. When you finally enter San José, turn right at a fork in the road following signs to Playa de los Genoveses.

Drive uphill and circle around the headland. The road soon becomes an easily

The Morrón de los Genoveses etches the coastline in Parque Natural de Cabo de Gata-Níjar.

negotiated dirt road, passing an old wind-mill on the left before descending to a sea of prickly pear cactuses and other more unusual flora. Turn off to enjoy **Playa de los Genoveses** ❷ or continue 2.5 miles (4 km) to **Playa de Monsul,** signaled by an enormous sand dune on the left. Both beaches are of fine yellow sand, and Monsul has a great view south to the Cabo de Gata light-house *(faro)* at Spain's extreme southeastern point. These beaches have been locations for numerous films, including *Indiana Jones and the Last Crusade* (1989) and *The Last Adventures of Baron Münchhausen* (1989). They become packed in high summer.

Retrace your tracks to the largest resort in the area, **San José** *(Visitor information, tel 950 38 02 99),* where you can stop for a drink. Continue to more authentic villages where local farmers and fishermen live in traditional houses. Follow the same

main road out for 2.5 miles (4 km) as far as Pozo de los Frailes, where you turn right at a sign for Rodalquilar and Isleta del Moro (5 miles/7 km) into yucca- and palm-studded hills. After passing the 18th-century coastal fort of **Los Escullos** (built to fend off pirates) and capriciously eroded cliffs nearby, watch for a turnoff to your right down to the promontory and islet of **Isleta del Moro** ❸. This tiny fishing village makes a relaxing spot for lunch.

Beautiful beach at the Playa de los Genoveses

See area map 261 F2

Níjar

70 miles (110 km)

2.5 hours (without stops)

Mojácar

NOT TO BE MISSED
- Níjar
- Isleta del Moro
- Rodalquilar gold mine

a cove containing the only freshwater spring in the entire nature reserve.

Return up the main road and drive straight on to Fernán Pérez, passing herds of goats as you rise into the sierra. In the village itself, watch for a sign on the right to Agua Amarga. This takes you through farmland, past almond trees, goats, prickly pears, and derelict houses before entering an area of lime quarries. As you emerge, the sea reappears in the distance beyond the stark, rocky hills. Ignore any side roads and keep going until you reach a junction with a paved road. Turn right and drive down past scattered white houses to eventually reach the fishing village of **Agua Amarga** ❻ nestling in its bay, a pleasant stop, with beach restaurants and a few craft-shops. For the more active, watersports and dive centers are found too.

Leave Agua Amarga by returning to the main road and turning right up into the hills. As you descend, you are confronted by huge cementworks that introduce the resort of **Carboneras** with its long palm-lined beach and marina. Follow signs for Mojácar (16 miles/26 km) that take you around the village and up into the hills. As you round the headland, the road skirts the beautiful **Playa la Galera** ❼, backed by dramatic clefts of high sierra. Spectacular switchbacks lead to a lookout point, where you can take in the stupendous coastal views north and south. Descending through rugged mountains, the road traverses the pretty village of **Sopalmo,** and soon passes the fort of Macenas in an area undergoing massive development. One more headland brings you to the long, built-up sweep of **Mojácar Playa,** and another 5 miles (8 km) leads to the turnoff up to the hill village of Mojácar (see p. 321). ∎

From here continue north, stopping at the **Mirador de la Amatista** for sweeping views, before arriving in the lovely valley of Rodalquilar. Lost in the hills to the west is the farmhouse of Cortijo de los Frailes, scene of the crime of passion that inspired Federico García Lorca's *Blood Wedding*, the story of a bride-to-be kidnapped by her ex-lover on the eve of her wedding. The groom's outraged cousin subsequently kills the ex-lover. Turn off into **Rodalquilar** ❹ village and drive up to the back, where you can look at the ruined remains of an old gold mine and maybe find a nugget, then return to the main road. You pass a turnoff to El Playazo, a secluded little beach between volcanic gullies, before reaching a junction. Turn right to the fishing village of **Las Negras** ❺ and drive straight down to the beach where you can stop for a drink and enjoy the lovely sea view. A walk along a path to the left brings you to **Cala de San Pedro,**

In & around Murcia

IT IS EASY TO OVERLOOK THE SMALL AUTONOMOUS community of Murcia, sandwiched between vast Andalucía and the coastal region of Valencia, but it does have points of interest. To the north lies the prolific wine-growing region of Jumilla. In the arid south is the attractive old market town of Lorca. If you are lucky enough to be there during Semana Santa (Holy Week), you can see one of Spain's finest and most traditional commemorations. Give the rather flat, overdeveloped coastline a miss: La Manga del Mar Menor is package-holiday heaven, and the airport is nearby, 23 miles (37 km).

Murcia has long flourished on oranges, mining, and industry. Its inhabitants have a proud, independent spirit that dates from its ninth-century status in the kingdom of al-Andalus: The name derives from the Arabic "Murshiya." Other Spaniards think Murcianos are inward-looking. During the Civil War Murcia backed General Franco's Nationalist forces, which did little for neighborly relations with anarchist Almería or republican Valencia. The city of Murcia, the prosperous modern capital, still has a distinctive feel. It shows little concern for the needs

Murcia's striking cathedral is an eclectic mix of styles, ranging from its Churrigueresque facade to its Gothic Los Vélez chapel.

Murcia

🅼 261 G3

Visitor information

www.murciaturistica.es

✉ Plaza Cardenal Belluga s/n

☎ 968 35 87 49

🕒 Closed Sun. p.m.

of visitors, but stop for lunch, as it is a renowned gastronomical center.

At the heart of the pedestrianized **old quarter** spreading north from the Segura River stands the **Catedral de Murcia** (*Plaza de la Cruz, tel 968 21 63 44*), notable for the lavish plateresque **Capilla de los Vélez** and exhibits of Gothic paintings, woodcarvings, and church silver in the museum. Follow Calle de Trapería north of here to the idiosyncratic **Casino,** now partly a restaurant. It is a 19th-century remake of Moorish style. To the west lies Murcia's main commercial street, **Gran Vía Escultor Salzillo,** named for the Murcian sculptor Francisco Salzillo (1707–1783). The **Museo Salzillo** (*Plaza San Agustín 1, tel 968 29 18 93, closed Sun. p.m. & Mon.*) displays his carved wooden figures for the Semana Santa *pasos* (Holy Week floats), carried on the shoulders of penitents during Murcia's spectacular processions.

Thirty-four miles (55 km) southeast of Murcia, the port of **Cartagena** was named for the Carthaginians from North Africa who captured it in 223 B.C. Their fortifications still look down on Spain's largest naval base. The diminutive submarine displayed in the old town center is an early prototype designed by Isaac Peral in 1888. The **Museo Nacional de Arqueología Marítima** (*tel 968 50 84 15, closed Sun p.m. & Mon.*) has Punic (Carthaginian), Phoenician, and Roman artifacts collected from the seabed, with models of boats. Cartagena is between Murcia's main beach resorts of Mazarrón and La Manga and has become a popular summer venue for concerts of contemporary music, well worth checking out.

LORCA

The coastal highway misses Lorca, by tunneling through the chalky hill crowned by the ruins of a Moorish castle. Its refurbished turrets and dungeons are now part of the **Fortaleza del Sol** (*tel 902 40 00 47, closed Mon.–Fri.*) medieval theme trail accessed from the **Antiguo Convento de la Merced** (*Puerta de San Ginés, tel 968 47 90 03*), one of Lorca's fine baroque mansions.

Head uphill from the main street to Plaza de España, dominated by the **Colegiata de San Patricio** (*Plaza de España, tel 968 46 99 66*), built between 1534 and 1780. The west facade teems with cherubim. Opposite, look at the former Casa del Corregidor with its corner carvings (1750) by Juan de Uzeta.

Downhill, don't miss the wonderful **Casa de los Guevara** (*Calle Lope Gisbert*), Lorca's most impressive example of domestic baroque architecture with an impressive entrance. This is the visitor information office. Inside, a number of reconstructed rooms include a well-stocked, wood-paneled 19th-century pharmacy, and an 18th-century ballroom with Venetian furniture. Close by, the **Centro Regional para la Artesanía** (*Closed Sun. p.m.*) is

Right: Interior of Murcia's unusual casino

Lorca
⊠ 261 G3
Visitor information
www.lorcatallerdel
tiempo.com
☎ 968 46 61 57
🕐 Closed Sat. &
Sun. p.m.

Alhama de Murcia
⊠ 261 G3
www.murciaturistica.es
✉ Plaza de la
Constitución 10
☎ 968 44 19 14
🕐 Closed Sat. &
Sun. p.m.

Murcianos enjoy good hiking in the hills of the Sierra de Espuña.

Sierra de Espuña
🄰 261 G3
Visitor information
www.sierraespuna.com
✉ Centro de Visitantes "Ricardo Codorniu," Sierra Espuña
☎ 968 43 14 30

Caravaca de la Cruz
Visitor information
www.caravacadelacruz.org
✉ Calle de la Monjas 17
☎ 968 70 10 03

housed in a starkly modern building by the Murcian architect Juan Antonio Molina. Handicrafts of local materials (clay, wood, glass, ceramics, bamboo) are for sale.

If you can't be here for Lorca's sensational Semana Santa processions, you can get an idea of them at the **Museo de Bordados del Paso Azul** *(Casa de las Cariátides, Calle Nogalte, tel 968 47 20 77, closed Sun. p.m. & Mon).* It is situated beside the church of San Francisco, which is itself worth a look for its dazzling baroque interior, full of gilded altarpieces. This restored late 19th-century house is the base of the Blue Brotherhood, one of the rival procession organizations. Upstairs is an embroidery workshop and a selection of the most finely worked costumes in silk and gold thread. The White Brotherhood, has an equally rich display in the **church of Santo Domingo** *(Calle Santo Domingo, tel 689 78 25 04, closed Sat. p.m. & Sun.–Mon.).*

SIERRA DE ESPUÑA

Rising abruptly from Murcia's plain, this sierra is best reached from

Alhama de Murcia, an 11th-century Moorish town with hilltop castle ruins and remains of Arab baths. From here the road twists through the sierra to Aledo and Totana, on the N340. The mountain range is named after its highest peak, Espuña (5,193 feet/1,583 m), and represents a miracle of repopulation and reforestation in what had become an arid desert by the 18th century, due to over-logging of the native oak forest. Hiking trails lead up the slopes to the Sierra's **pozos de la nieve** (snow wells). An example of real peasant ingenuity, these 16th-century domed brick structures were built to store snow during the winter months; this was subsequently hammered into crushed ice, and then transported on horseback at night, to keep it cool, to villages below. Just outside Aledo, look for the hermitage of **Santa Eulalia,** a tiny Mudejar chapel entirely covered in 17th-century frescoes by Juan de Ibáñez, a local artist.

CARAVACA DE LA CRUZ

Thirty-eight miles (60km) due west of Murcia, lost in the sierra, is this legendary medieval town, considered one of Catholicism's most holy places due to its possession of an alleged piece of the holy cross (the "vera cruz"). Caravaca's role kicked off in 1232 with the alleged conversion of a Moorish king, on witnessing a miracle. Since then the walled town has attracted streams of pilgrims, resulting in a plethora of convents and churches, including the Renaissance masterpiece, the **Iglesia del Salvador.** At its highest point looms the seventeeth century **Santuario de la Vera Cruz** *(Calle Monjas 9, tel 968 70 77 43).* Here, a side-chapel displays the holy relic though it is often mobbed by sick people desperate for a miracle. The museum *(tel 968 70 56 20, closed Mon.)* has an illuminating display on the history of the relic. ∎

Donkeys are still used for transport in Andalucía's more remote villages.

More places to visit in Andalucía & Murcia

CARMONA

This little town breathes history as far back as the 14th century B.C. Under the Romans it became their strongest settlement, and 500 years of Moorish rule left its mark too. High on a promontory 24 miles (38 km) east of Seville, Carmona is an atmospheric, easily-scaled destination. The main sight is the **Puerta de Sevilla Alcazar** where differing styles of arch point to its former rulers. Moorish *Qarmuna* lives on in the maze of narrow streets, a delight to roam around. Look out for the church of **Santa Maria,** built upon the former main mosque, and the noble mansions of the upper town. Tapas are strong too: try the *tagarninas con majao* (thistles with ground herbs and spices) or the more classic *gazpacho* (chilled vegetable soup). 🅰 260 C3, **Visitor information,** www.turismo.cardona.org ✉ Alcazar de la Puerta de Sevilla ☎ 954 19 09 55

JAÉN

Due north of Granada in a region of undulating olive groves lies Jaén, an unassuming yet prosperous town crowned by the hilltop castle of Santa Catalina. In the oldest quarter of La Magdalena is the **Palacio de Villardompardo,** a mansion housing two small museums built over an exceptional complex of Arab baths. Jaén's pride and joy is the massive Renaissance cathedral, but to plunge back into Jaén's Iberian past you need to visit the **Museo Provincal** in the new town. 🅰 260 E3, **Visitor information,** www.promojaen.es ✉ Calle Maestra 13 ☎ 950 61 50 25

MOJÁCAR

Once one of Andalucía's prettiest coastal resorts, Mojácar has succumbed to developers and lost much of its charm. Nothing, however, can detract from its spectacular site, high in the shadow of the Sierra Cabrera overlooking the Mediterranean. One mile (1.6 km) separates the pueblo from the *playa* (beach), the latter an unbroken white strip of low-rise development. In the village itself, cubelike white houses pile up the slopes to a main square with numerous craft shops and, just uphill, the sturdy, much restored **church of Santa María.** 🅰 261 G2 **Visitor information** ✉ Calle Glorieta 1, Edificio Servicios Multiples, Mojácar Pueblo ☎ 950 61 50 25

OSUNA

Osuna is one of Andalucía's many surprises, lost in agricultural plains north of the Serranía de Ronda. When you penetrate the old center, you enter a Renaissance and baroque world of elegant mansions, convents, and churches. The town's aristocratic character stems from the Dukes of Osuna who were among Spain's most powerful nobility. Overlooking the town are the old **university** and the interesting 16th-century **Colegiata**, which you can visit on a guided tour. It is a treasure trove of plateresque decoration and fine art works, including the "Expiración de Cristo" by José de Ribera (1591–1652) and a superb crucifixion by Juan de Mesa (1583–1627). Best of all is the lavish underground pantheon housing the tombs of the illustrious Dukes of Osuna.

260 C2 **Visitor information** Plaza Mayor 954 81 57 32 Closed p.m. & Sun.

Olive groves blanket much of eastern Andalucía's interior.

SIERRA DE CAZORLA

The mountains of the Sierra de Cazorla are the source of three major rivers: the Segura, the Guadalquivir, and the Borosa. The very beautiful biosphere reserve **Parque Natural de las Sierras de Segura y Cazorla** lies in Jaén's northwest corner near the border with Murcia. You can use several places as a base to visit the park. One of the nicest is the town of **Cazorla,** a postcard white village nestling in the shadow of a Moorish castle on the western side. From there you can take a stunning but dizzying road up to the **Puerto de las Palomas,** then drive north 25 miles (40 km) to Tranco, where you have a choice of onward routes. In between are hiking trails: Cazorla has 2,300 species of plants, and you might get a glimpse of wild deer, foxes, or stone marten. Overhead, look for birds of prey, including the royal eagle.

261 F3 **Visitor information** Paseo de Santo Cristo 17, Cazorla 953 71 01 02

VEJER DE LA FRONTERA

It is a precipitous drive up to the medieval village of Vejer, 10 miles (16 km) inland from the Costa de la Luz (see p. 278), but every invader from the Phoenicians to the Moors coveted its strategic hilltop site. Steep cobbled streets and immaculate whitewashed houses surround the old castle (now a hostel) and the attractive church of **San Salvador,** which combines Romanesque, Gothic, and Mudéjar styles. A well-preserved Jewish quarter is on **Calle Cobijadas,** by the walls. Relax on delightful Plaza de España, and admire the ornate fountain faced in 19th-century Sevillian ceramic.

260 C1 **Visitor information** Avenida de los Remedios 2 956 45 17 36

VÉLEZ BLANCO

This village lies in the rocky, semiforested Sierra de Maria, wonderful hiking territory west of Lorca (see p. 319). The towering castle was built for the local marquis in 1515, but to see its main patio (complete with Carrara marble columns) you must visit New York's Metropolitan Museum of Art. It emigrated in 1903 courtesy of George Blumenthal, an American millionaire who bailed out the bankrupt marquis. Other sights are the **Convento de San Luis,** on the opposite side of the village, and the nearby **Cueva de los Letreros.** This prehistoric cave contains faded paintings, including one known as the *indalo*—a stick figure holding a rainbow, adopted as the region's symbol.

261 F3 **Visitor information** Almacén del Trigo, Avenida del Marqués de los Vélez 950 41 53 54 ■

A rtists have long favored
the gentle Mediterranean
climate and landscapes of the
Balearics. Today high summer
sees floods of tourists, but go
off-season to discover a world
of prehistoric structures and
stunning coves.

Balearic Islands

**Another charter flight
arrives.**

Yachts and local fishing boats share the marina of Ciutadella in Menorca.

Balearic Islands

TAKE A FERRY FROM BARCELONA OR VALENCIA, A DOMESTIC FLIGHT FROM Madrid, Barcelona, Valencia, or Alicante, or a flight from almost any European capital, and you reach this jewel-like cluster of islands scattered over the Mediterranean azure. Mallorca, in particular, has been pulling in the package crowds since the 1960s, and Ibiza, formerly an artists' hideaway, is now one of the summer nightlife capitals of Europe. Mellow Menorca, after a sleepy existence on the fringe, is known by more discerning travelers, while tiny, rocky Formentera welcomes visitors in search of unadulterated nature.

Although widely perceived as a simple sun-and-sea destination, the Balearics have great beauty, and (especially Mallorca) a rich history set against an idyllic, rural interior. Their background is linked with Catalunya's, and the language is a close cousin of Catalan, although Castilian Spanish is also spoken. Carthaginians, Romans, Vandals, Moors, French, and British were all attracted to **2▷** these indented shores strategically located on Mediterranean trade routes, and they left contrasting historical imprints on the various islands. Mallorca is the most developed, but it is also the largest island and the one with the most varied landscapes and history. In recent years German investment has soared, and the result is a string of residential villas dotting the beautiful coves of the east coast. Palma, the capital, is very sophisticated. **▌▷** The island still retains extraordinary

beauty and unique points of historical interest, not the least megalithic structures, also a feature of other islands. Crafts have flourished on all the islands since the 1950s, when people came to the Balearics for alternative lifestyles. Eivissa-Ibiza became the hippie capital of

Europe in the 1960s and '70s, and crafts such as pottery and basket-making continue today, despite the islands' popularity, hot clubs, and rising prices. One of the main traditional industries in the Balearics is leatherware, from shoes to bags and belts, and it is a good place to stock up on labels such as Camper and Farrutx.

Artists have left major legacies, especially on Mallorca, which has the foundations of Joan and Pilar Miró, Miguel Barceló (Spain's leading contemporary artist, who was born in Felanitx), and Joan March. Military history is explored at length in Menorca, and Eivissa has an excellent archaeological museum. But most visitors come for the great outdoors. The mild

Mediterranean climate makes for wonderful hiking and cycling year-round. Swimming and other water sports are popular from May to October. Sailing and scuba-diving are widely available (the latter above all in Ibiza). Golf is another major attraction. The peak season for vacationers is July and August, when beaches are packed with roasting bodies and waters off the big resorts of Mallorca become polluted. Try to come outside this time, when the islands are less crowded and wildlife is more visible. Finally, food: It tends to be good, as the long cosmopolitan history of these islands has injected unusual influences that are combined with innovative Catalan refinement. ∎

Mallorca (Majorca)

MULTI-FACETED MALLORCA IS NO SECRET TO MILLIONS OF vacationers. Here you can switch your focus from rugged mountains to coves of crystalline water, white-sand beaches, underground caves, or lively Palma. Mallorca's popularity in summer extends even to the Spanish royal family, so an off-season visit is the best option.

Palma de Mallorca

▲ 325 C3

Visitor information

www.palmavirtual.es

✉ Carrer Sant Domingo 11

☎ 971 72 40 90

PALMA DE MALLORCA

Balearic's capital is an attractive, upbeat town with a lively cultural scene. More than half of Mallorca's 700,000 people live here. Waterfront palm trees, marinas, and elegant 18th-century mansions create a grand backdrop, while pedestrianized streets around Plaça Major hum with life. Scenically built around the secluded curve of the bay, Palma was founded by the Romans in 123 B.C., captured by the Moors in A.D. 903, and entered the Catalan net in 1229. Dominating the port is the **Almudaina** (*Carrer Palau Reial, tel 971 21 41 34, closed Sat. p.m. & Sun.*), the Moorish citadel. It acquired Gothic extensions as the palace of Jaume II, and it is still an official royal residence. You reach it by steps from the breezy **Parc de la Mar,** an elongated lake set in gardens.

Opposite stands the cathedral, **La Seu,** a massive Gothic edifice, bristling spires, and a towering belfry. The ornate southern portal, the **Portada del Mirador,** gives fine sea views. Vast proportions continue in the sober nave overlooked by **rose windows** designed by Antoni Gaudí (see pp. 172–75). One chapel contains an installation by Miguel Barceló. Kings Jaume II and Jaume III are buried in the lovely Mudejar chapel of **La Trinitat.**

Immediately to the east of the cathedral lies the **Museo de Mallorca** (*Carrer Portella 5, tel 971 71 75 40, closed Sun. p.m. & Mon.*), where archaeological exhibits and medieval artworks are displayed in a lovely 17th-century mansion. Just behind are the tenth-century **Baños Árabes** (*Arab Baths, Calle Serra 7, tel 971 72 15 49*), Palma's only complete relic of Moorish presence. From here, northwards, extends a network of over 150 patios, the heart of old Palma, also epitomized by a Roman arch and the **Calle Platería.**

Palma also has exceptional 20th century art collections. Northwest of the center, the **Fundació Pilar i Joan Miró** (*Carrer Joan de Saridakis 29, tel 971 70 14 20, www.a-palma.es/fpjmiro, closed Mon.*) was set up by the artist and his wife to preserve his studios where he had worked from 1956 until his death in 1983. Some of his works are displayed here and you can see more at the **Museu d'Art Espanyol Contemporani** (*Sant Miquel 11, tel 971 71 35 15, closed Sat. p.m. & Sun.*) alongside other Spanish greats such as Picasso, Juan Gris and Dalí. Behind the Almudaina is the **Palau March Museu** (*Calle Palau Reial 18, tel 971 71 11 22, www.fund bmarch.es, closed Sun.*). The highlight of this neo-baroque mansion is the panoramic sculpture terrace with pieces by Rodin, Henry Moore, Barbara Hepworth and Eduardo

Chillida. Palma's latest art venue, opened in 2004, is the stunningly designed **Museu Es Baluard** (*Plaça Porta de Santa Catalina, tel 971 90 82 00, www.esbaluard.org, closed Mon., $$*), slotted into the ramparts and again with great views, though a still limited international collection. You cannot miss Santiago Calatrava's sculpture on the terrace.

NORTHWESTERN MALLORCA

Avoid Mallorca's concentrated resort area, west of Palma between Magaluf and Santa Ponça, but don't miss the island's dramatic northern coastline. Here, the coast is backed by the Serra de Tramuntana and edged by a tortuous clifftop road (C710) with vertiginous views. Even when the granite sierra is blanketed in glowering clouds, the mountain villages and rocky cliffs are spectacular.

Just inland from the picturesque **Port d'Andratx,** a fishing harbor and in summer a yacht haven, is **Andratx** itself, dominated by a fort. From here a secondary road leads down to the extreme southwestern cove of **Sant Telm,** where boat tours take you past the island nature reserve of **Sa Dragonera.** The next place to stop is the Carthusian **monastery of Valldemossa** (*tel 971 61 21 06, closed Sun. p.m.*), nestling in the flanks of 3,490-foot (1,064-m) Tex. This monastery has never forgotten the winter of 1838–39, when the French writer Georges Sand and her lover, Frédéric Chopin, stayed there—their romance is recalled by hourly piano concerts.

The beautiful hilltop village of **Deiá,** discovered decades ago by writers and artists (including Robert Graves, 1895–1985, British author of *I, Claudius*), makes a bucolic stop. Farther north, the market town of **Sóller** is connected by a little train with a bay below that has expanded into a burgeoning resort. Boat tours

La Seu

www.mallorcawebsite.com/
    balearik/Cathedrali
    .html

✉ Carrer Palau
    Reial 29

☎ 971 72 31 30

🕐 Closed p.m. & Sun.

💲 $

Puerto Sóller

Ⓜ 325 C3

Visitor information

www.a-soller.es

✉ Canonge Oliver 10

☎ 971 63 30 42

go along the magnificent coast. It is worth making the detour from Sóller through the hills to see palm trees, oleanders, bougainvillea, and bamboo of the lush **Jardines de Alfàbia** (*Carretera Palma-Sóller, tel 971 61 31 23*), which surround a stately mansion. Inside you can admire an *artesonado* (carved coffered ceiling), saved from the original Moorish building.

The northern stretch of this road wiggles inland to finally reach **Pollença,** wedged between two hills. Down below is a sheltered bay, **Bahía de Pollença,** whose waters are perfect for waterskiing (but may be too polluted for swimmers). At the very end of the promontory, **Cap de Formentor,** a lighthouse is perched above a sheer 650-foot (200 m) drop down to the waves. From here, sweeping views take in the island of **Formentor** in the bay below. To reach its white-sand beaches, take a half-hour boat ride from the Bahía de Pollença. Overlooking the bay from the east is the charming walled town of **Alcúdia.** The **Museo de Pollentia** (*Carrer Sant Jaume 30, tel 971 54 70 04, closed Sat. & Sun. p.m. & Mon.*) is devoted to the outlying Roman site of Pollentia. To the east, the marshes of S'Albufera attract more than 230 bird species.

SOUTHEASTERN MALLORCA

The much flatter southeastern side of Mallorca unfolds in idyllic, pastoral splendor toward a string of coves, creeks, and breathtaking caves indenting the eastern coast. Beaches are fewer in the south, where salt flats and marshes give good bird-watching, and monasteries and megalithic sites dot the interior.

In the easternmost corner, just 9 miles (15 km) apart, Capdepera and Artà make a good starting point for exploring the nearby cave networks

of Coves d'Artà. **Capdepera** is a striking hill town topped by a 13th-century fortress, **Castillo de Capdepera** (*tel 971 81 87 46*), looking down on its marina. You can visit the castle though there is little to see other than sweeping views. **Artà,** too, rises in medieval fortified splendor from a high rock crowned by the church of **San Salvador.** Both towns have megalithic settlements on their outskirts.

Mallorcan scenic drama returns in the island's 800 limestone caves. Just beyond the **Canyamel,** a landmark 12th-century tower, the magnificent **Coves d'Artà** lie on the seashore. This cavernous underworld dripping with stalactites is spotlit to highlight the extraordinary formations: The so-called **Sala de las Banderas** (Hall of Flags) soars to an inspiring 148 feet (45 m). If you wish, continue south to the fishing village of **Porto Cristo** (*Visitor information, Calle Moll s/n, tel 971 81 51 03, closed in winter*) to reach the mile-long (1.6 km) chambers of the **Coves del Drac.** A tour of this awesome geological sight includes a boat ride across **Lago Martel,** the largest subterranean lake in the world, extending to 1 mile (1.6 km) and named for the French speleologist who stumbled across it in 1896. To add to its otherworldliness, boatloads of musicians play classical music in this eerie natural theater set.

South of here is **Felanitx,** an important ceramics center dotted with kiln chimneys and overlooked by windmills on the ridge above. The **main square** is a lovely place to relax and admire the unusually rich church, which mixes Gothic, Renaissance, and baroque decoration. Just south of town, a road switchbacks up through pine trees to the stunningly sited **Santuari de San Salvador** (*tel 971 82 72 82*), which has panoramic views and

Alcúdia

🅰 325 D4

Visitor information

www.alcudia.net

✉ Carretera Artà

☎ 971 89 26 15

Coves d'Artà

🅰 325 E3

www.arta-web.com
/cgi-bin/altres
/vven.cgi

☎ 971 84 12 93

💲 $$

Coves del Drac

🅰 325 E3

www.portocristo.com

☎ 971 82 07 53

💲 $$

The watchtower at Murador de ses Animis offers a splendid panorama over Mallorca's craggy coastline.

intriguing shrines. Together with Campos and Santanyí, Felanitx creates a golden triangle of delightful pastoral scenes where dry-stone walls edge fields of wheat, citrus, and olives. **Campos**, the market town, has traditional Mallorcan architecture, as does **Santanyí.** Look for the *talayot* **of Son Danus,** a megalithic watchtower that stands on the outskirts.

The coastline east of this triangle is a succession of stunning creeks of transparent water edged by white sand, with wooded hills rising above. **Cala d'Or** is one of the developed resorts but remains low key in comparison with those of the west coast. **Cala Figuera** still has the atmosphere of a fishing village. Tops in beauty comes **Cala Mondragó,** declared a nature reserve. Off the

south coast resort of Colònia Sant Jordi lies the **Cabrera archipelago** *(tel 971 72 50 10, permit required for overnight stays & mooring boats),* a national park with rich underwater life and bird-watching.

A last leap 28 miles (45 km) inland from the nudist beach of Es Trenc brings you north of Llucmajor to the **Santuari de Cura** *(tel 971 12 02 60),* which in many ways encapsulates Mallorca— this modernized medieval monastery has nonetheless conserved its 17th-century church, grammar school, and museum related to its didactic role. From the hilltop site you have magnificent views west toward Palma, the bay, and moody Serra de Tramuntana, and north toward the lighthouse of Formentor. ■

Turquoise waters surround the island of Formentera, a popular day-trip from Eivissa.

Eivissa (Ibiza) & Formentera

EIVISSA IS HOT IN TEMPERATURE AND MOOD. IT ATTRACTS planeloads of hip young things who come here purely for the nightlife. If clubs and street fashion are not your scene, then avoid July and August. Or head for quieter Formentera. Both islands are drier than Mallorca, lack its fertile meadows and mountains, but bask under clear blue skies virtually all year-round.

Eivissa (Ibiza)

🔼 324 A1

Visitor information

www.eivissa.org

✉ Calle Antoni Riquer 2

☎ 971 30 19 00

The old capital of Eivissa is perched on a promontory dominating the harbor of Eivissa and defined by the silhouette of the cathedral and Renaissance walls encircling the **Dalt Vila** (old town). Spectacular 16th-century ramparts, steep stone steps, and elegant mansions testify to its history, in contrast with the bars, restaurants, and boutiques that line the narrow streets of the "new town" below. To get an idea of the island's ancient past, look at the Carthaginian and other artifacts at the **Museo Arqueológico de Ibiza i Formentera** *(Plaça de la Catedral 3, tel 971 30 12 31, Sat. & Sun. p.m., & Mon.)* located beside the cathedral. Then take off into the interior of the island.

The traditional rural house of Eivissa is a simple, south-facing *casament,* a composition of white-washed cubes around a central, communal room, with verandas for storing crops. Beside these North African-looking houses are simple, fortified churches where inhabitants used to shelter from pirate attacks. **Sant Jordi, Sant Antoni de Portmany,** and **Sant Joan de Labritja** are all good examples.

Some of Eivissa's 56 beaches with transparent warm waters remain unspoiled. Both sandy and rocky **Cala Salada,** near Sant Antoni, is one of the more tranquil beaches in the developed area. (Sant Antoni is the capital of Ibiza's clubbing culture—so beware.) Less accessible Sant Joan to the northeast has **Cala d'en Serra** and **S'Illot des Rencli** along its vertiginous coastline. This wilder end of the island is a haven from the crowds. Santa Eulària des Riu is a booming high-rise resort yet with aging hippies at the Wednesday market. Head south to the nature reserve of **Ses Salines** to find surprising landscapes, extensive salt flats, and endless water sports.

FORMENTERA

The tiny little island of Formentera may seem a mere hiccup in the Balearics: Its 5,000 inhabitants occupy an area of just 31 square miles (80 sq km). But for faithful visitors it represents the last bastion of unadulterated tranquillity in the Mediterranean. Only 11 miles (18 km) from Eivissa it is easily reached by ferry. Cyclists and hikers revel in Formentera's untouched landscapes and well-marked trails; swimmers like the sandy beaches edged by crystalline water.

The Romans grew wheat extensively on Formentera, but constant pirate attacks made it uninhabitable in the Middle Ages,

and it recovered only in the late 17th century. If you are looking for culture, you are in the wrong place. The capital, **Sant Francesc de Formentera,** is not much more than an 18th-century fortified **church,** a small ethnological **museum** *(tel 971 32 26 40),* and

A "foam" party at the Club Amnesia in Eivissa

a cluster of hippy-style craft shops. Both Sant Francesc and the main tourist center, **Es Pujols,** lie on the shores of **Estany Pudent,** a large lagoon that attracts flocks of migrating birds and leads to a skinny promontory of land edged by beaches. To the west is **Estany des Peix,** a smaller lagoon protected as a nature reserve. On the northern bank stands the striking megalithic monument of **Ca na Costa.** The stone slabs are thought to be a prehistoric burial ground, dating from 4,000 years ago. At the eastern point of Formentera is **La Mola,** a lookout point with a lighthouse and a monument to Jules Verne (1828–1905), the French writer who wove the magic of this beautiful spot into a book. Views reach right across the island. ∎

Formentera
🗺 324 B1
Visitor information
www.guiaformentera.com
✉ Port de la Savina
☎ 971 32 20 57

Menorca (Minorca)

LONG OUTSHONE BY THE MORE OBVIOUS ATTRACTIONS of Mallorca and Eivissa, this peaceful, 274-square-mile (702 sq km) island is slowly gaining in popularity. Declared a biosphere reserve in 1993, it has a gently undulating landscape. A long history of occupation by a series of invaders, including a century of intermittent British rule, has given it a very distinctive flavor and gastronomy. North African couscous meets British puddings here, and Maó (Mahón) is the place where French mayonnaise was first created.

Outdoor seafood restaurants line Ciutadella's harbor.

Menorca (Minorca)
🗺 325 E4
Ciutadella
Visitor information
www.e-menorca.org
✉ Plaza de la
   Catedral 5
   Sa Rovellada de
   Dalt 24, Maó
☎ 902 92 90 15
   971 38 26 93

Menorca's only drawback is the wind—so be prepared. **Maó (Mahón),** the capital, lies at the end of a 3-mile (5 km) inlet and is one of the safest harbors in the Mediterranean. Life revolves around the cafés and restaurants of **Plaza del Ejercito,** and shops are concentrated in the streets between here and Plaza de España. Signs of sporadic British occupation from 1713 to 1802 are evident in older houses. In the town of Es Castell, 2 miles (3 km) along the inlet, well-conserved **Fort Marlborough** (Cala Sant Esteve, Es Castell, tel 971 36 04 62) gives you a picture of the period.

Far more memorable are the 500 **megalithic monuments** dotted over the island. Three main types of monument are talayots (conical stone mounds), taules (T-shaped structures), and navetes (upturned troughs resembling boats). They date from the second millennium B.C. and probably served as altars and funerary monuments. Two sites are outstanding: the settlement of **Trepucó** with its 16-foot-high taula, just outside Maó, and the **Naveta des Tudons,** 3 miles (5 km) east of **Ciutadella,** the delightfully scenic former capital.

The north coast beaches are pebbles and red-ocher sand backed by windy heath. Beaches of finer sand line the south coast creeks attracting the majority of visitors, but you can still find solitude at **Son Saura, Cala Mitjana** in the south, and **Platja d'en Torotuga** in the northeast. ∎

Closer to Africa than to Spain, these islands have year-round sun and are firm favorites for package vacations. Leave the high-rise resorts and you find volcanic landscapes, unique flora and fauna, and picturesque local architecture.

Canary Islands

Spain ... or Africa?

The dramatic volcanic cone of Taburient lords over the island of La Palma.

Canary Islands

CLUSTERED IN THE ATLANTIC OCEAN 620 MILES (1,000 KM) SOUTH OF mainland Spain, just below the Tropic of Cancer, these stark, volcanic islands are only 71 miles (115 km) from the African coast. The Spanish troops of Fernando and Isabel conquered the native Guanches in 1496 and quickly destroyed Europe's last Stone Age culture, but the archipelago's unique geological and biological features have proved more resilient. Today the Canaries' reputation as a budget sun-and-sea destination for northern Europeans tends to eclipse their other charms, but visitors with a bit of initiative find endless corners of astounding beauty and wonderful hiking territory.

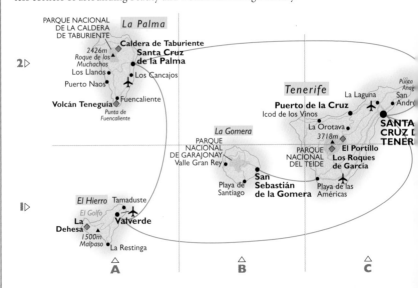

PARQUE NACIONAL DE LA CALDERA DE TABURIENTE

La Palma

Caldera de Taburiente
2426m
Roque de los Muchachos
Los Llanos
Puerto Naos
Fuencaliente
Volcán Teneguía
Punta de Fuencaliente
Santa Cruz de la Palma
Los Cancajos

2▷

Tenerife
La Laguna
Punta Anaga
San André
Puerto de la Cruz
Icod de los Vinos
La Orotava
3718m
SANTA CRUZ D TENER
PARQUE NACIONAL DEL TEIDE
El Portillo
Los Roques de García

La Gomera
PARQUE NACIONAL DE GARAJONAY
Valle Gran Rey
San Sebastián de la Gomera
Playa de Santiago
Playa de las Américas

El Hierro
El Golfo
La Dehesa
1500m
Malpaso
La Restinga
Tamaduste
Valverde

1▷

△ A   △ B   △ C

Seven main islands make up this archipelago. They all belong to one autonomous community, but there is considerable rivalry between the islands, and each one has a separate identity. The main bulk of tourists spills out onto the sands of Tenerife, the largest of the archipelago, dominated by the snow-covered peak of Teide. It is closely followed in popularity by Gran Canaria, the most populated island and the one with the greatest scenic diversity. La Palma has the greenest landscapes, in total contrast to Lanzarote's extraordinary lunar horizons of lava flows or Fuerteventura's desertlike dryness. Idyllic La Gomera has subtropical vegetation of laurel forest and palms, and tiny Hierro's abrupt, windswept slopes end in twisted juniper trees.

Much of the appeal of the Canaries lies in their mild, sunny climate. Temperatures hover between 66°F (19°C) in winter and 77°F (25°C) in summer. The other magnet is the sea. Deep-cobalt waters wash 930 miles (1,500 km) of coastline edged by dramatic cliffs and beaches. Huge high-rise resorts monopolize most of the beaches of Tenerife and Gran Canaria. If you want to escape the hordes, head out to the smaller islands. ∎

Flora & fauna

The ancient Greeks and Romans knew of the Canary Islands, but no outsiders settled there before the 15th century. This long isolation preserved an exceptional flora and fauna: Only Hawaii and the Galápagos islands have a comparable wealth of native species. The most famous is the chirping yellow canary itself, but the name of the islands probably stems from the fierce Verdino dog (from the Latin *canis,* meaning "dog"). Endangered species include the giant lizard, the hourbara bustard, the long-toed pigeon, and the blue chaffinch of Teide. Of the 2,000 species of flora, 600 are endemic. Evergreen laurel forests *(laurisilva)* that disappeared several millennia ago from the rest of the planet still thrive here. Laurisilva depend on specific conditions of humidity, temperature, and altitude, and can best be seen in Tenerife's Anaga highlands, at El Cedro in Gomera, and in La Palma's national park. ∎

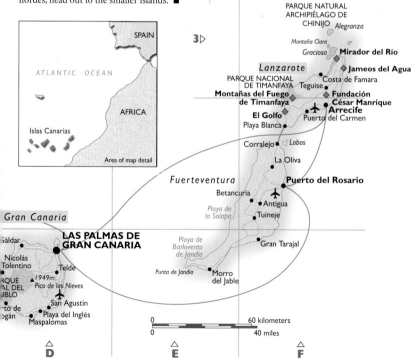

Tenerife

The popular beach resort of Playa de las Americas, in Tenerife

THIS MOUNTAINOUS, 780-SQUARE-MILE (2,000-SQ-KM) island divides into the highly developed southern coast with its drier climate and golden beaches, and the more humid, windier northern coast, where black-sand beaches beneath sheer cliffs remind you of Tenerife's volcanic origins. Between these areas is Spain's highest peak, permanently snowcapped Teide, rising 12,192 feet (3,718 m).

The capital and main port, **Santa Cruz de Tenerife,** lies in the southeastern corner with a dramatic bay setting. Its February carnival is Spain's most exuberant. This is now rivaled by Santiago Calatrava's $90 million **Auditorio** (opera house) with its 200-foot-high suspended canopy *(www.calatrava.com).* A new seafront promenade is the work of Swiss architects Herzog & De

Meuron, whose contemporary art center (the Instituto Óscar Domínguez) and a botanical garden are yet to be completed. Don't miss the converted hospital housing the excellent **Museo Arqueológico** *(Calle Fuente Morales, tel 922 53 58 16, closed Mon.).* Five miles (8 km) northeast is **Playa de Las Teresitas,** a pretty curve of golden sand from the Sahara, with good seafood

Santa Cruz de Tenerife
334 C2
Visitor information
www.cabtfe.es
www.webtenerife.com
Palacio Insular, Plaza de España
922 23 95 92
902 00 31 21

at the port of **San Andrés.** For historical background, head inland to **La Laguna,** Tenerife's first capital and now a university town, with several museums and fine mansions.

More upbeat in tone is verdant **Puerto de la Cruz,** Tenerife's oldest resort. It has mushroomed into a high-rise mirage built on black lava-stone rocks. Better still is **Lago Martiánez,** a series of saltwater pools by the Lanzarote artist César Manrique (see p. 339) to harmonize with the lush vegetation and volcanic rock. You can enjoy more subtropical plants at the **Jardín de Aclimatación de La Orotava** (*Calle Retama 2, tel 922 38 35 72*), a botanical garden created in the 18th century.

La Cruz's magnificent surroundings include the **Valle de la Orotava,** a cleft cutting to the water's edge from Teide. A 17-mile (27-km) drive up to the lookout point, **Mirador de Humboldt** (named after the German naturalist Alexander Humboldt) gives you stunning views over banana groves to the sea. The nearby town of **La Orotava** is a jewel of traditional timber houses with latticework balconies and leafy patios. Don't miss the baroque church of **La Concepción,** the beautiful **Casa de los Balcones,** actually two 17th-century mansions built of tea (a local pinewood), or the craft museum in a 17th-century monastery, **Museo de Artesanía Iberoamericana** (*Calle Tomás Zerolo 34, La Orotava, tel 922 32 17 76, closed Sat. & Sun. p.m.*).

Twenty-six miles (42-km) southwest from La Orotava, the road winds up to the **Parque Nacional del Teide,** declared a World Heritage Site in 2007, where you enter another lunar world. The immense Cañadas de Teide are a volcanic plateau and former crater of 50 miles (80 km) circumference. Here the vagaries of mineralogy have left luminous strata of turquoise iron oxide. Natural lava-stone sculptures, **Los Roques de García,** stand near the park's only building, the parador (hotel, see p. 379), which houses an information center. You can take a cable car from beside the C821 just below the peak or trek for 5 hours. You may see the Teide violet, the Teide marguerite, and the conspicuous Teide bluetit. Join daily treks from the visitor center at the pass of **El Portillo** (*tel 922 35 60 00, treks start at 9 a.m. & 1:30 p.m.*).

Fourteen miles (22 km) west of Puerto de la Cruz on the north coast is **Icod de los Vinos,** once famous for the production of Malvasía wine, which is being successfully revived after centuries of oblivion. The town also has traditional architecture, baroque churches, lush vegetation, good traditional restaurants, and a drago tree (dragon tree—named for its gnarled, monstrous appearance) that is thousands of years old. Sloth-like growth and a penchant for wild locations make it extremely rare—long may it survive. ∎

Parque Nacional del Teide

🗺 334 C1

Visitor information

www.reddeparquesnacionales.mma.es

✉ El Portillo

☎ 922 35 60 00

Puerto de la Cruz Visitor information

✉ Casa de la Aduana Calle Las Lonjas

☎ 922 38 60 00

Everything stops in Santa Cruz for the May festival procession.

Gran Canaria

Gran Canaria

📍 335 D1

www.grancanaria.com

Las Palmas

📍 335 D1

Visitor information

www.promocionlaspalmas
.com

✉ León y Castillo 17

☎ 928 21 96 00

TOURISM HAS A HIGH PROFILE ON THE MOST POPULATED island of the Canaries. This is partly due to 31 miles (50 km) of beaches, but another reason is its incredibly diverse landscapes.

Volcanic formations dominate the interior, making the cliff-edged north coast wetter, cloudier, and perfect for banana plantations. In contrast the most popular beaches fringe the almost desertlike terrain of the south coast. Canyons dominate the west, and the ravines of the central plateau vary from pine forests to stark volcanic rock.

An extensive network of hiking trails runs through these diverse landscapes. Naturalists head for the **Parque Rural del Nublo** on the flanks of Pico de las Nieves (6,393 feet/1,949 m), which has the largest number of endemic species of the archipelago.

Gran Canaria's biggest draw is the immense 5-mile-long (8 km) beach shared by three resorts: **San**

Agustín, Playa del Inglés, and **Maspalomas.** Innumerable facilities include water sports and hot nightlife but the greatest sight is the area of undulating sand dunes and oases of palm trees at Maspalomas. Smaller resorts are on the west coast, including the attractive fishing port of **Puerto de Mogán** (with good seafood) and secluded **Playa de Güigüi.**

Las Palmas de Gran Canaria, the sprawling capital and largest city of the Canaries, developed on a spit of land that gives sea access on both sides. This major Atlantic port was founded in 1478 by Isabel la Católica, and the historic **Vegueta** district survives among towering modern apartment blocks. Here you find the twin-towered **cathedral** and the lovely Renaissance **Casa de Colón** (*Calle Colón 1, tel 928 31 23 84, closed Sat. & Sun. p.m.*), which has exhibits on Colombus's four stopovers on the island and on the importance of the Canaries in the early voyages to America. At the **Museo Canario** (*Calle Doctor Chil 25, tel 928 33 68 00, closed Sat. & Sun. p.m.*) you get a picture of the indigenous Guanche culture. The **Centro de Arte Moderno** (*Calle Los Balcones 11, tel 928 31 18 24, closed Mon., & Sun. p.m.*) exhibits contemporary Spanish art in a converted 18th-century building. Overlooking the port is the **Castillo de La Luz,** built in the 16th century to fend off pirates and now an occasional exhibition venue. **Playa de las Canteras** is the buzzing city beach. ■

Peaks cradle the village of Tejeda, in the center of the island.

Lanzarote

DROMEDARIES, ARCHITECTURE THAT IS SENSITIVE TO the environment, and blinding white beaches are just some of the attractions of this 323-square-mile (836-sq-km) island, all of which is a biosphere reserve. Lanzarote is special for its otherworldly volcanic cover, the result of momentous eruptions in 1730–36 and 1824 that buried towns and fertile valleys under lava flows.

These events produced the awesome landscapes of the **Parque Nacional de Timanfaya** or **Montañas del Fuego o de Timanfaya,** which include 300 volcanic cones. Don't pass up on a bumpy dromedary-ride through this extraordinary national park, where the volcanoes still simmer.

The main port and town is **Arrecife,** named for the outlying reefs of this south coast and defended by the 16th-century **Castillo del San Gabriel.** This houses the **Museo Arqueológico y Etnográfico** *(tel 928 80 28 84, closed Sat. p.m. & Sun.).* Arrecife's other guardian, **Castillo de San José,** has been converted into the **Museo Internacional de Arte Contemporáneo** *(tel 928 81 23 21).* The latter was the brainchild of Lanzarote's greatest artist, César Manrique (1920–1992), who was almost solely responsible for the islanders' admirable attitude to their architecture and environment. You can enjoy more of Manrique's work at the **Jameos del Agua** (a saltwater lagoon in a volcanic cave) and the breathtaking, clifftop **Mirador del Río,** both in the north of the island, and at the **Fundación César Manrique** *(Taro de Tahíche, Teguise, tel 928 84 31 38).* This intriguing lava-top house was built by Manrique in 1968 to exemplify affinities between art and nature, and it houses a good collection of contemporary Spanish art.

On the southern edge of the park lies **El Golfo.** This spectacular emerald-green crater lake is at the base of volcanic cliffs and creates a startling contrast with the black-sand beach. More tormented rockscapes characterize **Los Hervideros,** farther south on this western coast, before the road reaches the **Salinas de Janubio.** This natural phenomenon is formed out of dazzling white salt mounds and salt pans within a crater. Some of Lanzarote's best beaches are the white sandy coves of **Papagayo** and the resort of **Playa Blanca,** both on the south coast. ■

Lanzarote
🗺 335 F3
www.turismolanzarote.com

Parque Nacional de Timanfaya
🗺 335 F3
www.mma.es/parques/lared/timan/index.htm
✉ Calle Laguneta 64, Pinajo
☎ 928 84 02 38
   928 84 02 40

Arrecife
Visitor information
www.webdelanzarote.com/arrecife.htm
✉ Parque José Ramírez Cerdá
☎ 928 81 18 60

A fiery photo opportunity in Lanzarote's national park

Other islands

LA GOMERA

For decades most visitors who came to this island with its rugged terrain were seeking to escape the rat race. The 40-minute hydrofoil ride from Santa Cruz de Tenerife has changed that, yet Gomera's deep ravines and bad roads have preserved its charms for hikers and cyclists. Terraced farming, date palms, and banana plantations surround the central plateau characterized by its ancient laurel forest often shrouded in mist. This is the **Parque Nacional de Garajonay,** where you find around 400 native species of flora that became extinct in Africa and Europe millions of years ago. There are well-marked trails, and guided treks are available. Accommodations are concentrated in the capital of **San Sebastián de la Gomera** (where Columbus prepared to cross to America), **Playa de Santiago,** and idyllic **Valle Gran Rey.**

Standing above the clouds on the edge of Caldera de Taburiente, La Palma

🅰 334 B1 **Visitor information** www.gomera-island.com ✉ Calle Real 4, San Sebastián de La Gomera ☎ 922 14 15 12

EL HIERRO

This somewhat bleak bump in the Atlantic Ocean has inspired numerous legends. As the westernmost island in the archipelago for Europeans it was the end of the known world —in fact it was once used by geographers as zero meridian until it was relocated through Greenwich. Fish, sheep, goats, pineapples, and vineyards are the islanders' main resources; tourism is limited to **Valverde,** the capital, and neighboring **Tamaduste** with its lava pool. **El Golfo,** a 15-mile (25 km) crescent-shaped depression on the north coast, is backed by a sheer rock face rising to 3,280 feet (1,000 m). The rest of the island slopes dramatically down from the peak of **Malpaso,** ending in curious rock formations and cliffs. 🅰 334 A1 **Visitor information,** www.el-hierro.org ✉ Dr. Quintero Magdaleno 4, Valverde ☎ 922 55 03 02

LA PALMA

Claiming to be the highest island in the world, and home to the Northern Hemisphere's largest astrophysical observatory on the summit of **Roque de los Muchachos** (7,957 feet/2,426 m), La Palma has a mellow, low-key atmosphere with an increasing accent on rural pursuits. This lush, well-irrigated island of only 80,000 inhabitants has two small resorts: **Los Cancajos,** near the capital on the east coast, and the black-sand beach of **Puerto Naos** on the sunnier west coast. Another center is at **Los Llanos,** close to the impressive **Caldera de Taburiente** and national park *(Visitor Center El Paso, tel 922 49 72 77)*. This gigantic volcanic crater (6 miles/10 km in diameter) is best seen from lookout points or explored on foot. La Palma's volcanic cones and craters ends at the southernmost **Volcán Teneguía,** scene of the island's last eruption in 1971.

The capital, **Santa Cruz de la Palma,** was once a major port and preserves a delightful **seafront quarter** of Renaissance buildings and picturesque houses with typical fretwork balconies. See the lovely church of **El Salvador** *(tel 922 41 32 50)*, then stroll uphill to charming **Plaza Santo Domingo.** Don't miss out on La Palma's handmade cigars, silk, embroidery, and basketwork, and taste its tea (pinewood) wine. 🅰 334 A2 **Visitor information,** www.lapalmaturismo.com ✉ Avenida Marítima 34 ☎ 922 42 33 40 ■

Travelwise

**Round the volcanic bend
in Tenerife**

TRAVELWISE INFORMATION

PLANNING YOUR TRIP

WHEN TO GO

Unless you wish to bask on the busy summer beaches or ski in the Pyrenees or Sierra Nevada in winter, the time to visit Spain is during spring or fall (March to mid-June, mid-September to November). Spring is perhaps the finest season, when the wild flowers burst into colorful life and the naturally social and gregarious locals return to the streets after the short and, in places, severe winter. Fall sees Spain return to life as scorching temperatures drop to a pleasant level and rain ends the summer drought. Although winter can be cold in some areas of the country, the Mediterranean coast, particularly near Valencia, has some of the highest winter temperatures in Europe. On the other hand, Spain also has some of the highest summer temperatures on the continent, resulting in an exodus from the cities to the coast. In August virtually the entire country is on vacation. Combined with the arrival of millions of (mostly European) foreign visitors, this makes the coasts, particularly the Mediterranean, terribly overcrowded.

CLIMATE

The geographical and geological diversity of the regions means that the climate varies greatly. The north coast is battered by the Atlantic over the winter, suffering cold, rain, and mist, but has hot summers marked by thunderstorms. The Mediterranean coast ranges from the deserts of Almería (Europe's lowest rainfall) to a subtropical climate in Granada to the pine-covered hills of Catalunya. To the north, the Pyrenees are permanently snowcapped. The center of the country is occupied by the high meseta, "the plain of Spain," that ranges in height from 1,310 feet (400 m)

to 3,280 feet (1,000 m). This region bakes in the summer and is swept by freezing winds in the winter. To the west, the meseta stretches to Extremadura and then on to the border with Portugal. In this verdant area of rivers and oak forests, moss and lichen thrive in the damp air.

Average temperatures (from the Spanish Meteorological Office):

Barcelona
Jan. 43°F/6°C–56°F/13°C
Aug. 70°F/21°C–83°F/28°C
Madrid
Jan. 34°F/1°C–49°F/9°C.
Aug. 63°F/17°C–88°F/31°C
Málaga
Jan. 49°F/9°C–63°F/17°C
Aug. 72°F/22°C–86°F/30°C

MAIN EVENTS

Spain has an enormous number of festivals and fiestas. Probably the best known of these is **San Fermín,** the running of the bulls in Iruña (Pamplona), July 6–14. Holy Week or **Semana Santa** (the week before Easter, see p. 272–73) is marked by spectacular processions in many towns, but most famously in Sevilla. If it's a party you want, then visit Valencia for **Las Fallas de San José** (March 12–19). More sedate are the fiestas of Madrid. During **San Isidro** (two weeks from May 15), many operas, concerts and ballets are performed. Other festivals are listed on pp. 388–89.

WHAT TO TAKE

You should be able to buy most things that you need in Spain. Clothing depends on the time of year and your destination. Spaniards tend to dress quite formally except at the coastal resorts during the summer months. Casual clothing and footwear (such as trainers) are quite acceptable during the day,

but you should dress up when going out at night.

Bring any essential prescription medication; for other medicines, Spanish pharmacy staff are helpful and knowledgeable, and dispense many drugs that in other countries might need prescriptions.

INSURANCE

Make sure you have adequate travel and medical coverage for treatment and expenses, including repatriation, baggage, and money loss. Keep all receipts for expenses. Report losses or thefts to the police and obtain a signed statement (una denuncia) from a police station to help with insurance claims.

FURTHER READING

Publishers are not included as many of these books have been reprinted by different companies.

For Whom the Bell Tolls by Ernest Hemingway. Perhaps the most famous book written on Spain and the Civil War.
The Sun Also Rises by Ernest Hemingway. This book put the San Fermín festival in Iruña (Pamplona) on the map.
South From Granada by Gerald Brenan. A fascinating account of life in rural southern Spain between the two World Wars.
The Spanish Temper by V.S. Pritchett. Perceptive portrait of Spain's people, landscape, history, and myth.
Homage to Barcelona by Colm Toibin. Firsthand account of modern life in Barcelona.
Voices of the Old Sea by Norman Lewis. The author looks back at the fishing village he knew in his youth from the unrecognizable place it has become today.
Spain by Jan Morris. A good general book on the country.
Our Lady of the Sewers by Paul Richardson. Pieces about "the ancient, perverse and eccentric" side of Spain that is becoming increasingly hard to find.

HOW TO GET TO SPAIN

ENTRY FORMALITIES

U.S., Canadian, and E.U. citizens may enter Spain without a visa and remain there for up to 90 days. Keep your identity card or passport on you at all times.

AIRLINES

The national carrier, Iberia, has direct flights from several North American cities to Madrid. U.S. airlines also offer direct flights, and several other European carriers have services to Spain.

Useful numbers & internet addresses
In the U.S. and Canada:
Air Europa, tel 888/238-7672
    www.air-europa.com/
Iberia, tel 800/772-4642
    www.iberia.com
British Airways,
    tel 800/247-9297
    www.ba.com
American Airlines,
    tel 800/433-7300
    www.aa.com
Delta Airlines, tel 800/241-4141
    www.delta.com

In Spain:
Iberia, tel 902 40 05 00
Air Europa, tel 902 40 15 01
American Airlines,
    tel 902 11 55 70
British Airways,
    tel 902 11 13 33
Delta Airlines,
    Madrid, tel 91 749 66 30
    Barcelona, tel 901 11 69 46
Vueling, tel 902 33 39 33
    www.vueling.com

ARRIVAL

BY AIR
Most intercontinental flights touch down at Barajas airport, Madrid. The airport is 10 miles (15 km) from downtown Madrid, a 20-minute taxi ride costing roughly 20 € ($31.50). Buses run every 10 minutes to Avenida de América, 5:36 a.m.–11:30 p.m. Tickets cost 1.00 €

($1.57). The underground train is slower and harder to use than the bus. If you arrive in Barcelona, a taxi ride into the center takes about 25 minutes and costs 25 € ($39.33). Buses leave every 6 minutes from 6:00 a.m.–1 a.m., and cost 3.90 € ($6.15). A train service runs from 6:00 a.m.–11:45 p.m. and costs 2.5 € ($3.93).

BY CAR
Arriving by car, you must choose between the Atlantic or Mediterranean coasts if you wish to travel on the motorways. Smaller roads cross the Pyrenees, but they may be blocked by snow in winter. The exception is the road through Andorra; it is closed only during extreme conditions.

BY SEA
Several ferries sail from the U.K. and France to the northern ports of Santander and Bilbo. Timetables change depending on the season. In the U.K.:
Brittany Ferries
    tel 08709 076 103
    www.brittany-ferries.com
P&O European Ferries
    tel 08705 980 333
    www.poferries.com

BY TRAIN
You can go by train from the U.K. via the Channel Tunnel, changing trains in Paris and passing the night on a *trenhotel*. The Madrid sleeper leaves Paris Austerlitz train station at 7:43 p.m. and arrives at Madrid Chamartín at 9:13 a.m. The train for Barcelona leaves at 8:32 p.m. and arrives at 8:24 a.m..

HEALTH

All visitors should take out adequate health insurance. EU citizens should bring a European Health Insurance Card (EHIC), which entitles them to free treatment by the Spanish health service. No vaccinations are required. Tap water is safe to drink though it may have a chlorine taste. Plastic bottles of mineral water are widely available. The primary health

concerns are sunburn and dehydration. Make sure to wear suitable clothing and put on sunscreen. During the hottest parts of the day in the summer you will notice few locals about on the streets.

GETTING AROUND

BY AIRPLANE

Most major cities in Spain have an airport for internal and international flights. The national airline Iberia (Tel 902 40 05 00) has the most frequent internal flights. Other airlines are Air Europa (Tel 902 40 15 01), Vueling (Tel 902 33 39 33), and Spanair (Tel 902 13 14 15).

BY CAR

Getting around by car is a good option, allowing you to get to out-of-the-way places that otherwise would be difficult to reach. Driving in the countryside is often a relaxing experience if you are used to the congested roads of northern Europe, but driving in the cities can be quite the reverse. Dual lane *autopistas* and the *autovías* link many provincial capitals and, outside of major cities and holidays, are relatively free of traffic. Tolls are paid in cash or with credit cards on exiting the autopista or, on short stretches, on entering. National roads, or *nacionales*, marked in red on the road maps, were the old main roads, now superseded by the motorways. They are still in constant use. Smaller roads marked in yellow are *comarcales*, regional roads, and are often picturesque and quiet, as are the local roads marked (white and often without any names or numbers).

Motoring information
European driving permits are valid in Spain. U.S. and Canadian citizens require an International Driving Permit, obtainable at any AAA or CAA office. If your permit does not include a photo,

you must carry ID that does—such as a passport. It is compulsory to carry two warning triangles, spare light bulbs, fuses, reflective jackets, and a spare tire. The minimum legal age for drivers is 18. You must be over 21 to rent a car. If entering Spain in your own car, make sure that you have appropriate insurance, including the green card available from your insurers. Using GPS/SatNav systems and cell phones while driving is prohibited.

Breakdown assistance
Freeways have emergency telephones at intervals. A tow truck from the nearest garage will be sent to help you. You must place a warning triangle behind your vehicle. If you belong to AAA, CAA, or AA you can get help in English from RACE, the Spanish motoring organization, tel 902 30 05 05, www.race.es.

Distances All distances are in kilometers (1 km=0.62 mile).

Drunk-driving The alcohol limit for drivers is 0.5g of alcohol per liter of blood or 0.25mg per liter breath alcohol concentration. The fine for exceeding this starts at 300 € ($471).

Fuel Fuel prices are controlled by the government and are slightly cheaper than in the U.K. but nearly twice those of the U.S. The types of fuel available are: Eurosuper 98, Premium, Eurosuper 95, Normal, Biodiesel, and Gasoleo (Diesel).

On-the-spot-fines Failing to wear your seat belt can range from 90 to 300 € ($142–471). Exceeding the speed limit results in a fine of between 300 and 600 € ($471–944). Non-residents must pay immediately; make sure you get a receipt (recibo).

Parking A yellow line on the road or pavement means no parking. A sign may indicate that you can park after a certain time.

Blue lines denote pay parking. Look for ticket-dispensing machines marked by a sign of a coin being pushed into a slot, and display the ticket in your car. If your car has been towed away, an orange sticker will give details of your car, the time it was taken, and the number to call. In cities it makes sense to use the underground car-parks, which now proliferate.

Seat belts Wearing seat belts is compulsory in the front seats and also in the back if the car is fitted with them.

Speed limits They are: freeways 75 mph (120 kph); nacional roads 62.5 mph (100 kph); C roads 56 mph (90 kph); towns and built-up areas 31 mph (50 kph). Stay alert: they may change.

Traffic circles Vehicles already in the circle have right of way unless it is marked otherwise.

RENTING A CAR
Renting a car in Spain is straightforward and relatively cheap. There are many local companies, and international ones such as Hertz and Avis. It is worth looking into fly-and-drive deals when booking your trip.
Avis, tel 902 18 08 54, www.avis.com
Hertz, tel 902 40 24 05, www.hertz.com
Europcar, tel 902 10 50 30, www.europcar.com
If you start in Madrid, bear in mind that road signs as you leave the city give road numbers rather than destinations.

BY TRAIN

RENFE (Red Nacional de Ferrocarriles Españoles) is the mainline national rail network. Outside the main holiday periods (summer and Easter Week), traveling by train is recommended, particularly on the Talgos (Tren Articulado Ligero Goicoechea Oriol) and the high speed AVEs (Alta Velocidad Española). Despite

being relaxed and reminiscent of an earlier age of train travel, Talgos are fast, comfortable, and reliable, and usually have a well-equipped snack bar. AVEs have telephones and other facilities.

Tickets can be bought at the station up to 15 minutes before the train departs; it is unwise to leave it so late as long lines form. Reserve your seat for longer journeys. Travel agents that display a RENFE sticker sell rail tickets, and RENFE also has offices in downtown areas in many cities, where you can purchase your ticket. For a long-distance rail journey, in the high season, book well in advance through your travel agent in your home country.

Trains are generally divided into 1st and 2nd class, but standards vary between the type of train and also between the trains themselves. You can get a 20 percent reduction on a round-trip ticket. There are special rates for those over 60 and children between 4 and 13, and for travelers with disabilities.

Inter Rail and Eurail passes are valid in Spain as they are elsewhere in Europe (www.inter railnet.com, www.eurail.com). Students should get an International Student Identity Card (ISIC), those under 26 an International Youth Travel Card (IYTC) and teachers an International Teacher Identity Card (ITIC)—all offer useful discounts (information on www.istc.org).

RENFE (www.renfe.es) has a comprehensive website with up to the minute details of prices, routes, and timetables in both Spanish and English.

TRANSPORTATION IN MADRID

TAXIS
Downtown Madrid teems with taxis (white, with a red stripe along their sides), and you rarely have to wait long before one appears. Madrid is a compact city, and taxis are not expensive, which makes them

an ideal mode of transport. A supplement is charged between 10 p.m. and 6 a.m. and for passing beyond the city limits.

METRO

The subway system is the most efficient and rapid mode of public transport. The distances between stops are short, so you tend to be near your destination when you exit the station. Punch your ticket as you start your journey. Most major attractions are within Zone A, for which single tickets cost 1 € ($1.57). The Metrobús ticket gives you ten journeys, either by subway or by bus, for 6.40 € ($10.07). The Tourist Travel Pass (Abono Turístico) gives you one day's subway and bus travel throughout Zone A for 3.50 € ($5.50) or seven days for 19.80 € ($31.15). To buy it you must show ID, and it cannot be shared. Lines are color coded and the train's direction is indicated by the terminal stations. Hold on to your ticket until exiting the system: Inspectors check for fare dodgers.

BUS

Madrid's bus network is extensive but confusing. On a short stay it may not be worth mastering. The price of a journey is the same as on the metro, and you can use tickets from your abono. If not, pay the driver, using small change rather than a note. Punch your ticket in the machine near the driver.

TRANSPORTATION IN BARCELONA

Barcelona has buses, cable cars, trams, and underground trains. If you plan to stay for more than a few days, buy one of the various targetes (similar to abonos in Madrid), either the T10 or the Travel Cards, which work on all forms of public transport. The Zone 1 T10 offers ten journeys, covers all of central Barcelona, can be shared and costs 6.90 € ($10.85). The Travel Cards offer unlimited travel for 2, 3, 4, or 5

consecutive days for 9.60, 13.70, 17.50, and 20.80 € ($15.10, 21.55, 27.53, and 32.72), discounts at some museums, sights, shows, and restaurants, and cannot be shared. They can be bought at the airport or at Tourist Information Offices.

TAXIS

Like Madrid, Barcelona abounds in taxis, only here they are black and yellow. They offer a cost-effective way of getting around the city, though much of the center is pedestrianized. The minimum charge is 1.80 € ($2.83).

METRO

Again, the quickest way of getting around the city is the metro. Smaller than Madrid's system, just five lines, it is open between 5 a.m.–12 p.m, until 2 a.m. on Friday, and all night on Saturday.

BUSES

The buses in Barcelona are color coded: red buses for the city center, yellow for cross-city, green for those that head out to the suburbs, and blue for the night buses.

PRACTICAL ADVICE

COMMUNICATIONS

E-MAIL

Most towns have an internet café that is easy to find.

Madrid

BBiGG Internet & Games www.bbigg.com, Calle Mayor 1, tel 91 531 23 64, metro Sol, 9 a.m.–12:30 a.m.; Calle Alcalá 399, tel 91 367 51 40, metro Pueblo Nuevo, 10 a.m.–12 p.m. Both cost 2 € ($3.15)/hour. **Café Comercial** Glorieta de Bilbao 7, tel 91 521 5655, metro Bilbao, 8 a.m.–1 a.m. Cost: 1 € ($1.57)/50 minutes.

Barcelona

Bornet Barra de Ferro 3 (by the Picasso Museum), tel 93 268 15 07, metro Jaume 1, open

Mon.–Fri. 10 a.m.–11 p.m., Sat.–Sun. & holidays 12 a.m.–11 p.m. Cost: 2.80 € ($4.40)/hour. **Ciber Condal** Basses de Sant Pere 26, tel 93 268 12 00, metro Arc de Triomf, open 10 a.m.–11 p.m. Cost: 1.50 € ($2.36)/hour. **EasyInternetCafé** Rambla del Capuchino 31, tel 93 301 75 07, metros Liceu & Drassanes, 9 a.m. –1 a.m. Cost: 2 € ($3.46)/hour.

Sevilla

Ciber No&do Plaza de San Francisco 19, open Mon.–Fri. 10 a.m.–2 p.m. & 5 p.m.–8 p.m. Cost: free for one hour. **Internetia** Avenida Menéndez Pelayo 43-5, tel 95 453 40 03, open 11 a.m.–11 p.m. Cost 2.20 € ($3.46)/hour.

POST OFFICES

To send a letter or postcard of less than 20 g costs 0.58 € within the E.U. and 0.78 € to North America. Registered mail, correo certificado, costs an extra 2.24 €. Stamps are available at post offices (correos), which in major cities are open Mon.–Fri. 8:30 a.m.–8:30 p.m. and Sat. 9:30 a.m.–1 p.m.

TELEPHONES

The country code for Spain is 34 followed by the provincial code, which starts with a 9. Codes to some provinces are: Madrid (91), Barcelona (93), Valencia (96), Sevilla (95), and Vizcaya (94). Many provinces have three-digit codes: Navarra (948) and Granada (958). Call boxes usually allow you to pay in cash or with a card (tarjeta telefónica). Tarjetas are sold at post offices and estancos (tobacconists, or tabacos), and come in denominations from 5 to 150 €. The access code to make an international call is 00. For collect calls, dial 1009. For national directory inquiries dial 11818, for international 11825. Spanish cell phone numbers start with 6. Calls to 900 numbers are free.

CONVERSIONS

1 kilo = 2.2 pounds

PRACTICAL ADVICE

1 liter = 0.2642 U.S. gallons
1 kilometer = 0.62 mile
1 meter = 1.093 yards

Women's clothing

U.S.	8	10	12	14	16	18
Spanish	36	38	40	42	44	46

Women's shoes

U.S.	6–6½	7–7½	8–8½	9–9½
Spanish	38	39	40–41	42

Men's clothing

U.S.	36	38	40	42	44	46
Spanish	46	48	50	52	54	56

Men's shoes

U.S.	8	8½	9½	10½	11½	12
Spanish	41	42	43	44	45	46

ELECTRICITY

The electricity voltage is 220 or 225 AC, not 110 V as in North America. Plugs are two pin. U.S. and Canadian appliances need adaptors.

HOLIDAYS

Spain has national, regional, and local holidays. It is not possible to keep track of all of them as each city, town, and village celebrates its own saint's day, and since all the days of the week have saints there is always a fiesta or festival going on somewhere. Most regions have at least seven others, but the main national holidays are:
January 1 & 6 (Epiphany)
Good Friday
Easter Sunday
Easter Monday
May 1 (May Day)
October 12 (National Day)
November 1 (All Saints)
December 6 (Constitution),
8 (Immaculate Conception),
& 25 (Christmas)

MEDIA

NEWSPAPERS

The most popular dailies are *El País, El Mundo,* and *ABC.* The left-leaning *El País* has the best international coverage. There are many regional English language papers on the Mediterranean

coast and the islands. In the tourist areas you find the same day *International Herald Tribune* and the British newspapers.

RADIO

The airwaves are full of local and national radio stations. The state-run Radio Nacional de España has four stations covering sports, pop, classical music, and current affairs, which are on the whole better than local stations. The Voice of America is broadcast on short-wave, but moves around according to the time of day: Try 9.700, 15.205, and 15.255 MHz. The same applies to the BBC World Service: Try 3.955, 7.150, 9.410, 15.070, and 15.400.

TELEVISION

Terrestrial Spanish television has good news coverage but tends to be a mess of game, quiz, audience participation shows, and Latin American soaps. Spaniards love their televisions and have them on constantly in bars and even restaurants.

There are two state-run channels, TVE1 and TVE2, and four independents as well as regional channels. Most hotels are equipped with satellite, cable, or digital television, offering international channels such as CNN, BBC World, and Sky.

MONEY MATTERS

Take a combination of traveler's checks and credit or debit cards that you can use to extract cash from the plentiful ATMs. Major credit cards are accepted in most establishments and all gas stations. Traveler's checks are a secure way to hold money (keep a list of their numbers separate from the checks) and can be changed in banks and exchange offices. Banks give you a better exchange rate but exchange offices are open longer hours.

Spain's currency is the Euro (€). The Euro comes in coins of 1, 2, 5, 10, 20, & 50 cents (céntimos) and of 1 & 2 Euros, and notes of 5, 10, 20, 50, 100, 200,

and 500 Euros. (At the time of printing 1 € = \$1.57.)

OPENING TIMES

Banks open 8:30 a.m.–2:30 p.m. (1 p.m. on Sat.).

Museums open 9 a.m.–7 p.m. Generally most close on Monday.

Shops and pharmacies, open 9:30 a.m.–2 p.m, and again between 4:30 p.m.–5 p.m., closing at 8 p.m.

Restaurants open around midday, close around 5 p.m., reopen around 7 p.m. and often serve food until past midnight.

Bars are open virtually 24 hours. Cafés open from 7 a.m. onward. Music bars open until between 3–5 a.m., and nightclubs often until 7 a.m.

PLACES OF WORSHIP

When visiting churches, remember that they are not meant as tourist attractions but places of worship; act accordingly.

REST ROOMS

Public toilets are rare outside tourist spots. Luckily, you are never far from a bar and it would be unusual if the owner did not let you use the toilet. Carry toilet paper with you as this is often in short supply.

TIME DIFFERENCES

Spain runs on CET (Central European Time), one hour ahead of Greenwich Mean Time, six hours ahead of Eastern Standard Time. The Canary Islands run on CET minus one. Noon in Spain is 6 a.m. in New York. EST.

TRAVELERS WITH DISABILITIES

Only in recent years has Spain begun to cater for the needs of people with disabilities. Newer buildings are more accessible than older ones, but there may still be problems. Check with hotels and restaurants before booking. Advice is available from:

Disabled Peoples' International (DPI)
748 Broadway, Winnipeg, MB R3G OX3, Canada, tel 204/287-8010, e-mail: dpi@dpi.org, www.dpi.org

RADAR (Royal Association for Disability and Rehabilitation) 12 City Forum, 250 City Road, London EC1V 8AF, U.K., tel 020-7250 3222, www.radar.org.uk

European Disability Forum Rue du Commerce 39-41, B-1000 Brussels, Belgium, Tel 32 2 282 4600, Fax 32 2 282 4609, e-mail: info@edf-feph.org, www.edf-feph.org

Mobility International U.S.A. P.O. Box 10767, Eugene, Oregon, U.S.A. 97440, tel 541/343-1284, e-mail info@ miusa.org www.miusa.org

ETIQUETTE & LOCAL CUSTOMS

The Spanish siesta is not a myth. Almost everything closes from 2–5 p.m., even later in summer. Lunch—the day's main meal—begins at 2 and often lasts until 5 p.m. Sunday lunch can go on longer. Dinner is a lighter affair, as it is considered unhealthy to eat a lot before going to bed.

TIPPING

Service is included on restaurant bills, so there is no need to tip. However, the Spanish service industry is poorly paid; a tip for good service would not be amiss. The Spanish themselves often leave their small change when paying for a drink and tip about 5 percent at restaurants. Tip taxi drivers and porters 2–3 €, depending on the distance and amount of luggage.

EMERGENCIES

EMBASSIES

Embassies are in Madrid, but larger cities have consulates.

United States
Serrano 75, tel 91 587 22 00, www.embusa.es
Canada
Núñez de Balboa 35, tel 91 423 32 50, www.canada-es.org
United Kingdom
Fernando Santo 16, tel 91 700 82 00, www.ukinspain.com
Consulate
tel 915 24 97 00, emergencies 606 98 76 26

Spanish embassies
United States
2375 Pennsylvania Ave. N.W., Washington, DC 20037, tel 202/452-0100, www.spainemb.org
Canada
74 Stanley Ave., Ottawa, Ontario K1M 1P4, tel 613/747-2252, www.embaspain.ca
United Kingdom
39 Chesham Place, London SW1X 8SB, tel 020-7235 5555, www.conspalon.org

EMERGENCY PHONE NUMBER

The central number for police, fire, and ambulance is 112.

POLICE

Spain has three distinct police forces. The Policía Local (or Municipal) are controlled by the local town hall and deal with minor matters such as traffic infringements. The Policía Nacional are the main crime-fighting force in the cities (except in the Basque country where they become Erzaintra and in Catalunya, Mossos d'Esquadra). The Guardia Civil operate in the countryside and on highways, in addition to controlling borders and prisons.

LOSS OF CREDIT CARDS

American Express España, tel 902 37 56 37 (24 hrs.)
Diners Club Español, tel 901 10 10 11 (24 hrs.)
Mastercard, tel 900 97 12 31 (24 hrs.)

VISA International, tel 900 99 11 24 (24 hrs.)

WHAT TO DO IN A CAR ACCIDENT

The Guardia Civil operates special units designed to deal effectively with anything other than minor accidents. If involved in an accident you should mark the position of your vehicle as accurately as possible, then move it to a safe place (call 112). and wait for the police. Place reflective triangles in front and behind. If it is a minor accident involving another vehicle, there is no need to call the police as long as both parties agree how it occurred. In this case, simply fill out the insurance details. For repairs, call from an SOS phone on freeways or call RACE (Tel 902 40 45 45).

HEALTH

Make sure that your health insurance covers you during your visit to Spain. E.U. citizens should complete and carry the EHIC form available from main post offices. Doctors are listed in the telephone directory, but in an emergency go to the nearest *urgencias*, call an ambulance on 112, or call the number for the nearest Red Cross (Cruz Roja). A hospital stay can be expensive, so make sure your insurance is valid and up to date.

International Association for Medical Assistance to Travellers (IAMAT) is a nonprofit organization that anyone can join free of charge. Members receive a directory of English speaking IAMAT doctors on call 24 hours a day, and are entitled to services at a set rate. www.iamat.org
United States
1623 Military Rd., Suite 279, Niagara Falls, NY 14304-1745, tel 716/754-4883
Canada
1287 St. Claire Ave. West, Toronto, Ontario M6E 1B8, tel 416/652-0137

HOTELS & RESTAURANTS

Spain has a wide variety of accommodations, ranging from the humblest of *fondas* or *casas de huéspedes* (guesthouses) to luxurious five-star hotels. A new interest in the countryside is reflected in the number of *casas rurales* (country houses) that have recently opened. Located in some beautiful and wild spots, they may be farm houses, country cottages, or restored palaces, and offer outdoor activities such as horseback riding, hiking, and bicycling. Facilities are reflected in prices, and in cheaper hotels you may not have a private bath. If in doubt check when making your reservation.

HOTELS

A number of hotels offer *media pensión* (includes breakfast and dinner) or *pensión completa* (includes lunch as well) at a competitive price. Inquire upon reservation or arrival. Spain is a noisy country and peace and quiet can be hard to come by. When reserving a room, mention that you would like one away from likely noise.

Paradors

Unique to Spain are the paradors, the nationally owned chain of hotels—some in historic buildings—often in national parks or other places of scenic interest.

Grading system

Spanish hotels are graded with a star system of one to five, five being top of the range. *Hostales* or *pensiones* have a different system of one to three stars. Standards may vary from region to region as the autonomous governments are responsible for their own classifications.

Some of the hotels in this guide fall out of the star rating system—this includes the *casas rurales* and *posadas*.

The following is a selection of hotels throughout the country, listed by location, price, then in alphabetical order. Hotels that are historically, architecturally, or aesthetically interesting have been chosen wherever possible.

Note, unless otherwise stated:
- Breakfast is not included in the price.
- The hotel has a restaurant. If the hotel restaurant is particularly good, a description is included.
- Smoking is now more strictly controlled. Hotels and larger bars and restaurants have non-smoking areas.
- Price categories are given only as guidance and do not take into account seasonal variations.
- The 7 percent I.V.A (Value Added Tax) is not included in the price categories.
- Prices are for a double room.

In high season always try to book in advance. You may be asked for a deposit or credit card number.

Credit & debit cards

Many hotels accept all major cards. Smaller ones may only accept some, as shown. Abbreviations used are: AE (American Express), DC (Diners Club), MC (Mastercard), and V (Visa).

Hotel chains & groups

www.solmelia.com (reservations: 00 34 902 14 44 40)
www.parador.es (reservations: 00 34 902 54 79 79)
www.nh-hotels.com (reservations: 00 34 902 11 51 16)
www.husa.es (reservations: 00 34 902 10 07 10)

Hotel groups or chains often have special offers, for example five nights in selected paradors at a fixed price that works out one-third cheaper than the normal price. Ask your travel agent or check their Web sites.

RESTAURANTS

By law, all restaurants have to provide a *menú del día* (starter, main course, dessert, and a drink), an economical option that is popular but usually offered only for lunch. More upscale restaurants may have a *menú degustación* (taster menu) that allows you to try small portions of several courses, including desserts. The price categories in the guide are for a meal à la carte, excluding wine. Some restaurants close on public holidays. Check before you go.

CAFÉS & BARS

Bars and cafés play a central role in Spanish social life. They open early in the morning and close late at night. It is common to have a *tapa* (a snack that can be anything from a small plate of olives or almonds to a tiny bowl of stew) with your beer or wine.
L= lunch D = dinner

PRICES

HOTELS
An indication of the cost of a double room without breakfast is given by **$** signs.

$$$$$	Over $300
$$$$	$220–$300
$$$	$160–$220
$$	$80–$160
$	Under $80

RESTAURANTS
An indication of the cost of a three-course dinner without drinks is given by $ signs.

$$$$$	Over $80
$$$$	$50–$80
$$$	$35–$50
$$	$20–$35
$	Under $20

IN & AROUND MADRID

ME MADRID
$$$$$ ★★★★
PLAZA DE SANTA ANA 14
TEL 91 701 60 00
E-MAIL memadrid@solmelia.com
www.mebymelia.com
The Hotel Reina Victoria is now the hip, ultra-fashionable ME Madrid. Once the home of the Counts of Teba, then the favored hotel of bullfighters and writers such as Ernest Hemingway, it has a beautiful facade and a rooftop bar and terrace with spectacular views.
192 Sevilla All major cards

HOTELS & RESTAURANTS

RITZ
$$$$$ ★★★★★
PLAZA DE LA LEALTAD 5
TEL 91 701 67 67
FAX 91 701 67 76
E-MAIL reservations@ritz.es
www.ritzmadrid.com
Built in 1910 for King Alfonso
XIII and Queen Victoria's
grandaughter's wedding
guests. The hotel is full of
beautiful antiques and elegant
chandeliers, and is surrounded
by luscious gardens.
🛏 167 🚇 Banco de España
🅿 ⬍ ❄ 🏋 🅒 All major
cards

SOMETHING SPECIAL

SANTO MAURO

Built in neoclassic style by the
Duke of Santo Mauro in
1894, this palace has interiors by
Josep Joanpere, combining the
original materials with the
contemporary. An intriguing
feature is the basement pool
with columns and vaulted
ceilings. La Biblioteca, the
restaurant, occupies the old
library. A modern, Basque-
Navarrese influenced cuisine
produces dishes such as scallop
and spider crab carpaccio with
vegetable tempura, monkfish with
cuttle-fish and mango tagliatelle,
and for dessert, chocolate mousse
with caramelized banana.
$$$$$ ★★★★★
ZURBANO 36
TEL 91 319 69 00
FAX 91 308 54 77
E-MAIL santo-mauro@ac-ho
tels.com
www.achotelsantomauro.com
🛏 51 🛏 42 🚇 Alonso
Martínez 🅿 ⬍ ❄ 🚕
🏋 🅒 All major cards

VILLA MAGNA
$$$$$ ★★★★★
PASEO CASTELLANA 22
TEL 91 587 12 34
FAX 91 431 22 86
E-MAIL villamagna@hyattintl.com
www.villamagna.park.hyatt.com
The modern facade contrasts
with the Charles IV-style inte-

riors. Major refurbishment took
place in 2008. It also has two
fine restaurants: The Berceo,
specializing in fish, and the Tse-
Yang, serving the highest quality
Chinese cuisine in the capital.
Gardens surround the hotel.
🛏 151 🚇 Núñez de Balboa
🅿 ⬍ ❄ 🏋 🅒 All major
cards

SOMETHING SPECIAL

VILLA REAL

A modern hotel built to blend
in with older surroundings.
The reception, salons, and bedrooms are decorated, in the
French style. Wonderful modern
and antique sculptures, paintings, tapestries, and other art,
include a collection of third-
century Roman mosaics. Guest
rooms have sitting areas with
mahogany furniture and bathrooms with Carrara marble.
Suites have balconies and saunas.
$$$$$ ★★★★★
PLAZA DE LAS CORTES 10
TEL 91 420 37 67
FAX 91 420 25 47
E-MAIL info@derbyhotels.es
www.derbyhotels.es
🛏 115 🚇 Sol 🅿 ⬍ ❄
🅒 All major cards

WESTIN PALACE
$$$$$ ★★★★★
PLAZA DE LAS CORTES 7
TEL 91 360 80 00 or 90 081 12 45
FAX 91 360 81 00
www.westin.com/palacemadrid
Inaugurated by King Alfonso
XIII in 1912, it has sumptuous
reception and main rooms,
with period decor. The stained-
glass cupola is a distinguishing
feature of this palace-hotel.
Bedrooms are small, but
interior furnishings and
bathrooms are impressive.
🛏 468 🅿 ⬍ ❄ 🏋
🅒 All major cards

LIABENY
$$$ ★★★★
SALUD 3
TEL 91 531 90 00
FAX 91 532 74 21

E-MAIL reserves@hotelliabeny.com
www.hotelliabeny.com
Large and modern, it is two
minutes from Puerta del Sol
and Gran Vía. It has marble
bathrooms and all the facilities
of a four-star hotel.
🛏 220 🚇 Sol 🅿 ⬍ ❄
🅒 All major cards

TRYP AMBASSADOR
$$$ ★★★★
CUESTA DE SANTO
DOMINGO 5
TEL 91 541 67 00
FAX 91 559 10 40
E-MAIL tryp.ambassador@sol
melia.com
www.trypambassador.solmelia.com
A 19th-century palace that
became a hotel in 1991. Right
in the heart of historic Madrid,
it retains some of the original
features, such as the sweeping
staircase and front door. The
elegant rooms are spacious
with mahogany furniture.
🛏 183 🚇 Santo Domingo
⬍ ❄ 🅒 All major cards

BEST WESTERN CARLOS V
$$ ★★★
MAESTRO VICTORIA 5
TEL 91 531 41 00
FAX 91 531 37 61
E-MAIL recepcion@hotelcarl
osv.com
www.hotelcarlosv.com
Two minutes walk from the
Puerta del Sol, the Carlos V
has an art nouveau entrance.
Rooms are large and simply
decorated, ask for one with a
balcony. The guest lounge also
has stucco ceilings and crystal
chandeliers. Cafeteria.
🛏 67 🚇 Sol ⬍ ❄ 🅒 All
major cards

INGLÉS
$$ ★★★
ECHEGARAY 8
TEL 91 4 29 65 51
FAX 91 420 24 23
E-MAIL comercial@ingleso
tel.com
www.ingleshotel.com
Virginia Woolf and other
writers and artists of her time
stayed at this hotel. No frills

but very well situated near Plaza Santa Ana and Puerta del Sol. No restaurant.

ⓘ 58 🚇 Sol 🅿 🛗 ⊠ All major cards

🏨 REGINA

$$ ★★★

ALCALÁ 19

TEL 91 521 47 25

FAX 91 522 40 88

E-MAIL info@hotelreginama drid.com

www.hotelreginamadrid.com

An unassuming historical building within walking distance of many of Madrid's sights. Spacious rooms for the tired sightseer. No restaurant.

ⓘ 142 🚇 Sevilla 🛗 🐾

⊠ All major cards

🍽 EL AMPARO

$$$$$

PUIGCERDÁ 8

TEL 91 431 64 56

www.arturocantoblanco.com

This restaurant serves adventurous modern Basque cuisine. Dishes that justify their reputation are puff pastry layered with apple, smoked fish, and foie gras and prawns tossed with creamy corn-filled ravioli. Exquisite desserts and wine.

🪑 80 🚇 Serrano 🕐 Closed Sat. L, Sun. & Easter 🐾

⊠ All major cards

🍽 JOCKEY

$$$$$

AMADOR DE LOS RÍOS 6

TEL 91 319 24 35

www.restaurantejockey.net

Among the top restaurants in Spain, it has an elegant decor. Start with the house aperitif, Gin Jockey. Specialties include the excellent *langostinos crudos al caviar con crema fresca* (prawns marinated and served with caviar cream.) Excellent selection of wines and ports. Jacket and tie are required.

🪑 100 🚇 Colón 🅿

🕐 Closed Sun. & Aug. 🐾

⊠ All major cards

🍽 LA TERRAZA DEL CASINO

$$$$$

ALCALÁ 15

TEL 91 532 12 75

www.casinodemadrid.es

Grand dining rooms and a fantastic summer terrace, but above all the original cooking of chef Paco Roncero, disciple of Ferrán Adriá, offers a wonderful combination of aromas and textures. Try the Thai lobster, knuckle of veal, or menu degustación (taster menu). One Michelin star. Jacket and tie are required.

🪑 65 🚇 Sevilla 🅿 🕐 Sat. L, Sun. & Aug. 🐾 ⊠ All major cards

🍽 LA TRAINERA

$$$$$

LAGASCA 60

TEL 91 576 05 75

www.latrainera.es

A long-established informal establishment with the best seafood in Madrid. Dishes are kept simple, generally either grilled or cooked on the hot plate. Many order the *salpicón de marisco* (various types of shellfish to share). Ham is the only meat on the menu. Wines include Albariño.

🪑 300 🚇 Serrano 🅿

🕐 Closed Sun. & Aug. 🐾

⊠ All major cards

🍽 ZALACAÍN

$$$$$

ÁLVAREZ DE BAENA 4

TEL 91 561 48 40

A pioneer of nueva cocina. Some dishes are Zalacaín classics, others more recent innovations. Specialties include cold cream of pumpkin with profiteroles, scallops and leeks in Albariño wine, and grilled sea bass with green olive vinaigrette. One of Spain's top restaurants. One Michelin star. Reservations are essential. Men must wear jacket and tie.

🪑 100 🚇 Gregorio Marañón 🅿 🕐 Closed Sat. L, Sun., Easter, & Aug. 🐾 ⊠ All major cards

🍽 EL OLIVO

$$$$

GENERAL GALLEGOS 1

TEL 91 359 15 35

Dedicated to the joy of olive oil, it offers some 40 varieties also sold in its shop. Its sherry bar features over 100 different brands. Its Mediterranean cuisine includes marinated sardines on caviar, warm lobster salad with herb vinaigrette, and outstanding desserts.

🪑 80 🚇 Cuzco 🕐 Closed Sun., Mon. D, & last 2 weeks Aug. 🐾 ⊠ All major cards

🍽 ENTRE SUSPIRO Y SUSPIRO

$$$$

CAÑOS DEL PERAL 3

TEL 91 542 06 44

www.entresuspiroysuspiro.com

This Mexican food is a must for aficionados. The corn quesadillas filled with *cuitlacoche* (corn mushrooms) and jalapeño chilies are very tasty, as is the *ensalada mandinga* (prawn, mango, onion, and coriander salad). Four hundred different tequilas to try. Reservations suggested.

🪑 65 🚇 Ópera 🅿

🕐 Closed Sat. L & Sun. 🐾

⊠ All major cards

🍽 NODO

$$$$

VELÁZQUEZ 150

TEL 91 564 40 44

www.restaurantenodo.es

The Japanese-Mediterranean cuisine here is so popular that you have to reserve weeks in advance. The red tuna is excellent, or try the tuna *tataki* with garlic; to sample various dishes go for the "bandeja nodo-box."

🪑 130 🚇 República Argentina ⊠ All major cards

🍽 OTTOCENTO

$$$$

LIBERTAD 16

TEL 91 521 69 04

www.ottocento.es

Once the Taberna Carmencita, open in 1850 and frequented by García Lorca, Dalí, and Buñuel. Now an Argentine-Italian restaurant. Try their beef sirloin ravioli.

🔆 40 🏊 Chueca 🔆 🖤 All major cards

🍴 PRÍNCIPE DE VIANA
$$$$

MANUEL DE FALLA 5
TEL 91 457 15 49
An old favorite with Basque-Navarrese cuisine. Try these specialties: *menestra de verduras de Tudela* (asparagus stewed with other vegetables); monkfish with clams in a green sauce. The ham croquettes are famous. Reservations essential.
🔆 80 🏊 Santiago Bernabéu 🅿 🕐 Closed Sat. L, Sun., Easter, & Aug. 🔆 🖤 All major cards

🍴 SAMARKANDA
$$$$

GLORIETA DE CARLOS V
TERMINAL DEL AVE
TEL 91 530 87 21
Set in the amazing location in the old Atocha train station, transformed into a tropical garden. The international cuisine includes caramelized duck crepes. Stop for a coffee break between museums.
🔆 350 🏊 Atocha–Renfe 🅿 🖤 AE, MC, V

🍴 CASA LUCIO
$$$

CAVA BAJA 35
TEL 91 365 32 52
www.casalucio.es
Casa Lucio keeps the dishes simple and focuses on quality ingredients. Try the Lucío potatoes, Madrid-style stewed tripe, and the rice pudding. The decor reflects the area's traditional Castilian houses.
🔆 120 🏊 La Latina 🅿 🕐 Closed Sat. L & Aug. 🔆 🖤 All major cards

🍴 LA VACA VERÓNICA
$$$

MORATÍN 38
TEL 91 429 78 27
It has antique chandeliers and walls covered with art work. Try the spinach, mushroom, and pancetta salad. Homemade desserts like white chocolate tart with raspberries. Reser-

vations suggested.
🔆 55 🏊 Antón Martín 🕐 Closed Sat. L. 🔆 🖤 All major cards

🍴 BOTÍN
$$

CUCHILLEROS 17
TEL 91 366 42 17
www.casabotin.com
Reputed to be the world's oldest restaurant—1725—and, according to Hemingway, the best. Legend has it that Goya once worked here as a dishwasher. Recommended are traditional roast suckling pig and the roast lamb.
🔆 260 🏊 Sol 🔆 🖤 All major cards

🍴 CUANDO SALÍ DE CUBA
$$

TERNERA 4
TEL 91 522 93 18
Hemingway's favorite place in the late 50s (when it was El Callejón de la Ternera). Serves unpretentious Cuban food and offers a reasonable lunch menu. Live music Wed.–Sat.
🔆 40 🏊 Callao 🅿 🕐 Closed Sun. 🔆 🖤 MC, V

🍴 MIRADOR DEL THYSSEN
$$

MUSEO THYSSEN-BORNEMISZA
PASEO DEL PRADO 8
TEL 91 429 27 32
The museum's garden-terrace full of palms and magnolias becomes a summer restaurant. Lots of candles provide an enchanting setting. Modern Mediterranean cuisine: grilled squid with pumpkin purée and mango noodles; oxtail with red peppers. Reservations needed.
🔆 150 🏊 Banco de España 🕐 Closed Mon. Sept.–June 🖤 All major cards

🍴 CASA MINGO
$

PASEO DE LA FLORIDA 34
TEL 91 547 79 18 or 547 58 45
www.sidramingo.com
Founded in 1888 by Asturian

railway workers, this cider tavern was probably the first in Madrid. Noted for its roast chicken, Asturian pork and bean stew (*fabada*), sausage, tripe and goat cheese. Friendly, and crowded—go early.
🔆 100 🏊 Príncipe Pío 🔆

🍴 LA BIOTIKA
$

AMOR DE DIOS 3
TEL 91 429 07 80
A cozy vegetarian place that makes delicious salads, soups and tofu-based dishes.
🔆 25 🏊 Antón Martín 🖤 All major cards

🍴 PARADIS THYSSEN
$

PASEO DEL PRADO 8
TEL 91 369 01 51
A cafeteria/restaurant open only 10 a.m.–6 p.m. The terrace is used in the evenings of July and August by the more upscale restaurant El Mirador.
🔆 40 🏊 Banco de España 🕐 Closed Mondays 🔆

ARANJUEZ 28300

🏨 EL COCHERÓRN 1919
$$ ★★

MONTESINOS 22
TEL 918 75 43 50
FAX 918 75 43 47
E-MAIL elcocheron1919@yahoo.com
www.elcocheron1919.es
By the Aranjuez Palace and its park, this small hotel is inviting, with a lovely interior patio.
🛏 18 🔆 🖤 All major cards

🍴 CASA JOSÉ
$$$$

ABASTOS 32
TEL 918 91 14 88
www.casajose.es
The imaginative and seasonally based cuisine that has won it one Michelin star. Specials include artichoke hearts glazed with sea urchin eggs and roe and deer chops in a cinnamon and caraway batter.
🔆 50 🕐 Closed Sun. D, Mon., & Aug. 🔆 🖤 All major cards

🍴 PALACIO DE OSUNA

$$$$
PRÍNCIPE 21
TEL 918 92 42 15

In a wing of the Duke of Osuna's old palace down by the river, choose from lamb or suckling pig roasted in a wood fired oven, and don't miss the Aranjuez asparagus in season.

🪑 260 🅿 🕐 Closed Sun. D & July 🛗 All major cards

CHINCHÓN 28370

🏨 PARADOR DE 🍴 CHINCHÓN

$$$ ★★★★
CALLE DE LOS HUERTOS 1
TEL 918 94 08 36
FAX 918 94 09 08
E-MAIL chinchon@parador.es
www.parador.es

A 17th-century monastery founded by the Augustinians. The cloister encloses a landscaped garden. Rooms are decorated in the Castilian style of dark wood and tiles; some have Renaissance murals.

ℹ 38 🅿 🔄 🛗 ♨ 🛗 All major cards

🍴 MESÓN DE LA VIRREINA

$$$
PLAZA MAYOR 28
TEL 918 94 00 15
www.mesonvirreyna.com

On a plaza that doubles as a bullring, the staples are Castilian dishes such as roast lamb or suckling pig. Try the local anise for which Chinchón is famous. Reserve if you want a table on one of the wooden balconies.

🪑 110 🅿 No parking on weekends 🛗 All major cards

SAN LORENZO DE EL ESCORIAL 28200

🏨 BOTÁNICO 🍴 $$ ★★★

TIMOTEO PADRÓS 16
TEL 918 90 78 79
FAX 918 90 81 58
E-MAIL hotelbotanico@valdesimonte.com
www.valdesimonte.com

A beautifully restored mansion set in gardens away from the bustle of the town. A peaceful place to spend the night.

ℹ 20 🅿 🔄 🛗 🛗 All major cards

🏨 MIRANDA & SUIZO

$$ ★★★
FLORIDABLANCA 18-20
TEL 918 90 47 11/43 58
FAX 918 90 13 12
E-MAIL reservas@hotelmirandasuizo.com
www.hotelmirandasuizo.com

One of many Victorian buildings. The interiors are functional and well kept. You can have meals in the hotel's wonderful *modernista* café.

ℹ 52 🔄 🛗 🛗 All major cards

NORTHWEST SPAIN

GALICIA

CAMBADOS 36630

🏨 PARADOR DE 🍴 CAMBADOS

$$$ ★★★★
PASEO DE LA CALZADA S/N
TEL 986 54 22 50
FAX 986 54 20 68
E-MAIL cambados@parador.es
www.parador.es

The ancestral home of the Bazán family, built in the 1600s, its beautiful rooms have views of the interior patio or across the countryside. The restaurant serves local dishes: *empanada de berberechos* (cockle pie); try the local Albariño wine.

ℹ 58 🪑 130 🅿 🔄 ♨ 🛗 All major cards

A CORUÑA (LA CORUÑA) 15000

🏨 HESPERIA FINISTERRE 🍴 $$$$$ ★★★★★

PASEO DEL PARROTE 2
TEL 981 20 54 00/04
FAX 981 20 84 62
www.hesperia-finisterre.es

Situated on the port at the edge of the old town. Wonderful views and a large sports complex with four heated seawater swimming pools, tennis, table tennis, basketball courts, and a gym.

ℹ 92 🅿 🔄 🛗 ♨ 🛗 All major cards

🏨 NH ATLÁNTICO 🍴 $$$ ★★★★

JARDINES DE MÉNDEZ NÚÑEZ
TEL 981 22 65 00
FAX 981 20 10 71
E-MAIL nhatlantico@nh-hotels.com
www.nh-hotels.com

A renovated 1960s building in the heart of the old town with views of the port. Spacious rooms with typical NH style.

ℹ 199 🅿 🔄 🛗 🛗 All major cards

🍴 CASA PARDO

$$$$$
NOVOA SANTOS 15
TEL 981 28 00 21/71 78
www.casapardo-domus.com

Near the port, this restaurant chooses ingredients carefully as befits its one-Michelin-star status. Try the *rape a la ajada gallega* (monkfish with a Galician sauce made by beating garlic, paprika, and oil together), scallops with ham and onion sauce, and game in season.

🪑 65 🅿 🕐 Closed Sun.,

PRICES

HOTELS

An indication of the cost of a double room without breakfast is given by **$** signs.

$$$$$	Over $300
$$$$	$220– $300
$$$	$160–$220
$$	$80–$160
$	Under $80

RESTAURANTS

An indication of the cost of a three-course dinner without drinks is given by **$** signs.

$$$$$	Over $80
$$$$	$50–$80
$$$	$35–$50
$$	$20–$35
$	Under $20

Mon. D & March 🔆 🔆 All major cards

LA PENELA
$$$
PLAZA MARÍA PITA 12
TEL 981 20 92 00
Housed in one of the finest *modernista* buildings in La Coruña, this elegantly decorated place offers traditional Galician dishes with class. Try the stuffed mussels, roast beef, or monkfish stew. Great value.
🔆 110 🔆 Closed Sun. & 2 weeks mid-Jan. 🔆 🔆 All major cards

NOIA (NOYA) 15200

PESQUERÍA DEL TAMBRE
$$ ★★★
SANTA MARÍA DE ROO
TEL 981 05 16 20
FAX 981 05 16 29
E-MAIL info@pesqueriadeltambre
www.pesqueriadeltambre.com
This lovely complex of stone buildings is on the site of an old Cisterian fishery. The restaurant serves good homemade Galician food. Fishing licenses available from May–Sept.
🔆 16 🔆 45 🔆 🔆 All major cards

OURENSE (ORENSE) 32000

ARNOIACALDARIA
$$ ★★★
VILA TERMAL 1
ARNOIA (2 MILES/3 KM FROM RIBADAVIA, 19 MILES/30 KM W. OF OURENSE)
TEL 902 49 24 00/01
FAX 988 49 24 22
E-MAIL reserves@caldaria.es
www.caldaria.es
A spa hotel along the Miño River. All types of health treatments are available, along with outdoor sports.
🔆 50 🔆 🔆 🔆 🔆 All major cards

ZARAMPALLO
$ ★
HERMANOS VILLAR 19
TEL/FAX 988 23 08 19/00 08

E-MAIL zarampallo@zarampall.com
www.zarampallo.com
An old house that has been modernized inside and decorated very elegantly. All the rooms look onto pedestrianized streets. The restaurant's Galician cuisine pays particular attention to vegetables.
🔆 14 🔆 60 🔆 Closed Sun. D 🔆 🔆 All major cards

MARTÍN FIERRO (CASA OVIDIO)
$$
SÁENZ DÍEZ 17
TEL 988 37 20 26
FAX 988 37 22 63
E-MAIL info@restaurantemartinfierro.com
www.restaurantemartinfierro.com
The owner lived many years in Argentina before returning to Ourense to set up this restaurant. The menu offers char-grilled Argentine cuts of meat and Galician seafood. Specialties include monkfish in asparagus sauce, beef entrecôte cooked in Ribeiro wine, and chestnut tart for dessert.
🔆 70 🔆 🔆 Closed Sun. 🔆 🔆 All major cards

PONTEVEDRA 36000

PARADOR DE PONTEVEDRA
$$$ ★★★★
BARÓN 19
TEL 986 85 58 00
FAX 986 85 21 95
E-MAIL pontevedra@parador.es
www.parador.es
A 16th-century palace in the historic heart of Pontevedra. The interior complements the grand stone facade with antiques and a hand carved stone staircase. Bedrooms look onto a rose garden. The dining room has antique mirrors and beautiful drapes.
🔆 47 🔆 140 🔆 🔆 🔆 All major cards

RÚAS
$ ★
PADRE SARMIENTO 20
TEL 986 84 64 16

FAX 986 84 64 11
E-MAIL hotelruas@terra.es
www.hotelruas.net
Most of Pontevedra's hotels are in the business part of the town, but Ruas is an exception. It has simple quiet rooms looking onto a lovely square (can be noisy on weekends), opposite the museum.
🔆 22 🔆 70 🔆 🔆 🔆 All major cards

CASA SOLLA
$$$$
AVENIDA SINEIRO 7
SAN SALVADOR DE POIO
(ON ROAD TO LA TOJA 2 KM)
TEL 986 87 28 84
www.restaurantesolla.com
A mile or so outside Pontevedra this bucolic restaurant boasts one Michelin star. An exciting mix of creative and traditional Galician cooking. Try the boned and crusted pork ribs, scallops with chard, or cod with asparagus and fresh garlic shoots.
🔆 50 🔆 🔆 Closed Mon., Thurs. & Sun. D, & 2 weeks Christmas 🔆 🔆 All major cards

DOÑA ANTONIA
$$$
SOPORTALES DE LA HERRERÍA 4, 1ST FLOOR
TEL 986 84 72 74
Galician cuisine using the freshest regional produce. The dining room looks onto the lovely Plaza de la Herrería.
🔆 35 🔆 Closed Sun. & Mon. D, except Aug.–Dec. 🔆 🔆 All major cards

SANTIAGO DE COMPOSTELA 15700

SOMETHING SPECIAL

PARADOR HOSTAL DOS REIS CATÓLICOS
Standing on the square by the cathedral, this parador is one of the great hotels. In 1499 Ferdinand and Isabella built it as a hostel for pilgrims. It still boasts an exquisite carved doorway, huge reception area looking into

the four superb courtyards, and a Gothic chapel. Rooms, many with canopied beds, have tapestries and antiques. Reserve well ahead.

$$$$ ★★★★★
PLAZA DO OBRADOIRO 1
TEL 981 58 22 00
FAX 981 56 30 94
E-MAIL santiago@parador.es
www.parador.es
[i] 137 [P] [⇄] [⚿] All major cards

🏨 MELIÁ ARAGUANEY
🍴 $$$ ★★★★★
ALFREDO BRAÑAS 5
TEL 981 55 96 00
FAX 981 59 02 87
E-MAIL melia@araguaney.com
www.araguaney.com
A modern building ten-minutes walk from the cathedral. The hotel has a disco, two restaurants, and a shopping center.
[i] 81 [P] [⇄] [⚿] [🚇] [⚿]
[⚿] All major cards

🏨 COMPOSTELA
🍴 $$ ★★★★
HÓRREO 1
TEL 981 58 57 00
FAX 981 58 52 90
E-MAIL hotel@hesperia-compostela.com
www.hesperia-compostela.com
Reproduction antiques adorn the spacious rooms in this historic building. By two main roads, so be sure to ask for one of the quieter rooms.
[i] 99 [⚿] [⚿] All major cards

🏨 VIRXE DA CERCA
🍴 $$ ★★★
VIRXE DA CERCA 27
TEL 981 56 93 50
FAX 981 58 69 25
E-MAIL vdacerca@pousadasdecompostela.com
www.pousadasdecompostela.com
This 18th-century building became a hotel in July 1999. Rooms in the old wing have sitting areas. The modern wing has more spacious rooms. Breakfast included.
[i] 43 [P] [⚿] [⚿] All major cards

🍴 DON GAIFEROS
$$$$
RÚA NOVA 23
TEL/FAX 981 58 38 94
An old-fashioned restaurant offering traditional Galician cuisine and international dishes. Try the griddled scallops, *veal a la gallega* (with a paprika sauce), and the hot chocolate ice cream.
[seats] 68 [🕐] Closed Sun. D & Mon. D [⚿] [⚿] All major cards

🍴 LA TACITA D'JUAN
$$$$
HÓRREO 31
TEL 981 56 20 41 or 56 32 55
www.latacita.com
This is the busiest place in town, providing hearty Galician food and a good selection of local wines. Specials include seafood filled crepes, conger eel pie, and ox entrecôte.
[seats] 100 [🕐] Closed Sun. & Aug. [P] [⚿] [⚿] AE, MC, V

🍴 MONCHO VILAS
$$$$
AVENIDA DE VILLAGARCÍA 21
TEL 981 59 83 87
E-MAIL monchovilas@mundor.com
www.monchovilas.com
The owner, Moncho Vilas, is keen to promote Galician fare and selects quality local produce. His traditional dishes include grilled sea bass with clams, fillet steak cooked in Oporto sherry, and *hake a la gallega* (with a paprika sauce).
[seats] 80 [🕐] Closed Mon. & Sun. D [⚿] [⚿] All major cards

🍴 TOÑI VICENTE
$$$$
ROSALÍA DE CASTRO 24
TEL 981 59 41 00
www.restaurantetonivicente.com
Toñi Vicente has won acclaim and one Michelin star. The innovative menu has a Galician flavor. Recommendations: the sea bass salad and grilled tuna on a bed of black olives and tomatoes.

[seats] 50 [🕐] Closed Sun. & 2 weeks Christmas [⚿] [⚿] All major cards

A TOXA (ISLA DE LA TOJA-O GROVE) 36991

SOMETHING SPECIAL

🏨 GRAN HOTEL LA
🍴 TOJA
Going to A Toxa (La Toja) is like going back in time. Originally constructed in 1907, this is a very luxurious hotel right on the waterfront with lavish interiors. The hotel has access to a sports complex with tennis, golf (9 holes), thermal baths, riding, and sailing.
$$$$ ★★★★★
TEL 986 73 00 25
FAX 986 73 00 26
E-MAIL hotel@granhotelhesperia-latoja.com
www.granhotelhesperia-latoja.com
[i] 197 [seats] 720 [P] [⚿] [⚿] [⚿] [⚿] All major cards

🏨 HOTEL LOUXO
🍴 $$ ★★★★
TEL 986 73 02 00
FAX 986 73 27 91
E-MAIL hotel@louxolatoja.com
www.louxolatoja.com
On the waterfront, but less spectacular than the Gran, the Louxo is next to the casino. Sumptuous rooms. Tennis, golf (9 holes), and sailing.
[i] 115 [seats] 350 [⚿] [⚿] / [⚿] [⚿] All major cards

TUI 36700

🏨 PARADOR DE TUI
🍴 $$$ ★★★★
AVENIDA DE PORTUGAL
TEL 986 60 03 00
FAX 986 60 21 63
E-MAIL tui@parador.es
www.parador.es
Built of granite and chestnut wood on the banks of the Mino river, right by the Portuguese border, this large country house offers a wide range of healthy activities, from swimming to tennis, as

well as hearty Galician food.
🛈 32 🅿 🔄 ❄ 🏊 🅂 All major cards

🍴 O NOVO CABALO FURADO
$$$
PLAZA DO CONCELLO 3
TEL/FAX 986 60 12 15/22 63
Excellent fresh fish and shellfish is served in the simply decorated dining room, or in summer, the small patio. Try the hake and monkfish stew, and, for dessert, hazelnut mousse. (The tapas bar of the same name is run by the owner's brother.)
🍴 60 ⏰ Closed Sun. July–Sept., Sun. D, & Mon. Oct.–June, Christmas–early Jan., & last 2 weeks June 🅂 All major cards

ASTURIAS & CANTABRIA

CASTRO URDIALES 39700

🍴 MESÓN EL MARINERO
$$$$
CORRERÍA 23 - BAJO
TEL 942 86 00 05/15 63
www.mesonmarinero.com
With a fantastic array of tapas and an upstairs dining room overlooking the port, this restaurant is a find. Choose from the selection of fresh fish cooked in the oven or in salt.
🍴 140 ❄ 🅂 All major cards

COSTA VERDE

🏨 AULTRE NARAY
$$ ★★★
PERUYES 33547, CANGAS DE ONIS (OFF CTRA N-634, KM 335)
TEL 985 84 08 08
FAX 985 84 08 48
E-MAIL aultre@aultrenaray.com
www.aultrenaray.com
A large 19th-century house in a beautiful spot looking out onto the mountains. The decor combines traditional and modern styles.
🛈 10 🅿 🅂 All major cards

🏨 CASA CONSUELO
$ ★★
CTRA. N-634, KM 511
OTUR (5 KM FROM LUARCA)
TEL 985 47 07 67 (hotel)
985 64 16 96 (restaurant)
FAX 985 64 16 42
E-MAIL info@casaconsuelo.com
www.casaconsuelo.com
A family-run hotel that is known for its restaurant. The traditional Asturian dishes depend on seasonal produce. Fresh fish and great desserts.
🛈 36 🍴 150 🅿 ⏰ Closed Mon., except in Aug. & Nov. 🔄 🅂 All major cards

🏨 LA CASONA DE PIO
$ ★★
RIOFRIO 3, CUDILLERO 33150
TEL 985 59 15 12
FAX 985 59 15 19
E-MAIL casonadepio@arrakis.es
This restored stone house-hotel right in the town center offers a comfortable stay in rustic style rooms. The restaurant serves locally caught fish including the Cudillero specialty, *curadillo* (dogfish).
🛈 11 🍴 50 🅂 MC, V, AE

LOS OSCOS

🏨 LA RECTORAL
$$ ★★★★
TARAMUNDI 33775
TEL 985 64 67 60/67
FAX 985 64 67 77
E-MAIL hotel@larectoral.net
www.larectoral.com
Typical of Spain's new wave of rural tourism, this hotel is set in beautiful countryside and offers lots of activities. The building is an 18th-century rectory with mountain views.
🛈 18 🍴 40 🅿 🅂 ⏰ Closed Mon. 🏊 🅂 All major cards

🏨 CABEZA DA VILA
$
SAN MARTÍN DE OSCOS 33777
TEL 985 62 60 19
FAX 985 62 61 34
www.cabezadavila.com
A 17th-century farmhouse restored by descendants of the original owners, and

almost like a museum. Large rooms furnished with antiques. No television in rooms. Separate house also available.
🛈 5 🅿 🅂 V

🏨 CASA RODIL
$ ★
AS POCEIRAS
2 KM FROM SANTA EULALIA DE OSCOS 33776 (CRTA. VEGADEO)
TEL 985 62 61 85
E-MAIL informacion@casarodil.com
www.casarodil.com
Surrounded by green fields and mountains this idyllically sited hotel has simple rooms with large baths. Delicious down-to-earth cooking uses local ingredients. No television.
🛈 4 🅿 🅂 All major cards

OVIEDO 33000

🏨 DE LA RECONQUISTA
$$$$$ ★★★★★
GIL DE JAZ 16
TEL 985 24 11 00
FAX 985 24 11 66
E-MAIL reconquista@hoteldelareconquista.com
www.hoteldelareconquista.com
Formerly a 1700s orphanage and hospital, this building has an arcaded courtyard and spacious, modern rooms.
🛈 142 🍴 60 🅿 🔄 🅂 🅂 All major cards

🍴 CASA FERMÍN
$$$$
SAN FRANCISCO 8
TEL 985 21 64 52/97
E-MAIL casafermin@almirez.com
www.casafermin.com
This glass-ceilinged restaurant in the old city center has been run by the same family since 1924. Excellent Asturian fare, both classic and avant-garde. Try their baked monkfish with squid noodles or a typical *fabada* (pork and bean stew).
🍴 120 ⏰ Closed Sun. 🅂 🅂 All major cards

PICOS DE EUROPA

🏨 HOTEL DEL OSO
🍽 $$ ★★★
COSGAYA 39582
CARRETERA DE POTES A
FUENTE DÉ, KM 14
TEL 942 73 30 18
FAX 942 73 30 36
E-MAIL info@hoteldeloso.com
www.hoteldeloso.com
In the heart of the Picos de
Europa beside the Deva River,
this hotel has warm and cozy
rooms with wooden bal-
conies. Hearty regional fare
such as river trout and stews.
🛏 50 🪑 90 🅿 🕐 Closed
Jan. 🏊 🅼 MC, V

SANTANDER 39000

**SOMETHING
SPECIAL**

🏨 REAL
🍽
This imposing French style
château was built by the
Botín family for royal guests. In
a spectacular location overlooking
the bay, the Real is surrounded
by gardens. A vaulted ceiling
graces the Royal Suite. The res-
taurant, El Puntal, offers modern
cuisine in distinguished rooms.
Try lobster salad with avocado
and mango or grilled duck's liver
with ginger and vodka.
$$$$ ★★★★★
PASEO DE PÉREZ GALDÓS 28
TEL 942 27 25 50
FAX 942 27 45 73
E-MAIL realsantander@husa.es
www.hotelreal.es
🛏 123 🪑 40 🅿 🔼 🕹
🅼 All major cards

🏨 RHIN
🍽 $$ ★★★★
AVENIDA REINA VICTORIA 153
TEL 942 27 43 00
FAX 942 27 86 53
E-MAIL rhin@gruporhin.com
www.gruporhin.com
Situated on El Sardinero
beach, the rooms are light
and spacious with traditional
furnishings. The restaurant, La
Cúpula, promotes modern
Cantabrian cuisine like crab-

filled hake with prawns and
clams. Desserts are elaborate.
🛏 89 🪑 40 🔼 🕹 🅼 All
major cards

🏨 CENTRAL
$ ★★★
GENERAL MOLA 5
TEL 942 22 24 00
FAX 942 36 38 29
E-MAIL reservas@elcentral.com
www.elcentral.com
Everything is blue in this
family-run hotel. No
restaurant.
🛏 41 🔼 🕹 🅼 All major
cards

🍽 DEL PUERTO
$$$$
HERNÁN CORTÉS 63
TEL 942 21 30 01
E-MAIL bdp@cantabrico.com
This traditional and reliable
restaurant maintains a high
standards and serves the best
shellfish in Santander. The bar
has a wonderful selection of
raciones (similar to *tapas*, but
larger portions).
🪑 130 🕐 Closed Sun. D &
Mon. 🕹 🅼 All major cards

SANTILLANA DEL MAR
39330

🏨 PARADOR DE
🍽 SANTILLANA
$$$ ★★★
PLAZA RAMÓN PELAYO 11
TEL 942 81 80 00
FAX 942 81 83 91
E-MAIL santillana@parador.es
www.parador.es
The dark wood pieces and
floors in this 18th-century
mansion are similar in style to
the original decor. The *parador*
has expanded to include a
new building across the plaza.
🛏 28 🪑 60 🅿 🔼 🅼 All
major cards

🏨 ALTAMIRA
🍽 $$ ★★★
CANTÓN 1
TEL 942 81 80 25 or
942 81 83 09
FAX 942 84 01 36
E-MAIL info@hotelaltamira.com
www.hotelaltamira.com

A former palace reconstructed in the 19th century and
since extended into the building next door. Rooms are
different shapes and sizes, all
with wood floors and ex-
posed stone walls. The restaurant has a growing reputation
for game, cod, and rice dishes.
🛏 32 🪑 270 🕹 Restaurant
only 🅼 All major cards

NORTHEAST SPAIN

EUSKADI &
NAVARRA

BERGARA 20570

🏨 ORMAZABAL
$ ★★
BARRENKALE 11
TEL/FAX 94 376 36 50
E-MAIL ormazabalreservas@in
fonegocio.com
www.gratisweb.com/hotelorma
zabal
In the center of Bergara, this
17th-century stone house
is full of period furniture.
No restaurant.
🛏 14 🅼 All major cards

BILBO (BILBAO) 48000

🏨 LÓPEZ DE HARO
🍽 $$$$ ★★★★★
OBISPO ORUETA 2
TEL 94 423 55 00
FAX 94 423 45 00
E-MAIL lh@hotellopezdeharo.com
www.hotellopezdeharo.com
A five minute walk from the
Guggenheim, this remodeled
1800s building has a classical
English feel. Rooms are lux-
urious and quiet—some non-
smoking. The restaurant, Club
Náutico, serves modern and
classical cuisine. Try the prawn
tails tossed with artichokes.
Wide choice of desserts.
🛏 53 🪑 60 🅿 🔼 🕹
🅼 All major cards

🏨 CARLTON
🍽 $$$ ★★★★★
PLAZA FEDERICO MOYUA 2
TEL 94 416 22 00
FAX 94 416 46 28

E-MAIL carlton@aranzazu-
hoteles.com
www.aranzazu-hoteles.com
On one of the prettiest
plazas, this elegant old hotel
has hosted bullfighters and
artists such as Hemingway
and Orson Welles. It was the
seat of the Republican Basque
government during the Civil
War. The renovated hotel
retains its charm despite.
① 144 **🛏** 40 **P** 🔁 **❄**
❖ All major cards

🏨 ITURRIENEA OSTATUA
$$ ★★
SANTA MARÍA 14
TEL 94 416 15 00
FAX 94 415 89 29
www.iturrieneaostatua.com
In Bilbao's historic center, this
old pension has appealing
interior decor that matches
the original facade colors. The
rooms have large beds and
artwork by local artists.
① 21 **❖** DC, MC, V

🍴 GORROTXA
$$$$
ALAMEDA URQUIJO 30
TEL 94 443 49 37
FAX 94 442 05 35
www.gorrotxa.es
A Bilbao classic by Carmelo
Gorrotxateg and his one
Michelin star, with superb
haute cuisine and traditional
Basque recipes. Try the wild
mushrooms with prawns and
the boned Bresse pigeon.
🛏 85 **🕐** Closed Sun.–Mon.,
Easter & July–early Aug. **❄**
❖ All major cards

🍴 ZORTZIKO
$$$$$
ALAMEDA DE MAZARREDO 17
TEL 94 423 97 43
www.zortziko.es
Daniel García is one of the
Basque region's top chefs. His
modern cuisine contrasts with
this historic early 20th-
century villa. Dishes include
cod risotto with truffles and
pigeon roasted in muscatel
grape juice. Great wine list.
This one-Michelin-star
restaurant is close to the

Guggenheim Museum.
🛏 120 **🕐** Closed Sun., Mon.
D, last fortnight Aug. & first
fortnight Sept. **❄** **❖** All
major cards

🍴 GUGGENHEIM
$$
ABANDOIBARRA 2
TEL 94 423 93 33
www.restauranteguggenheim.com
Under the guidance of the
famed Martín Berasategui, this
good-value restaurant offers
excellent avant garde cuisine
within the museum itself. Try
the rice with stewed wild
mushrooms and Idiazabal
cheese or indulge in a taster
menu. Reservations advisable.
🛏 100 **P** **🕐** Closed Sun.
D, Mon. & Tues. D **❄** **❖** All
major cards

DONOSTIA (SAN SEBASTIÁN) 20000

SOMETHING SPECIAL

🏨 MARÍA CRISTINA
🍴 An old-fashioned, luxurious
hotel, named after Queen
María Cristina who opened it in
1912, now restored to its belle
epoque glory. The bedrooms
and salons overlook the sea and
the Urúmea River. The restaurant, Easo, is on its way up.
$$$$$ ★★★★★
OQUENDO 1
TEL 94 343 76 00
FAX 94 343 76 76
E-MAIL hmc@westin.com
www.westin.com/mariacristina
① 136 **P** 🔁 **❄** 🏊
❖ All major cards

🏨 DE LONDRES Y DE
🍴 INGLATERRA
$$$$ ★★★★
ZUBIETA 2
TEL 94 344 07 70
FAX 94 344 04 91
E-MAIL reservas@hlondres.com
www.hlondres.com
This central belle epoque hotel
has superb sea views. The
casino is in the same building.
① 148 **P** 🔁 **❄** **❖** All
major cards

SOMETHING SPECIAL

🍴 ARZAK
Possibly the best restaurant in
Spain (three Michelin stars).
Chef Juan Mari Arzak and his
daughter, Elena, produce innovative cuisine that never loses
sight of traditional Basque
recipes. The entire menu is
superb: for example grilled
smoked tuna on a bed of melon
and spring onions. Reservations
suggested.
$$$$$
AVDA. ALCALDE ELOSEGUI 273
TEL 94 327 84 65
FAX 94 327 27 53
www.arzak.es
🛏 80 **P** **🕐** Closed Sun.,
Mon., June 17–July 4, & Nov.
4–28 **❄** **❖** All major cards

🍴 UREPEL
$$$$
PASEO DE SALAMANCA 3
TEL/FAX 94 342 40 40
www.urepel.net
Popular with San Sebastián's
upper crust, this one-Michelin-
star restaurant combines
classic dishes with modern.
Mainly fish, such as smoked
cod with roasted vegetables.
🛏 60 **🕐** Closed Sun., Tues.,
1 week Easter, & 2 weeks
Christmas **❄** **❖** All major
cards

🍴 BODEGÓN
ALEJANDRO
$$$
FERMÍN CALBETÓN 4
TEL 94 342 71 58
FAX 94 342 95 42
www.bodegonalejandro.com
Modern cuisine using simple
ingredients inspired by the
Basque maestro, Martín
Berasategui. Choose your
own fixed-price, three-course
menu for 30 euros.
🛏 70 **P** **🕐** Closed Sun. D,
Mon., Tues. D (Sept.–June), &
2 weeks Christmas **❄**
❖ All major cards

GASTEIZ (VITORIA) 01000

PARADOR DE ARGÓMANIZ
$$$ ★★★
CARRETERA N-1, KM 363
TEL 94 529 32 00
FAX 94 529 32 87
E-MAIL argomaniz@parador.es
www.parador.es
This stone Renaissance palace is only 7.5 miles (12 km) from Vitoria and worth the trip if you want a peaceful sleep. Spacious and light rooms with pine floors and balconies. Beautiful dining room.
🛏 53 🅿 🔁 🛗 🚇 All major cards

IKEA
$$$$$
PORTAL DE CASTILLA 27
TEL 94 514 47 47
www.restauranteikea.com
Traditional cuisine with innovative twists and a varied menu served in a sophisticated, modernized mansion. Recommended dishes include prawn carpaccio with gazpacho sorbet and suckling pig confit with grapefruit jelly.
🪑 279 🅿 🕐 Closed Sun. D, Mon., & 3 weeks Aug.– early Sept. 🛗 🚇 All major cards

HONDARRIBIA (FUENTERRABÍA) 20280

PARADOR DE HONDARRIBIA
$$$$ ★★★★
PLAZA DE ARMAS 14
TEL 94 364 55 00
FAX 94 364 21 53
E-MAIL hondarribia@parador.es
www.parador.es
This fortified castle was built in the 10th century by the Navarrese King Sancho Abarca. The *parador* has made the most of its wonderful building, leaving the beautiful thick stone walls exposed, even in the bedrooms. Some rooms have terraces overlooking the sea. No restaurant.
🛏 36 🅿 🔁 🚇 All major cards

RAMÓN ROTETA
$$$$
IRÚN 1, VILLA AINARA
TEL 94 364 16 93
FAX 94 364 58 63
www.roteta.com
Inventive Mediterranean fare. Try the shellfish salad and the monkfish in gooseneck barnacle sauce.
🪑 350 🅿 🕐 Closed Sun. D, Tues., & Feb. 🚇 All major cards

IRUÑA (PAMPLONA) 31000

IRUÑA PALACE TRES REYES
$$$$$ ★★★★
JARDINES DE LA TACONERA
TEL 948 22 66 00
FAX 948 22 29 30
www.hotel3reyes.com
Modern, luxurious surroundings offering spa-baths, a hairdresser, golf, and squash courts.
🛏 160 🅿 🔁 🛗 🚖 📺 🚇 All major cards

MAISONNAVE
$$ ★★★
NUEVA 20
TEL 948 22 26 00
FAX 948 22 01 66
E-MAIL informacion@hotel maisonnave.es
www.hotelmaisonnave.es
The French founded this hotel 100 years ago and since then personalities such as Hemingway, Valle-Inclán, and Ava Gardner have stayed here. Art exhibitions and musical recitals in the salons.
🛏 138 🅿 🔁 🛗 🚇 All major cards

JOSETXO
$$$$
PLAZA PRINCÍPE DE VIANA 1
TEL 948 22 20 97
FAX 948 22 41 57
A sober dining room is the setting for this classic establishment. Bull's meat is served here at the San Fermín festival. Try the pork sirloin flambéd in brandy or cod with peppers and lobster. Notable wine list.
🪑 125 🕐 Closed Sun. (except San Fermín), Easter, & Aug. 🛗 🚇 All major cards

ORREAGA (RONCESVALLES) 31650

LA POSADA
$
CARRETERA DE FRANCIA, S/N
TEL 948 76 02 25
FAX 948 76 02 66
www.laposadaderoncesvalles.com
This restored 16th-century inn is a historic monument. Delicious home-style cooking.
🛏 19 🪑 130 🅿 🕐 Closed Nov. 🚇 DC, MC, V

TUDELA 31500

RESTAURANTE 33
$$$$
CAPUCHINOS 7
TEL 948 82 76 06
FAX 948 41 10 08
www.restaurante33.com
Traditional cuisine using an abundance of vegetables. Specials include artichokes filled with foie gras.

PRICES

HOTELS
An indication of the cost of a double room without breakfast is given by $ signs.
$$$$$	Over $300
$$$$	$220–$300
$$$	$160–$220
$$	$80–$160
$	Under $80

RESTAURANTS
An indication of the cost of a three course dinner without drinks is given by $ signs.
$$$$$	Over $80
$$$$	$50–$80
$$$	$35–$50
$$	$20–$35
$	Under $20

🛏 130 🕐 Closed Sun. & first 3 weeks Aug. 🌀 🆑 All major cards

HARO 26200

🏨 HOSPEDERÍA SEÑORÍO DE BRIÑAS
$$$ ★★★
TRAVESÍA DE LA CALLE REAL 3, BRIÑAS (3 MILES/5 KM FROM HARO)
TEL 941 30 39 84
FAX 941 30 43 45
E-MAIL brinas@hotelesconen canto.org
www.hotelesconencanto.org
Set among vineyards, and the interiors of this 18th-century mansion have been restored with flare using frescoes and antiques. No restaurant.
🛏 20 🕐 Closed 2 weeks Dec.–Jan. 🆑 All major cards

🏨 LOS AGUSTINOS
🍴 $$ ★★★★
SAN AGUSTÍN 2
TEL 941 31 13 08
FAX 941 30 31 48
www.losagustinos.es
In a 14th-century convent, this hotel has been beautifully restored. Good restaurant.
🛏 62 🅿 🔁 🌀 🆑 All major cards

🍴 TERETE
$$$
LUCRECIA ARANA 17
TEL 941 31 00 23
A family-run establishment providing typical Riojan fare. The oven dates back to 1877 and specials include roast kid and vegetable stew.
🛏 120 🕐 Closed Sun. D, Mon., first 2 weeks July, & last 2 weeks Oct. 🌀 🆑 DC, MC, V

LAGUARDIA 01300

🏨 CASTILLO EL
🍴 COLLADO
$$$ ★★
PASEO EL COLLADO 1
TEL 945 62 12 00
FAX 945 60 08 78

E-MAIL hotel@hotelcollado.com
www.euskalnet.net/hotelcollado
This small castle dating from 1920 with an 18th-century chapel makes an enchanting hotel. The restaurant serves refined Riojan cuisine. Be sure to try the desserts.
🛏 8 🛏 60 🅿 🌀 🆑 All major cards

🏨 POSADA MAYOR DE
🍴 MIGUELOA
$$ ★★★
MAYOR 20
TEL 945 62 11 75
FAX 945 62 10 22
E-MAIL reservas@mayorde migueloa.com
www.mayordemigueloa.com
A hotel in a 1619 mansion. Interiors follow 17th-century Spanish style. All rooms are different and full of decorative details. Regional cooking includes homemade foie gras and delicious desserts.
🛏 8 🛏 120 🕐 Closed mid-Dec.–late Jan. 🆑 All major cards

LOGROÑO 26000

🏨 CARLTON RIOJA
🍴 $$ ★★★★
GRAN VÍA DEL REY JUAN CARLOS I, 5
TEL 941 24 21 00
FAX 941 24 35 02
www.hotelcarltonrioja.es
A modern building with a glass facade, central but not in the old town. Spacious rooms.
🛏 116 🅿 🔁 🌀 🆑 All major cards

SAN MILLÁN DE LA COGOLLA 26226

🏨 HOSTERÍA DEL MONASTERIO DE SAN MILLÁN
$$ ★★★★
MONASTERIO DE YUSO
TEL 941 37 32 77
FAX 941 37 32 66
E-MAIL hosteria@sanmillan.com
www.sanmillan.com
Restored wing of the Yuso Monastery with inviting and

warm rooms.
🛏 25 🅿 🔁 🌀 🆑 All major cards

SANTO DOMINGO DE LA CALZADA 26250

🏨 PARADOR DE SANTO
🍴 DOMINGO DE LA CALZADA
$$$ ★★★★
PLAZA DEL SANTO 3
TEL 941 34 03 00
FAX 941 34 03 25
E-MAIL sto.domingo@parador.es
www.parador.es
Part of the *parador* is in the 12th-century pilgrims hospital, next to the cathedral, built by Santo Domingo. Try the Riojan style cod in the restaurant.
🛏 100 🛏 61 🅿 🌀 🆑 All major cards

ALBARRACÍN 44100

🏨 CASA DE SANTIAGO
🍴 $$ ★★
SUBIDA A LAS TORRES 11
TEL 978 70 03 16
FAX 978 71 01 41
www.casadesantiago.net
A small hotel in a 16th-century building set in the old walled town. Colorful rooms with cane furniture and traditional baked clay floors.
🛏 9 🕐 Closed 3 weeks Feb. & Sept. 13–17 🆑 MC, V

DAROCA 50360

🏨 POSADA DEL ALMUDI
🍴 $$
GRAJERA 7
TEL 976 80 06 06
FAX 976 80 11 41
E-MAIL posadadealmudi@tele line.es
www.stararagon.com/posadadelal mudi
Intimate, hotel in a renovated 15th-century mansion. Warm yellows and patterned textiles enliven the rooms; there is a beautiful Renaissance courtyard. Breakfast included.
🛏 13 🌀 🆑 All major cards

HOTELS & RESTAURANTS

HUESCA 22000

🏨 HOSPEDERÍA DE 🍴 LOARRE
$$ ★★★
PLAZA MAYOR S/N, LOARRE
(30 KM FROM HUESCA)
TEL 974 38 27 06
FAX 974 38 26 65
www.hospederiadeloarre.com
A 16th-century palace in the
center of the village looking
to the church tower.
🛏 12 🅿 🔄 🌐 MC, V

🍴 LILLAS PASTIA
$$$$$
PLAZA DE NAVARRA 4
TEL 974 21 16 91
E-MAIL rest-lillas@terra.es
In the old casino, the dining
room is modernist and the
one-Michelin-star cuisine is
modern Aragonese.
🪑 170 🕐 Sun. D, Tues., &
Nov. 1–15 🔄 🌐 All major
cards

JACA 22700

🏨 GRAN HOTEL
$ ★★★
PASEO DE LA
CONSTITUCIÓN 1
TEL 974 36 09 00
FAX 974 36 40 61
E-MAIL ghotel@inturmark.es
www.inturmark.es/gransp.htm
This popular hotel is located
in the town's center. The
wood, stone, and glass
exterior conceals simple
warm rooms. No smoking.
🛏 165 🅿 🔄 🌐 🚉
🌐 All major cards

🍴 LA COCINA ARAGONESA
$$$$
CERVANTES 5
TEL 974 36 10 50
www.condeaznar.com
Regional cuisine with Basque
influences in a typical Aragon-
ese room. Game specialties
in season. Try the artichoke
hearts with foie gras or the
stuffed partridge.
🪑 150 🔄 🌐 All major
cards

SOS DEL REY CATÓLICO 50680

🏨 PARADOR DE SOS DEL REY CATÓLICO
$$$ ★★★★
SAINZ DE VICUÑA 1
TEL 948 88 80 11
FAX 948 88 81 00
E-MAIL sos@parador.es
www.parador.es
Set in the historic area of the
town, this *parador* is in the
characteristic Aragonese style.
Spacious, light rooms have
views of the countryside.
🛏 58 🅿 🔄 🌐 🌐 All
major cards

TARAZONA 50500

🏨 LA MERCED DE LA 🍴 CONCORDIA
$$ ★★★
PLAZA LA MERCED 2
TEL 976 19 93 44
FAX 976 19 93 45
E-MAIL hotel@lamerced.info
www.lamerced.info
Stylishly restored palace, built
in 1501, in the old town
center. The restaurant offers
good regional cooking.
🛏 7 🪑 90 🅿 🕐 Closed
first week Sept. 🔄 🌐
🌐 AE, MC, V

TERUEL 44000

🏨 REINA CRISTINA
$$ ★★★
PASEO DEL ÓVALO 1
TEL 978 60 68 60
FAX 978 60 53 63
E-MAIL reinacristina@gargallo
hotels.com
www.gargallohotels.com
On the edge of the old town,
this hotel has balconies with
views. Corner rooms are the
most spacious.
🛏 83 🅿 🔄 🌐 All major
cards

ZARAGOZA 50000

🏨 BOSTON
$$$ ★★★★★
AVENIDA DE LAS TORRES 28
TEL 976 59 91 92
FAX 976 59 01 96
E-MAIL reservas@sercotel.es
www.hotelboston.es
A large modern hotel opened
in 1992. The lobby and pano-
ramic lift are positively futuris-
tic and the rooms comfortable.
🛏 311 🅿 🔄 🌐 🌐
🌐 All major cards

🏨 NH GRAN HOTEL
$$ ★★★★
JOAQUIN COSTA 5
TEL 976 22 19 01
FAX 976 23 67 13
E-MAIL nhgranhotel@nh-hotels
.com
www.nh-hotels.com
Celebrities stay in this classical
and elegant hotel in Zaragoza.
Its restaurant, La Ontina, is
where modern Mediterranean
cuisine conjures up dishes
such as monkfish with partridge vinaigrette, and cuttle-
fish and mango spaghetti.
🛏 134 🪑 500 🅿 🔄 🌐
🌐 🌐 All major cards

BARCELONA

🏨 ARTS BARCELONA
🍴 **$$$$$ ★★★★★**
MARINA 19–21
TEL 93 221 10 00
FAX 93 221 10 70
E-MAIL rc.bcnrz.reservations@
ritzcarlton.com
www.hotelartsbarcelona.com
Occupying one of the Olympic
towers in Port Olímpic, one of
Barcelona's most impressive
buildings (44 floors), this hotel
offers superb views of the sea
and city. A little far from the
sights, but Sergi Arola's
restaurant is a must.
🛏 455 🪑 322 🅿 🔄 🌐
🚉 🌐 🌐 All major cards

🏨 CLARIS
🍴 **$$$$$ ★★★★★**
PAU CLARIS 150
TEL 93 4 87 62 62
FAX 93 215 79 70
E-MAIL claris@derbyhotels.es
www.derbyhotels.es
A hotel in a palace with over
400 works of art and archae-
ological artifacts in the rooms,
plus a Japanese garden.

① 123 P 🅿 🅢 🏊 🅗
🅢 All major cards

🏨 **LE MERIDIEN**
🍴 **$$$$$ ★★★★★**
LA RAMBLA 111
TEL 93 318 62 00
FAX 93 301 77 76
E-MAIL reservas.barcelona@le
meridien.com
www.lemeridien-barcelona.com
The top hotel on La Rambla
where stars such as Madonna,
Sting, and Julio Iglesias stay.
A 1900s building with neoclassic facade and modernized
interiors with fabrics by the
designer Kenzo.
① 233 P 🅿 🅢 🅢 All
major cards

🏨 **PALACE**
🍴 **$$$$$ ★★★★★**
GRAN VIA DE LES CORTS
CATALANES 668
TEL 93 510 11 30
FAX 93 318 01 48
www.hotelpalacebarcelona.com
Since it opened in 1919, this
classic grand hotel (formerly
the Ritz) has been offering
elegance and luxury. The suites
have bathrooms inspired by
Roman baths. Currently
undergoing refurbishment.
① 250 P 🅿 🅢 🅢 All
major cards

🏨 **REY JUAN CARLOS I**
$$$$$ ★★★★★
AVENIDA DIAGONAL 661–671
TEL 93 364 40 40
FAX 93 364 42 64
E-MAIL hotel@hrjuancarlos .com
www.hrjuancarlos.com
Built for the 1992 Olympics,
and designed in the shape of a
ship's bow, this hotel won the
National Architectural Prize.
The rooms are fully equipped.
① 412 P 🅿 🅢 🏊 🏊
🅗 🅢 All major cards

🏨 **AVENIDA PALACE**
🍴 **$$$ ★★★★**
GRAN VIA DE LES CORTS
CATALANES 605
TEL 93 301 96 00
FAX 93 318 12 34
E-MAIL avpalace@husa.es
www.avenidapalace.com

A distinguished hotel with
old-fashioned elegance
situated Eixample, close to
Gaudí's monuments.
① 151 P 🅿 🅢 🅢 All
major cards

🏨 **CONDES DE**
🍴 **BARCELONA**
$$$ ★★★★
PASSEIG DE GRÀCIA 73–75
TEL 93 445 00 00
FAX 93 445 32 32
E-MAIL info@condesdebarce
lona.com
www.condesdebarcelona.com
In the center Eixample, this is
one of the city's best hotels
with light, modernized rooms.
It has two magnificent
buildings (built in 1872 and
1890s) facing each other
across Carrer de Mallorca.
Gastronomy is overseen by
the Basque star, Martín
Berasategui.
① 235 P 🅿 🅢 🏊 🅗
🅢 All major cards

🏨 **ESPANYA**
🍴 **$$ ★★**
SANT PAU 9–11
TEL 93 318 17 58
FAX 93 317 11 34
E-MAIL hotelespanya@hoteles
panya.com
www.hotelespanya.com
This hotel is famous for its
modernista dining rooms
designed by Lluis Domenech i
Montaner. One has a sculpted
hearth by Eusebi Arnau and
sea life murals by Ramón
Casas. Rooms that look onto
the interior patio are quieter.
① 80 🅿 🅢 🅢 All major
cards

🏨 **GAUDÍ**
$$$ ★★★
NOU DE LA RAMBLA 12
TEL 93 317 90 32
FAX 93 412 26 36
E-MAIL gaudi@hotelgaudi.es
www.hotelgaudi.es
Modern rooms with views of
the Palau Güell roof. A café.
① 73 P 🅿 🅢 🅗 🅢 All
major cards

🏨 **GRAN VIA**
$$ ★★★
GRAN VIA DE LES CORTS
CATALANES 642
TEL 93 318 19 00
FAX 93 318 99 97
E-MAIL hgranvia@nnhotels.com
www.nnhotels.com
For old-fashioned charm and
elegance, this 19th-century
town house with an elaborate
modernista staircase and
incredibly high ceilings is a
good central option. Spacious
rooms, and roof terrace.
① 53 P 🅿 🅢 🅢 All
major cards

🏨 **RIALTO**
$$ ★★★
FERRÁN 40-42
TEL 93 318 52 12
FAX 93 318 53 12
E-MAIL reserve@gargallo-
hotels.com
www.hotel-rialto.com
The painter, Joan Miró, was
born here, in the heart of the
Barrio Gótico. Simple rooms
have pine floors and dark
wood furniture. Interior-facing
rooms are quieter.
① 202 🅿 🅢 🅢 All major
cards

🍴 **CA L'ISIDRE**
$$$$$
LES FLORS 12
TEL 93 441 11 39
E-MAIL info@calisidre.com
www.calisidre.com
This charming restaurant
serves traditional Catalan
dishes using local ingredients.
Popular with well-heeled
artists, on edge of Raval
district.
🍴 35 P Paral.lel 🕐 Closed
Sun., Christmas, Easter, & 3
weeks Aug. 🅢 🅢 AE, MC, V

🍴 **EL RACO D'EN FREIXA**
$$$$$
SANT ELIES 22
TEL 93 209 75 59
www.elracodenfreixa.com
Young chef, Ramón Freixa,
executes adventurous cuisine
here, north of the Diagonal.
Try the baked John Dory with
eggplant, wild mushrooms, and

sweet sausage or venison with leeks and polenta. Excellent desserts, and Spanish cheeses. One Michelin star. Reservations required.

🛏 50 🚇 Lesseps 🅿 🕐 Closed Sun., Mon., Easter, & Aug. 🛗 🏧 All major cards

🍴 GAIG
$$$$$
ARAGO 214
TEL 93 429 10 17
www.restaurantgaig.com
Now in the Hotel Cram, this classic restaurant (one Michelin star) has been run by four generations of the Gaig family. Carlos Gaig has developed a modern approach to the traditional recipes. Try the truffle cannelloni with truffle cream. Fantastic desserts.

🛏 60 🚇 Passeig de Gràcia 🅿 🕐 Closed Sun. & Mon. L 🛗 🏧 All major cards

🍴 LA DAMA
$$$$$
AVENIDA DIAGONAL 423
TEL 93 202 06 86
www.ladama-restaurant.com
Modern Catalan cuisine in a wonderful modernista building in the Eixample. The pastries, made here, are excellent.

🛏 80 🚇 Diagonal 🅿 🕐 Closed 3 weeks Aug. 🛗 🏧 All major cards

🍴 NEICHEL
$$$$$
BELTRAN I RÓZPIDE 1–5
TEL 93 203 84 08
www.neichel.es
A top restaurant in Barcelona, serving modern Catalan–French haute cuisine. Chef Jean Louis Neichel uses the freshest ingredients. Desserts and cheese are superb. One Michelin star. Reservations suggested.

🛏 60 🚇 Maria Cristina 🅿 🕐 Closed Sun., Mon., first week Jan., Easter, & Aug. 🛗 🏧 All major cards

🍴 VIA VENETO
$$$$$
GANDUXER 10

TEL 93 200 72 44
E-MAIL pmonje@adam.es
Noted for its elegance and awarded one Michelin star. Try the scampi tartare with salmon caviar or roast duck a la Bresse.

🛏 94 🚇 La Bonanova 🅿 🕐 Closed Sat. L, Sun., & Aug. 1–20 🛗 🏧 All major cards

🍴 JAUME DE PROVENÇA
$$$$
PROVENÇA 88
TEL 93 430 00 29
www.jaumeprovenza.com
Chef Jaume Bargués has won a Michelin star for his Catalan–French haute cuisine, such as rabbit Rossini with eggplant and orange sauce or monkfish with lobster. Reservations suggested.

🛏 60 🚇 Hospital Clinic 🅿 🕐 Closed Sun. D, Mon., Aug., & Christmas 🛗 🏧 All major cards

🍴 KRESALA
$$$$
SANTA TERESA 10
TEL 93 415 28 77
In a lovely town house in Gràcia that was once the designer Cristóbal Balenciaga's studio, Chef Manel Jiménez prepares an imaginative cuisine that has earned one Michelin star. Reservations suggested.

🛏 90 🚇 Diagonal 🅿 🕐 Closed Sun., Easter & 2 weeks Aug. 🛗 🏧 All major cards

🍴 OT
$$$$
CORSEGA 537
TEL 93 435 80 48
www.otrestaurant.net
Inventive Catalan cooking from Ferran Caparrós. Try the set menu with dishes such as acorn-fed pork fillet with seasonal fruit chutney and lavender. Reservations suggested.

🛏 32 🚇 Sagrada Familia 🕐 Closed Sun., Mon. D, 1 week Jan., & 2 weeks Aug. 🛗 🏧 DC, MC, V

🍴 SET PORTES
$$$$
PASSEIG ISABEL II, 14
TEL 93 319 30 33
www.7portes.com
This popular early 19th-century high-ceilinged establishment near the waterfront serves generous portions of traditional Catalan cuisine. Reservations suggested.

🛏 300 🚇 Barceloneta 🛗 🏧 All major cards

🍴 IL BELLINI
$$$
VIA AUGUSTA 201
TEL 93 200 50 99
www.ilbellini.com
One of Barcelona's best Italian restaurants with a small cozy dining room. From October to January the Italian chef prepares white truffle dishes.

🛏 80 🚇 Hospital Clinic 🕐 Closed Sun. D & 2 weeks Aug. 🛗 🏧 All major cards

🍴 BIOCENTER
$
PINTOR FORTUNY 25
TEL 93 301 45 83
For vegetarians this is a good option offering tasty hot dishes and a salad bar.

🛏 200 🚇 Liceu 🕐 Closed Mon.–Wed. p.m. & Sun. 🏧 MC, V

EASTERN SPAIN

CATALUNYA

COSTA BRAVA

🏨 MAS DE TORRENT
🍴 $$$$$ ★★★★★
AFORES S/N, TORRENT D'EMPORDA 17123
TEL 972 30 32 92
FAX 972 30 32 93
E-MAIL reservas@mastorrent.com
www.mastorrent.com
An 18th-century farmhouse with fantastic views of the coastline. The decor is a mix of sophisticated Catalan and rustic elements. The excellent restaurant offers traditionally

prepared food such as asparagus tossed with artichokes and foie gras. Notable wine list.

🚹 30 🅿 ⇄ 🄰 🌊 🄰 All major cards

🏨 DURÁN
🍴 $$ ★★★

LASAUCA 5
FIGUERAS 17600
TEL 972 50 12 50
FAX 972 50 26 09
E-MAIL hotel@portlligat.net
Formerly Dalí's Figueras base; the owner was a friend. Low-key, central, and a good value. It has a reputable restaurant.

🚹 65 🅿 ⇄ 🄰 🄰 All major cards

🏨 DIANA
$ ★★

PLAÇA D'ESPANYA 6,
TOSSA DE MAR 17320
TEL 972 34 18 86
FAX 972 34 11 03
E-MAIL info@diana-hotel.com
www.diana-hotel.com
Early 20th-century building by Antoni de Falguera with views of the sea and Platja Gran. No restaurant.

🚹 21 ⇄ 🄰 All major cards

🏨 PORT LLIGAT
$ ★★

PLATJA DE PORT LLIGAT
SALVADOR DALÍ S/N,
CADAQUÉS 17488
TEL 972 25 81 62
FAX 972 25 86 43
E-MAIL portlligat@intercom.es
www.costabravanord.com/hotel
portlligat
Next door to Dalí's last home. Some rooms have terraces and views of the sea. The mixture of furnishings adds to the general charm.

🚹 29 🅿 🌊 🄰 MC, V

SOMETHING SPECIAL

🍴 EL BULLI
T his is arguably the top restaurant in Spain and has three Michelin stars. Celebrity chef Ferran Adrià has created his own style, best sampled in the 12-course taster menu, an unforgettable experience. The

bodega matches the cuisine. Reservations far in advance.

$$$$$
CALA MONTJOI (6 KM FROM
ROSES), ROSES 17480
TEL 972 15 04 57
www.elbulli.com

🍴 50 🅿 🕐 Closed L except Sun. Apr.–June, Oct.–Mar., & Mon. & Tues. Apr.–June 🄰 🄰 All major cards

---

GIRONA (GERONA) 17000

🏨 CARLEMANY
🍴 $$$ ★★★★

PLAÇA MIQUEL SANTALÓ
TEL 972 21 12 12
FAX 972 21 49 94
E-MAIL carlemany@carlemany.es
www.carlemany.es
Good-value modern hotel with large rooms in the new part of town, but only a five-minute walk from the old. Good restaurant.

🚹 90 🅿 ⇄ 🄰 🄰 All major cards

🏨 COSTABELLA
$$$ ★★★

AVENIDA FRANÇA 61
TEL 972 20 25 24
FAX 972 20 22 03
E-MAIL reservas@hotelcosta
bella.com
www.hotelcostabella.com
Five minutes from the old town, this new hotel has non-smoking rooms and serves superior breakfasts.

🚹 49 🅿 ⇄ 🄰 🌊 🎽 🄰 All major cards

🍴 EL CELLER DE CAN ROCA
$$$$$

CARRETERA TAIALÀ 40
TEL 972 22 21 57
www.cellersanroca.com
Three Roca brothers have won awards including two Michelin stars. Joan Roca, a top Catalan chef, creates aromatic dishes such as clams with grapefruit sorbet and Campari. Outstanding wines. Reservations needed.

🍴 40 🅿 🕐 Closed Sun. & Mon., early July, & 2 weeks Christmas 🄰 🄰 All major cards

---

MONTBLANC 43400

🏨 DUCAL
$ ★★

FRANCESC MACIÀ 11
TEL 977 86 00 25
FAX 977 86 21 31
www.hotelducal.com
On the outskirts of the medieval town and not far from Poblet monastery, this is a warm and agreeable hotel.

🚹 41 🅿 🄰 All major cards

SANT CELONI 08470

🍴 CAN FABES
$$$$$

SANT JOAN 6
TEL 93 867 28 51
www.canfabes.com
Top restaurant in an old stone farmhouse. Sample Santi Santamaría's exquisite cuisine, which has won three Michelin stars, with the taster menu. Close by is the 5-bedroom Hotel Can Fabes and Santamaría's more relaxed, and slightly cheaper restaurant, the Espai Koch (Tel 93 848 43 84)—all part of his "Center of Gastronomic Enjoyment."

🍴 50 🅿 🕐 Closed Sun. D, Mon., 2 weeks Feb., & 2 weeks June–early July 🄰 🄰 All major cards

---

SITGES 08870

🏨 CELIMAR
$$ ★★★

PASSEIG DE LA RIBERA 20
TEL 93 811 01 70
FAX 93 811 04 03
www.hotelcelimar.es
Modernista hotel right on the seafront. No restaurant.

🚹 26 🅿 ⇄ 🄰 🄰 All major cards

TARRAGONA 43000

🏨 FARISTOL
🍴 $$ ★★

SANT MARTÍ 5, ALTAFULLA

43893 (7 MILES/11 KM FROM
TARRAGONA)
TEL 977 65 00 77
FAX 977 65 07 70
E-MAIL amarti@tinet.org
www.faristol.extendnow.com
The rooms in this 17th-
century mansion have been
furnished with period
furniture. The restaurant
serves grilled meats in its
cool interior courtyard.
🛈 5 🚭 DC, MC, V

🏨 IMPERIAL TARRACO
🍽 $$ ★★★★
PASSEIG DE LES PALMERES
TEL 977 23 30 40
FAX 977 21 65 66
E-MAIL hotelimperialtarraco
@husa.es
www.husa.es
The semicircle of this large
white 1960s block reflects the
remains of the Roman amphitheater. Rooms have balconies,
but ask for a sea view.
🛈 170 🅿 ⬍ 🚭 🚇
🚭 All major cards

🍽 MERLOT
$$$
CAVALLERS 6
TEL 977 22 06 52
www.restaurantmerlot.com
Occupying three floors of a
marvelously restored *modernista* building in the old town.
The Mediterranean cuisine is
based on regional products.
Try the fresh goat cheese and
tasty anchovy salad.
🔢 65 🚭 🚭 All major cards

TORTOSA 43500

🏨 PARADOR DE
🍽 TORTOSA
$$$ ★★★★
CASTILLO DE LA ZUDA
TEL 977 44 44 50
FAX 977 44 44 58
E-MAIL tortosa@parador.es
www.parador.es
An impressive tenth-century
fortress above Tortosa with
views of the Ebro plains and
Beceite Mountains, furnished
in keeping with its history.
🛈 72 🅿 ⬍ 🚭 🚇 🚭 All
major cards

VIC 08500

🏨 PARADOR DE
VIC-SAU
$$$ ★★★★
PARATGE BAC DE SAU
(14 KM FROM VIC)
TEL 93 812 23 23
FAX 93 812 23 68
E-MAIL vic@parador.es
www.parador.es
On the edge of the Sau
Reservoir, it resembles a
Catalan *masia* (farmhouse).
Some rooms overlook the
reservoir and mountains.
🛈 34 🅿 ⬍ 🚭 🚇 🚭 All
major cards

ALACANT
(ALICANTE) 03000

🏨 MELIÁ ALICANTE
🍽 $$ ★★★★
PLAZA PUERTA DEL MAR 3
TEL/FAX 96 520 50 00
E-MAIL melia.alicante@solme
lia.com
www.meliaalicante.solmelia.com
An enormous, plain hotel built
in the 1970s and stretching
along the port. The decor is
outdated but the rooms all
have balconies and sea views.
🛈 545 🅿 ⬍ 🚭 🚇
🚭 All major cards

🏨 TRYP GRAN SOL
🍽 $$ ★★★★
RAMBLA MÉNDEZ NÚÑEZ 3
TEL 96 520 30 00
FAX 96 521 14 39
E-MAIL tryp.gran.sol@solme
lia.com
www.trypgransol.solmelia.com
The only high-rise in the
center of Alacant near the sea.
🛈 123 🅿 ⬍ 🚭 🚇 🚭 All
major cards

🍽 NOU MANOLÍN
$$$$
VILLEGAS 3
TEL 96 520 03 68
www.noumanolin.com
Eat at the bar or in the dining
room. The *montaditos*, unique
to Alacant, are mini sandwiches
with fillings of your choice. The

rice dishes are delicious, as is
the *jamón ibérico*.
🔢 315 🅿 🚭 🚭 All major
cards

🍽 DARSENA
$$$
MARINA DEPORTIVA
MUELLE DE LEVANTE 6
TEL 96 520 75 89
www.darsena.com
Popular restaurant serving over
150 rice dishes. The poached
hake on a bed of cockles and
the black rice with broad beans
and mushrooms are favorites.
🔢 200 🅿 🚭 🚭 All major
cards

ALCOI
(ALCOY) 03803

🏨 MAS DE PAU
🍽 $$ ★★
CARRETERA ALCOY-
PENAGUILA, KM 9
TEL 96 551 31 11
FAX 96 551 31 09
Sheltered between mountains
in the Penaguila Valley, this
18th-century farmhouse is a
quiet retreat among the olive
and almond groves. Fine views
from the terrace, but bedrooms are somewhat cramped.
🛈 19 🅿 🚇 🚭 All major
cards

PRICES

HOTELS
An indication of the cost
of a double room without
breakfast is given by **$** signs.

$$$$$	Over $300
$$$$	$220–$300
$$$	$160–$220
$$	$80–$160
$	Under $80

RESTAURANTS
An indication of the cost of a
three-course dinner without
drinks is given by $ signs.

$$$$$	Over $80
$$$$	$50–$80
$$$	$35–$50
$$	$20–$35
$	Under $20

ALTEA 03590

🍴 MONTE MOLAR
$$$
PARTIDA MONTE MOLAR 38
TEL 96 584 15 81
Set in a villa with a spectacular terrace, the Monte Molar is known for its fashionable cuisine. Try the braised lamb in red wine with green beans.
🛏 60 🅿 🕐 Check for times 🟦 🚫 All major cards

CALP (CALPE) 03710

🏨 VENTA LA CHATA
$$ ★★
CARRETERA N 332 ALICANTE-VALENCIA, KM 172
TEL/FAX 96 583 03 08
EMAIL dgn@terra.es
Old-fashioned country house with rustic furniture and a garden. Simple, spacious rooms with views of Calpe.
🛏 17 🅿 🚫 All major cards

GUADALEST 03517

🍴 CASA PATRICIO
$$
ARRIBA 37, EL ABDET
TEL 96 588 53 10
Good local cuisine such as roast lamb.
🛏 55 🕐 Closed Mon., & 3 weeks July 🟦 🚫 MC, V

POLOP 03520

🏨 DEVACHAN
$$$ ★★★★
SAN FRANCISCO 13
TEL 96 689 56 40
FAX 96 689 62 33
EMAIL hoteldevachan@ctv.es
A magical little hotel in an 18th-century seignorial house in the mountain village of Polop. Sunny rooms in rustic style with attention to detail.
🛏 5 🛏 30 🟦 🚫 AE, MC, V

VALENCIA 46000

🏨 MELIÁ VALENCIA
🍴 PALACE
$$$ ★★★★★
PASEO DE LA ALAMEDA 32
TEL 96 337 50 37
FAX 96 337 55 32
E-MAIL melia.valencia.palace@solmelia.com
www.meliavalenciapalace.solmelia.com
Opposite the Palau de la Música and next to the Turia gardens, the modern facade of this hotel encloses state of the art design interiors.
🛏 248 🅿 🟦 🟦 🚤 🎾 🚫 All major cards

🏨 AD HOC
🍴 $MONUMENTAL
$$ ★★★
BOIX 4
TEL 96 391 91 40
FAX 96 391 36 67
E-MAIL adhoc@adhochotel es.com
www.adhochoteles.com
An 1880s house with combined modern design and antiques. The restaurant serves Mediterranean cuisine.
🛏 45 🛏 28 🟦 🟦 🚫 All major cards

🏨 REINA VICTORIA
$$ ★★★★
BARCAS 4
TEL 96 352 04 87
FAX 96 352 27 21
E-MAIL hreinavictoriavalencia@husa.es
www.husareinavictoria.es
Still the most elegant hotel in Valencia and refurbished in 2004. The rooms are classically decorated. Queen Victoria may have stayed here.
🛏 97 🅿 🟦 🟦 🚫 All major cards

🍴 TORRIJOS
$$$$$
DOCTOR SUMSI 4
TEL 96 373 29 49
www.restaurantetorrijos.com
A top restaurant with one Michelin star. Feature dishes include: *arroz con pintada y boletus* (rice with guinea fowl and porcini), and scallop salad with trout roe, basil, and lime.
🛏 60 🕐 Closed Sun.–Mon., last 2 weeks Jan., 2 weeks after Easter, last week Aug., & first week Sept. 🟦 🚫 All major cards

🍴 ALBACAR
$$$$
SORNÍ 35
TEL 96 395 10 05
The modern setting provides the atmosphere for this cuisine. Try oxtail and raisins stewed in Muscatel wine or red mullet with sea-urchins.
🛏 60 🕐 Closed Sat. L, Sun., Easter, & 3 weeks Aug. 🟦 🚫 All major cards

🍴 RÍAS GALLEGAS
$$$$
CIRILO AMORÓS 4
TEL 96 352 51 11
www.riasgallegas.es
This restaurant has its ingredients sent from Galicia. Sample the scallops and the Galician style turbot. Galician wines.
🛏 77 🅿 🕐 Closed Sun. & Aug. 🟦 🚫 All major cards

🍴 LA PEPICA
$$$
PASEO NEPTUNO 6–8, PLAYA MALVAROSA
TEL 96 371 03 66
www.lapepica.com
It's been dishing up exquisite seafood and rice dishes since 1898, either inside the cavernous restaurant or out on the breezy terrace. Hemingway and the King of Spain both ate here.
🛏 450 🕐 Closed Sun. D & last 2 weeks Nov. 🚫 All major cards

XÀBIA (JÁVEA) 03730

🏨 EL RODAT
🍴 $$$ ★★★★
DE LA MURCIANA 9
CARRETERA CABO DE LA NAO
TEL 96 647 07 10
FAX 96 647 15 50
E-MAIL info@elrodat.com
www.elrodat.com
Surrounded by gardens of pine, palm, and bougainvillea, this elegantly furnished hotel offers views of the Montgó mountains and the coast.
🛏 42 🅿 🟦 🟦 🚤 🎾 🚫 All major cards

🟦 Air-conditioning 🏊 Indoor/🏊 Outdoor swimming pool 🎾 Health club 🚫 Credit cards   **KEY**

XÁTIVA (JÁTIVA) 46800

🏨 HOSTERÍA DE 🍴 MONTSANT
$$ ★★
SUBIDA AL CASTILLO S/N
TEL 96 227 50 81
FAX 96 228 19 05
E-MAIL mont-sant@mont-sant.com
www.mont-sant.com
This restored Cistercian monastery dating back to 1320 has simple elegant rooms and is surrounded by a huge garden. Breakfast included.
🛏 16 🅿 🛗 🏊 📺 🏧 All major cards

CASTILLA Y LEÓN

ÁVILA 05000

🏨 PALACIO DE LOS 🍴 VELADA
$$ ★★★★
PLAZA DE LA CATEDRAL 10
TEL 920 25 51 00
FAX 920 25 49 00
E-MAIL recepcion.avila@veladahoteles.com
www.veladahoteles.com
A restored 16th-century palace opposite the cathedral. The rooms are airy, spacious, and attractively decorated. Amazing interior courtyard.
🛏 145 🅿 🛗 🛗 All major cards

🏨 HOSPEDERÍA DE 🍴 BRACAMONTE
$ ★★
BRACAMONTE 6
TEL 920 25 12 80
FAX 920 25 38 38
E-MAIL hospederia@hospederiadebracamonte.com
www.hospederiadebracamonte.com
This 16th-century mansion near the Plaza del Ayuntamiento and close to the cathedral is charming place. Good-value restaurant where lamb roasted in a wood-burning oven is a specialty.
🛏 22 🪑 200 🅿 🛗 DC, MC, V

🍴 EL ALMACÉN
$$$
CARRETERA DE SALAMANCA 6
TEL 920 25 44 55
FAX 920 21 10 26
On the outskirts of town with views of the Adaja River, this restaurant may serve the most refined cuisine in Ávila. Try the gilt-head bream fillet with mussels al pil-pil (sizzling oil with garlic and chili).
🪑 75 🛗 🅿 🕐 Closed Sun. D, Mon., & Sept. 🏧 All major cards

BURGOS 09000

🏨 LANDA
$$$$ ★★★★★
CARRETERA N1 MADRID-IRÚN, KM 235
TEL 947 25 77 77
FAX 947 26 46 76
www.landahotel.com
For luxury and the best food in Burgos, stay in this former palace with its Gothic tower. The restaurant serves seasonal specialties and tasty rice dishes. Delicious desserts shouldn't be missed.
🛏 42 🅿 🛗 🛗 🏊 🏊 📺 🏧 MC, V

🏨 LA POSADA
$ ★★★
LANDELINO TARDAJOS 3, CASTROJERIZ 09110 (25 MILES/40 KM FROM BURGOS)
TEL 947 37 86 10
FAX 947 37 86 11
This restored 16th-century inn on the Camino de Santiago offers a quiet alternative. Filled with rustic furniture the posada has medieval bodegas and a glass-covered patio.
🛏 21 🅿 🕐 Closed 2 weeks late Sept.–early Oct. 🛗 🏊 MC, V

CIUDAD RODRIGO 37500

🏨 PARADOR DE CIUDAD RODRIGO
$$$ ★★★
PLAZA CASTILLO 1
TEL 923 46 01 50
FAX 923 46 04 04
E-MAIL ciudadrodrigo@parador.es
www.parador.es
This 14th-century castle on the banks of the Águeda river surrounded by well-kept gardens. Some rooms have fantastic views—one is circular with a domed ceiling. Check the tower views.
🛏 35 🅿 🛗 🏧 All major cards

🍴 LA BRASA
$$
AVENIDA DE SALAMANCA 32
TEL/FAX 923 46 07 93
A straightforward restaurant for quality meats grilled over an open fire, homemade sausages, and other Castilian recipes such as huevos con farinato. Exceptional wine list, and reasonable prices.
🪑 100 🕐 Closed Sun. D & Tues. 🛗 🏧 All major cards

LEÓN 24000

🏨 PARADOR DE LEÓN
$$$$ ★★★★★
PLAZA SAN MARCOS 7
TEL 987 23 73 00
FAX 987 23 34 58
E-MAIL leon@parador.es
www.parador.es
This stunning parador, built by King Ferdinand in the 16th century for pilgrims, has an ornate plateresque facade and is filled with antiques and works of art. Ask for a room in the medieval part. Splendid dining room where regional dishes such as frog legs, river eel stewed with potatoes, and cecina (dried beef) are served.
🛏 226 🅿 🛗 🛗 🏧 All major cards

🏨 LA POSADA REGÍA
$$ ★★★
REGIDORES 9–11
TEL 987 21 31 73
FAX 987 21 30 31
E-MAIL posada@regialeon.com
www.regialeon.com
A small hotel in a town house that dates back to 1370. Rooms in rustic fashion are in

---

HOTELS & RESTAURANTS

reds and blues with wooden floors and beamed ceilings. The restaurant, Bodega Regía, serves regional cuisine.
🔒 19 ⊞ 120 🅢 DC, MC, V

🍴 VIVALDI
$$$$
PLATERÍAS 4
TEL 987 26 07 60
www.restaurantvivaldi.com
Creative modern cuisine uses local produce. Specials include suckling pig confit with chestnut and kumquat jelly.
⊞ 115 ⊞ Closed Sun. D & Mon. Sept.–June & Sun. July–Aug. 🅢 🅢 All major cards

SALAMANCA 37000

🏨 RECTOR
$$$ ★★★★
PASEO RECTOR ESPERABE 10
TEL 923 21 84 82
FAX 923 21 40 08
E-MAIL hotelrector@tele fonica.net
www.hotelrector.com
A grandiose 1940s building of Villamayor stone with elegant interiors and bedrooms. The breakfast here is excellent, but there is no restaurant.
🔒 13 🅿 🔄 🅢 🅢 All major cards

🏨 SAN POLO
🍴 $$$ ★★★
ARROYO DE SANTO DOMINGO 2
TEL 923 21 11 77
FAX 923 21 11 54
E-MAIL hotelsanpolo@hotelsan polo.com
www.hotelsanpolo.com
Modern hotel built among the 11th-century Romanesque ruins of San Polo church. Many rooms look over the old town.
🔒 37 🔄 🅢 🅢 All major cards

🏨 PALACIO DE
🍴 CASTELLANOS
$$ ★★★★
SAN PABLO 58–64
TEL 923 26 18 18
FAX 923 26 18 19

E-MAIL nhpalaciodecastellanos @nh-hotels.com
www.nh-hotels.com
The most stylish place to stay in Salamanca near the Plaza Mayor. The original cloister is a fantastic example of Hispanic-Flemish architecture.
🔒 62 🅿 🔄 🅢 🅢 All major cards

🍴 CHEZ VÍCTOR
$$$$
ESPOZ Y MINA 26
TEL 923 21 31 23
Owner Victór Salvador offers creative French-Spanish cuisine. The goat cheese charlotte is delicious and desserts are phenomenal, with a menu just for chocolate ones.
⊞ 50 ⊞ Closed Sun. D, Mon., & Aug. 🅢 🅢 All major cards

🍴 VÍCTOR GUTIÉRREZ
$$$$
SAN PABLO 66–80
TEL 923 26 29 73
E-MAIL restaurantevictorgutierrez @yahoo.com
www.victorgutierrez.321.cn
The fresh and inventive cooking of this Peruvian chef has rapidly won him a Michelin star for this recently-opened restaurant opposite the San Esteban convent. Try his marinated tuna with apple ice, or boletus mushrooms confir with scallops and fresh pasta.
⊞ 20 ⊞ Sun. D & Tues. D 🅢 All major cards

🍴 EL BARDO
$$$
COMPAÑÍA 8
TEL 923 21 90 89
www.restauranteselbardo.com
Just off the Calle Mayor, this small place has a lively ground floor tapas bar and a first floor dining room. Recommended dishes include lamb chops with vegetables and arroz negro (squid with rice cooked in its ink). Many vegetarian dishes.
⊞ 50 🅢 🅢 All major cards

SEGOVIA 40000

🏨 LOS LINAJES
$$ ★★★
DOCTOR VELASCO 9
TEL 921 46 04 75
FAX 921 46 04 79
E-MAIL loslinajes@terra.es
www.loslinajes.com
Within city walls, on a narrow, quiet street, this hotel occupies part of the medieval palace of the Falconi family. Some of the older rooms have views of the Eresma Valley.
🔒 62 🅿 🔄 🅢 🅢 All major cards

🏨 PARADOR DE SEGOVIA
🍴 $$$ ★★★★
CARRETERA DE VALLADOLID
TEL 921 44 37 37
FAX 921 43 73 62
E-MAIL segovia@parador.es
www.parador.es
A modern parador filled with contemporary art and furniture. The views of Segovia are stunning, but it is far from the center city. The restaurant serves some of the city's best roast suckling pig and other more imaginative dishes.
🔒 114 🅿 🔄 🅢 🅢 🅢 🅢 All major cards

🍴 MESÓN DE CÁNDIDO
$$$
PLAZA AZOGUEJO 5
TEL 921 42 59 11
www.mesondecandido.es
Under the aqueducto these quaint dining rooms—now a national monument—have functioned since 1786. The cuisine is traditional Castilian.
⊞ 420 🅢 🅢 All major cards

🍴 MARACAIBO–CASA SILVANO
$$$
PASEO EZEQUIEL GONZÁLEZ 25
TEL 921 46 15 45
www.restaurantemaracaibo.com
Chef Óscar Hernándo offers a fine mix of traditional Castilian dishes and up-to-the-minute creative cooking. Try the wild mushrooms with foie gras and

grated black truffle or cod *pil-pil* (white garlic sauce).
 70 🔟 All major cards

SORIA 42000

🏨 PARADOR DE SORIA
🍴 $$$ ★★★★
PARQUE DEL CASTILLO S/N
TEL 975 24 08 00
FAX 975 24 08 03
E-MAIL soria@parador.es
www.parador.es
A modern *parador* in the park dedicated to poet Antonio Machado. Wood floors and furnishings. Ask for a room overlooking Soria and the Duero River. The restaurant offers garlic soup and beans.
🛏 67 🅿 🔟 All major cards

TORDESILLAS 47100

🏨 LOS TOREROS
🍴 $$ ★
AVENIDA VALLADOLID 26
TEL 983 77 19 00
FAX 983 77 19 54
E-MAIL toreros@hotellostoreros.com
www.hotellostoreros.com
A family-run hotel in a former country house with small but cozy rooms.
🛏 34 🅿 🔟 All major cards

TORO 49800

🏨 JUAN II
🍴 $ ★★★
PASEO DEL ESPOLÓN 1
TEL 980 69 03 00
FAX 980 69 23 76
E-MAIL info@hoteljuanii.com
www.hoteljuanii.com
A very good value hotel next to the Colegiata with views over the plains of Zamora. The rooms are spacious with tiled floors and rustic decor.
🛏 42 🅿 🔟 🚇 All major cards

VALLADOLID 47000

🏨 MOZART
🍴 $$ ★★★
MENÉNDEZ PELAYO 7
TEL 983 29 77 77

FAX 983 29 21 90
E-MAIL hotelmozart@hotelmozart.net
www.hotelmozart.net
In a city-center house, dating from 1872, this hotel has attractive wood balconies. The rooms are of ample size and functionally equipped. Ask for a balcony. No restaurant.
🛏 38 🅿 ⬆ 🔟 AE, MC, V

🍴 MESÓN DE ANGEL CUADRADO
$$$$
MARINA ESCOBAR 1
TEL 983 30 16 73/30 70 19
FAX 983 30 70 19
E-MAIL meson@mesonangelcuadrado.com
www.mesonangelcuadrado.com
Castilian cooking, both traditional and creative. Try the wild boar stew or crab pancakes. Excellent wine list. Reservations suggested.
 60 🕐 Closed Sun. July–Aug., & Sun. D Sept.–June 🔟 All major cards

ZAMORA 49000

🏨 HOSTERÍA REAL DE ZAMORA
🍴 $$ ★★★
CUESTA PIZARRO 7
TEL/FAX 980 53 45 45/22
E-MAIL hostzamora@hosteriasreales.com
www.hosteriasreales.com
This delightful hotel occupies the Palacio de la Inquisición, a historic monument, on a quiet street with a terrace and walled garden. The small rooms open onto the 16th-century interior patio.
🛏 26 🔟 All major cards

🍴 LA POSADA
$$
BENAVENTE 2
TEL 980 51 64 74
www.restauranteposada.com
The *menú turístico* is a good choice at this classically decorated restaurant.
 50 🕐 Closed Sun. D, & Mon. 🔟 All major cards

PRICES

HOTELS
An indication of the cost of a double room without breakfast is given by $ signs.
$$$$$ Over $300
$$$$ $220– $300
$$$ $160–$220
$$ $80–$160
$ Under $80

RESTAURANTS
An indication of the cost of a three-course dinner without drinks is given by $ signs.
$$$$$ Over $80
$$$$ $50–$80
$$$ $35–$50
$$ $20–$35
$ Under $20

CASTILLA-LA MANCHA & EXTREMADURA

ALARCÓN 16214

🏨 PARADOR DE ALARCÓN
🍴 $$$$ ★★★★
AVENIDA AMIGOS DE LOS CASTILLOS 3
TEL 969 33 03 15
FAX 969 33 03 03
E-MAIL alarcon@parador.es
www.parador.es
Once Moorish, then a fortified medieval castle with 14 rooms. Turret rooms have narrow slits for windows; some have four-poster beds. Dine on typical local fare including *morteruelo* (a hash of mixed meats including game and liver) or leg of lamb.
🛏 14 80 🅿 ⬆ 🔟 All major cards

ALMAGRO 13270

SOMETHING SPECIAL

🏨 PARADOR DE ALMAGRO
This 16th-century Franciscan convent, built around 14 courtyards, is a peaceful place, decorated with naive paintings

and beautiful old tiles. Rooms were monks' cells. The restaurant serves traditional Manchegan fare such as *mojete*, (cold roasted onions and peppers), and *tiznao*.

$$$ ★★★★
RONDA SAN FRANCISCO 31
TEL 926 86 01 00
FAX 926 86 01 50
E-MAIL almagro@parador.es
www.parador.es
🛈 54 🅿 🔁 🌀 🏊 🚫 All major cards

🍽 EL CORREGIDOR
$$$$
GERÓNIMO CEBALLOS 2
TEL 926 86 06 48
www.corregidordealmagro.com
A delightful restaurant in an old house with original tiling. The food is modern Manchegan—try cod in eggplant sauce or lamb ribs confit.
🍴 130 🅿 🕐 Closed Mon. & last week July 🌀 🚫 All major cards

BADAJOZ 06000

SOMETHING SPECIAL

🏨 MONASTERIO DE 🍽 ROCAMADOR
Built by Franciscan monks in the 16th century. No two rooms are alike in decor or size, and some are built into the rock. Basque-Extremaduran cuisine is served in the former chapel.

$$$ ★★★★
CARRETERA NACIONAL BADAJOZ-HUELVA, KM 41.1, ALMENDRAL
TEL 924 48 90 00
FAX 924 48 90 01
E-MAIL mail@rocamador.com
www.rocamador.com
🛈 26 🅿 🏊 🚫 All major cards

🏨 HUSA ZURBARÁN
$ ★★★★
PASEO CASTELAR S/N
TEL 924 00 14 00
FAX 924 22 01 42
Attentive service and recently modernized decor at this

hotel overlooking Castelar Park and the Guadiana River.
🛈 215 🅿 🔁 🌀 🏊 🚫 All major cards

🍽 ALDEBARÁN
$$$$
AVENIDA ELVAS S/N URBANIZACIÓN GUADIANA
TEL 924 27 68 37
www.restaurantealdebaran.com
Elegant and charming, this is the city's best restaurant. Fernando Bárcena uses the freshest local produce to create the Basque-influenced menu of Extremaduran haute cuisine. Dishes include fresh anchovies marinated with truffles, *solomillo de cerdo ibérico* (Iberian pork-fillet steak) with truffle purée, and Casar cheese salad.
🍴 100 🅿 🕐 Closed Sun. & Mon. D & 2 weeks Aug. 🌀 🚫 All major cards

🍽 LA TOJA
$$$
SÁNCHEZ DE LA ROCHA 22
TEL 924 27 34 77
www.restaurantelatoja.com
On the outskirts of town, this classy restaurant provides Galician seafood: *chipirones en su tinta* (tiny squid in their own ink), *pulpo a la gallega* (octopus stewed with potatoes, parsley, and paprika), and sorbets. Paella on Sundays.
🍴 75 🅿 🕐 Closed Sun. D, & first 2 weeks Feb. 🌀 🚫 AE, MC, V

CÁCERES 10000

🏨 PARADOR DE 🍽 CÁCERES
$$$ ★★★★
ANCHA 6
TEL 927 21 17 59
FAX 927 21 17 29
E-MAIL caceres@parador.es
www.parador.es
The Torreorgaz family built this 14th-century palace in the heart of medieval Cáceres. A small, pretty interior patio leads to reception. The restaurant Torreorgaz offers fine local fare including: *migas* (fried bread

crumbs) with quail eggs and venison with Casar cheese.
🛈 33 🅿 🔁 🌀 🚫 All major cards

🏨 MELIÁ CÁCERES 🍽 BOUTIQUE
$$ ★★★★
PLAZA DE SAN JUAN 11
TEL 927 21 58 00
FAX 927 21 40 70
E-MAIL melia.caceres@solmelia.com
www.meliacaceres.solmelia.com
In a renovated 16th-century palace in the old town, next to Cáceres' commercial center. The rooms are spacious with modern decor. The restaurant, bar, and some bedrooms have beautiful brick-vaulted ceilings.
🛈 86 🅿 🔁 🌀 🚫 All major cards

🍽 ATRIO
$$$$$
AVENIDA DE ESPAÑA 30
TEL 927 24 29 28
FAX 927 22 11 11
E-MAIL info@restauranteatrio.com
www.restauranteatrio.com
Since 1986, this elegant restaurant has served classical and modern cuisine, winning two Michelin stars. Dishes include roast scallops with truffle purée, rib of lamb stuffed with boletus mushrooms, *bacalao monacal* (cod with spinach and potatoes) and bananas sautéed with brown sugar on caramel and ginger cream.
🍴 60 🕐 Closed Sun. D, & first 2 weeks Sept. 🌀 🚫 All major cards

🍽 CHEZ MANOU
$$$
PLAZA DE LAS VELETAS 4
TEL 927 22 76 82
One of the few restaurants in the historic walled town, near the museum. A small cozy place specializing in French cuisine and regional dishes.
🍴 50 🕐 Closed Sun. D & Mon. 🌀 🚫 MC, V

HOTELS & RESTAURANTS

CUENCA 16000

🏨 PARADOR DE CUENCA
🍴 $$$ ★★★★
SUBIDA A SAN PABLO S/N
TEL 969 23 23 20
FAX 969 23 25 34
E-MAIL cuenca@parador.es
www.parador.es
In the restored 1500s monastery of San Pablo, the *parador* sits in the Hoz del Huécar gorge. The restaurant in the old refectory has an interesting menu: *morteruelo* (Cuencan game gruel), *pisto con lomo de orza* (ratatouille with pork loin), and *alajú* (almond, walnut and honey dessert).
🛏 63 🪑 150 🅿 🛗 🔲 🏊
📺 🗝 All major cards

🏨 LEONOR DE AQUITANIA
$$ ★★★
SAN PEDRO 60
TEL 969 23 10 00
FAX 969 23 10 04
E-MAIL reservas@hotelleonord
eaquitania.com
www.hotelleonordeaquitania.com
A hanging house overlooking the gorge, one of two hotels in the old town. It combines traditional design with contemporary decor.
🛏 49 🛗 🗝 All major cards

SOMETHING SPECIAL

🏨 POSADA DE SAN JOSÉ
In the heart of the old town, this hanging house was home to Velázquez's daughter. The rambling 17th-century building is filled with antiques. Simple rooms; without televisions or telephones—not all have bathrooms. A bar-dining area serves breakfast and tapas but no restaurant. Reserve early.
$ ★★
JULIÁN ROMERO 4
TEL 969 21 13 00
FAX 969 23 03 65
E-MAIL info@posadasanjose.com
www.posadasanjose.com
🛏 21 🗝 All major cards

🍴 FIGÓN DE PEDRO
$$$
CERVANTES 13
TEL 969 22 68 21
www.figondepedro.com
A modest but lively restaurant in the business district owned by Pedro Torres, who runs the Mesón Casas Colgadas. The menus are almost identical—less expensive here. Specials include a Moorish sweet, *alaju* (made with honey, almonds, and walnuts).
🪑 55 🕐 Closed Sun. D, & Mon. 🔲 🗝 All major cards

🍴 MESÓN CASAS COLGADAS
$$$
CANÓNIGOS S/N
TEL 969 22 35 09
www.mesoncasascolgadas.com
Enjoy the magnificent panorama, in one of the hanging houses next to the Museum of Abstract Art, as you dine on game and Manchegan specialties. Worth sampling are the *ajo arriero* (a paste made from salted cod, garlic, parsley, and paprika), venison, and roast suckling pig.
🪑 100 🕐 Closed Mon. D & Tues. 🔲 🗝 All major cards

GUADALUPE 10140

🏨 HOSPEDERÍA DEL
🍴 REAL MONASTERIO
$$ ★★
PLAZA DE JUAN CARLOS I S/N
TEL 927 36 70 00
FAX 927 36 71 77
www.monasterioguadalupe.com
An imposing 16th-century monastery of Gothic, Renaissance, and Baroque style. Part of the building is still used by monks who also run the hospedería. Comfortable rooms surround the cloister. The restaurant serves hearty fare such as tomato soup and goat *caldereta* (stew). For weekends reserve two months ahead.
🛏 47 🅿 🕐 Closed 4 weeks Jan.–Feb. 🛗 🔲 🗝 MC, V

PRICES

HOTELS
An indication of the cost of a double room without breakfast is given by $ signs.

$$$$$	Over $300
$$$$	$220–$300
$$$	$160–$220
$$	$80–$160
$	Under $80

RESTAURANTS
An indication of the cost of a three-course dinner without drinks is given by $ signs.

$$$$$	Over $80
$$$$	$50–$80
$$$	$35–$50
$$	$20–$35
$	Under $20

🏨 PARADOR DE
🍴 GUADALUPE
$$$ ★★★★
MARQUÉS DE LA ROMANA 12
TEL 927 36 70 75
FAX 927 36 70 76
E-MAIL guadalupe@parador.es
www.parador.es
Built in the 15th century, this *parador* was the pilgrims' hospital and a noted medical school. Orange and lemon trees in the courtyard, enhance the Moorish atmosphere.
🛏 41 🅿 🛗 🔲 🏊 🗝 All major cards

JARANDILLA DE LA VERA 10450

🏨 PARADOR DE
🍴 JARANDILLA DE
LA VERA
$$$ ★★★★
AVENIDA GARCÍA PRIETO 1
TEL 927 56 01 17
FAX 927 56 00 88
E-MAIL jarandilla@parador.es
www.parador.es
The Counts of Oropesa and the Marquises of Jarandilla built this fortified summer palace in the 1400s, a perfectly proportioned and elegant building. Good selection of typical Extremeduran dishes.

---

① 53 ⊞ 50 🅿 ⑤ ⌇
⊗ All major cards

JEREZ DE LOS CABALLEROS 06380

⊞ LOS TEMPLARIOS
⬤ $$ ★★★
CARRETERA DE VILLANUEVA
TEL 924 73 16 36
FAX 924 75 03 38
E-MAIL templarios924@hotmail
.com
www.hotellostemplarios.net
A simple three-star hotel in a
town with few choices.
① 48 🅿 ⊟ ⑤ ⌇ ⊗ All
major cards

MÉRIDA 06800

⊞ PARADOR DE MÉRIDA
⬤ $$$ ★★★★
PLAZA CONSTITUCIÓN 3
TEL 924 31 38 00
FAX 924 31 92 08
E-MAIL merida@parador.es
www.parador.es
Founded by Franciscans in the
18th century, this building is in
the heart of Mérida. Some
rooms give onto a pretty
interior courtyard and there
are also Mozarab gardens. The
restaurant provides reliable
regional gastronomy: *gazpacho
extremeño* (chilled soup),
caldereta extremeña (stewed
lamb with red peppers, fried
bread crumbs, and the
regional sausage), and truffles.
① 82 🅿 ⊟ ⑤ ⌇ ⑦
⊗ All major cards

⊞ NOVA ROMA
$$ ★★★
SUÁREZ SOMONTE 42
TEL 924 31 12 61 /31 12 01
FAX 924 30 01 60
E-MAIL reservas@novaroma.com
www.novaroma.com
Only a two-minute walk from
the Roman ruins and the
museum, this modern building
has a white marble reception
area and cafeteria. The rooms
have large beds and arm
chairs. Breakfast is expensive.
① 55 🅿 ⊟ ⑤ ⊗ AE,
MC, V

⬤ RUFINO
$$
PLAZA DE SANTA CLARA 2
TEL 924 31 20 01
A wide selection of tapas and
solid Extremaduran fare such
as partridge stew.
⊞ 45 🕒 Closed Sun. & 3
weeks Sept. ⑤ ⊗ All major
cards

SIGÜENZA 19250

⊞ MOLINO DE ALCUNEZA
$$ ★★★
CARRETERA DE ALBORECA,
KM 0.5 ALCUNEZA
TEL 949 39 15 01
FAX 949 34 70 04
E-MAIL informacion@molinodeal
cuneza.com
www.molinodealcuneza.com
A 15th-century flour mill on
the banks of the Henares
River has been converted into
a comfortable hotel.
① 11 🅿 ⌇ ⊗ All major
cards

TOLEDO 45000

⊞ ALFONSO VI
$$$ ★★★★
GENERAL MOSCARDÓ 2
TEL 925 22 26 00
FAX 925 21 44 58
E-MAIL info@hotelalfonsoVI.com
www.hotelalfonsoVI.com
Probably the most luxurious
hotel in Toledo, the Alfonso is
situated opposite the Alcazar.
Rooms have Castilian decor
① 83 ⊟ ⑤ ⊗ All major
cards

SOMETHING SPECIAL

⊞ HOSTAL DEL
⬤ CARDENAL
This beautiful hotel was built
as a summer palace for
Cardinal Lorenzana in the 18th
century. Rooms are decorated in
Castilian style with dark wood
headboards, big old mirrors, and
hand-painted bathroom tiles.
Reserve early. Mainly local dishes
such as oven-baked sea bass and
lamb stew.
$$ ★★★

PASEO DE RECAREDO 24
TEL 925 22 49 00
FAX 925 22 29 91
E-MAIL cardenal@hostaldel
cardenal.com
www.hostaldelcardenal.com
① 27 ⊞ 200 🅿 ⑤ ⊗ All
major cards

⊞ PARADOR DE TOLEDO
$$ ★★★★
CERRO DEL EMPERADOR S/N
TEL 925 22 18 50
FAX 925 22 51 66
E-MAIL toledo@parador.es
www.parador.es
A fine example of a *cigarral*, a
Toledan country home, built
beside the Tajo River. Rooms
are spacious, some with
magnificent views of the city.
① 77 🅿 ⊟ ⑤ ⌇ ⊗ All
major cards

⊞ PINTOR EL GRECO
$$ ★★★
ALAMILLOS DEL TRÁNSITO 13
TEL 925 28 51 91
FAX 925 21 58 19
E-MAIL info@hotelpintorel
greco.com
www.hotelpintorelgreco.com
In the heart of the old Jewish
quarter next to El Greco's
house-museum, this pretty
17th-century bakery became
a hotel in 1989. The interior
courtyard and facade are well
preserved. Airy rooms off the
three galleries have ironwork,
tiles, and lanterns.
① 33 🅿 ⊟ ⑤ ⊗ All
major cards

⬤ ADOLFO
$$$$
LA GRANADA 6
TEL 925 22 73 21/25 24 72
www.adolforestaurante.com
A classic establishment, in a
beautiful building with Mudejar
workmanship, offering both
innovative cuisine and traditional dishes. Try the sautéed
wild mushrooms with ham,
saffron hake, or partridge stew.
Excellent wine cellar.
⊞ 100 🕒 Closed Sun. D,
Mon., & last 2 weeks July ⑤
⊗ All major cards

HIERBABUENA
$$$
CALLEJÓN DE SAN JOSÉ 17
TEL/FAX 925 22 39 24
www.restaurantehierbabuena.com
Good-value food served on a covered Moorish patio with lots of natural light. Seasonal menu: octopus and mango salad or boar and venison sirloin with Calvados sauce.
🔲 80 🕐 Closed Sun. D, & Sun L July–Aug. 🗝 All major cards

LA LUMBRE
$$$
REAL DEL ARRABAL 5
TEL/FAX 925 28 53 07
www.lalumbre.net
Regional and national dishes: leeks and asparagus soufflé, confit of wild boar in honey, or hake with peppers.
🔲 40 🕐 Closed Sun. & first 2 weeks July 🛗 🗝 All major cards

MILLE GRAZIE
$$
CADENAS 2
TEL/FAX 925 25 42 70
www.millegrazie.es
This Italian place, owned by brothers, makes excellent pizzas and pastas. Veer away from the familiar and you will be pleasantly surprised: crepes Talaggio, *lenguado a la parmigiana* (sole with parmesan).
🔲 72 🕐 Closed Sun. D & Mon. 🛗 🗝 All major cards

TRUJILLO 10200

PARADOR DE TRUJILLO
$$$ ★★★★
SANTA BEATRIZ DE SILVA 1
TEL 927 32 13 50
FAX 927 32 13 66
E-MAIL trujillo@parador.es
www.parador.es
The old town's only hotel occupies the 16th-century convent of Santa Clara. The rooms lead onto the cloister (now glassed in) and the courtyard. Try the wild boar.
🛏 48 🅿 🛗 🗺 🗝 All major cards

FINCA SANTA MARTA
$$
CARRETERA TRUJILLO-GUADALUPE, KM 89.5
TEL 927 31 92 03
FAX 927 33 41 15
E-MAIL henri@facilnet.es
www.fincasantamarta.com
This hotel on the Trujillo-Guadalupe road was an olive farm and is still surrounded by acres of olive, cherry, and almond trees. Rustic feel with wood beams and stone floors. Order meals in advance.
🛏 14 🅿 🗺 🗝 MC, V

MESÓN LA TROYA
$$
PLAZA MAYOR 10
TEL 927 32 13 64
Huge portions and low prices make this a popular place. You can have tapas at the bar. The chaotic noisy atmosphere and general friendliness are reason enough to dine here. You will be served a tortilla, salad, and sausage to start whether you ordered them or not!
🔲 250 🛗 🗝 All major cards

ZAFRA 06300

PARADOR DE ZAFRA
$$$ ★★★★
PLAZA CORAZÓN DE MARÍA 7
TEL 924 55 45 40
FAX 924 55 10 18
E-MAIL zafra@parador.es
www.parador.es
This castle, built by Arab masons in the 15th century, has nine towers. Hernán Cortés stayed here before going to Mexico. The rooms are off the central white marble courtyard, and are rather somber, but the marble bathrooms are luxurious.
🛏 51 🅿 🛗 🗺 🗝 All major cards

HUERTA HONDA
$$ ★★★
LÓPEZ ASME 1
E-MAIL info@www.hotelhuertahonda.com
www.hotelhuertahonda.com
TEL 924 55 41 00

FAX 924 55 25 04
Rooms here are decorated with differing colors and textiles, resulting in a country manor style. The restaurant serves regional and national cuisine with a strong Basque influence. Specials: artichokes filled with salmon, fresh goat cheese with sherry vinaigrette, and roast suckling pig with a fruit sauce.
🛏 49 🔲 40 🅿 🛗 🗝 All major cards

LA CABAÑA
$$
RECINTO FERIAL S/N
TEL 924 55 21 06
Straightforward cooking of fresh produce, either meat or fish, grilled, fried, or roasted. Try sea bass or partridge.
🔲 30 🕐 Closed Sun. & Mon. D 🗝 DC, MC, V

ANDALUCÍA & MURCIA

ALMERÍA 04000

AM TORRELUZ
$$ ★★★★
PLAZA FLORES 5
TEL 950 23 49 99 or 902 23 49 99
FAX 950 23 47 09
E-MAIL torreluz4@amhoteles.com
www.amhoteles.com
The most comfortable place to stay in Almería. Roof terrace and wonderful views of the sea. Nearby are two other Torreluz hotels, one has two stars and the other three.
🛏 94 🅿 🛗 🗝 🗺 🗝 All major cards

MARTÍN FIERRO
$$$
CARRETERA DE RONDA S/N
TEL 950 27 68 53
Next to the train station this Argentinian restaurant serves delicious grilled steaks, empanadas, and *ravioles con tuco* (raviolis with tomato and onion). Desserts include a pancake filled with caramel sauce.
🔲 150 🅿 🛗 🗝 All major cards

CASA PUGA
$
JOVELLANOS 7
TEL 950 23 15 30
www.barcasapuga.es
Open since 1890, this thoroughly Almerian bar in the old town center serves excellent tapas and *raciones* (larger portions), including *jamón de jabugo* (ham from acorn-fed pigs), smoked cod with roasted peppers, and fried fish of the day. Good wine list.
🔲 50

ALPUJARRAS

ALQUERÍA DE MORAYMA
$ ★★★
CADIAR 18440
TEL 958 34 32 21
Nice rustic rooms in a wonderful setting with fantastic views of the Sierra Nevada. The restaurant serves local food.
🛏 24 🔲 50 P ≋ 🅲 V

CASA MEZCUA
$
CUESTA SAN MIGUEL
184391 CÁSTARAS
TEL 958 85 55 26
E-MAIL info@casamezcua.com
www.casamezcua.com
Delightful guesthouse in a tranquil, unspoilt village. Two self-catering apartments (sleeping four) with terraces and garden access, and two comfortable guest rooms in main house. Superb views, and excellent food with advance notice.
🛏 4 🅲 All major cards

ANTEQUERA 29200

PARADOR DE ANTEQUERA
$$ ★★★
PASEO GARCÍA DEL OLMO, S/N
TEL 95 284 02 61
FAX 95 284 13 12
E-MAIL antequera@parador.es
www.parador.es
A modern *parador*: luminous rooms with wood floors and leather furnishings. Quiet and surrounded by gardens.
🛏 55 P 🅲 ≋ 🅲 All major cards

CASTILLA
🏨 $ ★★
INFANTE DON FERNANDO 40
TEL/FAX 95 284 30 90
E-MAIL vidal@castillahotel.com
www.castillahotel.com
In the historic center, a new hotel in a restored building.
🛏 18 🅲 🅲 All major cards

EL ANGELOTE
$$$
PLAZA COSO VIEJO S/N
TEL 95 270 34 65
Traditional cooking in a restored 17th-century building with an interior courtyard opposite the Nájera Palace.
🔲 70 🕐 Closed Sun D., Mon., & last 2 weeks July 🅲 🅲 MC, V

BAEZA 23440

EL MERCANTIL
$
PORTALES TUNDIDORES 18
TEL 953 74 09 71
This atmospheric *cafetería/bar de tapas* has been running continuously since 1886. Once the favorite hang-out of the poet Antonio Machado before he fled into exile at the end of the Spanish civil war. Try the rabbit and *jamón de jabugo*.
🔲 150 🅲 All major cards

CABO DE GATA 04150

CORTIJO EL SOTILLO
🏨 $$ ★★★★
CARRETERA DE SAN JOSÉ S/N
TEL 950 61 11 00
FAX 950 61 11 05
www.cortijoelsotillo.es
An 18th-century ranch-style building with large rooms and cool marble floors; used in the film, *A Fistful of Dollars*. Horseriding available.
🛏 20 🔲 45 P 🅲 ≋ 🅲 All major cards

LA OLA
$
ISLETA DEL MORO
TEL 950 38 97 58
A simple restaurant, with a terrace over the water where you can dine year-round. Menu depends on the day's catch.
🔲 35 P 🕐 Closed Sun. 🅲 No credit cards

CÁDIZ 11000

PARADOR DE CÁDIZ
$$$ ★★★★
AVENIDA DUQUE DE NÁJERA 9
TEL 956 22 69 05
FAX 956 21 45 82
E-MAIL cadiz@parador.es
www.parador.es
One of the modern *parador* located opposite the Santa Catalina castle. All rooms have views of the Atlantic.
🛏 149 P 🅲 🅲 ≋ 🅲 🅲 All major cards

EL FARO
$$
SAN FÉLIX 15
TEL 902 21 10 68
www.elfarodecadiz.com
Specializes in seafood. A fantastic spread of *raciones* at the bar in this chic spot.
🔲 215 P 🅲 🅲 All major cards

CARMONA 41410

CASA DE CARMONA
🏨 $$$ ★★★★★
PLAZA DE LASSO 1
TEL 95 419 10 00/414 41 51
FAX 95 419 01 89
E-MAIL reserve@casadecarmona.com
www.casadecarmona.com
This elegant 16th- to 17th-century house is an example of Mudejar architecture. It has three interior courtyards and a couple of regal sitting rooms. Rooms have antiques.
🛏 34 🔲 60 P 🅲 🅲 All major cards

PARADOR DE CARMONA
$$$ ★★★★
ALCÁZAR S/N

TEL 95 414 10 10
FAX 95 414 17 12
E-MAIL carmona@parador.es
www.parador.es
Built within the 14th-century
fortress walls, this *parador* has
spectacular views of the
Corbones plains. Spacious
rooms, some with balconies,
others with huge windows.
The medieval refectory makes
an impressive dining room.
① 63 P ⬆ ⧉ ⧉ All
major cards

🍴 **SAN FERNANDO**
$$
SACRAMENTO 3
TEL 95 414 35 56
FAX 95 414 35 57
In a grand house on one of
Carmona's plazas. The duck
with blue cheese is very good,
as is the *menú degustación*.
Game in season.
⬚ 60 ⧉ Closed Sun. D
Mon., & Aug. ⧉ ⧉ All
major cards

CÓRDOBA 14000

🏨 **AMISTAD CÓRDOBA**
🍴 **$$$ ★★★★**
PLAZA DE MAIMÓNIDES 3
TEL 957 42 03 35
FAX 957 42 03 65
E-MAIL nhamistadcordoba@nh-
hotels.com
www.nh-hotels.com
Córdoba's most stylish hotel is
in the heart of the Judería, and
backs onto the Arab city
walls. Two beautifully restored
mansions plus the annex date
back to the 18th century.
① 84 P ⬆ ⧉ ⧉ All
major cards

🏨 **MACIÁ ALFAROS**
🍴 **$$$ ★★★★**
ALFAROS 18
TEL 957 49 19 20
FAX 957 49 22 10
E-MAIL alfaros@maciahote
les.com
www.maciahoteles.com/alfaros
A quiet modern hotel built
over a convent in the heart
of old Córdoba. Some rooms
have terraces and look onto
the patio.

① 144 ⬚ 180 P ⬆ ⧉
⧉ ⧉ All major cards

🏨 **ALBUCASIS**
$$ ★★
BUEN PASTOR 11
TEL/FAX 957 47 86 25
www.hotelalbucasis.com
This hotel off a quiet street is
centered on a pretty courtyard. Simple rooms and
spacious tiled bathrooms.
① 15 P ⧉ ⧉ DC, MC, V

🏨 **MEZQUITA**
$ ★★
PLAZA SANTA CATALINA 1
TEL 957 47 55 85
FAX 957 47 62 19
www.hotelmezquita.com
Opposite the mosque, this
mansion has two patios. The
rooms and halls have antique
furniture and paintings. Each is
different, but all are spacious
with white-marble floors.
① 21 ⧉ ⧉ All major
cards

SOMETHING SPECIAL

🍴 **ALMUDAINA**

A beautiful 16th-century
house that originally be-
longed to Bishop Don Leopoldo
de Austria is now Córdoba's top
restaurant. Elegant dining rooms
lead off the covered interior
patio. The cuisine puts a modern
twist on local recipes: smoked
salmon, crab and melon salad,
sea bass with a sauce of asparagus, and wild mushroom and
tiny squid. If you are up to it try
the *rabo de toro* (bull's tail).
$$$
PLAZA CAMPO SANTO DE LOS
MÁRTIRES 1
TEL 957 47 43 42
FAX 957 49 03 18
www.restaurantealmudaina.com
⬚ 182 ⧉ Closed Sun. D &
Sun. mid-June–Aug. ⧉
⧉ All major cards

🍴 **BODEGAS CAMPOS**
$$
CALLE DE LOS LINEROS 32
TEL 957 49 75 00
www.bodegascampos.com

PRICES

HOTELS
An indication of the cost
of a double room without
breakfast is given by **$** signs.
$$$$$ Over $300
$$$$ $220–$300
$$$ $160–$220
$$ $80–$160
$ Under $80

RESTAURANTS
An indication of the cost of a
three-course dinner without
drinks is given by $ signs.
$$$$$ Over $80
$$$$ $50–$80
$$$ $35–$50
$$ $20–$35
$ Under $20

This complex, typical Córdoba
courtyards, was founded as a
bodega in 1908. Superb
collection of fair posters and
rows of oak barrels signed by
famous visitors. Rustic decor
and leafy patios for dining in
summer. Traditional local
cuisine with modern touches.
⬚ 600 P ⧉ Closed Sun. D
⧉ ⧉ All major cards

GRANADA 18000

🏨 **PARADOR DE**
🍴 **GRANADA**
$$$$$ ★★★★
REAL DE LA ALHAMBRA S/N
TEL 958 22 14 40
FAX 958 22 22 64
E-MAIL granada@parador.es
www.parador.es
An exquisite *parador*—a 15th-
century Franciscan convent
built by the Catholic Monarchs
in the Alhambra gardens—with
privileged access and views.
The old wing has rooms with
antiques and rugs. A popular
place, so reserve a year in
advance. Good restaurant.
① 36 P ⧉ ⧉ All major
cards

🏨 **ALHAMBRA PALACE**
🍴 **$$$$ ★★★★**
PLAZA ARQUITECTO

GARCÍA DE PAREDES 2
TEL 958 22 14 68
FAX 958 22 64 04
E-MAIL reservas@h-alhambra
palace.es
www.h-alhambrapalace.es
An over-the-top imitation of
the Alhambra. Most rooms
have fine views over the
Alhambra, the city, and out
to the Sierra Nevada.
🛈 126 🅿 ⬌ 🌀 🗝 All
major cards

🏨 PALACIO DE SANTA
INÉS
$$ ★★★
CUESTA DE SANTA INÉS 9
TEL 958 22 23 62
FAX 958 22 24 65
E-MAIL sinespal@teleline.es
www.palaciosantaines.com
A small 16th-century palace
in the Albaicín with a
plateresque facade and 35
rooms, all off an interior
patio. Ask for a room with
views of the Alhambra. No
restaurant.
🛈 35 🌀 🗝 All major cards

🏨 AMÉRICA
$$$ ★
REAL DE LA ALHAMBRA 53
TEL 958 22 74 71
FAX 958 22 74 70
E-MAIL reservas@hotelamerica
granada.com
www.hotelamericagranada.com
An old house with a pretty
Andalusian patio and rooms
set within the Alhambra
precincts. Reserve months in
advance.
🛈 17 🕐 Closed Dec.–Feb.
🌀 🗝 All major cards

🏨 CARMEN DE SANTA
INÉS
$$ ★★★
PLACETA DE PORRAS 7
TEL 958 22 63 80
FAX 958 22 44 04
E-MAIL sinescar@teleline.es
www.carmensantaines.com
In the Albaicín and run by the
same family as the Palacio de
Santa Inés, this old Arab house
on the Alcazaba wall has
rooms filled with antiques,
and views of the Alhambra.

Quiet. No restaurant.
🛈 9 🅿 🌀 🗝 All major
cards

🏨 REINA CRISTINA
🍴 $$ ★★★
TABLAS 4
TEL 958 25 32 11
FAX 958 25 57 28
E-MAIL clientes@hotelreina
cristina.com
www.hotelreinacristina.com
This was the poet Luís
Rosales' home. It is a grand
19th-century town house
with an elegant reception and
traces of an interior patio—
fountain, columns, and plants.
Simple rooms. Try the
restaurant for local and
innovative dishes, and the
café for delicious cakes.
🛈 58 🍽 150 🅿 ⬌ 🌀
🗝 All major cards

🍴 CUNINI
$$$
PLAZA DE LA PESCADERÍA 14
TEL/FAX 958 25 07 77/26 75 87
Near the cathedral, and popu-
lar for its superb seafood
spread at the tapas bar. Good
fish stew. Reservations needed.
🍽 45 🕐 Closed Sun. D, &
Mon. 🌀 🗝 All major cards

🍴 HORNO DE SANTIAGO
$$$$
PLAZA DE LOS CAMPOS 8
TEL/FAX 958 22 34 76
www.hornodesantiago.com
Modern cuisine based on
regional recipes and market
availability. Warm chick pea
and prawn salad is a good
option. Excellent wine list.
🍽 120 🕐 Closed Sun., &
Aug. 🌀 🗝 All major cards

🍴 SEVILLA
$$$
OFICIOS 12
TEL 958 22 12 23
www.restaurantesevilla.es
Since 1930, it was frequented
by García Lorca and fellow
poets. It has character with
a wonderful tapas bar, four
dining rooms, and a terrace.
Traditional and creative
cooking.

🛏 40 🕐 Closed Sun. D 🌀
🗝 All major cards

GUADIX 18500

🏨 HOTEL COMERCIO
🍴 $$ ★★★★
MIRA DE AMEZCUA 3
TEL 958 66 05 00
FAX 958 66 50 72
E-MAIL hotelcomercio@
moebius.es
www.hotelcomercio.com
A sophisticated hotel for
Guadix, with simple,
comfortable rooms. Prize-
winning restaurant serves
regional dishes: Try the roast
lamb with honey, raisins, and
pine nuts.
🛈 42 🅿 ⬌ 🌀 🎽 🗝 All
major cards

JAÉN 23001

🏨 PARADOR DE JAÉN
🍴 $$$ ★★★★
CASTILLO DE SANTA
CATALINA
TEL 953 23 00 00
FAX 953 23 09 30
E-MAIL jaen@parador.es
www.parador.es
Built in the style of the nearby
13th-century Arab fortress,
the rooms here have fantastic
views, and one salon has high-
crossed arches. The restaurant
serves local dishes; try the
pipirrana salad, spinach, and
egg, Jaén-style, with the local
red wine—Duque de Bailén.
🛈 45 🅿 ⬌ 🌀 🏊 🗝 All
major cards

JEREZ DE LA
FRONTERA 11400

🏨 JEREZ-SPA
$$$ ★★★★★
AVENIDA ALCALDE ÁLVARO
DOMECQ 35
TEL 956 30 06 00
FAX 956 30 50 01
E-MAIL reservas@jerezhotel.com
www.jerezhotel.com
One of Jerez's few hotels, set
on a wide avenue near the
Real Escuela Andaluza de
l'Arte Ecuestre. The unusual

garden is tropical. .

🛏 127 **P** 🔁 🌀 ⛰
🏧 All major cards

🏨 PALACIO GARVEY
$$$ ★★★★
PLAZA RAFAEL RIVERO
TEL 956 32 67 00
FAX 956 32 73 40
E-MAIL palaciogarvey@sfera
hoteles.com
www.sferahoteles.net
In old town, by the casino, this
1850s mansion was built for
the Garvey sherry dynasty.
Exclusive feel, well modern-
ized, arty, and light.
🛏 16 **P** 🔁 🌀 ⛰ 🏧 All
major cards

🍴 LA MESA REDONDA
$$$
MANUEL DE LA QUINTANA 3
TEL/FAX 956 34 00 69
Decorated with antiques and
art, it serves traditional Andalusian specialties and game in
season. Try the Iberian pork
cutlets with foie gras in sherry
sauce. Reservations essential.
🍽 45 **P** 🔁 Closed Sun.,
Easter weekend, & mid-
July–mid-Aug. 🌀 🏧 All
major cards

MÁLAGA 29000

🏨 PARADOR DE MÁLAGA
GIBRALFARO
$$$ ★★★★
CASTILLO DE GIBRALFARO S/N
TEL 95 222 19 02
FAX 95 222 19 04
E-MAIL gibralfaro@parador.es
www.parador.es
The best accommodation to
be found in Málaga is the
parador, a stone building with a
view of Málaga and the bay.
Reserve well ahead.
🛏 38 **P** 🔁 🌀 ⛰ 🏧 All
major cards

🏨 DEL PINTOR
$$ ★★★
ÁLAMOS 27
TEL/FAX 952 06 09 80/81
E-MAIL info@hoteldelpintor.com
www.hoteldelpintor.com
Close by the Picasso Museum
in the town center, this modern

hotel opened in 2005. Decorated in red, white and black
by the local painter Pepe
Bornoy.
🛏 17 🔁 🌀

🏨 MOLINO DE
SANTILLÁN
$$
CARRETERA DE MACHAR-
AVIAYA, KM 3, RINCÓN DE LA
VICTORIA 29730 (12 MILES/
20 KM FROM MÁLAGA)
TEL 902 12 02 40
FAX 95 240 09 50
www.molinodesantillan.com
This idyllic spot is reached via a
dirt road from the coast. The
colonial-style villa nestled in the
hills is surrounded by gardens,
avocados, and custard apples.
Although small the rooms are
comfortable and quiet.
🛏 22 **P** ⛰ 🏧 All major
cards

SOMETHING
SPECIAL

🍴 ANTIGUA CASA
DE GUARDIA

Málaga's oldest bar probably
hasn't changed much since
1840. Packed with locals, it is a
lively place. Try Málaga wines,
made from muscatel grapes and
dispensed from large wood
barrels. The Seco Añejo (matured
for a year) is less sweet than the
new season Pedriot, accom-
panied by a plate of ice cold
prawns. No tables, standing only.
$
ALAMEDA PRINCIPAL 18
(CORNER OF CALLE PASTORA)
TEL 95 221 46 80
www.antiguacasadeguardia.net
🔁 Closed Sun. except
Easter week & Dec. 🏧 No
credit cards

MOJÁCAR 04638

🏨 CORTIJO DE LA MEDIA
🍴 LUNA
$$
PARAJE DE LAS MARINAS 36
TEL 950 47 88 13
E-MAIL info@cortijodelamedia
luna.com
www.cortijodelamedialuna.com

Recently restored and
extended farmhouse, between
the village and the beach. Great
views and excellent restaurant.
🛏 6 **P** 🌀 🏧 All major
cards

MURCIA 30000

🏨 ARCO DE SAN JUAN
🍴 $ ★★★★
PLAZA DE CEBALLOS 10
TEL 968 21 04 55
FAX 968 22 08 09
E-MAIL info@arcosanjuan.com
www.arcosanjuan.com
In a recently-restored 18th-
century building in Murcia old
town, by the cathedral, this
hotel is well-equipped and has
a good restaurant.
🛏 94 **P** 🔁 🌀 🏧 All
major cards

🍴 MORALES
$$$$
AVENIDA DE LA
CONSTITUCIÓN 12
TEL/FAX 968 23 10 26
A popular intimate dining
room serving Murcian fare.
Try the *verduras de la huerta
murciana* (Murcian vegetables).
🍽 60 🔁 Closed Sat. D,
Sun., & last 2 weeks Aug. 🌀
🏧 All major cards

RONDA 29400

🏨 PARADOR DE RONDA
🍴 $$$ ★★★★
PLAZA DE ESPAÑA
TEL 95 287 75 00
FAX 95 287 81 88
E-MAIL ronda@parador.es
www.parador.es
Once the town hall and
located in a central spot. Ask
for a room overlooking the
spectacular Tagus gorge.
🛏 78 **P** 🔁 🌀 ⛰ 🏧 All
major cards

🏨 DON MIGUEL
🍴 $$ ★★★
VILLANUEVA 4 & 8
TEL 95 287 77 22 or
95 287 10 90 (restaurant)
FAX 95 287 83 77
E-MAIL info@dmiguel.com
www.dmiguel.com

Opposite the *parador* and on the edge of the gorge, with spectacular views, particularly in the restaurant. Local dishes.
🏠 30 🛏 100 🅿 ⬆ ❄
🏧 All major cards

SEVILLA (SEVILLE) 41000

ALFONSO XIII
🍽 $$$$$ ★★★★★
SAN FERNANDO 2
TEL 95 491 70 00
FAX 95 491 70 99
www.alfonsoxiii.com
The grandest place to stay in Sevilla was inaugurated in 1929 by King Alfonso XIII. It is neo-Mudejar built around a large courtyard. The salons are ornately decorated with Moorish lamps and Sevilla tiles.
🏠 147 🅿 ⬆ ❄ 🏊 💪
🏧 All major cards

CASA IMPERIAL
$$$$ ★★★★★
IMPERIAL 29
TEL 95 450 03 00
FAX 95 450 03 30
E-MAIL info@casaimperial.com
www.casaimperial.com
This 16th-century palace adjoins the Casa de Pilatos. The hotel is arranged around three courtyards painted in Sevilla white and yellow.
🏠 24 🅿 ⬆ ❄ 🏧 All major cards

LAS CASAS DE LA JUDERÍA
$$$$ ★★★★
CALLEJÓN DE DOS HERMANAS 7
TEL 95 441 51 50
FAX 95 442 21 70
E-MAIL juderia@casasypalacios.com
www.casasypalacios.com
In the heart of the Barrio de Santa Cruz, this magical hotel occupies three palaces, each with an inner courtyard full of plants. The rooms are spacious, minimalist, and quiet.
🏠 112 🅿 ⬆ ❄ 🏊
🏧 All major cards

LOS SEISES
🍽 $$$$ ★★★★
SEGOVIAS 6
TEL 95 422 94 95
FAX 95 422 43 34
E-MAIL losseises@husa.es
www.hotellosseises.com
This 16th-century palace is now a smart, stylish hotel incorporating the Renaissance, Roman, and Moorish materials discovered during restoration. Airy rooms, roof terrace and a restaurant serving cuisine with Arabic touches.
🏠 43 🛏 200 🅿 ⬆ ❄
🏊 🏧 All major cards

DOÑA MARÍA
$$$ ★★★★
DON REMONDO 19
TEL 95 422 49 90
FAX 95 421 95 46
E-MAIL reservas@hdmaria.com
www.hdmaria.com
Opposite the cathedral and Giralda, this is a large stately mansion. All the rooms have a different decor. Top floor terrace. No restaurant.
🏠 65 ⬆ ❄ 🏊 🏧 All major cards

SOMETHING SPECIAL

TABERNA DEL ALABARDERO
The poet Antonio Cavestany was born and died in this early 1900s house, a pure Andalusian place around a central patio. This popular and elegant restaurant serves modern Mediterranean cuisine. Try Sanlucar prawn carpaccio and Alabardero style partridge.
$$$ ★★★★
ZARAGOZA 20
TEL 94 450 27 21
FAX 95 456 36 66
E-MAIL hotel.alabardero@hotmail.com
www.tabernadelalabardero.com
🏠 7 🛏 225 🅿 🕐 Closed Aug. ⬆ ❄ 🏧 All major cards

PLAZA DE ARMAS
$$ ★★★
MARQUÉS DE PARADA
TEL 95 490 19 92
FAX 95 490 12 32
E-MAIL nhplazadearmas@nh-hotels.com
www.nh-hotels.com
A modern structure of steel and glass contains functional rooms. The breakfasts can be a disappointment.
🏠 262 🅿 ⬆ ❄ 🏊
🏧 All major cards

EGAÑA ORIZA
$$$$
SAN FERNANDO 41
TEL 95 422 72 11 or 95 422 72 54
www.restauranteoriza.com
This simple, elegant restaurant backs on to the old city walls. Basque-influenced recipes include game in season. Try the smoked eel with asparagus. Reservations needed.
🛏 150 🕐 Closed Sat. L, Sun., & Aug. ❄ 🏧 All major cards

LA ALBAHACA
$$$$
PLAZA SANTA CRUZ 12
TEL 95 422 07 14
E-MAIL la-albahaca@terra.es
www.andalunet.com/la-albahaca
Right in the center of the Barrio de Santa Cruz, this restaurant occupies a lovely old Andalusian house built by the architect Juan Talavera.
🛏 60 🕐 Closed Sun. ❄
🏧 All major cards

SIERRA NEVADA 18196

EL LODGE
🍽 $$$$
MARIBEL 8, MONACHIL
TEL 958 48 06 00
FAX 958 48 13 14
E-MAIL ellodge@ellodge.com
www.ellodge.com
Log cabin interiors with cozy, warm rooms covered in Finnish pine. In the winter guests can ski to the hotel.
🏠 20 🅿 💪 🏧 All major cards

TARIFA 11380

SOMETHING SPECIAL

🏨 HURRICANE HOTEL
🍴

Close to Tarifa the Hurricane stands in a luscious palm-filled garden. The modern building has a design in keeping with local architecture. Interiors are minimalist with potted plants and earthy tones; the laid-back atmosphere is popular with kite-surfers. The candlelit restaurant is known for its modern cuisine with eastern influences. Try the fish of the day with basmati rice. Horse riding available.

$$ ★★
CARRETERA N-340 CÁDIZ-MÁLAGA, KM 77
TEL 956 68 49 19
FAX 956 68 03 29
E-MAIL info@hotelhurricane.com
www.hotelhurricane.com
🛏 33 🅿 🏊 🍷 🦽 All major cards

ÚBEDA 23400

SOMETHING SPECIAL

🏨 PALACIO DE LA RAMBLA

This exclusive, peaceful hotel in the center of Úbeda is a 16th-century palace with a Renaissance cloister. Each of the rooms has palatial dimensions, some four-poster beds, and all contain interesting antiques. No restaurant. Breakfast included.

$$$ ★★
PLAZA DEL MARQUÉS 1
TEL 953 75 01 96
FAX 953 75 02 67
www.palaciodelarambla.com
🛏 8 🅿 🕐 Closed mid-July to mid-Aug. 🦽 AE, MC, V

🏨 PARADOR DE ÚBEDA
🍴 **$$$ ★★★★**
PLAZA DE VÁZQUEZ MOLINA
TEL 953 75 03 45
FAX 953 75 12 59
E-MAIL ubeda@parador.es
www.parador.es
A grand 16th- to 17th-century

Renaissance palace. Around the two interior patios are rooms with high beamed ceilings.
🛏 36 🦽 All major cards

🏨 ALVAR FAÑEZ
$$ ★★★★
JUAN PASQUAU 5
TEL 953 79 60 43
E-MAIL hotel@alvarfanez.com
www.alvarfanez.com
In the heart of the historic center. A pretty covered courtyard leads to rooms with wooden floors. Roof terrace.
🛏 11 🅿 🦽 All major cards

VEJER DE LA FRONTERA 11150

🏨 V
$$$
ROSARIO 11-13
TEL 956 45 17 57
FAX 956 45 00 88
E-MAIL info@hotelv-vejer.com
www.hotelv-vejer.com
Strikingly converted in mini-malist style, a well-equipped hotel in a 17th-century manor house with an internal court-yard and three rooftop ter-races with views of Morocco.
🛏 12 🕐 Closed in Jan. 🦽 All major cards

🏨 ESCONDRIJO
$$
CALLEJÓN OSCURO 3
TEL 956 44 74 38
E-MAIL info@escondrijo.com
www.escondrijo.com
A lovely guest-house in old quarter with Moorish touches (once the Chapel of Vera Cruz), a galleried internal courtyard and views from the ample terrace. Large, rooms with character and style.
🛏 5 🕐 Closed Dec. & Jan. 🦽 MC, V

🍴 TRAFALGAR
$$$
PLAZA DE ESPAÑA 31
TEL 956 44 76 38
www.miraalsur.com/trafalgar
A rather sophisticated establishment for Vejer, the dining room is in warm colors,

with lovely old floor tiles. Mediterranean cuisine using fresh local produce.
🍽 100 🕐 Closed Mon. & Jan. 🦽 All major cards

BALEARIC ISLANDS

MALLORCA (MAJORCA)

PALMA DE MALLORCA 07000

🏨 CONVENT DE LA
🍴 MISSIÓ
$$$$ ★★★★
CARRER DE LA MISSIÓ 7A
TEL 971 22 73 27
FAX 971 22 73 48
www.conventdelamissio.com
Stunningly converted 17th century monastery in the heart of the old town. Exclusive, minimalist feel includes an art gallery. Some rooms with terraces. The restaurant serves seasonal cuisine.
🛏 14 🦽 🏊 🦽 All major cards

🏨 SAN LORENZO
$$$ ★★★★
SAN LORENZO 14
TEL 971 72 82 00
FAX 971 71 19 01
E-MAIL info@hotelsanlorenzo.com
www.hotelsanlorenzo.com
A 17th-century mansion with each room unique. There is no parking nearby.
🛏 9 🦽 🏊 🦽 All major cards

🏨 HOTEL BORN
$$ ★★
SANT JAUME 3
TEL 971 71 29 42
FAX 971 71 86 18
www.hotelborn.com
This 16th-century palace has spacious, traditional rooms with a classical Palma-style patio. No smoking.
🛏 30 🦽 🦽 All major cards

🍴 KOLDO ROYO
$$$$$
PASEO MARÍTIMO 3

TEL 971 73 24 35
www.koldoroyo.com
Modern Basque cuisine with Mallorcan influences is served in the dining room overlooking the bay. Good taster menu and desserts.
🔲 80 🕐 Closed Sat. L & Sun. 🔵 🏊 AE, MC, V

🍴 PARLAMENT
$$$
CONQUISTADOR 11
TEL 971 72 60 26
www.restaurantparlament.com
Inside Palma's parliament building, this old-fashioned establishment with high ceilings serves inventive Mediterranean cuisine
🔲 140 🕐 Closed Sun. 🔵 🏊 MC, V

🍴 CELLER SA PREMSA
$$
PLAZA OBISPO BERENGUER DE PALOU 8
TEL 971 72 35 29
www.cellersapremsa.com
A tavern full of old wood wine barrels and walls covered in faded feria posters. Basic food in a great setting.
🔲 200 🏊 All major cards

NORTHWESTERN MALLORCA

🏨 L'HERMITAGE
🍴 $$$$ ★★★★
ORIENT, CARRETERA ALARÓ BUNYOLA, KM 8
TEL 971 18 03 03
FAX 971 18 04 11
E-MAIL info@hermitage-hotel.com
www.hermitage-hotel.com
A peaceful 17th-century convent with grand tower and baroque cloister. Four rooms are in the convent itself; others are in a terraced building.
🛈 24 🅿 🏊 🏊 All major cards

NORTHEASTERN MALLORCA

🏨 PETIT HOTEL CASES DE PULA
$$

CARRETERA SON SERVERA-CAPDEPERA, KM 3
TEL 971 56 74 92
FAX 971 56 72 71
EMAIL petithotel@pulagolf.com
www.pulagolf.com
Warm and full of character, this little hotel occupies the Finca de Pula (1581). Modernized rooms have internet connection. Suites are spacious with Italian marble floors and rustic decor.
🛈 10 🅿 🔵 🏊 🍸 🏊 All major cards

EIVISSA (IBIZA)

🏨 EL CORSARIO
🍴 $$$ ★★
PONIENTE 5, IBIZA
TEL 971 30 12 48
FAX 971 39 19 53
E-MAIL elcorsario@ctv.es
www.ibiza-hotels.com/corsario
At the highest point inside the city walls, this lovely hotel occupies a 17th-century building. The best rooms overlook the town and harbor; although some lack air-conditioning. The restaurant offers a short and expensive menu, but the food is superb.
🛈 14 🔲 45 🏊 DC, MC, V

🏨 LA VENTANA
$$$
PLAZA SA CARROSSA 13, IBIZA
TEL 971 39 08 57
FAX 971 39 01 45
E-MAIL info@laventanaibiza.com
www.laventanaibiza.com
This small hotel has simple rooms, each different. For a quiet night ask to be as far from the terrace as possible. When reserving, you are asked for a 50 percent deposit on a credit card.
🛈 14 🔵 🏊 AE, MC, V

MENORCA

MAÓ (MAHÓN) 07700

🏨 PORT MAHÓN
$ ★★★★
FORT DE L'EAU 13
TEL 971 36 26 00
FAX 971 35 10 50

E-MAIL portmahon@sethotels.com
www.sethotels.com
A colonial-style building decorated with reproduction furnishings and a terrace looking on to the sea. Quiet, well-equipped rooms.
🛈 82 🔵 🏊 🏊 All major cards

🍴 JÁGARO
$$$$
MOL DE LLEVANT 334
TEL 971 36 23 90
E-MAIL jagaromenorca@hotmail.com
Right on the port shore, this Menorcan institution serves excellent fish and seafood. Menorcan lobster is famed: try the caldereta (stew) or fried with egg. Their fritada de pescado (fry-up of assorted fresh fish) is also memorable.
🔲 200 🕐 Closed Sun. D & Mon. (Oct.–Mar.) & month before Easter 🔵 🏊 All major cards

🍴 LA CARABA
$$
S'UESTRÀ 78, SANT LLUÍS
TEL/FAX 971 15 06 82
In a lovely old Menorcan house, inventive Mediterranean cooking and a friendly local atmosphere. Fine terrace and garden. Reserve in high summer.
🔲 60 🕐 Closed L & Nov.–May

CANARY ISLANDS

TENERIFE

PARQUE NACIONAL DE LAS CAÑADAS DEL TEIDE 38300

🏨 PARADOR DE
🍴 CAÑADAS DEL TEIDE
$$$ ★★
LAS CAÑADAS DEL TEIDE, LA OROTAVA
TEL 922 37 48 41
FAX 922 38 23 52
E-MAIL canadas@parador.es
www.parador.es

HOTELS & RESTAURANTS

The *parador* stands at 6,500 feet (2,000 m) above sea level with views of the Pico del Teide. Not an attractive building, but the location compensates. Some rooms have balconies.
🛏 37 🅿 ⬆ 🖥 📺 🌐 All major cards

PUERTO DE LA CRUZ 38400

🏨 MONOPOL
🍴 $$ ★★★
QUINTANA 15
TEL 922 38 46 11
FAX 922 37 03 10
E-MAIL monopol@interbook.net
www.monopoltenerife.com
A long-established hotel in a 1742 building, with impressive stylish rooms and a leafy Canarian courtyard.
🛏 93 ⬆ 🖥 All DC, MC, V

SANTA CRUZ DE TENERIFE 38000

🏨 MENCEY
🍴 $$$ ★★★★★
AVENIDA DOCTOR JOSÉ NAVEIRAS 38
TEL 922 60 99 00
FAX 922 28 00 17
E-MAIL mencey@sheraton.com
www.sheratonmencey.com
The most expensive hotel in town occupies a grandiose marble and stucco building in a quiet residential section. Colonial-style interiors and wonderful gardens.
🛏 286 🅿 ⬆ 🖥 🌐 All major cards

🍴 EL COTO DE ANTONIO
$$$$
GENERAL GODED 13
TEL 922 27 21 05
This restaurant uses local produce to create the Basque and Canarian cuisine with its modern influences. Try a kid goat in almond sauce or baby squid with pasta.
🍽 40 🕐 Closed Sun. D, & first 3 weeks Aug. 🖥 All major cards

🍴 MESÓN DEL DUQUE
$$$
TEOBALDO POWER 15
TEL/FAX 922 27 49 09
Tasty *raciones* at the old wood bar with wine barrel tables, or go through to the restaurant for local fare.
🍽 28 🕐 Closed Sun. & Aug. 🖥 MC, V

LAS PALMAS 35000

🏨 SANTA CATALINA
🍴 $$$ ★★★★★
LEÓN Y CASTILLO 227
TEL 928 24 30 40
FAX 928 24 27 64
www.hotelsantacatalina.com
Set in the middle of the palm park, this is Las Palmas' classiest hotel with the air of another era. The casino is in the same building.
🛏 202 🅿 ⬆ 🖥 🌐 All major cards

🏨 APARTAMENTOS PLAYA DORADA
$$
LUIS MOROTE 61
TEL 928 26 51 00
FAX 928 26 51 04
There are no hotels in the mid-price range in Las Palmas, but these apartments are an alternative with sitting rooms and balconies.
🖥 MC, V

🏨 EL REFUGIO
$$
CRUZ DE TEJEDA (SAN MATEO)
TEL 928 66 65 13
FAX 928 66 65 20
www.hotelruralelrefugio.com
At the foot of volcanic rocks this Canarian-style hotel has stone and red-tiled roofs. Views of the native pine trees. Cozy rooms; breakfast includes delicious homemade bread.
🛏 17 🅿 🖥 🌐 All major cards

🍴 CASA JULIO
$$$
LA NAVAL 132
TEL 928 46 01 39
FAX 928 46 60 02
Excellent fresh fish and seafood, Canarian soup or stew prepared daily. Try the *cherne* (sea bass) in a white wine clam sauce. The dining room is decorated like the inside of a boat.
🍽 75 🕐 Closed Sun. 🖥 All major cards

🍴 EL CUCHARÓN
$$$
RELOJ 2
TEL 928 33 32 96
Typical local food with modern touches is served in this simple restaurant.
🍽 50 🕐 Closed Sat. L, Sun., & mid-Aug.–mid-Sept. 🖥 All major cards

🏨 FINCA DE LA FLORIDA
$$
EL ISLOTE 90, SAN BARTOLOMÉ
TEL 928 52 11 24
FAX 928 52 03 11
E-MAIL reserva@hotelfincadela florida.com
www.hotelfincadelaflorida.com
Outside San Bartolomé, this rural hotel has a mainly German clientele. Traditional whitewashed farmhouse with an attractive garden: simple but comfortable rooms. Ask for directions when reserving.
🛏 16 🅿 🖥 🌐 📺 All major cards

🏨 FINCA DE LAS SALINAS
$$
LA CUESTA 17, YAIZA 35570
CARRETERA YAIZA-ARRECIFE
TEL 928 83 03 25
FAX 928 83 03 29
E-MAIL fincasalinas@hotmail.com
www.fincasalinas.com
Restored grand 18th-century mansion with elegant, spacious interior and quiet bedrooms. Breakfast included.
🛏 19 🅿 🖥 🌐 📺 All major cards

SHOPPING

A number of goods are particularly associated with Spain, such as leather (shoes, handbags, wallets, belts), ceramics, embroidery, fans, and certain foods including olives, almonds, hams, olive oil, honey, wines, and sherry. You come across these items all over Spain, though more so in their place of origin, where often prices are lower and the quality is higher. Spain is still full of those fantastic old-fashioned shops with service to match that are disappearing fast from the rest of Europe. Some of the most beautifully laid out are those that sell everything from cheese to apple liquor to dish detergent. However, the chain stores are encroaching. You find the same names in northern Spain and another set in the south. The department store that you'll find in all the major cities is El Corte Inglés. It is a very comprehensive store that carries absolutely everything. Big hypermarkets like Pryca on the outskirts of the towns and cities, are useful for bulk shopping including good wines, cheeses, bread, clothes, newspapers, and film; they also have gas stations. Smaller shops are in town centers, which are often pedestrianized. Hardware stores *(ferreterías)* are packed with interesting kitchen utensils and other unusual items.

MARKETS

Everywhere, from the smallest village to the largest city, there's at least one weekly market where you can find everything from clothes to pottery and food. Markets usually start early in the morning and last until around 2 p.m. For the pick of the produce go early, although you won't find it really bustling until around 10 a.m. Often there will be a stand where you can buy freshly made *churros* (fritters) accompanied by coffee for breakfast. A lot of the produce on sale is locally grown and you can recognize local farmers by the woven baskets they use for weighing produce. Buy things that are in season and that are more expensive at home, such as almonds, strawberries, avocados, and wonderful red and green tomatoes. Look also for local delicacies like cheeses, honey, olives, dried peppers and tomatoes, hams, and herbs. When buying cheeses it is quite acceptable to ask to taste a small portion first.

Spain has few secondhand markets *(rastros)* or flea markets *(mercadillos)* and you are more likely to come across them, apart from Madrid and Barcelona, in places where there are communities of other nationalities, for instance on the Costa Blanca and Costa del Sol.

OPENING HOURS

Apart from bakeries *(panaderías)* that open at 8 a.m., other shops open at 9:30 a.m. or 10 a.m. They close for lunch between 1:30 p.m. or 2 p.m and 4 p.m or 5 p.m., and then stay open until 8 p.m. or 8:30 p.m. Supermarkets and stores like El Corte Inglés stay open all day, often until later than 8:30 p.m. Some shops close on Mondays, and bakers are open on Sunday mornings.

PAYMENT

Supermarkets, El Corte Inglés, and other chains accept credit cards backed by ID, which you should carry. Check the signs on the door before you go in and always ask before paying.

EXPORTS

VAT (value-added tax), known as IVA *(impuesto sobre el valor añadido)*, is 16 percent, included in the price of most retail goods. Visitors from outside the E.U. are entitled to claim back the 16 percent IVA if they have spent more than 100 euros in any one shop and will be taking the goods out of the E.U. within three months. Ask the shop for an invoice *(factura)* showing the price and the IVA paid for each item and identifying the vendor and the purchaser (you have to show your passport). When you leave Spain, present the invoice to the IVA booth in the airport for customs to stamp, then hand it in at a Banco Exterior (there's one at Madrid's Barajas airport), or mail it back to the vendor. The vendor will then mail the refund to you.

RETURNS

If you have any complaints about a purchase, return it to the shop as soon as possible with the receipt as proof of purchase. Anything bought in a sale is usually not refundable.

IN & AROUND MADRID

CAKE SHOPS & DELI

Casa Mira Carrera de San Jerónimo 30, tel 91 429 88 95. Excellent handmade *turrones,* marzipans, and other pastries. Open since 1842.

Lhardy Carrera de San Jerónimo 8, tel 91 521 33 85. Open since 1839. You can buy pastries, cakes, cold meats, and cheeses. Also has a restaurant.

La Mallorquina Puerta del Sol 8, tel 91 521 12 01. Incredible selection of delicious cakes to take away, or eat at tables upstairs with a coffee.

CIGARS

Cava de Puros Barquillo Barquillo 22, tel 91 522 02 22. Excellent selection of cigars.

CLOTHES & SHOES

Ágatha Goya 6-8, tel 91 577 63 11 or Arturo Soria, tel 91 759 13 15. Contemporary jewelry.

Camper Gran Vía 54, tel 91 547 52 23. Trendy shoes for men and women. All over Spain, 15 shops in Madrid alone.

El Corte Inglés Preciados 3; Plaza Callao 2; Goya 76 & 87; Princesa 42; Serrano 47; and others. Madrid's largest department store, found all over the country.

Purificación García Serrano 19 and 28, tel 91 435 80 13. Designer clothes for women.

Zara Serrano 61, tel 91 575 63 34; Gran Vía 34, tel 91 521 12 83. Stylish clothes and

SHOPPING

accessories chain with reasonable prices. All over Spain, 23 shops in Madrid alone.

EMBROIDERY
Artesanía Reyes Preciados 11, tel 91 531 81 48. Embroidered shawls, sheets, and tablecloths.
Gil Carrera de San Jerónimo 2, tel 91 521 25 49. Beautifully embroidered silk shawls and fans, plus flamenco dresses and accessories. Open since 1880.

HATS & UMBRELLAS
Casa de Diego Puerta del Sol 12, tel/fax 91 522 66 43. Opened in 1858, this shop specializes in umbrellas of every design.
Casa Yustas Plaza Mayor 30, tel 91 366 50 84. Specializes in hats.

MARKETS
In Madrid:
El Rastrillo Marqués de Viana, Sun.
El Rastro Ribera de Curtidores, Sun.
Mercado de Monedas y Sellos Plaza Mayor, Stamps and coins. Sun.
Mercado de San Miguel Plaza de San Miguel, Permanent covered food market. Mon.–Sat.

Around Madrid:
Alcalá de Henares Mon.
Aranjuez Sat.

NORTHWEST SPAIN

CHEESES
La Casa de los Quesos Artesanos Rúa Bautizados 10, Santiago de Compostela, tel 98 158 50 85. All types of Galician cheeses: Arzua-Ulloa, Tetilla, Cebreiro, and San Simón.
La Masera Párroco Camino 29, Luarca, tel 98 547 09 47. Cheeses from the region, and vacuum-packed ingredients for making the famous *fabada* (Asturian bean stew).
Viuda de Macrino Suárez Párroco Camino 4, Luarca, tel 98 564 02 84. Combination of food and hardware store.

CHOCOLATE AND CANDY
El Metate Preguntoiro 12, Rúa San Payo, Santiago de Compostela. The best chocolate in Santiago. Located in what used to be a chocolate factory.

JEWELRY
Marín & Durán Huérfanos 11, Santiago de Compostela, tel/fax 981 58 17 83. Jewelry made from silver and jet stone.
Regueira Rúa da Azabachería 9, Santiago de Compostela, tel 981 58 36 27. Jewelry made from jet stone.

LACE & EMBROIDERY
Bolillos Rúa Nova 40, Santiago de Compostela, tel 981 58 97 76. Handmade lace and embroidery made by several women in the shop, using traditional methods.

MARKETS
Cudillero	Fri.
A Coruña (La Coruña)	Tues.
Luarca	Wed.
Noia (Noya)	Thurs. & Sun.
Ourense (Orense)	7th & 17th each month (if Sun., nearest Sat.)
Oviedo	Thurs. & Sun.
Pontevedra	1st, 8th, 15th, 23rd each month (if Sun., nearest Sat.)
Santander	Mon.-Sat.
Santiago	Mon.-Sat.

POTTERY & CERAMICS
A Mouga Rúa Xelmírez 26, Santiago de Compostela, tel 981 56 07 96. Locally made handicraft including traditional Galician pottery.
Sargadelos Rúa Nova 16, Santiago de Compostela, tel 981 58 19 05. Modern designs and variations on the traditional blue-and-white pottery.

NORTHEAST SPAIN

ANTIQUES
Eduardo Borrás Barriocepo 44, Logroño, tel 941 20 10 83.

Través del Espejo Iturrioz
Leza Portales 7, Logroño, tel 941 25 33 63.

FOOD
Aitor Lasa Aldamar 12, Donostia (San Sebastián), tel 94 343 03 54. Specializes in cheeses and all varieties of mushrooms (fresh, dried, and frozen). Also walnuts and Tolosa beans.
La Koxkera Fermín Calbetón 34, Donostia, tel 943 42 45 99. Famous old deli, specializing in salted and unsalted cod, cheeses, patés, and Basque specialties

MARKETS
Bilbo (Bilbao)	Mon.–Sat.
Calahorra	Thurs.
Daroca	Thurs.
Haro	Tues. & Sat.
Huesca	Mon. & Tues. clothes market; Thurs. flower market
Hondarribia (Fuenterrabía)	Daily fish market
Jaca	Fri.
Laguardia	Tues. & Fri.
Logroño	Sun.
Nájera	Thurs.
Oñati (Oñate)	Sat.
Iruña (Pamplona)	Sun. & first Sat. each month (secondhand)
Donostia (San Sebastián)	Sun.
Santo Domingo de la Calzada	Sat.
Sos del Rey	Fri.
Teruel	Thurs.
Gasteiz (Vitoria)	Thurs. & Sat., first Sat. each month furniture market
Zaragoza	Wed. & Sun

POTTERY
Arte y Artesanos, León XIII 18, Zaragoza, tel 976 21 20 51. Pottery from all over Spain.

WINE
Bodega Nuestra Señora del Romero Carretera Tarazona 33, Cascante (4.5 miles/7 km from Tudela), tel 948 85 14 11. Wines from Navarra.

Bodega Vinícola Real
Carretera de Naida, Km 9,
Albelda de Iregua, Logroño, tel
941 44 42 33. Regional wines
and foods. Also functions as a
12-room hostel.
**C.V.N.E. (Compañía
Vinícola del Norte de
España)** Barrio de la Estación,
Haro, tel 941 30 48 00. Rioja
wines.
Mi Bodega Santo Tomás 13,
Haro, tel 941 30 40 03. Rioja
wines and other regional
products.
Vinacoteca Ezkerra Beato
Tomás de Zumarraga 27 bajo,
Vitoria-Gasteiz, tel 945 24 95
51. A wide selection of Rioja
wines, and their own wine from
Leza.

BARCELONA

CAKES & PASTRIES
Farga Diagonal 391, tel 93 416
01 12. Delicious homemade
pastries that you can sample in
the tearoom. Many other stores.

CHOCOLATES
Petit Plaisir Ganduxer 33, tel
93 414 41 93. Belgian chocolate.
Xocoa Petritxol 11, tel 93 301
11 97. Swiss chocolates and
homemade candies.

FOOD
Cafés el Magnífico, Argenteria
64. Open since 1919. Over 30
freshly toasted coffees to try
and buy.
Fira Artesana Plaça del Pi 1.
First Fri.–Sat. of each month 10
a.m. to 10 p.m. Homemade
cheeses, pâtés, and various
candies with honey and
almonds.
La Cansaladería Alsina
Canalejas 29, Sants. Open since
1880. Honors the pig in all its
edible forms.
Semon Ganduxer 31, tel 93
240 30 88. Excellent smoked
fish, caviar, and pâtés.

GADGETS
Beardsley Petritxol 12, tel 93
301 05 76. Kitchen utensils,
gadgets, and cook books.

El Corte Inglés Plaça de
Catalunya 14, Diagonal, 617,
Plaça Francesc Macià, 20, Portal
de L'Angel 19 and more.
Konema Rambla Catalunya 43,
tel 93 488 33 25. Designer
gadgets for the kitchen.
Vinçon Passeig de Gràcia 94,
tel 93 215 60 50. Sophisticated
designer store, from sofas to
kitchen knives.

JEWELRY
Puíg Doria Diagonal 612, tel
93 201 29 11, Rambla Catalunya
88.

MARKETS
Feria Artesanía Rambla Santa
Mónica. Sat. & Sun. all day. Arts
and crafts.
**Mercadillos de Anticuarios
de la Catedral** All day Thurs.
Antiques in the Plaça Nova
opposite the cathedral.
Mercat de Sant Josep or de
la Boquería. Rambla de Sant
Josep. Mon.–Sat. all day. A
spectacular array, one of Spain's
best food markets.
Mercat dels Encants Plaça de
les Glories Catalanes. Mon.,
Wed., Fri., & Sat., 8 a.m.–7 p.m.
Secondhand and sometimes
antique market, and new stuff.
Anything from furniture to
fabrics.
Mercat de Sant Antoni
Comte d'Urgell. Mon., Wed.,
Fri., & Sat., 8 a.m.–8 p.m. Flea
market. Old books, collector
cards, movie posters, and comics
on Sun. a.m.
Mostra D'Art
Plaça del Pi and Plaça Sant Josep
Oriol. All day and Sat. & Sun.
mornings. Art on show and on
sale at reasonable prices.

WINE
Celler de Gelida Vallespir 65,
tel 93 339 26 41. A wide
selection of Catalan wines and
cavas, Rioja, Rueda, armagnacs,
and more. Opened in 1885.
Lafuente Juan Sebastián Bach
20, tel 93 201 15 13. Wines
from all over Spain including
rare Reservas. Opened since
1905.

Vila Viniteca Agullers 7, tel
93 268 32 27. An outstanding
collection of Spanish wines, also
wines from France, and port
from Portugal.

EASTERN SPAIN

FOOD
La Garriga Espalter 9, Sitges.
Hams and other meats.
La Granadina Girona
(Gerona) 7, Alacant (Alicante),
tel 96 521 11 51. A selecton of
about 70 cheeses, hams, pâtés,
and caviar.

MARKETS

Alcoi (Alcoy)	Wed., Thurs., & Sat.
Alacant (Alicante)	Thurs. & Sat.
Altea	Tues., Sat. & Sun.
Bégur	Wed. & Sun.
Cadaqués	Mon.
Calp (Calpe)	Sat.
Dénia	Mon.
Elx (Elche)	Mon. & Sat.
Girona (Gerona)	Tues. & Sat.
Xàtiva (Játiva)	Tues. & Fri.
Montblanc	Tues. & Fri.
Palafrugell	Sat. & Sun.
Ripoll	Sat.
Sagunt (Sagunto)	Wed., Thurs., & Sat.
Sitges	Sat.
Tarragona	1st & 3rd Fri., Sat. & Sun.
Tortosa	Mon.
Tossa de Mar	Thurs.
Valencia	Sun.

CASTILLA Y LEÓN

BASKETWORK & ANTIQUES
Antiquaria Rúa Mayor 47,
Salamanca, tel 923 26 72 99.
Antiques and reproductions.

FOOD
Artesa Ordoño II 27, León, tel
987 25 18 55. Regional products
such as meats, sausages, Bierzo
wines, cheeses, and chocolates
from Astorga.

La Casa de los Quesos
Plegarias, León. Cheeses from
Spain and abroad.
La Despensa Ramos Carrión
6, Zamora, tel 980 53 68 16.
Local products.
La Quesería Alcalde Miguel
Castaño 1, León, tel 987 26 44
24. Spanish cheeses including
some produced by the shop;
particularly appetizing is the
Campo de Oro.

LEATHER GOODS
Calzados San Luis Plaza
Mayor 5, Ciudad Rodrigo, tel
923 46 03 65. Make and sell
shoe leather wine bottles.

MARKETS
Ávila	Fri.
Burgos	Thurs.
Ciudad Rodrigo	Tues.
El Burgo de Osma	Sat.
León	Sat.
Peñafiel	Thurs.
Salamanca	Sun.
Segovia	Thurs.
Soria	Daily
Tordesillas	Tues. & 1st Sun. Oct.
Valladolid	Sun.
Zamora	Tues.; livestock market on the 12th of each month

POTTERY
Luisa Pérez Fermoselle 79,
Zamora, tel 980 53 06 02. A
traditional pottery workshop.
MJ Cerámica Balborraz 13
Zamora, tel 980 53 44 45.
Traditional pottery with
interesting modern influences.

CAKE & CANDY
Convento de las Dueñas In
front of Iglesia San Esteban,
Salamanca. Cakes and marzipan
made by the nuns.
Convento de Santa Teresa
Plaza Santa, Ávila. Spain's best
yemas (yellow cakes, named
after the egg yolks used to make
them and which they resemble).

WINES
Bodegas Fariña Camino del
Palo s/n, Toro, tel 980 57 76 73.
Toro wines. Guided tour of the
bodegas, wine tasting, and wines
for sale, including their own
Gran Colegiata.
Bodegas Protos Calle
Bodegas Protos 24-28, Peñafiel,
tel 983 87 80 11. Wines from
the Ribera del Duero region.
Pecados Originales Pasaje
Gutierrez 6, Valladolid, tel 983
39 23 26. Regional, national, and
international wines.

CASTILLA-LA MANCHA & EXTREMADURA

FOOD
Gabriel Mostazo San Antón
6, Cáceres, tel 927 24 54 93.
Regional products and
Extremaduran wines, including
those from the Monasterio de
Tentudia.
La Almazara Plaza Mayor 4,
Trujillo, tel 927 32 28 56
Regional products such as hams,
wine, cheeses, honey, and oil.
Santo Tomé Santo Tomé 3, tel
925 22 37 63 & Plaza de
Zocodover 7, tel 925 22 11 68,
Toledo. Marzipan makers since
1856, and cakes too.

KNIVES
Cuchillería Gómez La Feria
52, Albacete, tel 967 22 01 61.
Traditional family business, near
the bullring.
Simón Cuchillería Marqués
de Molíns 14, Albacete, tel 967
21 03 67. Old-fashioned
hardware in the center of town.

MARKETS
Albacete	Sun.
Belmonte	Mon.
Cáceres	Wed.
Cuenca	Thurs.
Mérida	Tues.
Plasencia	Tues.
Sigüenza	Sat.
Toledo	Tues. 1st Sat. of month
Trujillo	Thurs.
Zafra	Thurs.

POTTERY
**Centro de Artesanía Iglesia
Santa Cruz** Santa Catalina s/n,
Cuenca, tel 969 23 31 84. Very
good arts and crafts.
Cerámica Rosi Padre Juan de
Mariana 15, Talavera de la Reina.
Fourth-generation potter,
producing traditional and
imaginative ware.
DAM—Diseño—Decoración
Adarve del Padre Rosalio 14,
Cáceres, tel 927 24 46 92.
Furniture, pottery.

ANDALUCÍA & MURCIA

BOOKS & ANTIQUES
Antigüedades Juan Carlos I,
Juan Ruíz González 20, Úbeda,
tel 953 75 76 37. All sorts
of antiques.
Librería Atlántida Gran Via
de Colón 9, Granada, , tel 958
22 44 03. Bookshop that stocks
books in English.

CARPETS & ARTS & CRAFTS
**ACA Zoco—Artesanía
Cordobesa** Judíos s/n,
Córdoba, tel 957 20 40 33, e-
mail: asociación@aca-zoco.com.
Jewelry, leather crafts, and
ceramics all made by local
artisans.
Lorca Artesana Río
Guadalentín 9, Lorca, tel 968 46
61 97. Traditional carpets and
rugs from Lorca.

FOOD & WINE
Convento de Santa Paula
Santa Paula 11, Sevilla (Seville),
tel 95 442 13 07. These nuns
make delicious jams and
marmalades using Sevilla
oranges, plus other sweet-
meats and candies.
COVAP Barqueros 2, Córdoba,
tel 957 49 85 05. Modern shop
selling legs of ham, sausages,
cheeses, and vacuum-packed
packages of ham, etc. Ideal for
taking home.
Galería de Vinos Caldos
Cerón 12, Jaén, tel 953 23 59
99. A wide selection of wines,
including the very good Duque
de Bailén from Jaén.

La Flor de Toranzo Jimios 1, Sevilla, tel 95 422 93 15. Very good quality cheeses, ham, and cod. This is also a popular bar, offering traditional tapas for a tasty light lunch.

Las Campanas Plaza del Socorro, Ronda, , tel 952 87 22 73. *Yemas* (small sweet yellow cakes made with egg yolks).

Rincón de Baco Madre de Dios 9, Murcia, tel 968 22 34 40. Prizewinning local wine seller, and food to go with it.

HATS

El Sombrero de Tres Picos Plaza de Cuba 8, Sevilla, tel 95 428 34 58. Specializes in sombreros as well as bags and belts.

Sombreros Padilla Crespo Avenida de la Constitución 2, Sevilla, tel 95 422 24 55. The proprietors have been making hats here since 1935 and have very stylish selection of Sevilla sombreros.

LEATHER GOODS

Arcab Paseo Cristóbal Colón 18, Sevilla, tel 95 421 81 30. Everything to do with horses and horseback riding, from saddles to boots.

Curtidos Varo Alfaros 5, Córdoba, tel/fax 957 47 87 03. Leather goods, including boots made to measure and everything to do with horseback riding and hunting. This fascinating old-fashioned shop has been open since 1917.

MARKETS

Almería	Tues., Fri., Sat., & Sun. (airport)
Antequera	Daily except Sun., Tues. flea market.
Baeza	Tues.
Cádiz	Sun.
Córdoba	Sun.
Carmona	Mon. & Thurs.
Granada	Wed. & Sat., Sun. flea market.
Guadix	Sat.
Jerez de la Frontera	Sun. flea market, except in summer.
Lorca	Thurs.
Málaga	Sun. flea market.
Mojácar	Wed. & Sun.
Murcia	Thurs. & last Sun. of month
Níjar	Wed.
Sevilla	Arts & crafts daily; antiques & paintings Thurs.; general Fri. & Sat.; secondhand & antiques Sun.

OLIVE OIL

La Tienda del Aceite Avenida de Castro del Río 96, Baena, tel 957 69 20 31. Quality olive oils from the region in bottles and tins. Balsamic vinegar.

POTTERY & TILES

Alfarería Melchor Tito Valencia 44, Fuenteseca 17, Úbeda, tel 953 75 36 92. Pottery.

Azulejos Santa Isabel Alfarería 12, Sevilla, tel 95 434 46 08. Hand-painted tiles.

Cerámica Fajalauza Fajalauza 2, tel/fax 958 20 06 15. Famous Granada pottery.

Cerámica Triana Antillano Campos 14, Sevilla, tel 95 433 21 79. Traditional handmade pottery and ceramics.

Diego Lozano Jiménez Arco de las Escuelas 2, Baeza., Jaén, tel 953 74 14 71. Pottery including the green designs particular to Baeza. The owner in his spare time has also sculpted all of Baeza's monuments in miniature in marble. Ask to see them and make a small contribution.

Hermanos Almarza Valencia 36, Úbeda, Jaén, tel 953 75 00 63. Pottery.

La Tienda de los Milagros Pocico 9, Níjar, Almería, tel 950 36 03 59. Pottery with very colorful and original designs, each one different. Higher prices but better quality than many.

SHERRY BODEGAS

Domecq San Ildefonso 3, Jerez de la Frontera, tel 956 15 15 00, www.bodegasfundadorpedrodomecq.com. Reserve in advance for a tour.

González Byass Manuel María González 12, Jerez de la Frontera, tel 956 35 70 16, www.gonzalezbyass.es. Call ahead for a tour and tasting.

BALEARIC ISLANDS

S'Alambic Andén de Poniente 33-36, Maó (Mahón), tel 971 35 03 03. Local pottery from Paco Lora, and textiles as well.

Colmado de la Montaña Jaime II 27, Palma de Mallorca, tel 971 71 25 95. Good local cheeses and the popular *sobrasada* (soft, raw, red pork sausage with paprika and a lot of fat).

MARKETS

Eivissa (Ibiza Town)	Daily
Maó (Mahon)	Tues. & Sat.
Palma	Mon., Fri., & Sat. arts & crafts; Sat. flea market

CANARY ISLANDS

El Rincón del Fumador Albareda 23, Las Palmas de Gran Canaria, tel 928 27 82 15, fax 928 22 46 10, www.step.es/rincon. An immense selection of tobacco and cigars from the Canaries, Cuba, and the Philippines; pipes, and other smoking accessories.

Mercado de Nuestra Señora de África Plaza Mercado, Santa Cruz de Tenerife. Cheeses from all the islands and other food.

Pabellón de Ventas del Cabildo Insular Plaza de España, Tenerife, tel/fax 922 29 15 23. Goods made by local artisans.

MARKET

Santa Cruz de Tenerife Secondhand market Sun.

ENTERTAINMENT

Madrid and Barcelona are packed with bars, cafés, and things to do in the evenings. Madrileños tend to stay up the latest, often until sunrise, and really know how to enjoy themselves. Barcelona is very good for classical music and avant-garde theater and designer bars. The weekly *Guia del Ocio* in Madrid and Barcelona is an excellent guide to what is on. In these and other places you can also pick up information on entertainment and events from visitor information centers, and this is often in English.

For tickets all over Spain and phone/online reservations:
El Corte Inglés tel 902 40 02 22, www.elcorteingles.es
ServiCaixa tel 902 33 22 11; www.serviticket.es
Caixa Catalunya tel 902 10 12 12; www.telentrada.com
For tickets in Madrid only:
Localidades Galicia Plaza del Carmen 1, tel 91 531 91 31/27 32, www.eol.es/lgalicia
Entradas.com tel 902 22 16 22 (movies) or tel 902 48 84 88 (other events) www.entradas.com

MADRID

FLAMENCO
Café de Chinitas Torija 7, tel 91 547 15 02/01, www.chinitas .com, 9:30 p.m.–2 a.m. Metro Santo Domingo. Geared to vacationers.
Corral de la Morería Morería 17, tel 91 365 84 46, www.corral delamoreria.com. From 9:30 p.m.. Metro Ópera.
La Soleá Cava Baja 34, tel 91 365 52 64, Mon.–Sat. 10 p.m. until late. The last of the genuine flamenco bars. Metro La Latina.
Taberna Casa Patas Cañizares 10, tel 91 369 04 96. Flamenco 10:30 p.m., Fri. & Sat. midnight. Top singers, dancers, and guitarists. Reservations suggested. Metro Antón Martín.

THEATER
Madrid's Theater Festival, from late Oct.–late Nov. features all forms of theater including dance.
Teatro de Bellas Artes Marqués de Casa Riera 2, tel 91 532 44 37. Metro Banco de España. Classical theater.
Teatro Pavón Embajadores 9 (Plaza de Cascorro), tel 91 528 28 19. Metro La Latina. *Modernista* theater where the Compañía Nacional de Teatro Clásico

currently performs classic drama.

OPERA & CLASSICAL MUSIC
Auditorio Nacional de Música Príncipe de Vergara 146, tel 91 337 01 40, www.auditorio nacional.mcu.es. Metro Cruz de Rayo. Classical music.
Teatro de la Zarzuela Jovellanos 4, tel 91 524 54 00, www.teatro delazarzuela, Metro Banco de España & Sevilla, www.te atrodelazarzuela.mcu.es. Spanish genre of light opera, *la zarzuela.*
Teatro Monumental Atocha 65, tel 91 429 81 19, Metro Antón Martín. Classical music.
Teatro Real Plaza de Oriente, s/n, tel 91 516 06 06, www.tea tro-real.com. Metro Ópera. Grand theater for opera and ballet.

POP, ROCK, WORLD & JAZZ
Advance tickets from Madrid Rock, Gran Vía 25, Calle Mayor 38, and the FNAC store, Calle de Preciados. Cash. Venues include:
Café Central Plaza del Ángel 10, tel 91 369 41 43, Metro Sol & Antón Martín. 1:30 p.m.–3 a.m. Live jazz.
Calle 54 Paseo de la Habana 3, tel 91 561 43 12, Metro Nuevos Ministerios. Jazz, Latin, fusion, Cuban. Reserve to eat.
Clamores Alburquerque 14, tel 91 445 79 38, www.salaclamores .com, Metro Bilbao. 6 p.m.–3 a.m. Jazz, world music, flamenco.
Honky Tonk Covarrubias 24, tel 91 445 61 91, www.clubhonky .com, Metro Alonso Martínez. Rock, funk, pop joint. Live acts, DJs, and restaurant. All week.
La Boca del Lobo Echegaray 11, tel 91 429 70 13, www.labocadellobo.com, Metro Sevilla. Music, including reggae, singer-songwriters, flamenco, rumba, film, and theater.

Populart Las Huertas 22, tel 91 429 84 07, www.populart.es, Metro Sevilla & Antón Martín. From 6 p.m.–2:30 a.m. (3:30 a.m. at weekends). Jazz.

CINEMA
These central cinemas show films in their original language:
Alphaville Martín de los Heros, 14, tel 91 559 38 36, Metro Ventura Rodríguez y Plaza de España.
Cine Doré (Filmoteca Nacional) Santa Isabel 3, tel 91 369 11 25, Metro Antón Martín. Old and new films.
Ideal Yelmo Cineplex Doctor Cortezo 6, tel 91 369 25 18, Metro Sol.
Renoir Cuatro Caminos Raimundo Fernández Villaverde 10, tel 91 534 60 18, Metro Cuatro Caminos.
Renoir Plaza de España Martín de los Heros, tel 91 541 39 14, Metro Plaza de España.
Renoir Princesa Princesa 3, tel 91 541 41 00, Metro Plaza de España.
Renoir Retiro Narváez 42, tel 91 541 41 00, Metro Ibiza.
Verdi Bravo Murillo 28, tel 91 447 39 30, Metro Quevedo.

CASINO
Casino Gran Madrid Carretera de La Coruña, km 29, Torrelodones, tel 91 856 11 00, www.casino granmadrid.es, open 4 p.m.–5 a.m. Playing rooms, restaurant, buffet, disco, and live acts. Passport or driver's license required to get in.

BULLFIGHTING
Plaza de Toros Monumental de las Ventas Alcalá 237, tel 91 356 22 00, www.las-ventas.com. Metro Ventas. The biggest bullring in Spain. The main season starts in mid-May for the San Isidro feria. Must reserve for this; best seats are in the shade. Tickets from the bullring, www.lostaquiladores.com or 902 15 00 25 (by credit card).

CAFÉS & BARS
Here is a short list worth visiting:
Café de Oriente Plaza de Oriente 2, tel 91 541 15 64,

ENTERTAINMENT

Metro Ópera. An elegant old-fashioned café-bar and restaurant.
Café Gijón Paseo de Recoletos 21, tel 91 521 54 25, Metro Banco de España & Colón. Good regional fare.
Círculo de Bellas Artes Marqués de Casa Riera 2, tel 91 360 54 00, Metro Banco de España. Elegant surroundings.
La Venencia Echegaray 7, tel 91 429 73 13, Metro Sevilla. A dusty old bar with six different sherrys.
Los Gabrieles Echegaray 17, tel 91 429 62 61, Metro Sevilla. Covered in beautiful tiles; you can have tapas with your drink.
Viva Madrid Manuel Fernández y González 7, tel 91 429 36 40, Metro Sevilla. Lively place, but go early as it gets very crowded.

BARCELONA

THEATER

Barcelona is full of theaters and stages—mainly in Catalan and sometimes in Spanish. Check in the *Guía del Ocio*. Some groups mix miming, special effects, and modern theater such as La Fura dels Baus, Els Joglars, and Els Comediants. These show modern work unless otherwise indicated.
Mercat de les Flors Lleida 59, tel 93 426 18 75, www.mercatflo rs.org, Metro Poble Sec. At foot of Montjuïc, this venue shows drama, dance, and concerts.
Teatre El Molino Vila i Vila 99, tel 93 215 00 69, Metro Paral.lel. Musical cabaret.
Teatre Llantiol Riereta 7, tel 93 329 90 09, www.llantiol.com, Metro Paral.lel. Concerts, comedy, theater, movies, musicals.
Teatre Lliure Plaça Margarida Xirgu 1, tel 93 289 27 70, www.lliure.com, Metro Plaça Espanya. Theater, musicals, dance. The refurbishment of their home in Carrer Montseny is due for completion in Sept. 2009.
Teatre Poliorama La Rambla dels Estudis 115, tel 93 317 75 99, www.teatrepoliorama.com, Metro Catalunya. Theater, opera, flamenco, and more.
Teatre Romea Hospital 51, tel 93 301 55 04, www.teatrer

omea.com, Metro Liceu.
Teatre Tivoli Casp 10, tel 902 33 22 11, www.grupbalana.com. Musicals and dance shows.
Teatre Victoria Paral.lel 67, tel 93 329 91 89, www.teatrevic toria.com, Metro Paral.lel. Ballet, modern dance, and musicals.

OPERA & CLASSICAL MUSIC

The monthly *Informatiú Musical* leaflet from tourist offices has listings of classical music.
Gran Teatre del Liceu La Rambla 57–59, tel 93 485 99 98, www.liceubarcelona.com. Metro Liceu. The Liceu that burned down in 1994, reopened 1999. Opera and dance.
Palau de la Música Catalana Palau de la Música 4–6, tel 93 295 72 00, www.palaumusica.org. Metro Urquinaona. Classical and choral music.

POP, ROCK, WORLD, & JAZZ

Apolo Nou de la Rambla 113, tel 93 441 40 01, www.sala-apolo.com, Metro Paral.lel. Rock, flamenco, reggae, jazz, movies.
Bikini Deu i Mata 105, tel 93 322 08 00, Metro Les Corts. Rock, funk, hip hop, and a late disco.
La Paloma Tigre 27, tel 93 317 79 94, www.lapaloma-bcn.com, Metro Catalunya or Sant Antoni. Lovely old dance hall. Live tango, paso doble, salsa and more.
Harlem Jazz Club Comtessa Sobradiel 8, tel 93 310 07 55, Metro Drassanes. Nightly (except Mon.) 8 p.m. –2 a.m. Jazz, Latino, rock, African.
Jamboree Plaça Reial 17, tel 93 301 75 64, Metro Liceu. Jazz and funk every night starting at 11 p.m. Admission includes drink.
La Boîte Diagonal 477, tel 93 319 17 89, Metro Diagonal. Jazz or blues jam sessions usually start around midnight.
Tarantos Plaça Reial 17, tel 93 319 17 89, www.masimas.com/ tarantos, Metro Liceu. Historic flamenco joint, now also welcoming singer-songwriters.

CINEMA

The following cinemas show films

in their original language with Spanish subtitles:
Casablanca-Gràcia Girona 173–175, tel 93 459 03 26. Metro Verdaguer.
Casablanca-Kaplan Passeig de Gràcia 115, tel 93 218 43 45, Metro Diagonal.
Filmoteca de la Generalitat Cine Aquitania, Avinguda de Sarrià 33, tel 93 410 75 90 Metro Hospital Clinic. Old and new films.
Malda Carrer Pi 5, tel 93 317 85 29, Metro Liceu.
Renoir Les Corts Eugeni D'Ors 12, tel 93 490 53 10, Metro Les Corts.
Verdi Verdi 32, Gràcia, tel 93 238 79 90, Metro Fontana.
Verdi Park Torrijos 49, tel 93 238 79 90, Metro Fontana.
Yelmo Icaria Salvador Espriu 61, tel 93 221 79 12, Metro Carlos I.

CASINO

Casino de Barcelona Marina 19–21, Port Olímpic, tel 93 225 78 78. 1 p.m.–5 a.m. Gaming room and machines. Restaurant. Passport or driver's license to get in.

CAFÉS & BARS

Bar Pastis Santa Mónica 4, tel 93 318 79 80, Metro Drassanes. Old bar with a French cabaret theme.
Café de l'Ópera La Rambla 74, tel 93 317 75 85, Metro Liceu. One of Barcelona's classiest cafés.
Café Salambo Torrijos, 51, tel 93 218 69 66. An unpretentious designer bar.
El Paraigua Pas de L'Ensenyança 2, tel 93 302 11 31, Metro Jaume I. Classical music on the lower floor, jazz/blues above.
El Xampanyet Montcada 22, tel 93 319 70 03, Metro Jaume I. Cava and French champagne. Good tapas.
La Cava del Palau Verdaguer I Callis 10, tel 93 310 09 38, Metro Catalunya. Cava bar and tapas.
The Quiet Man Marqués de Barbera 11, tel 93 412 12 19, Metro Liceu. Irish pub. Live music some nights.
Torre Rosa Frances Tárrega 22, tel 93 340 88 54. Metro Congrés. Cocktail bar and terrace.

ACTIVITIES

Spain is a large mountainous country with huge tracts of land turned into national parks. It also has thousands of miles of coastline—from rugged and spectacular cliffs to gentle beaches. Consequently, it is a delight to anyone seeking outdoor activities, whether skiing, climbing, diving, golf, or walking. The Canary Islands offer excellent diving and hiking, the golf courses on the Costa del Sol are among the finest in the world, and the endless mountains on the peninsula have some of the wildest countryside in Europe for hiking.

Below are various central federations and some individual venues for a variety of activities, but it is by no means a complete list. For comprehensive information on local activities and events, contact the local tourist offices.

GOLF
Real Federación Española de Golf tel 91 555 26 82, www.golfspainfederacion.com

HORSEBACK RIDING
Real Federación Hípica Española tel 91 436 42 00, www.rfhe.com.

POLO
Real Federación Española de Polo tel 95 499 93 65, www.rfepolo.org

MOUNTAINEERING
Federación Española de Deportes de Montaña y Escalada tel 93 426 42 67, www.fedme.es

SAILING
Real Federación Española de Vela tel 91 519 50 08, www.rfev.es

SCUBA DIVING
Scuba Schools International tel 96 152 22 97, fax 96 153 74 09, www.ssispain.com

THERMAL SPRINGS
Asociación Nacional de Balnearios tel 91 549 03 00, www.balnearios.org

MADRID

CLIMBING
Federación Madrileña de Montañismo tel 91 527 38 01, www.fmm.es.

HIKING
Espacio Acción tel 91 326 72 92, www. espacioaccion.com

HORSEBACK RIDING
Federación Hípica de Madrid tel 91 477 72 38, www. federacionhipicamadrid.com

PARAGLIDING
De Madrid al Cielo Escuela de Parapente tel 91 552 84 33, www.madridalcielo.com

NORTHWEST SPAIN

FESTIVALS
Feast of St. James July 25, Santiago de Compostela. Mock cathedral burning and fireworks.
Festival Internacional de Santander all August. Music from across the board, tel 942 21 05 08 www.festivalsantander.com

GENERAL
Los Cauces Avenida de Covadonga 23, Cangas de Onis, Asturias, tel 98 594 73 18, www.loscauces.com. Canoeing, horseback riding, quad biking, hiking, spelunking, and more.

GOLF
Club de Golf de La Coruña La Zapateira, A Coruña (La Coruña), tel 981 28 52 00, fax 942 50 04 21, www.clubgolfcoruna.com
Real Golf de Pedreña Santander, tel 942 50 00 01, www.realgolfdepedrena.com

HORSEBACK RIDING
Benjamín Cobrana Valle de Lago, Somiedo, Asturias, tel 985 76 39 52

SCUBA DIVING
Buceo Galicia, A Coruña, tel 981 21 22 06, www.buceogalicia.com

NORTHEAST SPAIN

FESTIVALS
Festival de Cine de San Sebastián second half of September. www.sansebastianfestival.com
Fiesta de San Fermínes Running of the bulls in Iruña (Pamplona).
Fiesta de San Mateo Around September 21 for harvest and Logroño grape crushing.
Festival de Jazz Late July in Donostia (San Sebastián). www.jazzaldia.com

GOLF
Club de Golf Larrabea Legutiano, Álava, tel 94 546 54 82, www.larrabea.com

HORSEBACK RIDING
Club Hípico del Zaldiaran Armentia, Álava, tel 94 514 53 67
El Rancho de Boca la Roca Benabarre, Huesca, tel 974 54 35 65, www.rancho.de

KAYAKING & CLIMBING
TT Aventura Avenida Pirenaica 10, Ainsa, Huesca, tel 974 51 00 24, www.ttaventura.com

SCUBA DIVING
Buceo Euskadi Puerto, Mutriku, Guipuzkoa, tel 94 319 50 88, www.buceo euskadi.com

WHITE-WATER RAFTING
Aguas Blancas Avenida de Sobrarbe 11, Aínsa, Huesca, tel 974 51 00 08, www.aguasblancas .com

BARCELONA

CLIMBING
Travessa Barcelona, tel 93 491 49 98, www.travessa.net

GOLF
Club de Golf La Mola Matadepera, Barcelona, tel 93 730 05 16, www.golflamola.com
TREKKING
Tarannà Nòmades Vallespir 174, Barcelona, tel 93 411 83 73, www.tarannanomades.com

EASTERN SPAIN

FESTIVAL
Las Fallas de San José
Valencia March 12–19. Mix of
fireworks, bonfires, and music.

GOLF
Club de Golf de Girona Sant
Julià de Ramis, Girona (Gerona), tel
972 17 16 41, www.golfgirona.com

HIKING
Els Frares Quatretondeta
Alacant (Alicante), tel 96 551 12
34, www.mountainwalks.com

HORSEBACK RIDING
Club Hípico Lloret Lloret de
Mar, tel 972 36 86 15

RAFTING & KAYAKING
Deportur Les Lleida (Lérida),
tel 973 64 70 45, www.deportur
.com/rafting.htm

PARACHUTING
Skydive Empuriabrava
Costa Brava Aeroclub
Empuriabrava, Girona, tel 972 45
01 11, www.skydiveempuria
brava.com

SCUBA DIVING
Dive Paradís Port de la Clota,
L'Escala, Girona, tel 972 77 31 87,
www.diveparadis.com
Diving Center Cadaqués Moll
d'es Poal, De la Miranda, Cadaqués, tel 93 484 23 49 www.diving
cadaques.com

SKIING
Estación Baqueira-Beret
Vielha, Lleida, tel 973 63 90 10,
www.baqueira.es

CASTILLA Y LEÓN

GOLF
Club de Golf Villar de Olalla
Cuenca, tel 969 26 71 98

CASTILLA-LA MANCHA & EXTREMADURA

FESTIVALS
WOMAD (World of Music,
Arts, and Dance) Cáceres at
beginning of May. International
bands. www.womad.org/caceres
Festival de Teatro Clásico
Mérida, Badajoz in July. Classics
staged. tel, 924 00 94 80
www.festivaldemerida.es

GOLF
Norba Club de Golf Carretera,
N630, Km 558, tel 927 23 14 41,
www.norbagolf.com

PARAGLIDING
Parapente Extremadura
Sergio Sánchez 4, Cáceres, tel
927 22 68 46

ANDALUCÍA & MURCIA

**Nevadensis Guías de
Montaña** Plaza de la Libertad,
Pamoaneira, Granada, tel 958 76
31 27, www.nevadensis.com.
Activities in the Sierra Nevada.

FESTIVALS
Carnaval in Cádiz a month
before Easter. www.carnavalde
cadiz.com
Feria del Caballo (Horse Fair)
April or May, Jerez de la Frontera, Cádiz. Expect crowds.
www.jerez2020.com/aFeria.htm
**Festival Internacional de
Guitarra** early July, Córdoba.
www.guitarracordoba.com
Corridas Goyescas, early
September, Ronda, Málaga. Top
matadors fight in 19th-century
costumes. www.rmcr.org
Semana Santa Easter
processions in Sevilla (Seville).

GOLF
Mijas Golf Fuengirola, Málaga, tel
95 247 68 43, www.mijasgolf.org
La Manga Club Los Belones,
Cartagena, Murcia, tel 968 17 50
00, www.lamangaclub.es
**Real Club de Golf
Sotogrande** Sotogrande, Cádiz,
tel 956 78 50 14, www.golfsoto
grande.com
Real Club de Golf Las Brisas
Marbella, Nueva Andalucía,
Málaga, tel 95 281 08 75,
www.lasbrisasgolf.com

HORSEBACK RIDING
Club Hípico de Cordóba
Carretera de Trasierra Km 32,
Córdoba, tel/fax 957 27 16 28,
www.clubhipicodecordoba.com
**Club Hípico de
Benalmádena** Benalmádena,
Málaga, tel 95 256 84 84,
www.clubhipico.com

SCUBA DIVING
Granada Sub La Herradura,
Granada, tel 958 64 02 81,
www.granadasub.com
Tribal Sub Club Náutico El
Candado, Málaga, tel 95 229 78
00, www.tribalsub.com

BALEARIC ISLANDS

GOLF
Golf Club de Ibiza Santa
Eulália, Eivissa (Ibiza), tel 971 19
60 52, www.golfibiza.com

HORSEBACK RIDING
Federación Hípica Balear
Reverend Francesc Sitjar 1,
Palma de Mallorca, tel 971 75 67
54, www.hipicabaleares.com

SCUBA DIVING
Ibiza Diving Santa Eulália,
Eivissa, tel 971 33 29 49,
www.ibiza-diving.com

CANARY ISLANDS

GOLF
Golf Costa Teguise Lanzarote,
tel 928 59 05 12, www.lanzarote
-golf.com
**Real Club de Golf Las
Palmas** Las Palmas, tel 928 35
10 50, www.realclubdegolfdela
spalmas.com. Also has horses.

HORSEBACK RIDING
Club Hípico La Atalaya San
Cristobal de la Laguna, Santa
Cruz, Tenerife, tel 922 25 14 10,
www.clubatalaya.com

SCUBA DIVING
Diversity Local 125, Centro
Comercial, Playa de las
Américas, Santa Cruz de
Tenerife, tel/fax 922 71 71 29,
www.divingtenerife.net

LANGUAGE GUIDE

USEFUL WORDS & PHRASES

Excuse me *Perdón*
Hello *Hola*
Goodbye *Adiós*
Please *Por favor*
Thank you *Gracias*
You're welcome *De nada*
Good morning *Buenos días*
Good afternoon/evening *Buenas tardes*
Good night *Buenas noches*
today *hoy*
yesterday *ayer*
tomorrow *mañana*
now *ahora*
later *más tarde*
this morning *esta mañana*
this afternoon/this evening *esta tarde*
Do you speak English? *¿Habla inglés?*
I am American *Yo soy americano*
I don't understand *No entiendo*
Where is…? *¿Dónde está…?*
I don't know *no sé*
At what time? *¿a qué hora?*
when? *¿Cuándo?*

Do you have…? *¿tiene un…*
a single room *una habitación individual?*
a double room (double bed) *con cama de matrimonio?*
a double room (twin beds) *una habitación con dos camas?*
for one night *para una noche?*

I need a doctor/dentist *Necesito un médico/dentista*
Can you help me? *¿Me puede ayudar?*
hospital *hospital*
police station *comisaría de policía?*

I'd like *Me gustaría*
How much is it? *¿Cúanto es?*
Do you accept credit cards? *¿Se aceptan tarjetas de crédito?*
cheap *barato*
expensive *caro*
post office *el correo*
visitor information center *la oficina de turismo*
open *abierto*
closed *cerrado*
every day *todos los días*

MENU READER

breakfast *el desayuno*
lunch *el almuerzo/la comida*
dinner *la cena*
I'd like to order *Me gustaría pedir*
Is service included? *¿Está incluido el servicio?*

la carta menu
menú del día fixed priced three-course meal including a drink
a la carta ordering anything other than *menú del día*
lista de vinos wine list
la cuenta check

tapa small snack taken with a drink
ración portion, helping
a la parrilla grilled
a la plancha grilled on a hot plate
crudo raw
ahumado smoked
estofado stew
frito fried
horno oven
empanada savory pastry
tortilla Spanish omelet made with potatoes and often served cold

un agua mineral mineral water *sin gas* (still) *con gas* (sparkling)
el azúcar sugar
un café americano large black coffee
un café con leche large white coffee
un café descafeinado decaffeinated coffee
un café solo short black/ espresso
una cerveza beer
cubiertos knives and forks
la leche milk
el pan bread
la sal salt
un té tea
un vino tinto red wine
un vino blanco white wine
vino de la casa house wine
un zumo de naranja fresh orange juice

cabra goat
callos tripe
cerdo pork
chorizo spicy sausage
conejo rabbit
cordero lamb
hígado liver
jamón ham
lomo loin (usually of pork)
pato duck

pavo turkey
pollo chicken
perdiz partridge
riñones kidneys
salchichas sausages
ternera beef

atún tuna
caballa mackerel
chanquetes whitebait
dorada bream
lenguado sole
lubina sea bass
merluza hake
pescadilla whiting
rape monkfish
salmonete red mullet

almejas clams
calamares squid
camarón shrimp
cangrejo crab
chipirones small squid
gambas prawns
langosta lobster
mejillones mussels
ostra oyster
pulpo octopus
vieira scallop

alcachofa artichoke
arroz rice
berenjena eggplant
calabacín zucchini
cebolla onion
champiñones mushrooms
col cabbage
espárragos asparagus
espinacas spinach
guisantes peas
habas broad beans
judías beans
lechuga lettuce
patatas fritas french fries
pepino cucumber
puerro leek
seta wild mushroom
zanahoria carrot

albaricoque apricot
cereza cherry
ciruela plum
frambuesa raspberry
fresa strawberry
limón lemon
mandarina tangerine
manzana apple
melocotón peach
naranja orange
sandía watermelon
uva grape

CREDITS

ILLUSTRATIONS CREDITS

Abbreviations for terms appearing below: (t) top; (b) bottom; (l) left; (r) right

Cover (l), Jose Fuste Raga/Corbis. (m) M. L. Stephenson/Corbis UK Ltd. (r), Gettyone/ Stone. Back Cover inset, G. Milverton/ Impact Photos. Spine, M. L. Stephenson/ Corbis UK Ltd. 1, M. Chaplo/Andalucia Slide Lib. 2/3, AA Photo Library/A. Molyneux. 4, M. Chaplow/Andalucia Slide Lib. 9, P. Thompson/Eye Ubiquitous. 11, M. Chaplow/Andalucia Slide Lib. 12/13, Steve McCurry. 14, N. Egerton/Travel Ink. 15, G. Azumendi/Vision Photo. 16/17, A. Guinart/ Vision Photo. 18/19, G. M. Azumendi/ Vision Photo. 20/21, Index Fototeca. 23, Age Fotostock. 24/25, Glen Allison/Getty Images. 26, M. Chaplow/Andalucia Slide Lib. 29, Index Fototeca. 30/31, Age Fotostock. 32/33, Godo-Foto. 35, Index Fototeca. 36, Bett- mann/Corbis UK Ltd. 38, Age Fotostock. 39, Index Fototeca. 40/41, Index Fototeca. 42/43, Vision Photo. 44, Index Fototeca. 45, Index Fototeca. 46/47, H. Gruyaert/Magnum Photos. 48, AA Photo Lib./S. Day. 49, Hulton Archive/Getty Images. 50/51, M. Chaplow/ Andalucia Slide Lib. 52, Lalo Yasky/Wire- Image/Getty Images. 53, AA Photo Lib./R. Strange. 55, AA Photo Lib./J. Edmanson. 56, J. Lawrence/Travel Ink. 57, R. Roberts/ Impact Photos. 58, M. Chaplow/Andalucia Slide Lib. 60t, M. Chaplow/Andalucia Slide Lib. 60b, P. Enticknap/Travel Lib. 61, M. Chaplow/Andalucia Slide Lib. 62, Philippe Desmazes/AFP/Getty Images. 63, Prado, Madrid, Spain/Bridgeman Art Lib., London. 64, Age Fotostock. 65t, G. Wright/Axiom. 65b, S. Black/Travel Lib. 66,Tino Soriano/ National Geographic Image Collection. 67, Godo-Foto. 68, Museo Thyssen-bornemisa, Madrid. 69, Thyssen-Bornemisza Museum/ AKG - London. 70, M. Chaplow/Andalucia Slide Lib. 71, Thyssen-Bornemisza Museum/AKG - London. 72, AA Photo Lib./J. Edmanson. 73, Godo-Foto. 74, Robert Frerck, Odyssey Productions. 75, Steve McCurry/NGS Image Collection. 76, Museo de America, Madrid, Spain/Index/ Bridgeman Art Lib., London. 77, R. Duaso/ Vision Photo. 78, A Guinart/Vision Photo. 79, H Schmidt/Travel Lib. 80, A Guinart/ Vision Photo. 82, R. Duaso/Fototext. 83, Age Fotostock. 85, Eye Ubiquitous. 86, Age Fotostock. 87, G. Azumendi/Vision Photo. 88, D. Cumming; Eye Ubiquitous/Corbis UK Ltd. 89t, M. Alavedra/Fototext. 89b, A Guinart/Vision Photo. 91, Age Fotostock. 93, A Guinart/Vision Photo. 94, Age Fotostock. 95, Index Fototeca. 96, Age Fotostock. 97, Age Fotostock. 98, Age Fotostock. 99, F. Dunlop. 100, Age Fotostock. 101, Travel Lib. 102, Index Fototeca. 103, M. Alavedra/Foto- text. 104, Age Fotostock. 105, G. M. Azumendi/Vision Photo. 106/107, P. Enticknap/Travel Lib. 107, M. Alavedra/ Foto-text. 108, G. M. Azumendi/Vision Photo. 108/109, G. M. Azumendi/Vision Photo. 109, M. Holford. 110, G. M.

Azumendi/Vision Photo. 111, Gettyone/ Stone. 114, Age Fotostock. 115, G. M. Azumendi/Vision Photo. 116/117, E. Barahona Ede/Museo Guggenheim Bilbao. 117, E. Barahona Ede/Museo Guggenheim Bilbao. 118t, E. Barahona Ede/Museo Gug- genheim Bilbao. 118b, G. M. Azumendi/ Vision Photo. 119, Age Fotostock. 121tl, G. M. Azumendi/Vision Photo. 121tr, A. Arzoz/Axiom. 121b, Age Fotostock. 122/123, Index Fototeca. 123, Alex Segre/Alamy. 124/125, Age Fotostock. 126, Age Fotostock. 127, F. Dunlop. 128, G. M. Azumendi/Vision Photo. 129, Godo-Foto. 130, M. Alavedra/ Fototext. 131, G. M. Azumendi/Vision Photo. 132/133, Age Fotostock. 133, G. M. Azumendi/Vision Photo. 134, M. Chaplow/ Andalucia Slide Lib. 135t, Age Fotostock. 135b, C. O'Rear/Corbis UK Ltd. 136, C. Bowman/Robert Harding Picture Lib. 137, K. Gillham/Robert Harding Picture Lib. 138, Age Fotostock. 139, A. Guinart/Vision Photo. 140, F. A. Lopez/Vision Photo. 141, Expo Zaragoza 2008. 142/143, A. Guinart/ Vision Photo. 143, Vision Photo. 144, G. M. Azumendi/Vision Photo. 145, G. M. Azumendi/Vision Photo. 147t, M. Hamblin/ Oxford Scientific Films. 147b, Vision Photo. 148, Age Fotostock. 150t, G. M. Azumendi/ Vision Photo. 150b, H. Reinhard/Bruce Coleman. 151, Age Fotostock. 152, A. Guinart/Vision Photo. 153, Gettyone/Stone. 155, K. Russell. 156, Age Fotostock. 157, A. Blomqvist/The Seeing Eye. 159, AA Photo Lib./S. Day. 160-61, Robert Frerck, Odyssey Productions. 161t, R. Duaso/Fototext. 162, AA Photo Lib./S. Day. 163, Edifice/CORBIS. 164, AA Photo Lib./M. Jourdan. 164/165, AA Photo Lib./M. Jourdan. 166, S. Black/Travel Lib. 167tl, K. Russell. 167tr, S. Maze/Corbis UK Ltd. 167b, R. Duaso/Vision Photo. 168, Rosmi Duaso/Time Life Pictures/Getty Images. 169, AA Photo Lib./M. Jourdan. 170, K. Russell. 171t, AA Photo Lib./M. Jourdan. 171b, Tom Thistlethwaite/Corbis. 172, AA Photo Lib./S. Day. 173, K. Russell. 173b, AA Photo Lib./S. Day. 174, Gettyone/Stone. 175, A. Blomqvist/The Seeing Eye. 176, Richard Klune/CORBIS. 177, Archivo Gallen/Godo- Foto. 178, M. Chaplow/Andalucia Slide Lib. 180, A. Guinart/Vision Photo. 181, M. Chaplow/AA Photo Lib. 182, M. Chaplow/ Andalucia Slide Lib. 183, M. Chaplow/ Andalucia Slide Lib. 184, Sipa Press/Rex Features. 185t, Vision Photo. 185b, Robin Townsend/AP Photo/EFE. 186/187, M. Alavedra/Fototext. 187, A. Guinart/Vision Photo. 188, J. M. Escofet/Vision Photo. 189, R. Duaso/Vision Photo. 191, G. Milverton/ Impact Photos. 192, James Davis Worldwide. 193, Kord Photographics/Images Colour Lib. 194, R. Manent/Corbis UK Ltd. 194/195, M. Alavedra/Fototext. 196t, F. Dunlop. 196b, M. Alavedra/Fototext. 197, M. Alavedra/Fototext. 198, M. Alavedra/ Fototext. 199, Eye Ubiquitous. 200, A. Guinart/Vision Photo. 202, A. Guinart/ Vision Photo. 203, A. Guinart/Vision Photo. 204, Age Fotostock. 205, D. Waugh/ Gettyone/Stone. 206, A. Guinart/Vision Photo. 207, AA Photo Lib./M. Chaplow 208,

Age Fotostock. 209, P.A. Thompson/Index Stock Photography Inc. 211, H. G. Schmidt/Travel Lib. 212, Godo-Foto. 213, Alberto Paredes/Alamy. 214, Age Fotostock. 215, R. Vanni/Corbis UK Ltd. 216/217, A. Guinart/Vision Photo. 218, Peter Adams/ Corbis. 220, Index Stock Photography Inc. 221, R. Richardson/Travel Lib. 222, M. Busselle/Corbis UK Ltd. 223, Travel Lib. 224, Index Stock Photography Inc. 225, R. Richardson/Travel Lib. 226, A. Guinart/ Vision Photo. 227, A. Guinart/Vision Photo. 228, F. Dunlop. 229, Index Stock Photo- graphy Inc. 230, Age Fotostock. 231, J. Miller/Robert Harding Picture Lib. 232, A. Guinart/Vision Photo. 233, B. Barbey/ Magnum Photos. 235, M. Henley/Impact Photos. 236, J. Cornish/Gettyone/Stone. 237, Age Fotostock. 238, Salvador Dali, El Quijote, 1945, © Kingdom of Spain, universal heir of Salvador Dali/DACS 2001. 238/239, C. Penn/Impact Photos. 241, N. Egerton/Travel Ink. 242, M. Busselle/Corbis UK Ltd. 243, Godo-Foto. 244, James Davis Worldwide. 246, R. Frerck/Odyssey/Chicago/ Robert Harding Picture Lib. 247, G. M. Azumendi/Vision Photo. 248, Robert Harding Picture Lib. 249, F. Dunlop. 250/251, Robert Harding Picture Lib. 251, Age Fotostock. 252, H. Gruyaert/Magnum Photos. 253t, Private Collection/Bridgeman Art Lib., London. 253b, A. Guinart/Vision Photo. 254/255, A. Guinart/Vision Photo. 255, A. Guinart/Vision Photo. 256, Age Fotostock. 256/257, H. Gruyaert/Magnum Photos. 258, Age Fotostock. 259, C. Coe/Axiom. 262/263, M. Alavedra/Fototext. 264/265, C. Caldicott/Axiom. 265, C. Coe/Axiom. 266, P. Seheult /Eye Ubiquitous. 267, AA Photo Lib./A. Molyneux. 268, C. Caldicott/Axiom. 269t, H. Sitton/Gettyone/ Stone. 269c, C. Coe/Axiom. 269bl, M. Chaplow/Andalucia Slide Lib. 269br, Iranzo/ Index Fototeca. 270, Godo-Foto. 271, M. Chaplow/Andalucia Slide Lib. 272, A. Williams/Axiom. 273t, S. Greenland/Eye Ubiquitous. 273bl & br., M. Chaplow/ Andalucia Slide Lib. 274/275, M. Alavedra/ Fototext. 276, P. Enticknap/Travel Lib. 278, A. Guinart/Vision Photo. 279, S. Black/ Travel Lib. 280, B. Battersby/Eye Ubiquitous. 281, C. Caldicott/Axiom. 282, M. Chaplow/ Andalucia Slide Lib. 283, AA Photo Library/ M. Chaplon. 285, Travel Lib. 286/287, JTB/drr.net. 288/289, D. Codina/Fototext. 289, M. Chaplow/Andalucia Slide Lib. 290, P. Ward/Corbis UK Ltd. 291, M. Chaplow/ Andalucia Slide Lib. 292, AA Photo Lib./D. Robertson. 293, H. G. Schmidt/Travel Lib. 294, M. Chaplow/Andalucia Slide Lib. 295, M. Chaplow/Andalucia Slide Lib. 296/297, A. Guinart/Vision Photo. 298, F. Dunlop. 299, R. Duaso/Fototext. 300t, L. Miles/Eye Ubiquitous. 300b, Godo-Foto. 301, L. Miles/ Eye Ubiquitous. 302, R. Westlake/Travel Ink. 303, A. Blomqvist/The Seeing Eye. 304, James Davis Worldwide. 304/305, Age Fotostock. 306, L. Miles/Eye Ubiquitous. 308, M. Chaplow/Andalucia Slide Lib. 309, M. Chaplow/Andalucia Slide Lib. 310, F. Dunlop. 311, M. Chaplow/Andalucia Slide

Lib. 312, D. Contantine/Axiom. 313, F. Alda/Corbis UK Ltd. 314, Ch. Hermes/Travel Lib. 315, T. Mata/Vision Photo. 316, T. Mata/Vision Photo. 318/319, M. Rubio/James Davis Worldwide. 319, A. Guinart/Vision Photo. 320, M. Chaplow/Andalucia Slide Lib. 321, M. Chaplow/Andalucia Slide Lib. 322, M. Chaplow/Andalucia Slide Lib. 323, S. Benbow/Axiom. 324, J. Balanya/Vision Photo. 326/327, Ch. Hermes/Travel Lib. 328/329, AA Photo Lib./K. Paterson. 330, James Davis World-wide. 331, S. Ben bow/Axiom. 332, Age Fotostock. 333, AA Photo Lib./J. Tims. 334, S. Black/Travel Lib. 336, S. Black/Travel Lib. 337, AA Photo Lib./R. Moore. 338, AA Photo Lib./J. Tims. 339, AA Photo Lib./C. Sawyer. 340, D. Robertson/Travel Lib. 341, A. Arzoz/Axiom.

Founded in 1888, the National Geographic Society is one of the largest nonprofit scientific and educational organizations in the world. It reaches more than 285 million people worldwide each month through its official journal, *National Geographic*, and its four other magazines; the National Geographic Channel; television documentaries; radio programs; films; books; videos and DVDs; maps; and interactive media. National Geographic has funded more than 8,000 scientific research projects and supports an education program combating geographic illiteracy.

For more information, please call 1-800-NGS LINE (647-5463) or write to the following address: National Geographic Society 1145 17th Street N.W. Washington, D.C. 20036-4688 U.S.A.

Visit us online at www.national geographic.com/books

For information about special discounts for bulk purchases, please contact National Geographic Books Special Sales: ngspecsales@ngs.org

For rights or permissions inquiries, please contact National Geographic Books Subsidiary Rights: ngbookrights@ngs.org

Order *Traveler* today, the magazine that travelers trust. In the U.S. and Canada call 1-800-NGS-LINE; or 813-979-6845 for international calls. Or visit us online at ww.nationalgeographic.com/traveler and click on SUBSCRIBE.

Travel the world with National Geographic Experts: www.nationalgeo graphic.com/ngexpeditions

Printed in China

Published by the National Geographic Society

John M. Fahey, Jr., *President and Chief Executive Officer*

Gilbert M. Grosvenor, *Chairman of the Board*

Tim T. Kelly, *President, Global Media Group*

John Q. Griffin, *President, Publishing*

Nina D. Hoffman, *Executive Vice President, President, Books Publishing Group*

Kevin Mulroy, *Senior Vice President and Publisher*

Marianne Koszorus, *Director of Design*

Leah Bendavid-Val, *Director of Photography Publishing and Illustrations*

Elizabeth L. Newhouse, *Director of Travel Publishing*

Carl Mehler, *Director of Maps*

Barbara A. Noe, *Senior Editor and Series Editor*

Cinda Rose, *Art Director*

Jennifer A. Thornton, *Managing Editor*

R. Gary Colbert, *Production Director*

Richard S. Wain, *Production Project Manager*

Bridget English, Caroline Hickey, Michael McNewy, Meredith Wilcox, Christina Solazzo, Ruth Thompson, and Mapping Specialists *Contributors to 2008 edition*

Edited and designed by AA Publishing (a trading name of Automobile Association Developments Limited, whose registered office is Norfolk House, Priestley Road, Basingstoke, Hampshire, England RG24 9NY. Registered number: 1878835).

Rachel Alder, Marilynne Lanng, *Project Managers*

David Austin, *Senior Art Editor*

Betty Sheldrick, *Senior Editor*

Keith Russell, *Designer*

Inna Nogeste, *Senior Cartographic Editor*

Richard Firth, *Production Director,*

Steve Gilchrist, *Prepress Production Controller*

Cartography by AA Cartographic Production; Drive maps drawn by Chris Orr Associates; Cutaway illustrations by Maltings Partnership, Picture Research by Zooid Pictures Ltd. and Liz Wells, AA Photo Library

Third edition 2008

Copyright © 2001, 2005, 2008 National Geographic Society. All rights reserved. No part of this book may be reproduced or transmitted in any form or by any means, electronic or mechanical, including photocopying, without permission in writing from the National Geographic Society, 1145 17th Street N.W., Washington, D.C. 20036-4688.

The Library of Congress has cataloged the first edition as follows: Library of Congress Cataloging-in- Publication Data

Dunlop, Fiona, 1952-
    The National Geographic traveler. Spain/Fiona Dunlop.
        p. cm.
    Includes index.
    ISBN 0-7922-7922-0
    1. Spain--Guidebooks. I. Title: Spain. II. Title.

DP14 .D86 2001
914.604'83--dc21   00-052681

National Geographic Traveler: Spain. **Third edition. ISBN 978-1-4262-0250-6**

The information in this book has been carefully checked and to the best of our knowledge is accurate. However, details are subject to change, and the National Geographic Society cannot be responsible for such changes, or for errors or omissions. Assessments of sites, hotels, and restaurants are based on the author's subjective opinions, which do not necessarily reflect the publisher's opinion. The publisher cannot be responsible for any consequences arising from the use of this book.

NATIONAL GEOGRAPHIC

TRAVELER

A Century of Travel Expertise in Every Guide

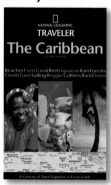

- **Alaska** ISBN: 978-0-7922-5371-6
- **Amsterdam** ISBN: 978-0-7922-7900-6
- **Arizona** (3rd Edition) ISBN: 978-1-4262-0228-5
- **Australia** (3rd Edition) ISBN: 978-1-4262-0229-2
- **Barcelona** (2nd Edition) ISBN: 978-0-7922-5365-5
- **Beijing** ISBN: 978-1-4262-0231-5
- **Berlin** ISBN: 978-0-7922-6212-1
- **Boston & environs** ISBN: 978-0-7922-7926-6
- **California** (3rd Edition) ISBN: 978-1-4262-0324-4
- **Canada** (2nd Edition) ISBN: 978-0-7922-6201-5
- **The Caribbean** (2nd Edition) ISBN: 978-1-4262-0141-7
- **China** (2nd Edition) ISBN: 978-1-4262-0035-9
- **Costa Rica** (2nd Edition) ISBN: 978-0-7922-5368-6
- **Cuba** (2nd Edition) ISBN: 978-1-4262-0142-4
- **Dominican Republic** ISBN: 978-1-4262-0232-2
- **Egypt** (2nd Edition) ISBN: 978-1-4262-0143-1
- **Florence & Tuscany** (2nd Edition) ISBN: 978-0-7922-5318-1
- **Florida** ISBN: 978-0-7922-7432-2
- **France** (2nd Edition) ISBN: 978-1-4262-0027-4
- **Germany** (2nd Edition) ISBN: 978-1-4262-0028-1
- **Great Britain** (2nd Edition) ISBN: 978-1-4262-0029-8
- **Greece** (2nd Edition) ISBN: 978-1-4262-0030-4
- **Hawaii** (2nd Edition) ISBN: 978-0-7922-5568-0
- **Hong Kong** (2nd Edition) ISBN: 978-0-7922-5369-3
- **India** (2nd Edition) ISBN: 978-1-4262-0144-8
- **Ireland** (2nd Edition) ISBN: 978-1-4262-0022-9
- **Italy** (3rd Edition) ISBN: 978-1-4262-0223-0
- **Japan** (3rd Edition) ISBN: 978-1-4262-0234-6
- **London** (2nd Edition) ISBN: 978-1-4262-0023-6
- **Los Angeles** ISBN: 978-0-7922-7947-1
- **Madrid** ISBN: 978-0-7922-5372-3
- **Mexico** (2nd Edition) ISBN: 978-0-7922-5319-8
- **Miami & the Keys** (3rd Edition) ISBN: 978-1-4262-0323-7
- **New York** (2nd Edition) ISBN: 978-0-7922-5370-9
- **Naples & southern Italy** ISBN 978-1-4262-0040-3
- **Panama** ISBN: 978-1-4262-0146-2
- **Paris** (2nd Edition) ISBN: 978-1-4262-0024-3
- **Piedmont & Northwest Italy** ISBN: 978-0-7922-4198-0
- **Portugal** ISBN: 978-0-7922-4199-7
- **Prague & the Czech Republic** ISBN: 978-0-7922-4147-8
- **Provence & the Côte d'Azur** (2nd Edition) ISBN: 978-1-4262-0235-3
- **Romania** ISBN: 978-1-4262-0147-9
- **Rome** (2nd Edition) ISBN: 978-0-7922-5572-7
- **St. Petersburg** ISBN 978-1-4262-0050-2
- **San Diego** (2nd Edition) ISBN: 978-0-7922-6202-2
- **San Francisco** (3rd Edition) ISBN: 978-1-4262-0325-1
- **Shanghai** ISBN: 978-1-4262-0148-6
- **Sicily** (2nd Edition) ISBN: 978-1-4262-0224-7
- **Spain** (3rd Edition) ISBN: 978-1-4262-0250-6
- **Sydney** ISBN: 978-0-7922-7435-3
- **Taiwan** (2nd Edition) ISBN: 978-1-4262-0145-5
- **Thailand** (2nd Edition) ISBN: 978-0-7922-5321-1
- **Venice** ISBN: 978-0-7922-7917-4
- **Vietnam** ISBN: 978-0-7922-6203-9
- **Washington, D.C.** (3rd Edition) ISBN: 978-1-4262-0225-4

AVAILABLE WHEREVER BOOKS ARE SOLD